Political
Legitimacy in
Southeast
Asia

EAST-WEST CENTER
SERIES ON

CONTEMPORARY ISSUES IN ASIA
AND THE PACIFIC

Series Editor, Bruce M. Koppel

Political Legitimacy in Southeast Asia

THE QUEST FOR MORAL AUTHORITY

Edited by Muthiah Alagappa

STANFORD UNIVERSITY PRESS
STANFORD, CALIFORNIA
1995

Stanford University Press
Stanford, California

© 1995 by Stanford University Press
Printed in the United States of America
CIP data are at the end of the book

Stanford University Press publications are
distributed exclusively by Stanford
University Press within the United States,
Canada, Mexico, and Central America;
they are distributed exclusively by
Cambridge University Press throughout
the rest of the world

A New Series from
Stanford University Press and the East-West Center

CONTEMPORARY ISSUES IN ASIA AND THE PACIFIC

Bruce M. Koppel, Editor

A collaborative effort by Stanford University Press and the East-West Center, this new series addresses contemporary issues of policy and scholarly concern in Asia and the Pacific. The series will focus on political, social, economic, cultural, demographic, environmental, and technological change and the problems related to such change. A select group of East-West Center senior fellows—representing the fields of political science, economic development, population, and environmental studies—serves as the Advisory Board for the series. The decision to publish is made by Stanford.

Preference will be given to comparative or regional studies that are conceptual in orientation and emphasize underlying processes and to works on a single country that address issues in a comparative or regional context. Although concerned with policy-relevant issues and written to be accessible to a relatively broad audience, books in the series will be scholarly in character. We are pleased to offer here the first book in the series, *Political Legitimacy in Southeast Asia: The Quest for Moral Authority*, edited by Muthiah Alagappa.

The East-West Center, located in Honolulu, Hawaii, is a public, non-profit educational and research institution established by the U.S. Congress in 1960 to foster understanding and cooperation among the governments and peoples of the Asia-Pacific region, including the United States.

Preface

THIS book was conceived in 1990–91 when I was teaching a course on comparative politics of Southeast Asia at Columbia University. The question of political legitimacy surfaced many times during the course, both as an issue in itself and in relation to the effectiveness of domestic governance, regime change, and the international conduct of governments. Yet the issue appeared to have been little explored directly in relation to Southeast Asia. My interest in the subject was further stimulated by the growing nexus between domestic politics and international relations—my primary area of interest until this time.

Because it constitutes the core of political organization, the right to rule affects all political activities and is crucial to our understanding of the politics of any country. In addition to affecting the structure of domination, the "language of legitimacy" provides the reference framework for competing centers of power to articulate and mobilize resistance to the incumbent power holders. Thus the issue of legitimacy lies at the heart of the political discourse and many of the political crises in the Southeast Asian countries. Acknowledging its centrality to state-society relations, this book is devoted to an explication and elaboration of the concept and to the study of political legitimacy in seven Southeast Asian countries. What is the meaning and nature of legitimacy? What are its constituent elements? Who is seeking to legitimate what? Which groups are crucial for political legitimation? On what basis is authority claimed, acknowledged, contested? Why do legitimation projects succeed or fail? Can any patterns be observed? These are some of the questions we shall explore here.

In designing the project I decided to invite younger scholars to write the country chapters and to involve more established scholars in an advisory capacity to review, discuss, and comment on their work. Apart from concentrating some of the best minds on the subject, this approach, I believe, facilitates interaction between the younger and senior scholars, fosters the development of Southeast Asian studies, and makes the East-West Center better known among scholars of Southeast Asia. The authors and the project advisory group—drawn from Southeast Asia, the United States, the United Kingdom, and Australia—met in two stimulating and productive workshops: first in August 1992 in Honolulu and subsequently in February 1993 in Chiang Mai. I found the project enormously demanding as well as enriching. Indeed, the other authors and I hope the reader will find this book useful and as stimulating as it has been for us. We consider our work to be not the final word but the beginning of the study of political legitimacy in Southeast Asia—a subject we commend to others for further inquiry.

Many people have helped in this undertaking. As members of the advisory committee Benedict Anderson, Michael Aung-Thwin, Rodney Barker, Donald Crone, Harold Crouch, William Duiker, Benedict Kerkvliet, Bruce Koppel, Michael Leifer, Kenneth Liberthal, William Liddle, Chai-anan Samudavanija, and James Scott gave generously of their time and expertise. In addition to suggesting suitable younger scholars, each read and reread several chapters. Many of their comments and insights have been incorporated into the conceptual and case study chapters. Taufik Abdullah, John Badgley, Suchit Bungbongkarn, Chuah Beng Huat, Diane Davis, Wimal Dissanayake, Bernard Gordon, Carolina Hernandez, Paul Kreisberg, Andrew Nathan, Kim Ninh, Murugesu Pathmanathan, Kristin Pelzer, Douglas Ramage, Biswapriya Sanyal, Kusuma Snitwongse, Loekman Sutrisno, Carlyle Thayer, and Geoffrey White commented on one or more chapters. Substantial parts of the manuscript were also read and commented upon by Christopher Clapham, Christopher Collier, John Girling, Charles Morrison, and Yaacov Vertzberger. Clark Neher read and commented upon the entire manuscript. To all of these scholars I express my deep appreciation. I would also like to thank the case study authors. Their knowledge—not only of the country of their specialization but of the Southeast Asian region as a whole—and their ability to integrate area studies and theory are remarkable. They are a talented and diligent group of young scholars. It is my pleasure to have had the opportunity to work with them.

Thanks are also due to the Henry Luce Foundation for providing funding support, the Chaiyong Limthongkul Foundation for cohosting the second workshop in Chiang Mai, Michel Oksenberg, Bruce Koppel, and Charles Morrison of the East-West Center for their support, Don Yoder for his copyediting, Deborah Forbis and David Wolff for their proofreading, Anne Stewart for her liaison with Stanford University Press, Christopher Collier for providing invaluable aid as my research intern during the

latter part of the project, Kelly Kanetani and Jeannie Hamasaki for organizing the two workshops, Ann Takayesu for so efficiently word processing the entire manuscript and preparing the bibliography for several chapters, and Dorothy Villasenor, Marilu Khudari, and Catherine Blickos for
their secretarial assistance during the various phases of the project.

Finally I would like to express my greatest appreciation and admiration
for my wife, Kalyani, without whose forbearance and support this book
would not exist.

Muthiah Alagappa

Contents

Contributors   xiii

A Note on Thai and Vietnamese
Names   xv

Introduction   1
Muthiah Alagappa

PART I
Legitimacy: Explication and Elaboration

1. The Anatomy of Legitimacy   11
Muthiah Alagappa

2. The Bases of Legitimacy   31
Muthiah Alagappa

3. Contestation and Crisis   54
Muthiah Alagappa

PART II
Legitimacy: Case Studies

4. Malaysia: Aspects and Audiences of
Legitimacy   69
William Case

5. Singapore: Political Legitimacy Through
Managing Conformity   108
Cho-Oon Khong

6. The Philippines: The Languages of
    Legitimation   136
    John T. Sidel

7. Burma: The Depoliticization of the
    Political   170
    Chao-Tzang Yawnghwe

8. Thailand: The Evolution of Legitimacy   193
    Saitip Sukatipan

9. Indonesia: Historicizing the New Order's
    Legitimacy Dilemma   224
    Mochtar Pabottingi

10. Vietnam: The Changing Models of
    Legitimation   257
    Thaveeporn Vasavakul

PART III
Conclusions and Observations

11. Seeking a More Durable Basis of
    Authority   293
    Muthiah Alagappa

    Notes   337
    Bibliography   397
    Index   433

Contributors

MUTHIAH ALAGAPPA is senior fellow in the Program on International Economics and Politics at the East-West Center. Previously he was visiting professor at the East Asian Institute and the Department of Political Science at Columbia University, senior fellow at ISIS (Malaysia), and adjunct faculty at the University of Malaya and National University of Malaysia. He received his Ph.D. from the Fletcher School of Law and Diplomacy, Tufts University. His research interests include international relations theory, international relations of the Asia-Pacific region, and comparative politics of Southeast Asia.

WILLIAM CASE is lecturer at University College, University of New South Wales, Australian Defence Force Academy. Previously he was a postdoctoral fellow at the Research School of Pacific and Asian Studies, Australian National University, research associate at the Faculty of Economics and Administration, University of Malaya, and lecturer in the Institut Teknologi MARA in Shah Alam, Selangor. He received his Ph.D. from the Department of Government, University of Texas at Austin. His research interests include interelite and elite-mass relations, regime change and continuity, and Southeast Asian politics.

CHO-OON KHONG is currently senior economist with Group Planning, Shell International Petroleum Company, London. He has taught at the School of Social Science, University of Bath, and at the National University of Singapore and was Laski Senior Scholar, St. John's College, Cambridge. He received his Ph.D. in international relations from the London School of Economics. His research interests include the international political economy and the political development of East and Southeast Asia.

MOCHTAR PABOTTINGI is director of the Center for Political and Regional Studies, Indonesia Institute of Sciences, in Jakarta. Previously he was head of the Department of Development and Comparative Politics in the same institute. He received his Ph.D. from the Department of Political Science, University of Hawaii at Manoa. His research interests include Indonesian politics broadly defined to include culture, economics and history, nationalism, and egalitarianism.

JOHN T. SIDEL is lecturer in Southeast Asian politics in the Department of Political Studies, School of Oriental and African Studies, University of London. He received his Ph.D. from the Department of Government, Cornell University. His research interests include local politics, political economy, and human rights issues.

SAITIP SUKATIPAN is assistant professor in the Faculty of Political Science, Thammasat University. She received her Ph.D. from the Department of Political Science, University of Hawaii at Manoa. Her research interests include the political economy of Southeast Asia and political communication.

THAVEEPORN VASAVAKUL is postdoctoral fellow in political and social change at the Research School of Pacific and Asian Studies, Australian National University. She received her Ph.D. in government from Cornell University. Her research interests, focusing on Southeast Asia, include comparative revolutions, ideological state apparatuses and the making of economic and political cultures, and state formation in the twentieth century.

CHAO-TZANG YAWNGHWE is a Ph.D. candidate in the Department of Political Science, University of British Columbia. Previously he served in various political-military capacities in the Shan State army. His research interests include comparative politics of Southeast Asia with an emphasis on political regimes, state-society relations, and democratization.

A NOTE ON THAI AND VIETNAMESE NAMES

According to scholarly convention, Thai names are cited and alphabetized by family name (the last name) in the Notes, Bibliography, and Index. After the first appearance of the full name in the text, however, the given name is used because Thai people are more commonly known by their first name.

Vietnamese names are likewise cited and alphabetized by family name (the first name in Vietnamese order) in all reference matter. After the first appearance of the full name in the text, Vietnamese people are generally referred to by their better-known given name.

Political Legitimacy in Southeast Asia

Introduction

MUTHIAH ALAGAPPA

> The strongest man is never strong enough to maintain his mastery at all
> times unless he transforms his strength into right and obedience into duty.
> —Jean-Jacques Rousseau, *The Social Contract*

IN the early morning of May 18, 1992, the Royal Thai Army using machine guns and tanks fired indiscriminately on tens of thousands of antigovernment demonstrators at the Phanfa bridge in Bangkok. During the
next three days, 52 people were killed and an estimated 167 were missing.[1]
Material damage was extensive and the crisis had short-term economic
consequences as well. The image of the Thais as a benign nonviolent
people and the reputation of Thailand as politically stable and on a fast
track to becoming a newly industrializing country (NIC) were stained.
This political crisis was by far the worst in Thailand since 1973.

At the heart of it was the conflict between the military—which was
trying to regain its prominent political role through the appointment of
the army chief, General Suchinda Kraprayoon, as the unelected prime
minister—and the "new" sociopolitical groups (a broad cross section of
Bangkok's politically active middle and working classes led by students,
academics, politicians, and business leaders) that resisted this attempt
and clamored for a more participatory political system. The crisis ended
with the intervention by the much revered King Bhumipol Adulyadej,
who commanded General Suchinda and opposition leader Chamlong Srimuang to end their confrontation and draft a new constitution to meet
the needs of the country.[2] Suchinda resigned on May 24; an amendment
was passed to the effect that future prime ministers should be elected; and
Anand Panyarachun, a respected former bureaucrat and businessman
and the interim prime minister from March 1991 to April 1992, was

appointed caretaker prime minister with the task of organizing new elections.

Burma experienced a similar political crisis in 1987–88 that continues at the time of this writing. Years of political frustration and severe economic problems (stagflation, unemployment, demonetization of high-denomination bills) culminated in widespread mass political demonstrations against the military in 1988.[3] The military responded with ruthless suppression, killing between 4,000 and 5,000 people and arresting tens of thousands in 1988 alone. On the brink of collapse, the military launched a coup d'état against itself in September 1988 and has since ruled the country under martial law in the name of the State Law and Order Restoration Council (SLORC). To shore up its domestic and international legitimacy, the military organized tightly controlled elections in May 1990. Much to its dismay, the opposition National League for Democracy (NLD) won a landslide victory. But the military, determined to hold onto power, has refused to convene the elected assembly and transfer power to the NLD.[4] It continues to detain Aungsan Suukyi, leader of the NLD, and seeks to destroy the government in exile set up by several elected members of the NLD in Manerplaw in the Karen territory.

The Philippines was engulfed in a political crisis for much of 1985–86. The attempt by President Ferdinand Marcos to hold onto office, despite his poor showing in the fraudulent elections he organized to shore up his domestic and international legitimacy, was thwarted by the mutiny of key segments in the Armed Forces of the Philippines (AFP) and the EDSA demonstration by hundreds of thousands of ordinary Filipinos. These developments, as well as the United States' decision to withdraw its support, convinced Marcos of the futility of his bid to hold onto power.[5] Lacking a moral basis and the necessary domestic and international support to govern, he fled the Philippines on February 26, 1986. The termination of the crisis brought about a change in the presidency as well as a change in the political system.

At the core of each of these three crises was a conflict over political legitimacy, or the "right to rule." Political legitimacy may be defined as "the belief in the rightfulness of a state, in its authority to issue commands, so that the commands are obeyed not simply out of fear or self-interest, but because they are believed to have moral authority, because subjects believe that they ought to obey."[6] The legitimation of power relies on the conviction of the governed that their government (whether democratic, monarchic, communist, theocratic, or authoritarian) is morally right and they are duty-bound to obey it. In the absence of such conviction there can only be relations of power, not of authority, and political legitimacy will be contested.[7]

In the three situations cited here, the governments failed to gain or sustain the right to rule. The Thai military's attempt to regain and institutionalize its predominant political role—and the efforts of the Burmese military and of Marcos to perpetuate their political control—diverged sharply from that of other political groups in these countries, which increasingly emphasized participatory politics. Poor performance and the repressive nature of the governments in Burma and the Philippines also undermined public confidence in the political system. Other centers of power, with the support of politically significant sections of the population in all three countries, resisted the incumbents' claim to the right to rule and rejected the type of government they represented.

Although relatively recent and certainly dramatic, these developments have by no means been confined to these countries of Southeast Asia.[8] Legitimacy was chronically contested in South Vietnam and Laos from 1954 through 1975 and in Cambodia from 1970 to the present time. Malaysia suffered a setback after the race riots in 1969. The legitimacy of the Marxist-Leninist regimes in Vietnam and Laos, despite their longevity, has become strained. Developments in China (June 1989), the South Asian countries, the successor states of the Soviet Union, and the Eastern European countries indicate that political legitimacy is contested in many other countries as well.

Significance of Political Legitimacy

The right to rule is fundamental. Constituting the core of political organization, it affects all political activities.[9] This is especially so in the modern state, which, claiming supreme and comprehensive authority within the territory under its jurisdiction, seeks to regulate the vital interests and actions of its citizens through binding commands, rules, and laws backed by force.[10] As Weber argues, the basis on which legitimacy is claimed will influence the structure of domination. "The type of obedience, the kind of administrative staff developed to guarantee it, the mode of exercising authority"—all depend on the kind of legitimacy claimed.[11] Apart from influencing the structure of domination, legitimacy also frames the discourse among strategic groups—and between these groups and the public—in their endeavor to control the use of state power.[12] As the "language of legitimacy" often defines what is and what is not legitimate political activity, it provides a reference framework for articulating and mobilizing resistance against the incumbent government.[13] Thus it is crucial to the understanding of politics in any country.

Legitimacy also shapes the effectiveness of governance, the scope, pace, and method of political change, and the international conduct of the state. By maximizing political obligation, legitimacy greatly enhances the viability of rulership.[14] If acceptance of commands issued by authorities is based solely or even largely on naked force, then the right to rule will be challenged and political change will be sought through resistance, rebellion, and revolution. The government's survival will consume the bulk of its resources, and its effectiveness will be considerably reduced. If the government is perceived as legitimate, however, the social, political, and economic cost of governance will be low and the government's capacity to promote its political and socioeconomic goals will be enhanced.[15]

From the rulers' viewpoint, legitimacy is not just a stratagem to secure more effective control or perpetuate themselves in office. Self-justification in moral terms is crucial for most rulers. They need to believe they are serving the national interest or a moral cause even if it necessitates a "noble lie."[16] By enhancing self-esteem, such a belief justifies domination and enjoyment of the privileges of power. Defense of the government, including the use of coercion, against rival claimants to power also becomes accepted as necessary and justified in the eyes of the public. Thus all rulers, even the most tyrannical, wish to appear legitimate and seek to cultivate belief in their legitimacy. Moreover, there is moral pressure from the governed to convert relations of power into relations of authority. A perception that power is exercised on the basis of moral considerations and for the benefit of the governed softens the hard edges of inequality and subordination—two concomitant features of power relations—and justifies obedience to the ruled.

Despite its centrality, political legitimacy in developing countries has rarely been studied explicitly.[17] A number of reasons account for this situation, but only two will be considered here. First, state-society relations were not a primary concern of the three main currents (the political development, Marxist, and dependency schools) in the comparative scholarship on Third World politics.[18] Political development theories have been concerned with the goals of economic growth, distribution, preconditions for democracy, political order and stability, and, more recently, the transition to democracy.[19] Implicitly or explicitly, the development theory posits a linear model in which traditional societies develop into modern ones. As advocates of modernization, some proponents of these theories have endorsed a strong autonomous center with domination based on power. Marxists, by contrast, view the state as an instrument of class rule, as a guarantor of production relations, or as an arena for class struggle. Their theories generalize about "features or functions shared by *all* states within a mode of production, a phase of capitalist accumulation, or a position in the world capitalist system."[20] The dependency school, which attempts to marry Marxism and nationalism, emphasizes the dependent character of the economies of the less developed countries and the need to break the bonds with the capitalist order.[21] A central claim of the dependency school, according to Robert Packenham, is that "nations, classes, class 'fractions,' groups, regions and other units of analysis are constrained and conditioned by the international capitalist system in ways that have either created underdevelopment . . . or brought about distorted, inappropriate development."[22] The resolution of the linked problems of class exploitation and imperialism that this school advocates requires the overthrow and replacement of capitalism by socialism.

The development school assumes democracy and modernization as the ultimate goals and views economic growth as the primary means of creating the necessary preconditions to achieve these goals.[23] Marxists advocate the overthrow of the sociopolitical order and its replacement with the more egalitarian socialist system. The dependency school aims at the same outcome but proposes to achieve it by breaking the bonds of international dependency. All three approaches have deterministic tendencies and focus on universal goals and processes. Explicitly or implicitly, they view the political systems in developing countries as inherently unstable, in transition to Western or universal models, and unworthy of consideration in their own right.[24] Consequently local political traditions, languages, and contexts receive little attention; differences are explained as deviations.[25]

The view that political systems in developing countries are in transition to Western or universal models has not been borne out in practice. The relative durability of one-party political systems and the economic success of such regimes in East Asian countries refute some of the central assumptions of the three approaches cited earlier, giving rise to new theorizing about political institutions in developing states. Samuel Huntington, for example, suggests that the interaction of Asian cultures and economic growth has produced a distinctive Asian form of democratic institutions.[26] The basic point, from the perspective of this study, is that politics in developing countries has its own dynamics.[27] And these dynamics will determine the political system in each country, a system that may or may not approximate those of the West. Even if the claim that the political systems of developing countries are in transition to Western models proves to be correct in the long term, the evidence from the last four decades suggests that it will be a slow process with no predetermined path.[28] At present, diverse sociopolitical arrangements—including Leninism, military regimes, monarchy, personal dictatorships, quasi-democracies, and democracies—characterize the Southeast Asian political landscape. It is necessary to study these systems in their own right with due attention to local norms, values, and circumstances.

The second reason why legitimacy has been understudied—and this applies to the general study of legitimacy—relates to the alleged shortcomings of the "theory of legitimacy."[29] Criticisms of legitimacy usually highlight its weakness as a social science concept: its limited explanatory power and the difficulty of operationalizing the concept. Because every political order rests on a combination of coercion, expediency, and a belief in legitimacy, it is argued that there is no way to ascertain the degree of belief in legitimacy that is required to classify a regime as legitimate or illegitimate. Problems of tautology, difficulty in identifying the elements of legitimacy, and finding the required evidence to support cause-and-effect propositions are the other shortcomings commonly cited.[30] That legitimacy or the lack of it is more easily explained during a crisis or after the displacement of a particular government or regime than during periods of stability, that the explanation must be distinguished from what is to be explained, and that research into the shared beliefs and consent of the governed will be problematic, particularly in countries with nondemocratic systems—these charges are difficult to refute.[31]

It is, however, pertinent to note here that as "the production of society is a skilled performance, sustained and 'made to happen' by human beings," theory building as envisioned in positivism has made little progress.[32] This is not to imply that social life is without patterns or that generalizations are impossible, only that such patterns cannot be conceived as "elements of a transhistorical order of uniformities."[33] Generalizations cannot be universal and valid for all times; they are limited to a determinate range of conceptual issues in temporally and contextually bounded collectivities and processes. It is in this context that the impact of legitimacy on political behavior must be analyzed.

Further, while a direct cause-and-effect relationship may be difficult to establish, this difficulty does not imply that legitimacy has no explanatory power. Legitimacy and the legitimation project do affect political relations, and, along with other variables, they have been used widely to explain domestic conflict, political reform and revolution, and regime survival and change.[34] Recent literature on the national security of developing countries, for example, convincingly traces one key aspect of this problem to the issues of political identity and authority.[35] Similarly, political change—including the collapse of communism in the Soviet Union and Eastern Europe, the transition from authoritarianism to democratic rule, and political revolution in developing states—has been explained in terms of the erosion of legitimacy.[36] While legitimacy cannot predict precisely when a regime change will occur, it is nevertheless useful in drawing attention to trends in the degree of support enjoyed by particular governments and regimes. Even critics of the concept concede this. Huntington, for example, while characterizing legitimacy as a "mushy" concept, admits that it is essential to our understanding of the problems confronting authoritarian regimes in the late twentieth century. In his schema, the "deepening legitimacy problem of authoritarian systems" is one of the five independent variables advanced to explain the Third Wave of democratization.[37] Thus legitimacy is not without explanatory value. By establishing a frame of meaning, it can contribute to the "clearing up of puzzles or queries."[38]

Legitimacy in social practice is complex, multifaceted, and contested. Any attempt to give it greater conceptual certitude and rigor is bound to be unrealistic. Thus while the difficulties cited earlier draw attention to the problems associated with theory building and underscore the need for much greater discipline in employing legitimacy as a social science concept, these shortcomings in no way refute the importance of legitimacy.[39] The foregoing discussion has dealt mostly with the weakness of legitimacy as a social science concept. The focus has been on the question of "what legitimacy can do for us." But legitimacy is important in its own right. Political authority and the basis on which it is constituted are core issues meriting inquiry for their own sake. As noted earlier, even the most tyrannical government seeks to depict itself as legitimate, and the claim to the right to rule is frequently contested by other groups. The claim to legitimacy and its contestation are a central feature of politics and worthy of study independent of their impact on stability, performance, and such variables. Approached in this way, legitimacy is both cause and effect.[40]

Purpose, Structure, Method

Because of its centrality in state-society relations and its fundamental importance to political domination and organization, the focus of inquiry in this book is on legitimacy itself. What is the meaning and nature of legitimacy? What are its constituent elements? Who is seeking to legitimate what? Which groups are crucial for political legitimation? On what basis is authority claimed, acknowledged, resisted? Did the legitimation projects succeed? Why or why not? Why is legitimacy contested? Can any patterns be observed? This book explores such questions with reference to Southeast Asia.

The study is structured in three parts. Part I is devoted to explication and elaboration of the concept. The meaning of legitimacy, its constituent elements, the referent objects of political legitimation, and the critical audiences are explored in Chapter 1. Chapter 2 examines the various bases on which authority may be claimed, acknowledged, or resisted, their interrelationships, and their significance for political legitimation in developing states. The contested nature of legitimacy and the recurrence of legitimacy crises in developing countries are examined in Chapter 3.

Part II comprises seven country studies: Burma, Indonesia, Malaysia, the Philippines, Singapore, Thailand, and Vietnam. These studies, informed by the conceptual discussion of legitimacy in Chapters 1, 2, and 3, address the following questions: Who is seeking to legitimate what? On what basis is authority claimed, acknowledged, or resisted? What accounts for the success (or failure) of the legitimation projects? While these studies conform to a common framework, the authors have been allowed wide latitude in expanding and enriching the core approach in a manner they consider appropriate to their respective countries. Thus while all of them address common questions, there are variations in details of the approach that have been tailored to account for the special circumstances of each country. Drawing upon the country studies and other published material, Chapter 11 in Part III offers specific conclusions with reference to political legitimacy in Southeast Asia.

PART I

LEGITIMACY

Explication and Elaboration

The Anatomy of Legitimacy

MUTHIAH ALAGAPPA

POLITICAL legitimacy, as noted in the Introduction, is the belief by the governed in the rulers' moral right to issue commands and the people's corresponding obligation to obey such commands. The first three chapters seek to develop a conceptual framework for the analysis of political legitimacy. What is the meaning and nature of legitimacy? What are its constituent elements? What are the referent objects of political legitimation? Which audiences are critical for political legitimation? These are the central questions that will be examined in this chapter. It begins by exploring the meaning of legitimacy with a view to highlighting two key points. First, legitimacy is a social practice, an outcome of the interaction between ① ruler and ruled; hence it must be framed in the sociopolitical and economic context of a specific society at a specified time. Second, legitimacy is multifaceted, highly contingent, and a dynamic feature of government; ② hence its cultivation must be unending.

The Meaning and Nature of Legitimacy

Weber's formulation of legitimacy has been a dominant thread in the literature and provides a good starting point for discussion.[1] According to Weber, "the basis of every system of authority, and correspondingly of every kind of willingness to obey, is a belief, a belief by virtue of which persons exercising authority are lent prestige."[2] For authority to be confirmed, he says, the claim to legitimacy should "to a significant degree and according to its type [be] treated as valid."[3] In other words, authority can exist only when the ruler "possesses an acknowledged right to command" and the ruled have "an acknowledged obligation to obey."[4] The idea of belief and the notion of acknowledgment by the governed are the two key elements in Weber's formulation of legitimacy. They underpin the ruler's claim to authority and validate the structure of domination.

This formulation has been criticized on a number of counts.[5] One relates to the idea of belief—which has been criticized for equating legitimacy with emotion and popular opinion, for misrepresenting the relationship between people's belief and legitimacy, for making legitimacy a product of government manipulation, and for providing no objective criteria for evaluating legitimacy. The second basic criticism relates to the specific societal and temporal bounds of the Weberian approach—which, it is argued, ignore independent or universal values that are posited as more appropriate in the evaluation of legitimacy. The third charge relates to incompleteness—for Weber has been criticized for ignoring other elements that contribute to legitimacy. These basic criticisms are reviewed here primarily as a way of emphasizing the need to root discussions of legitimacy in the political discourse of the society and to highlight the dynamic and contested nature of legitimacy.[6]

The interpretation of belief as fleeting popular opinion, as well as the depiction of the Weberian social scientist as depending on public opinion polls, rests on a misreading of Weber and is quite easily dismissed. The critics disconnect belief from the motives and basis for belief. This view is contrary to Weber's formulation, however, which links belief in authority to deeply held beliefs based on tradition and legality.[7] More fundamental is the criticism that the Weberian approach is not objective or scientific, as well as the accompanying claim that, in Peter Stillman's words, "the legitimacy or illegitimacy of a government is a matter not of public opinion nor of belief about the appropriateness or good title to government" but of "the objective compatibility between the value pattern of society and government output."[8] Stillman defines value pattern as "the generalized criteria of desirability, the standards for evaluations, and the normative priorities for the society."[9]

Stillman's objective formulation is not substantially different from the Weberian formulations that emphasize shared beliefs between ruler and ruled. His claim to objectivity turns out to be more a matter of style and degree than one of fundamental difference. Further, as noted in the Introduction, scientific rationality is not suited for the study of social practices that are predicated on motivation, knowledge, judgment, choice, and negotiation and are therefore highly contingent. The danger in Stillman's approach is that it seeks to remove legitimacy from the domain of the belief of the governed. In arrogating to themselves the power to decide what the society's value pattern should be, analysts may be tempted to smuggle in their own beliefs.[10]

This brings us to the second set of criticisms: the argument that the Weberian approach empties legitimacy of independent moral content and therefore lacks evaluative criteria. Weber clearly states that legitimacy may "derive from a rational belief in the absolute validity of the order as an expression of ultimate values, whether they may be moral, esthetic, or any other type."[11] He also contends that such an order is more stable than one based on pure expediency or custom.[12] Thus norms and values are important in the analysis of legitimacy, but only as part of the belief of the governed at the time under consideration. Society cannot conform to some extraneous truth. The task of the social scientist is to explain in terms of the society's beliefs at the time, not in terms of extraneous ideals. Moreover, so-called independent or universal ideals usually embody a strong element of ethnocentrism and cultural bias. Such ideals, however, are not totally irrelevant.[13] They may help to explain changing norms and their consequences: the erosion of legitimacy and, ultimately, a legitimacy crisis. But for this to happen, the so-called universal values must permeate and inform the domestic discourse on legitimacy. At this point, however, they can no longer be considered extraneous.

At the heart of the legitimacy issue is the discourse (persuasion through argument and reason) between ruler and ruled at the various levels (nation, province, district, village)—a fact that should not be obscured by the methodological requirements of scientific rationality or the introduction of extraneous ideals. If one accepts that "every social actor knows a great deal about the conditions of social reproduction of the society in which he or she is a member,"[14] and this must be true unless actors are perceived as "judgmental dopes," then, contrary to the claims of the critics, legitimacy must be explicitly framed in terms of the society's "mutual knowledge."[15] In the context of this study, mutual knowledge may be conceived as a series of tacitly understood norms, rules, and procedures that, on the basis of rights and obligations, establish the appropriate and inappropriate ways for the acquisition and exercise of state power—thereby enabling one to judge the legitimacy or otherwise of specific institutions and acts in this regard. The task of the social scientist is then to discern locally accepted frames of meaning and use them to evaluate specific practices and outcomes.

Legitimation of power is an interactive and therefore dynamic process among the government, the elite groups, and the politically significant public: those in power seek to legitimate their control and exercise of that power; the subjects seek to define their subordination in acceptable terms. This process is characterized by projections and counterprojections of legitimacy, by contestation of meanings, and by deployment of resources including coercion, negotiation, and possibly suppression and elimination. Recognition of authority is one possible outcome; resistance, rebellion, and revolution are also possible. The potential for conflict inherent in this process is, as we shall see, accentuated by the contested nature of the political institutions in developing countries. As the terms of the interaction between ruler and ruled are defined and redefined continuously, legitimacy, conceived as an outcome of this process, will be subject to continuous redefinition as well. Although more durable in some cases than others, legitimacy is a dynamic feature in need of constant cultivation.

Elements of Legitimacy

As noted earlier, the two key elements in Weber's formulation of legitimacy are the notions of belief and acknowledgment by the governed. David Beetham criticizes Weber for making legitimacy primarily a matter of belief and ignoring other elements such as legal validity and consent that, according to him, have nothing to do with belief but nevertheless contribute to legitimacy.[16] But Weber does not exclude considerations of legal validity and consent. He advances belief in legality (that is, a readiness to conform with rules that are formally correct and have been imposed by accepted procedure) as one of the bases of legitimacy and the most common in modern states.[17] One can charge that Weber does not develop a structure of legitimacy with legal validity as one of its dimensions, as Beetham has done, but this is to criticize Weber for being incomplete rather than for being wrong. In asserting the need for acknowledgment, Weber also recognizes the role of consent although he does not address this element in any depth. Contrary to Beetham's assertion, legal validity and consent are not independent of belief. Law differs from belief in terms of its formal standing and enforceability, but its authority derives from the beliefs that underscore the political order. If law is not well grounded in the beliefs of society, its validity and ability to confer legitimacy on governments will be suspect. Similarly, consent is influenced by belief and hence is not independent of it. Belief, legal validity, and consent are interrelated elements of legitimacy. Do these three elements exhaust the structure of legitimacy, or are there others? And how do these elements relate to each other?

A further element—proper and effective use of power—is necessary to complete the structure of legitimacy. This element refers to the effective use of state power within accepted rules for the promotion of the collective interest and welfare of the political community. The significance of this element will be discussed later. Analytically, distinguishing the exercise of power from the rules that govern its acquisition makes it possible, for example, to inquire into the legitimacy of a government in a less well established regime where the rules for acquiring power do not matter much, to examine the eroding legitimacy of a government that acquired power by conforming with accepted rules, or to investigate the continued legitimacy of a government despite poor performance.

Thus legitimacy comprises four key elements: shared norms and values, conformity with established rules for acquiring power, proper and effective use of power, and consent of the governed. Based on these four elements, an expanded definition of legitimacy can be advanced: A command-obedience relationship may be defined as legitimate if the political order in which it is rooted is based on shared norms and values, if the government in concern acquired power in conformity with established rules, if that power is exercised within prescribed limits for the promotion of the community's collective interest, and if the governed have given their consent to the incumbent government. Now let us explore these four elements of legitimacy in greater detail.

Shared Norms and Values

Norms and values in the context of this study are essentially belief systems or ideologies that specify how things ought to be.[18] They determine the type of political system and hence the structure of domination. Shared norms and values can be interpreted as normative regulation of society on the basis of universal consensus.[19] As internalized moral values can exert a powerful impact on the determination of goals and the means to achieve them, institutionalization of such values in society through a central value system contributes to social cohesion, which, from the perspective of this study, in turn leads to agreement on the rules governing the acquisition of state power and its use.

This formulation, however, suffers from three limitations.[20] First, it overemphasizes the role of norms in regulating behavior. Not all behavior is governed by normative beliefs. People's everyday conduct is likely to be grounded much more in habit, pragmatism, and expediency than in commitment to normative ends—especially if these people are in subordinate positions and unable to influence the basis for political organization. Shared norms and values are more relevant for dominant groups that have the power to sanction legitimate orders.[21] Second, it fails to consider asymmetry in power and its implications for legitimation. Power has considerable potential to legitimate itself. Political institutions, through their role in determining rules and allocating resources, structure the social context for action and mold behavior. The application of these rules and resources, over and over, creates standards of behavior that are internalized and routinized. In this way institutions influence social reproduction, including the development and perpetuation of legitimating norms. Although the salience of this socialization dimension in legitimation must be recognized, care must be taken to avoid structural determinism.[22] As noted by Anthony Giddens, structure is both medium and outcome of the reproduction of practices. It can be transformed by the actions of agents.

Third, the emphasis on consensus obscures the pervasiveness of conflict in society. Shared norms and values do not simply obtain; they have to be created. This is especially so in developing countries where there is no established normative framework. In this situation, hegemonic groups seek to sustain their domination of society by projecting sectional interests as universally beneficial and valid. At the same time, other groups will seek to limit this hegemony on the basis of competing norms and values. The various rationales that may be deployed by these competing groups are explored in Chapter 2. The point here is that the legitimation of a political order is an outcome of ideological struggle among what may be termed strategic groups.[23] This does not imply that shared norms and values are unimportant—only that they do not imply universal normative consensus, that they are more important among strategic groups, that they have to be created, and that power plays a significant role in their creation.

Although formulated in the context of Marxist theory, Gramsci's concept of hegemony can provide useful insights and is relevant to the discussion of the production of a shared value system.[24] In a hegemonic system, the dominant group exercises political, intellectual, and moral leadership on the basis of ideological unity (a common worldview). To gain the consent of subordinate groups, the dominant group has to broaden its basic corporate interests and build upon those that coincide with the interests of other groups in order to forge universal or "popular national" interests. It has to be "coordinated concretely with the general interests of the subordinated groups," and an equilibrium must exist in which "the interest of the dominant group prevails, but only up to a certain point."[25] Gramsci's conception of hegemony comprises two overlapping layers. One relates to political leadership of an alliance among groups. This alliance is born of pragmatic considerations and is purely instrumental in character: each group maintains its own individuality, as well as its own ideology, but the demands of the subordinate groups are articulated to those of the fundamental group. The second and more significant layer is the intellectual and moral leadership that provides political direction. Here hegemony involves a "higher synthesis" that fuses all the elements into a "collective will" forging ideological unity.

There are two routes to the creation of ideological unity: imposition and transformation.[26] In the first the ideology of the dominant group is imposed on other groups. Unity is achieved through absorption and neutralization of the interests of the other groups with the aim of preventing them from opposing the hegemony of the dominant group. The subordinate groups are neutralized or excluded and prevented from making demands. This route is not Gramscian. In the Gramscian conception, hegemony relies on the creation of "collective will" through transformation. It involves the disarticulation of the ideologies of subordinate groups and rearticulation of the relevant elements into the ideology of the dominant group. In other words: the hegemonic ideology includes ideological elements from all groups, but the unity comes from the articulating principle, which is always provided by the hegemonic group.

The unity forged is active and direct, resulting from genuine adoption of the interests of the other groups by the dominant group. This gives rise to a genuine "national popular will," making for the advancement of the whole society. Ideological unity is the product of a constant struggle between, and synthesis of, the ideologies of the dominant and subordinate groups; the unity derives from the articulating principle of the dominant group. A successful hegemony is one in which the dominant group appears to represent the general interest.

Further, production of shared values, if it is to be successful, must draw upon history and culture.[27] A polity, notes Bhiku Parekh, "is not a chance and fluctuating collection of individuals but has a history and a character."[28] All institutions exist in historical continuity, as do all social practices. Hence historical contextualization is important in the construction and analysis of norms and values. So too is culture. Because it conveys "a sense of antiquity and continuity," culture can be a potent force in the construction of legitimating norms.[29] The analysis of culture's role in the creation of shared norms, however, is complicated by the tension between two different conceptions of culture. One views culture as an implicit, integrated, consensual symbolic system that orders behavior and events. The other conceives culture as dependent, dynamic, "actively and continuously constructed."[30]

In the former conception, culture is a given and an independent variable; in the latter, it is essentially a resource (or weapon) to be used for political purposes. According to the latter view, moreover, cultures are multiple and plural and the reading of the past is always tailored to serve contemporary political aspirations.[31] As culture is invariably interpreted to serve some contemporary political need, it is difficult to deny the argument of selective construction. But in order for this construction to be potent it must resonate in the body politic—that is, it must be part of the society's mutual knowledge. Thus in order to be a resource, culture must also be a given, although not static. As noted by Marshall Sahlins, "things must preserve some identity through their changes, or else the world is a madhouse."[32] Hence the past is an inextricable part of the present; the two conceptions are not mutually exclusive. "Events are ordered by culture but in the process culture is reordered. Reproduction leads to transformation when worldly circumstances do not conform to received categories."[33] The latter is then revalued and functionally redefined. This continuity and change in culture—its impact on social practices including legitimation—may be got at through historicization.

To the extent that power holders are successful in fusing all elements into a collective will and appear to represent the general interest, the government and the regime it represents will be perceived as legitimate. Resistance and contestation of hegemony, on the other hand, indicate failure. Several indicators—including conflict over the organizing ideology, the use of force in securing compliance, and the degree of public support for the system—may signify the presence or absence of shared norms and values in the society.

The presence of groups advocating political organization on the basis of different ideologies may be viewed as evidence of the lack of shared norms. Such groups will always be present, however, and their participation legitimizes the existing system to some extent. What is critical is their support base and their potential to capture power through legal and extralegal means. It is this that defines their significance and the challenge they pose to the legitimacy of the existing government and hence the regime. If they command substantial and growing support, the legitimacy of the incumbent regime can be construed as weak and eroding; the converse demonstrates a high level of commitment to the regime.

Ideological competition leading to conflict could issue from a number of developments: from different constructions of the political identity of the state, from ideational changes (resurgence of religion as a significant political force, for example, or growing salience of the notion of popular sovereignty), or as an outgrowth of economic development or failure to perform. Conflict has been particularly intense in developing countries because of the newness of the nation-state and the consequent need to define its political identity, the intense competition for state power because of the access it provides to state resources, and the global ideological conflict that permeated national political discourse. Demands for autonomy and secession by communities that do not identify with the nation-state may also feed ideological conflict. Ideological and nationality conflicts are frequently accompanied by political violence and extensive use of force.

Force is an integral part of authority. It is necessary both to demonstrate law and to consolidate trust in it. While laws together with custom are the primary means of regulating society, the "abstract availability of physical violence" is necessary to ensure their efficacy.[34] By ensuring that those who violate socially accepted norms will be punished, physical force makes for clear outcomes and increases the security of expectations. This, in turn, makes for greater regularity in social interaction.[35] To qualify as legitimate, however, the use of force must satisfy two conditions. First, the institution employing force must itself be legitimate; second, the use of force must be within the law and limited to the pursuit of the collective interest of the political community. In a legitimate political order, most citizens will comply on normative grounds and force will play a largely symbolic role. A massive use of force reflects the ineffectiveness of coercion and the weakness of the government's legitimacy. It can further undermine legitimacy even from the perspective of those who are not its target. While the use of force is always illegitimate from the perspective of the target, it can be deemed legitimate to the extent that most of the other citizens, who do not have to be coerced to secure compliance, view its use as justifiable in the public interest.[36]

Difficulty arises, however, with respect to the use of force by governments whose legitimacy is weak or contested—especially by groups that do not identify with the nation-state as constituted. Will the use of force by such governments enhance their legitimacy or further undermine it? No clear-cut answer is possible. The impact upon legitimacy will depend on the context and purpose as well as the extent of the force. If force is used to restore order and stability, the government's legitimacy may well be enhanced, at least temporarily, from the perspective of those who are not the targets of coercion. A massive use of force, on the other hand, to impose an ideology or to sustain a government against the will of the people—as, for example, is currently the case in Burma—will be perceived as illegitimate. From the perspective of groups that seek to secede from the state and view terror and instability as a means of realizing their goal, the government's use of force to restore order will be counterproductive and therefore illegitimate. Yet certain people in such disaffected communities may welcome the use of force to restore order. Hence the relationship between force and legitimacy is much more complex in countries in which the legitimacy of the nation-state, regime, and government is weak and contested. Nevertheless, the purpose, context, and extent of the use of force can be useful indicators of the degree of legitimacy enjoyed by the government and perhaps the regime.

Similarly, the degree of public participation in the political system and the public's compliance with the commands of the incumbent government may reflect the level of commitment to the system. To be viewed as commitment, both support and participation must be voluntary and embrace most of the system's principles, institutions, and procedures. Participation in elections alone, for example, even if the voter turnout is high, is not sufficient to demonstrate public commitment to a democratic system. Fear, profit, and expediency could account for the impressive voter turn-out. To be meaningful, participation in elections must be part of involvement in a broad range of activities connected with the democratic system: membership in interest groups and political parties, support for specific causes and policies, belief in the efficacy of the judicial system, compliance with government policies even when there is an attendant cost. When this is not the case, public support for the system must be inferred to be luke-warm or lacking. Routine disregard of the judicial system, widespread evasion of government orders, extensive political disobedience, and, more generally, skepticism and cynicism indicate a lack of public trust in the political system and therefore a lack of shared norms and values. As we shall see, the level of shared norms and values has a substantial impact on the legitimating potential of the next element: conformity with established rules for acquiring power.

Conformity with Established Rules

The creation of shared norms and values contributes to the development of a well-established regime in which the rules for acquisition of political power are clearly specified, commonly accepted, and scrupulously observed. In this situation, the formal provisions governing the acquisition of political power are unlikely to be contested except at the margins. A government that acquires power by conforming with such provisions will be viewed as legitimate; one that disregards them will be viewed as illegitimate. Although the situation is not always clear-cut, by and large the legitimacy of a government can be judged by widely recognized rules and standards.

When norms and values are keenly contested, however, invariably the regime and its provisions relating to the acquisition of power will be contested as well. This is the case in many developing countries where conformity with the rules does not necessarily confer legitimacy. It should be noted here that while developing countries desire to don the mantle of the modern state, traditional attitudes toward power continue to inform governance in many of them.[37] These countries may be described as traditional states in modern garb, states in which "relationships of a broadly patrimonial type pervade a political and administrative system which is formally constructed on rational-legal lines."[38] Power in such countries derives from official positions as well as intrinsic personal qualities, but it is exercised predominantly in traditional ways without distinction between private and public property. The gap between the formal system and the actual conduct of politics in these countries may be substantial. When this is the case, satisfying the formal requirements of the political system will not carry much weight in conferring legitimacy. Rival claimants to power can contest the legitimacy of the incumbents on the basis of traditional sources of power (big man, patron-client relations), especially at the local level. Further, arbitrary manipulation of the system to serve the interests of the power holders, a common practice in such situations, is likely to undermine public confidence and reduce the legitimating value of the system. Public recognition of the government's claim to the right to rule in such cases is more likely to rest on the government's performance.

There are, however, two occasions when a government may enjoy initial legitimacy even when the regime is not well established. One situation is when a government assumes power in the wake of a politically defining ① moment.[39] Such a moment, by its very nature, carries enormous moral authority, a revolutionary mandate, that can legitimize certain norms and values—as well as the government that seeks to represent and foster them—while delegitimating the earlier system. The second situation relates to charismatic authority: here the charisma of an individual leader, ② either alone or in conjunction with other bases of authority, usually a politically defining moment, is deployed to legitimate a government. The politically defining moment and charismatic authority can only be mobilized to gain initial legitimacy, however. In the long run, other resources capable of creating more durable institutions and procedures will have to be mobilized to sustain legitimacy.

In the absence of an established regime or special situations (politically defining moment and charisma), the manner in which a government acquires power will not count for much in its legitimation. A coup d'état, for example, is not necessarily an illegitimate means of acquiring power in such a situation, although it may appear so to the outside observer.[40] The proper and effective use of power is more important. Before discussing this element, however, it is necessary to point out that conformity with established rules is much more relevant for the legitimation of governments than regimes. As rules emanate from a regime, conformity with them may indicate, but does not constitute, the regime's legitimacy.

Proper Use of Power

There are two aspects to the proper use of power. The first is government operating within the law or other tacitly accepted rules and procedures; the second is the effective use of power to promote the collective interest of the community—that is, performance. Although it has received less attention, the criterion of government operating within the law is a prerequisite for the continued legitimacy of governments deriving their authority from conformity with well-established rules. Further, such powers must be exercised only for the pursuit of the public good (security, welfare, justice) and not for private gain. Violation of the spirit or letter of the formal provisions or tacit understandings, as well as the use of public means for private gain (corruption), will undermine the legitimacy of the government even if it acquired power in accordance with established rules. The Watergate affair called into question the legitimacy of the Nixon administration in the United States, for example, while corruption undermined the legitimacy of the Tanaka and Takeshita governments in Japan. Abuse of power undermined the legitimacy of the Chatichai government in Thailand. Where abuse of power is enabled by the political system, it can erode the legitimacy of the regime—as reflected, for example, in the growing demand for political reform in Japan.

Definitions of legitimacy tend to exclude the issue of performance. Weber, for example, excludes "purely material interests and calculations of advantages" as a basis of authority because, in his view, they "do not form a sufficiently reliable basis for a system of imperative coordination."[41] Rodney Barker, arguing that legitimacy and the duty to obey are based on certain values and acknowledgment of authority, excludes "the substance of what [governments] do or what they wish to do" from his definition of legitimacy.[42] He rejects rational choice, performance, and superior skills as a basis of legitimate authority. David Held restricts the term "legitimacy" to normative agreement, excluding tradition, pragmatic acquiescence, and instrumental acceptance.[43]

Exclusion of performance as a basis of authority is primarily a consequence of viewing it as "authority by inducement." However, effective performance can be deployed to generate moral authority.[44] The enormous concentration of power in the state cannot be justified except in terms of its use in the pursuit of the collective interests of the political community. And success or failure in this endeavor affects the legitimation of government and the regime in which it is rooted.[45] Recognition of this potential has led all types of governments to claim the right to rule on the basis of their competence and achievements (or promised achievements).[46] Further, the realization of fundamental political, civil, and economic rights is also related to performance in guaranteeing the "collective will" of the community and enhancing the cultural and material welfare of the citizens. Thus performance, conceived broadly, as it should be, can be an effective resource in the cultivation of legitimacy.

Its importance, however, depends on the type of regime. Performance is less important in well-established democratic regimes because of their capacity for self-renewal. While an ineffective government can be turned out of office by the electorate, the issue is its effectiveness, not its legitimacy. In this regime, legitimacy is a function of conformity to established rules. Although George Bush was defeated in the 1992 elections because of a poor economic track record, at no time was the legitimacy of his administration in question. Prolonged ineffectiveness, however, may undermine the legitimacy of even relatively well established democratic regimes or at least some of their institutional aspects. Governments in regimes that lack the capacity for effective self-renewal will have to rely much more on effective performance to establish their right to rule.

The ends for which the state's power is used, as well as its success in achieving them, will undoubtedly influence the public's attitude, including allegiance toward the incumbent government, and define the substance of everyday political discourse. This discourse may be viewed as "latent" ideology, providing a link to the more abstract or "forensic" level of normative beliefs.[47] Viewed in this way, performance transcends the purely instrumental dimension and becomes a crucial element in the analysis of legitimacy. By emphasizing the practical level and connecting it to the abstract level, it ensures that discussion of legitimacy is firmly embedded in the reality of everyday discourse.

Consent of the Governed

Consent, the fourth element in the structure of legitimacy, "is a way of binding oneself, of creating self-assumed commitments."[48] Consent is given by individuals.[49] In the political realm, to give consent is to recognize the government's right to issue commands and to assume a duty to obey them. Duty-bound obedience should be distinguished from instrumental acceptance.[50] The commitment to obey is based on allegiance; instrumental acceptance is based on rewards. In practice it may be difficult to separate the two. Further, instrumental acceptance over the long term may become duty-bound obedience. Apathy and fearful obedience do not constitute consent.

Consent is crucial, for without public recognition there can be no authority. The nature, significance, and role of consent, however, depend on the type of regime. In a participatory regime, for example, an action must be free, informed, and intentional to qualify as consent. It must be active and performative—that is, it must create and support values. Participation in elections, while important, does not itself constitute consent. Such participation must be grounded in a firm belief in the underlying principles and must be coupled with active participation in the related institutions and procedures that constitute the system. The evidence for this must be established independently. Consent is especially significant in a participation-oriented regime; it is not irrelevant in other regimes, but it may be difficult to identify.

Consent of the administrative staff and strategic groups is critical for the legitimation of authoritarian and totalitarian regimes. Public consent relates more to the legitimation and execution of goals and policies than to the constitution of government.[51] Such consent, in these two regimes, is secured through mobilization. In theocratic and monarchical regimes, God's will and divine right constitute the basis of authority. Consent in both of these systems is passive. Obligation to obey is not incurred by agreement or participation but is presumed to exist unless withdrawn. In an Islamic state, for example, the duty to obey issues from religious obligation. But the follower is not required to obey a ruler who does not faithfully uphold the Islamic system. In this situation consent can be withdrawn with substantial delegitimating potential. In such systems the presence of consent is difficult to verify, but not its withdrawal.

Consent in general is given to the formal source of commands, not to their content. A person cannot make his obedience contingent upon his personal evaluation of the merits or demerits of the specific commands or their outcome. Sometimes a command may contravene religious and moral principles that have a higher standing in the individual's value hierarchy.[52] These cases, however, are exceptions. In general, consent implies a duty to obey the government in matters under the jurisdiction of the state irrespective of the content and outcome of commands. This, however, is not the same as blind obedience.[53] External conformity (following the command) must be distinguished from internal assent (believing in the command). When political disobedience appears on a massive scale, it reflects a lack of consent and erosion of the incumbent government's legitimacy and, depending on the underlying reasons, perhaps that of the regime as well.

The Hierarchy of Elements

For ease of reference, the four elements of legitimacy may be labeled as normative (shared norms and values), procedural (conformity to established rules), performance (proper and effective use of state power), and consent elements. While the four elements may be distinguished for analytical purposes, in practice they are closely interconnected. The normative element, for example, affects the validity of the rules that govern access to power. Without institutionalization, however, shared norms and values cannot have a practical impact. Similarly, the procedural element has an impact on the government's exercise of power and its performance. The latter, in turn, can reinforce, mitigate, or negate the legitimacy derived from conformity to rules. Consent is an integral part of the other three elements. Further, a weakness in one, so long as it is not fundamental, may be compensated by strength in another. Thus one must consider all four elements together in evaluating legitimacy.

A hierarchical layering may be discerned among the first three elements. As norms and values and the degree to which they are universalized determine the structure of domination as well as the relative strength of the regime, they affect the legitimating potential of the procedural and performance elements. When the normative element is strong, it will have the potential to legitimate the regime as well as the government that acquires power in conformity with the rules of the regime. Hence shared norms and values is the fundamental element. Further, in a well-established regime, because of the capacity for self-renewal, the procedural element is usually more important than performance. This hierarchy, however, does not always hold. In less well established regimes, performance is more important in the legitimation of governments. It can also contribute to a regime's legitimacy in the long run, although it cannot itself constitute the basis of a regime.

Satisfaction of all four elements confers a high degree of legitimacy on governments. In this situation, might is converted to right and obedience becomes duty. If certain elements are met less than satisfactorily, legitimacy will be strained. If the shortfall is acute or the violation flagrant, elite and public confidence in the government and the political system it represents will be undermined, a crisis may ensue, and the political institution may cease to be legitimate.

This discussion of the constituent elements reinforces a point made earlier: legitimacy is a complex, dynamic, variegated feature and a matter of degree rather than a simple dichotomy of legitimacy/illegitimacy. Indeed, all four elements of legitimacy are subject to change. Norms and values may change as a result of political, socioeconomic, and ideational changes—in Western Europe, for example, the basis of authority changed gradually from kingship to contractarianism to popular sovereignty. Similarly, the legitimacy of governments may vary over time—the same government may be more legitimate during certain periods, for example, and less so at other times. The reasons for obedience, too, may vary with different audiences in society—some may comply on normative grounds, while others may comply on the basis of calculation of advantages, others out of fear, and yet others out of lack of preferred alternatives. This is especially likely to be the case in multiethnic societies. Even a person's reasons for compliance may vary from issue to issue. Thus change is a constant and no political institution is permanently legitimate, although the legitimacy of some may be more durable than that of others. The legitimacy/illegitimacy dichotomy is only applicable with regard to governments in a well-established regime. In all other cases, legitimacy cannot be so concretely established. It is likely to be subjective and may be judged to be strong or weak—except of course during a crisis when a government and possibly the regime may be deemed to have been delegitimated.

Referent Objects of Legitimation

As legitimation of power is the goal of legitimators, it is useful to distinguish the political institutions that are connected with the concentration, regulation, and exercise of state power, for these institutions are usually the objects of legitimation exercises. In the literature on legitimacy, the state is usually cited as the referent object of legitimation. But it is too abstract and in practice is seldom the specific object of legitimation of power holders. Further, the term has many meanings, and the differences are substantial.[54] In this book the term 'state' is used in its generic conception and may be defined as "a structure of domination and coordination including a coercive apparatus and the means to administer society and extract resources from it."[55] In this generic conception the state is not in need of political legitimation. But three associated institutions—which are concerned with expressing political identity (nation-state), type of government (regime), and the actual control and exercise of state power (government)—do require legitimation and are usually the referent objects of legitimation projects undertaken by claimants to power.[56]

Nation-state refers to a political community whose territorial and juridical boundaries coincide with the boundaries of a nation.[57] According to Ernest Renan, a nation is a "living soul, a spiritual principle" constituted by two things: "One is the common possession of a rich heritage of memories; the other is the actual consent, the desire to live together, the will to preserve worthily the undivided inheritance which has been handed down. The nation, like the individual, is the outcome of a long past of efforts, and sacrifices, and devotion."[58] The nation is imagined, limited, and sovereign.[59] The idea that the nation should constitute the basis for political community, as well as the accompanying principle of national self-determination, while Western European in origin, now has universal appeal. As noted by Benedict Anderson, the idea of nation is now firmly entrenched and "nationalism is virtually inseparable from political consciousness."[60] Nation-state has become the ideal, and it is commonly assumed that every effort must be made to realize it—hence the emphasis on nation building, national integration, and the like.

Regime (or political system) refers to "the formal and informal organization of the center of political power, and of its relations with the broader society. A regime determines who has access to political power, and how those who are in power deal with those who are not."[61] In other words, it refers to the type of government, such as democracy, totalitarianism, and authoritarianism. In operational terms, regime refers to the principles, institutions, and procedures that constitute the political system. In the case of a democratic system, for example, the operational referents will include the principles of participation and contestation, the associated institutions (the constitution, legal system, political parties, elections, accountable executive and legislature, and independent judiciary), and procedures relating to the acquisition of power through elections and its exercise in accord with constitutional and legal provisions. Hence a change of regime requires a substantial change in the relationship between ruler and ruled and the manner of access to power. A mere change in the holders of office—for example, through a coup d'état in a military regime—does not qualify as a regime change. This characterization specifically excludes applying the label "regime" to specific holders of office (the Soeharto regime or the Thatcher regime).

Government refers to the actual exercise of political power within the framework of the regime and, more specifically, to those organizations and people charged with the duty of governing.[62] In operational terms, the government refers to the individuals, political parties, and other institutions such as the military and the bureaucracy that are in control of state power. Regimes, if they are well established, are more durable than governments. A well-established regime is one in which the rules for the acquisition and exercise of political power are clearly specified, commonly accepted, and scrupulously observed. In such a regime, governments come and go without affecting the nature of the regime itself. While this distinction between regime and government can be made with relative ease in advanced democratic states (as well as in some monarchies and certain authoritarian and Marxist-Leninist regimes), the low level of institutionalization in most developing states makes such distinctions more difficult but not impossible.[63] In Thailand, for example, there were several changes of government under the military regime from 1947 to 1973. More commonly the two institutions are fused: a change in government brings about a change in regime as well. Nevertheless this distinction has its analytical uses, especially in evaluating the progress made in legitimating power over

a long period. In reality, all three referent objects of political legitimation—nation-state, regime, and government—are relatively new in developing states, thus accentuating the contested nature of political legitimacy.

Critical Audiences

That consent by the public is vital for the legitimation of power today is
beyond doubt. The public, however, is not one entity but many individuals and groups "with different levels of engagements, values, intensities,
and weight."[64] As the elite groups have greater control over power resources and are more engaged in the political process, shared norms and
consent among the elite are more important than among the general public. And groups that have an effective capacity for articulation and mobilization are even more crucial because of their multiplier effect. Without
their leadership, grievances remain localized; rarely will they have the potential to undermine the legitimacy of a national government. The crucial
role of the elite is emphasized in the definition of legitimacy advanced by
Arthur L. Stinchcombe: "A power is legitimate to the degree that, by virtue
of the doctrine and norms by which power is justified, the power holder
can call upon sufficient other centers of power, as reserve in case of need,
to make his power effective."[65] The limiting condition according to this
definition is not acceptance of the norms and values by the public at large
but by the other centers of power.
  This condition is particularly relevant to communist and authoritarian
regimes. While acceptance by the citizens would enhance the moral basis
and self-esteem of such regimes, their legitimacy depends on acceptance
by state institutions or "political forces to be found within the circle of
power."[66] Thus Weber's emphasis on the solidarity of the administrative
staff is not irrelevant to the legitimacy of certain contemporary regimes.[67]
Semidemocratic and democratic regimes, on the other hand, will require
broad-based support. Even here, however, because of the low level of political participation, acceptance by the elite groups and state institutions
such as the armed forces and civilian bureaucracy continues to be critical.
  The key role of power centers suggests that a high degree of normative
integration among strategic groups is crucial for the legitimation of government. Insofar as a stake is created for most if not all groups, conflict is
internalized. Seymour Martin Lipset captures the critical role of strategic
groups in his argument that a crisis of legitimacy will ensue if, in the
course of transition to a new social structure, the status of major conservative institutions is threatened or access to politics is denied to new
groups.[68] This argument suggests that an inclusionary approach by a

dominant group with a unifying vision for the country as a whole and the capacity to incorporate the demands of other strategic groups in society is likely to be more successful in legitimating itself than an exclusionary one—especially in countries experiencing a rapid increase in social and political mobilization, as well as in multiethnic states where ethnicity continues to be a strong contender for the construction of political identity.

Although the masses are less important than elites and strategic groups, the salience of popular mandate is growing. Incumbents as well as competing groups increasingly seek to justify or challenge the right to domination in the name of the people.[69] Increased opportunities for voluntary political association and participation, along with the development of civil society, will further enhance the legitimating role of the masses. Where civil society is more developed, the interests, expectations, demands, and support of the masses will count for much more in the political process. The accompanying necessity to respond to their demands reduces the power and autonomy of strategic groups. Instead of being merely passive and facilitative, the public will begin to influence strategic groups and create new ones to serve its interests and expectations.

The interplay between mass-level predisposition and elite-level political initiatives will become more significant. Although initially the interaction may center on exchange relationships of a utilitarian kind, in due course it is likely to affect public attitudes toward the system of government as well. The masses can play a critical role in the delegitimation of government and regime. Faced with massive protests and uprisings, the incumbents are rendered morally bankrupt and impotent. This development could lead to the collapse of the government and perhaps the regime. And if governments respond with repression, their moral authority is likely to be further eroded.

Key Points

This chapter may be summarized in six key points. First: Legitimacy is the belief by the governed in the ruler's moral right to issue commands and the people's corresponding obligation to obey such commands. Political legitimation is an interactive process between ruler and ruled. Conceived as an outcome of this process, legitimacy is contingent, dynamic, and continuously defined. Its cultivation must therefore be unending. As the interaction between ruler and ruled lies at the heart of the legitimacy question, it must be framed in the context of a specific society at a specified time.

Second: A command-obedience relationship is legitimate if the political order in which it is rooted is based on shared norms and values, if the government acquired power in conformity with established rules, if it exercises that power within prescribed limits for the promotion of the community's collective interest, and if the governed have given their consent to the incumbent government. While these four elements of legitimacy may be distinguished for analytical purposes, in practice they are interrelated and must be considered together.

Third: Because of its potential to influence procedure, performance, and consent, the normative element is fundamental. In an established regime, the procedural element is usually more significant than performance. These hierarchies do not hold, however, if the norms and values are not widely shared. In this case, performance and the other elements discussed in the next chapter will become more significant for political legitimation of the incumbent government.

Fourth: In light of the plurality of referent objects, critical audiences, and constituent elements, political legitimacy is necessarily complex and variegated. Further, except in a well-established regime and during moments of political crisis, legitimacy is likely to be a matter of degree (strong/weak rather than legitimate/illegitimate).

Fifth: The nation-state, the regime, and the government are the three political institutions that power holders commonly seek to legitimate. Shared identity is crucial for the legitimation of the nation-state, shared norms and values for regime legitimation, and conformity with established rules and performance for government legitimation.

Sixth: Allegiance of the administrative staff, strategic groups, and the elite is crucial for political legitimation, especially in authoritarian, totalitarian, and monarchical systems. The significance of the masses for political legitimation is especially great in a participatory system. The masses have substantial delegitimating potential in all political systems.

2

The Bases of Legitimacy

MUTHIAH ALAGAPPA

AUTHORITY may be claimed on the basis of one or more elements of legitimacy discussed in the preceding chapter. Two of the three types of authority cited by Weber (belief in the sanctity of tradition and belief in legality) relate essentially to the procedural element of legitimacy.[1] The force of authority derived from conforming with established rules, however, depends in large measure on a high level of commitment to the norms and values in which it is rooted. As noted by Weber himself, reliance on procedure is more suited to societies in which a normative framework has been sanctioned or is contested only at the margins.[2]

This is not the case in many developing countries. Their political systems are still weak and contested and embryonic. Normative frameworks about how things ought to be—and the incorporation of relations of power into these frameworks—are still being worked out, often through struggle including the use of force.[3] Consequently the level of institutionalization is low and the preconditions for employing the procedural element as the basis of domination are absent or present only in rudimentary form. Conformity with institutions and procedures in this situation cannot confer legitimacy. In the absence of a well-established regime, the emphasis in political legitimation shifts to the normative and performance elements. In the first case—the normative element—the concern is with prescribed goals or values for society on the basis of which the incumbent power holders seek to construct a normative framework. In the second case—performance—the concern is less with the use of power within the law and more with its effective use for promotion of the collective welfare. In addition to normative goals and performance, authority may also be claimed on the basis of charisma, a politically defining moment, and international support.

These rationales—normative goals, performance, charisma, politically defining moment, and international support—are better viewed, at least initially, as resources that may be mobilized in support of the legitimacy claim.[4] Their conception as resources ensures that the role of power in legitimation is incorporated into analysis. Resources may be deployed manipulatively to advance certain interests by presenting them as an idealized vision for the whole society or by using them to structure the rules and regulations.[5] Only when the claim to domination has been acknowledged by the other strategic groups and the public should these resources be viewed as a basis of authority. This chapter examines the potency of these various rationales for the legitimation of power and their institutionalization potential.

Normative Goals

Prescribed goals for a society can cover a broad spectrum. At one end are ideological goals such as building a democratic (the Philippines under Aquino) or socialist state (Vietnam). As a system of beliefs and attitudes associated with social groups and having the potential to determine political, economic, and moral objectives, ideology can be mobilized to justify domination. Moreover, such goals have the potential to constitute a specific political system. As there is a necessary link between the goal posited and the political system, these goals, for ease of reference, may be called system-defining goals.

At the other end of the spectrum are goals like national liberation (North Vietnam until 1975), ethnic protection (Malaysia), or survival (Singapore) that can be deployed to justify domination but do not themselves define a specific political system. They can, however, be linked to a particular political system on the grounds that only this system can facilitate attainment of the goal. A socialist system of government was presented by the Communist Party of Vietnam as inseparable from the goal of national liberation. In Singapore, the curtailment of certain key features of democracy has been presented as essential for the survival of a small island-state. The modification of the democratic system in Malaysia has also been presented as necessary to ensure Malay dominance, which in turn has been claimed as essential for national survival given the ethnic makeup of that country. As there is no necessary conceptual link between the goal and the political system advocated, these goals may be called non-system-defining goals.

At this end of the spectrum one also finds goals like building a good society (the Burmese Way to Socialism) or a new society (the Philippines under Marcos) or a Pancasila state (Indonesia). Although they have been presented as system-defining goals, their potential in this respect is limited. Because of the emotional benefits that attach to commitments to raise not only the nation's living standards but also its profile in the international community, the nexus between economic goals and nationalism in the form of "national" economic goals like "catching up with the West" (Japan in the interwar and postwar periods) or achieving developed country status (Malaysia's Vision 2020, Singapore's Next Lap, Next Century) may also be used to mobilize support for legitimacy claims.

As it would be impossible to cover every conceivable goal or value here, we confine our discussion to those that are particularly relevant to the countries studied in this book: goal-rational ideologies, popular sovereignty, and religion. The following sections outline the nature and content of these resources, the grounds on which their deployment may be contested, and their institutionalization potential.

Goal-Rational Ideologies

While all ideologies may be deployed as goals, certain ideologies such as communism envision specific goals for the society. The ultimate goal prescribed for society underpins the claim to authority in goal-rational systems. Institutions and persons claim their authority on the basis of the rational relationship between the ultimate goal and the roles assigned to them in the system. Thus the prescribed tasks and roles form the basis for evaluating their actions. Task achievement takes precedence over process and rule compliance.

This is the case with Marxist-Leninist governments in Vietnam, Laos, and until recently Cambodia, governments that have justified their domination on the basis of salvation through communism and the virtue of building a communist society.[6] The tasks and roles of the communist party, the government, and social organizations are legitimated in terms of their relationship to this ultimate goal.[7] Monopoly of knowledge—that is, "its infallible insight into the course and goals of history"—legitimates the party.[8] The party is the authoritative interpreter of the works of Marx, Engels, Lenin, Mao, Deng, and Ho. Government authority in Marxist-Leninist regimes is legitimated in terms of its role as an instrument of the party to realize the ultimate goal, as well as through the principle of popular sovereignty. When these two methods of legitimation are found to be incompatible, the issue is resolved in favor of the party.[9]

Building an ideal national society is particularly appealing and frequently employed in support of the claim to legitimacy in developing countries. In Southeast Asia, the "Burmese Way to Socialism" and the goal of building a "new society" in the Philippines both fit the mold of goal rationality. Burma's "System of Correlation of Man and His Environment," which underpinned the state ideology, justified the role of the Burma Socialist Program Party (BSPP) and the state (government) and provided the framework for analyzing, implementing, and evaluating the achievements of these two institutions.[10] The role of the BSPP was justified on the basis of the historical role of the working people; the role of the party and the state was to provide leadership in the pursuit of progress and "good."[11] In the Philippines, Ferdinand Marcos justified the martial law regime on the basis of the presumed need to save the republic and create a new, more egalitarian society.[12] According to Marcos, only a revolution from the center could lead to the creation of this new society. This, in his view, justified the break from the "old system" and its replacement by a new "constitutional authoritarian" system in which the style and tenure of "leadership will depend not upon the wiles and manipulations of oligarchs and political lords but upon its own performance, upon its ability to justify the people's faith in democratic government."[13]

Although national ideologies like Pancasila (Indonesia) and Rukunegara (Malaysia) fall short of goal rationality, they nevertheless seek to establish principles and values that the incumbents deem vital for the development of a viable polity. These governments have not sought to justify specific institutions in the name of these ideologies, but they have used them to justify, at least in part, the general structure of domination and their policies. As self-appointed custodians, the incumbents frequently seek to control the content and the "true" or "correct" interpretation of national ideologies. Contrary interpretations and alternative ideologies are labeled subversive. National ideologies are employed to delegitimate opposition groups and policies.

In claiming the right to rule on the basis of a certain societal goal, the legitimator usually seeks to persuade others to accept its sectional values as those of the community as a whole. This strategy may be pursued at the level of discourse (the discursive mode) as well as at the level of practical social conduct (the institutional mode).[14] Expediency and manipulation characterize the discursive mode; the connection of signification to legitimation in favor of existing social relations characterizes the institutional mode. In presenting sectional interests as universal values, contradictions are denied or their locus is obscured; existing social relations are presented as having always existed: fixed, immutable, and therefore natural.[15]

As noted by James Scott, however, "the very process of attempting to legitimate a social order by idealizing it always provides its subjects with the means, the symbolic tools, the very ideas for a critique that operates within the hegemony."[16] Expediency and manipulation can easily be penetrated and prevent the achievement of hegemony, while the knowledge of social actors and the contingent character of social practice can minimize if not negate the effects of structure. Audiences can draw upon other resources, paradigms, and subaltern traditions to resist and contest the claim to legitimacy. Success in realizing hegemony, as discussed in the preceding chapter, depends on the dominant group's ability to transcend its corporate interests and integrate the interests of the other social groups into its own. Only by fusing all elements into a "collective will" can the dominant group credibly claim to represent the interests of the entire community.[17] Further, the dominant group must satisfy the interests of the other social groups if it is to secure their support and compliance. Failure to satisfy these conditions is likely to lead to resistance and contestation of the incumbent government's authority.

The legitimacy of a government claiming authority on the basis of goal rationality may be contested on several grounds: the correctness of the goal itself, rival interpretations of the substance of the goal, alleged deviation from a specified goal or value, or failure to attain the goal. Any combination of these factors—as well as the presence and vitality of competing norms at the international level—may contribute to a crisis of faith in the goal-rational ideology. Giuseppe Di Palma, for example, argues that such a crisis of faith on the part of the rulers in Eastern European states was a key factor in the rebounding of society and the collapse of communist regimes. According to Di Palma, the loss of confidence opened the gate for venting of popular resentment, which, in turn, confirmed to the communist rulers that they had lost the right to rule. This recognition further broadened the appeal of resistance and sped the mobilization of society.[18]

Although Weber discusses goal-rational legitimacy as a type of authority, he does not regard it as being on a par with his three pure types of legitimate domination.[19] His supporters have justified this exclusion on the grounds that domination of this type is achieved on the basis of some principle that is not within the exclusive domain of the state.[20] Thus while the government may enjoy power on the basis of the value in question, legitimacy is not inherent in the state but derives from an external body that has command of the legitimizing value. The state is merely an agent.

This difficulty may be resolved by indigenizing universal ideologies (Burmese Way to Socialism, Pancasila democracy, Confucian democracy) and claiming unique authority for the government in the interpretation of the "new" or "national" ideology—as continues to be the case in many developing countries including the remaining communist countries as well as theocratic states like Iran.[21] As this claim does not preclude challenges to the legitimacy of governments on the basis of rival interpretations, however, it is a less satisfactory form of legitimation than that based on accepted rules and procedures.

The legitimating and institutionalization potential of goal-rational ideologies depends on a number of considerations. First the goal must be accepted by all or most of the strategic groups as relevant and valid for the whole society. The conditions for this were outlined earlier. Second, progress must be made in realizing the goal. If reality is substantially different from the posited goal, then belief in the goal and the associated political system will decline. Third, the goal must have the potential to constitute a specific political system. While this is the case with universal ideologies, it is not necessarily so with many indigenous ones. As noted earlier, goals like national liberation, ethnic protection, and survival do not themselves necessarily define a political system. Thus even when there is agreement on a goal, this need not translate into agreement on the nature of the political system. Further, goal attainment often takes precedence over rule compliance in goal-rational systems. In fact the rules may be continuously amended on the ground that this is required for goal attainment. Frequent changes, especially if they are perceived as self-serving, are likely to hinder institutionalization, thus preventing the procedural element from becoming the primary basis for political legitimation.

Popular Sovereignty

The belief that sovereignty resides in the people is now widely acknowledged. Although the origins of this essentially Western notion can be traced to earlier periods,[22] the English and particularly the French revolutions in the seventeenth and eighteenth centuries mark the beginning of the modern development of the idea of popular mandate. The French Revolution destroyed royal authority and instituted the new principle that sovereign authority emanates from the people or the nation and that "the central government is the only legitimate executor of that authority."[23]

The English and American revolutions and the later French one have had a powerful resonance throughout the world. Nationalism, anticolonialism, social revolution, secession, and other political movements have been waged on the principle that people are the ultimate source of authority. Commercialization, industrialization, integration of national economies into a global market economy, higher levels of education, the accompanying growth of the middle and working classes and a civil society, the dramatic collapse of authoritarian and communist regimes in other countries, the growing international ethos in favor of democracy and human rights—all have the power to sharpen the public's political consciousness and fuel demands for political participation. Thus the political significance of popular sovereignty in developing countries appears likely to increase. This trend is reflected in the growing number of governments that seek to justify their rule by claiming a popular mandate or portraying their rule as serving the people. Opposition, too, is often framed in the name of the people.

The idea of popular sovereignty may be conceived in two ways: as the collective will of the people (outcome-oriented conception) or as a power relationship among individuals in arriving at outcomes (process-oriented conception).[24] The notion of collective will has been criticized on a number of counts: the difficulty in identifying a popular will, the difficulty of devising suitable institutional arrangements to give effect to such a will even if one can be identified, the incapacity of the many to make sound judgments, and the potential for anarchy and totalitarianism.[25] J. L. Talmon contends that the idea of popular sovereignty, because of its potential to provide "a theoretical expression of the will of the people that gains a voice (through the program of a vanguard party or by the leaders of a mass movement) independent of the outcomes of voting or the actual preferences of the members of society," contains the seeds of totalitarian democracy.[26]

Because of its emphasis on the collective will and its inattention to the mode of expressing the people's will, democratic theorists have refrained from using the idea of popular sovereignty conceived as a collective political will.[27] Instead the emphasis in defining democracy has been on the procedural dimension. In the process-oriented conception of popular sovereignty, relationships of power and background conditions are emphasized along with a focus on political decision making. Citizens must be independent and they must have access to equal resources to affect the process for making a social choice. Julie Mostov observes: "The degree to which constitutional law and the distribution of resources support this relationship [independence and equality] indicates the degree to which a people is sovereign."[28]

The democratic system of government is closely associated with popular sovereignty, but the two must be distinguished. As noted earlier, definitions of democracy tend to ignore the collective will aspect of popular sovereignty and focus instead on the procedural dimension—stressing participation, contestation for office, processes that affect policymaking, and accountability of policymakers. Nevertheless, democracy (regardless of the variations in institutional arrangements) ultimately rests on the idea that it is government of, for, and by the people as opposed to government of, for, and by an individual or a few people.

Popular sovereignty, particularly the collective will interpretation of it, can be mobilized to support the legitimacy claims of other regimes—communism, authoritarianism, and monarchy—as well. Its role varies from system to system. Government authority in Marxist-Leninist regimes is formally proclaimed on the principle of popular sovereignty. The purpose, however, is not to offer political choice but to encourage popular identification with the system. Mass mobilization, moreover, is used to suppress opposing viewpoints. Further, popular sovereignty in communist regimes is restricted to the working class. In authoritarian regimes, popular sovereignty is not the basis for constitution of government, but it is deployed to increase the self-esteem of rulers, silence domestic opposition, ward off international pressures, gain international legitimacy, and generally to consolidate the position of the incumbents. Elections are controlled and, where necessary, rigged to demonstrate that the government has the support of the people. Often, authoritarian governments opt for nominated parliaments on the ground that elected ones are less legitimate because of the corruption and vote buying that characterize elections. Some claim that nominated parliaments have greater potential to be inclusive and therefore to be more representative of people from all walks of life—and hence will be in a better position to determine the "true" interests of the people. Authoritarian governments may also seek to justify their hold on power by claiming that they can better serve the interests of the people. An extension of this argument is that "ordinary" people are not in a position to decide what is good for the country as a whole. Out of concern for their immediate interests, laypeople may behave "irrationally." Hence they must be guided and this requires limitations on participation and contestation.[29]

While popular sovereignty may be harnessed to support the legitimation claims of nondemocratic regimes, this principle can also be mobilized to contest their legitimacy. This has been the experience of countries with authoritarian and Marxist-Leninist regimes. Exposure to beliefs and practices associated with popular sovereignty, however restrictive they may be, inculcates belief in them, thus increasing their significance in the long run. Such factors appear to have been crucial in the political protests and revolutions in Burma, the Philippines, and Thailand, to cite just a few examples. Despite the close association, a democratic system is not spared contestation on the basis of the principle of popular sovereignty. It has to contend with difficult questions like who should have voting rights and whether the present legal and social conditions do in fact provide for independence and equality of citizens. Rapid political mobilization on the basis of popular sovereignty by contributing to excessive demands, polarization of society, and breakdown of law and order may overburden the democratic system and undermine its legitimacy—as, for example, in the Philippines in the 1960s, in Thailand during the 1973–76 period, and in India, particularly during the premierships of Indira and Rajiv Gandhi.

Popular sovereignty can be deployed both to challenge and to sustain existing power relations.[30] Beginning in the seventeenth century, popular sovereignty was deployed to challenge and ultimately displace the principle of hereditary monarchy as the basis of government in many countries. While popular sovereignty is not the only consideration, its growing significance suggests that the remaining monarchies and authoritarian governments will, in varying degrees, be vulnerable to challenges on the basis of this principle. Marxist-Leninist movements have challenged the legitimacy of incumbent power holders, in part, on the basis of their claimed representation of the proletariat and have used the same principle to justify the subsequent enormous concentration of power in the state. At another level, the right to "national" self-determination, which is closely linked to popular sovereignty, was deployed to challenge and displace the authority of colonial powers. In the postindependence era, however, the same groups, now governments, have in the interest of self-preservation and stability sought to restrict the application self-determination to those people under white or foreign domination. This, however, has not prevented other indigenous communities from deploying the same principle to contest the legitimacy of the nation-state, regime, and government. In light of the multifaceted aspects of popular sovereignty, its role and significance cannot be confined within prescribed limits. Hence the legitimacy of regimes in which popular sovereignty plays a significant but subordinate role or no role at all, as well as regimes in which popular sovereignty is the mainstay, is likely to be subject to continuous contestation and change.

Religion

Religion is not the primary basis for political domination in any Southeast Asian country at present, but its political significance is growing, especially in Malaysia, Indonesia, and Brunei. Religious sanctions have long been mobilized to legitimate kingship as well as rule by clergy. Authority derived directly from God (divinity and divine right) has served to justify the rule of monarchs, whereas deputization and custody of the moral and material heritage of the prophets have underscored the clergy's claim to legitimacy. With the growth of secularism in the Western European states and its extension to other parts of the world through colonialism, the potency of religion as a legitimating resource has declined in most countries. Of late, however, its political significance appears to be on the rise. While attention has focused largely on Islam, other religions (Buddhism, Hinduism, Catholicism) have also become politically more significant. Huntington, for example, cites the "striking changes in the doctrines and activities of the Catholic Church . . . and the transformation of national

churches from defenders of the status quo to opponents of authoritarianism" as one of the key changes that contributed to the Third Wave transition from authoritarian to democratic rule.[31]

In the contemporary period, the significance of religion for political
legitimation is twofold. First, the moral authority of religion and the
"church" may be employed to delegitimate and bring about a regime
change without altering the secular character of the state—the role of the
Philippine Catholic church in the removal of Marcos is an example.[32] Second, religion may be deployed to define the political community and
structure of domination. Religion has been successfully employed to establish theocratic states in the contemporary era. The effort to constitute
authority on the basis of religion is the focus of this section—especially
Islam, which explicitly combines religion and politics and which has been
mobilized by political groups in several Southeast Asian states.

The legitimacy of the command-obedience relationship in Islam derives
from the common acknowledgment by both ruler and ruled that Allah is
the only source of authority, that it is the ruler's duty to respect and en-
force the holy laws and create the conditions necessary to fulfill the precepts of Islam, and that it is the believer's duty to obey God, his prophet,
and those in authority.[33] The duty to obey derives from religious obligation. Disobedience is therefore a sin and a crime. Rulers in Islamic states
have emphasized the duty to obey with a view to consolidating and enhancing their position. Such obligation, however, is not unlimited. Drawing upon the earlier career of the Prophet Muhammad when he was engaged in opposing the pagan regime in Mecca, the radical tradition in
Islam emphasizes that obedience is owed only to just rulers—that is, those
who rule in accord with the holy laws.[34] Disobedience and revolution
against those who are deemed unjust are justified. As there are no clearly
defined rules to determine who is just or unjust, different interpretations
giving rise to religious and political tensions are relatively common. Islam,
like other religions, has been harnessed to support a variety of regimes
ranging from absolute monarchy in Saudi Arabia and Kuwait to a full-
blown theocratic state in Iran.

The existence of different schools of thought, the inherent potential for
conflicting interpretations, and the clear demarcation of political community in Islam have several consequences for political legitimation. First,
authority claimed on the basis of Islam will not be free of disputation.
Rival claimants to political power can contest the legitimacy of the incumbent government on the ground that the latter's version of Islam is not
authentic. The Ayatollah Khomeini, for example, supported revolutions
abroad on the basis that his was the only true, authentic, and universal
form of Islam: all other models were "falsifiers of Islam." Second, in coun-

tries with a majority Muslim population in which the authority of government derives from secular beliefs, Islam will remain a formidable competing basis for political authority. While Islam can be employed in a supplementary fashion, such coexistence is likely to be uneasy, tension-ridden, and, over the long run, difficult to confine within prescribed limits. This is not to argue that coexistence is impossible or that secularism cannot take root in states with Muslim majorities; it is only to point out that there are basic incompatibilities which can be exploited by rival claimants to power. Third, an increase in the significance of Islam as the source of political authority in such countries is likely to be accompanied by an erosion in the political position of religious minorities, leading in the worst case to disenfranchisement.[35] Fourth, in states where there is a significant Muslim minority, Islam can be mobilized to reject the authority of the political center and fuel demands for autonomy and secession (as in southern Thailand and the southern Philippines).

Performance

As elaborated in Chapter 1, proper and effective use of power to promote the collective well-being of the political community can generate moral authority. Indeed it has been widely employed by governments to justify their control of state power, while poor performance is frequently advanced by those contesting the incumbent's right to rule. Performance here is defined to encompass the security, welfare, and justice functions of government and not just economic performance. Although performance is a key resource, it suffers a number of limitations.

First, legitimation on the basis of performance is highly contingent—and therefore, as pointed out by Weber, it is unreliable as a long-term basis of authority.[36] Apart from the fact that governments must continuously do better in order to meet rising expectations ("what have you done for me lately?"), performance, especially economic performance, is not fully within the control of present-day governments. Growing internationalization and the dependent character of the economies of nearly all developing countries imply that while governments have the power to mismanage their economies, good performance depends on the state of the global economy as well. Legitimation, to the extent that it can be based on economic performance, then becomes a function of the global economy. As this relationship is imperfectly understood by the lay public, opposition groups may manipulate the situation to contest the legitimacy of the incumbent government.

Second, while good performance may enhance legitimation, it can also

undermine the legitimacy of certain governments.[37] Authoritarian governments face a perpetual "performance dilemma." Both good and bad performance can undermine their legitimacy. Success in addressing an external security problem or in restoring law and order in the country, while
enhancing initial legitimacy, will in the long run make this rationale less
salient and force governments to search for alternatives. The fear of domestic turmoil, however, may continue to make this rationale salient in
some countries, especially multiethnic ones.[38] Economic growth and industrialization give rise to new socioeconomic and political groups and
demands that cannot be accommodated without a change in the nature of
the regime, as demonstrated by the experience of Taiwan and South Korea
as well as that of Thailand.[39] Moreover, economic growth can be counterproductive if the costs and benefits are not shared equally and the growth
accentuates inequalities along ethnic, religious, and regional lines. To enhance legitimacy, good economic performance must be accompanied by
distributive justice.

Third, although good performance can generate moral authority, it is
quite instrumental in character. Thus performance itself is too narrow a
basis of authority. Governments relying excessively on performance will
be vulnerable to challenge on the basis of greater rewards as well as force.
While force is an integral part of authority, it cannot by itself constitute
the basis of authority. Rule by force alone will be challenged, and power
holders will experience a perpetual state of insecurity. Thus even in totalitarian regimes, where terror and intimidation are used extensively to
control the society at large, solidarity must characterize relations among
personnel in the top echelon if trust and stability are to be maintained. A
political order that relies entirely on force will collapse as soon as greater
force can be mobilized against it.

Fourth, since performance relates directly to the actual exercise of
power, it is more relevant to the legitimation of governments than regimes.
Even for governments, performance is of major importance only when the
normative and procedural elements of legitimacy are weak. The capacity
for self-renewal makes performance less significant for government legitimation in well-established regimes. The consequences of performance for
a regime's legitimacy will be greater if the government and the regime are
fused, as is the case in many developing states, or if a change in government is unlikely to bring about the required effectiveness. Sustained good
performance over a prolonged period will engender confidence in the regime; a persistently bad record will have the reverse effect—as illustrated
by the recent experiences of the Soviet Union and the Eastern European
countries. Fledgling democratic regimes, by and large, are unable to survive poor performance. In Latin America, for example, poor economic

performance often provides the necessary cause for opposition forces, usually the military, to oust democratic governments.[40] Only well-established democratic regimes appear to be capable of weathering poor performance without a significant impact on their legitimacy. While performance may credit or discredit a regime, it cannot itself provide the basis for articulation of a new regime. Only political belief systems have this potential.

Finally, while performance affects legitimation, the reverse is also true. A legitimate government, because it can formulate and implement policies independent of the vested interests of other powerful groups, is better able to undertake long-term policies and mobilize greater resources for productive use.[41] This course will further enhance its legitimacy, creating a virtuous cycle. In this situation, performance can make a significant contribution to a regime's institutionalization. A government whose legitimacy is contested, on the other hand, will have to invest scarce resources in keeping itself in power—thus negatively affecting performance. Poor performance further undermines its legitimacy. The government becomes locked in a vicious cycle, discrediting the regime in which it is rooted.

Thus the nexus between performance and legitimation is both complex and dynamic. While good performance can be vital for legitimation of governments, it is highly contingent in character and can in some cases undermine legitimacy. On balance, the delegitimating potential of poor performance would appear to be much greater than the legitimating potential of good performance. Further, performance cannot substitute for political beliefs and thus has only an indirect impact on a regime's legitimacy. Nevertheless, it has the power to promote or hinder a regime's institutionalization.

Other Legitimation Resources

In addition to normative goals and performance, other resources—charisma, a politically defining moment, and international support—may also be deployed to support legitimacy claims.

Charisma

Weber uses the term charisma (a gift of divine grace) to refer to those who are "set apart from ordinary men and treated as endowed with supernatural, superhuman, or at least specifically exceptional powers or qualities."[42] He views charismatic authority as a revolutionary type for exceptional situations.[43] Although many leaders may lack charisma as

Weber defines it, they do command power and authority that may be used as a resource in support of their claim to the right to rule. In Southeast Asia political leaders like Sukarno and Soeharto in Indonesia, Aung San and Ne Win in Burma, Ho Chi Minh in Vietnam, Marcos in the Philippines, Lee Kuan Yew in Singapore, and Tunku Abdul Rahman in Malaysia have commanded substantial power and authority that they have deployed to legitimate their governments.[44] The deployment of such power and authority for political legitimation will be explored here.

Explanations of the power and authority of leaders invariably draw upon history and political culture. It has, for example, been argued that in precolonial Southeast Asia power and authority were not sharply distinguished, that power was customarily concentrated in the ruler, and that this continues to be the case today.[45] As power in these countries did not have a negative connotation, there was no reason to control it. In fact, concentration of power in the ruler, as opposed to separation and checks and balances of power, appears to have been the norm. Indeed, this practice was viewed as a mark of stable rule. While individual leaders could be judged as good or bad in terms of their conduct measured against ethical codes, power itself was seen as a positive or at least neutral good that accrued to persons with merit. Power conferred status, and deference was owed to persons of high status. Despite the many political changes (Dutch colonialism, Japanese occupation, the national revolution) and the socioeconomic changes they brought about, Benedict Anderson argues that "the cultural grip of this traditional perspective remains strong" in Indonesia.[46]

In a similar vein, Lucian Pye contends that although Europe succeeded in imposing its legalistic concept of the nation-state, traditional cultures remain decisive in determining the course of political developments in Asia.[47] In Pye's view, the widespread persistence of authoritarian rule in Asia can be explained by Asia's political cultures, which "share the common denominator of idealizing benevolent, paternalistic leadership, and of legitimizing dependency." The authority of leaders and the political system in certain Southeast Asian states has been explained in terms of patron-client relations as well, a concept rooted in traditional ideas about power and societal relations. Some have argued that a vast network of such ties linking the various levels from the barrio to the national level, with the president as supreme patron, underpins the legitimacy of the political order in the Philippines.[48] It has also been argued that personal rulership in developing states relies on a new kind of patrimonialism where authority is based not on traditional regimes or belief in the ruler's unique qualities but on personal loyalties, material incentives, and rewards.[49]

If these propositions are accepted, the procedural element of legitimacy can be deemed less important in Asian countries. This indeed appears to have been the case in precolonial Southeast Asia.[50] While rules for accession to the throne did exist, they were frequently violated. Usurpation, which was common, was readily legitimized through court rituals involving only palace officials. The question here is the relevance of this practice in the contemporary period.

As pointed out in Chapter 1, history and political culture are crucial in the construction of norms and values and offer important insights into power and authority in contemporary states.[51] Care must be taken, however, to avoid the tyranny of history and a static conception of culture that commits one to an ideological conservatism making it difficult to explain change. In light of the numerous layers that constitute "national" political culture, clearly it can support more than one way of life.[52] Only if this proposition is accepted does it become possible to explain political conflict and change.[53] Further, as noted earlier, culture is a resource that can be selectively employed to support or contest the right to rule. So-called traditions may be of quite recent vintage—invented to establish the authenticity of communities, to legitimize political institutions and status relationships, and to inculcate value systems and behavior.[54] The notion of invented tradition is particularly relevant here as many of the political institutions in the developing countries are unprecedented.

As Clifford Geertz cautions, "in [this] garden of metaphors almost any hypothesis discerning a form of thought in a piece of action has a certain logic. . . . The main temptation to be resisted is jumping to conclusions."[55] Our task is to historicize the links between cultural themes and political development rather than to apply deductive logic. In light of these considerations, an approach that views culture as a dynamic force rooted in the past but also adapting to changing times and constructed to serve present needs will be more helpful in exploring the role of personal authority for legitimating government and regime in the modern state. Note, too, that the accumulation of power by individuals is facilitated not only by political culture but also by the circumstances of the situation, their leadership role in advocating a new belief system, and the low level of political institutionalization that is characteristic of many developing countries.

Weber's discussion of charismatic authority is relevant in exploring the significance of personal authority for political legitimation. When a leader is believed to have charisma, this alone may suffice as the basis of authority. Yet this is not always the case. Sukarno, despite his charisma, had to enter into a coalition with the army and the Communist Party to consolidate his position. Very few leaders have charisma of the type defined by Weber. Thus personal authority, while important, is usually insufficient. Other resources—popular sovereignty, performance, international support—are also harnessed to bolster the right to rule. These resources are not necessarily complementary, however, and could, in the long run, because of their potential to provide a competing basis for legitimation, be harnessed by competing groups to contest the legitimacy of government founded on personal authority.

Legitimation based on personal authority is less durable because it is vulnerable to collapse if the leader dies or suffers setbacks that raise doubts about his or her charisma. In light of the difficulty of solving the succession problem, personal authority can rarely be institutionalized and is therefore transitory. It can, however, be employed to institutionalize a political system based on ideology. For this to happen, the leader must be committed to the ideology and earnestly pursue routinization.[56] As this strategy involves a reduction in their own authority, very few leaders have been willing to adopt it. In fact it is highly likely that leaders may deliberately seek to weaken institutions to shore up their own position and power.[57] There is a tension between personal authority and institutionalization that more often than not, because of the leader's self-interest, is likely to work against institutionalization.

Politically Defining Moment

A politically defining moment is one of high political consciousness that can generate deep emotion and galvanize enormous support for a cause. The moment may be a single event or, more likely, the culmination of a string of related events such as national independence, revolution, civil war, holocaust, and international warfare. Inevitably there are differences over which moments are politically defining and why. Their significance may be contested as well. Nevertheless, some moments achieve a widely if not universally accepted political definition.

By its very nature, a politically defining moment has enormous moral authority that can legitimate certain causes while delegitimating others. Political institutions may be legitimated or delegitimated by these moments. If the event is inspired by a specific belief and waged by a united movement, as was the case with the Islamic revolution in Iran, it can legitimize that belief as the basis of the succeeding regime. But if the event is a consequence of a movement against the existing political system and government but is not inspired by commitment to a specific belief—or, worse, if it is waged by an ad hoc coalition of convenience—the government that follows may enjoy legitimacy, but not for long. Its legitimacy is likely to be contested by others who took part in the event. This was the case with several of the postindependent governments whose legitimacy was short-lived. Nationalism in these states was essentially a reaction to

foreign domination and was not rooted in a common past. As the euphoria surrounding independence evaporated, religious, ethnic, linguistic, and
regional grievances eroded the will to live together in harmony. Other
groups and leaders who took part in the struggle for independence but did
not succeed to power challenged the government—drawing upon the
same politically defining moment.

Likewise, the February 1986 political revolution in the Philippines was
primarily an opposition to Marcos waged by a broad ad hoc coalition
made up of groups (segments of the military, conservative politicians in
UNIDO, a segment of the business elite, progressives and traditional
elements in the PDP-Laban, the Catholic church) with divergent interests.[58] Public perception of the developments in early 1986 as miraculous,
coupled with the victory of Corazon Aquino in the elections and the triumph of people power over tanks, did initially confer enormous moral
authority on Aquino and legitimated the democratic system.[59] This authority, however, was soon subject to erosion and contestation. Aquino
had to accommodate many groups in her administration. While this did
in one respect enhance her government's legitimacy, it also made the setting of priorities extremely difficult and contributed to an immobility that
undermined faith in her government—both from the perspective of the
public, which had high expectations, and from the perspective of several
crucial groups (the military, progressives, traditionalists, conservatives)
that had all hoped to pursue their agendas through the Aquino government. The most potent challenge came from the politicized military. Indeed, Defense Minister Juan Ponce-Enrile, who sought to use the military
as a vehicle for his presidential ambitions, claiming credit for and authority from the same defining moment, sought to oust the Aquino government on several occasions. The conservative politicians were disenchanted
with the reformist tendencies of Aquino while the progressives were frustrated with the superficiality and slow pace of reform. These developments, in part, account for the constant threat faced by Aquino's government throughout its six years in office. The February 1986 political
revolution and the charisma of Aquino, however, were not without effect.
They enabled a return to constitutionalism and the victory of the government coalition in the May 1987 elections, though with time and new challenges their legitimating effect is likely to decline.

Thus legitimation based on a politically defining moment is not free of
disputation and will not be durable unless, as in the case of personal authority, it is institutionalized on the basis of an ideology. With the passage of time, politically defining moments are likely to lose force and suffer
a corresponding decline in their legitimating potential—especially with
later generations that had no direct experience of them. Although the de-

fining moment may become sanctified and invoked to justify domination, such invocation will not be enough to ensure domination. At best, they are only a supplementary basis of legitimacy.

International Support

For Weber the question of legitimacy is driven exclusively by domestic forces. International considerations do not enter into his discussion. Today, however, extranational developments have a significant impact on ruler and ruled and their interaction. The salience of this dimension is clear from the efforts of governments and dissident groups to secure international support for their causes. One should be careful, however, not to exaggerate its significance: in the final analysis, the problem of political authority is a domestic issue. International dynamics are relevant only to the extent that they influence domestic discourse on the norms for legitimation and affect the power resources of the domestic contestants.

The international dimension may shape the domestic discourse on legitimacy in several ways. The dominant international ethos can provide ideological security—or create insecurity—for fledgling governments. During the Cold War, affiliation with one of the two principal ideological blocs or the nonaligned movement provided such security, enhancing the domestic legitimacy of governments. With the end of the Cold War and the collapse of the communist bloc, the West is promoting democracy, human rights, and capitalism as the dominant ethos of the international system. The Western countries have applied the test of "good governance" (specified in terms of democracy, human rights, and a free market economy) in their response to domestic developments in countries such as China (the Tiananmen incident), Burma (the 1988 political uprising), Thailand (February 1991), and in a limited way Indonesia (East Timor). Usurpation of power through military coup d'état—for example, in Peru and Thailand—has been condemned. Conditions are being imposed on bilateral and multilateral economic relations and assistance with a view to promoting good governance. The content of these international norms and their linkage to economic relations have been contested by certain developing countries, especially those in East Asia.[60]

The vitality of competing norms in the international system can erode the confidence of leaders and cause them to lose faith in their own ideology.[61] The remaining Marxist-Leninist and authoritarian regimes, for example, must now function in an international system characterized to a substantial degree by the ethos of capitalism and, to a lesser degree, by democracy. This creates in them a sense of isolation and vulnerability. Moreover, international norms can provide an alternative model for the ruled. Revolutionary developments in technology (telecommunications and transportation), educational exposure in foreign countries, and international institution building (global and regional) have dramatically increased international interaction and hence detailed knowledge of other political systems, including their merits and demerits.[62]

International actors can affect the power resources of domestic contestants in a number of ways. Acceptance by the international community or by superpowers like the United States and the former Soviet Union—as well as access to the resources of international organizations like the United Nations, International Monetary Fund, International Bank for Reconstruction and Development, General Agreement on Tariffs and Trade, and regional organizations—confers prestige with the potential to increase state capacity, enabling leaders and their governments to consolidate their domestic base. Nonrecognition not only reduces the standing of the incumbent government and its capacity; it also enhances the status of rival claimants to power. The net effect of the denial of international recognition is to intensify domestic conflict, making it difficult for the incumbent government to convert power into authority—witness the situation in South Africa until the end of apartheid and in Cambodia until the conclusion of the Paris Peace Accords in October 1991. Sanctions and conditions imposed by international financial institutions can also deprive the government of much needed economic assistance.

In sum, then, the end of the Cold War, the commitment of the only remaining superpower to promote democratic values, the growing economic interdependence, and the growing porousness of the state impede the institutionalization of regimes based on norms that are grossly at variance with those of the international community. International developments in other countries—as, for example, the collapse of authoritarianism and the return to democracy in Latin American countries and the Philippines—can stimulate domestic political action in support of alternative systems as was the case in South Korea, Burma, and China. This, however, does not alter our earlier contention that the international dimension plays only a contributory role in domestic legitimation.[63] The institution and legitimation of democratic regimes in South Korea and Taiwan were primarily a consequence of domestic developments.[64] Despite the overwhelming support of the Western countries, the legitimacy of Boris Yeltsin's democratic government continues to be contested in Russia. And the inability of international disapproval to bring about political change in China and Burma, except on the margin, indicates the limited effect of the international dimension.[65] Further, nationalism can be invoked to justify resistance to the policies of the "imperial" powers and enhance domestic legitimacy of the government and the regime.

Significance of the Rationales

The preceding discussion suggests a number of observations. First, most of the rationales are vulnerable to dispute and contestation at both the conceptual and operational levels. Except for a few universal ideologies, there is no direct correspondence between a specific rationale and a particular type of government. Each can be deployed to justify a wide variety of domination. Islam, for example, has been deployed to justify regimes ranging from kingship to theocratic state. Even charisma, usually linked to personal rule, can be harnessed to justify other types of domination. Hence, based on different interpretations, most goals as well as the other rationales—politically defining moment and international support, for example—can be mobilized in support of the incumbent government as well as its opponents.

Second, no single resource appears adequate in itself. Even when popular sovereignty is given maximum expression, as in democracies, performance is not unimportant. Persistently poor performance (insecurity, a declining standard of living, growing inequality, incompetence, abuse of power) can undermine its legitimacy. Similarly, popular sovereignty and performance cannot be ignored even in a theocratic regime. Normally a number of resources must be employed for the legitimation of governments in less well established regimes. The right mix depends on the sociopolitical context, the type of regime, as well as the stage in the government's evolutionary dynamic. In an authoritarian regime, for example, negative legitimacy, nationalist credentials, a politically defining moment, and personal authority may be important to begin with, but in time the salience of these resources will decline and performance becomes more important. In the long run, even performance may not be sufficient.

The strategy of deploying multiple rationales has both advantages and disadvantages for the legitimation of government. If the rationales are correctly selected to appeal to the many and different audiences at a particular point in time as well as over a period of time, this strategy can enhance legitimation—especially in multiethnic/multireligious countries and those undergoing rapid socioeconomic and political change. In both cases, the audiences are heterogeneous. Choosing the right mix will allow the ruler to simultaneously deploy the legitimation resources considered most appropriate for each target group.[66] Religion, for example, can be stressed to one group, popular sovereignty to another, performance to yet another, and coercion imposed to suppress the residual group. Such a mix also allows the government to emphasize the rationale that it considers most valuable in its international dealings—which, as noted, are not without consequence for domestic legitimacy. If the rationales are complementary, the multiple strategy may also make it possible to compensate for weakness in one resource with strength in another, thus avoiding a rapid erosion of legitimacy. This, together with the absence of alternatives and state coercion, may help explain the long gestation period before the ouster of an unpopular government.

Nevertheless, the strategy of multiple rationales may also provide opportunities for contestation of legitimacy. If the rationales are not complementary, their application will give rise to tension and conflict—providing opportunities for exploitation by rival claimants to power. A government that deploys the rationales of popular sovereignty, religion, and economic development to legitimate itself, for example, will be confronted with the problem of reconciling the conflicting demands of these three resources. This issue can be exploited by opposition groups, which, arguing the primacy of a particular rationale (religion, democracy), may accuse the government of insincerity and manipulation. Moreover, the dynamic nature of these rationales implies that their role cannot be contained within prescribed limits. Competition (and possibly conflict) among groups advocating the primacy of certain rationales will be a persistent feature of regimes claiming legitimacy on the basis of multiple justifications.

This leads us to the third observation: there is a hierarchy among the rationales. While all of them can be deployed in support of legitimation, some have a primary quality, while others are essentially supportive and are usually deployed in a supplementary role. Further, some are less contingent and therefore more durable than others. Because of their power to constitute a political system and durable institutions, normative goals rank at the top of the hierarchy and are usually deployed as the primary basis of the claim to authority. Some goals (ideology-based) have greater power than others to create a regenerative political system.

Beetham cites popular sovereignty as the most important and stable ideology, and he advances a developmental model on this basis.[67] Because of the potential of the process-oriented conception of popular sovereignty to satisfy all four elements of legitimacy and because it is internal to the state, popular sovereignty is certainly a satisfactory basis of authority. Religion is perhaps less satisfactory in this regard. Theocratic regimes are open to contestation on the basis of rival interpretations as well as their record of performance and the lack of a popular mandate. Moreover, their institutionalization potential in the contemporary era is unclear. Other goals—national liberation and survival, for example—are similarly less satisfactory. They do not define a specific political system, although they can foster the institutionalization of an ideology-based system.

To accept Beetham's developmental model in full, however, implies acceptance of the end-of-history and linear progress theses.[68] No belief system is permanent. Forces of change, both visible and subterranean, are always at work. Indeed, institutions closely linked to popular sovereignty—capitalism, liberalism, and democracy, for example—may carry the seeds of their own destruction. As noted by John Hall, liberalism is ill equipped to satisfy spiritual, psychological, and emotional needs.[69] He contends that the "consolidations of democracy open up rather than close down historical possibilities."[70] Just as popular sovereignty supplanted the idea of contractarianism, it too may be supplanted by another norm or become incorporated into a political model that can limit its expression. A long view of history would suggest caution in such matters. Further, as noted earlier, the collective will interpretation of popular sovereignty can be deployed to justify totalitarian and authoritarian regimes as well. These clearly are not stable and enduring regimes.

Personal authority comes next in the hierarchy. It may constitute a distinctive political system (personal rule) and can also legitimate political systems based on ideologies. But because of its very nature, as well as the succession problem, personal rule cannot be routinized and institutionalized. Performance, politically defining moments, and international support, unlike normative goals and personal authority, cannot constitute a political system on their own and thus are not associated with a specific political system. They are essentially supplementary rationales, although performance may sometimes be deployed as a primary rationale. Their relevance for legitimation depends on the continued salience of a defining moment, good performance, conformity to international norms, or international support and is highly contingent. They occupy the bottom rung in the hierarchy.

This routinization-cum-institutionalization hierarchy, however, must be qualified. It applies much more to the legitimation of regimes than governments. A government may be legitimated on the basis of any of these rationales. Further, although ideology-based goals rank high in the hierarchy, the realization of their institutionalization potential hinges on the other resources—especially performance, personal authority, and international support. Good performance, as noted earlier, can create a virtuous cycle engendering confidence in the political system. Personal authority can be important, as well, as demonstrated by the role of leaders like Mohandas Gandhi and Jawaharlal Nehru (India), Ho Chi Minh (Vietnam), and Lee Kuan Yew (Singapore) in the institutionalization of regimes in their countries. Similarly, a favorable international climate, by enhancing ideological security and performance, may also facilitate institutionalization. This hierarchy also does not rule out the possibility of deploying ideologies in a subordinate role in political systems constituted on another basis of authority.

Finally, the hierarchy of constituent elements of legitimacy, the hierarchy of rationales, the requirements of successful hegemony, and the distinction between regime and government provide a framework for evaluating progress made in the legitimation of power in the long run. To the extent that there is ideological unity between ruler and ruled, and the incumbent government appears to represent the general interest of the whole society, progress will have been made in creating shared norms and values that in turn will enhance the legitimating value of the procedural element. Thus increasing reliance on the procedural element as the basis of authority indicates growing strength of the regime and progress in legitimation. Government and regime become more distinct in this situation; a change in government has little impact on the legitimacy of the regime. Crisis tendencies disappear or become manageable.

Signs of such progress include the growing prominence of rules, stable and effective government, an ability to make controversial decisions without losing the support of key groups, the declining significance of antisystemic forces, the system's capacity to accommodate new power centers, the limitation of coercion to a largely symbolic role, and the peaceful succession of governments within the framework of the regime. An expansion of the state's capabilities (penetration, regulation, extraction, and appropriation) and its monopoly of force, because of their contribution to effective governance, are also key indicators.[71] As stability can also mask the erosion of legitimacy, progress in legitimation must be judged on the basis of a wide variety of indicators.

We have seen that the various rationales—projected goals and values, performance, charisma, politically defining moment, and international support—have less legitimating power than that of the procedural element in a well-established regime. These rationales are open to contestation on the basis of rival interpretations, success as well as failure in attaining projected goals and performance standards, and loss of charisma or external support. Moreover, their legitimating value may decline with the passage of time. These rationales are highly contingent, as well, and, with the exception of a few ideology-based goals, do not have the power to define or regenerate a system. Even in the case of the system-defining ideologies, the construction of a shared normative order must satisfy stringent conditions and is likely to be prolonged and open to contestation. Thus political legitimation in developing countries, as well as in many others, is likely to face formidable challenges.

3

Contestation and Crisis

MUTHIAH ALAGAPPA

THAT the control of state power requires legitimation is universally recognized, but success in this endeavor has eluded many governments. Legitimacy, as noted by David Beetham, appears to be "as much the exception as the rule."[1] It is frequently contested, and legitimacy crises are not uncommon. Why is political legitimation difficult? Why is legitimacy contested? Why do legitimacy crises occur? These questions are explored in this chapter.

Challenges to Political Legitimation

Political legitimation faces formidable challenges in nearly all modern states. These challenges relate to the difficulties associated with self-regulation in a sovereign state, the government's incapacity to satisfy the ever increasing demands on it, and the dynamic nature of legitimacy itself.[2] The norm of sovereignty, a distinctive feature of the modern state, places a premium on self-regulation in all domestic matters, particularly the political domain. But the concentration of power in the state required to realize the notion of supreme authority makes self-regulation exceedingly difficult, especially in relation to the acquisition and exercise of political power (the second and third elements of legitimacy). Since political power is the key to the control of state resources and since it is concentrated in the state (especially in an interventionist state), competition for the control of state power is intense—making self-regulation vulnerable to disruption.

Effective self-regulation in a democratic state, for example, requires satisfaction of a number of conditions. At the normative level, the political leaders must be committed to democratic ideals and their institutionalization. In particular the military, as the repository of state coercive power with the means to be disruptive, must be firmly committed to the ideal of civilian control. Otherwise, the leaders are likely to resort to extralegal means to seize and maintain political power. At the substantive level, the political, legal, and socioeconomic conditions must provide for the independence and equality of citizens. Moreover, there must be a balance of power among the various strategic groups, a strong civil society to limit the government's power, and a strong party system to mediate among conflicting demands.[3] Finally, international geopolitical and economic considerations should not favor other forms of rule (authoritarian, totalitarian) as was the case during the Cold War. These conditions are far from satisfied in many countries that claim to be democratic. Democracy in these countries is often only a thin veneer, making democratic self-regulation very susceptible to challenge and disruption.

The demands on government have continued to proliferate. In addition to its traditional functions—political identity, law and order, external security—government is increasingly expected to undertake social and economic functions that involve it ever more deeply in extractive and distributive tasks. The net effect has been to expand government's role in the provision of public goods. Further, the principle of popular sovereignty has substantially widened political participation—creating broad and variegated sets of interests and demands that must be satisfied. Although government's control of the national economy has increased through modern administrative systems and its ability to raise revenues, its capacity to perform the various functions has not kept pace with demands and, moreover, has been constrained by the growing salience of the international environment. Above all, the health of the national economy, which bears upon the government's capacity to provide social and material benefits, has become greatly dependent on specialization at the international level and access to the markets of other countries over which most governments have little control. The growing gap between demand and capacity may, when it becomes acute, contribute to a "crisis of governability" affecting the consent element with the potential to undermine the legitimacy of the government and the political system in which it is rooted.[4]

As observed in Chapter 1, shared norms often have to be created. The ideological struggle that is associated with the attempt to create unity among the various strategic groups imputes a dynamic character to social relations and hence to the legitimation project. This dynamic nature of legitimacy, combined with the changing relevance of the bases on which authority is claimed and acknowledged, compounds the difficulty of achieving political legitimation. As an outcome of the interaction between ruler

and ruled, legitimacy is subject to continuous negotiation. Thus governments, even when they acquire power in accord with widely accepted rules
and procedures, cannot take their legitimacy for granted. Illegal use of
power—as well as a crisis of confidence in the political leadership, which
can issue from any number of sources, both domestic and international—
can undermine their legitimacy. Changes in values as well as persistent
poor performance, both of which may be beyond the control of governments, may in the long run call into question the legitimacy of even a well-
established regime. While these challenges are common to all modern
states, they are particularly acute in developing countries. The contested
nature of the referent objects of legitimation,[5] the rapid pace of socioeconomic change in many of these countries, and weak state capabilities further aggravate the tension in the relationship between ruler and ruled,
making the cultivation of legitimacy ever more difficult.

As stated in Chapter 1, the idea of the nation as the basis of political
community and the related construct of nation-state have now become
universal norms. But the "imagined" nations are relatively new, strange,
and not deep-rooted in many developing countries.[6] In many cases, colonial states have been transformed into nation-states and nationalism has
been essentially anticolonial in character.[7] The arbitrary state boundaries
drawn by the colonial powers—and the mass internal and international
migration they encouraged in pursuit of extractive and commercial goals—
have resulted in "multiethnic territorialisms" that have no political rationale for existence other than as dependencies of the metropolitan powers.[8]
With the dissipation of the unity fostered by anticolonial nationalism and
experience of "internal colonialism," ethnic, racial, linguistic, and religious consciousness has been on the rise, contributing to disenchantment
with the new nation and nation-state.[9] Concerned that even minor revi-
sions will lead to the collapse of their nation-states, political leaders have
rejected any further right to national self-determination.[10] They seek to
forge nations on the basis of their present territorial boundaries. In this
task some have sought to indigenize the nation and nation-state by inventing links with the precolonial past. The projected national community
usually incorporates a disproportionate share of the values of the *Staatsvolk*, the dominant ethnic group that controls state power, displaying
strong overtones of cultural, ideological, and economic imperialism.

This hegemonic attempt to forge a national political community undermines the political-economic position and sociocultural identity of other
indigenous (minority) communities, leading to their alienation from the
nation and nation-state as some identify themselves as separate nations
and seek to form new nation-states. The end of the Cold War and its bipolar global order appear to be contributing to a decline in international

support for the norms of juridical statehood.[11] Concurrently there is growing international acceptance of ethnicity as the basis of political community and therefore the major legitimator of states. This trend could further accentuate the legitimacy problem. A new wave of ethnic and religious nationalism may be in the making. Yugoslavia is the extreme case, but declining support for the norms of juridical statehood may also be detected in Russia and the Eastern European states and could become the case in certain African and Asian states as well. In Southeast Asia, the legitimacy of the nation and nation-state continues to be contested by elements of minority communities in Burma, Thailand, Indonesia, and the Philippines. It could also become an issue in Malaysia with reference to the East Malaysian states, particularly Sabah.[12] With the exception of Burma, however, this problem is not as acute in Southeast Asia as in other developing regions.

Challenges to the legitimacy of the nation and nation-state quite logically extend to the other realms of political organization as well. Disaffected groups reject the legitimacy of the regime and government on the ground that they have no desire to become part of the nation-state or, alternatively, they seek changes in the nature of the regime that will accommodate their values and interests. While ethno-nationalism undoubtedly affects support for the political system in multiethnic states, the issue of a regime's legitimacy is not confined to this situation alone. It may be a problem even in countries where the nation and nation-state are not contested (Cambodia, perhaps Vietnam in the future) and also among the *Staatsvolk* of multiethnic countries (China, the Philippines, Thailand, Burma).

The problem of regime legitimacy can be traced to the newness of these states as modern states and to the lack of shared values for political organization. There were no established systems from which the political leaders of the postcolonial states could derive their legitimacy. Except for a few cases, colonial rule destroyed or marginalized the traditional basis of domination.[13] In any case, these bases were not directly acceptable to most of the elite that waged the struggle for independence. The removal of colonial rule, the imposition of new ideas and political institutions, the resort in some cases to traditional ideas, and the activation of the population through nationalist struggles caused serious dislocations. The new leaders had the gargantuan task of legitimating the nation and nation-state, as well as creating shared norms and institutionalizing them. Different ideologies were espoused by competing groups as the basis for political organization. In some cases this competition became violent and was exacerbated by the global ideological conflict during the Cold War. The recent resurgence of religion and the promotion of democracy and human rights by the West as universally valid norms may also complicate the issue of legitimation.

As noted in earlier chapters, the forging of a shared identity (required to legitimate the nation-state) and the forging of a shared normative order (required to legitimate the regime) are difficult, long-drawn-out, conflict-prone processes. In the absence of a shared normative order or a weak one, governments claim the right to rule on the basis of other rationales. These rationales, as noted in Chapter 2, are open to rival interpretations and are less enduring. Further, as situations change, their relevance may weaken, subjecting the government and regime to periodic contestation.

Political legitimation is further complicated by the rapid pace of socio-economic change, the growing salience of popular sovereignty, and the government's unwillingness or inability to accommodate the political consequences of such developments. The new groups that emerge from economic growth, for example, seek to participate in the political process and share in the exercise of power to promote their interests. Their effort, however, has been resisted by the incumbents, who seek to preserve the government's exclusivity and autonomy by citing a number of reasons—including national unity and security threats from within and without—that are usually a cloak for self-serving interests. This clash of interests leading to conflict has been especially characteristic of authoritarian regimes, although it is not confined to them. Many governments are also weak in terms of what has been called social control.[14] Consolidation of state power is a prerequisite for institutionalization, but the powers of penetration, regulation, extraction, and appropriation are limited in many developing countries, primarily by the existence of strong local societies. The political center is often unable to extend its writ throughout the country. When power is not concentrated in the state, the government's authority can be challenged by other centers of power, and the role of power in legitimating itself through the institutional mode will be severely circumscribed.

Since these considerations and the conflicts of interest they give rise to are enduring, the nature of the regime will continue to be contested. In postindependence Southeast Asia, challenges to regime legitimacy have been mounted by communist movements, by military establishments, and by ethnic, religious, and prodemocracy groups. Regime changes have occurred in Burma (1962), Thailand (1973, 1976, 1991–92), Indonesia (1959, 1965), the Philippines (1972, 1986), Cambodia (1970, 1975, 1978), and Laos (1975). Today legitimacy is openly contested in Burma and Cambodia and, to a lesser degree, in Indonesia and Vietnam. The potential for such challenges is present in most other Southeast Asian countries as well.

Because of the fusion of regime and government, contestation of a regime's legitimacy will translate into contestation of the government's legitimacy. A government's legitimacy may be contested for a number of other reasons as well: abuse of power, rivalry among personalities and institutions, intense competition for state power because of easy access to state resources through public office, and regional grievances. Often the incumbent government must concern itself with not only its own legitimation but also that of the nation-state and the regime it seeks to establish and consolidate. This burden, combined with weak state capabilities, may lead to the erosion of legitimacy, a legitimacy crisis, and perhaps the government's collapse.

Because of the conflation of nation-state, regime, and government in many developing countries, conflict over the legitimacy of one institution is likely to affect the others as well. We have seen how disaffection with the nation-state can affect the legitimacy of regime and government. Similarly, disaffection with the government or regime may create disenchantment with the nation-state—as has been the case, for example, with several minority communities in Burma, the Tamils in Sri Lanka, and the Sikhs in India. In sum, then, political legitimation in developing countries is intimately connected with state-building and nation-building processes that are likely to consume decades or more before achieving maturity. These processes are likely to be subject to reversals and may, in some cases, collapse altogether.

Legitimacy Crisis

A legitimacy crisis is a situation in which the basis on which authority has been claimed or acknowledged is under such severe stress that there is a strong possibility of its destruction and transformation. The legitimacy crisis of a regime must be distinguished from that of a government or individual leader, although at times the two may be conflated. In the first case, the conflict is over the basic values that constitute the political and social order. In the second case, the conflict is over the acquisition and exercise of power focused on specific institutions—government, individual power holders—or policies; the basic norms and hence the political system itself are not contested.[15] Further, a legitimacy crisis must be distinguished from a legitimacy strain. In the latter case, the commitment to underlying norms may be weak to begin with, or perhaps the commitment has eroded for whatever reason, but the erosion has not reached crisis proportions.[16]

Legitimacy or the lack of it becomes more obvious during periods of crisis, making clear-cut determination of illegitimacy and legitimacy possible. At other times, legitimacy is much more difficult to discern. Instrumental acceptance, apathy, and coercion may sustain governments for relatively long periods, giving the appearance of stability and obscuring the erosion of legitimacy. Nevertheless, a careful analysis on the basis of the four elements of legitimacy and the other bases of political legitimation advanced earlier can provide valuable insights into the degree of legitimacy enjoyment by an incumbent.

Relevant Theories

Three theories—capitalist development, crisis of the capitalist state, and overloaded government—are relevant in explaining the erosion of legitimacy and the crisis tendencies of authoritarian, democratic, and Marxist-Leninist regimes. The thrust of the capitalist development theory is that capitalist development promotes democracy.[17] From the perspective of this study, the significance of the theory lies in its assertion that capitalist development changes the power of groups, their interests, and their alignments. This in turn affects the balance of power among the various classes, as well as the relationship between the state and society, and creates pressures for political change with consequences for the struggle among groups over the right to rule.[18] If a group believes the rules of the game to be disadvantageous, its commitment to them will erode and set in motion demands to alter the rules in its favor. This contributes to the erosion of legitimacy. If the demands are strong enough and the power holder refuses to accommodate them, the resulting tension can lead to conflict and possibly a legitimacy crisis of the government or the regime itself.

The crisis of the capitalist state theory focuses on the inability of the capitalist state to survive insoluble contradictions.[19] These contradictions are presumed to issue from increasing state intervention in the economy, the capitalist concern for economic freedom, and the conflicting demands of the capital-owning class and the population at large. The state, it is argued, cannot reconcile the demand for economic freedom of the capital-owning class, which it is presumed to represent, with the welfare demands of the population at large from which it draws its legitimacy. This insoluble contradiction strains legitimacy and makes the survival of the advanced capitalist state highly problematic. William Connolly, drawing on the work of Habermas, posits a conflict between the growth imperative and democratic ideals—a conflict that, he argues, gives rise to a legitimacy dilemma.[20]

The overloaded government theory posits that fragmentation of power, rising expectations, declining deference to authority, appeasement strategies by self-interested political parties and governments, expansion of the state, restriction of the private sector, and the state's inability to meet expectations set in motion a vicious circle that contributes to the erosion of legitimacy.[21] This theory assumes a pluralist starting point and contends that a firm, decisive political leadership that is less responsive to democratic demands and procedures is necessary to break the vicious cycle.

Two additional factors not fully captured by these three theories may also contribute to the erosion and crisis of legitimacy. The first is the failure to deliver on promised goals, deviation from them, or their irrelevance: the growing gap between claim and reality is likely to undermine legitimacy. This is particularly salient with regard to governments that claim authority on the basis of goal rationality. Second, values change over time. This change may be an outcome of capitalist development, but it might also be a response to sociopolitical change that is quite independent of economic forces. With the communication and transportation revolutions, transnational ideological and cultural flows have become particularly salient in this regard. Changing political values will call into question the legitimacy of the existing regime. The growing salience of religion, for example, may challenge the legitimacy of secular political systems. The capitalist development theory, failure to achieve projected goals, and changing values are particularly relevant in explaining the erosion and crisis of legitimacy in authoritarian regimes.

Authoritarian Regimes

Authoritarian governments usually acquire power through negative legitimacy: the military—or a civilian leader with the support of the military—usurps power with the declared purpose of saving the country or its revered institutions in order to clean up the mess, to restore law and order, or to protect the country from a security threat.[22] This intervention will be supported by groups that have been (or expect to be) disadvantaged by the policies of the former government. Disenchantment with the former government usually, though not always, makes for public acquiescence if not approval of the intervention.

Invariably, authoritarian governments seek to base their claim to rule on performance (restoration of law and order, delivery of material goods) and the personal authority of leaders. Excessive reliance on performance, however, creates a dilemma for them.[23] Good performance removes the purpose that justified the initial intervention—if the law and order problem has been effectively dealt with, for example, it can no longer be cited as a reason for continuation in power. On the other hand, failure to maintain law and order will quickly discredit the government. Effective economic performance may strengthen authoritarian rule in the short term, but in the long run it creates tension between the government and the new groups (the middle and working classes and the evolving civil society) unleashed by such development. The new groups, particularly the working class, demand their political incorporation and at a minimum the accommodation of their interests. Since these run counter to the interests of the power holders, challenges lead to the contestation of authoritarian rule. Economic failure, on the other hand, will discredit the authoritarian government for failing to deliver on its promise of material welfare.

The crucial problems, however, relate to the lack of a moral justification for continued authoritarian rule and the limited capacity for self-renewal. While physical security and rice are important—and delivering them does create moral authority—the social and political aspirations of the governed must also be satisfied if authority is to endure. Ideals such as popular mandate may be temporarily co-opted by authoritarian regimes. But in the long term, because of their potential to present alternative bases for legitimation, they are likely to undermine the legitimacy of authoritarian rule. Further, the procedures for transferring power in authoritarian regimes, even when they do exist, are seldom observed. The transfer is usually accompanied by the threat or use of force leading to political breakdown.

Apart from the dynamics within a country, authoritarian rule is also affected by political and economic developments at the international level. Support from the United States and the Soviet Union during the Cold War was a key factor in the staying power of a number of authoritarian regimes. Beginning with the Carter administration and gaining greater force since the end of the Cold War, the United States and Western Europe have intensified their support for groups and governments advocating human rights and democratic values.[24] The growing dominance of these so-called universal values can embolden groups advocating these values, undermine the confidence of authoritarian leaders, and call into question the legitimacy of their rule. Participation in the international market economy—which is vital today if the government is to make good its promise of material welfare—may also have negative consequences for the legitimacy of authoritarian governments in the long run—but only to the extent that they alter the distribution of power among the various groups in society and the balance of power between state and society.

Authoritarian regimes by their very nature are prone to legitimacy crisis. Their legitimacy is based on rationales (charisma, performance, international support) that are difficult to sustain over a long period of time and, moreover, are subject to challenge on the basis of greater reward or greater force. Sustained capitalist development contains the seeds that can destroy authoritarian rule. Combined with a capacity for limited self-renewal, these considerations contribute to the erosion of legitimacy and, eventually, to a crisis.

Democratic Regimes

The theory of overloaded government in a modified form is relevant in explaining the erosion and crisis of legitimacy in a democratic system. Overload occurs in developing democratic countries because of intense politicization and radical political and socioeconomic demands focused on the government and the latter's incapacity to address these demands effectively. As noted earlier, many of the new nation-states are deeply divided along ethnic, religious, and regional lines. Invocation of primordial loyalties by political leaders for their own ends, combined with the extreme demands that these and other radical factions make without due consideration for the "national" good, place a heavy burden on the system.[25] This intense politicization is compounded by the key features of the democratic system (universal suffrage, freedom of association, free expression, participation, and contestation)—making for bitter conflict, turmoil, and generally a zero-sum political game in these countries. Further, the government's prominent role in promoting socioeconomic development makes it the focus of socioeconomic grievances.

Competition for political power becomes even more intense because of the enormous resources controlled by an interventionist state. In this situation, elections become a battleground. Campaigns arouse hatred and are frequently accompanied by violence, killings, and fraud. The system is unable to carry the burden of so many insoluble political problems. The net result is a fragmentation of the political center that contributes to weak government. The many political problems confronting the weak government further divert attention and scarce resources away from more productive uses. Performance suffers. This situation may be aggravated by bad economic policies, mismanagement, and corruption. Growing disorder and inequality may also reinforce the public's disenchantment with the democratic system. Atul Kohli explains the growing crisis of governability in India in terms of "rapid political mobilization of diverse groups, a de-institutionalizing role of leaders, and, more broadly, a situation in which institutions fail to keep pace with growing demands."[26] Internal political tensions and economic problems may be aggravated by global developments—transnational conflicts, pressures from international financial institutions to meet their conditions in order to qualify for loans and assistance, and adverse international economic developments (a rise in the price of oil, a revaluation of major currencies, a recession in major markets) over which these countries have little control.

In the absence of a deep commitment to democratic values and associated institutions and procedures, strong middle and working classes, a significant civil society, and strong political parties, the temptation to subvert the system to serve the immediate political needs of incumbent leaders or to seize power through nondemocratic means is substantial. As these conditions are absent (or present only in rudimentary form), the democratic system in many developing countries is vulnerable to easy displacement. The great political and economic burdens borne by democratic regimes in many developing countries may contribute to a collapse from within. As noted by Samuel Huntington: "Under a democratic regime, radicalism, corruption and disorder reach unacceptable levels and the military overthrow it to considerable popular relief and acclaim."[27]

Marxist-Leninist Regimes

In hindsight it is clear that Marxist-Leninist regimes in the Soviet Union and Eastern Europe experienced a deep legitimacy crisis that led to their collapse in the late 1980s. Several reasons have been advanced to explain the collapse of these regimes, including a crisis of faith in ideology at the elite level, moral bankruptcy, a failure to perform, and the removal of external constraint.[28] From the perspective of this study, the key point is that the Marxist-Leninist regime is not an attractive political model at present. The remaining Marxist-Leninist governments, most of which are in Asia, while seeking to maintain a Leninist political system, have embarked upon economic reform and, in effect, are on the way to becoming market economies. Shorn of ideological and nationalist credentials and in the absence of charismatic figures, these governments are increasingly staking their claim to rule on performance. In essence these regimes are little different from the authoritarian regimes discussed earlier. The dynamic that erodes the legitimacy of authoritarian rule is likely to affect these regimes as well in due course. The central question is this: Can these governments continue to maintain Leninist political systems while liberalizing their economies and pursuing capitalist development?

The foregoing discussion suggests that in the setting of developing countries, all three regime types are prone to legitimacy strain and crisis. The logic of authoritarian and, to a lesser degree, Marxist-Leninist regimes contains the seeds of self-destruction. The socioeconomic and political problems, as well as the peripheral position of the developing states in the international economic order, impose a heavy burden and sap the vitality of democratic regimes. In all regime types, incumbent governments may have substantial legitimacy to begin with, but this legitimacy is progressively eroded and may culminate in a legitimacy crisis. Very few governments seem able to escape this pattern. The democratic model, because of its capacity for self-renewal and the orderly transfer of power, may have the potential to break out of this vicious cycle. For this to happen, however, there must be a strong commitment to democratic values among the elite, strong political parties and civil society must exist, economic growth must be sustained, the benefits of development must be widely distributed, and the heavy political burdens placed on the system must be reduced. And although many have suggested how these burdens might be eased, in practice this has proved to be difficult.[29] Even if these suggestions are workable, democratic development is likely to be gradual and checkered. Thus it appears that, in the short to medium term at least, legitimacy crisis is likely to be a recurrent feature in the politics of developing countries.

PART II

LEGITIMACY

Case Studies

4

Malaysia

Aspects and Audiences of Legitimacy

WILLIAM CASE

> We have always contended in this country that when everybody is un-
> happy, then we are doing well. It means that we are not giving any
> community all that they ask for. Everybody feels deprived. The Malays
> are not happy, the Chinese are not happy, the Indians are not happy.
> They all say the government is not doing enough, which means we are
> being fair.
> —Prime Minister Mahathir Mohamad, interview in *Newsweek* (May 2, 1988)

WHILE mindful of the self-congratulatory tone and mildly convoluted
logic of the prime minister's statement to *Newsweek*, one can nonetheless
appreciate the thrust of his assessment. Such perceptions about the fair
use of state power lead swiftly to a discussion of political legitimacy. In
examining legitimacy in Malaysia, this chapter begins by outlining some
of its features, indicating which audiences find the political arrangements
legitimate (governing elites, most business elites, much of the new Malay
middle class, incorporated populations of Malay workers and peasants,
and dispersed groups of Indian estate laborers) as well as those that are
more equivocal in their judgments (some Islamic elements in the Malay
middle class and among rural populations in the peninsula's northern
states, many middle-class Chinese and Indians, most urban Chinese workers, and many indigenous Iban and Kadazan communities in East Malaysia). I also propose a mechanism through which the government's legitimacy among specified audiences can be shown and examine ways by
which the government has sought to blunt perceptions of *illegitimacy*
among others.

Second, the chapter notes traditional, colonial, and ethnic factors that have shaped the criteria by which the legitimacy has been evaluated in Malaysia, helping to define the claims to legitimacy made by governing elites and the ways in which mass audiences have responded to them. While these claims have often cited electoral mandates and the rule of law, featured an indigenous ideology (*Rukunegara*) and nationalist slogans ("Buy British Last"), relied on a socializing school system, patriotic holidays, and inspiriting anthems (such as *Lagu Setia*, the "Loyalty Song"), and proclaimed a strong developmentalist mission ("Malaysia Inc.," "Look East," and "Vision 2020"), variants of such bases of legitimation have been deployed in nearly all contemporary Southeast Asian states. Thus it is of greater interest to explore what is unique to Malaysia, the historical and sociocultural forces that have given rise to such claims, as well as the attraction or alienation this has created among the diverse audiences.

Third, drawing upon Malaysia's political experience since independence, the chapter tries to show the relative success with which the UMNO-led government has established its authority. This success accounts for the mass compliance and political stability that have generally prevailed in Malaysia, a record that has not been matched elsewhere in the region. Accordingly, little attention is given here to audiences that have contested the rightness of the country's political arrangements and the exercise of state power. Because my concern is with explaining political stability (rather than sketching out scenarios of destabilizing pressures) and because the grievances of alienated communities are easily recorded, a more useful and indeed challenging exercise lies in demonstrating government authority among key elites and mass audiences.

Finally, the chapter considers how rapid economic growth and evolving identities seem to be modifying the contours of political legitimacy in Malaysia. The UMNO-led government may need to recast its claims in order to retain relevance. In doing so, however, the government may also discover a momentary slippage between structural changes and societal outlooks, opening some scope for political innovation. Put simply, the government might begin to incorporate more audiences into the country's political life as well as upgrade the criteria for what constitutes legitimacy. While Malaysia's trajectory has been impressive to date, governing elites might now make more egalitarian, even democratic, progress.

Contemporary Features and Audiences

Documenting political legitimacy in Malaysia might seem easy to accomplish. The governing United Malays National Organization (UMNO), through the Barisan Nasional (National Front) coalition, has regularly renewed its control over state power through at least "semidemocratic" procedures. It operates a stable regime with little use of force, and it oversees a nation-state whose validity is contested, if anywhere, only on the regional edges. Such restraint has in most other Southeast Asian countries been usually short-lived or entirely absent. But it is precisely because of this benign configuration in Malaysia that political legitimacy is empirically difficult to verify. Audiences rarely celebrate legitimacy when it serves as "the quiet accompaniment of stable government."[1] Rather, it is when people oppose an existing government and its regime that they most readily engage in observable, cross-the-grain conduct, thereby enabling analysts "negatively" to establish the presence of legitimacy in other periods. One has little trouble, for example, highlighting the early authority of the Aquino government in the Philippines by showing the commitment with which the people sought to eliminate Marcos's rule. Such efforts to bring down one government or regime may evince the legitimacy of another.

Thus the absence of such situations in Malaysia—indeed, the very stability of its politics—makes it difficult to establish legitimacy's presence. Stability may, after all, subsist on no more than a low diet of habitual self-interest, widespread indifference, or stark public fear. To test for legitimacy in such circumstances, one can focus on strain points—periods during which political relations and economic conditions have ground down. Specifically, when self-interested audiences have long been denied material benefits, yet their fear of government coercion remains low, their sustained inaction, or actions stopping short of full-blown crisis, point strongly to perceptions of the government's authority.

Of course, the success of this approach hinges partly on showing that even during strain points public fear of coercion has indeed remained low in Malaysia. Skeptics can recite a crushing miscellany of emergency statutes, detention orders, and "draconian amendments" with which the UMNO-led government has enforced the social order and its primacy within it. Preventive arrest under the Internal Security Act (ISA) has been the sharpest instrument in its arsenal.[2] But without entering into difficult debate over the relationship between coercion and legitimacy (that is, that they may covary until reaching some threshold beyond which they vary inversely), one notes that the UMNO-led government has resorted to it sparingly. When placed in the larger setting of Southeast Asia, marked by "salvagings," disappearances, mysterious gunmen,[3] and killing fields, UMNO emerges as comparatively restrained. In short, though audiences in Malaysia have had opportunities to resist the government violently—as mass audiences have done in Burma, Thailand, Indonesia, and the Philippines, even though facing far greater risks—they have seldom made use of them.

Elite and Mass Audiences

Implicit in this thesis is legitimacy's relational aspect: its sense of obligation and reward among elites, as well as between them and mass audiences. Most accounts of elite-level interaction in Malaysia, at least before
the May Thirteenth rioting in 1969, emphasize consociational patterns of
party behavior converging tightly over ethnic lines in a national director-
ship.[4] Less noted is the extent to which elites have persisted in this mode
since 1969. In brief, while much political dynamism has shifted in recent
decades from an interethnic to a mainly intra-Malay arena, UMNO
leaders have never cut their economic ties to the Chinese. Indeed, today's
trustees of UMNO's business assets and the new generation of Chinese
capitalists appear to collaborate even more fully than in the past. Moreover, though greater Malay dominance over politics has spurred new factionalism in UMNO—giving rise to clusters of "old guards," "new orders," "ultras," and "teams"—it has not been waged at all costs. Even as
elite persons and factions have pushed past party rules in order to weaken
some leaders, their competitions have finally been contained by their belief
that they can legitimately wield state power only through an UMNO-led
government.

In terms of elite-mass relations, governing elites in Malaysia have vigorously sought legitimacy among various mass audiences. UMNO has
turned first to the Malay community, recognizing that collective identity
is central to validating political control. It is on the basis of "nation, race,
and faith"[5] that a leader declares before followers, "I am one of you,"
gaining the trust that anchors his or her standing as defender of communal
prerogatives. In doing this, UMNO has asserted the Malays' indigene
standing against other communities, founding its right to rule on "prior
occupation" and "ownership of the country."[6] Put simply, UMNO governing elites have proclaimed "Malay dominance" (*ketuanan Melayu*)
over the "land of the Malays" (*tanah Melayu*).[7] Further, to alloy this legitimacy with ordinary support, the UMNO-led government has fulfilled
Malay notions of birthright and entitlement with material rewards. During the first decade after independence, this effort consisted mainly of providing rural Malay populations with small-scale development projects,
agricultural subsidies, and settlement schemes. After the May Thirteenth
rioting, however, UMNO vastly augmented this approach, adopting the
New Economic Policy (NEP) in order to urbanize Malay audiences and
upgrade their socioeconomic status. A stream of state contracts and corporate restructuring thus carried aloft a very visible segment of "Malay
millionaires"—evidence of UMNO's commitment to an ethnic ascendancy that the community could more broadly, vicariously share. A new

Malay middle class was also developed through state scholarships, professional qualifications, managerial positions in state enterprises, and employment quotas thrust upon multinational and Chinese-owned businesses. And, finally, low-cost housing projects, amenities, and hiring requirements paved the way for Malay workers to enter urban production centers and services.

At the same time, while depending on tensions with other ethnic communities to make sense of its Malay guardian role, UMNO has tried to justify its primacy before non-Malay audiences as well. It has leavened its message of Malay dominance by gathering subordinate ethnic parties into its Barisan coalition, relying on them to magnify UMNO's forbearance on certain issues into an image of power sharing. The Chinese community, roughly one-third of Malaysia's population, has thus been offered representation in the cabinet through the Barisan's "number two" party, the Malaysian Chinese Association (MCA), and through the Gerakan Rakyat Malaysia (GRM, the People's Movement of Malaysia), a largely regional party based in Penang and Perak. The Indian community, about 8 percent of the country's population, has been represented in government by the Malaysian Indian Congress (MIC), while the views of certain indigenous groups in East Malaysia have been articulated at the federal level by such parties as the Parti Bangsa Dayak Sarawak (PBDS) and the United Sabah National Organization (USNO). Together with other party components—many of them "mosquito" organizations that have flitted in and out of the coalition—the Barisan Nasional has had generally a membership of about ten parties. Its campaign symbol is an evenly balanced scale.

This conciliatory message has also been expressed on an economic plane. While dedicated to strengthening the Malay presence in modern business sectors, the UMNO government has tried simultaneously to portray the NEP, through its mitigation of Malay bitterness, as beneficial to non-Malay mass audiences. In short, this appeal contains an implicit offer of protection against new rounds of May Thirteenth violence. More positively, perhaps, the NEP has also been grounded in certain material incentives for support. While publicly facilitating Malay access to Chinese-owned enterprises, loose implementation of the NEP has enabled even small and medium-sized Chinese firms to seek out state contract work through Bumiputra ("sons of the soil") front men. The NEP can even be read as having insulated the Chinese role in these exchanges, specifying that within an essentially market economy 40 percent of the country's total equity ownership should remain in non-Malay hands.

Finally, in terms of cultural appeals, the UMNO-led government has sought legitimacy, however disingenuously, by stressing the importance of a Malaysian identity and national unity. At one level, of course, this lan-

guage has taken a pernicious turn, as the government has pushed sporadi-
cally its National Culture Policy (NCP) of "one language, one culture"
weighted heavily toward the values of the indigenous race. But at other
times it has declared tactically its respect for a multiracial Malaysia.[8]
Overall, the government has thus refrained from waging a campaign of
zealous assimilation of non-Malay customs and educational practices by
claiming that policy decisions on such racially sensitive issues have been
reached in the consultative spirit of the "Barisan way."

Most non-Malays, however, have remained skeptical of these government pledges of comity. It is thus doubtful whether non-Malay support
for the Barisan—oscillating with the business cycle and the government's
sporadic ethnic concessions—has translated even during peak periods
into perceptions of legitimacy. One finds instead that below the elite level
these audiences have habitually maligned UMNO rule, sharply complain-
ing that "everything is for the Malays." Many Chinese have denigrated
the MCA's role in the cabinet as nominal, tokenist, or even traitorous
(while MCA leaders themselves sometimes let slip their frustrations over
UMNO decisions).[9] Indian businessmen and professionals have remained
equally aloof from the MIC, repelled by its image of boisterous leadership
and factional indiscipline. Within these communities, middle-class audiences have been especially resentful over the inability of non-Malay government parties to abolish NEP quotas, believing them to have hindered
their personal occupational advancement and their children's educational
opportunities. Indeed, during the 1970s, government proposals to restrict non-Malay tertiary education overseas, even when privately funded,
prompted many middle-class Chinese and Indians to migrate to Canada,
Australia, and New Zealand.[10] Such flight from "Malay dominance" un-
derscores the extent to which these audiences doubted the rightfulness of
government policies during this period or the utility of trying to change
them through existing regime procedures.

Nonetheless, in the Barisan's approach, best characterized overall as
"hegemonistic with accommodationist elements,"[11] it is clear that regardless of ethnic affiliation, most elite-level and middle-class audiences in Malaysia have been awarded a genuine, if uneven, piece of the action. Thus,
in taking the major ethnic communities together, it can probably be said
that the UMNO-led government has forged legitimacy among most Malays without utterly sacrificing all support among non-Malays—or at least
without disturbing a non-Malay acquiescence born of the recognition that
things could be worse. During the early 1990s, one might even push this
assessment further. While it has often been suggested that middle-class
non-Malays have at best viewed the government with a hard-bitten pragmatism, attitudes seem recently to have graduated into a more nuanced

understanding of the UMNO government's activities, or at least the prime minister's leadership. During campaigning for the 1990 general election, the *Far Eastern Economic Review* reported that Mahathir had "largely overcome his former Malay chauvinist image, and Chinese [were] for the first time turning out to shake his hand when he [made] political forays around the country." [12]

In surveying Malaysia's social terrain, however, we discover other audiences that may have slipped through the government's legitimacy net. Galvanized by the Iranian Revolution and global Muslim resurgence, the Parti Islam Se-Malaysia (PAS, the Pan-Malaysian Islamic Party) replaced its nationalist Malay leadership during the early 1980s with one that was even more avowedly theistic. Party leaders then began to denounce UMNO officials as *kafirs* (infidels)—"an extremely serious and emotional charge to be levelled at a fellow Muslim"—and they publicly challenged Mahathir to a televised debate over his religiosity. [13] Indeed, their "profound ideological distance" was shown by the PAS's rejection of UMNO's secular and ethnic appeals, professing loyalty to Allah rather than to any racial grouping. [14] Consequently, the simmering, often ancestral divisions between PAS and UMNO followings grew so inflamed that throughout the decade many Malay villagers refused to share mosques and burial grounds or permit their children to marry across party lines. UMNO responded by banning PAS *ceramahs* (political meetings) in the peninsula's northern states, claiming that PAS leaders were organizing an antigovernment *sabil* (crusade). Moreover, federal development assistance was withheld from PAS-controlled *kampongs*, while *imams* (religious teachers) appointed by UMNO refused to preach to them.

In these circumstances, the "Memali incident" erupted in northern Kedah in 1985. Seeking to prevent the arrest of a charismatic Muslim leader who had once been a PAS branch official, the villagers of Kampong Memali clashed with police in a daylong siege during which eighteen people were killed, marking an unusually violent confrontation in Malaysia's postcolonial history. Memali became the battle cry of PAS campaigners for the 1986 general election. [15] One further observes that with the election in 1990 of a mainly PAS government in Kelantan, resistance has intensified in the peninsula's northeast. Indeed, that PAS officials in Kelantan have repudiated the federal government's moral authority over them is shown by their insistence on forging an Islamic state founded on *shari'ah*—the divine law of Islam—and the *hudud* codes of punishment.

Equally, many urban Chinese workers, hawkers, and petty business operators have questioned the government's authority and withheld their support. More uniformly educated in Mandarin than middle-class Chinese are, these audiences have been deeply alienated by their inability to thread past official barriers to state benefits or to avoid state controls on their cultural practices. Evidently preferring their traditional business relationships and folkways, they remain suspicious of government intentions toward the webwork of Mandarin schools, shophouses, temples, and cultural displays that still clings to the country's Chinatowns. Further, while these groups have little appetite for armed revolt (recalling, perhaps, the emergency period during the 1950s and army conduct during the May Thirteenth rioting), they have nonetheless registered their disapproval of the Barisan by voting overwhelmingly against it. After the 1990 election, opposition leaders of the largely non-Malay Democratic Action Party (DAP) estimated that even the president of the MCA received only 10 to 15 percent of the ethnic Chinese vote in his district of Labis, while other MCA parliamentarians were able to win office only in Malay-majority districts suitably prepared for them by UMNO.[16] The opposition DAP has thus been able to assert that it is Malaysia's second-largest political party and the lone guardian of parliamentary accountability, socialist values, and cultural pluralism.

But even among these audiences, the UMNO-led government has headed off grave legitimacy crises through timely concessions and semi-democratic openness. Briefly, UMNO has alleviated Islamic grievances since the mid-1980s by burnishing its own religious character (chartering an interest-free Islamic bank and an Islamic university, requiring an undergraduate course in Islamic Civilization in universities, and presenting itself as the world's largest Islamic party), and it has in some measure dispersed Chinese resentments by permitting the DAP to articulate and give vent to them.[17] On this score, strongly Islamic Malays and working-class Chinese may doubt, even deny, the government's authority, but they seem at another level to accept the worth of the regime. Though these audiences vote regularly for opposition parties that contest the very purpose of government in Malaysia, their participation suggests they still value electoral procedures. Similarly, while the PAS and the DAP go further in calling for basic regime changes—the PAS wishing to eradicate liberal British residues in order to concentrate power among eminent Muslims in a consensus-seeking *syura* (Islamic council) and the DAP pressing conversely for greater political access and competitiveness (even while tightly enforcing leadership prerogatives within its own organization)—both parties have avoided electoral boycotts. In state assembly elections, moreover, they sometimes even contemplate coming to power, the PAS in Kelantan, Trengganu, and possibly Kedah and the DAP in Penang.

Thus, with doubts over the regime fairly limited among these audiences, fewer still have sifted down to challenge the rightfulness of the nation-state. PAS leaders have not questioned the country's borders so much as the sanctity of the political arrangements within them. Working-class Chinese, though denied the migratory options of the middle class, are so dispersed throughout the country's urban areas and "new villages" that they have never sustained coherent notions of secession. Indeed, DAP leaders sought in one instance to embarrass the Gerakan before the Chinese community by exposing what were alleged to be the plans of one of its top officials to obtain permanent residence in Australia.

Much more problematic today are the assessments of legitimacy made in the East Malaysian state of Sabah. Perhaps one-third of the state's population consists of ethnic Kadazans (a new, more nationalist term for the previous category of Dusun, a pejorative Malay word connoting "country hick").[18] The Kadazans, frequently Roman Catholic, often intermarry with the Chinese who make up about 20 percent of Sabah's population. Various other groups classified loosely as Muslim (Bajaus, Bugis, Brunei Malays, migrants from the southern Philippines) comprise approximately 40 percent. For two decades after Sabah's incorporation into Malaysia, UMNO was able to maintain Muslim parties in power in the state's legislative assembly. But in 1985, surging Kadazan resentments swept the Parti Bersatu Sabah (PBS, the United Sabah Party) into office. Though it entered the Barisan a year later, relations with UMNO remained tense. Kadazan grievances arose over UMNO's refusal to allow Sabah a state university or local television station, to increase Sabah's share of local oil revenues or the proportion of Sabahans working in local branches of federal agencies, or to stem the flow of Muslim migrants from the Philippines. This resentment was more generally expressed as indignation over UMNO's dismissal of the Twenty Points, a series of assurances offered to Sabah when it joined Malaysia in 1963.[19] Finally, just days before the 1990 general election, the PBS abruptly abandoned the Barisan Nasional in order to join an opposing coalition. Prime Minister Mahathir termed this action "a stab in the back," and after the Barisan's electoral victory he began to wage near-open warfare against the PBS state government.[20] This campaign succeeded finally in weakening the PBS during state elections in February 1994, then prompting enough defections from the party that it collapsed a month later.[21]

But the replacement of the PBS government has probably only deepened the resentment of many Kadazans about "Malay-Muslim hegemony" in Sabah. Indeed, through cultural associations, the recovery of collective myths and memories, and the revival of traditional festivals, Loh Kok Wah describes how ethnic leaders have forged a distinct, transclass sense of shared Kadazan identity in opposition to the UMNO-led government.[22] Many analysts thus fear that perceptions in Sabah of political illegitimacy may go beyond the government level to challenge the regime and nation-state, fueling strong antifederalist sentiments, even separatist actions. These attitudes may eventually accumulate in Malaysia's first legitimacy crisis, even if it is one limited to regional dimensions. Doubts over legitimacy could emerge also among some Iban groups in Sarawak,[23] some parties and movements that have operated in the past in Malaysia, and a few trade unions, media organizations, and public interest associations whose activities have been suppressed.

Great Moments and Strain Points

Thus far we have explored the ways in which elite and mass audiences may vary their perceptions of legitimacy as they move through concentric arenas of government, regime, and nation-state. Briefly, the UMNO-led government has established its legitimacy among most Malays and attracted their electoral support. It has also softened perceptions of illegitimacy among many Islamic groups and non-Malay communities, even purchasing some support through ad hoc co-optation or program fillips. Moreover, even when these audiences have rebuffed government appeals, their voter participation has seemed to signal that they perceive the regime as legitimate, a useful avenue for displaying their grievances. Finally, while we have noted growing perceptions in Sabah of the nation-state's illegitimacy, they are regional in scope and new in their intensity. Thus what stands out most is the extent to which the UMNO-led government has perpetuated its legitimacy across nearly the whole board, obtaining societal compliance without massive force.

In focusing more closely on UMNO's moral claim to state power, it is helpful to think in terms of "goal-rational legitimacy," a concept introduced by Muthiah Alagappa in Chapter 2. By this he means that while a government may project shades of personal or procedural legitimacy, it may more importantly claim that it incarnates society's most profound aspirations, thereby establishing its uniquely deserved right to rule. Marxist-Leninist governments have probably been the best example of this claim, boasting of scientific insights into capitalist contradictions, heavy industrialization, and social classlessness. But in Malaysia the UMNO-led government has also presented itself as able to rule matchlessly, fathoming special Malay needs, yet respecting essential non-Malay interests—all the while driving steady, sometimes rapid, economic growth that has been enjoyed by both sets of audiences.

Alagappa also discusses "politically defining moments," a collective reference to the great moments and strain points that respectively regenerate or run down legitimacy. At these junctures, cultural forces, mass attitudes, and elite decisions intersect in sharp reinforcements of, or decisive departures from, existing patterns of politics. Thus in charting the overall progress of legitimacy in Malaysia (by turns lineal, dialectical, and atavistic), one can identify a rough alternation of great moments and strain points, each set in the context of the milestone laid before it. In this way, one observes too that if legitimacy is relational, it is variable and dynamic. As governments typically leak their legitimacy away, they recast their claims in order to recapture it.

We have placed the UMNO-led government at the center of this analysis. Thus UMNO's founding marks the first great moment in the government's goal-rational legitimacy. Shortly after World War II, returning British forces sought to rationalize administration over the four Federated Malay States and the five Unfederated Malay States that together made up the protectorate known as British Malaya. As part of this scheme, colonial officials removed the "special privileges" enjoyed traditionally by the indigenous (and thus sovereign) Malays, abruptly putting the community on an equal political footing with the more entrepreneurial overseas Chinese. The result was an outpouring of Malay demands for protection that took British officials by surprise. It provided also the vital mass sentiments that Dato' Onn bin Jaafar, an aristocratic district officer from Johor, was able to amalgamate under the new UMNO in 1946.

After establishing itself as the leading Malay vehicle in politics, UMNO effectively pressed the British to restore many Malay privileges. It thus grew strong enough to forge a favorable relationship with the MCA, coalescing in 1952 in order to contest a series of elections that staked out the route to national independence. In making this arrangement—the basis for the Alliance party coalition formed in 1953—UMNO and MCA leaders acted on some assumptions about ethnic roles and their relative strengths. These understandings then cohered swiftly in another moment of legitimation and were encoded in the Merdeka Constitution. Informally labeled "the bargain," this document parceled out most state positions and power to UMNO leaders while preventing them from intruding in Chinese business dealings.

As a formula for legitimation, "the bargain" was oligarchic and communalist and therefore in keeping with the quiescent mass attitudes and rigid ethnic encapsulation prevailing at independence. Throughout the 1960s, however, economic growth eroded mass deference while entrenched inequalities began to galvanize Malay grievances. In the 1969 election, some Malay constituencies thus abandoned the Alliance coalition, splitting the Malay vote between UMNO and the PAS. Together with gains made by opposition Chinese parties, the election results created sudden uncertainties over Malay political dominance, triggering much elite-level maneuvering and the May Thirteenth rioting—a deep strain point in the UMNO-led government's legitimacy. UMNO acted quickly, however, to reenergize its standing. By turning from the interethnic bargain to reverse discrimination under the New Economic Policy, UMNO acquired directly, or through new government agencies, top positions and assets in many foreign and Chinese-owned companies, then either shifted them to key Malay insiders or held them in trust for mass Malay audiences. As we will see, however, this policy constituted less the break in elite relations that is often supposed than another moment in UMNO's quest to retain legitimacy.[24] While strengthening its primacy and ties to the Malays, UMNO continued at some level to cooperate with the non-Malays, replacing the Alliance coalition with the more loosely accommodative Barisan Nasional in 1974.

But in this new environment of greater Malay political power and economic participation, UMNO factions emerged in opposition to one another. During the 1970s, then, cleavages within the Malay community began to overshadow the country's interethnic rivalries, producing a second strain point in Malaysia's political record. Limited mainly to competing UMNO elites, this episode was marked by party purges, televised confessions, detentions under the Internal Security Act, and long terms of imprisonment. It was never capped, however, by any reformulation of policy and explicit new moment in legitimation. Rather, it was gradually wound down through expedient deals, key pardons and early releases, and the resumption of political and business careers.

Perhaps because of this irresolution, a third strain point occurred ten years later that had similar origins.[25] There were also important differences, however, in that conflict this time took place amid a sharp economic downturn affecting Malay elites and the middle class, and it threatened eventually to spill over into interethnic arenas. Accordingly, this outbreak grew vastly more complex and raged far more destructively than the previous one, even splitting UMNO and leading to its formal deregistration. Malaysia's dramatic economic recovery during the late 1980s, however, resuscitated UMNO, giving it the resources with which again to embrace many Malays and some space in which to treat the Chinese more permissively. This episode may amount to a new legitimating moment. Specifically, the government replaced the New Economic Policy in 1991 with the New Development Policy (NDP), which seemed to scale back the government's role in the economy and its enforcement of preferentialist Malay quotas. Many Chinese have thus welcomed the NDP, at least tentatively, recognizing that the next round of economic contraction and scarcity should clarify its status as a durable moment of legitimation.

Let us conclude by returning to a point made at the start of this section. While the UMNO-led government's legitimacy has fluctuated in great moments and strain points, it has never slipped into legitimacy crises. And because the government has avoided such crises, it is difficult to show comparatively that legitimacy has at other times existed. The best way, then, is to focus on strain points, making use of the difference between moral legitimacy and ordinary support. During these episodes, the government's economic or distributional performance fell seriously below the expectations of critical Malay audiences, thereby weakening support based on self-interest. The extent to which audiences remained uncoerced, yet refrained from challenging the UMNO-led government, may then reasonably be ascribed to their acceptance of its authority. This is not to say that they continued faithfully to follow UMNO elites during these strain points or that these elites honored UMNO procedures unflinchingly. Indeed, personal standings eroded and game rules were broken (helping, paradoxically, to make the case that attitudes were not deadened by indifference). Rather, it is to suggest that deeper perceptions about "goal-rational legitimacy"—in the Malaysian context, the ethnic claims that mark the UMNO-led government as the rightful holder of state power—have unequivocally endured.

Ethnic and Colonial Bases of Legitimacy

Government appeals for legitimacy must bear strong relevance to the identities and outlooks of key audiences. In this section, then, we will focus more closely on the historical development of audiences and attitudes in Malaysia, tracking their formation and demonstrating their significance for perceptions of legitimacy today. At the most fundamental level, of course, Malaysia's audiences have been ethnically delineated. It is not enough, however, to take this as given and then simply say that the UMNO government's appeals have resonated strongly among the Malays and other audiences have been variously appeased or left alienated. Rather, the emergence and tenacity of ethnic linkages themselves must be explored. One should also take account of other forms of cleavage that seem increasingly to intersect ethnic lines and stake out new segments, combining in complex new patterns of intraethnic tension and, occasionally, cross-ethnic tolerance.

Debate continues to swirl around ethnic identification—the extent to which it is deeply primordial, merely "false consciousness," or collectively rational.[26] Moreover, while ethnicity is at least partly manifested in culture, its adjustable character robs it of lasting cultural markers. Ethnic identities may thus be multiple, even nested, abruptly changing as contexts and reference communities change, or they may be evolutional, gradually and subtly unfolding. But, as is the case with political legitimacy, one no sooner determines that static, watertight ethnic cultures do not objectively exist than one sees their emotional power in historical processes of social affiliation and conflict. Donald Horowitz ascribes this power to an individual quest to share in ethnic "group worth." [27] Judith Strauch and Judith Nagata respectively emphasize "psychic comfort" and "reflected glory." [28] And Clive Kessler writes about finding "personal authenticity" in a collective identity; he also observes that "familiar, ancient, and deeply rooted cultural elements [have] the power to confer legitimacy." [29]

Ethnic Malay Perceptions

Interelite and elite-mass relations may be legitimated (or denied legitimacy) by ethnically framed cultures. With respect to the Malay community, authority (*kewibawaan*) traditionally rested on a rigid, intricate system of stratification that was traceable to the fifteenth-century Melaka Sultanate and recorded in the *Malay Annals* (*Sejarah Melayu*), various histories (*hikayat*), and court texts. The supplementary myth of Hang Tuah (*Hikayat Hang Tuah*) also helped solemnize knowledge about the virtues of royal greatness and mass deference, disseminating it across a patchwork of Malay kingdoms (*kerajaan*) even after Melaka's collapse. [30]

Uppermost in this status system was a hereditary patriarch—the ruler, rajah, or sultan—"the repository of Islamic authority and supernatural power." [31] Possessing legendary *kedaulatan* (sovereignty) and sacred regalia, as well as claiming the sanction of Islam, the rulers succeeded generally in performing an unimpeachable role as "protector." [32] The relational quality of this authority, however, was also made plain by the annals: "If any ruler puts a single one of his subjects to shame (*memberi 'aib*), that shall be a sign that his kingdom will be destroyed by Almighty God. Similarly it has been granted by Almighty God to Malay subjects that they shall never be disloyal or treacherous to their rulers, even if their rulers behave evilly or inflict injustice upon them." [33]

The ruler had therefore to consult first with local elites. Ensconced in the capital of his respective state the ruler met in an open hall with the noblemen, engaging them in consensual decision making and validating their statuses with a medley of high titles and court offices. He also shared power and statuses with nonaristocratic chiefs in the hinterland, presenting them with the honorific "*datuk*," necessary insignia, and letters of credit (*surat tauliah*). Further, the ruler relied on these chiefs to broaden his authority over mass Malay audiences. [34] Even at this level, however, the ruler's powers were limited and his authority relational. The annals admonish: "Subjects are like roots and the ruler is like the tree; without roots the tree cannot stand upright."[35] One notes also the "traditional concern for manpower in the lightly populated lands of Southeast Asia,"[36] as well as the dissipating effects of great physical distances and impassable terrains. In sum, then, the Malay rulers' governing status, their transfer of that status through monarchic regimes, and their assertion of power over the *negeri* could never be morally contested. It could, however, be moderated or avoided, revealing its relational, rather than absolutist, nature.

In time, however, these cultural assumptions about royal authority eroded. During the nineteenth century in particular, wealth from an accelerated tin trade in the peninsula "wrecked Malay political culture" as the rulers were challenged by their newly enriched chiefs.[37] Royal status, in short, was quickly hollowed out as chiefs struck separate deals with Chinese miners and set up their own riverine tollways. John Gullick records that "quarrels over power and money led to turbulence. In 30 years from 1839 every state of the peninsula had suffered . . . a usurpation of the throne or a civil war or both."[38] In these unsettled circumstances, even peasants often abandoned their rulers, migrating freely around the peninsula.

But from the late nineteenth century until World War II, Malay political culture was in many ways reconstituted through British colonialism. As is well known, the British sought to legitimate the power they seized in Malaya by propping up and adorning the rulers' ceremonial visages, celebrating them with palaces, incomes, and honors modeled on Victorian England's own newly innovated rituals and Mogul-Indian pageantry.[39] It is less well known that the British residential system and various state councils fostered genuine discussion on certain issues. This involved, for example, the appointments of district headmen (*penghulus*) and religious magistrates (*kathis*), Malay pensions, peasant farming, and Muslim personal law.[40] Thus one could argue that indirect rule—at least as it was applied in Malaya—preserved, even elevated, some of the rulers' traditional authority. Gullick has recently written that "there were sometimes disagreements, and in the last resort the resident could insist on having his way. But it suited both parties to avoid an open confrontation, and so the ruler had some power to restrain or postpone unwelcome changes."[41] He observes also that the rulers were strengthened by the British settlement of succession disputes and the containment of chiefs and that their communication was facilitated through colonial conferences and *durbars* (formal, high-level meetings). Further, they were given more formal authority in their respective *negeri* over Islam and culture. Indeed, the greater resilience that the British imparted to the rulers was made clear by their inability to do away with royal privileges under the Malayan Union scheme in 1946.[42]

As decision making in the protectorate grew more routinized, however, much of it was shifted from the rulers and residents to new bureaucratic arenas. Owing partly to shortages of European personnel, the Malays were not overlooked in this matter. Rather, they were trained for new bureaucratic roles at the Malay College at Kuala Kangsar, and they were recruited after 1910 into a subsidiary stream called the Malay Administrative Service. Moreover, some argue that this policy brought an important "acculturation process" to bear, further converting the regional loyalties and family rivalries of dispersed Malay elites into a sense of corporate unity.[43] For our purposes here, it is the revival and projection of traditional status into a deeply rule-ordered context that deserves attention.

Put simply, Malay cultural attitudes toward authority were revitalized, yet updated, through colonial experience.[44] Authority was thus made more explicitly rule-bound and transferable, changing hands from the rulers to aristocratic civil servants and eventually to top UMNO politicians. One recognizes in this progress from regional sultanism to Malay nationalism much continuity in elite-level relations. After World War II, the rulers and Malay aristocrats acquired still more layers of court protocol and ceremony, even as their protector role shrank to a symbolic importance. UMNO, having defended Malay "special rights" against British attempts to repeal them, then rapidly took precedence as the community's substantive protector.[45] Yet the overlap and reciprocity between these elites was made clear by the annual shower of royal titles upon UMNO leaders, coupling noble *kedaulatan* (sovereignty) and secular authority in a dual concept of protector.[46]

At the same time, in their appeal to mass audiences for legitimacy, A. C. Milner notes that the new Malay ideologues appropriated the language of the royal courts: "Loyalty and service to the race were described in precisely the same terms as had been used for centuries to convey devotion to a sultan."[47] Accordingly, the basic principle of UMNO's governing authority remained that it must not be openly challenged. Many have noted the persistence of "feudal" or patrimonial organization of Malay political power, an "unquestioning loyalty," a "culture of deference," and "obligatory followership."[48] But we also observe that individuals and cliques remained able to maneuver in oblique and anonymous ways. Through elliptical speeches and slights, criticisms veiled in proverbs and Malay poems, *surat layang* ("flying" or poison pen letters), whispering campaigns, and extraordinary levels of rumormongering, followers acted on their ambitions through techniques characterized as the traditional shadow play (*wayung kulit*).[49] Further, even when followers erred in posing too direct or public a challenge, cultural norms suggested that leaders mete out a moderate punishment—a posting abroad or a transfer to the interior—and that followers unhesitatingly accept it. This overall restraint in interelite and elite-mass relations was an important element in what has widely been described in Malaysia as the "Malay way."[50]

Ethnic Chinese Perceptions

Ethnic Chinese culture was also disposed toward vertical authority patterns and stark stratification. Lucian Pye attributes this tendency to Confucian assumptions: in the classical Chinese ideal, they were crystallized in an authority structure overseen by an imperial patriarch and upheld by the landed gentry and scholarly bureaucratic elites.[51] This configuration was in some ways reproduced in colonial Malaya. British officials formalized the status of Chinese headmen (*kapitan Cina*) who then incorporated their workers in clan houses (*kongsi*) and secret societies (*hui*). Strauch observes that in these circumstances, "workers [were] bound through secret-society ritual to their elite leaders who filled authority roles modeled in part on those of lineage heads in China."[52]

But the absence in Malaya of an authentic Chinese patriarch meant that authority relations never solidified fully in traditional ways. Restrictions on Chinese smallholdings and bureaucratic employment exacerbated this condition, producing upstart leaders who looked upon commerce as the main source of status despite its "low evaluation in their native land."[53] Thus, in ungoverned competitions for wealth, the Chinese "genius for combination" was converted into a disunifying force as the *kapitan Cina* mobilized rival lineages in violent struggles over tin fields, triggering uprisings in Perak and contributing to the civil war in Selangor. In the late nineteenth century, then, the British abolished the *kapitan Cina* system and outlawed secret societies, regularizing their functions under an office called the Chinese Protectorate. During subsequent decades, marked by periods of great market prosperity, the nature of Chinese leadership changed. Business leaders replaced the secret society headman and war chief.[54]

After World War II, these new tycoons (*towkay*) made their political authority manifest in the Malayan (later Malaysian) Chinese Association (MCA) while continuing culturally to underpin it through philanthropic aid to Chinese schools and social organizations (*shetuan*).[55] Although they avoided violent confrontation, they still played out their rivalries against a backdrop of lingering subethnic identities. Hence, in contrast to the Malays who held Islam and Malay languages in common, Chinese segmentation bristled with sharp linguistic differences, especially after the emergence of English-educated Chinese. Further, while the Malays generally muted their subethnic regional identities—traceable to various peninsular Malay states and Indonesian islands—many Chinese leaders and followers cherished their distinct provincial, county, and prefectural roots in South China through native-place associations (*tongxiang huiguan*).[56] Even as some Chinese grew more attuned to the Malaysian setting, this seemed only to splinter the community more seriously, creating groups that were unevenly assimilated and committed to their new homeland.[57]

Finally, while the Malays had a strong political incentive to claim indigenous Malay status and preferentialist state benefits—first from the British and later from UMNO—the rewards of an overarching identity were less obvious to the Chinese. Though intuitively it might seem that they could wrest better terms from UMNO by uniting and bringing their full numbers to bear, this would probably have raised Malay suspicions, thereby forcing UMNO's hand. Indeed, for many Chinese, the futility of seeking either to conciliate or confront UMNO has been made plain since independence by the limited efficacy of both the MCA's participation in government and the DAP's role in opposition. This configuration of Malay dominance has bred cultural confusion among the Chinese, weakening their conformity to cultural rules about legitimate political conduct. Pye observes that "Confucian political culture does not contain any guidelines for minority leadership in a community dominated by a non-Confucian culture. . . . Any Chinese who acts as a leader must be an impostor if he is subservient to the Malay majority leadership."[58] In consequence, factions of young bloods, Young Turks, and "Chinese Firsters" have challenged the authority of MCA leaders regularly and openly, sparking brawls that variously fascinated and alienated their followings.

This brief overview of cultural attitudes toward authority suggests that through colonial experience Malay elite and mass audiences reestablished much agreement over hierarchical status. These contours were reinforced by political incentives and shared language and religion, ensuring that intra-Malay competitions were moderately waged. In these circumstances, Malay leaders were popularly credited with an ethos of ethnic unity and fair play. Taken in isolation, classical Chinese culture seemed equally to value inviolate status and consensus among followers. But in the distant context of Malaysia, the lack of traditional, unassailable Chinese patriarchs encouraged elite rivalries. Such behavior, moreover, flourished in an unfamiliar condition of Malay hegemony that sowed doubts about Confucian culture and activated narrow subethnic loyalties. While colonial experience probably restrained MCA leaders from competing violently for power, they were nonetheless impelled to play rough, repeatedly bogging down in factional impasses that drained their authority.

Interethnic Relations and Legitimacy

After independence, one might expect that this skewed distribution of power would tempt the Malays to seek more of it, commensurably worsening tensions among the Chinese. Indeed, such assumptions inform most recent studies of Malaysia's political economy.[59] But it is more interesting to ask why ethnic imbalances and political strain points have not grown more severe still, thereby concentrating authority patterns more tightly and marking out sharp breaks in legitimacy. In asking this question, we begin by returning to the colonial record. What did the colonial experience mean in terms of fusing ethnic leaders in common attitudes toward authority? To be sure, the British forged "the epitome of the plural society,"[60] closely juxtaposing the Malays and Chinese and concretizing their differences in an ethnic division of responsibilities and reward. This approach has often been judged a colonial strategy of divide and rule, imposing gross ethnic labels upon audiences in British Malaya in order to heighten their differences.[61] With the removal of colonial control, one would have expected ethnic elites and mass publics to erupt in uncorked communalism.[62]

But with the brief though important exception of the ethnic rioting in 1969, destabilizing eruptions did not occur, suggesting that the motivations and effects of British colonialism were more complex. One could argue that in pursuing a sophisticated self-interest against what they expected was a limitless time horizon, the British avoided separating Malaysia's ethnic elites into conflicting functions and antagonistic cultures. By consulting with the rulers through the state councils over certain issues, the British fashioned a contractual basis for their control over the protectorate and opened a conduit to mass sentiments. More to the point, however, state council membership was broadened to incorporate ethnic Chinese. Thus while the *kapitan Cina* and *towkay* who attended the state councils were preoccupied with tin mining, tariffs, revenue farms, and the immigration of coolies, they learned swiftly to collaborate with the rulers in mutually beneficial ways. By gaining from the rulers necessary "resolutions in council," the Chinese were authorized to develop the industries upon which royal pensions depended (a pattern, we have noted, that persists today). Moreover, Emily Sadka records several cases involving land usage and leases wherein Chinese councillors supported the rulers in successfully opposing the British resident.[63]

As the pace of economic activity quickened and power fell to the bureaucracy, Malay aristocrats gained new prominence through the Malay Administrative Service. Though the Chinese were prevented by the rulers from entering this service in the protectorate's Federated Malay States, they were able to join the Straits Settlements civil service in the crown colony encompassing Singapore, Malacca, and Penang. Presumably the bureaucratic acculturation process for Chinese officers was in many ways the same as for Malays, thereby projecting across ethnic lines some common notions about the legitimate use of state power. It also made plain that in parting with some of this power, the British greatly favored the "sovereign" Malays but did not bluntly shut out the Chinese.

During the decade between World War II and Malaysia's independence, the British tried to equilibrate representation across ethnic elites and, further, to broaden it among mass audiences with democratic procedures. Even more strikingly, this process involved efforts to undo tight ethnic loyalties. The British tried to level ethnic standings by inaugurating the Malayan Union scheme in 1946, convening the Communities Liaison Committee (CLC) during 1949–50, and backing the multiethnic Independence of Malaya Party (IMP) in several democratic elections.[64] Three points stand out. First, lest we mistake this for a wholly altruistic departure from sophisticated self-interest, we are reminded that the British sought through the union scheme to punish the rulers for their wartime amity with the Japanese, as well as to resuscitate the Chinese businesses that would hasten economic recovery.[65] They also hoped that by promoting open politics they could keep markets open and thus the place of British firms within them. Second, the British were only partly successful on each of these counts. After long perpetuating beliefs about Malay sovereignty, the British met with firm Malay resistance over their sweeping attempts to equalize ethnic statuses. They thus retreated behind the federation agreement that restored Malay privileges and reopened legal questions over Chinese citizenship. In the CLC meetings, moreover, while the British succeeded in building a bond of trust between Malay and Chinese leaders,[66] they were unable to root out Malay notions of "special rights" or the inclination to align in ethnic parties. This became clear as early as the Kuala Lumpur city council elections in 1952 when UMNO and the MCA, forming an alliance but refusing to merge more deeply, soundly defeated the Independence of Malaya Party. Analysts have since observed that attempts to form multiethnic parties in Malaysia have either failed outright or tilted in ethnic directions, highlighting the value that audiences have continued to place on their ethnic identities and cultures. Finally, one notes that although Malaysia's elections took on a Westminster gloss, their competitiveness was belied by UMNO's perennial use of district malapportionment and patronage in order to win them. Thus, from the start, Malaysia's regime must be classified as no more than quasi-democratic.

On the other hand, the British were able to block changes to existing political and social orientations they considered desirable. During the Malayan Emergency between 1948 and 1960, they took strong actions against leftist forces, banning certain Malay associations influenced by Sukarno's vision of socialism and defeating militarily the Malayan Communist Party, made up largely of Chinese. Passivity due to government coercion should not be mistaken for legitimacy, however. When coercion stops, the lack of legitimacy may be made plain by the recurrence of suppressed behavior driven by contrary ideals. But the withdrawal of most British troops from Malaysia toward the end of the emergency did not result in any new surge of leftist sentiments and organizing. This silence can be partly explained by the UMNO government's continuing use of preventive detention against socialist parties—in particular, the Malay-led Parti Rakyat (People's Party) and the Chinese-oriented Labor Party, which combined in 1957 as the Socialist Front. But the inability of the Parti Rakyat to mobilize the Malays is better understood by the extent to which it was overshadowed by traditional kinds of authority and protection: the rulers' noblesse oblige and UMNO's patrimonialism. Equally, the Labor Party's attractiveness for the Chinese lay less in its class-based prescriptions than in its commitment to ethnic defense. This was shown when the Socialist Front finally fractured in disputes over establishing Malay as the country's official language.[67]

Overall, then, this interplay between colonial designs and long-standing structures served greatly to modify, yet contrarily to reinforce, traditional assumptions about leadership, ethnicity, and class relations. This outcome provided congenial soil for UMNO government authority, even while creating a space in which non-Malay business elites could operate. Thus, in terms of elite-mass relations among the Malays and inter-elite relations across both communities, one can conceptualize a moment of legitimation coinciding with independence. Moreover, this initial moment was formalized by the Merdeka Constitution and the interethnic bargain it contained. As noted earlier, this agreement posited that Malay leaders would hold the lion's share of state power but would refrain from using it to impinge upon corresponding Chinese control of the economy.[68] To close the deal, these elites exchanged enough of their resources that they all enjoyed something of both worlds. UMNO leaders, granting in the manner of the sultan in council the state licenses and contracts that sustained Chinese businesses, received campaign contributions, secret funds, and memberships on the boards of Chinese-owned companies. Top Chinese businessmen, in turn, were given a political voice through the MCA in the governing Alliance. One also notes that the Malayan Indian Congress (MIC) was brought into the Alliance in 1954, thereby incorporating the leadership of the small Indian community.

In this configuration, UMNO imbued the Alliance with indigenous Malay status, thereby grounding its claim to be the "predominant partner."[69] UMNO had to clarify this predominance just once—when its standing was challenged briefly during the July crisis of 1959 by an MCA faction of "Chinese Firsters."[70] Thereafter, the UMNO president held even firmer sway over the Alliance, allocating candidacies among its component parties and approving their selections. Reserved for the MCA, however, were ministerial appointments in finance and in commerce and industry, enabling its leaders to block fiscal policies that threatened Chinese business interests. These same terms were also reflected in broad political and cultural contexts. Malay dominance was enshrined in the rotating monarchial position of *yang dipertuan agong*, the official status of Islam, and privileged Malay access to state hiring, licenses, and scholarships. In adopting an accommodative posture, however, UMNO leaders retained non-Malays in technical units of the bureaucracy, permitted the observance of non-Islamic religions, and delayed in designating Malay as the official language. R. S. Milne thus concludes that "when the whole scene [was] surveyed, in its political, economic, and social aspects, it [became] clear that a kind of short-term rough justice between the claims of the communities [was] in fact attained."[71]

To sum up this section: Plainly history—and historicization—matter. Citing the importance of the Melaka Sultanate and its portrayal in the *Sejarah Melayu*, Barbara and Leonard Andaya write: "Even today elements of earlier statecraft can be discerned in modern Malay political relationships and in the functioning of Malay society itself."[72] Long periods of continuity—or, conversely, sharp breaks in the record—can thus be understood as set in a trajectory of earlier events, variously perpetuating its momentum or reacting deliberately against it. We began by noting that traditional orientations among the Malays focused on strong, even supernatural, leadership tempered by protection, leniency, and geographic distances. These expectations similarly characterized the Chinese. When juxtaposed in the colonial setting of Malaya, however, these ethnic lineages began to evolve in reference to one another. At the elite level, British policies did much to harmonize these identities and roles, cultivating a reciprocity across distinct spheres of competence. But within these communities, while colonialism strengthened mass Malay perceptions of the rulers' authority, it did not concretize equivalent patterns among the Chinese. Traditional Chinese outlooks had transferred imperfectly to Malaya, distorted by the slippage of elite status from classical emperors, bureaucrats, and scholars to upstart *towkay*-politicians. Moreover, while Malay outlooks persisted after independence, even while gravitating from the rulers to UMNO, mass Chinese audiences remained distant from the MCA, disillusioned by its inability to pursue their ethnic needs.

Malay Views of UMNO Authority

This section articulates more precisely the fit between Malay expectations and the governing UMNO's appeals. This correspondence has produced among many Malays an unbroken perception of government legitimacy during the postcolonial period—a claim that we shall test in the light of some serious strain points.

Many cursory accounts of Malaysian politics and socioeconomic structures still dwell on the country's "plural," "divided," or "communal" makeup as its most salient feature, suggesting that any serious study of legitimacy must be cast relentlessly along these lines. Yet political and even economic dynamism has been flowing steadily from interethnic to intra-Malay arenas since the 1970s. Hence, in today's context of undoubted Malay dominance, there is good reason to give special attention to Malay assessments of UMNO authority, testing them amid the new party rivalries that have erupted quite independently of fears of the non-Malays. Indeed, the most recent strain point in the country's political record only belatedly took on a "communalist" tone; at other times it featured some contingent, interethnic alliances.

The selection of strain points—in 1969, the mid-1970s, and the late 1980s—enables us to chart this flow of power to UMNO and the rising salience of intra-Malay issues. While the May Thirteenth rioting in 1969 hinged clearly on ethnic hostilities, later strain points must be thought of primarily as intra-Malay competitions. In analyzing UMNO conflict during the 1970s, surging atop unusually high growth levels and redistributive benefits, one learns first that the personal authority of UMNO leaders and the procedural legitimacy of UMNO game rules were nearly exhausted. Moreover, this erosion set precedents for further attacks on the prime minister and deeper violations of UMNO traditions during the 1980s, especially when catalyzed by the economic contraction of that period. That these strain points stopped short of full-blown legitimacy crises, however, suggests the hardy character of UMNO's goal-oriented legitimacy, the basis for its recovery of Malay support.

Finally, while analysts naturally differ in their interpretations of these strain points, most would nonetheless agree that they mark the most severe tests in the country's political life. These junctures, therefore, offer good opportunities for isolating the governing UMNO's authority before many Malay audiences and investigating its precise nature. This approach also makes for an intrinsically challenging exercise: verifying implicit perceptions of legitimacy among the Malays is methodologically more difficult than cataloging the less favorable sentiments expressed by the non-Malays.

The decade after the July crisis in 1959 can be thought of as an age of high political culture in UMNO, the period during which its leader's personal authority, its procedural traditions about incumbency and succession, and its cultural and symbolic underpinnings were consolidated and most reliably infused with legitimacy and support. Such a description of

high culture is more than caricature. When many of today's UMNO leaders refer wistfully to party leadership and traditions—usually lamenting
the regularity with which they have come to be challenged—they appear
to have in mind the easy compliance and sense of order in the party that
reached their apogee during the 1960s. What they have never had cause
to lament, however, is any serious loss of UMNO's legitimacy, its ultimate
right to rule. Although ordinary support for the party has in recent decades sometimes grown thin, and even personal and procedural legitimacy
has seriously declined, the party's "infallible" insights about how best to
affirm Malay dominance and unity, to manage the non-Malays through
the Barisan way, and to uplift all communities through development have
perpetuated its standing among most Malaysian audiences.

Tunku Abdul Rahman, a prince from the northern Malay state of
Kedah, served during the 1950s and 1960s as UMNO president (and
hence Malaysia's prime minister). Habituated in colonial experience, he
seemed to merge an aristocratic outlook with modern beliefs, marking his
rule as highly personalist in a severely bureaucratized setting.[73] While publicly adopting a strong "Malaya for the Malays" attitude,[74] he spent his
leisure time in un-Malay ways, gambling and playing mah-jong with the
Chinese. The Tunku was autocratic, true; yet he was often permissive, tolerant of Malay cronies and Chinese monopolies.

But it is less the Tunku's decisional style and indulgence of the Chinese
that some Malays admire today than the autonomy with which he was
able to take these actions. Indeed, his leadership was shaped, though
largely unchecked, by the formal institutions of party and state. The
Tunku thus dominated the UMNO Supreme Council meetings,[75] person-
ally selected *mentri besars* (chief ministers), and appointed his followers
to the party's state liaison committees. At UMNO's annual general assem-
blies, compliant delegations of Malay civil servants and schoolteachers
broadly respected the Tunku's leadership autonomy, leaving most top
party posts for him to fill. Accountability, then, involved no more than
weakly phrased "chiding," "furtive" opposition, and unfocused resolutions growing from mysterious cliques operating loosely in the states.[76]

In sum, then, the Tunku reflected, yet set his stamp upon, syncretic Malay attitudes toward support and authority. He lacked the brassy charisma
specified by Weber, perhaps, but operated still with a resonant persona
and leadership style. Thus while the substance of his decisions might now
and then be personalist and unpopular (his admission of Singapore into
the federation followed by its summary expulsion, his ouster of Sarawak's
chief minister, and his temporizing over the National Language Bill), this
expressed, to a point, the UMNO president's personal authority and autonomy from procedures. Overall, one concludes that patrimonial lead-

ership and power in UMNO—informed by the traditional Malay role of protector, colonial experience, and new organizational modes; clouded in ceremony though solidly undergirded by beliefs in hierarchy, seniority, orderly succession, and patience (and the proximity of a menacing non-Malay community); and tempered by exchange relationships, however unequal, democratic procedures, however insincere, and scope for low-level factionalism and criticisms, however informal and nonideological—established a baseline of legitimacy in the party's political culture. It is against this standard that subsequent strain points and their effects on legitimacy may be measured. As we shall see, strains in support for UMNO—cutting even into its personal and procedural elements of legitimacy—indicate the goal-rational authority that UMNO has more broadly retained. Indeed, this legitimacy appears to have been revitalized at certain other historical moments as well.

The May Thirteenth Riots

Although there was modest economic growth in Malaysia during the 1960s, analysts agree that many Malays were increasingly frustrated by their inability to share in it.[77] Chinese control over credit, tight trading networks, keen motivation, and experience—enclosed in ethnic culture and family loyalties—presented formidable barriers to Malay participation. Moreover, in abiding by "the bargain," Tunku Abdul Rahman did little to remedy these imbalances with state power. While his government funded agricultural support schemes and rural development projects, it stopped short of promoting Malay entry into urban sectors of the economy or even consolidating the ascendancy of Malay cultural symbols. Thus, after a decade during which "the high expectation the Malays had of 'their' government helping them failed to be realized,"[78] support for UMNO began to wane. Moreover, their grievances began to center directly on the Tunku, a protector perceived finally as unwilling to protect them. After he compromised with MCA leaders in producing the National Language Act in 1967, for example, students at the Muslim College sharply dramatized his loss of personal authority by burning him in effigy.[79]

These attitudes were also made manifest in Malaysia's 1969 general election as Malay support slipped away to the Parti Islam Se-Malaysia (PAS). During this period, the PAS articulated a fairly straightforward Malay nationalism. Thus most accounts frame the election and the May Thirteenth rioting that followed in terms of raw communalist parties that ignored, or were oblivious of, the power-sharing arrangements of "the bargain."[80] By respectively galvanizing Malay grievances over the economy and non-Malay resentments about their inferior political and cultural status, these parties succeeded in gravely weakening the Alliance government. Many Chinese then organized processions in Kuala Lumpur to celebrate the gains made by the opposition Democratic Action Party and the Gerakan, inflaming Malay resentment over the loss of their birthright and provoking them finally to engage in several days of sharp ethnic violence.[81]

These events should not, however, be construed as a legitimacy crisis for UMNO. Although failure to promote Malay interests had eroded support for UMNO as well as the Tunku's personal authority, the underlying, goal-based authority was unaffected and even strengthened. Many Malays in Kuala Lumpur—confronted by the consequences of their support for the PAS and the tide of Chinese euphoria—turned again to UMNO. Rallying outside the residence of the UMNO chief minister of Selangor, Datuk Harun Idris, they sought reassurance over their identity and moral coherence for their protests. The Malay counterdemonstrations organized by Harun, and perhaps even the rioting they precipitated, can be interpreted as a mass-level acknowledgment of UMNO authority. Similarly, at the elite level, while some UMNO leaders continued to scorn the Tunku's personal leadership, they too declared their belief in the party's greater legitimacy. For example, a UMNO Supreme Council member, Dr. Mahathir Mohamad, having been defeated in the election by the PAS, circulated an open letter to the Tunku demanding that he stand down because "the Malays . . . hate you for giving [the Chinese] too much face."[82] But rather than leaving UMNO in order to work against it, Mahathir led a group of "ultras" in seeking its renewal, urging that the MCA be dropped from the government, that parliament be closed permanently, and that UMNO set up, in essence, a one-party state.[83]

While UMNO's primacy was quickly renewed, the tough methods prescribed by Mahathir were avoided (leading even to his brief expulsion from the party), highlighting significant aspects of continuity. Most accounts ascribe a watershed quality to the May Thirteenth rioting, citing the rupture of elite relations across ethnic lines, the steady closure of politics, the removal of the Tunku, and heightened factionalism in UMNO. But despite the fury of mass Malay action and UMNO's response, the riots cannot be conceptualized as a deep break in Malaysia's political record after which everything ineluctably changed. Ethnic cooperation, though greatly adjusted under the New Economic Policy, persisted at the elite level. Parliament was reopened and democratic procedures were reintroduced, if in truncated form. Moreover, the Tunku was peacefully eclipsed by his deputy, Tun Abdul Razak, rather than forcibly ousted, and hence he was able to play a prominent role at later political strain points.

In seeking to regain support and reinforce its legitimacy, UMNO began after May Thirteenth to meet more of the Malays' material aspirations. It extolled Malay indigenousness by dusting off the Bumiputra ("sons of the soil") legal classification and vastly upgraded special rights through the NEP. But while this policy's aim "to bring up the Malays" appears straightforward,[84] its operations and consequences grew highly complex. First, the UMNO government created new trust agencies, such as the National Trading Corporation (Perbadanan Nasional Bhd., or Pernas) and the National Equity Corporation (Permodalan Nasional Bhd.), which carved out holdings in foreign and Chinese-owned companies. By then releasing these assets to the Malays through cooperative schemes, UMNO projected that the community's total capital ownership could be boosted from the existing 6 percent to 30 percent over a twenty-year period.[85]

Some UMNO leaders sought to move even beyond this traditional, patrimonialist approach in order to foster greater self-reliance among the Malays. Many state enterprises were thus formed that either prepared infrastructure and financing for new Malay-owned companies or went into business directly. Few of these bodies were profitable. But they were justified nevertheless as acquainting the Malay directors and managers they recruited with modern business operations and skills. Training was also imparted on a broad scale through scholarship programs and tertiary education overseas. Hence, through a stream of executive postings, funding, and programs, UMNO sought vigorously to "breed Malay capitalists,"[86] proclaiming that they would one day be able to compete with the Chinese.

This imperative was most thoroughly exploited, however, by UMNO itself. Starting up shell companies and "two-dollar" firms, inflating them with state contracts and licenses, and rotating capital under holding companies and investment arms, UMNO penetrated deeply during the 1970s into financial services, property development, light manufacturing, and media ownership. Analysts generally agree, however, that businessmen sprung from UMNO in this way amounted to little more than well-positioned trustees and proxies.[87] Moreover, they note that these individuals grew powerful enough to feed back into UMNO's decision making—bidding for nominations and influencing its policies—thereby fusing government and business in Malaysia's distinct brand of money politics.

It remains an open question whether this finely developed political savvy will ripen into true business viability.[88] Meanwhile, most studies have focused critically on UMNO's business dealings, citing the corruption, economic inefficiencies, and violations of shareholders' rights that were perpetrated under the guise of the NEP. What they have overlooked, however, is that the promotion of "Malay millionaires," the patronage of the Malay middle class, and the deepening of money politics to village-level branches probably enhanced the community's overall sense of group worth. Notions of tainted money and the suggestion made by many non-Malays (and certain Malay liberals) that special rights in fact belittled recipients were thus swept away in exultation over the NEP's rightness. Moreover, by giving the Malays an enlarged economic stake, the NEP probably eased the potential for violence in interethnic encounters. Looking back on the May Thirteenth rioting, Wan Azmi Wan Hamzah, a central beneficiary of NEP restructuring during the 1980s, observed: "Now Malays have to hesitate before they torch a business. They may own part of it."[89]

At the same time, in consolidating its hegemony over politics and moving forthrightly into the economy, UMNO buttressed its legitimacy with enough new Malay support that it was free to maintain certain bare-bones understandings with the Chinese. Although UMNO diluted the MCA's role in government by broadening the three-member alliance into the Barisan Nasional and, further, loosening the Chinese grip on financial and trade ministries, it continued to offer MCA leaders at least some service portfolios. Similarly, while UMNO forced Chinese businessmen to take on quotas of Malay partners and earmark discounted Bumiputra shares, enough exemptions, appeal processes, and oversights cropped up during the NEP's implementation that they continued to accumulate vast wealth.[90] The uninterrupted business expansion of Robert Kuok's Perlis Plantations, the Hong Leong Group, and Lim Goh Tong's Genting Bhd. during this period offer three very visible examples of this. Finally, this same skewed, though calibrated, approach to policymaking was projected at a cultural level. In 1971, UMNO began to outline its National Culture Policy (NCP) "based on the cultures of the people indigenous to the region,"[91] leading the Ministry of Education to cease funding secondary schools that used non-Malay languages for instruction. But one also notes that the ministry continued to assist Mandarin and Tamil primary schools and, moreover, permitted Chinese secondary schools to operate independently. Hence in surveying the impact of ethnic rivalries upon cultural integrity in Malaysia, Harold Crouch concludes that "far from assimilation into the Malay community, the main threat to Chinese and Indian cultures came from Westernization rather than Malay-ization."[92]

In sum, the 1969 elections and May Thirteenth rioting prompted UMNO to extend its control over politics, the economy, and national culture. This was expressed through UMNO's greater centrality in an enlarged governing coalition, as well as its formulating the NEP and the NCP. Taken together, these adjustments to the interethnic terms of "the bargain" probably mark a second historical moment in UMNO legitimation, one that greatly reenergized it with mass Malay support. Of course, this same moment quickly eroded the UMNO government's support before non-Malay audiences. But as UMNO's policy advanced, a porousness and leniency set in, bracketing the oft-heard lament that "everything is for the Malays" with a grab bag of "Ali Baba" deals, share swaps, and sub-contracts for Chinese businessmen, as well as permits (however grudgingly offered) for non-Malay schools, churches, and temples. Thus, while few Chinese during the 1970s would publicly have conceded that the UMNO government was legitimate, they were not so alienated that they opposed it through violent behavior. Indeed, by voting regularly for the opposition DAP, they greatly enlivened the regime that helped to verify the legitimacy of UMNO's hold on state power.

Old Guards, Politicos, and the New Order: 1975–78

Audiences generally withdraw their support over a ruling party's declining performance—its inability to deliver the goods. When a party has too many goods to deliver, however, its performance may be taken for granted, thus also reducing the urgency of ordinary support. Such weakening of the material basis for support describes a second strain point in Malaysia's political record that occurred during the mid-1970s. Amid clear ethnic dominance and perhaps economic surfeit, party elites could contemplate factional ambitions with less fear of dishonoring old shibboleths of "Malay unity." Such calculations, further, grew into challenges to the party leader's personal authority that in their directness ran afoul of procedural traditions. Nevertheless, the goal-rational legitimacy of UMNO endured. Indeed, one could argue that the intensity with which elites competed for party positions during this strain point—rather than going outside the party to form breakaway groups or antisystem movements—evinced their continuing recognition of UMNO's morally unassailable right to rule.

Three distinct factions can be identified during this period. First, the new prime minister, Tun Abdul Razak, recruited a coterie of Malay intellectuals and advisers he considered able to carry out the NEP. This group included Hussein Onn, who was appointed deputy UMNO president (and hence deputy prime minister), and Mahathir Mohamad, Musa Hitam, and Tengku Razaleigh—widely regarded as Malay "ultras." Characterized by high education and keen ethnic motivations, this faction was labeled the "new order." Resentment toward this group's preeminence grew among a second faction of "politicos" headed by Harun Idris, the chief minister of Selangor. While the men who made up this faction were also guided by ultra-Malay ideals, Tun Razak dismissed them as unsophisticated: their old-time populism, charismatic appeals, and unrestrained use of patronage and corruption were unsuitable for new technocratic planning and restructuring.[93] These politicos then joined a third faction of "old guards" in opposing the new order. Led by Tunku Abdul Rahman, this resurgent group of notables was bound by warm recollection of the Tunku's "easy-going style."[94] One observes, however, that this alliance between the politicos and the old guard was one of extreme convenience: Harun Idris had earlier supported Mahathir in harshly denouncing the Tunku over the May Thirteenth rioting and his government's neglect of Malay interests.

As the struggle between the new order, politicos, and old guard unfolded, deep strains appeared in UMNO traditions. When Tun Razak tried to confirm the new order's ascendancy by virtually naming, rather than artfully positioning, his preferred slate of vice-presidential candidates at the 1975 UMNO general assembly, his actions wounded the delegates' sense of participation, however vacuous, and drew a sharp challenge from Harun Idris. Tun Razak responded by offering Harun an overseas posting, which Harun refused—a clear violation of norms about vertical loyalties and soft punishments. Tun Razak then brought corruption charges against Harun, but died suddenly a month later in January 1976. Tun Razak was succeeded peacefully by Hussein Onn. The new order was itself soon divided, however, when Hussein reached over the heads of more senior officials to choose Mahathir as his deputy. Hussein also clashed with Harun, leveling more corruption charges, deposing him as chief minister, and finally expelling him from the party—measures that were strikingly public and severe. Hence the UMNO Supreme Council, already shaken by the Tunku's allegations that the government was infested with "socialists," overruled Hussein by readmitting Harun to the party. Factional advantages then undulated in new purges, jailings, and televised "confessions." The conflict persisted until 1978 when the Tunku was mollified by an invitation to address the general assembly and Harun was given six years in prison, thus finally ending challenges to Hussein's leadership of UMNO.[95]

Several conclusions can be drawn from this account of a deep and protracted strain point. First, support for UMNO weakened—not because of inadequate material performance, as had characterized the Tunku's tenure, but because of the easy abundance of benefits under the NEP. There was, quite simply, much more to fight over and less reason to maintain discipline while doing it. Second, while Tun Razak and Hussein Onn were not pushed forcibly from office, their personal authority was undermined by factional rivalries. Further, as this factionalism mounted (driven, perhaps, by pressures to pare the party's winning coalition to its minimum size),[96] the traditional procedures were more broadly ignored. Certainly there was a quickening tendency in UMNO toward unprincipled competition and casual coalescence. Tun Razak's new order was not so evenly technocratic as the categorization implied, nor was Harun Idris without administrative skills, suggesting that their factionalism had more to do with positions and power than true policy differences. Moreover, the joint challenge to the new order mounted by Harun and the Tunku was motivated by obvious expedience, its brittleness made plain by the Tunku's silence over Harun's long prison sentence.

But however uncertain ordinary support had become and however much the personal and procedural elements of legitimacy had declined, Malay audiences never doubted UMNO's final authority or its status as the country's paramount political institution. The resolve with which factions sought to expel each other from the party or to battle their way back into it clearly demonstrates their refusal to conceptualize any other route to power. Hence this strain point may be viewed as a crisis in interelite relations, but hardly one of UMNO's goal-based legitimacy. Finally, as the full framework of UMNO game rules was restored, elite relations improved. After Mahathir succeeded Hussein Onn as prime minister in 1981, he arranged a royal pardon for Harun Idris and ordered the release of others who had been jailed during the struggle, enabling them to resume their careers in politics and business. These measures resuscitated the popular belief that the Malays, more easily than other communities, were able to patch up their differences after serious quarreling.

Old UMNO vs. New UMNO: 1987–88

As Mahathir's tenure as prime minister unfolded during the 1980s, he appeared to depart from customary patterns of UMNO leadership. While insulating his personal prerogatives in politics, he sought gradually to liberalize business by lessening state patronage and controls so that new Malay businessmen might contribute more independently to economic growth. Some analysts thus contend that Mahathir tried to replace UMNO's heritage of economic patrimonialism with a vigorous new commercial culture—one administered by efficient state bureaucrats, driven by dynamic Malay entrepreneurs, and undergirded by a disciplined workforce.[97]

Two related features, however, frustrated this progress, perhaps paving the way in Malaysia for an ethnic permutation of Habermasian crisis in state capitalism. First, the suspension of patronage was not uniformly imposed, for a network of partners and protégés centering conspicuously on the finance minister was spared. Second, the jealousies this policy sparked were worsened by a steep economic downturn during the mid-1980s and the ruin of many small and medium-sized businesses owned by Malays.

Under the NEP, these Malay businessmen had joined mid-ranking civil servants in displacing rural schoolteachers as the most vibrant cohorts in UMNO, and they grew into the largest delegations attending the UMNO general assembly. Thus when UMNO held its election in 1987, many of them directly opposed Mahathir's candidacy for president, reopening gaps in personal and procedural elements of UMNO legitimacy.

This extraordinary challenge was led by Tengku Razaleigh Hamzah, a Malay aristocrat from the northern state of Kelantan who had been pivotal in fashioning Bumiputra trust agencies and lending institutions. Hence, in augmenting familiar patrimonialism with new organizational skills, Razaleigh won the allegiance of many Malay businessmen imperiled by recession as well as salaried bureaucrats uninspired by Mahathir's visions of entrepreneurialism. The assembly election, however, marred by high bidding over "floating" voters and irregular ballot counting, resulted in Razaleigh's narrow defeat. His followers then took action in the Parliament, the media, and the judiciary in order to force a new election. Mahathir quickly parried their advances, jailing MPs, shutting down newspapers, and purging judges from the Supreme Court. In early 1988, Razaleigh's confrontational legal strategy drew a "kamikaze defense" from Mahathir's lawyers,[98] leading the High Court abruptly to order UMNO's deregistration. This outcome shocked Malaysian audiences and cast the country's politics onto wholly uncharted terrain.[99]

Recognizing the veneration with which many Malays had looked upon UMNO, Mahathir and Razaleigh—their supporters respectively marking time in factions labeled "Team A" and "Team B"—sought publicly to portray each other as responsible for destroying it. Mahathir also maneuvered to annex UMNO's intrinsic legitimacy by forming a successor party, UMNO (Baru)—that is, New UMNO—while warning that "those who worked against UMNO's interests" would be barred from joining.[100] Razaleigh, for his part, though claiming still to be committed to reviving UMNO (Lama)—that is, Old UMNO—began to gather his supporters into another vehicle, the Semangat '46 (Spirit of '46), avowing that it embodied UMNO's true founding ideals.[101] Mahathir countered by dropping "(Baru)" from his new party's name and modifying its logo and flag so that they resembled the original symbols. In these ways, Mahathir and Razaleigh, their personal authority uncertain, put forth competing claims as "heir" to the UMNO legacy.[102]

During 1989, however, it became clear that Malaysia's economy was embarked on a startling recovery. This resurgence quickly replenished Mahathir's patronage resources and support, enabling him to renew his prime ministership in the 1990 general election. Razaleigh's challenge was thus pushed back to his native Kelantan, and it was soon superseded by the Islamic resurgence in that state. These fluctuations in support give weight to the earlier observations about strain points in politics and their meaning for legitimacy. Malaysia's evolving demographic structure and UMNO's maturing middle-class membership implied more qualified support for the party, particularly when audiences were ruffled by recession. Further, this skepticism began to gnaw at the personal authority of Mahathir and Razaleigh. These leaders, in turn, even while cloaking themselves in UMNO's status and symbols, broke its traditions about orderly succession, mild challenges, and soft disciplines—to the point of cleaving the party's formal organization. What stands out most during this strain point, however, is the consistency with which Mahathir and Razaleigh evoked UMNO's symbols and cultural promises. Their rivalry over the party, therefore, hinged on their pledges in some manner to restore it.

One cannot conceive that Mahathir would finally have prevailed, or that Razaleigh's challenge would have lasted so long, had they cast the memory of UMNO aside in order to establish fresh, ahistorical parties. Thus the intensity with which Mahathir and Razaleigh struggled to authenticate themselves—sounding the UMNO horn of Malay unity and dominance, blaming each other for the party's demise, proclaiming their duty to resurrect it—underscored dramatically UMNO's unique resonance with Malay sentiments. If anything, the tug-of-war over the party between Team A and Team B makes this point even more persuasively than the earlier outbreaks, deeply shaking the legitimacy of individual leaders, provoking their violations of UMNO procedures, yet failing to precipitate a legitimacy crisis. In short, though elite rivalries and mass disloyalties grew unusually strong at this strain point, they did not diminish UMNO's goal of ensuring Malay dominance and the authority that flowed from it. Agreement at this most fundamental level, then, prevented wholly unrestrained, politically destabilizing actions.

After Mahathir's reassertion of national leadership, catalyzed by economic recovery and consolidated through general election, he returned to his long-term policy aims. In brief, he again sought to ease Malay businessmen off state benefits, hoping to make good on their lengthy "apprenticeships" under the NEP. At the UMNO general assembly in 1992, Mahathir thus called for "a new culture which is relevant to the present business climate, which is more risky and sophisticated."[103] Such policies, however, met with resistance from UMNO conservatives, especially in the bureaucracy, who still measured their performance by fulfilling Bumiputra quotas and requirements. Mahathir's government was therefore obliged to set Malay businessmen down gently by privatizing state assets on generous terms and prolonging their lines of state credit.

In these circumstances, Mahathir's efforts to activate Malay entrepreneurialism hardly constituted an onerous policy demand, and Malay support for UMNO remained strong. And because the economic recovery greatly increased the scope of Chinese business activities, the Barisan's support (or at least Mahathir's personal standing) seemed to brighten across ethnic lines. Put simply, in a context of easy money Mahathir was able to relax the NEP's rhetoric and priorities through its successor plan, the New Development Policy. As one example of the shift in policy direction that might follow, the Majlis Amanah Rakyat (Council of Trust for Indigenous People), a key Bumiputra trust agency, was ordered to open an investment scheme to non-Malay participation.[104] On a wider plane, Mahathir began to highlight the value of learning non-Malay languages, and, incredibly, he officiated at several Chinese lion dance competitions in Kuala Lumpur's national stadium.[105] If it could be shown that this will be reciprocated by Chinese audiences acknowledging Mahathir's personal authority and, further, that this will deepen into greater Chinese appreciation of the UMNO-led government, the New Development Policy can then be said to have signaled another moment in legitimation: by striking this interethnic deal—more integrated than "the bargain" and more balanced than the NEP—UMNO's authority would at last be made more comprehensive.

The three distinct strain points, taken together, seem to trace a trajectory of mounting complexity. In the first case, the May Thirteenth rioting, mass Malay audiences were galvanized by their awareness of their ethnic deprivation, prompting them to shift their support from UMNO. They also showed that they no longer perceived the party leader as unerring, thus encouraging elite factions to defy a high political culture of seniority and deference. That UMNO retained a deeper legitimacy, however, was displayed by the determination with which elite and mass audiences later returned to it. The second strain point, set during the mid-1970s, was in many ways different. Its seriousness is suggested by its originating at the elite level and its occurring despite—or more likely because of—the New Economic Policy's easy provision of material benefits. Its lessons were much the same, however. While elites showed new readiness to act on factional ambitions at the expense of the party leader and traditions— entering into soft alliances and adopting confrontational postures— they were resolved to uphold the party. Finally, during 1987–88, Prime Minister Mahathir's use of political power to accelerate socioeconomic changes doubled back in larger political challenges. The strain point that resulted was the most complex of the three. Not only did it test relations among elites and between them and mass audiences, raging through political, business, and ethnic arenas, but it eroded personal and procedural legitimacy to the extent that UMNO was juridically wrecked. But more striking than UMNO's deregistration were the continued efforts to draw on its authority, leading finally to its renewal as UMNO (Baru). It is difficult to imagine clearer evidence of the legitimacy with which the party has been perceived. In sum, then, during each of these conflicts, elite and mass audiences stopped well short of challenging UMNO's right to rule.

Progress in Legitimation

Legitimacy is a relational concept involving claims about the moral worth of political arrangements and the judgments that diverse audiences then make about the validity of those claims. This interplay between appeals and perceptions ranges over three concentric arenas: the government's use of state power, the regime through which it acquires or extends that power, and the breadth of the nation-state over which it asserts jurisdiction. In focusing on the first of these arenas, audiences assess the persona and style of the governing leader, the regulatory traditions and procedures within the governing party, and the goals and value patterns (perhaps culminating in an ideology) that the government contends it is uniquely able to pursue.

This chapter has argued that if perceptions of legitimacy are to persist, they must at some point be underpinned by substantive performance and material benefits. Thus while legitimacy possesses a distinctive, high moral tone, it is nonetheless related to the simple support that governments must ordinarily earn. At the same time, the differences between legitimacy and support are great enough that the strains in one can be used to reveal the perpetuity of the other. Indeed, this method has been critical to investigating authority in Malaysia, for its political record lacks the crises and public sacrifices that flag the legitimacy of contrary arrangements. We have proceeded, therefore, by plotting the alternation of strain points and great moments. Such strain points, by eroding support, strip legitimacy bare, enabling one plausibly to attribute public inaction amid serious material shortfalls to the residual legitimacy of the UMNO-led government.

Legitimacy has also to do with identity—a perception by culturally, socioeconomically, or regionally bounded audiences that a government's makeup is reflective of their own. In Malaysia, identity has hinged on ethnicity, which, though transfigured by rapid economic growth, has scarcely been eliminated. Accordingly, this chapter has sought to trace the development of Malay attitudes toward political power, showing its correspondence first with the regional protection provided by the sultans and later with the nationalist unity overseen by UMNO. We have also seen that while the UMNO government's ordinary support—and even its personal and procedural elements of authority—have been tested episodically since independence, its goal-rational legitimacy has endured. This final, moral claim to state power has rested on UMNO's "infallible" knowledge about how best to promote Malay unity, protection, and dominance, a mission that itself derives morally from the community's indigenous standing in *tanah Melayu* (land of the Malays).

This ethnic rationale was made urgent and authoritative by the presence of rival communities against which to define it. But even among these audiences, the UMNO government has sought to cultivate broader perceptions of rightfulness, professing its deep understanding of life in a multiracial society. In brief, even as UMNO proclaimed before Malay followings its defense of their birthright, it tried to persuade the Chinese and Indians that it responsibly checked Malay chauvinism. The institutional basis for striking this balance—redressing Malay grievances while at some level respecting non-Malay identities and property rights—was, of course, the consultative "Barisan way."

While it has managed to attract ordinary support from middle-class Chinese and Indians, it is doubtful that this formula ever inspired higher perceptions of legitimacy. Though accepting the grudging concessions and half-measures that have been given them, these audiences have retained long memories of their second-class political citizenship and the many barriers that were put up to their educational and occupational advancement. Even more problematic were the grievances displayed by strongly Islamic Malays, working-class Chinese, and certain communities in East Malaysia. But these attitudes, though significant, should not cloud the overall analysis. One is struck more by the country's evident record of political stability—or, more precisely, by the government's legitimacy and support that have upheld that stability. In short, the government's fairly reliable provision of elite-level patronage, middle-class comfort, rural development, and urban amenities, as well as some keen Islamic programs alongside timely cultural compromises, did much to supplement Malay perceptions of legitimacy with cross-ethnic support. Deeper, lingering grievances, moreover, were dispersed either through quasi-democratic opportunities for protest or, as a last resort, through various degrees of coercion. But even here the relationship between legitimacy and coercion was hardly inverse. While government force may be perceived as illegitimate by those against whom it is applied, it may commensurately heighten perceptions of legitimacy among the audiences who are its beneficiaries.

If ethnic perceptions are relational, however, they are also variable, shifting as elite and mass audiences adjust their identities over the years. Among the Malays, patrimonialist outlooks and ethnic rivalries traditionally encouraged a vertical sense of identity and allegiance, shaping attitudes toward authority that militated against autonomous organizing and class-based formations. Accordingly UMNO was founded upon, and tirelessly iterated, a defense of Malay unity against non-Malay interlopers. But as the party then rounded out its hegemony over politics and made much headway in business, the need for such a defense perhaps became less obvious. The successes of the NEP unleashed new, more complex expectations and discontent. Some Malay audiences were prompted to demand even greater access to state largesse, for example, while others, recoiling from the corruption this tendency spawned, looked increasingly to Islam for release.[106] Such conflicting motivations also characterized middle-class Malays who favored greater democratization of the country's politics during the late 1980s.[107] While some viewed democracy as a way to turn out UMNO and seize patronage benefits for themselves, others considered it useful for exposing and curbing such "money politics." Rural Malay audiences began to send equally shifting signals. Many villagers decried UMNO's "infidel" character, even as their neighbors readily accepted remittances from urbanized relatives involved in UMNO business deals or government programs. Still other rural groups clamored for entry into the Federal Land Development Authority's resettlement schemes, while settlers already on the estates resisted the tight administration and terms of land tenure.[108]

In sum, then, because the UMNO government has given many Malays new positions and confidence, their identities may eventually shift out from under UMNO's patrimonialist weight. This is not to suggest, of course, that working-class solidarity has achieved sudden salience in Malaysia. It is instead the new middle class upon which most scholarly attention is now focused. Nor is it to say that ethnic identification is fully evaporating in modernity. Indeed, even as much of the Malay middle class grasps at an "international lifestyle," it is busily engaged in reviving (or reinventing) regional places of origin, village folkways and entertainments, the significance of Islam, and other cultural markers.[109]

This new assertiveness, then, may present the UMNO government with long-term difficulties, making less relevant its claim to goal-rational legitimacy founded on ethnic protection. Insofar as one can gauge, many middle-class Malays appear to have grown confident sharing work experiences with non-Malays (even if remaining uninterested in meeting with them outside the workplace).[110] The UMNO government may thus have to find new ways to address Malay attitudes and the larger, changing patterns of identity in which they are embedded. Some argue that UMNO has thus far responded largely with force—tightly containing political participation throughout the 1980s while dampening the "unauthorized" construction of Malay culture.[111] But to the extent that political controls have hardened during the past decade (and this has not been a consistent trend), there is little evidence that they have extended to issues of ethnic Malay culture and identity. Indeed, UMNO has sought to legitimate its political actions by keeping pace with evolving ideas about what it means to be Malay, using state power less to halt this process than to keep up with it. And in a clear attempt to sanctify its strong accent on business, the UMNO government has recently formed the Malaysian Institute for Islamic Understanding (IKIM) to "refocus the ethos of Islam and give progressive principles embodied in the religion more attention." [112]

Curiously, this revival of everyday culture and reinterpretation of Islam has largely overlooked the Malay rulers, traditionally the guarantors of Malay *adat* (custom) and *ugama* (religion). Seeking more fully to assume the mantle of protector, UMNO has begun to diminish royal statuses, while middle-class Malays have become more receptive to steps that weaken royal advantages in tendering for state contracts. Hence the UMNO government was able to trim the political prerogatives of the king during the constitutional crisis in 1983 and to remove even the rulers' immunity from prosecution ten years later. In short, while UMNO drew heavily in the past upon the rulers' traditional authority, it has sought more recently to cast them aside in its rush to consolidate state power and generate new forms of legitimation.

In pursuing these aims, the UMNO government has been bolstered during the early 1990s by its electoral victory and the country's economic recovery. It has been able, then, to participate in the complex Malay quest for new identities and traditionalist grounding, even while shifting its appeals for legitimacy from simple protection to an exhilarating developmentalism—an exhortation to "go for growth." Thus even as Malay audiences are becoming more socially variegated and politically insistent, UMNO has probably retained its authority among them (although this assessment awaits testing in yet another strain point). Moreover, these same circumstances may encourage the UMNO government to make new overtures to other ethnic communities—in particular, by reassuring the Chinese about their business activities and "cakemaker" status. The New Development Policy appears to relax the hiring and ownership quotas that encumbered Chinese business planning. Thus UMNO's longstanding claim that the Barisan is not so hard for overseas Chinese to live with, especially when they ponder their lot elsewhere in Southeast Asia, may become more convincing.

In seeking perhaps to stretch its authority across the board, the UMNO-led government enables speculation about some "progress" in legitimation. If societal attention in Malaysia is indeed slipping slowly from bipolar ethnic identities and sharp faceoffs—diluted by new business feuds, sundry cultural revivals, and new class and gender fissures that open *within* ethnic communities—government appeals for legitimacy may be framed in a looser, more progressive idiom. Further, because these new concerns are probably more pliant than the raw ethnic tensions they overshadow, contestation may more safely take place in a context of openness. A. C. Milner reports that in the three-cornered struggle for Malay allegiances, top UMNO leaders, the rulers, and the *ulama* confide that despite their very different agendas, they are at base politicians who are learning the practice and customs of politics: "They have begun to share a political discourse." At the same time, "as the Chinese and Indians of Malaysia engage more openly in the same public sphere, they too might not so much aggravate the pluralization of Malaysia as unwittingly contribute to the establishment of this specific form of unity."[113] A steady fragmentation of Malaysian society, in short, may distract from the animosities of the traditional core communities. Audiences may then express their demands through common political terms, even democratic procedures, as the easing of ethnic hatreds makes more democratization possible. Such an opening of the regime might also win governments of the day more authority.

Such interest in retaining or expanding legitimacy makes clear its desirability. Indeed, just when one is about to conclude that it is neither politically necessary nor analytically fruitful, one confronts the lengths to which governments everywhere go to legitimate their power. Thus while this chapter has stressed that the UMNO government's authority has resided primarily in its fidelity to the icons of indigenousness, protection, Malay unity, dominance, and Islam, another study might start with the assumption that ethnic cultures are hardly static entities to which governments must closely and unfailingly respond. Cultures are reinterpretable and take on new values—a process in which ruling persons and parties may in some instances take the lead. Farseeing leaders can thus innovate within the parameters of cultural familiarity, couching initiatives in enough palliatives that they can nudge cultural change along a desired (or at least less determinist) trajectory.

In Malaysia, Prime Minister Mahathir has oscillated sharply between farsightedness and recklessness. In often stepping over the line between the culturally familiar and the starkly innovative, he has juxtaposed competing strands of sentimental and dynamic Malay culture, producing a tense amalgam of communal protection and cross-ethnic compromise, top-down imposition and grassroots democracy, and rural contemplation amid high-flying entrepreneurialism. One watches with much interest to discover whether his government will encounter new strain points, perhaps even buckling under Islamic resurgence, a new wave of Chinese bitterness, or East Malaysian separatism. Alternatively, the UMNO government's authority might simply persist among loyal Malay audiences, or it might be dramatically rekindled in still another great moment.

5

Singapore

Political Legitimacy Through Managing Conformity

CHO-OON KHONG

IN any comparative study of political legitimacy in Southeast Asia, the inclusion of Singapore provokes a range of powerful yet contradictory responses. At the level of institutions and procedures we see, apparently, a great deal of legitimacy: a sense of duty to obey based on acknowledgment of constitutional authority. There is a strong, decisive, and charismatic political leadership determined to institutionalize, and hence to safeguard, its form of rule. The positive achievements of this leadership in nation building have been widely recognized. Yet there is a problem in evaluating legitimacy in Singapore, a problem that arises from the perceived vulnerability of the tiny city-state's achievements: an insecurity that engenders contradictory and ambiguous impulses in the state of mind of both leadership and citizenry. Certainly there is a sense (felt more acutely and continually expressed by the political leadership itself) that the degree of legitimacy engendered by the political leadership's institutionalizing process still rests on shallow foundations. What appears to be a manifest sense of the citizenry's duty remains critical, not unconscious, and therefore translates into a fragile allegiance to the nation-state. Obedience to authority is based on rational calculations of immediate self-interest.[1] And if legitimacy only emerges over the long haul, Singapore, unlike its neighbors, cannot draw on a long-established national identity to reinforce its short history as an independent nation-state within the contemporary international system. The record itself is too short to permit a definitive assessment of the problem of legitimacy in Singapore, and no conclusive measure of its extent is possible. For the leadership, there remains an ongoing need to buttress as well as broaden the shallow foundations on which its political legitimacy is sustained.

If an assessment of political legitimacy in Singapore is clouded with ambiguity, one key to its understanding may lie, as has been suggested, in the singular nature of the state of Singapore compared to that of other countries in the region. The circumscription imposed by Singapore's physical parameters—its limited size and its geopolitical setting squeezed in between two much larger and ethnically dissimilar countries who view it with a certain proprietary regard—immediately marks it out as different. All concerned, within the state and without, remain acutely conscious of Singapore's unique status as the only Southeast Asian state with a predominantly ethnic Chinese population. While geographic circumstances facilitate the political control of the ruling regime, they simultaneously feed its obsession with its own legitimacy.

A sense of separateness therefore underlies any evaluation of the problem of legitimacy in the politics of Singapore. It is felt most keenly by the country's political leadership, inducing a profound sense of vulnerability. And if we understand legitimacy to be a two-way process—claiming the right to rule, on the one side, and acknowledging it, on the other—we can also identify a similar concern within the population at large. Indeed, a deep-seated fear of pregnability coupled with an appreciation of the transience of its own achievements—both characteristic of that immigrant mentality common to leadership and populace alike—lies at the heart of the country's political experience. It has driven the leadership coalition to brook no compromise in reinforcing its dominance over all other potential rival social groups. And, most important from the point of view of legitimacy, this same outlook has herded the population into accepting a range of peremptorily imposed government policies deemed necessary for national survival.

These policies have succeeded in transforming the sense of isolation and vulnerability into a powerful driving force that has achieved substantial economic growth, generally (though unevenly) shared.[2] Yet however much the government's outstanding economic record may have strengthened its hold on power, recognition of its claim to power was based originally on a shared perception of external threat. Indeed, the government's growing concern with ensuring the legitimacy of the political regime it has set in place arises from an awareness that, whatever the government itself might publicly claim, popular acceptance of its right to rule originally derived from beliefs and considerations that predate its economic achievements. That the political regime has been extremely effective in achieving results from government policies is not in doubt. Yet we are examining not effectiveness but legitimacy, and we therefore should not allow our awareness of one to cloud our assessment of the other. Certainly the political leadership evinces no such misperception in its increasing attempts to institutionalize the political process and foster a sense of national identity to legitimate its particular form of rule. In this sense, Gramscian methods were tried only when the political leadership began to fear a divergence of views between itself and society, but these methods have achieved only a tenuous success.

An additional implication follows from this understanding. It becomes difficult to argue the case for a Gramscian ideological hegemony imposed by the political leadership over society, in the sense of an alien mode of thought that in time becomes accepted as the societal norm. Relations between government and society (whether we characterize them as a series of tacit agreements or as an imposition) were worked out from an implicitly shared ideational base that accorded the leadership, at least initially, a significant degree of legitimacy. Of course, legitimacy in this sense in no way implies an unconscious long-term allegiance to the state. Yet the point remains that the societal outlook that gave the leadership the political room to act, using direct force only sparingly, was not extraneously imposed. The leadership has indeed subsequently striven to impose certain ideologies on the collective mind-set of society, but, as we shall see, these ideologies and the manner of their imposition have achieved only qualified acceptance.

In examining political legitimacy in Singapore, it therefore becomes important to understand the initial agreement that gave the leadership the political authority to act. We can then assess, later in the chapter, the distinctive domestic political arrangements that have ensued, as well as their implications for the legitimacy of the political regime. Like all anomalies, Singapore excites great interest, especially among other elite groups, within the region. Its political experimentation has been watched with close attention. The political leaders in Singapore, for their part, have come to regard their particular form of rule as a compelling exemplar—rather in the manner of those revolutionary states that seek to validate their domestic political arrangements by winning adherents abroad. While in this case they base their claim on the performance record of their administration, we must also assess the quality of the legitimacy that accrues to the political system if we are to form an opinion of its potential demonstration effect for other ruling groups who might wish to continue to resist the blandishments of Huntington's Third Wave.[3]

Establishing a Political Consensus

At the establishment of a training center for civil servants in 1959, Prime Minister Lee Kuan Yew declared: "The mass of the people are not concerned with legal and constitutional forms and niceties. They are not interested in the theory of the separation of powers and the purpose and function of a politically neutral civil service under such a constitution. . . . If the future is not better, either because of the stupidities of elected ministers or the inadequacies of the civil service, then at the end of the five-year term the people are hardly likely to believe either in the political party that they have elected or the political system that they have inherited."[4]

Lee and his People's Action Party (PAP) had just come to power in a newly autonomous, if not yet quite independent, Singapore. At one level, Lee Kuan Yew's speech reflected the political conditions of the time and the particular circumstances of his ruling party. Yet his words provide a revealing insight into his political beliefs. They set out a political creed that was to inform the process of creation and construction on which Lee Kuan Yew was then to embark, a process whose end result is the modern city-state that is Singapore today.

A conventional interpretation of Singapore politics may well characterize the period of the late 1950s and early 1960s as an era of democratic mass politics in the sense that one can identify apparently autonomous party political leaders, open party competition, and free elections. Certainly various social groups openly organized around specific economic or ethnic identifications and then moved to articulate and promote their particular interests. The political system was democratic insofar as it allowed these groups to bargain freely and negotiate with each other, in this way enabling them to play a part in shaping government policy as well as controlling the government's power. But this carefully drawn parallel with the characteristics of a civil society fails at a crucial point, for the different groups contending with each other did not see themselves as acting within a commonly accepted democratic framework. Indeed, the question of the political system's legitimacy did not arise. There was no commonly accepted structure based on shared values that set limits to permissible behavior. However democratic the system may have been in form, this democratic character was not commonly acknowledged by its participants. Hence there was no way of reaching a consensus by negotiating trade-offs between the participants.

The apparent democracy of that time, in fact, had Hobbesian parallels. Various groups maneuvered, plotted, and struggled against each other in order to capture the institutions of state for their own exclusive use and establish political and ideological dominance over their rivals.[5] Only then would they be required to justify, and hence seek to legitimate, the governing position they had acquired.

As it turned out, it was Lee Kuan Yew who achieved power at the head of a small Western-educated group of individuals, quite atypical of Singapore society at the time, and with a mass following of workers and Chinese middle school students gained only through a tactical alliance with left-wing communist forces. On coming to power, Lee moved swiftly to distance himself from his radical populist support. In consequence, his overriding concern became the need to create a base of legitimacy that would justify the state, which he now controlled, in the eyes of society. While establishing his own authority, Lee sought simultaneously to break down the political bases of rival claimants for power.

Cutting his links with the populist sector, which itself continued to nurture rival claimants for power, and without a mass base of his own, Lee addressed the urgent need to legitimate his rule through the promise of economic performance, which in turn required policies aimed at critical social problems if it was to achieve tangible results. As such a course of action presupposed efficient administration, the logic of the situation led Lee and his small coterie to forge a tactical alliance with certain social groups, most notably the civil service. This group, in particular, comprised technocrats who had little sympathy for political conflict and viewed the bargaining and competition of the earlier democratic process as irrelevant distractions, potentially destabilizing for the process of economic growth. The result, in effect, was a governing elite that could secure its political survival only by persuading the people that, despite its unrepresentative, indeed distinctly different, composition, it nevertheless represented their interests. There was a difficult balance to maintain here: on the one hand, the need to establish a common identity with society by expressing a substantive purpose that its members recognized; on the other, the need to maintain its autonomy to act, essential if it was to achieve that purpose, by remaining apart from and indeed above those same members of society. The conditions of the time allowed that balance to be kept.

The period may be characterized as a time of national crisis: social unrest, high unemployment, and uncertainty over the nature and dimensions of the state, with political arguments over Singapore's ability to forge an independent course, over whether or not it should join the proposed new Malaysian federation, and if so on what terms. Such turbulent conditions gave the PAP leadership a contingent legitimacy, allowing it to use its command of the instruments of state to suppress political opposition while continuing to retain, albeit on a conditional basis, a high degree of allegiance from the populace. The people were prepared to rationalize their beliefs in such a way as to accept, even if temporarily, the cost of the leadership's authoritarian control for the sake of restoring political stability.

If we are to cite a politically defining moment in the course of Singapore history, an obvious point would be August 9, 1965, when Singapore separated from Malaysia. It was a moment of catharsis both for Lee Kuan Yew and for his people. In a celebrated incident, Lee was so gripped by frustration and fury that he broke into tears at a press conference on that day. The people evinced general relief that the two-year Malaysian interregnum, marked by communal tensions and increasingly strained relations between the Singapore administration and the federal government, was at last over. Lee's tears, however, were as much a manifestation of his concern over Singapore's uncertain political future as an expression of his inability to prevail in the political struggle, now past, with the Malaysian government. Independence had been forced on him and, once achieved, took a form that had not been originally envisaged. Independent Singapore was an island nation-state and an enclave within Southeast Asia. Singapore's political leadership was therefore seized with the overriding imperative of securing the political viability of a country placed, as they saw it, in such an anomalous position. Again—but this time over the question of the survival of the state—they chose the same solution. The way to achieve political viability was to seek economic viability through a nation-building program that emphasized modernization and economic development.

In the domestic context, too, the political leadership believed initially that its legitimacy would be more securely anchored through seeking economic growth and social reform. A determination to show its effectiveness in achieving results would, in its view, provide a more durable basis for the contingent legitimacy so far ceded to it. The leadership has essentially never lost this belief, though (as we shall see) political and economic developments in the 1980s forced a recognition of the fragility of such legitimation, which was to require reinforcement through ideological imposition and political institutionalization and also some limited compromise to take account of increasingly variegated social demands.

The principal political rival that had been destroyed—the Barisan Sosialis (in fact, a splinter group of the PAP)—had been avowedly populist. But Lee Kuan Yew and his technocratic colleagues deliberately avoided taking up the populist mantle in their style of rule. Instead the PAP government sought to base its legitimacy, first, on the establishment of political order through an efficient and relatively, if not entirely, incorrupt government and, second, on its commitment to securing the welfare of its citizenry through a benevolent, if not entirely benign, paternalistic govern-

ment. This approach led to a style of political rule that may be characterized as a kind of predestined determinism. The ruling elite set the goals to
be achieved and the means by which they might be pursued. And in doing
so, it set the distinctive feature of its form of rule by removing freedom of
choice for individual citizens in the economic, social, and political arenas.
If the practice of politics is essentially concerned with the making of
choices, then the process of political change initiated by the ruling elite
may be characterized as one of systematic depoliticization, a term that
may be open to some misinterpretation.

Most obviously, of course, Singapore no longer has open negotiation
between competing groups, the hallmark of a pluralist liberal democracy.
But this is not to suggest that because social groups no longer compete,
they have therefore been thoroughly repressed, though an element of repression cannot be ruled out. We have a situation in which ordinary
people as members of society no longer have—or, perhaps more important, no longer feel they have—access, however imperfect, to state power
and therefore have no ability to influence the actions of government in any
meaningful way. Although this statement must be qualified in the light of
developments in the 1980s—the government's response to the loss of its
parliamentary monopoly in 1981, for example, and the shift in its economic strategy after the 1985 recession—it remains essentially true.

When ordinary people perceive a separation between themselves and
the decision-making institutions of state, a sense of alienation ensues, a
further consequence of the depoliticizing process. Depoliticization does
not, of course, necessarily imply alienation. Indeed, as we shall see, support for the political leadership was appreciably strengthened at the
founding moment of the state because of a consciousness of external
threat. But depoliticization can readily lead to alienation should this consciousness become less intense and the political leadership seem no longer
to respond to the concerns of the people.

Even alienation, as a lack of positive support, does not necessarily imply opposition to the state. Indeed, as Rodney Barker argues, the state can
get by with the acquiescence of a large part, up to a majority, of the population, even if it is not seen as directly representing their interests, provided
it does not excessively provoke them.[6] Nevertheless, the political leaders,
as cultivators of their own legitimacy, must obviously ask themselves how
long this state of affairs can prevail and to what degree they can count on
habitual compliance with government policy, especially with government-
imposed constraints.

While the process of depoliticization in Singapore may have led to a de
facto elimination of choice in the political arena, we must ask where the
politics has gone in such a situation. The simple answer is that power, and

hence effective decision making, becomes even more concentrated in the structures of the state and the hands of the ruling elite, formed (as we have seen) by a coalition between political leadership and the civilian bureaucracy. Indeed, a seminal work on the politics of Singapore, in answering this very question, concludes that the polity has changed to an "administrative state."[7] To the extent that there is a loss of accountability in this system, its politics—the interplay of interests that leads to a political decision—becomes concealed. But it is submerged within the structures of government, not outside. The population itself remains depoliticized; across the broad swath of society, there are no concealed political bargains because there is no effective political power to strike such bargains. The question may then be posed, What is the nature of governmental authority given this political development?

To answer this question, we must return to the politically defining moment of Singapore's inadvertent independence. The period of union with Malaysia had raised the political profile of the PAP leadership as it fought to maintain its separate identity, to promulgate its own ideology within the wider Malaysian polity, and also to avoid being subordinated to Malaysian politics based (as the PAP leadership saw it) on assumptions of Malay dominance. In this power struggle between Singapore and Kuala Lumpur, Lee Kuan Yew clearly emerged as the standard-bearer of Singapore interests. If domestic political strife had originally conceded a contingent legitimacy to the PAP leadership, this fragile legitimacy was considerably strengthened by a popular view of this leadership as defender against external threat, a perception that was to be skillfully cultivated by the PAP leadership in its subsequent nation-building efforts. The moment of independence therefore gelled popular support behind Lee Kuan Yew and his PAP leadership. Indeed, with no other alternative leadership available, Lee's domestic political position was at this point secure and the legitimacy of his leadership unquestioned.

The circumstances surrounding independence also provided a unique opportunity for the PAP leadership to create, as if on a tabula rasa, a political regime in its own desired image, untroubled by any effective challenge. It may be argued that the chief criterion for distinguishing between the concept of regime and that of government is the degree of institutionalization. But when the process of institutionalization, creating a particular political regime, is closely identified with a particular ruling group (if not, indeed, a particular individual), and when the institutions thus created are commonly perceived to serve that ruling group's political ends, we have, in the Singapore case, an especially close connection between regime and government. The framework of the regime was created by simple amendment of the constitution, a procedure readily carried out through a parliament dominated by the ruling party, whose members owe their position and hence allegiance to the ruling leadership and none of whom has any longer a personal power base either within the party or without. Any challenge to the legitimacy of government therefore becomes inevitably a challenge to the nature of the political regime.

Equally, although it may be possible in normal circumstances to distinguish between nation-state on the one hand and regime and government on the other, this differentiation, while still possible, requires qualification in the case of Singapore. The problem with the multiethnic immigrant community of Singapore has been that different sections of the community held different conceptions of the "nation" to which they belonged; even Lee Kuan Yew's spirited defense of Singapore within Malaysia was, for many of the majority Chinese community, a defense of Chinese interests. The boundaries of the Singapore "nation" remained indistinct for some considerable time and indeed became crystallized only with the creation of the Singapore state in its present form in August 1965. Instead of an existing nation preceding the formation of a state, the borders of the newly independent state defined the nation within it. And insofar as the state was the creation of a particular political leadership, questions of legitimacy directed at the government and impinging on the political regime may possibly extend even further to the nation-state itself. The fault lines of the Singapore nation, as the political leadership is well aware, lie worryingly close to the surface of Singapore society, even if they have become less distinct after 30 years of fostering a feeling of national identity.

Bases of Support

Even if we understand the legitimacy of the political leadership to be broad-based and without challenge at the onset of independence, we still need to delineate the shape and structure of that legitimacy as it arises in Singapore society. The legitimate exercise of political power requires public recognition and consent, but the public itself is divided into various groups, each with its own aims and values, each involved to a different degree in the political process. If, however, consent is of greatest relevance to elite groups within society, we may confine ourselves to identifying those elite groups on whose support the political leadership is most dependent.

In the case of Singapore, the leadership began its rule by seizing the initiative, setting out its own political vision, and enforcing cooperation from, if not indeed coercing, all other social groups. It did not allow itself to be restricted by striking accommodations with critical social elites. In its subsequent drive toward depoliticization, it moved to create a political regime in which the state consciously sought to insulate itself from society. The regime may be characterized as inclusionary in the sense that various elites were co-opted by the political leadership to form a governing coalition and therefore attached themselves to the institutional structure of the state. But in this attachment they lost their own independent identity even as their aims coalesced with those of the political leadership.

While the political regime may be characterized as inclusionary, this does not necessarily qualify it as democratic in the sense of mobilizing popular participation in decision making. Indeed, the political regime may well be regarded as oligarchic, as decision making is effectively confined to the political leadership. The point is this: while there was an element of coercion in directing society as a whole, the political leadership still made a conscious effort to link itself with certain elites and through this conjunction to incorporate them into the system of legitimation that justifies the political structure of the state.[8]

The most prominent of these groups was the civil service, whose senior members merged with and to a large degree even supplanted the political leadership. In Singapore, civil servants have long played a key role in the political process. Lee Kuan Yew exhorted them: "Your role as civil servants is not only to help the Government well, but to help the Government in carrying the bulk of the people along with it."[9] The civil service must therefore do more than work with the government: it must help mobilize popular support and build a consensus in favor of government policies.

As the ruling elite co-opted the civil service, so the civil service in turn became politicized to serve the ruling elite. As noted earlier, the two were naturally inclined to share the same values, and a close identification of interests developed between them. For both of them, economic development was essential for national survival, and this aim would be best achieved through rational management untrammeled by political compromise. Indeed a technocratic approach, it was believed, would allow the political leadership to depoliticize contentious issues by arguing that they may be treated in a neutral and objective manner. Insofar as technocrats are generally accepted by the people as suitable instruments for implementing the growth policies of the political leadership (in fact they occupy a position of considerable status in society), the alliance, based on a convergence of interests between an increasingly technocratic civil service and the political leadership, has played a vital role in conferring legitimacy on the government.

Initially the bureaucracy was subservient to the political leadership. But as the civil service gradually became politicized to aim at the objectives set by the political leadership and (as we shall see) as the armed forces became in effect part of that civil service, effective decision-making power passed into civil service hands. Meanwhile the civil service itself became the principal recruiting ground for political leadership—both sets of people congenially sharing the same cast of mind—and the ruling party was bypassed in consequence. Civil servants who have followed this course, moving readily to assume political power and ministerial responsibility, include Goh Chok Tong, the current prime minister, and much of his present "second-generation" cabinet.

These bureaucrats-turned-politicians retain a close identity of interests with the original founding political leadership. Nevertheless, this trend to bypass the ruling political party in the course of merging the higher echelons of the civil service with the political leadership, when combined with a predilection for removing political choice from individual citizens, has had profound implications for the political structure. The evolution of this structure is conventionally described as a move from a multiparty system to a single dominant party.[10] More accurately, in essentially political terms, the structure has shifted to a nonparty system in the sense that no political party, not even the ruling one, plays a decisive political role today. As Sinnathamby Rajaratnam (a former senior minister and one of the PAP's founding fathers) once remarked: "It did not take long before we established a close link between us and the civil service. In fact, after the first two elections, the PAP became really an administration. It was no longer a party. And the civil service became a part of that."[11]

Effective power within the government has flowed away from the dominant party to accumulate within an institutional bureaucracy; the only check on that power comes from a political leadership that increasingly consists of co-opted members of that same bureaucracy. As the dividing line between the two groups dissolves, political participation effectively becomes confined to the institutional bureaucrats who succeed to positions of leadership within the government.

Given this characterization of the political structure, it should be noted that the party still exists as a cadre-based institution. Indeed, the party does not disappear as an effective institution under these political circumstances, but it is transformed into an institution of a different kind. It provides a channel for dispensing government patronage, it guides the implementation of government policy, and it provides the mechanism through which the political leadership is represented in elections. In fulfilling all these functions, the party is now subordinate, not dominant as before. It no longer plays a part in shaping policy, nor is it concerned with the competition for power within the ruling administration.[12]

Other elite groups, however, remain clearly subordinate to the political leadership. Both the armed forces and the police have been progressively integrated with the overall aims of government—indeed as James Minchin observes, "in a real sense . . . [they] constitute a modern equivalent of clergy who guard the faith."[13] Compulsory military service provides an effective means of transmitting the objectives and values of the political leadership to the younger generation of Singaporeans. The officer corps includes a significant component of "scholars," university graduates educated abroad on armed forces scholarships. These officers have risen rapidly to positions of leadership within the military and have then moved on to the civil service administration and even to the political leadership itself. Lee Kuan Yew's son, Lee Hsien Loong, though his political career was temporarily interrupted after a diagnosis of cancer, is a case in point. Before his unexpected illness forced a halt to his political advancement, Lee Hsien Loong reached the rank of second deputy prime minister within the cabinet, having previously risen to the rank of brigadier-general in the army at the age of 32. During his military service he also managed to incorporate a distinguished academic career at Trinity College, Cambridge, and at Harvard University. Some observers claim there is a division in the officer corps between the scholars and the nonacademic "farmers," a breach that constitutes a source of tension. This division, if it exists, appears less significant than the erasure of the dividing lines between military, civilian bureaucracy, and political elite.[14]

The military elite comes increasingly, by this means, to be linked to the economic growth that provides the rationale for the state's policies. Guillermo O'Donnell argues that, in the Weberian sense, there is an "elective affinity" between such a technocratic elite and what he calls situations of high modernization. If this is indeed the case, the military elite loses its separate identity as it increasingly identifies with and merges into the administrative framework of the state. Rather as in the eighteenth-century chemical theory, it destroys itself in the process of coming together with its apparently antithetical counterpart.[15]

The local business community, based largely on the Mandarin-speaking part of the Chinese population, was effectively bypassed by the economic development strategy of the political leadership, which forged an alliance between foreign capital, in the shape of transnational investment, and the state, allowing the latter to reinforce its autonomy against the domestic private sector. The demands of local business elites on the political leadership were vitiated by their inability to organize on a scale that can compete effectively with foreign transnational enterprises. The irony of their position is that in their desire for stability they had originally supported the bureaucratic-authoritarian state. That support, however, turned into a resentful and increasingly weak defense of a declining immigrant commercial order whose assets have dissipated away, in the face of the new bureaucratic–foreign business coalition built up by the ruling elite. Recent attempts to shift the Singapore Chinese Chamber of Commerce and Industry away from its old clan-based structure have been justified on the grounds that the change will modernize that institution and hence make it more relevant; yet there are concerns that the move may result in the eventual co-optation of local business interests by the bureaucratic state (the same way other social groups have lost independent power). It remains to be seen if local business interests can regroup to retain an independent identity; it would seem increasingly unlikely that they could ever provide a focal point for a possible alternative political grouping in the future.[16]

Indeed, as noted earlier, the lack of access of social groups to state power has changed to some degree, though not substantively, since the 1980s. Most notably, government recognition of local business interests underwent an apparent renaissance after the economic recession of 1985. A subcommittee on local businesses provided significant contributions (as well as trenchant criticism of government policies) to the report of the Economic Committee, under the chairmanship of Lee Hsien Loong, aimed at charting a course of action to end the recession.[17] In the event, however, the recession was overcome largely as a consequence of external developments—in particular, an influx of Japanese investment brought about by a rapid appreciation of the yen and encouraged by government-imposed cuts in local employment and operating costs.

After local business views were given a due airing, the strategies mapped out by the Economic Committee, while giving some voice and increased state support to domestic entrepreneurs, still placed a greater weight of reliance on foreign transnational corporations to spearhead a reemphasized economic shift from manufacturing to services. Even the government's aim of emphasizing the private sector as the new engine of growth has not led to any decline in the dominant state corporatist mentality. (Indeed, the drive to privatize parts of the public sector, currently a worldwide trend, does not itself create local entrepreneurial capitalists, as Singapore is not alone in discovering.) Apparently local business remains disenchanted with what is perceived to be economic domination by multinational companies.[18]

It therefore appears that the role of external elites also requires consideration. While not all analyses of leadership-elite relations incorporate an international dimension, external elites could assume critical importance in certain instances. In the case of Singapore, the management of transnational enterprises played a key role in influencing the decisions of the political leadership and in acting in partnership with state-owned com-

panies run by the civil service bureaucracy. These state companies together with multinational enterprises provided the main thrust for the economic development that was the leadership's primary objective. The
foundations of a much expanded role for transnational investment in the
domestic economy were laid by the labor legislation of 1968, which, by
establishing the rights of managers while limiting the employment protection of labor, shifted the balance of power between employers and employees. In particular, the Industrial Relations (Amendment) Ordinance
set out the prerogatives of management and removed a range of contentious issues from labor-management negotiations.[19]

The aim of the new labor laws was to assure employers, especially potential employers from transnational companies, that labor in Singapore
was effectively controlled and provided a reliable low-cost resource. In the
view of the political leadership, these laws did not leave labor unpro-
tected. Rather, given the critical importance of export-oriented investment
in their development strategy, trade unions could not be trusted to carry
out their labor protection function while giving due regard to the government's, and hence the country's, wider interests. Labor interests were
therefore yet another responsibility that the government arrogated to itself, using a corporatist, rather than a legalistic, approach to managing
relations between employers and labor.

Given the conjunction of foreign multinational and state-owned companies as the spearhead of the leadership's economic development
strategy, the success of this strategy, generally acknowledged by society at
large and widely recognized abroad, placed the management of transnational enterprises in a position that legitimated the PAP political leadership both domestically and internationally. These transnational managers,
though not part of the central political-bureaucratic alliance, found themselves playing a more significant role in government policy formulation,
through their links with government statutory boards and state-owned
companies, than they might have expected to play in most other countries.

Within the ruling coalition itself, it was the civil service that saw its role
dramatically expand as a result of more state intervention in the economy.
A range of statutory boards was set up, largely over the course of the
1970s, to guide government involvement in the economy. Three large
holding companies were established that have since set up several hundred
subsidiaries of their own as vehicles for direct government economic participation. As Lawrence Krause argues, "there appears to be no ideological barrier preventing the government from entering any economic activity."[20] These organizations, staffed by government employees and
directed by top-level civil servants with direct access to the prime minis-

ter's office, have played a key role in enhancing the power of the civil service within the Singaporean administrative state and in impelling the coalescence between political leadership and high-level bureaucrats.

As suggested earlier, the trade union movement was organized in line with the overall state corporatist ethos and brought together under the umbrella of the National Trades Union Congress (NTUC), which is closely affiliated with the PAP and led by a technocratic elite co-opted from the government. The current president of Singapore, Ong Teng Cheong, was previously a deputy prime minister and concurrently secretary-general of the NTUC. His successor as NTUC head is Lim Boon Heng, a senior minister of state who will remain a minister without portfolio. The NTUC's purpose appears to be to explain government policy to union members and mobilize their support behind government initiatives. The wage-negotiating function of trade unions has been appropriated by the National Wages Council, which meets in closed-door sessions with employers and the government. Although there was for some time a problem with declining union membership (workers see little point in joining), the situation has stabilized since 1985. Larger trade unions have been broken up, first into smaller industry-based unions and then into even smaller in-house unions with management participation. These changes were embodied in the Trade Union Act as amended in 1983.[21]

Finally the role of the intelligentsia as a source of legitimation for the political leadership should be noted. Chan Heng Chee writes: "One feature of establishment and especially establishment in a small place is that the same groups relate to each other very intensely. The same books are read and language and perceptions are standardized. After a while the consensus denies new ways of seeing things and doing things, the denial of which renders the country poorer."[22] Such closeness is unlikely to give rise to an intellectual Aufklärung, especially when the ruling elite seeks from the intelligentsia a theoretical justification of government policies in order to legitimate them. Consequently the record of the ruling elite resembles Jane Austen's Emma: faultless despite its faults.[23]

It would appear, then, that in the Singapore polity, despite apparent compromise in the 1980s, the political leadership has not allowed itself to be fenced in by a network of bargains with certain strategic groups. All significant areas of society are effectively controlled by the leadership through its bureaucratic administration. Indeed, in many instances these social groups may be seen to be themselves creations of the governing elite. Under such conditions it is difficult for the rulers to accept that their legitimacy may be called into question, that they need to seek support from the people because they are accountable to the people. Instead it is the people who are judged by their leaders and the people who are therefore required to adapt by yielding to the dictates of their leaders.[24] What, then, is the basis of the legitimacy that ensues?

Ideology as a Basis of Legitimacy

There is a high degree of apparent legitimacy of government, regime, and state in the Singapore polity, if the critical test is the widespread acceptance of governmental authority. Yet political support is predicated on the narrow base of the government's record of economic performance, which necessitated limited compromise with societal interests in the economic sphere after the 1985 recession. In the political sphere, we may, accepting a minimal procedural definition of democracy, identify a structure of democratic procedures in the Singapore polity. But these procedures have been so constrained by a range of restrictions and limitations (and, perhaps even more important, by a fear, held by many in society, of actively supporting opposition politics) that the democratic nature of these procedures loses much of its validity.[25]

Nevertheless, if we understand the political culture to comprise a summary of that part of social reality concerned with how people think they ought to be ruled—the political culture encompassing people's values, beliefs, and emotional attitudes—it may even be possible to adopt a definition of democracy that, although sufficiently inclusive to embrace non-liberal beliefs and practices, is nevertheless based on a restrictive interpretation of the term. These beliefs and practices are included insofar as they can be set within a constitutional structure that more or less satisfies the formal and procedural requirements of democracy.[26] The problem lies in determining whether people believe that authoritarian practices are essential to maintaining order and are in the general interest of society (as we have suggested was the case in the initial period of PAP rule) or whether that belief has been superseded by a suspicion that authoritarian practices have been imposed by political leaders to ensure their hold on power.

Political developments in the 1980s seemed to indicate a shift in the popular perception: an opposition candidate was returned in a by-election in 1981 to break the PAP's parliamentary monopoly, and the PAP's vote fell to 62.9 percent in the 1984 general election, with two opposition candidates returned.[27] While these results did not themselves threaten the political hegemony of the ruling elite, they nevertheless raised questions about the social pressures that were beginning to emerge and the direction in which these pressures might propel the political process in the future. For the political leadership, the obvious response would be to allow greater participation in the political process and a closer engagement between policymakers and society's expressed interests. Yet the resulting proximity would be at the expense of that autonomous position from which the leadership has been able to override sectional interests and advance those policies responsible for the country's success.

To preserve its political autonomy, the political leadership has therefore been extremely reluctant to tread this particular path, although it is equally reluctant to be seen not to address social demands. Its response, therefore, has been threefold: first, to preserve its control over political discourse through ideological hegemony; second, to preserve the essential features of the political system through institutionalization; and third, to add mobilizing agencies to the existing system that will secure greater participation (or rather a sense of greater participation) within strictly defined limits. We shall assess each of these measures in turn.

The attempt to use ideology to strengthen political legitimacy is particularly interesting, indeed ironic, in the Singapore case. The country's political elite and its intellectual acolytes have long argued that their "pragmatic" approach to government excludes the influence of any ideology whatsoever. It may be hard to accept that there is no body of beliefs informing the actions of government. Yet as Ow Chin Hock, chairman of the feedback unit, argues, "The government is not shackled by any particular ideology or dogma" (a statement that calls to mind Keynes's famous dictum about the frenzied distillations of madmen in authority).[28]

While denying the influence of ideology on its actions, the political leadership has become increasingly concerned that an ideology is needed to guide the beliefs and actions of its citizenry. Official formulations of a national ideology have a long history in Singapore—not only as a legitimizing device for the political leadership (which may be seen to conform to the values being promulgated), but also as an attempt to shape social norms in a way that supports the leadership's objectives. As is only to be expected where value systems are introduced from above, these ideologies often strike little resonance in the people at whom they are aimed. (Indeed, the people's actions sometimes reveal startlingly contrary values and beliefs.) Nevertheless, official ideologies provide insight into the thinking of the political leadership itself.

The ruling elite began by promulgating a "survival" ideology that emphasized discipline and organization, values that have been subsequently dredged up on occasion for public attention. Concern that the citizenry was being increasingly exposed to ideas seeping in from abroad, influences that were difficult for the ruling elite to monitor and control, led to a long officially inspired debate over the relative merits of "Asian" values (good) versus "Western" values (bad). The "Asian" values are the alleged values of Chinese culture, though they bear an uncanny resemblance to Weber's Protestant work ethic; the "Western" values appear to be an agglomeration of undesirable traits that few would have any hesitation in rejecting, though they also include some ideas, such as individualism, that would obviously be inimical to a disciplined, compliant, and organized labor force.[29]

This Asian-Western debate has rumbled on for some time. In the course of the debate, Confucianism has been singled out by the political leadership as exemplifying the Asian values they regard as praiseworthy and threatened.[30] Hence the ruling elite sought to sponsor a study of Confucian ethics in order to acquaint its immigrant citizenry (more precisely, the Chinese immigrants) with their cultural heritage. In this ideological drive, an Institute of East Asian Philosophies was set up within the university and staffed by eminent academics brought in from abroad to define Confucianism for the citizens of Singapore. (In a revealing transmutation, this institute, since renamed, is now devoted to the study of the so-called East-Asian economic miracle, presumably achieved with Confucian values.)

In the Singapore context we therefore need to evaluate ideology not by its substance, but by the intention behind its use. The Confucian campaign was instituted by the ruling elite not because the citizenry was seeking a deeper understanding of its heritage, but rather because the leadership wanted to establish a set of cultural values it believed would further its policies. The meaning of this philosophy would be relevant only insofar as it could be adapted to fit a specific view of society and polity that the ruling elite wished to promulgate and believed to be in the general interest. The leadership's interpretation is therefore selective. The problem for the citizenry is to divine the government's intentions (not always spelled out) and then shape their actions and, ideally, their beliefs accordingly.

A similar process may be discerned in the officially guided debate over the formulation of a national ideology, much of which appears to be a reiteration of previous discussions. In the national ideology debate, which emerged in response to the political developments of the 1980s, the government propounded a set of five "shared values": "nation before community and society above self; the family as the basic unit of society; respect and community support for the individual; consensus instead of conflict; and racial and religious harmony."[31] The emphasis on "shared values" implies some notion of a national or public interest that overrides sectional concerns. It may be used to serve several functions.

To begin with, "shared values" bridge the gap between the select few, associated with the ruling elite, and the mass of common people. Even though the ruling elite may then choose to implement a narrowly based policy, emphasizing unity helps the elite to identify its policies with the nation at large. Opposition to these policies is by definition partisan, for it involves going against the nation as a single entity. The ruling elite is at one with the nation; opposition only represents particular interests at best and is antinational at worst.

Such self-promotion should not, however, be regarded as a cynical gesture by the ruling elite. Even the most well-meaning leadership may have difficulty in separating its own aims from the concerns of the people over whom it rules—especially where the leadership is convinced that it knows the best interests of its subjects. The danger in establishing a set of common icons binding rulers to ruled is that the leadership may end up misleading itself as to what it truly intends.

An emphasis on commonality also sets the boundary between legitimate and illegitimate thought and action. In using commonality to identify itself with a unitary national interest, the leadership raises an ideological umbrella over itself, the state apparatus, the regime it has created, and the nation. The possibility is thus open for any political activity outside this umbrella to be regarded as illegitimate—especially if that activity is critical of any part of the expressed common national will.

In Singapore's multiethnic society, such commonality masks ethnic divisions by including minority racial groups within the core identity of the majority Chinese population. While making it clear that it regards minorities as separate and distinct groups with unique characteristics, the leadership has never sought to exclude them from its intended common society, despite occasional worries about the minorities' reliability or supposedly fractious inclinations. Yet elements within the Malay and Indian communities remain suspicious of an imposed Asian identity that extends elements of Confucian philosophy to all racial groups.[32] The ruling elite is especially concerned over opposition based in a particular ethnic minority and likely to oppose the values defined by the elite. "Shared values," therefore, are also an attempt to define such opposition as illegitimate.

Within Singapore society the degree of attachment to the professed "shared values" can be expected to vary. As they represent an idealized image promoted by the leadership, not everyone will be attracted to the picture. Loyalty will be strongest at the top among the chosen few and more variable (though in places perhaps strong as well) at the bottom among the common people. As an ideal, what we have here is a self-justification presenting a perfect image that people may contemplate to their own satisfaction. We may even expect to find a gap between the idealized image represented by "shared values" and the actual behavior of at least some of the people attracted to it. Those at the bottom who are unconvinced will behave in ways that fall short of the ideal, though they may find it necessary to put on a show of conformity.

The image does not necessarily bear probing as a rational, internally consistent body of thought, however, for it is not intended to serve as an object of critical examination. As James Cotton argues: "It is possible to consider the regime's embrace of the present 'core values' as a device akin to Plato's 'noble lie': notions philosophically meaningless . . . and politically vacuous but sufficient to appeal to the understanding of ordinary citizens."[33] The problem for the leadership remains: it must secure real changes in behavior from people perfectly prepared to declare allegiance to a set of vague generalities, but not necessarily ready to accept a particular interpretation of those elastic terms.[34]

The fervor with which the ideological campaign has been pressed calls into question (at least in the Singapore case) Lucian Pye's assertion that the persistence of authoritarian rule in Asia can be attributed to an indigenous political culture that idealizes benevolent paternalistic leadership and legitimizes dependency.[35] While Singapore's largely Chinese immigrant population may still hold residual beliefs deriving from the Confucian culture of the country from which they departed (reflected, perhaps, in a ready disposition to accept, in times of crisis, a central organization and a central authority figure who sets the moral behavioral pattern), the weakness with which these residual beliefs are held requires constant reinforcement from the political leadership.

As we have seen, the political leadership was initially accorded legitimacy contingent on its restoring order to a turbulent society and polity; a further basis of legitimacy was provided at independence by a shared perception of an external security threat. Legitimacy was strengthened—and to some degree supplanted, though not replaced—by the government's successful economic record. People's political calculations traded off a continuously rising standard of living against the irksomeness of authoritarian social control, and the force of political opposition was muted.

The problem for the leadership today lies in the calculations of an increasingly better-educated and affluent population, especially when centralized control is seen to be not just irksome but also economically inefficient.[36] Singapore's small size and openness to the powerful formative influences of transnational forces have hastened this process, encouraging people to judge the practices and institutions of the domestic political regime against the international standards espoused by those countries with whom the local leadership is quick to draw economic (though not political) comparisons. If the leadership is preoccupied with its own legitimacy, it is as a victim of its own success, for social order has been firmly established and a sense of external threat much diminished.[37]

The Institutionalization of Leadership

The question of political culture also raises the issue of personal leadership as a factor in a regime's legitimation. Singapore is remarkable for the extent to which the practice of politics bears the imprint of one man. Indeed, as James Cotton has pointed out, the terms of political discourse in the city-state have been molded from the beginning by Lee Kuan Yew.[38] Lee's personal conception of politics wrote the ground rules and set the limitations of its exercise, determined the nature of the political regime, and shaped the character and objectives of government policy. Lee provided forceful leadership for his colleagues, and together, as the founding fathers of modern Singapore, they offered strong, decisive, and charismatic rule.

The success of his government's strategy, however, gave Lee Kuan Yew's rule a legitimacy that has proved impossible to bequeath to his second-generation successors. Over the course of the 1980s, many Singaporeans came to regard Lee's patrician style and increasingly elitist policies as excessive. Most notably the "graduate mothers" policy, which gave priority to the schooling of children whose mothers had university degrees, had to be abandoned in 1985 after overwhelming public opposition even from the beneficiaries of the scheme. Lee's public pronouncements on eugenics and his government's other genetically based policies were not well received either, and these policies were withdrawn or modified.

Yet however intemperate or intolerant he may be perceived, Lee has never lost the respect of the people. To them he has earned the right, through his considerable accomplishments in building the country, to rule by injunction, and in a way that some might characterize as peculiarly Confucian, he is always heard with respect, even if not with total agreement. But those of Lee's younger successors who have sought to emulate their master's tough impatient style—without any record of achievement to back them up—have won no popular regard.

Presumably aware of his own substantial personal achievements, Lee in public statements reveals little confidence that his people will act responsibly in the absence of firm direction and little confidence that his political successors can maintain and build on his legacy. The recent constitutional change creating a new political office of elected president needs to be seen in this light. The move to a less centralized system of rule, with checks against personal inadequacies and individual abuses of power, represents not a desire to shift the political regime to a more pluralistic form, but actually an attempt to preserve its essential character through institutionalization. The new presidency comes with substantial powers, ranging widely over key areas of government policy, that put its incumbent in a powerful position not just to counterbalance the prime minister and executive but to shape political decisions in a preferred direction. Yet restrictions on eligibility for the presidency effectively limit the incumbent to someone who is a product of the present political establishment and therefore ideologically compatible with it.[39]

It is, however, unclear to what extent such institutionalization can secure the accomplishments and perpetuate the present political regime. The elected presidency bore the stamp of Lee's thinking and was first proposed by Lee himself. Yet it will obviously function differently without him. Under a politicized independently elected presidency without Lee's overarching presence to guarantee the consensual style of the present political establishment, current practice may well begin to erode, with policy debates played out increasingly in public, rather than in private.

In this sense, fundamental change to the political regime will have to await Lee's demise, and while new constitutional forms indicate the potential for change, the direction in which politics will go may eventually differ from what the present arrangements are intended to provide. Any legitimacy that Lee has secured through his personal authority will pass with him.

Issues of Ethnicity

Before turning to participation, we should deal with several issues raised by ethnic considerations. Here the official multiracial ideology ostensibly fulfills a unifying function in this multiethnic state, even if analysis of its practice reveals an agenda hidden by the political leadership. The problem of legitimacy arises over the extent to which certain ethnic groups identify with and support the prevailing political regime.

Although the majority Chinese community encompasses a number of different dialect groups, the government insists on Mandarin as the mother tongue to define a common, unifying identity for them. Yet the Chinese community may also be divided linguistically in another way: between the English-educated, who dominate the professions and the government bureaucracy (many of whom are not fluent in Mandarin), and the Chinese-educated, who remain largely within the private sector. This division has significant political implications: with the Chinese-educated feeling relatively more isolated from the government, the political leadership has become increasingly anxious over their allegiance to the regime.

There are clear signs that official efforts to promote Chinese cultural characteristics have intensified because of an increasing concern over the influence of Western culture. Efforts to promote Mandarin have intensified;[40] the government has indicated a possible reversion to Mandarin rather than English as the first language in schools for those who want it;[41] and the Chinese identity of Singapore has been emphasized by holding an international conference for overseas Chinese in August 1991.[42] Measures to promote the Chinese community have received greater urgency from the second-generation leadership associated with Goh Chok Tong, though these leaders have inevitably been motivated by concerns expressed by Lee Kuan Yew himself.

The gap between English-educated and Chinese-educated should not be overemphasized, however. The strength of the opposition vote in the August 1991 general elections was blamed by the political leadership on the grievances of Chinese-educated voters.[43] Yet the pattern of voting for the opposition could, with perhaps more justification, be explained in economic rather than social or cultural terms. The introduction of government policies based on an "antiwelfare" political philosophy, intended to reduce government subsidies and raise revenue, particularly affected lower-income voters in an economically polarized society.[44] These policies, introduced in such basic social areas as health, education, housing, and transportation, affected the livelihood of all and were popularly viewed as being motivated by money-making considerations (though the government, like its counterparts elsewhere in the world, stressed the economic rationality and quality of services that paid their way).[45]

In Singapore, the Malay community is of special political significance because of the country's geopolitical situation. The Malays show an increasing awareness of their relative backwardness educationally and occupationally compared with the Chinese, though ironically the significant gap in living standards between the two communities has begun to close even as Malay consciousness of that gap has risen.[46] Furthermore, while Malays are now conscripted into the armed forces along with other races (they had initially been excluded from the draft), they are still kept out of senior positions in the army, an indication of lingering distrust over their loyalty to the state.[47] Research within the Malay community reveals a deeply held belief that their disadvantages have been imposed on them on a racial basis by the Chinese.[48] Although Malays reject cultural deficiency as an explanation for their backward position, Malay leaders, together with their Chinese counterparts in the ruling elite, argue that Malay values are the primary reason for their backwardness—a discrepancy that may lead some to question the legitimacy of these Malay leaders, who were appointed from above by the ruling elite rather than having arisen from within their own community.[49]

Participation and Alienation

Could a more participatory political culture take root in Singapore society, whatever the intentions of the ruling elite? Proponents of a civic culture approach to development would argue that the embourgeoisement of society comes about through economic growth.[50] Within the resulting civil society, separate groups of independent economic and political forces arise and influence the government; in the process, they limit the government's independence of action by curbing its behavior.

In Singapore, such changes in political attitudes have not been systematically studied, though the extent of electoral support for a weak and divided opposition rose to 37 percent in the 1984 general elections, 38 percent in the 1988 general elections, and over 40 percent in the 1991 general elections. This shift may indicate that general attitudes are changing—that people are less ready to accept without question the dictates of an autonomous leadership. But in the absence of direct empirical evidence, it is unclear whether support for the opposition (in a political system where voting is compulsory) truly implies a desire for more active participation in the political process and for greater involvement in decision making.

Jon and Stella Quah make an educated guess: "Singaporeans as a whole seem to prefer the comfortable position of leaving the affairs of state and the nation's policies in the hands of a reliable, strong government. At the same time, they also want to be reassured that they will be consulted by the political leadership."[51] Indeed, leaving the affairs of state to the political leadership with its attendant bureaucracy may well be a comfortable attitude to take, provided that the leadership's policies are seen to meet the political demands placed on them. Yet making demands on government (however effective that government may be) without the clear responsibility that comes with the people's shouldering of political choice is a dangerously immature attitude. It certainly does not represent a society's move toward gaining popular access to state power.

If the Quahs' educated guess is correct, pluralistic domestic forces are likely to remain weak. People will continue to behave according to their position in the hierarchy of domestic society: the lower down the hierarchy, the more constrained their behavior, leaving the elite at the top to dominate—even if in principle the elite must ensure the welfare of its subordinates.

The problem may be that people do not feel competent to act. Certainly they have had little opportunity to participate in decision making. A civil society not only requires people who believe in their ability to make independent decisions, but also needs an organizational structure that allows individual participation, one that coordinates action while simultaneously preserving autonomy.

Yet, as noted earlier, the political system is effectively oligarchic, dominated by a technocratic elite who regard political debate as "dysfunctional," an obstacle to the achievement of "rational" solutions. In this view the practice of politics is not an art but a science in which the technocratic power of the elite, rather than its ability to mobilize the citizenry, becomes the critical factor. Government is characterized as an exercise in the rational management of the state. Elite rule then provides an intellectual justification for assuming decision making: separating the expert from the ignorant. The elite may yet argue their democratic credentials on the assumption that while common citizens may not be able to provide expertise, they are able to provide a modicum of judgment on elite rule.

In this situation, elections become something other than contests for power between formally organized political parties. They remain a desirable, if not essential, legitimizing device: a public demonstration of undivided support for the government's policies. Indeed, the leadership has at times characterized support for the opposition as irresponsible.[52] Hence elections are at best a referendum to gauge public opinion, at worst a test of loyalty to the ruling regime. But in neither case are elections a means of asserting popular choice between rival party platforms, given the lack of effective opposition. Michael Leifer observes: "In this mixed political culture, democracy is conceived as a process which permits periodic electoral judgement on the record of government. In effect, the exercise is designed to secure a renewal of a mandate that enables policy to be enunciated in a didactic manner and without challenge in a parliament where competent opposition has not been seen for over a generation."[53]

This situation gives rise to a political culture that is essentially dependent and derivative, unable to formulate or express coherent alternatives of its own to set against the official truth. Instead of expressing alternatives, the culture results in the making of demands on the ruling elite. To the extent that these demands are satisfied, further demands are then made on the leadership. Indeed, the concern of the elite is that these demands can grow quite insatiable through feeding on themselves.

A further implication follows from a situation in which citizens are encouraged to leave decision making to the political leadership: people are likely to feel no close attachment to the leadership's institutions, an attitude reinforced perhaps by the traditional Chinese (indeed Confucian) concern to keep a distance between oneself and one's family on the one side and a morally dubious predatory state on the other. Detachment then leads to alienation from the power-wielding structures of state, as people withdraw even from the token show of participation the political process asks of them.[54]

In Singapore, the government's claim to moral authority is based on public recognition of its performance record, tangible proof of the effectiveness of the ruling elite. But the people's conscious attachment to autonomous civilian institutions, the mark of a civil society, is absent. From a democratic viewpoint, the social soil of Singapore is not conducive to growing independent clusters of economic and political forces, each with its own aims and abilities, each with its own intentions of shaping the objectives and limiting the autonomy of the state. From a legitimization point of view, we see public alienation and withdrawal from the legitimizing institutions set up by the political leadership, even while at bottom there is general recognition of the government's sovereign authority. The legitimacy of the government may therefore be widespread, but the basis of this legitimacy in society remains shallow because societal interests are not engaged as part of the political regime.

The implication must follow that the public's compliance, even complacency, with the leadership and its political regime is not based on a deep-rooted recognition of the legitimacy of the civil procedures and institutions of the regime. What now appears to be social consensus reflects instead the capacity of the ruling elite to neutralize conflicting interests in society and to nurture a broad-based recognition that politics is the business of the government, not of the people.

What, then, may be inferred about the actual extent of legitimacy in society? We have examined various hypotheses, but hard evidence is difficult to adduce in the absence of serious social crisis since 1965. The level of emigration may be taken as a test of legitimacy. Certainly, it is an issue of concern to the political leadership; a survey carried out in 1989 revealed a close correlation between people's sense of political alienation and their attitude toward emigration.[55] What emigration does not do, however, is indicate the pattern of alienation within society. Emigration is largely a middle-class phenomenon: this group has the professional skills that gain entry into other countries. Emigration is on the whole not even a consideration of the working class, for unskilled and semiskilled workers are fully aware that they lack the skills and financial resources to move abroad. Yet while a degree of alienation may be readily perceived within the middle class, the dissatisfaction of the much larger working class is of more immediate political consequence for the ruling elite.

The 1991 elections showed substantial rises in votes cast against the PAP in constituencies with both working-class and middle-class electorates. But the three additional seats the government lost to the opposition were in areas with large public housing estates and a less privileged electorate, and the sole constituency that has remained with the opposition since 1984 is in a traditional working-class area. The extent of opposition participation in elections is not, however, an indication of widespread legitimacy of the political system; opposition parties operate under considerable restrictions and have great difficulty finding candidates prepared to stand against the ruling party. Moreover, they are not generally regarded as providing viable alternatives to the political establishment, even by many who vote for them. The pattern of votes cast in elections needs to be viewed in this light.

The ruling elite itself is concerned to secure greater participation, but only on closely circumscribed terms. To begin with, the leadership succession in November 1991 from Lee Kuan Yew to Goh Chok Tong was seen as an opportunity for the bureaucratic elite (exemplified by Goh) to show a more human face by assuming a more common and sympathetic manner.[56] This different style of leadership, it was believed, would help check the rising alienation by bridging the gulf between rulers and ruled. The change of manner has not yet led to any substantive change of policy. Goh declared his intention to work toward a "kinder, gentler society" and to introduce policies that have "a human face." He then quickly added that "this does not mean that the society under Mr. Lee has not been kind and gentle."[57]

Some measures aimed at obtaining greater popular participation in the political process have indeed been introduced in recent years. The political system has taken on a baroque hue and is now embellished with Citizens' Consultative Committees, Residents' Committees, and a Feedback Unit. These new bodies may serve a social mobilization function, but they also help the leadership obtain a more accurate sense of popular sentiment by monitoring opinion, and this may be their primary function. Indeed, a prominent second-generation leader once declared: "The important point is that we have to be seen to be consulting the people. The inadequacy of consultation with the people is only a minor problem. . . . But I don't believe that consultation with the people is a very productive exercise. People, even with education, tend to be irrational."[58]

In fact, the new-generation leadership that came to power with Goh was responsible, while operating earlier under the premiership of Lee Kuan Yew, for a range of restrictive measures that effectively clamped down on the emergence of independent tendencies evinced by various social groups. Amendments to the Newspaper and Printing Presses Act in September 1986 to restrict foreign publications were initiated by Wong Kan Seng, a prominent "liberal" member of the new order regime and current leader of Parliament. Lee Kuan Yew observed that these younger political leaders would be less tolerant of the foreign news media than he and his older-generation colleagues had been.[59] The attempt by the Law Society to comment on these amendments was attacked by Wong and Goh Chok Tong and led to curbs on the Law Society and a reorganization of the legal profession.[60]

The arrest of sixteen people in May 1987 and a further six in June— on the grounds that they were involved in a Marxist conspiracy within the Catholic church to overthrow the ruling regime and establish a communist state—was again a decision taken by the new generation of leaders, as Goh was at pains to emphasize.[61] In April 1992 Goh announced that the implementation of a refurbishment program for public housing would be linked to the voting patterns of the different constituencies—a "political loyalty test," as it was termed.[62]

The efforts to manage participation do not represent real political change. The present stasis results precisely because the new leadership, like the old, fears for the fragility of the Singapore polity and economy. The analogy may have shifted, in Goh Chok Tong's words, from "refugees on a small sampan . . . [which needs] a strong captain" to "a trawler or hovercraft going at high speed. . . . The boat can still capsize."[63] But the leadership's perception remains the same: there is no margin for error. Hence its policies presuppose a permanent atmosphere of crisis. Singaporeans are constantly warned that the country is vulnerable, and this air of crisis is used to close off alternatives within the polity and to emphasize discipline and conformity. In the mind-set of the political leadership, rationality can be maintained only through rigid control of society to prevent its ravagement by an unreasoned and unsound populism.

As the state's corporatist organization of society comes under increasing strain, the state finds it difficult to keep its co-opted organizations under control. Coordination of policy becomes more difficult too, as does winning compliance.[64] In the Singapore case, moreover, the legitimacy of the political regime remains open to criticism of partiality to certain social groups; further, legitimacy has yet to break decisively from performance and personal authority. While the legitimacy of the leadership, regime, and state currently appears secure, Singapore's leadership must discover a more durable basis of legitimacy if the regime's viability is to be maintained over the long term. Indeed, it is certain to need those new means of ensuring its legitimacy as social and economic change in the future is likely to create new—and possibly more serious—challenges to its authority.

6

The Philippines

The Languages of Legitimation

JOHN T. SIDEL

In Barrio Dungo-an, Danao City, just a 45-minute drive north from Cebu City, lies the Philippines' twentieth-century answer to Borobodur, Pagan, and Angkor Wat: the burial grounds of the late Ramon M. Durano, Sr. (1905–88). Covered with fresh flowers replenished every week, his tomb lies in a tiny chapel, almost encircled, like a stupa, not by lingams with Sanskrit inscriptions but rather scores of busts representing all the popes in the history of Christianity, each facing the late Durano. Framing the chapel and this collection of popes, life-size dioramas of various biblical scenes—the Last Supper, the Nativity—fill out the grounds of the Ramon M. Durano Sr. Home for the Aged, adjacent to the church and orphanage that also bear his name, and just across the street from his publishing house and bakery.

Surrounding these monuments to Durano's beneficence and position in the Catholic cosmology, substantial landmarks of his remaining this-worldly empire radiate out in the four cardinal directions: saltbeds stretching east to the coastline; several hectares of sugarcane plantation lining the highway back south toward Cebu City; the "industrial welfare estate"—a sugar mill, ice plant, and cement factory—on the northbound road; mines and extensive landholdings to the mountainous west. In the neighboring towns, mayors and other local notables remain to this day beholden unto the late Durano, having benefited handsomely from his long tenure as representative and political kingpin of Cebu's former first congressional district. Elsewhere in the province, in Cebu City (and, to a lesser extent, the nation's capital, Manila), scores of Durano relatives and protégés are still in place—in Customs, the Port Authority, the Bureau of Internal Revenue, the ranks of the police, and among various law firms and construction companies. From its metaphysical, religious, and political center and source at his gravesite, Durano's empire still emanates its ebbing power.[1]

Yet however impressive in scope and remarkable in style, this monument's projection of Durano's authority claims little in the way of an attentive audience. The burial grounds remain almost entirely empty, the church has fallen into disrepair, and the old age home and orphanage are virtually deserted. Only the caretaker, Durano's longtime personal bodyguard, maintains a permanent vigil, standing by the memory of the boss whose life he had protected for so many years.

In its contemporary context, this monument to Durano, though not as centrally located as, for example, Jakarta's Taman Mini, may say as much about Philippine democracy as Ibu Tien's pet project does about the nature of Soeharto's New Order regime in Indonesia.[2] Indeed, the case of Durano, who as congressman and acknowledged power broker in Cebu outlasted six presidents and survives today in dynastic form through his politically active children, exemplifies certain contradictions apparent in the projection of political authority throughout the Philippines. On the one hand, Durano manifested a visible commitment to the Catholic religion—through generous donations to churches, sponsorship of numerous priests, and his own elaborate burial arrangements. On the other hand, in the course of his political career he earned a reputation for relying on violence, intimidation, and fraud during elections, allegedly ordered several murders, and sponsored and protected in his own hometown a cottage industry in homemade firearms. Similarly, though careful to build up his name as a great patron and philanthropist, Durano made his fortune through pilfered government funds, fixed contracts and concessions, behest loans, land grabbing, and reliance on low-wage labor and union busting. Moreover, while he donned shorts and carried a bolo when in Danao in a flamboyant display of his populist local "big man" credentials, Durano was a six-term congressman who spent considerable time in Manila attending to legislative matters and whose patronage and power emanated largely from his position within the state apparatus.[3] Finally, while avowedly Catholic, fluent in English, seemingly quite westernized, and supposedly an outstanding legislator, Durano made claims to leadership—as the bizarrely fashioned monument to his "superior death status" suggests—that were in some ways strikingly reminiscent of those made by precolonial "men of prowess" throughout Southeast Asia.[4]

Durano himself captured some of these contradictions well in the dedication he wrote to his autobiography on December 24, 1986 (his eighty-first birthday):

> "CIC
> Godfather
> Warlord
> Killer
> Boss
> Indian
> Caesar of Cebu
> Political Kingpin"
>
> They call me these names.
> But I say:
>
> > I am a repentant Sinner,
> > I love God and my Neighbor,
> > I die for this Love,
> > > This is my Name forever,
> > > This is my Title for all
> > > generations.
>
> Signed, Ramon M. Durano[5]

Though clearly idiosyncratic, the case of Durano highlights a number of important issues surrounding the nature of political legitimacy throughout the Philippines. Most prominent, perhaps, is the role of patronage and paternalism in the legitimation not only of political leadership but of an entire social order and system of governance. Moreover, the efforts to legitimize political and economic power on a personal basis, as well as the deemphasis of the formal institutions and laws of the Philippines' constitutional democracy, underline the need to distinguish between the legitimation of individual holders of political and economic power, on the one hand, and the legitimation of the nation-state and the regime on the other. Moreover, the readily apparent distance between the observable behavior of a successful politician such as Durano and the Western norms embedded in Catholicism, legality, and constitutional democracy suggests the significance of other, indigenous, local, "Filipino," or possibly "Southeast Asian" elements in the legitimation formula. Finally, the elaborate monument to the late Durano serves as an apt reminder that the process of legitimation is played out not in suspended animation but against the backdrop of time, as memories and dreams, nostalgia and hope, always impinge on the present.

Moreover, the Durano case raises troubling methodological issues for the discussion of legitimacy in the Philippines. First of all, any attempt at

generalization must somehow contend with the significant religious, ethnic, linguistic, geographic, and class diversity of the contemporary Philippines. Further, a discussion of legitimacy must likewise deal with the local-
to-national continuum and address the variation in the modes of
legitimation observed in local and national arenas. Finally, such a discussion must also problematize both the efficacy of legitimation claims and
the role of legitimacy in Philippine society, assessing to what extent legitimacy—rather than coercion, expediency, apathy, the "dull compulsion of
economic relations," and "the absence of preferable alternatives"—sustains the political order.[6]

While legitimacy as a fixed quality may in fact hold little predictive
value, the "languages" in which legitimating claims are expressed and
evaluated define in three important ways the essential facts of power and
domination in a society. First, the grounds on which legitimacy is claimed
often reveal precisely what they are designed to mystify or obscure: essential realities about the nature of political and economic power. Read back-
wards, legitimacy claims specify what exactly, in a given setting, is considered dangerously *illegitimate*. Second, the mode by which power is
legitimated must in some way shape the very structures of domination. As
Max Weber argues:

> Experience shows that in no instances does domination voluntarily limit itself to
> the appeal to material or affectual or ideal motives as a basis for its continuance.
> In addition, every such system attempts to establish and to cultivate the belief in
> its legitimacy. But according to the kind of legitimacy which is claimed, the type of
> obedience, the kind of administrative staff developed to guarantee it, and the mode
> of exercising authority, will all differ fundamentally.[7]

> For a domination, this kind of justification of its legitimacy is much more than a
> matter of theoretical or philosophical speculation; it rather constitutes the basis of
> very real differences in the empirical structure of domination. The reason for this
> fact lies in the generally observable need of any power, or even of any advantage
> of life, to justify itself.[8]

Third, the basis on which appeals to legitimacy are made provides a language for voicing resistance to domination. As James C. Scott has noted,
all claims to legitimacy "must, by definition, represent an idealization,
which therefore inevitably creates the contradictions that permit it to be
criticized *in its own terms*. The ideological source of mass radicalism is, in
this sense, to be sought as much *within* a prevailing ideological order as
outside it."[9]

To summarize: however wretchedly corrupt, exploitative, and illegitimate the existing political order in the Philippines may be, its pretensions
to the contrary offer tools for understanding and challenging the status

quo. As E. P. Thompson, concluding a study of eighteenth-century British society, remarks:

The rhetoric and the rules of a society are something a great deal more than sham. In the same moment they may modify, in profound ways, the behavior of the powerful, and mystify the powerless. They may disguise the true realities of power, but, at the same time, they may curb that power and check its intrusions. And it is often from within that very rhetoric that a radical critique of the practice of the society is developed: the reformers of the 1790s appeared, first of all, clothed in the rhetoric of Locke and of Blackstone.[10]

Though a comparison between eighteenth-century England and the postwar Philippines is beyond the scope of this essay, Thompson's essential theoretical thrust is its guiding spirit. By tracing the structure of legitimation at the levels of nation-state, regime, and individual claimants to political authority, this chapter constitutes a reexamination of the nature of power in Philippine society.

Democracy and the Paternalist Past

Popular understandings of the overall structure of power in the Philippines revolve around two distinct constructions of legitimate governance. First, the modern, Western institutions of the nation-state and constitutional democracy serve as the formal models and goals of "progress" and "national development," as well as standards by which to evaluate the political realities of today. Second, widespread nostalgia for an idealized golden age of what may loosely be described as paternalism provides another vantage point for evaluating the shortcomings of the contemporary political and social order. For many Filipinos, the structure of power relations in Philippine society is seen as caught between these two ideals: between a lost past and an as yet unattainable future.

At its most grandiose, the language of legitimation in the postwar Philippines has centered on the claims and pretensions of a modern nation-state and constitutional democracy. Like its counterparts in Southeast Asia, the Philippine state claims sovereignty over a fixed territory and the population within it, enjoys the same juridical status as other nations in the international arena (in the United Nations and International Monetary Fund, for example), and boasts its own version of what scholars have described as "official nationalism."[11] Schoolbook lessons on Philippine history, monuments to various national heroes, periodic assertions of the Philippines' historic claim to Sabah, and an evolving national language policy promoting "Pilipino" exemplify the modern state's efforts to advance the legitimacy of the Philippines as a nation. The state apparatus also justifies its existence as an agent of national development and public administration. The very names of national state agencies—the Department of Public Works and Highways, the Department of Justice, the National Economic Development Authority—convey their purposiveness: the notion of an indivisible (national) public good is put forth as the yardstick of government performance.

Moreover, the country's system of laws, most notably the Philippine Constitution, represents a corollary set of claims to authority, based on the familiar rational-legal basis cited by Weber. Formally, political authority is structured along legal lines: laws and statutes define the contours of power; a bicameral legislature, a multitiered court system, and a variety of law enforcement and regulatory agencies impose the rule of law upon Philippine society. Since independence in 1946, moreover, the government has, except during the 1972–86 authoritarian interlude, claimed legitimacy according to its formal adherence to democratic procedures, regularly held local and national elections, and frequent alternation of rival political parties in power.[12]

These claims to modern nation-statehood and constitutional democracy have in real ways structured and constrained the exercise of power in the contemporary Philippines. The state devotes substantial resources to the maintenance of formal diplomatic relations with other nations, to the advancement of an official Philippine culture, language, and history, and to the elaboration of national administrative capacities from Batanes to Tawi-Tawi. Meanwhile, legislators in the two houses of Congress engage in passionate debates, the Supreme Court and lower judicial bodies hear cases on a continual basis, law schools and bar associations are filled with aspiring attorneys, and citizens frequently file lawsuits, earning the Philippines a reputation as an extremely litigious society. Political officeholders issue a steady stream of laws, regulations, and administrative orders, shrouding even their most nefarious actuations with assertions of legal and constitutional legitimacy. President Marcos's proclamation of martial law in 1972, for example, included explicit claims as to its basis in the 1935 Constitution, gained further legal strength through a subsequent Supreme Court decision, and preceded the ratification of a new constitution in 1973. Again and again, Marcos claimed that his dictatorship amounted to "constitutional authoritarianism."[13]

Finally, democratic procedures regulate political succession at the national level and determine local executive and legislative authority throughout the entire Philippines. The frequency of elections and the enormous number of available elective positions permit considerable political turnover, a measure of pluralism, and a broad geographical distribution of power, thus giving Filipinos all over the archipelago an interest in the persistence of formal democracy. Indeed, even President Marcos, who declared martial law and abolished Congress in 1972, held numerous plebiscites to legitimize his continuation in power and assumption of extraordinary powers and even called local (1980), parliamentary (1978 and 1984), and presidential elections (1981 and 1986) in the course of his dictatorial rule.[14]

The modern standards and claims of nation-statehood and constitutional democracy have shaped not only the structure of domination but also the contours of resistance in the contemporary Philippines. For example, a variety of popular movements have protested against the shortcomings and injustices of the Philippines' identity as a sovereign nation. Ethnic minorities, facing the encroachment of state and capital, have fashioned their struggles in terms of insurgent subnationhood, whether fighting for secession like the Moro National Liberation Front (MNLF) or for autonomy like the Cordillera People's Liberation Army (CPLA).[15] Radicalized segments of the urban intelligentsia, angered by such encroachments on Philippine sovereignty as U.S. military bases and foreign debt, have, since the late 1960s, waved the banner of nationalism.[16] Even the Communist Party of the Philippines (CPP), though radical in its revolutionary goals of social transformation, seeks to gain national power as defined by the regime.[17] The CPP and its front organization, the National Democratic Front (NDF), claim that only a social revolution can defeat U.S. imperialism and bring genuine independence to the archipelago.[18]

Meanwhile, legality provides a basis for criticizing abuses of power—a language for legitimating protest and resistance. Legislative and judicial bodies serve as arenas for promotion of reform, restriction on abuses of power, and protection of civil liberties. Union leaders denounce illegal strike-breaking tactics,[19] peasants demand enforcement of agrarian reform statutes,[20] and urban poor resist demolition of their settlements through restraining orders obtained in municipal courts.[21] Aspiring local politicians level graft and corruption charges against incumbent town mayors or provincial governors; losing presidential candidates file election protests before the Supreme Court. Among the most prominent anti-Marcos opposition forces were lawyers' groups (such as MABINI) avowedly engaged in protecting civil liberties and human rights.

Finally, democratic procedures tend to encourage opponents of those in power to work through electoral means. Elections tempt even the most disaffected citizens—whether local gangsters, communist guerrillas, Muslim rebels, or military putschists—to run for office and thus to participate in Philippine democracy. The ideal of democracy also played a role in the dramatic events of February 1986, in which thousands of Filipinos took to the streets in nonviolent protest against electoral fraud perpetrated by the Marcos dictatorship. Even those most eager to subvert or discard formal democratic procedures—Ferdinand Marcos, the Communist Party, military rebels—claim to oppose not democracy per se but rather those forces—oligarchy, corruption, patronage, disorder—that interfere with the workings of democracy in practice. The chairman of the Central Committee of the Communist Party of the Philippines, for example, claimed in 1970 that a "People's Democratic Revolution" would serve the "genuine national and democratic interests of the entire Filipino people" by vanquishing "U.S. imperialism, feudalism and bureaucratic capitalism now regnant in the present semi-colonial and semi-feudal society."[22] Similarly, President Marcos published in 1974 a volume in his name—titled *The Democratic Revolution in the Philippines*—which argued that the declaration of martial law two years earlier would save democracy from "the rightist and leftist rebellion, the secessionist movement in the South, private armies, political overlords, economic oligarchs, criminal syndicates, and the feudalistic economic system."[23]

Although there appears to be considerable consensus on the desirability of Philippine nation-statehood and constitutional democracy, it is unclear how broadly or how deeply this consensus permeates Philippine society. The strength of nationalist sentiment in the Philippines, for example, is hard to gauge. Ethnic minorities have voiced support for "independence" or "autonomy" at different times, a million Filipinos have allegedly signed a petition in support of the Statehood Movement U.S.A., and a considerable portion of the country's population has chosen to live and work abroad.[24] Jokes about the long lines for visas at the U.S. embassy, about hiring former Singapore prime minister Lee Kuan Yew to run the Philippines, and about the likely overwhelming victory of a referendum making the Philippines the fifty-first state are legion. Meanwhile, anthropologists have concluded, "the roots of the Philippine national legal system do not run deep. Much of the rural population in the Philippines, for instance, does not share in the emphasis of the national legal culture on procedural justice. In addition, the Western-style courts are only one among a variety of mechanisms—ranging from self-help to informal mediation by community leaders—by which people in the lowland Philippines process their disputes."[25]

Finally, the extent of popular commitment to democracy remains open to dispute: few Filipinos actively took to the streets to resist Marcos's abolition of Congress and declaration of martial law in 1972 or the various military coup attempts in the 1986–91 period. In the early 1970s and mid-1980s, authoritarianism supposedly enjoyed considerable popular appeal as a possible solution to the Philippines' economic and political

problems. In fact, nation-statehood and constitutional democracy are institutions that were imposed—rather than indigenously created—in the
course of the Philippines' subjugation to American colonial rule and rest
ultimately on modern *American* notions of political legitimacy.[26] Moreover, to this day, appeals to the sanctity of "democracy" are in considerable measure geared to foreign (most prominently American) observers,
commentators, and critics, while the "developmental" actuations of government technocrats play largely to the staffs of USAID, JICA, ADB, IMF,
World Bank, and other foreign donors and creditors.[27]

The extent to which the imported Western constructs of nation-state
and constitutional democracy enjoy legitimacy among Filipinos deserves
closer consideration. Certainly those Filipinos most clearly involved in, or
dependent upon, the formal institutions supposedly embodying these
ideals are likely to hold them dear. The state apparatus as a whole is the
single largest employer in the Philippines and—through its glossy publications and statistical performance reports, its internal surveillance agencies (Commission on Audit, Office of the Ombudsman), and its subcon-
tracted technocratic subsidiaries (University of the Philippines College of
Public Administration, Development Academy of the Philippines)—systematically promotes the notions of "public administration," "national
development," and "the Philippines" among hundreds of thousands of
civil servants. The legal system likewise sustains thousands of judges, public prosecutors, court stenographers, attorneys, law school professors, and
publishers of law journals, not to mention the officials of the state's various law enforcement agencies, all of whom rely on and daily affirm the
notion of authority based on the legal order as legitimate. Finally, elections
spawn politicians and political parties, a seasonal cottage industry run by
newspaper editors, TV and radio commentators, polling groups, and political scientists, as well as the apparatus of the Commission on Elections,
all geared toward the propagation and performance of the election ritual.
With an extremely high number of government positions open to electoral
competition, "democracy" means a great deal to many ordinary Filipinos.

Yet millions of Filipinos may very well vote, go to court, seek government assistance, and even attend Independence Day parades out of expediency and lack of preferable alternatives—or out of beliefs unrelated to
those legitimacy claims formally propagated by the state. The Philippines,
after all, is neither ancient Athens nor contemporary Kansas: its population remains overwhelmingly poor, ethnically diverse, and unlikely to interpret—to translate—foreign notions of legitimate governance in a uniform or simplistic fashion.

Alongside the promise of Philippine nation-statehood and constitutional democracy, there lingers in the popular imagination what has been

described as a "generalized nostalgia for patron-client relationships,"[28] that is, the fading memory of a lost paternalist age typical of a predominantly agrarian society in the process of capitalist transformation.[29] The legitimacy of this fondly remembered sociopolitical order rests not on the institutional integrity of "public administration," "the law," and "democracy," but on an imagined—but typically quite localized—social harmony in which personal relationships and obligations bind together individuals of unequal status, wealth, and power.[30] The legal system and the bureaucracy serve essentially as patronage resources. Judicial decisions and legal enforcement, appointments of schoolteachers, policemen, and customs officials, allocations of artesian wells, roads, public works contracts, and import licenses—all flow forth as provisions from patrons to their clients. In this paternalistic setting, some scholars have concluded that "the legitimacy of the government derives in large part from the legitimacy accorded patrons by clients."[31]

In the contemporary Philippines, the wealthy and powerful look back fondly on the days when they enjoyed the loyalty, affection, and deference of tenants, workers, and followers, even as the poor sometimes idealize the generosity and accessibility of earlier generations of landlords and local politicians.[32] The daughter of a longtime congressman, for example, recalled in a mid-1970s biography of her father that in his later years the aging politician, his eyes "filled with nostalgia," would reminisce: "During those times, my leaders would even vie with each other in picking up the bill for the expenses incurred. They would spend their own money, kill their own chickens, butcher their own pigs and cows, and not ask anything in return. They were not only my leaders, they were my true friends."[33] A rice-farming tenant in central Luzon interviewed in the 1970s recalled his former landlord with similar fondness: "General Tinio was my *kompadre* because he was the godfather [*ninong*] of my eldest child. Actually, he was a sponsor at weddings and baptisms of many tenants I knew. He even came to my house occasionally just to see how things were."[34] In scholarly and journalistic accounts, memoirs, and contemporary conversations, such memories abound: the "beloved mayor" of a Visayan fishing village remembered as a "benign patronal figure" who provided free medical services to the needy;[35] the Mindoro congressman remembered as a "generous road-builder, legal counselor, recommendation-maker, job-giver, and guardian angel."[36] In Danao City, Cebu, more than just the spectacular monument described earlier remains of the late congressman Ramon Durano, Sr. The churches he built, the baptisms, weddings, and burials he sponsored, the jobs, loans, and handouts he provided from cradle to grave: such is the stuff of local nostalgia.

Memories of this idealized paternalist past continue to shape the contours of both domination and resistance in the Philippines. Politicians, ever conscious of popular expectations, still devote enormous time, energy, and resources to what has been described as the "simulation of patronage."[37] A recently published handbook for aspiring politicians emphasizes the three vital elements of "KBL"—*Kasal* (weddings), *Binyag* (baptisms), and *Libing* (burials)—as ceremonies of great religious and symbolic importance that deserve a would-be politico's frequent attendance and sponsorship.[38] Even in Makati, the Metro Manila municipality known as the nation's financial center and most exclusive residential district, such practices live on. The mayor "provides" free medical care for poor residents at Makati Medical Center, donations at funerals, and Christmas gifts.[39]

The language of paternalism informs not only the claims that poor Filipinos make upon those with greater status, wealth, and power, but also the resistance they wage against oppression. The bonds that are said to have once held society together—kinship, ritual coparenthood, clientship—form the bases upon which demands for material assistance are still made on the rich and powerful, whose previously demonstrated generosity, pity, and noblesse oblige are also conveniently recalled (or reconstructed).[40] As plantations, logging concessions, tourist resorts, industrial estates, and reclamation projects increasingly intrude upon the landscape, resistance to "progress" and "development" is voiced in the precapitalist idiom of custom, tradition, ancestral domain, subsistence rights, and the social use of property.[41] Wealth and power, it is made clear, were once linked to personal obligations and responsibilities; violations of these norms, labeled by social scientists as the breakdown or erosion of patron-client relations, are recognized as the prelude to class conflict and rebellion.[42] Over the years, a wide variety of rural insurgency movements—from the Huks to the MNLF, the CPLA, and the New People's Army (NPA)—have enlisted peasant support against those who exploit land and labor without regard for the welfare of the population. Even today, above the artillery charges of the NPA's socialist revolution, one can hear the crackle of "small arms fire" in the class war.[43]

In contemporary Philippine political discourse—today's structure of power relations—the regime appears caught somehow betwixt and between, lost on the road from a degenerated paternalist past to an imagined Americanized future, and dominated neither by personal loyalties nor formal institutions but, rather, by money, violence, and a predatory state. From the vantage point of the early 1990s, it is nearly impossible to discern to what extent the paternalist past was ever experienced as a paternalist present, for scholarly accounts, elite politicians' biographies, and informants' reminiscences suspiciously locate the lost golden age of high paternalism as far back as the colonial 1920s. Moreover, while Filipinos today often trace a fall from grace stretching from the Philippines' 1950s status as Southeast Asia's "showcase of democracy" into what many commentators, both Filipino and foreign, describe as the region's "basket case," newspaper and magazine articles from the highly mythologized Magsaysay period (1953–57) bear witness to a familiar and longstanding sense that democracy as practiced in the Philippines is not quite, not really, well, democracy. Yet a visitor to the Philippines in 1992—as perhaps in 1972 or even 1952—quickly encounters a widespread sense of loss, betrayal, decline, and disillusionment with *pulitika*,[44] expressed in jokes and anecdotes, cartoon strips and tabloid headlines, radio dramas and movie scripts. An elusive future, it seems, has haunted the Philippines for as long as its paternalist past.

For the millions of Filipinos who read newspapers, listen to radio commentaries, or engage in street-corner gossip, the nation-state by and large appears neither as an agency of public service nor as an arena for patron-client relationships but, rather, as a complex set of predatory mechanisms for the private exploitation and accumulation of resources originally in the public domain. From top to bottom, as daily life and newspaper scandals make clear, the state's enforcement of regulations, provision of licenses and permits, and appointment of personnel all amount to petty rentier instruments for the extraction of *tong* (fixed bribes) and *lagay* (grease money), practices popularly referred to with derision as *pangungurakot*. The revenue-generating agencies of the state (Bureau of Customs, Commission on Immigration and Deportation, Bureau of Internal Revenue) provide ample opportunities for extortionary activities or serve as "milking cows" (the Philippine Amusement and Gaming Corporation, the Philippine Charity Sweepstakes Office). Moreover, money and *palakasan* (influence) bear upon the titling of lands, the awarding of logging and mining concessions, and access to loans from government financial institutions. Government contracts (for construction, reclamation, and provision of supplies, for example) and franchises (electric power, cockpits, stevedore services), it is widely understood, fall to bidders on a similar basis. Thus private wealth and state power are seen as closely intertwined, and "oligarchs" and "cronies" abound.[45]

The legal system, according to a variety of sources, is widely regarded with skepticism: the law is seen less as an instrument of justice than "a means of manipulation, complication, stratagem, and violence" by which those with power and influence further their interests.[46] A 1967 NBI study found that an average of 48 policemen every month were directly implicated in the commission of crimes, for example, while a survey of Manila newspapers from January to December of that year revealed a total of 97 headlines reporting police offenses.[47] In a late-1960s random survey of 1,000 Manila residents, one anthropologist discovered that "only two persons felt *any* policeman was honest."[48] Today, popular opprobrium

for law enforcement officers is evident in various derisive slang terms and
common references to policemen as *buaya* (crocodiles),[49] and it is common knowledge that most bank robberies are the work of police and
military-led syndicates. As for the judicial system, it is widely appreciated
that *palakasan* (influence peddling) and *pera* (money) play decisive roles
in the filing, prosecution, and settlement of cases. One anthropologist conducting fieldwork in rural areas in the Visayas in the early 1980s reported
a "widespread conviction that judges, witnesses, and other legal officials
may be bought."[50]

Philippine democracy in practice reflects less the popular will, or even
the dynamics of patron-client relations, than the interplay of money, violence, and the manipulation of state resources. Per capita election expen-
ditures in the Philippines have long been estimated as surpassing those in
the United States and are said to rank among the highest in the world.[51]
Vote buying, in both houses of Congress, at party conventions, and on
election day, is known to be pervasive. As one scholar noted in the 1950s:
"Candidates are not unwilling to pay for votes and electors are not reluctant to sell their ballots. . . . An amazingly large portion of Filipino voters
have acquired the habit of looking up to campaign periods for free transportation, food, drinks and to realize quick money."[52] The exchange of
money—rather than enduring loyalty—also serves as the basis for frequent party switching and shifting alliances between aspiring and
incumbent mayors, congressional representatives, provincial governors,
senators, and presidents.[53]

Moreover, elections are occasions for the surfacing of warlords, goons,
and private armies in the popular imagination—through newspaper accounts, radio commentaries, police reports, and gossip. Indeed, coercion
serves several crucial functions in the electoral process: enforcement of
illegal monetary transactions (such as vote buying and bribery), intimidation or elimination of unsympathetic voters, candidates, and election
officials, and actual physical interference with the electoral process
(ballot-box stuffing and ballot grabbing, for example). Thus elections are
associated with frequent incidents of violence and terrorism: according to
the latest reports, election-related violence in 1992 left 105 wounded and
104 killed, as well as 5 kidnapped.[54]

Finally, money and violence combine to facilitate systematic electoral
fraud through the manipulation of state resources. Campaign funds derive
largely from "dirty money"—protection received from various criminal
rackets,[55] kickbacks on contracts and franchises awarded or promised,[56]
and skimmed off or diverted government revenues and appropriations.[57]
The processes of voter registration, casting of ballots, and tallying and
canvassing of votes at the precinct, municipal, provincial, and national

levels are all marred by fraud committed with the collusion of government officials intimidated, bribed, and otherwise pressured by candidates and their henchmen.[58]

By and large the attitude of much of the population toward the workings of Philippine democracy is, understandably, one of great skepticism: the "blasé attitude" associated with the monetization of transactions and human relationships.[59] Thus some scholars examining the electoral process in the post-Marcos era have concluded:

> Cynicism about elections and politicians is common. Poor people . . . are often too preoccupied with making ends meet to pay much attention to elections which, in any case, they believe are frequently riddled with cheating. Similarly, a pronounced sentiment is that elections are essentially contests among candidates with little genuine interest in the problems of the poor majority; hence who wins is not terribly important to most people. Finally, they see office holders more often than not using public office for their own purposes rather than for public service. This negative appraisal helps to explain why people may treat elections in instrumental ways—selling their votes, participating in a nominal way to please a relative or friend who is campaigning, or in other ways "working the system."[60]

As a former provincial governor recently commented after reeling off the prices of votes for sale in his home province: "[Voters] reason out that since this political exercise is a circus, someone has to pay. But this time, it shall be the circus performers, not the audience. To all candidates, HURRY!"[61]

Charisma, Money, and the State

While legitimation of the regime—the overall structure of power relations in the Philippines—is expressed in terms of the state's formal claims and society's collective memory, the authority of individual claimants to power is propagated in terms that appear to defy generalization. Indeed, as the introductory remarks about the late Ramon Durano suggest, both social diversity and the multitiered structures of the democratic state problematize any simplistic understanding of the "audience" or "arena" within which legitimacy claims are voiced and heard in the Philippines. Nonetheless, an analysis of the grounds on which individual aspirants to power assert claims to legitimacy—within local and national arenas—in Philippine society reveals a clear pattern in the legitimation of political power. This pattern must be understood as reflecting the historical processes of state formation and capitalist transformation experienced by Philippine society.

In the precolonial Philippines, political authority was entirely personal and charismatic, based on the belief in power located in certain innate qualities of certain individuals: magical powers, oratorical skills, spiritual refinement, bravery in battle. Power could not be stored or stabilized through money, lineage, defined political offices, hierarchies, rules, or geographical units; it had to be reaffirmed through continuous demonstrations of personal prowess and "inner soul stuff" and provision of protection and material rewards to dependents and followers. Upon this indigenous structure of political leadership and economic power, historical developments in Philippine state formation superimposed derivative authority in the early Spanish colonial period, proprietary wealth (land and money) in the nineteenth century, and a national state apparatus in the twentieth century.

In precolonial Philippine societies, authority was essentially charismatic, dependent on belief in the inherent personal power possessed by individuals. Such power, known in Tagalog as *kapangyarihan*, was understood as "the spiritual substance that 'animates' the universe and is often concentrated in certain power-full beings and objects."[62] Male *datus*, much like "big men" or "men of prowess" elsewhere in Southeast Asia,[63] settled local disputes, extracted tribute (*buwis*) from subjects, controlled trade, led raids on neighboring settlements as well as efforts to defend against such raids, and amassed and sustained surpluses of material resources with which to cement the manifold relationships of dependence that bound followers to them. Tattooing their bodies "in proportion to their prowess,"[64] *datus* affirmed—through supernatural feats and bravery in battle, provision of sumptuous feasts, and prodigious generation of offspring—their *kapangyarihan*.[65] Meanwhile, female (or effeminate/transvestite male) shamans known as *catalona* in Tagalog and *babaylan* in Visayan also claimed *kapangyarihan*, affirmed through healing and mystical practices, based on privileged access to the spirit world of preternatural deities and spirits.[66]

In the course of state formation, external forces superimposed upon Philippine society alternative bases for political legitimation to those provided by personal, charismatic authority.[67] The Spanish colonial regime supplanted *kapangyarihan* with *puwesto*—"position"—by introducing a form of derivative political power whose force and legitimacy lay outside the realm of locally affirmed personal leadership and resided instead in a supralocal, quasi-legalistic political order. Colonial administration formally empowered the native *datus* as village headmen (*cabezas de barangay*) and petty governors (*gobernadorcillos*), determining ascension to these posts first according to hereditary succession and later through a closely supervised and restricted municipal election process whose form was defined "by a long series of laws, decrees, and circulars, designed at once to promote the selection of able candidates and also to inject the proper doses of dignity and probity into the proceedings."[68] Henceforth these native local authorities enjoyed—within formally demarcated geographical units—discretion over the enforcement of Spanish colonial legal statutes. Their power rested essentially in law and *puwesto*: position within the state.[69]

The advent of capitalism in the Philippines provided another basis for the exercise of power. In the nineteenth century, the opening of the Philippines to international trade and the ensuing commercialization of agriculture created a new path for the accumulation of economic, social, and ultimately political power—proprietary wealth—that lay outside the colonial state apparatus and was more enduring than tenure as *gobernadorcillo* or *cabeza de barangay*. The economic opportunities offered for those cultivating export crops such as sugar and abaca encouraged acquisition of land—a solid, lucrative economic base for the assertion of social and political power.[70] Emerging landed elites, if not occupying them themselves, deemed local positions of political authority worth influencing or controlling (through stooges).[71] In short, now land and money facilitated access to *puwesto* and hence *poder* (power).

Finally, twentieth-century American colonial rule entailed a further elaboration of the structure of power in the Philippines: the construction of a bureaucratic state of national proportions. The transfer of provincial-level powers to local hands and the linkage of municipal and provincial government to a Manila-based legislature and bureaucracy staffed by Filipinos created a newly accessible source of political and economic power.[72] Empowered by the Americans to supervise the rapidly Filipinized and ever expanding bureaucracy, the national legislature (and through it provincial and municipal politicians) gained control over the extensive resources devoted to the expansion of health care, education, transport, public works, and the rule of law throughout the archipelago. Eventually, with the inauguration of the commonwealth in 1935, the American governor-general was replaced by an elected Filipino president. Access, direct or indirect, to the enormous resources flowing from a national state apparatus centered in Manila—through discretion over government projects and funds as well as control over the appointment and transfer of government officials—became a primary factor of political and economic power.[73] In sum, then, the American colonial era witnessed the introduction of a new form of power, one neither dependent on personal charisma nor based simply on the delegation of privileges by external agencies but, rather, achieved by tapping into the generous supply of national state patronage radiating out of Manila.

As the preceding analysis suggests, the historical process of state formation in the Philippines superimposed upon an indigenous structure of localized charismatic authority alternative sources of power: defined political offices (*puwesto*), money, and the resources of a national state. Displaced but not dissolved, *kapangyarihan* still constitutes an essential basis for the legitimation of powerful individuals' authority in Philippine society. From bandits and priestesses to provincial bosses and presidents, in highly localized settings as well as the national arena, legitimacy is asserted through claims to *kapangyarihan*, even as the close connections between power, money, and the predatory state are obscured.

Chiefs, Priestesses, and Outlaws

Philippine history is replete with colorful figures enjoying leadership status outside and often opposed to the state apparatus and instead basing their authority on charisma, privileged access to the spiritual world, and provision of material welfare. As successive waves of colonization and capitalist penetration extended Christianity, the commercialization of agriculture, and the rule of law to new frontiers, various manifestations of resistance sprang up in the expanding "outlaw" sphere. Countless uprisings and instances of banditry and witchcraft in the Catholicized lowlands throughout the Spanish era paralleled the recalcitrance encountered in pagan highland and Islamicized areas.[74] The revolution against the Spaniards, continuing disturbances and various rebellions against American rule, and formation of guerrilla units during the Japanese occupation followed, representing more recent continuations of this much celebrated tradition.

In the postwar Philippines, the continuing strength of this form of authority is evident in three distinct manifestations: the chief, the priestess, and the outlaw. First of all, indigenous forms of leadership have persisted in those parts of the archipelago least affected by Spanish and American colonial rule. In the Islamicized parts of Mindanao and the Sulu archipelago, *datus* and sultans still claim a significant degree of authority over the local population.[75] In the Gran Cordillera of northern Luzon, in Mindoro and Palawan, in upland areas of Mindanao, and in other parts of the archipelago, numerous ethnolinguistic groups to this day retain their own variegated structures of community-based authority outside the realm of the Philippine state.[76] Residing in remote upland stretches of public land and practicing subsistence-oriented and often swidden agriculture, these people are typically "discovered" by Western anthropologists or intrusive logging and mining companies, agribusiness ventures, and state agencies. Understood as "tribal peoples" or "ethnic minorities," these groups have increasingly found themselves forced to deal with lowland incursions on

their domain, their chiefs sought out—and built up or done in—by outsiders eager for influence and mediation. The late Kalinga *pangat* Macliing Dulag,[77] who was assassinated in 1980 while leading resistance to government dam projects in the cordillera, is probably the most famous
example of the "tribal chief."

Second, lowland Philippine society, while nominally the domain of the
male-dominated Catholic church hierarchy, plays host to numerous spirit
mediums, faith healers, mystics, shamans, and cult leaders reminiscent of
the precolonial *babaylans*.[78] Popular religious sects of widely variegated
orientations hold revival meetings in cities, lead pilgrimages and establish
communes on remote mountaintops, and hold sway over large patches of
rural Mindanao.[79] Catholic charismatic groups reach millions through radio and television programs; bumper stickers all over Manila advertise "El
Shaddai," a movement supposedly 7 million strong.[80] The leaders of most
of those groups whose activities have been well documented are—as in
the precolonial Philippines—women. Through prayer, oratory, and healing, these "priestesses" claim privileged access to the spirit world—to
kapangyarihan.[81]

And third, the persistence of precolonial charismatic authority in contemporary Philippine society is evident in the popular figure of the "outlaw," celebrated in numerous folk tales, novels, *komiks*, radio shows, and
movies.[82] "Social bandits"—highwaymen, pirates, and urban gang
leaders—are found in every corner of the archipelago.[83] More sporadic
are groups overtly engaged in organized rebellion—the Huks in the 1940s
and 1950s and the NPA and MNLF from the 1970s to the present—
whose purposiveness and internal solidarity inevitably atrophy in time.

Despite the enormous variety observable in these "outlaw" elements,
certain common features explain the considerable popular legitimacy they
have enjoyed in Philippine society. Such outlaws, for example, often portray themselves quite successfully as providing both protection and material rewards to their followers and the local population at large. Famous
bandits, pirates, and urban gang leaders are well remembered among poor
farmers, fishermen, and slum dwellers for their alleged Robin Hood qualities. These outlaws, it is claimed, administer a widely appreciated form of
local justice by protecting the population from cattle rustlers, local
toughs, petty extortionists, and wife-beaters. A recent newspaper account
of a funeral captures the flavor of the alleged social bandit's popular
appeal:

Hailed as "The Hero of the New Age," public enemy number one Alfredo de Leon
alias Ka Benjie/Joey/Boyet was escorted to his grave by at least 2,000 sympathizers
in Karuhatan, Valenzuela.

Thousands of others lined the narrow streets of the working-class town where he was regarded as a Robin-Hood-like figure, who reportedly shared with residents the proceeds of his ransom kidnapings.

De Leon, a former communist hit man who broke away from the insurgent movement to form his own Red Scorpion Group and turned to crime, was killed in an alleged shootout with police on Feb. 17 in Calumpit, Bulacan.

Romy, 20, said, "*Mahal siya ng mga tao dito kasi para ba siyang Robin Hood na matulungin*" [He was loved by the people because he was like a helpful Robin Hood].[84]

Village fiestas to celebrate pirate raids, cases of beer drunk after bank heists, killings of predatory cattle rustlers or policemen—such is the stuff of local legend. Similarly, those marked as "communist terrorists" in the military lexicon became well known as "NPA" in the popular imagination—not as members of the New People's Army, but as "Nice People Around," who resisted the predatory encroachments of plantation owners, logging companies, and military platoons.[85]

Moreover, the legitimacy of these outlaws rests to a considerable extent on beliefs in their intrinsic personal power, most commonly expressed through references to their martial prowess and possession of amulets or magical powers known as *anting-anting*. The outlaw constructs his reputation through acts of violence that establish his personal visibility, his singularity, and his bravery and willingness to risk his life in combat.[86] Residents of Cebu City, for example, date the beginning of Isabelo "Beloy" Montemayor's widely acclaimed career as a pirate back to a 1950s fight in which he killed, with a small hunting knife, a drunken assailant armed with a bolo. A wound he suffered in this contest forever marked him with a lopped-off earlobe, earning him the Cebuano nickname of "Palong." Paradoxically, the outlaw's singularity often involves magical powers of polymorphism—the ability to change his form. Legendary Cavite bandit Leonardo Manecio, for example, remains widely known as "Nardong Putik" for his reputed ability to turn into mud (*putik*) and thus disappear when surrounded. Popular accounts of the Cebuano pirate Beloy Montemayor feature numerous episodes in which he evaded the agents of the law by donning various disguises. Fishermen's wives on far-flung Visayan islets still claim that Montemayor was dressed as a woman when he was fatally shot by the police in 1975 and that a crowd of onlookers cut open his bloodied torso to examine the size of his heart. The corpse of many an urban gang leader has been found covered with elaborate tattoos, which, as was true of precolonial Philippine "men of prowess," encode the wearer's body with marks of bravery and magical powers.[87]

These *anting-anting* absorb, tap into, or afford privileged access to external sources of power but ultimately depend on the inner qualities—the *loób*—of the bearer. According to numerous accounts, various items associated with Holy Week rituals in the Catholicized lowlands—icons, scapulars, rosaries, crosses, holy water—are frequently used as *anting-anting*, while Latin verses or *orasyon* are recounted to empower the amulets.[88] In Muslim areas, verses from the Koran similarly serve as empowering *ajimat*.[89] Though often derived from the paraphernalia of organized religion,[90] *anting-anting* serve merely as a mode of access to intrinsic power or *kapangyarihan*, and their efficacy depends on the state of the bearer's inner self or *loób*:[91]

For the power that is concentrated in an amulet to be absorbed by its wearer, the latter's loób must be properly cultivated through ascetic prayer, controlled bodily movements and other forms of self-discipline. For an amulet to take effect, the loób of its possessor must have undergone a renewal and purification.[92]

According to popular belief, the bearer of an *anting-anting* must be "helpful, devout, humble, and quiet, but brave if put to the test. . . . There is a close connection between an *anting-anting* and the *loób* of its bearer and the sturdiness and beauty of his or her character."[93]

Finally, the legitimacy of the charismatic outlaw lies in his—often violent—opposition to the predatory forces of the state. Rebellion starts with a refusal to pay off the corrupt policeman, a bloody encounter with a soldier, or a knife fight with a local smuggler protected by the authorities. Numerous Tagalog movies scripted along similar lines have enjoyed considerable commercial success. Commenting on the films of Ramon Revilla, best known for his portrayal of "Nardong Putik" and other Cavite bandits, one scholar concluded: "Revilla's themes do not vary: a man with his back against the wall has no choice but to fight those he perceives to be the perpetrators of injustice. This is the reason why all the heroes in Revilla's films turn their back on society to lead the life of a fugitive, killing policemen and other government agents with impunity."[94]

While reminiscent of precolonial charismatic authority, these claims to legitimacy often obscure the close links of these putative outlaws to the predatory state against which they purport to counterpose themselves.[95] The provision of protection and material rewards, that is, may mask the extent of extraction facilitated by a local monopoly on violence maintained with the connivance of policemen and politicians. Expressions of belief in *anting-anting* allow local folk and policemen alike to explain away unsuccessful law enforcement efforts and permit the outlaw to claim authority on the basis of popularly acclaimed intrinsic—rather than derivative—power. Self-styled social bandits double as the hired guns, bodyguards, and election campaigners of local politicians, the extortion collectors of corrupt policemen, or the security guards and "muscle" of logging companies, plantation owners, and city slum syndicates.

That "Robin Hoods" abound—in legends, *komiks*, novels, radio
shows, and movies as well as real life—reflects not only their popular legitimacy but also the ease with which these outlaws are incorporated as
subcontractor-agents of the predatory state. Similarly, the government's
counterinsurgency strategy in the 1980s involved the enlisting of various
religious cults and tribal groups against the communist rebels.[96] Ironically,
today even local contingents of the New People's Army will, for a price,
facilitate illegal logging or deliver votes to a mayoral candidate, while erst-
while "comrades" serve in vigilante squads, paramilitary forces, and politicians' armed coteries.[97] In the May 1992 elections, a lucky few even ran
in various municipalities as candidates for mayor and won.[98]

Local Politicians

Unlike the ephemeral outlaw figure, the archetypal Philippine local
politician tries to establish his legitimacy on a more enduring basis than
that provided by *anting-anting* and Robin Hood myths. Indeed, Philippine politicians are well known for their efforts to cast themselves in the
timeless idiom of the family and to establish bonds with their constituency
that stretch toward eternity. Though the local politico may be less dependent on popular legitimation than the outlaw, his appeals to legitimacy
themselves reveal much about the nature of his power.

As numerous scholarly and journalistic accounts have shown, the local
politician typically expresses his claims to legitimacy in terms of family.
Indeed, the town mayor often represents the interests of a particular clan,
and it is not uncommon for mayorships to be passed down within a family
or rotated. In Cebu, for example, the province's longest-running small-
town dynasty—the Escario clan of Bantayan—has for nearly half a century passed a municipal mayorship from father to mother, then to two
sons, and now back to the mother, Remedios Escario, known to all as
"Ma Mediong." Moreover, ties of consanguinity and affinity allow a politician to activate a network of relatives, even as his coalition partners (the
vice mayor, municipal councillors, *barangay* captains) do the same on his
behalf. In many towns, the ratio of elective positions to voting population
is such as to encompass the entire population through direct and indirect
kinship ties. The following account of a *barangay* captain in a town in
Nueva Ecija is instructive:

Being from large, well-established extended families gave Tomas Gregorio a res-
ervoir of supporters and advocates or campaigners (*mga lider*). Recalling how he
organized his campaigns in 1960 and 1964, Tomas pointed toward that area of
San Ricardo lining the road leading to the village of Bagong Sikat and named
several cousins, nieces, and nephews, in addition to his brothers and sisters, whom

he had asked to campaign for him. "I have so many relatives there, it was easy to get help and votes."[99]

Ritual kinship ties—forged by sponsoring baptisms and assuming roles as godfathers/mothers (*ninong/ninang*) for various children—create a secondary network of *kumpare*, *kumare*, and *inaanak* (ritual coparents and godchildren) that can likewise be activated. In sum, as in the precolonial setting, lineage provides a means to identify family connections and thus potential allies.

In addition, local politicians propagate the notion of small-town society as an enlarged family by capitalizing on opportunities for what anthropologists call liminal moments. Such moments, which involve the experience of "communitas" through a temporary suspension of hierarchy and structure, are most frequently achieved on ritual occasions—baptisms, funerals, weddings—and through common feasting activities.[100] As observed elsewhere in Southeast Asia, contemporary Philippine "feasts of merit" affirm the fertility and potency of the sponsor even as communitas is achieved.[101] Other events in which the local politician typically assumes a similar role include local beauty contests, Holy Week processions, and both town and barrio (*barangay*) fiestas. Significantly, these occasions involve large public feasts: the common ritual of eating reaffirms the image of an undifferentiated community.[102] Accounts of election campaigns reveal how local politicians try to capitalize on such shared experiences:

Rallies were staged in important barrios and the old folks, the pillars of the community, would be there. And after the speeches a big jar of *basi* [wine made from nipa palm or sugarcane] and a glass . . . would be brought out. The people would drink from that same glass, being passed around from one to another. . . . [The congressman] as guest of honor and speaker would start the ceremony by taking a sip from the glass, which would be the symbol of their unity.[103]

Some politicians run their campaigns as continuous feasts for hordes of followers invited to eat in the candidate's house.[104]

In various other ways, the local politician tries to establish his personal prowess. As throughout precolonial Southeast Asia, where "the achievement of founding a line of descent [was] emphasized rather than that of perpetuating an old one,"[105] the prodigious generation of offspring is valorized as a sign of the local politician's intrinsic powers. Pablo Cuneta, Pasay City mayor for nearly 40 years and father to some twenty children by over a dozen mothers, is a prominent example. Though he is more than 80 years old, his prowess is still alleged to be intact and allows him to pose as "father of Pasay City": with all his well-heeled "wives" and children, he claims to have offspring on every street.[106]

Often the local politician works hard to establish his reputation as a successful *sabungero* (cockfighting aficionado) by owning a *sabungan* (cockpit) and sponsoring extravagant cockfighting tournaments often followed by lavish feasts.[107] He imports, breeds, and trains his roosters, investing hundreds of thousands of pesos in feeding and conditioning. With a well-paid professional breeding and training staff, formalized routines, elaborate diets, and various *anting-anting* at hand, the local politician with serious *sabungero* credentials has much to impart to his followers. He lines up their bets, shares his expert knowledge and the resources of his cock farm, and helps to arrange cockpit licenses for his protégé mayors—invariably *sabung* enthusiasts too—with the Gamefowl Commission. Hovering over his prize fighting cock in the ring at the center of the *sabungan*, with his protégés and fellow *sabungeros* lining up their bets behind him, the politico reaffirms his authority before this exclusive audience in a bloody celebration of "big man" prowess. The victories of the politico's fighting cock vividly reflect his privileged command of fate or luck—*suwerte*—while the selective sharing of some of the bounty—a practice known as *balato*—binds supporters closely to him.[108]

Like precolonial *datus*, local politicians also have a great stake in their control of language.[109] Aside from the esoteric lingo of the *sabungan*, the local tongue for radio commentary,[110] and the Tagalog of Manila, the local politician must tap into the languages of power. Whenever possible, he flaunts his eloquence in English or pontificates in crisply enunciated legalese: "according to paragraph three, section two, chapter five of the Revised Penal Code . . ." Often he drops casual asides peppered with intimate references—*brod*, *'pare*, or the most personal nickname—to powerful figures in Manila.[111] Moreover, the politico's command over his audience requires adeptness in the performative function of political speech.[112] At a preelection luncheon hosted by the provincial governor, for example, a mayoral candidate nodded approvingly as "Gub," hamming it up considerably, lamented the disloyalty of a previous follower. A successful politician, the aspiring town executive explained, must know how to do four things: to womanize, to gamble, to cheat, and, he stressed, to cry.

Through language the local politician thus projects his personal power. The ease with which he switches from one tongue to another displays "not the ability to say what one wants to say, but the ability to replace one's 'own' words, the words one would ordinarily use, with others."[113] Moreover, his skilled use of various languages of power reaffirms his indispensability: he alone can explain the subtleties of the rooster's plumage, crack witty jokes on the radio talk show, successfully defend the errant mayor in court, converse intelligently with a visiting foreign official, and whisper sweet nothings into the ear of the president's brother.

Moreover, much as the bandit relies on church paraphernalia or *oras-*

yon, the local politician affirms his privileged access to the spiritual world of *kapangyarihan* through identification with the institutions of organized religion. The late congressman Ramon Durano, who sponsored the construction of numerous churches as well as the elaborate Catholic theme park where he is buried today, is an extreme case, but other examples abound. In Bantayan, Cebu, the Escarios are famous for their elaborately decorated *carroza* in Holy Week processions, while elite clans' floats dominate fiesta parades in many towns elsewhere in the archipelago. In Taluksangay, Zamboanga del Sur, perhaps the most beautiful Muslim mosque in the Philippines bears testimony to the dominant local clan's special connection to Allah: a plaque—obtained from the National Historical Institute through political allies in Manila—proclaims (in Tagalog) Hadji Abdullah Mas Nuño as the founder of the religious center "from whence Islam bore fruit throughout Mindanao." Contemporary Nuños lay claim to the surrounding fishponds and mangrove swamps, control the village's seaweed trade, provide security to a nearby pearl farm, and occupy positions in the municipal council, local electric cooperative, Islamic bank, and nearest branch of the Philippine Charity Sweepstakes Office.

As he does with the provision of spiritual resources, the local politician poses as the source of material welfare too. In assuming the role of the grand patron, the local politician frequently passes off public resources, funds, and prerogatives as flowing from his personal powers and magnanimity. The account of Congressman Francisco "Pacoy" Ortega's beneficence to a barrio in La Union is instructive:

Pacoy gave them everything. Name it, they had it. . . . You might notice the term "Pacoy gave." Actually, this is the wrong phrase for he did not give something he owned. But during those times when the Congressman was powerful, where all public work releases had to pass through them, called "pork barrel," where nothing happened in their district without their blessings, this term was commonly used. In a sense, he did. He gave what was entrusted to him and for every project gave a part of him too—in terms of sleepless nights, of planning, exerting efforts in making them realities. The discretion was his as to whom to give these releases.[114]

Thus various public works projects, however modest, are portrayed as evidence of the local politician's generosity toward his constituents. A memorial book for Mandaue City captures this tactic quite aptly:

Island inhabitants stood witness to the dedication with which the late Mayor Dimataga gave during his time. The circumferential road known as the Quezon National Highway, asphalting of city streets, construction of several school buildings in the different barrios, the construction of the Mactan International Airport, the Opon Emergency Hospital now known as Opon District Hospital, the

Mactan-Mandaue Bridge are but a few of Mayor Dimataga's tangible accomplishments as municipality and later as city mayor.[115]

Bridges, public markets, *barangay* basketball courts, funds for fishermen's
cooperatives, repairs of public school buildings—all flow forth as the gifts
of the congressman or governor to his constituency. "His" rural irrigation
and electrification programs bring light and water to the homes and farms
of the population. "His" roads bring constituents to the nearest urban
center, their goods to market, their children to school. While skimmings,
kickbacks, and the profits of favored construction companies circulate
among the select few, signs and cornerstones fill the landscape with the
local boss's presence: "Project of Congressman Puey," "Montano Hall,"
"Governor's Drive," and so forth.

Overall, the local politician's claims to legitimacy amount to the elaboration of a myth that locates him as the center and source, exemplar and
embodiment, of the community while scrupulously obscuring the derivative nature of his power. Through the idiom of the family, the mayor, governor, or congressman defines his relationship to his constituency as inherent, permanent, and primordial. By consanguinity, affinity, ritual
coparenthood, and ritual feasting, he purports to incorporate the community into his extended family, obscuring the impersonal and contractual aspects of the various relationships of dependence linking poor villagers, local *liders*, *barangay* captains, and municipal councillors to him
while stressing their putatively personal and permanent nature. Officiating
at baptisms and burials, weddings and processions, the local politico su-
pervises birth and death and sanctifies the unity of the community and its
members. As aspiring family patriarch, godfather, provider of succor and
guidance in times of distress, donor of artesian wells and temporary jobs,
he poses as the source of all life and death, wealth and power. With his
family name engraved on numerous local monuments and stenciled on the
signs of various establishments, the local boss strives to achieve and sustain his status as both symbol and root of his bailiwick's very essence.

Thus town and mayor, province and governor, public and private, fuse.
Masking derivative authority and state resources as personal prowess and
beneficence, the local politician situates himself as the center and original
source of the power that flows through his office. Government contracts,
jobs, various public resources—all are dispensed to favored clients as to-
kens of the governor's generosity, even as he lines his own pockets with
kickbacks, percentages skimmed off provincial funds, and grease money
from various illegal activities. The town's small-time private monopolies
(ice plant, bus company, rural bank, cockpit, gas station, general store,
and rice mill), while invariably owned by the mayor and his allies, figure

unproblematically as "public utilities." The local elite's properties and businesses, like the politician's power and influence, allegedly provide land, employment, and sustenance to the rest of the community. Such claims in essence appeal to precapitalist norms and popular arguments for what some scholars call the "social use of property,"[116] while obfuscating the extraction of monopoly rents, exploitation of labor, and expropriation of scarce resources (land, coral reefs, forests, quarries) from the broad mass of the population.

Yet the efforts of local politicians to project their legitimacy as latter-day "big men" fail to produce a reliably receptive audience outside the close circle of their henchmen and dependents. As the extensive reliance on violence, vote buying, and fraud in Philippine elections implies, politicians themselves have very little faith in their hold on the hearts and minds of constituents. As suggested earlier, widespread cynicism—and, where possible, resistance—is the response of society at large to local politicians' claims to authority.

National Contenders

In terms of audience, the national arena was once the provincial *sabungan* (cockpit) writ large. The broad mass of the population was overwhelmingly rural, inaccessible to even the most ambitious campaigner, unlikely to read a national newspaper, and largely indifferent to events in Manila. Aspirants to the Senate and the presidency thus addressed the provincial bosses who delivered the votes and the Manila fat cats who supplied the funds as their most important customers; appeals to popular legitimacy before an unassembled national audience were feeble and half-hearted. Male bonding rituals (gambling, cockfighting, whoring, drinking, and feasting)—elaborated first in Quezon's crony circles and gradually institutionalized in party conventions—defined the terms of "big man" performance in the national arena.[117]

Yet in time the interrelated processes of national integration, industrialization, urbanization, social differentiation, expansion of education and literacy, and elaboration of national media networks changed the terms for the legitimation of national power in the Philippines in two crucial yet conflicting ways. On the one hand, the projection of intrinsic personal power—*kapangyarihan*—became possible on a national level. On the other hand, "reform" and the notion of an impartial, technocratic-developmental state came to enjoy legitimacy among a broad audience.

The elaboration of an extensive media network throughout the archipelago created new possibilities for the projection—before a national audience—of authority based on indigenous notions of personal power. In this context, Ferdinand and Imelda Marcos's great innovation in the 1960s was to conduct, for perhaps the very first time, politics as spectacle on the national stage and for a national audience. For while Marcos had "gunned, gooned, and golded" his way into Congress and horsetraded and extorted his way up the ladder to Senate president much like others before him, he addressed not just the old boys' club that Quezon had established but also the millions of men—and women—voters in the hinterlands beyond. By 1965, when he first ran for president, the number of radio listeners and television watchers who heard his distinctive, deep-toned voice, of newspaper and magazine readers who read about his bachelor adventures and beautiful wife, must have stretched well into the hundreds of thousands. Hence the new style of political campaigning exemplified by Ferdinand and Imelda's singing duets on provincial stages and the publication of a commissioned biography—*For Every Tear a Victory*—in 1964.[118]

Once elected, Marcos continued to elaborate the myth of the "big man" writ large on the national stage. Whispered stories of his amorous adventures, official lies about his wartime exploits, scattered reports of his privileged access to Yamashita's treasure, and occasional references to his possession of *anting-anting* continued to flow out of Malacañang palace over the years.[119] Paintings depicting President and Mrs. Marcos as seminude and emerging from a forest of bamboo stalks, identifying them with the Philippine legend of Malakas ("Strong") and Maganda ("Beautiful"), adorned the palace's grand staircase, while a commissioned academic revision of this myth circulated in outlets of the national bookstore.[120] A national infrastructure program of grandiose scale dwarfed congressional and gubernatorial pork barrel projects; Don Mariano Marcos State University and the Marcos Highway soon outshone Montano Hall and Governor's Drive.[121] Reinvigorating the Presidential Arm for Community Development, Marcos short-circuited the provincial bosses' patronage networks in the 1969 elections by handing out checks for various "development projects" directly to barrio captains throughout the country.[122]

Paralleling Ferdinand's elaboration of his national "big man" image was Imelda's prominent role as supreme matron. Like her dashing husband, Imelda promoted the notion of her intrinsic power. As she confided to her biographer: "Before I go to sleep, I have to go through the correspondence I received during the day . . . usually 2,000 letters a day. This one asking for a job, that one telling about a child that has to be hospitalized, this one asking for a picture, that one for an autograph. It takes me one or two hours just signing letters: *they all want your real signature.*"[123] As one keen observer noted: "'They' ask not only favors, but for the 'real' marks of her person: her photograph and signature."[124] Moreover, Imelda's numerous cultural projects—collectively derided as evidence of an "edifice complex"—served as a counterpart to the president's development programs:

She sought to complement these moves by turning state power into a series of such spectacles as cultural centers, film festivals, landscaped parks, five-star hotels, and glitzy international conferences which seemed to be present everywhere yet whose source was infinitely distant from those who viewed them. These spectacles cohered less around egalitarian notions of nationhood than on the fact that they all originated from her and reflected her initiatives, which in turn had been explicitly sanctioned by the president. Whether on the campaign trail for Ferdinand or as first lady, Imelda was in a unique position to remake Philippine culture into the totality of the marks of the regime's patronage. National culture was construed as a gift from above that circulated to those below.[125]

Yet the Marcoses' projection of their intrinsic personal power on the national stage was constrained by their simultaneous efforts to legitimate themselves before an international audience. Unlike the classic "big man" or "social bandit," Marcos was forced to promote his own legitimacy in more impersonal, national, and developmental terms and to identify himself with the state apparatus. The international lending institutions, commercial banks, and foreign aid donors upon which the Marcos regime was so heavily dependent required such a veneer, at least for their accounting books.[126] Thus technocrats trained at the Development Academy of the Philippines and Harvard Business School were on prominent display in the cabinet, while cronies prospered through such ill-named institutions as the Construction and Development Corporation of the Philippines, the Development Bank of the Philippines, and the Philippine Sugar Commission. Indeed, the state expanded, but in national and developmental guise: instead of "Meldy's homes," the Ministry of Human Settlements; in place of "Kids for Marcos," the Kabataang Barangay (Barangay Youth); in lieu of "Ferdy's Army," the Integrated National Police and an expanded Armed Forces of the Philippines to suppress Muslim separatists and communist "terrorists" in preservation of national integrity. Under such banners as "anti-oligarchy" and "developmental journalism," the National Development Corporation, Department of Agrarian Reform, and Ministry of Information selectively seized key assets from Marcos enemies and transferred them to friendly hands.

Marcos made efforts, of course, to obscure the derivative nature of his resources and powers and to establish the myth of his organic ties to the Filipino people. In particular, he obfuscated the extent of his dependence on the United States while exaggerating American reliance on the Philippines and validation of his legitimacy. Imelda pioneered the Philippines' debut in the international arena—through well-publicized maverick diplomacy with China, Libya, and the Soviet Union—while Ferdinand won official visits to Washington and arranged papal tours of the archipelago in 1970 and 1982. Domestically, an effort to "indigenize" the state apparatus emphasized its putative organic roots and authenticity: Marcos was linked by destiny, according to revisionist history,[127] to the *datus* of the precolonial era. The Tagalog term *barangay* replaced the Spanish *barrio* for the primary administrative unit; Pilipino came to complement English; the Batasang Pambansa (National Assembly) replaced the American-style bicameral Congress; ministries supplanted executive departments. Marcos also tried to cloak the predatory and exclusionary "stateness" of his regime through the creation of a popular constituency. Samahang Nayon (Farmers' Cooperatives), Kabataang Barangay, Cocofed (a coconut farmers' federation), and the Trade Union Congress of the Philippines (TUCP) all emerged in quasi-corporatist fashion as pillars of support for Marcos's political machine, now called the New Society Movement (Kilusang Bagong Lipunan).[128]

As the increasingly transparent emptiness of Marcos's claims set the tone for his downfall in the mid-1980s, his attempted projection of *kapangyarihan* on the national stage provided the basis for the legitimation of those who aspired to succeed him. The assassination of Benigno Aquino, Jr., in 1983 created a martyr whose apparent courage and self-lessness—viewed by the thousands of Filipinos who filed by his open funeral casket—contrasted sharply with the aging despot closeted in the palace. Aquino's defiant martyrdom established beyond a doubt his authenticity and thus created a spiritually potent icon; meanwhile, increasing signs of Marcos's deteriorating health, mounting revelations about his ill-gotten wealth stashed overseas, and compelling evidence of his fraudulent war exploits exposed the president's supposed personal aura of power as a cruel and pathetic farce.[129] Thus Marcos's leading opponent, Corazon Aquino, styled herself as a simple housewife whose authority derived not—as did Marcos's—from the agencies of the state, the support of the United States, or the power of money and violence, but from her authenticity, her Marianesque womanhood,[130] and her privileged access to the powerful icon—an *anting-anting* of sorts—that the memory of her slain husband had become. The four-day nonviolent "People Power Revolution" that ousted Marcos and catapulted Aquino to power in February 1986 allegedly drew much of its strength from participants' faith in their command of sacral power, as the prominence of crucifixes and images of the Blessed Virgin in the crowds made clear.[131]

Yet as "Cory" Aquino assumed the presidency, routinization of her charismatic authority set in and soon opponents of her administration were reclaiming *kapangyarihan* in their attacks on the predatory state.

The dashing army colonel Gregorio "Gringo" Honasan, for example, whose prowess in the overthrow of Marcos and other exploits was widely popularized in numerous magazine articles and TV talk shows, led various coup attempts, made daring escapes from custody, and occasionally resurfaced after stints in hiding. Allegedly sheltered by his numerous mistresses, "Gringo"—like legendary bandit Nardong Putik with his *anting-anting*—was everywhere and nowhere at the same time. Though the spate of coup attempts abated, national elections in May 1992 provided an alternative arena for charismatic claims to power. Famed movie action star Joseph "Erap" Estrada captured the vice presidency, while the classic cinematic portrayer of Philippine bandits, Ramon Revilla, won a top Senate seat on the slogan "Agimat Ng Masa"—Amulet of the Masses. Several TV and movie stars were elected to the Senate, while numerous other media personalities won various local and congressional seats in Manila and other urban centers.[132]

Over the years, a national audience has also emerged for the projection of authority based not on personal power but on the formal institutions of the modern nation-state. In the course of postwar Philippine history, the themes of progress, national development, good government, law and order, and reform—idealizing an "impartial, rationalizing, bureaucratic State power, above and outside the predatory game"—have found a growing domestic social base in the emerging, largely urban, middle class.[133] The first shades of this gradual transformation were visible in the 1953 presidential campaign of Ramon Magsaysay, which projected the—largely American-inspired—notion of reform on the national level.[134] Though with his death in 1957 the presidency reverted quite easily to a colorless machine politician, in post-Magsaysay elections various reformist third parties made regular bids for the presidency. Indeed, Marcos justified the imposition of martial law in 1972—before foreign and domestic audiences alike—as a "revolution from the center" aimed at eliminating corruption, oligarchy, and patronage politics. His administration advertised through an impressive technocratic veneer its "developmental" orientation; the Aquino and Ramos administrations have done likewise. Presidential candidates in the May 1992 election all paid lip service to the ideals of progress and national development, and in various cities and suburban provinces, aspiring and incumbent officials settled on campaign slogans similarly inspired.

In fact, the post-Marcos period has borne ample testimony to the prominent role of reformist credentials in the legitimation of national political power. Counterposing themselves to the omnipresent *trapos* (a shorthand term for traditional politicians that also means "dust rag" in Tagalog), a number of prominent public figures have emerged as the putative champions of the growing urban middle classes and hence of the overall national interest. Many of these figures are women. President Aquino, for example, based part of her appeal on claims that she would clean up a corruption-ridden state;[135] one of her first executive orders created the Presidential Commission on Good Government. More recently, Elections Commissioner Haydee Yorac, a former law professor, made daily headlines in the months leading up to the May 1992 elections for her efforts to curb election fraud and violence through stringent enforcement of the Commission on Elections' statutes and regulations. Most noteworthy, however, is Miriam Defensor Santiago, the former judge, law professor, and head of the Commission on Immigration and Deportation, who ran as the People's Reform Party's presidential candidate in the May 1992 elections. Lacking a political machine, she campaigned on the strength of her zealous crusade against graft and corruption and placed a strong second. Though "Miriam" may fade from the scene, the appeals on which she based her campaign are certain to remain fixtures of the national scene for years to come.

Conclusion

In the weeks preceding the May 11, 1992, election, sightings of *manananggal* and *aswang*—the evil creatures of Philippine folklore—in various slum areas of Metro Manila filled the Tagalog tabloids and dominated local radio shows and gossip.[136] Such reports, it might be argued, offer clear evidence of "ritual slippage" in the 1992 elections. Indeed, for years scholars have portrayed the secular breakdown of patron-client relations, elite politicians have claimed to be "peeved by the growing demands of the electorate,"[137] and townsfolk have reminisced about a fabled yesteryear of prosperity, beneficent paternalism, and close-knit social harmony. Perhaps the recent tabloid headlines are simply expressions of what one scholar of Philippine politics has called a generalized nostalgia for patron-client relationships and a "longing for a notion of patronage . . . which harked back to more traditional concepts of hierarchy."[138]

But perhaps a more profound disenchantment is in evidence. Indeed, Spanish reports of "disturbances" in some of the same locations in the seventeenth century speak not of *manananggal* or *aswang* but rather "a gang of disreputable *Catolona* women [Tagalog priestesses] . . . who secretly held the town almost in their power."[139] The elections, it may be argued, betrayed the weakness or absence of *kapangyarihan* in the contemporary political context.

A third interpretation might instead link such phenomena to a longstanding—and widespread—popular skepticism and indifference toward a form of politics in which, as scholars have noted, money turns elections into markets and crassly commodifies the common good. Perhaps the *manananggal* stories in fact respond to the "craving today for excitement, for extreme impressions, for the greatest speed in its change. . . . The search for mere stimuli in themselves is the consequence of the increasingly blasé attitude through which natural excitement increasingly disappears. This search for stimuli originates in the money economy with the fading of all specific values into a mere mediating value."[140] Perhaps the billions of pesos spent on bumper stickers, billboard posters, bribes, and votes elicited not bewilderment and dejection but simply boredom and disgust.

In any case, these phenomena suggest that popular understandings of the political order are not exhausted by the language of "constitutional democracy." In fact, as the preceding analysis has suggested, we must distinguish between the nation-state's formal claims and society's collective nostalgia and then examine the ways in which individual claimants to authority legitimate their power in various arenas and before various audiences. Only thus can we hope to illuminate what legitimating claims and mechanisms often obscure: the essential nature of power in Philippine society.

As we have seen, much of the effort devoted to legitimating political power in various arenas within Philippine society is geared toward claims that power is not simply reducible to money. The *anting-anting* of the local bandit, the family-style feasts and fiesta processions sponsored by the local politician, the movie-star looks of the national senator—all locate the source of power in the intrinsic personal qualities of the aspiring power holder: in his innate *kapangyarihan*. These various mechanisms thus represent claims that power—unlike money—does not circulate and that the "big man" is essentially irreplaceable and indispensable.

Moreover, legitimation along these lines also obscures the derivative nature of power, its origin in the predatory state, and its role in the process of capital accumulation. Through the bandit's Robin Hood escapades, the mayor's funeral donations, the congressman's public works projects, and the president's national highways, power is equated with personal benevolence even as its source in the state apparatus and the cash economy remains hidden. Big man/little people, public/private, monopoly/common property: such distinctions thus fade from view. Extracting monopoly rents, exploiting low-wage labor, and expropriating the country's scarce natural resources, these predators pose as the providers of land, employment, and sustenance.

To be sure, coercion, expediency, apathy, "the dull compulsion of economic relations," and "the absence of preferable alternatives" have—

more than any belief in legitimacy—sustained the existing order. The gap between the projection and the reception of legitimacy claims in the Philippines is clearly considerable. Yet, as noted throughout this chapter, the legitimation of both the regime and the individual claimants to authority involves certain concessions and constraints upon domination and the exercise of power. Moreover, the very process of capital accumulation has generated various forms of resistance that appropriate the languages of legitimation. In the agrarian setting and among the urban poor, recalcitrance or rebellion are thus commonly framed in appeals to precolonial and precapitalist norms in which power and property serve a purely social use. Among the emerging urban middle class and within the national business elite, the hallmarks of successful capitalist development—good government and rapid economic growth—form the basis for an insurgent reformism.

At root, the question of legitimacy in Philippine society concerns both power and wealth, predatory state and capitalist economy. In a society with such gross economic disparities, with money and influence mutually reinforcing, with violence and guile the currencies of social mobility, the situation could hardly be otherwise. Above all, in the "rent-seeking society," the legitimacy of capitalism itself is at stake: "If income distribution is viewed as the outcome of a lottery where wealthy individuals are successful (or lucky) rent seekers, whereas the poor are those precluded from or unsuccessful in rent seeking, the market mechanism is bound to be suspect."[141] In the Philippines, where voting is like betting, elections are like cockfights, and *jueteng* (an illegal numbers game) is ever popular, the metaphor of the rigged lottery is certainly appropriate. General Alfredo Lim, for example, stunned TV watchers just a few years back, when, in full public view, he picked the winning million-peso prize number for himself out of the Philippine Charity Sweepstakes Office (PCSO) jackpot. Lim, who as director of the National Bureau of Investigation was in the process of investigating charges of PCSO anomalies, waited out the ensuing public outcry and kept the loot. In 1992, as candidate of the People's Reform Party, he earned the support of a key religious group (the Iglesia Ni Cristo) through a lucky coin toss and went on to win the mayorship of Manila.

Though few dare cross the ruthless General/Mayor Lim, the overall popular sentiment in favor of "free and fair lotteries" is clearly on the rise. While no popular protests were mounted against the numerous instances of fraud and violence in the May 11, 1992, elections, expressions of outrage followed allegations of cheating in another contest that was apparently valued more highly. Indeed, Pepsi-Cola's retraction of number 349 as the winning number in its much-publicized sweepstakes caused one of the most violent riots in recent Philippine history. Crowds formed outside

Pepsi-Cola plants and offices in various cities, throwing rocks and chanting angry slogans. In their rage, some irate "349ers" appealed to a higher source of justice, respected Elections Commissioner Haydee Yorac: "Mrs. Yorac," one poster read, "Help us, we were cheated." [142]

Though seemingly bizarre and unrelated, the *manananggal/aswang* scare, General Lim's jackpot, and the Pepsi protest help us to place the official results of the May 1992 elections in perspective. Perhaps, at some grand symbolic level, Fidel Ramos's victory in the presidential race signals the triumph of technocracy, development, and an impartial state over personalism and patronage politics. Yet Ramos only narrowly defeated the zealously reformist Miriam Defensor Santiago and would certainly have lost if the two *sabungero* (cockfighting) machine politicians of the old school—Ramon Mitra, Jr., and Danding Cojuangco—had combined forces. Moreover, swashbuckling action-film star Joseph "Erap" Estrada won the vice presidency by a margin dwarfing that of Ramos: a clear victory for the classic "big man."

To interpret these rather ambiguous election results as reflections of the popular will would be both naive and unfair to the ordinary Filipino, whose vote was constrained by the available alternatives as well as by the coercive and monetary pressures long associated with electoral contests in the Philippines. Instead, the May 1992 elections should perhaps be read as a script or a screenplay, whose various characters and multiple subplots speak out to a potentially indifferent audience through competing languages of legitimation. Today, in the face of widespread cynicism and disillusionment, these languages of legitimation continue to structure the complex discourse of Philippine democracy.

7

Burma

The Depoliticization of the Political

CHAO-TZANG YAWNGHWE

BURMA is in the midst of a deep political crisis. Indeed, the State Law and Order Restoration Council (SLORC), which constitutes the present government, is confronted with a grave legitimacy crisis on two basic counts. First, it seized power in a bloody coup d'état following the "people power" uprising in September 1988 and the collapse of the 26-year-old military-socialist regime.[1] Second, the military-supported, state-funded National Unity Party (NUP) was defeated overwhelmingly in the May 1990 general elections.[2] SLORC refused to acknowledge the verdict, however, and appears determined not to transfer power to the victorious National League for Democracy (NLD) of the popular opposition leader, Aungsan Suukyi.[3]

As the 1988 "people power" uprising and the May 1990 elections have far-reaching consequences for the legitimacy of both government and regime, they are worth recounting here. The 1988 uprising was sparked off by protests of students at the Rangoon Institute of Technology (RIT) following a clash with local Mranmaa Soshei-lit Lanzin and police officials at a teashop named "Sanda Win."[4] With no channels for airing and redressing grievances, resentment against the military's domination of politics and its repressive rule had in fact been building up for a long time—resentment exacerbated by the economic mismanagement and corruption pervading the entire system. Further, two demonetization measures carried out in fairly quick succession (in 1985 and 1987) wiped out almost all savings in the country.[5] As a result of this accumulation of grievances and the brutality of Sein Win's *lon-htein* (special riot police), the RIT students protesting the handling of the "Sanda Win" incident were soon joined by students from other campuses, followed by the Rangoon public and general urban populace.[6] The flames of outrage were fanned by two open letters to Ne Win from retired Brigadier Aung Gyi, once the number-two man, criticizing the Lanzin establishment and its policies as well as condemning *lon-htein* brutality.[7]

In July 1988, faced with a determined countrywide demand for change, Ne Win vaguely promised a multiparty system but inexplicably appointed the much despised Sein Lwin to head a "new" government. No mention was made thereafter, by Ne Win or anyone else in the military, of the 26-year-old military-socialist regime and government, the BSPP, or the national ideology: they disappeared without a trace. The military's excision of its own ideology and institutions on the basis of which it claimed the right to rule for nearly three decades indicates the gravity of the legitimacy problem confronting SLORC. As Sein Lwin's appointment sparked further public protests,[8] Dr. Maung Maung, a civilian, was appointed to head another new government. He promised multiparty elections, but it was too little too late. Although Maung Maung was a well-known legal scholar, he was Ne Win's longtime crony and hence was viewed by the public as part of the failed military-socialist regime. Huge protest rallies, attracting people from all walks of life, including civil servants and navy and air force personnel, sprang up in Rangoon and most of the towns. The main attraction was Aungsan Suukyi, the daughter of the fabled Bogyoke Aungsan, whose name and fame Ne Win and the military had long exploited to bolster their claim to the right to rule.[9]

It seemed at the time that the February 1986 People Power Revolution in the Philippines was about to be repeated in Burma. As in the Philippines, an immensely popular opposition leader emerged. Like Corazon Aquino, Aungsan Suukyi was a political figure linked by bloodline to a national martyr-hero, lending her an aura of great legitimacy. Not only did she project a fresh, clean, democratic image, but she also enjoyed the support of the Buddhist clergy. Many believed, too, that Bama (ethnic Burmese) soldiers would not fire on the mainly Bama protesters in Rangoon and elsewhere.[10] Moreover, the public believed that the international community, especially the UN and Western governments, would somehow intervene on their behalf, since the military-socialist regime had collapsed and the people had clearly expressed their desire for change.

The military, however, was not about to relinquish power. When General Saw Maung declared that the military had staged a "coup" to save Burma, troops moved in shooting to kill. No one knows exactly how many were killed, but the number was certainly in the thousands.[11] Despite the bloodbath, the international community did not act in the manner the Burmese public expected. While the Western world and India condemned the massacre and froze or cut back on economic relations,[12] neighboring countries, particularly China, Thailand, and Singapore, recognized SLORC, led by Saw Maung and Khin Nyunt, head of the Military Intelligence Service.

Many Burmese believe that had the international community, including Burma's neighbors and the UN system, withheld recognition, the coup would have collapsed; certainly the coup makers were most vulnerable in the first few weeks after the "coup." The counterargument—that the alternative to SLORC was an inexperienced government that would have been unable to govern or stem the tide of anarchy—is a circular argument to justify the status quo. The same argument could have been employed to support Marcos against Aquino's People Power Revolution.

Burma's "people power" uprising can be viewed as a social revolution that failed.[13] The movement articulated the society's demand for a radical change in the nation-state form, the political system, and especially the composition of government. Although it was partially successful in that the "Burmese Way to Socialism" is no longer the official ideology, the movement failed to achieve its main goal, the displacement of the military regime. Despite this failure, the Burmese people were, it seems, more determined than ever to dislodge the military and replace it with new leaders and groups representing society at large. They took full advantage of SLORC's promise to hold a general election in 1990, a promise that was prompted by the erosion of domestic legitimacy and the military's desire to refurbish its international image after the 1988 massacres.

The 1990 elections can be looked upon as a clear contest for the mandate to rule. The military sought to demonstrate that it had the people's support. The opposition parties sought to demonstrate that the military had lost its mandate to rule and the people desired a new political system and government. The election was certainly viewed by the opposition, as well as by the military, as a test of legitimacy. *Both accepted the electorate as the final arbiter*: the "sovereign people" would decide who had the right to rule.

SLORC and indeed many international observers believed that the military-backed NUP would almost certainly win the elections. The NUP was, after all, composed of powerful former government and Lanzin party officials who had long wielded state power and influence. Moreover, the military spruced up its image with an eye to winning the election: it "beautified" Rangoon and other towns, widened roads, planted trees and flowers, upgraded parks, and put fresh paint on the country. NUP candidates and organizers went to the countryside and spent vast amounts on local projects such as digging wells and repairing bridges, monasteries, and schools.

The opposition, in contrast, was divided into almost two hundred political parties. Unlike the NUP, they lacked organizational structures and funds; they had no resources to distribute and no power to dispense favors. Further, they were prevented from holding rallies except with SLORC's permission—which was granted only on condition that the government and the military would not be criticized in any way. Opposition candidates, organizers, and leaders were harassed; many were detained and tortured; some simply disappeared.[14]

Given the NUP's preponderance of resources, organizational cohesion, and power as well as the restrictions placed on the opposition, the chances of any opposition party winning, much less by a landslide, were very slim. Nonetheless, even though its most valuable asset, Aungsan Suukyi, was placed under house arrest and barred from participation, the National League for Democracy (NLD) handily defeated the NUP. Indeed, the NUP won only 14 of the 425 seats. Its candidates lost even in the military constituencies—in Mingaladon, Hmawbi, Maymyo, and Coco-gyun (an island naval base). SLORC, however, chose to ignore the outcome. Instead it has attempted to redefine the purpose of the elections and to continue to claim legitimacy on a number of bases, old and new, that will be explored later in the chapter.

In sum, then, the present government in Burma is clearly illegitimate. SLORC does not have the moral right to govern the country. Nevertheless, despite its grave legitimacy problem, SLORC continues to enjoy international recognition. Indeed, some analysts even argue its legitimacy. To understand why this is so, we must turn to the literature on Burma and examine conventional approaches to legitimacy.

Legitimacy in Burma: A Critical Overview

What constitutes legitimacy in Burma? This question is important because it has been generally ignored in the literature, or observers have simply assumed that the incumbent government possesses legitimacy simply because it is at the power center—that is, in physical occupation of the formal structures and edifices of state power. This uncritical assumption may have its roots in the works of earlier Western scholars who, to avoid ethnocentrism, emphasized tradition and opposition to colonialism.[15] These scholars assumed that the Anti-Fascist People's Freedom League (AFPFL), which inherited power, enjoyed full legitimacy by virtue of its leadership in the independence struggle—an assumption that coincided with the self-image and claims of the new AFPFL power holders. While this approach to legitimacy is not unique to the literature on Burma, in Burma's case it has become entrenched. Analysts have uncritically assumed that successive governments were legitimate. This, however, has not been the case. Rebellions, insurgencies, and civil unrest have figured prominently since 1948 and have more or less become a permanent political feature of Burma. This pattern strongly suggests that the legitimacy of the nation-state, regime, and government in Burma is highly contested.

Instead of reexamining their assumptions, analysts have attempted to reconcile the contradiction between presumed legitimacy and widespread resistance to the incumbent institutions by squaring the circle. Until the 1988 "people power" uprising, the Bama opposition was portrayed as nothing more than the handiwork of unruly, ill-informed, and highly politicized hotheads (students, unemployed urban youths, young Buddhist monks, and the like); it was communist-inspired; it was the work of selfish politicians. As for the non-Bama opponents, they continue to be marginalized as troublesome tribal isolates who are being led by misguided, reactionary, self-interested, local and traditional notables bent on dismembering the "union" (*Pry-Htaung-Zu*) at the behest of foreign powers.[16] In short, incumbent institutions (nation-state, regime, and government) are viewed, in the Huntingtonian mold,[17] as representing the solution to national problems. Politics and political opposition are consequently seen as an impediment to development and the achievement of national goals.

A recent illustration of this approach to legitimacy in Burma, in which only one side of the state-society equation is given weight, is the quickness and ease with which the international community, including the United Nations, accepted the change of the country's name to Myanmar. At issue here is not merely semantics. The name change is an attempt by SLORC to claim what it considers to be a more authoritative international legitimacy. In other words, the outside world's acceptance of the name change is meant to convey to the populace that SLORC, despite the developments of 1988 and 1990, is considered legitimate by international acclaim.[18]

Notwithstanding SLORC's almost unintelligible reasons for the name change,[19] it is improper on at least two counts. First, it was effected by a government that gained power after a bloody coup d'état. The key question that should be posed here is: what right has a handful of armed men to unilaterally change the country's name? Second, the term "Mranmaa" is an adjective rather than a noun. Strictly speaking the new name should be "Mranmaa-Pry," or "Myanmarland" (as in "Thailand"). Acceptance of this name change by the international community illustrates the unthinking acceptance, even by the knowledgeable, of a ruling group's self-assumption of legitimacy. More important, it indicates a failure to understand the fundamental political and conceptual problem of legitimacy.

Among the few scholars with a genuine interest in the question of legitimacy in Burma, Robert H. Taylor and Michael Aung-Thwin in particular have equated legitimacy with the possession of state power. In other words, legitimacy is determined by the state—specifically, by those controlling its power centers and structures. They alone, it is argued, know what is best for "the nation" and provide "the state" with an essential historical-structural continuity. Conversely, all resistance to the state is deemed illegitimate because it is an expression of trends that contradict tradition and the trajectory of history and, besides, is antinational and perhaps foreign-inspired.[20]

Taylor's approach has enjoyed some currency among academics.[21] He presents the state as dominant in its relationship to nonstate institutions and moreover asserts that the state shapes the relationship between itself and civil society as well as the structures of crucial relationships within civil society.[22] Using this reasoning, Taylor implies that the establishment of state hegemony vis-à-vis society—and the limitations imposed by the state on political, economic, and social behavior as in precolonial kingdoms in Burma and under the post-1962 military government—is legitimate. A further inference invited by Taylor's formulation is that any action that opposes the hegemony of the state is illegitimate.

In keeping with this highly statist and elitist position, Taylor treats the government and nation-state, during both the colonial interregnum (roughly 1885–1942) and the period of AFPFL rule (1948–1962), as essentially corrupted and weakened by the intervention of self-interested, particularistic social forces in the sphere of the state.[23] Any force that acts autonomously or opposes the power holders is, by his definition, illegitimate; any participation of society in "the political" (even in the colonial state) is dysfunctional because it not only compromises the state's integrity but interrupts its historical trajectory as well.[24]

Taylor's formulation legitimizes the highly statist (even fascistic) model of state and society envisioned by the military in Burma. This formulation is a conceptual confusion, however, as it can be inferred that resistance even to the colonial state is illegitimate. To overcome this confusion Taylor implies that because the colonial state is illegitimate, resistance to it is legitimate.[25] This argument therefore raises the question: how did the military-socialist government become so legitimate that any resistance to it is illegitimate? His reply seems to be that the military-socialist government is highly legitimate because it is rooted in the Burmese tradition.[26]

Similar to Taylor's argument is Michael Aung-Thwin's view of the Burmese state as a historically constituted final arbitrator of "meaningful political order."[27] He defines this order as one in which society is meaningfully ordered by power holders in a hierarchical arrangement and the populace (especially the non-Bama segments) is kept in its "proper place" with reference to the superordinate Bama center. His model is that of a presumably happy, harmonious world that he imagines characterizes the precolonial pax Burmanica order. Legitimacy is thus defined by Aung-Thwin in terms of submission by all to the power holders engaged in the task of recreating "order *with* meaning," based on traditional ways, using traditional symbols, and so on.[28]

Like Taylor,[29] Aung-Thwin views political participation by societal actors—especially resistance by non-Bama actors (the Karen, Kachin, Shan, and so on)—as artificial, unnatural, and, by implication, illegitimate. He argues that extrastate political activities are colonial in nature, or invented and encouraged by colonial rulers, because these activities did not exist in the harmonious, well-ordered, hierarchically arranged traditional Bama polities.[30]

There are several flaws in Aung-Thwin's conception of legitimacy, which he claims is based on Bama historical traditions. One is that he sweepingly dismisses all political changes in Burma from 1885–86 onward as manifestations of a "meaningless" political order. Indeed these changes may be meaningless to those who romanticize the past as a perfect golden age. The fact remains, however, that such changes cannot be so easily dismissed in the real world. Further, it is doubtful whether any ruler, no matter how powerful or ruthless, can re-create past traditions in totality, especially in the realm of politics.

Moreover, Aung-Thwin's view that non-Bama ethnic nationalism and resistance to Bama "colonialism" are the invention of colonial rule is problematic, to say the least. While it may be possible, by extending Leach's work on the Kachin back in time,[31] to claim that the Bama precolonial political system served as a "higher" model for other ethnic entities, this does not mean that a "nation-state kingdom" was established under Bama-Buddhist hegemony or that the Bama model was the only one. The Rakhine, Mon, and Shan kingdoms and principalities had access to other models as well.[32] Not only were they constantly engaged in tributary or other political relations with neighboring kingdoms (India/Bengal, China/Yunnan, Siam, and other Tai kingdoms and principalities), but they often, even chronically, contested the Bama kings' claims as superordinate rulers.[33] As for the notion that non-Bama ethnic consciousness resulted from Western intrusions, this idea will long be debated. The crux of the matter is that the Bama were themselves not immune from colonialism and its accompanying (i.e., Western) thoughts and models that affected their inspirations, aspirations, and identity.

Finally, despite Aung-Thwin's belief that traditional Bama kingship and power were accepted by all as meaningful and legitimate, the traditional view of rulers and kings (or *min*) from below was quite the contrary. Rulers and *min* were, because of their capricious despotic practices and unrestrained extortions, regarded as one of the fundamental evils afflicting mankind in Burmese political tradition. They were not esteemed as benefactors and protectors of the common person.[34] They were to be avoided at all cost. Indeed, there is another Burmese-Buddhist tradition of rulership. This is the tradition of the *miṇ-tara*, a just king, who is chosen by the people and whose power and authority derive from a compact with the ruled whereby the ruler is required to govern justly and to be highly moral.[35] The implication of this other tradition is that, in the final analysis, it is the governed who determine the legitimacy, or otherwise, of rulers. Taylor dismisses this legitimacy concept, also rooted in tradition, as merely explaining the "unequal division of rights between the king and the populace."[36]

The existence of these two traditions regarding politics, authority, and legitimacy highlights the problem inherent in using tradition to justify a certain system of rule. Taylor and Aung-Thwin are seemingly unaware of the politics embedded in the very act of defining, creating, and re-creating tradition—an act that requires one to select and interpret what constitutes tradition.[37] Thus their insistence on an all-meaningful, organic, timeless, tradition-cum-political order is flawed.

From this critical overview it is evident that political legitimacy in Burma has not been treated as an outcome of the interaction between ruler and ruled that is embedded in contemporary politics. On the one hand, legitimacy is simply inferred by virtue of a deeply embedded tradition; on the other, it is viewed as inherent in the control of state power. In both cases, politics is immaterial since legitimacy is a given. Although it might appear that the question of political legitimacy in Burma is irrelevant in practice, the ramifications of control over state power without legitimacy cannot be ignored. Illegitimate rule can and often does lead to neglect of the search for solutions to fundamental national problems. This was clearly the case in Burma—as can be judged from academic analyses from 1962 onward. They all seem to contain the same litany of woes: the hardship of the people has increased; armed conflicts continue; the real economy (not the official one with its impressive figures) continues to decline; rulers continue to fear the ruled; the populace continues to endure the mounting difficulties in silence.[38] More than 30 years of illegitimate rule has not resolved any of Burma's outstanding problems.[39]

Thus one begins to see the importance of legitimacy for the effectiveness of power and achievement of national goals, order, and stability. Paradoxically, however, because legitimacy is a complex (and variable) concept, illegitimate rule can under certain conditions—such as coercive repression—create an illusion of purpose, strength, and unity.[40] But in the final analysis it often results in tragedy, as in Burma.[41] Thus if the political dynamics between ruler and ruled is taken into account, order and prog- ress will not be mindlessly attributed to authoritarian rule. Conversely, the removal of authoritarian rule would not be seen as inviting chaos and anarchy or, as SLORC now emphatically stresses, the balkanization of the country, as in Yugoslavia.[42] Apart from these practical consequences of illegitimate rule, a government without legitimacy, as Gordon Clark and Michael Dear point out, is no different from an organization like the Ma- fia.[43] Legitimacy, therefore, is not just the icing on the cake. It is a crucial line that separates rulers of nation-states from gun-toting thugs. Political legitimacy is an outcome of the interaction between the incumbents and their political opponents in particular, and the populace in general, with reference to the nation-state, the regime, and the government. In sum, it involves the political process and the dynamics through which legitimacy is claimed, imposed, won, maintained, consolidated, contested, or lost.

Contested Political Institutions

In investigating the legitimacy problem in Burma, it is important to grasp the broad outline of the basic political arrangements from its inception as a modern state in 1948. From 1948 to around 1958 Burma was a quasi- federal (or semiunitary) state. The political system, based on parliamen- tary rule within a more or less liberal democratic framework, was presided over by the ruling, left-leaning AFPFL, composed of civilian political leaders (Thakins) deemed to have led the country to independence as young nationalists.[44] In the second period, from 1962 to 1988, Burma continued to be formally a quasi-federal state, but in practice it became a unitary state. The political system—based on the "national" ideology of the "Burmese Way to Socialism," similar to Marxist-Leninist regimes of the Soviet bloc—was presided over by the party dominated by Ne Win, commander of the armed forces.[45] From 1988 to the present, the nation- state and the political system have been in limbo. SLORC, ruling without ideology or constitution, is composed of "sons and successors" of Ne Win, which makes it an integral part of the pre-1988 ruling military estab- lishment.[46]

Yet counterposed to the formally constituted political arrangement in Burma there have always been significant well-organized forces operating outside the officially sanctioned framework of politics. In official jargon, they are collectively termed "multicolored insurgents" (*Yaungzon Thu- bon* or *Yaungzon-Thaunggyan-thu*). "Multicolored" is certainly apt: the rebel forces are as different from one another as they are from the ruling government.[47] Although they are delegitimized by power holders, it would be rash to dismiss them as bandits or criminals, for they too are supported, in varying degrees, by constituencies they claim to represent, especially in instances of ethnic-based political-military organizations—particularly in post-1962 Burma with the establishment of a military-dominated one-party political system that arbitrarily delegitimized voices outside the formal political framework.

The earliest challenge to the new state in Burma took place in Rakhine, the western coastal strip. It was led by a monk, U Seinda, who had in World War II led a Rakhine guerrilla force against the Japanese. The next challenge came from the Red Flag "Trotskyite" communists led by Thakin Soe.[48] But the most formidable and best organized was the White Flag communist party.[49] The White Flag (BCP/CPB) was led by Thakin Than Tun—brother-in-law (their respective wives were sisters) of Thakin Aung-san, the now mythologized architect of independence and father of the armed forces, the Tatmadaw—until his death in 1968.[50] It launched its armed struggle in 1948 a few months after independence.[51] Next came the challenge from the Karen resistance movement and its allies, the Mon and Pa-O rebels. Open warfare broke out between the Karen and the AFPFL government in 1949, and the Karen have been fighting Rangoon ever since.[52] In 1959, when the White Flag and Karen insurrections were simmering down, an armed uprising involving nearly all ethnic groups erupted in Shan State.[53] This uprising was followed in 1960 by the Kachin resistance movement.

In addition to the more or less organized rebel groups and "armies," urban-based opposition has persisted, especially since the 1962 coup. Until 1988 these urban protests occurred in and around Rangoon (the modern capital) and Mandalay (the second-largest city and former capital). These uprisings were usually initiated by university students who were later joined by the general student population and in time by ordinary people from all walks of life. The largest and, relatively speaking, most successful protest against the ruling military establishment was the "people power" uprising in 1988.[54]

The crucial question is this: are these acts of opposition to be looked upon as irrational outbursts by disorderly and unruly misfits, or are they symptoms of something fundamentally wrong? It is easy and indeed tempting to attribute both armed and unarmed opposition to factors only marginally related to the legitimacy problem—the rapid pace of mobilization, rising expectations, religious and ethnic sentiments, regionalism, social banditry, the "plural society" legacy of colonialism.[55] It is even possible to attribute this opposition to the collapse of law and order. While these explanations may be relevant, they do not tell the whole story. Given the persistence of rebellions in Burma, it is not easy to dismiss them as chronic but politically insignificant outbursts of lawlessness. In fact, it is difficult not to view them as integral to the most basic problem facing all political organizations: the problem of legitimacy. The persistence of rebellion illustrates the problems that power holders confront in justifying their claim to power. It also underlines the problems inherent in establishing a nation-state and a political system that will be acceptable to key actors on the Burmese political stage.

The AFPFL Period

Upon assuming power, the first set of power holders in independent Burma, the AFPFL leaders, had to project their legitimacy in multiple ways because the nation-state they inherited encompassed diverse cultures, traditions, histories, experiences, and, most important, personalities who had recently fought on different sides in World War II.[56] That is, they were confronted with a complex task of projecting their legitimacy messages to a wide audience. They also had to project to the international community an image of being responsible, mature leaders capable of administering the country and honoring international obligations, especially vis-à-vis the departing British.[57] This legitimating message to the external world was crucial since its projection and subsequent acceptance enabled the AFPFL not only to succeed to power but to buttress its domestic position as well. International legitimacy enabled it to obtain much-needed resources to cope with domestic contenders and challengers.[58]

Domestically, AFPFL leaders staked their claim to authority foremost as nationalists who had fought for freedom from British colonial rule and the Japanese invaders. Like many other "democratic and modern" national leaders, they claimed popular sovereignty as the source of their power and legitimacy. They also attempted to legitimate their rule in terms of a soon-to-be-achieved goal: a prosperous, just, and equitable democratic-socialist Burmese society. Furthermore, the new state, the Union of Burma, was created on the basis of the 1947 Panglong Agreement, cosigned by the AFPFL supreme leader Bogyoke Aungsan and Sao Shwe Thaike, the Yawnghwe prince,[59] as well as other non-Bama leaders—Shan princes, or *chaofa* (Lords of the Sky), Kachin *duwas* (great leaders), and Chin chiefs. Hence the AFPFL leaders had to project a federalist image: they had to appear as fair-minded leaders who harbored no hidden Bama imperial intention to subjugate the minority nationalities (the Taingyintha).

In keeping with their legitimation messages, AFPFL leaders sought to consolidate their legitimacy vis-à-vis the non-Bama by laying down the political framework for the new Union of Burma as embodied in the 1947 Constitution. The new state was in theory a federal one, in keeping with the Panglong spirit and Aungsan's promise of full equality and noninterference by the Bama government and leaders in the affairs of the constituent states and in their diverse traditions, customs, and culture. Aungsan's promise of full equality and autonomy is remembered to this day by the non-Bama groups in the form of a slogan attributed to him: *Bama ta-kyat, Shan ta-kyat* (Bama one Kyat, Shan one Kyat). In practice, however, the federation was weighted in favor of Rangoon. The constituent units were in essence semiautonomous satellites of the Bama "mother" state (*Mranmaa Pry-Ma*).[60] This imperfect federalism was nonetheless accepted as legitimate by the non-Bama on the understanding that the terms were open to future adjustment. An important adjunct to the acceptance of the union was the assurance, provided in the constitution, for the right of the Shan, Karenni, and Kachin states to secede.[61] The political system, also in accord with AFPFL's legitimacy message, was founded on principles associated with liberal democracy, entrusting ultimate power to the sovereign people via the parliament. A more or less pluralistic, inclusive, and competitive political system was established with provisions for freedom of expression, political association and organization, party politics, periodic elections, and parliamentary rule.

The first and gravest challenge to the AFPFL regime's legitimacy came from the BCP/CPB, which was AFPFL's most important partner—or, rather, its ally-cum-rival—in the anticolonial nationalist movement.[62] The BCP/CPB was led by Thakin Than Tun, an able administrator, excellent organizer, and effective leader.[63] After Aungsan and U Nu (the first prime minister), he was the most respected figure nationally. During the 1945–48 period, the BCP/CPB had its sympathizers and cadres in key positions in almost every political organization, from government service unions (including the police union), labor unions, student unions, and peasant organizations to various informal political organizations like the *Pyithuyebaw*, the People's Volunteer Organization (PVO).[64] It was the BCP/CPB that in 1945–47 orchestrated the highly emotional and effective strikes, marches, and rallies that forced Britain to grant independence sooner rather than later.[65] Moreover, it had deeply infiltrated the Bama units of the newly reformed Burma Army.

The BCP/CPB questioned the legitimacy of the political system because of its "bourgeois" liberal democratic form. It perceived the political system as a capitulation by Aungsan and the AFPFL to British imperialist interests. It accused the AFPFL of abandoning revolutionary goals and argued that the 1948 independence was a sham. It also contested the AFPFL leaders' right to rule on the grounds that they represented foreign and domestic capitalist interests, not the people.[66] Thus in 1948 the BCP/ CPB openly challenged what it considered an illegitimate regime and government. In this effort it was joined by a major faction of the AFPFL "army," the PVO, which owed loyalty only to the late Aungsan.[67] Moreover, three out of four Burma Rifles units composed of Bama nationals joined the BCP/CPB. Only Ne Win's 4th Burma Rifles did not defect. Its officers became the core of a power center within the state that was later to oust the AFPFL in 1962.

An equally serious challenge to the legitimacy of AFPFL power holders came from the Karen, led by the Karen National Union (KNU) and its armed wing, the Karen National Defense Organization (KNDO). According to Maung Maung Gyi, the Karen were treated by the Bama elites in precolonial Burma as "no better than wild animals."[68] The Karen's situation improved, however, with the arrival of the British. A large percentage of the Karen converted to Christianity, benefiting from schools and other changes introduced by missionaries.[69] Because of these educational advantages, the Karen (like the Tamils in Sri Lanka and the Ibos in Nigeria) came in time to staff the lower and middle echelons of the colonial state as clerks, superintendents, schoolteachers, policemen, and soldiers.[70] Contrary to widely held perceptions, they were not a favored, collaborating ethnic group lording it over the downtrodden majority Bama.[71] Since Burma was part of India until the mid-1930s, the British depended more on Indian than Karen troops to pacify and police the colony.

Politically more significant was the emergence of a new elite group as a result of colonial development in the fertile, accessible, resource-rich Irrawaddy basin and delta, which was home to both the Bama and the Karen. With Britain's introduction of a modified liberal political framework (albeit within a colonial framework) from the 1920s onward, this new group—consisting of landowners, rice mill owners, teak merchants, general traders, brokers, moneylenders, barristers, doctors and nurses, the salaried, and *pinnya-tat* (those with education)—was drawn onto the political stage. Since both the Bama and the Karen operated within the same geographical area, their proximity led to ethnic politics, as leaders appealed to their respective ethnic groups for support. Others (the British, Indians, Eurasians, and to a lesser extent the Chinese) were also drawn into the political arena. They too claimed to represent the interest of their respective ethnic groups. The Bama elites came to resent the political participation of the non-Bama minorities. Colonial-inspired development created not only a new capitalist market economy but also a consequent plurality of groups, classes, sentiments, and interests. One result, especially among the Bama urban poor, was a resentment of foreigners—a sentiment that gave rise to serious anti-Indian and anti-Chinese riots, heightening Bama "nationalism."[72]

The Bama elites' resentment of the Karen reached a new level when World War II broke out. The Karen were loyal to the British for many reasons, but it is probable that they simply viewed the British administrators as legitimate, as did many nonpolitical Bama.[73] The young, impatient Thakins, however, embraced the Japanese as their deliverers from colonial bondage. During the war, units of the Burma Independence Army (BIA) indulged in a series of bloody atrocities against the Karen. Thus was sown the Karen's deep distrust of the Bama, especially of the political and military Thakins who constituted Burma's new rulers after 1948.[74]

In the Karen perception, it was the British and the loyal Karen who won the war, not the Bama Thakins, whose mentor, the Japanese, was defeated. In peace, however, it was the Thakins who obtained the fruits of victory—power over the entire country. In the few years before and immediately after independence, renewed massacres and atrocities by armed Bama bands further exacerbated the Karen's distrust and Karen-Bama tension.[75] For the Karen, therefore, the post-1948 nation-state and the AFPFL's status as national rulers were both illegitimate. Thus the Karen felt driven to what they considered justifiable violence against oppressive rule by illegitimate rulers—namely, the AFPFL-Thakin "traitors."[76]

In the early years of independence, therefore, AFPFL power holders were confronted and nearly toppled by the combined forces of two challengers situated at opposite ends of the ideological spectrum: the BCP/CPB communists and the anticommunist Karen National Union. Fortunately for the AFPFL leaders, their legitimation message (the Panglong Spirit, federalism, and anticommunism), addressed to the Shan, Kachin, Chin, and others, found a receptive audience. The staunch support of these groups bolstered the AFPFL's legitimacy,[77] which, in turn, reinforced its international legitimacy and brought in much-needed foreign assistance and military aid.[78] This assistance enabled both the AFPFL and the new state in Burma to weather a deadly legitimacy crisis.

The liberal-democratic political system proved effective as well in consolidating the legitimacy of both the nation-state and the AFPFL. By the middle to late 1950s, the AFPFL's adherence to the parliamentary system was paying off. Ironically, the good performance of the leftist coalition, the National United Front (NUF), and its allies in the 1956 elections convinced those allied to the BCP/CPB or Red Flag that the path of armed struggle was not the only option.[79] They began to view the parliamentary system as an alternative means to unseat the AFPFL and also as an avenue to initiate and implement the reforms they favored. Consequently, many rebel "armies" and organizations responded positively to U Nu's 1958 "Arms for Democracy" program.[80]

This period, when the liberal-democratic parliamentary framework of politics was growing stronger and gaining greater legitimacy, has unfor-

tunately not been adequately analyzed.[81] Many portray this as a time of
AFPFL incompetence, weakness, and unruly politics or as a time when
"crypto-communists" and secret allies of the BCP/CPB gained parliamentary seats and votes, endangering democracy and freedom.[82] Such observations not only reflect the sentiments of the Burmese military in 1958,
but are also in line with the anticommunist, Cold War posture of the West.
Parliamentary politics was accordingly dismissed by Western academics
as detrimental to democracy; at the same time, military intervention—to
maintain law and order and, incongruously, to preserve democracy—was
given an aura of legitimacy. Ne Win's caretaker government of 1958–60,
for example, was acclaimed a success in restoring law and order.

The two-year interlude of military rule (1958–60), when the country
was run by Ne Win and his caretaker government, does not constitute the
delegitimation of the AFPFL and the parliamentary system. It was a consequence of the split within the ruling AFPFL and a degree of immobili-
zation at the top. The handover of power to General Ne Win by Prime
Minister U Nu was effected within the parliamentary framework and in
accord with constitutional procedures.[83] Moreover, no structural change
in the political system was instituted by the military caretaker government, especially with regard to center-periphery arrangements. Governments of the non-Bama constituent states, for example, continued to be
staffed by non-Bama officers and were presided over by non-Bama leaders
who were essentially collaborators rather than subordinates of the military commanders, as they became after the 1962 coup.[84]

The 1961–62 federal movement was a sign of the growing confidence
of non-Bama in the federal structure and parliamentary system of Burma.[85]
It represented a search by both the governments and opposition groups of
the non-Bama states for a constitutional solution to the problem of military abuses in their home territories.[86] The reformers sought to renegotiate
the terms of association. Their main concern was with what they considered the unfair division of powers between the government in Rangoon
and the non-Bama states.[87] A careful study of the 1961 Taunggyi Federal
Conference records shows that the movement was not a rejection of the
federal structure and was not aimed at secession.[88] Nor was it connected
to the transfer of power from the *chaofa* to the Shan State government, an
issue already settled in 1952.[89]

The 1962 coup makers depicted the federal movement as part of a secession plot by Shan *chaofa*, Karen rebels, and regional notables to wrest
power. Many have consequently lost sight of its constitutionality as *a political interaction among legitimate actors at national and subnational levels*. For the non-Bama the 1962 coup represented a violation of the Panglong Spirit and hence the dissolution of the union.[90] The Shan view,

therefore, is that any legitimate future nation-state must be renegotiated among the interested ethnoterritorial units.[91]

Just as the federal structure and parliamentary political system were beginning to gain legitimacy, they were negated by two developments. First, the AFPFL splintered, as mentioned earlier, into squabbling factions;[92] second, Ne Win's military faction of the AFPFL establishment began to dispute the rightfulness not only of the control of power by civilian Thakins but also of the federal structure and parliamentary system.[93] Soon after U Nu's faction, the *Pry-daungzu* (Union Party), won a landslide victory in the 1961 general elections, the military Thakins staged a coup.[94] They declared that civilian leaders were incompetent and corrupt, that "aboveground communists" were about to gain power on behalf of their "underground" masters via parliamentary politics, that the union was about to disintegrate because of constitutional accommodation with Shan *chaofa*s and other "disloyal" non-Bama leaders, and that the parliamentary system was defective.[95]

This indictment represents a condemnation by the military of politics based on the notion that power rests ultimately with the people. The many weaknesses of AFPFL leaders and parliamentary politics cited by the military are not failings particular to Burmese or Third World politics and politicians. They are found in the democratic political systems of the West as well.

The Military-Socialist Regime

The coup makers sought to legitimate their usurpation of power first by delegitimizing the political system they displaced. They directed a relentless stream of attacks against inept and corrupt politicians, divisive parliamentary practices, and alien ideologies; they warned, too, of national disintegration and foreign-instigated plots by feudal elements, a code word for non-Bama leaders.[96] Second, they claimed the right to rule on the basis of their historic role as restorers of Burmese nationhood and saviors of the country. They drew heavily on the alleged pivotal role of the Tatmadaw in the independence struggle;[97] they also stressed their role in stemming the communist tide and restoring law and order in post-1948 Burma. Third, they portrayed themselves as the true heirs of Aungsan, the mythologized "father" of the Burmese revolution.[98] Finally, they projected the goal of the new regime as the establishment of a one-party socialist state and economy in a "*Mranmaah-nee, Mranmaah-han*" form (that is, in a Burmese way and Burmese form). At the core of this socialism is the doctrine known as the "System of Correlation of Man and His Environment

(SCME)," or the *Anya-manya Th'baw-tra*, supposedly a synthesis of Buddhism and socialism.[99]

For most Burmese, both Bama and non-Bama, the coup makers' legitimation message was neither inspiring nor credible. The *Anya-manya* doctrine, for example, did not impress Burmese conversant with Buddhist philosophy or with socialist and Marxist concepts because it appeared to them to be rooted in neither.[100] Moreover, it was known to be cowritten by an ad hoc group under the guidance of U Ba Nyein, a civil servant and alleged wizard in Marxist economics.[101] This group included some communist turncoats, a heretical monk (U Okkata), and a soft-porn author.[102] Thus the so-called Burmese socialist doctrine was not highly esteemed. In Burma, as elsewhere, the message is only as credible as its messenger. Furthermore, the military's legitimating messages contained nothing new. Claims of having won independence or created Burmese nationhood had, like the socialist goal, become the stock in trade of every political aspirant by 1962.

There was also one significant factor that outside analysts missed entirely: Ne Win, chairman of the Revolutionary Council, had few admirers outside the military. His public image was that of a gambler and playboy. In contrast to Aungsan and even U Nu, he was never looked up to as a role model; indeed, he was considered a political lightweight, especially by politicians who gravely underestimated his considerable skills as a politician and keen instinct for survival. What also seems to be forgotten is that U Nu's Pry-daungzu party won the 1960 elections on an antimilitary platform. Its rival, the stable AFPFL, which voters saw as backed by the military, was overwhelmingly defeated—like the NUP 30 years later. Nonetheless, outsiders welcomed the 1962 coup, holding that military rule somehow satisfied Burmese criteria of legitimacy as inferred from what they thought was Bama political culture and rulership traditions.[103] The military's seizure of the state was also in line with the "modernizing military" thesis in vogue in the 1960s.

As noted in Chapter 1, the rationale for authoritarian rule is founded on the promise of resolving the political and performance crises of the displaced democratic regime. Military rule aims at solving the problematic features of democratic politics by simply abolishing them and immunizing the state from the problems of society by elevating the state (and by implication, power holders) above society and politics. But having abolished popular participation in politics, the military faces the grave problem of how to deal with the principle of popular sovereignty, one that no postcolonial ruler can ignore. Even if it is successful (a rare outcome for military rule) in achieving national goals, the military cannot claim to derive its authority from the people.

With the establishment of the military-socialist political system, all forms of political articulation outside the Lanzin Party were declared illegitimate. Everything related to politics had to be encapsulated within the Lanzin Party and the 1974 Socialist Constitution. On paper this political system was similar to Soviet-style Leninist regimes.[104] In reality, however, and unlike the parties of the Soviet bloc, the Lanzin Party was not supreme. It was hollow: unempowered to operate as a ruling party.[105] Frequent purges by Ne Win kept it off balance and prevented it from developing institutional integrity or organizational autonomy.[106] In time the Lanzin Party deteriorated. Most party positions became sinecures for former military officers known as *baungbee-khyots*.[107] All positions were filled with loyal men appointed by a group of military officials absolutely loyal to Ne Win. The party as such had no meaningful function other than as a stamp of approval.

With the "ruling" Lanzin Party made politically redundant, organs of the state such as the administrative councils (*Prythu-Gaungsee*) at all levels as well as the national parliament (*Prythu-Hluttaw*) also became redundant. Civilian party and state functionaries were likewise marginalized. Real power rested with active or retired military officers—specifically, with Military Intelligence (MI) personnel responsible only to Ne Win.[108]

At the national level, power resided in the hands of Ne Win alone—who, in the fashion of rulers possessing only doubtful legitimacy, employed "the process of terror" in the service of power.[109] In the final analysis, the political system became a facade hiding a system of patrimonial rule.[110] Politics in Burma became the sole preserve of one man who exercised unlimited power with the help of an all-powerful staff of MI agents and a network of terrorizing and terrorized spies and informers.[111]

Since the Lanzin Party–based political system remained moribund, it did not and could not serve as it might have to legitimize Ne Win's control and exercise of state power.[112] Hence the White Flag, the KNU, and other ethnoregional "armies" who had contested the pre-1962 political system continued their political activities as outsiders. Ne Win's attempt to negotiate with armed rebels in 1963 was perfunctory: they were told to surrender and cooperate in building Burmese socialism or face extinction.[113] In the late 1960s the regime introduced the Ka-Kwe-Ye (KKY, or Homeguard) program in Shan State, whereby local warlords and former insurgents were permitted to engage in cross-border trade (in narcotics and contraband) in exchange for fighting communist and other rebels.[114] This expedient deal allowed "economic insurgents" to make money and provided military and Lanzin Party officials with further opportunities for investment and extortion.[115] SLORC's current ceasefire with the former communist warlords of the Border Areas New Democratic Army (BANDA) is a similar arrangement.

Those who had actively participated in the pre-1962 political system,

Bama and non-Bama alike, were pushed aside.[116] They became nonpersons living the rest of their lives in fear-ridden obscurity. Civilian administrators, the backbone of the state, were all subordinated to unqualified military officers. Burmese civil servants thereafter lived by the dictum *Ma-lup, Ma-shup, Ma-prot*, meaning: "Don't work, don't get involved, won't be fired."[117]

After a few years of spectacular rallies and conventions, the working people, in whose name the military claimed the right to rule, were likewise shunted aside. In 1967 and 1974 workers from state enterprises were taught a costly lesson in submission when they staged a series of protest strikes in Insein, the Chauk oilfield, and Simalaik.[118] As for the peasants, instead of being liberated from landlords, they were put at the mercy of a more powerful landlord: the government. Instead of prosperity, 86 percent of rural families lived below the poverty level and 25 percent became landless.[119] Thus the military rulers, by their delegitimization of workers' aspirations and exploitation of peasants, failed even to win over those whose interests and welfare they claim to promote.

Ne Win and the military did, however, succeed in dismantling the protocapitalist economy with their spate of nationalization. Compounding the enormous economic dislocation this caused, the military outlawed all private economic activities, creating a new type of criminal: the "economic insurgent." Since everyone was by necessity an "economic insurgent," everyone became criminally liable and hence vulnerable to harassment by the state. Thus resentment against the repressive military-socialist regime grew and festered, periodically bursting out in the open in the form of urban uprisings (1962, 1963, 1964, 1965, 1966, 1967, 1970, 1974, 1975, 1976, and so on). Another significant effect of Ne Win's socialism was the emergence of a vast underground economy based on domestic and cross-border trade in scarce goods. These illegal but essential economic activities (even diplomats and international agency personnel were involved) circumvented the "socialist" controls and regulations imposed by the military regime.[120]

Although Lanzin socialism was a fiction, it nonetheless resulted in real suffering throughout society, affecting all but the top echelon of the military hierarchy and the better-connected "economic insurgents." It led Burma down the slope of poverty and bankruptcy to least-developed-country status in 1987—clearly the opposite effect to that intended by the power holders, who calculated that the Burmese Way to Socialism was a world-class legitimation formula.[121] The end result was a mass country-wide protest movement in 1988 that caused the whole formidable edifice to collapse almost overnight, silently and unmourned. The "people power" uprising of 1988 can be regarded as an act of delegitimization, by a significant segment of the public and the nonmilitary elite, of military power holders and their political system.[122]

SLORC: New Legitimacy or Old?

Notwithstanding the collapse of the military-socialist regime, military officers are still in political command. Burma's present legitimacy crisis may be viewed as a continuation of the crisis that confronted the previous regime made more acute by the repression and atrocities committed by SLORC since 1988. By firing on fellow Bama and killing thousands, they have done the unthinkable.[123] To circumvent the illegitimacy of the military-socialist regime of which it is the de facto successor, SLORC has linked its right to rule to the legitimacy of the armed forces: the Tatmadaw.

The military's view, expressed by SLORC leaders like Than Shwe, Khin Nyunt, and Saw Maung before his mental breakdown, is that the Tatmadaw, and the Tatmadaw alone, has the right to rule. To the military, this right is inherent in its historic responsibility as the protector and defender of national sovereignty. Only the Tatmadaw, according to them, is capable of keeping the country together, maintaining order, and ensuring a suitable climate for economic development. SLORC as the "convener" of the National Convention in February 1993 further argues that even in a democratic system, the Tatmadaw must continue to enjoy a leadership role.[124] This claim is obviously aimed at formalizing and entrenching the political role of the military as in Indonesia. In sum, then, SLORC's goal is to legitimize the military as a constitutional but extrapolitical institution with the power to define the bounds of politics—in other words, the right to delegitimize politics, to depoliticize the political. Yet the Tatmadaw's own legitimacy and credibility as a patriotic institution have been gravely compromised. The 1988 massacres by the Tatmadaw and its treatment of the Bama populace afterward—mass relocation, the imposition of "porter" or unpaid coolie service for the military, open repression directed against the Bama populace—have seriously eroded the Tatmadaw's legitimacy in the eyes of the Bama themselves.

In view of the widespread belief that SLORC still represents the discredited pre-1988 military establishment and remains beholden to Ne Win, Sein Lwin, and Maung Maung,[125] it will not be easy for SLORC to sell its legitimation message domestically. If it is to be favorably received in the new political environment, SLORC's leaders must first convince the public that they are a new breed of patriot-soldiers. This means at the very least that they would have to disown the 1962–88 political arrangement as well as its many leaders. It is doubtful that SLORC could do this; such an exercise might lead to fractures within the Tatmadaw and hence to its downfall.

SLORC's legitimacy problem is compounded in that its only allies— the former BCP/CPB, the ethnic Chinese BANDA warlords,[126] and a host of foreign-based and well-connected former "economic insurgents"—are of dubious political standing.[127] The ethnic Chinese BANDA warlords had formerly served under the BCP/CPB flag. After their mutiny against the communist leadership in 1988 they agreed to stop fighting Rangoon in exchange for a free hand in trade and other economic matters, especially in the now legalized informal "free enterprise" economy based on narcot-ics and cross-border transactions with China and Thailand.[128] The agree-ment is an informal one motivated, on the one hand, by SLORC's need for latitude in dealing with the Bama-based democratic opposition led by Aungsan Suukyi and, on the other, by the BANDA warlords' need to ac-cumulate wealth to ensure their personal survival and that of their armies. The BANDA-SLORC alliance is purely expedient and inherently unstable. For the economic opportunistic elements—the BANDA warlords and "economic insurgents"—to be transformed into productive entrepreneurs supportive of the military, a modicum of rationality must be introduced into the economic and related political sphere so that they will be allowed some say in policy matters affecting their commercial interests. This would mean power sharing and certain democratic trappings. One model that might serve this purpose is Indonesia's military-dominated "Pancasila democracy."

This transformation is easier said than done, however, for power shar-ing is not the Bama military's strong point. The earlier military-socialist system could have worked as a legitimizing vehicle had the military been willing to share some power with bureaucrats, technocrats, academics, and selected non-Bama leaders and thus become more inclusive. Such an approach, as noted in Chapters 1 and 2, requires a unifying vision that is lacking in the case of the Burmese military. The military has failed in the past to come up with a power-sharing institutional arrangement. Whether it is now more willing or able to adopt an inclusive approach remains to be seen. SLORC's leaders are haunted by fears of popular retribution for the 1988 massacres and past crimes as well as the possibility of future confiscation of their wealth, mainly property and land,[129] accumulated since 1988. It seems unlikely, therefore, that SLORC will institute sub-stantial reform.

Enjoying no legitimacy at home, SLORC has trumpeted its legitimacy abroad. Consider, for example, its declaration in regard to the National Convention: "The SLORC is governing the nation as a military govern-ment [that] has been accepted as such by the United Nations and the respective nations of the world."[130] This message is meant to impress on the ruled that the junta is legitimate by the acclaim of more powerful, external entities. The emphasis on international legitimacy is also intended to boost the morale of its immediate constituency, the Tatmadaw elite. SLORC has been relatively successful in garnering external support. China has provided moral and material support, especially military hardware, and the ASEAN governments' "constructive engagement" policy—postulated on the premise that SLORC would liberalize if given economic and trade incentives—has reinforced SLORC's regional standing.[131] Furthermore, ASEAN's position on human rights and democracy, which argues that economic development and each country's specific "background, history [and] culture" are more important than human rights,[132] has helped SLORC to ignore internal and Western demands for political change while simultaneously gaining access to hard currency and other external resources. These resources have enabled it in turn to buy the loyalty of military subordinates, who are most vital to its continued survival. The crux of the matter, however, is that Burma's ongoing crisis is not about human rights per se but legitimacy. It seems that SLORC's external supporters, in their concern about the possible impingement of human rights on national sovereignty, have overlooked the question of legitimacy.

Despite SLORC's international legitimacy, its move to legitimize its control of state power at home via the National Convention has not been successful. Its attempt to transform elected members of Parliament into mere convention delegates is resented. It is also doubtful that SLORC will be able to win support in its attempt to legitimize the political dominance of the military via the constitutional route. Opposition groups have become even more confident of their greater legitimacy, further undermining the confidence and legitimacy of SLORC. This change is due partly to the 1990 election verdict and, more important, to the internal and international legitimacy of Aungsan Suukyi.

SLORC's legitimacy problem and the present political impasse show that the collapse of the military-socialist regime in 1988 has not changed anything with regard to Burma's legitimacy crisis. The current military leaders are faced with the same legitimacy problem as their predecessors. In 1962 military leaders confronted the problem by closing off the sphere of politics from society at large. Yet the political system set up to depoliticize the political collapsed precisely because it could not legitimize itself or its creators.

There is little doubt about the enormous, almost insurmountable, difficulties confronting SLORC's leaders in legitimizing their grip on power and constructing a new political system. Nevertheless, given the prevalence of factors in their favor, they may be able to hang onto power for quite some time. This favorable position rests mainly on two factors: the "sovereign people" of Burma are not recognized as such by the outside world, and SLORC enjoys a preponderance of physical force and has relatively easy access to external resources and the support of neighboring countries. A new constitution, together with all its formal paper institutions, is likely to satisfy the United Nations and perhaps even the West. In academic circles, those who continue to look at Burma from the outside and from the top down will no doubt be happy to explain away the systemic dysfunctions and attendant tragedies stemming from the legitimacy problem in terms quite unrelated to it.

Yet legitimacy will continue to pose a serious problem for rulers in Burma, be they military or civilian. More than three decades of illegitimate and repressive military rule has greatly damaged the fabric and culture of politics in Burma. Political reality since 1962 has been characterized by the decay of government institutions and political infrastructures, the erosion of the norms of legality and rationality, and the habit of violence. The resolution of the crisis requires a process of mutual relegitimization and the deinstitutionalization of coercion, especially with regard to the ethnoterritorial segments whose legitimate constitutional aspirations have been delegitimized by force, provoking a violent response.[133] In other words, the resolution of Burma's legitimacy crisis requires the political will of those in power to relegitimize politics itself, offering the forces in society at large a framework for the articulation of their diverse interests. The damage already inflicted on the political culture will make this a difficult task even for Aungsan's daughter; for SLORC and other military leaders, the task will be impossible.

8

Thailand

The Evolution of Legitimacy

SAITIP SUKATIPAN

FOR a few days in the middle of May 1992, Thailand captured the world's attention as government troops opened fire indiscriminately on thousands of its citizens. The violence on the streets of Bangkok during those three days exceeded even what one might expect from a macabre movie. How does a country like Thailand, after a decade of quasi-democracy and economic liberalism and apparently on its way toward the status of newly industrialized country, become engulfed in such a political crisis? Underlying the series of conflicts that led to the showdown between the military and the prodemocracy forces was the question of political legitimacy. This chapter examines three key aspects of political legitimacy in Thailand: the nature of the legitimacy problem, the substance of legitimizing principles, and the social groups whose consent is crucial to the legitimation of regime and government.

The Nature of the Problem

In contrast to the generally uncontested legitimacy of the Thai nation-state (except in southern Thailand),[1] the legitimacy of regimes and governments has been the subject of periodic and at times violent contention among strategic groups competing for control of state power. Since 1932 Thailand has wavered seemingly endlessly between the two opposing poles of military authoritarianism and parliamentary democracy. There have been as many as fifteen constitutions, seventeen military coups, and two popular uprisings (in 1973 and 1992). Many Thai political scientists have viewed the conventional pattern—the usurpation of power through a coup, the promulgation of new constitutions, the holding of elections, followed by political conflict among the elite groups leading to government collapse—as a recurrent cycle in Thai politics.[2]

The origins of the regime legitimacy problem can be traced to the displacement of the approximately 500-year-old absolute monarchy by the People's Party through a coup d'état in 1932. This coup was in large part the outcome of the conflict between the royal-aristocratic elite and the newly emerging commoner-bureaucratic elite.[3] Rapid centralization and bureaucratization of Siam during the reign of King Rama V to modernize and protect the kingdom in the face of encroaching colonialism spawned a new elite whose conception of legitimacy was no longer based on divinity or other ascriptive qualifications of the ruler.[4] In its view, political legitimacy had to be grounded in the principle of egalitarianism and merit. Dissent over tradition as the source of authority first surfaced among the younger generation of princes, nobles, and intellectuals, most of whom had gone to school in Europe. In 1885, a group of young princes in London and Paris submitted a petition to King Rama V outlining the problems facing Siam, criticizing the excessive centralization of power, and calling for modernization of the state by transforming the absolute monarchy into a constitutional one.[5]

This exposure of the nobility to Western political ideas, the creation of a modern bureaucracy, and the spread of modern education among commoners planted the seeds of political change in Thai society. The legitimacy of absolute monarchy began to erode soon after it peaked in the reign of King Rama V. To be successful, an absolutist regime requires a capable, responsive, and tactful monarch with political skill and charisma. The king must be able to utilize and control the huge and powerful bureaucracy and cope with increasing demands from the modernized sectors of the society. King Rama V was adept at this. His successors, however, were not. Hence the tension between, on the one hand, the princes and nobles who filled the top positions of the royal administration and, on the other, the civilian-military bureaucrats whose influence grew steadily after the demise of King Rama V. This tension was aggravated by the worldwide depression in the 1920s, which affected Thailand as well. With the rapid decline in state revenues, the government had to undertake financial retrenchment. The number of government employees was reduced from 90,239 in 1926 to 72,351 in 1932. Economic depression also brought great hardship for the poor in Bangkok and the countryside. Yet they did not take part in the 1932 coup. Fewer than 500 civilians and military officers located in Bangkok participated in the 1932 coup. It was by no means a revolt of the middle class, industrial workers, mass-based political parties, or other nongovernment groups.

From this period onward, personal and factional rivalries among the Bangkok elite continued to be the dominant cause of political change in Thailand. Change in government was frequently accomplished through bloodless coup d'état.[6] The elite perception of legitimacy and the support of strategic groups have been crucial for political legitimation during the first 40 years of modern Thai politics. Before the 1970s, the masses did not play a substantial role in these politics. Unlike the experiences shared by most other countries in Southeast Asia, historically the Thai people have not been mobilized into large-scale resistance efforts against colonial powers or their own repressive rulers. Seven successful coups (1932, 1933, 1947, 1951, 1957, 1958, and 1971) were neither opposed nor supported by the public at large. The Thai people seemed to accept whichever government was in power. Thus it is usually concluded that the public does not matter in political legitimation in Thailand. This, however, has changed with time. Not only has the politically aware Bangkok public widened substantially, but the rural people have also been brought into the political process in terms of electing the government. The different bases on which the rural masses and the urban elite and middle classes confer legitimacy, as well as its implications, have now become a crucial issue in political legitimation and will be explored later in the chapter.

In essence Thailand has had four political systems since 1932: a military regime with brief interludes of democratic government from 1932 to 1973;[7] a democratic regime from 1973 to 1976; a quasi-democratic regime from 1978 to 1988; and a post-1988 democratic regime (with the military's attempt in 1991–92 to regain political power). Within each regime there have been changes in government. The ensuing sections discuss the principles and practices of political legitimation in each of the four regimes with particular attention to the changing bases and constituencies of legitimacy.

The 1932–73 Military Regime

To replace the centuries-old regime based on tradition and a patrimonial network, the new power holders had to find alternative legitimizing principles, make compromises, and exploit the prestige of traditional institutions while at the same time employing force to suppress other contenders for power.

A New Basis of Legitimacy

The principles of democracy, with an emphasis on political equality and constitutional rule, were advanced by the coup's promoters as the ideal to replace absolute rule, which was denounced as arbitrary and in the selfish interest of royalty and conservative aristocrats.[8] In reality, democracy and constitutionalism became symbolic weapons rather than the basis for defining the institutions and procedures of the political system. They were employed to consolidate the new leadership's power and protect their interests in the face of threats from those ousted in the power struggle. The first constitution of the country, "granted" by the king, empowered the 1932 coup leaders to appoint half the members of the unicameral parliament in order to ensure their control over elected members. Moreover, the military as well as civilian bureaucrats were allowed to assume political offices concurrently. Nevertheless, the 1932 democratic spirit did have an impact on the military as well as civilian leaders in the pre–Sarit Thanarat period. They recognized that at least the trappings of parliamentary democracy were important for political legitimation. Hence restricted political contestation was allowed periodically, and the 1932 constitution was not abrogated until 1947. Even after 1947, Phibul Songkram, prime minister during 1938–44 and 1948–57, deployed democratic devices to buttress his position vis-à-vis his rivals—Sarit Thanarat and Phao Sriyanon, commander of the army and police director-general respectively.

In addition to constitutionalism, the 1932 coup's promoters sought to legitimize their control of political power by pledging support for the three key pillars of Thai society: the institutions of the monarchy (*phra mahak-asat*), nation (*chart*), and religion (*satsana*). Though the legitimacy of the absolute monarchy had eroded significantly among the urban classes, the overwhelming majority of the people who resided in the provinces could not conceive of any alternative to the rule of the "Lord of Life" that had continued from time immemorial. Thus the monarchy continued to be an important institution. In their quest for legitimacy, the coup's promoters sought royal pardon and the king's approval of the constitution. A number of princes suggested to the king that he resist the People's Party by using his loyal troops to fight back. King Prachathipok (Rama VII), however, was already sympathetic toward democratic reform even before the coup. To avoid bloodshed he decided to accept his new role as constitutional monarch. King Rama VII's approval of the 1932 constitution was significant in legitimating the new regime. Benjamin Batson quotes the following interview of Chiang Mai residents reported in the *Bangkok Times* of February 16 and 18, 1933: "The people cared only for the King, and as the King had given his approval to the new order it was therefore acceptable to the people."[9] Despite the initial accommodation, relations between the coup's promoters and the king deteriorated over the issues of appointment of members to the national assembly, the economic plan drafted by Pridi

Banomyong, and the 1933 countercoup attempted by Prince Bowaredt. The king went into self-exile and eventually abdicated in 1935.[10] Although a new king (Ananda Mahidol—Rama VIII) was installed, the coup's promoters, viewing the monarchy as a rival, paid only lip service to the institution. The political fortunes and influence of the monarchy declined until its revival under Sarit in 1957.

Phibul placed much greater emphasis on the other two institutions (nation and religion) to buttress the military's claim to authority. He changed the name of the country from Siam to Thailand and emphasized the Thai nation itself as the paramount institution. He introduced a vigorous campaign to promote nationalism and patriotism.[11] His government also embarked on an irredentist policy by engaging in a small-scale war against French Indochina to reclaim territories lost to France in the late nineteenth century. Phibul's success in this war made him popular and glorified the military establishment. Nationalism was now linked to militarism. Phibul insisted that the armed forces were the most important national institution and should never be slighted.[12] The monarchy, the House of Representatives, and the cabinet, according to him, could not persist without the support of the armed forces. Ultranationalism and militarism, widely inculcated in various forms, reached their peak during World War II. Allied with Japan, Phibul declared war against the West.[13] He made no secret of his admiration for Japan as the Asian country that had modernized itself and emerged as a great military power of the world.[14]

The military exploited its own prestige to enhance its claim to state power. Historically, the military had enjoyed high status in Siamese society as guardian of the kingdom and later the Thai nation. The frequent wars and border conflicts between Siam and its neighboring kingdoms led to an extensive role for the military in government affairs. Before 1887 there was no clear distinction between military and civilian organizations. The official versions of Thai history are the stories of war heroes and heroines who sacrificed their lives to defend the independence of the kingdom. Standing armed forces were created during the reign of King Rama V. The most able princes and nobles served in the army or the navy.

In the Thai conception, independence and security related mostly to defending the territorial integrity of the state against external attack. Burma, Cambodia, and Vietnam were the traditional adversaries, then the Western colonial powers, and more recently the "communist menace" during the Cold War. In light of these past roles, the military claims to be the sole guardian of the Thai nation and claims the right to intervene in any issue that in its view falls within the domain of national security. Preserving national independence and security have thus been key justifications for continued military domination of Thai politics. In conjunction with the disproportionately large resources allocated to the military and the opportunity it provided for upward social mobility, this historic role contributed to high public esteem for the military, at least until the 1970s. The uniform was symbol of both honor and power. Each year thousands of young men applied to enter cadet schools whose entrance requirements were high and the process very selective.

Buddhism "is the most important symbol of, and primary base for, . . . national and cultural identification. . . . The prosperity of the nation is thought to be related to the prosperity of Buddhism and vice versa; and the stability of the nation and religion cannot be separated." [15] Thus Thai rulers have always been concerned with the protection and promotion of Buddhism. To harness the symbolic value of religion, Phibul portrayed himself as the champion of Buddhism. His government gave financial assistance for the restoration and construction of a large number of temples during the 1950–56 period and also celebrated the twenty-fifth centennial of the Buddhist era in grand style. [16] Though Phibul's support for Buddhism was made nominally on behalf of the king, who is the nation's religious leader, in effect it was an attempt to delink the two institutions and make his government the official sponsor of the national religion. [17]

In addition to exploiting the role of religion, Phibul sought to legitimize his government on the basis of an external security threat and the support of the United States. Projecting an international communist threat to Thailand, Phibul sought economic and military assistance from Washington. With the outbreak of the Korean War in June 1950, he abandoned the traditional flexibility of Thailand and offered to provide troops and rice in support of the U.S.-led war effort in Korea. The support and praise of the United States enhanced Phibul's domestic position vis-à-vis his contenders (Sarit and Phao). Indeed, many leaders came to view him as essential in securing American aid and World Bank loans and for the promotion of Thailand's international trade. During Phibul's rule, Thailand enacted the Anticommunist Act in 1952 and joined the Southeast Asian Treaty Organization in 1954.

Apart from these bases of support, a crucial factor in helping the military to secure its dominant position from 1947 through 1973 was its ability to stage or suppress coup attempts and its effective use of force to control political opposition. When the military so desired, elected parliaments were dissolved and political parties and activities were banned. Laws and decrees were enacted to provide the executive with the necessary powers to arrest and detain suspects without trial. Press censorship was common. Under the long and direct rule of Phibul (1938–44, 1948–57), Sarit Thanarat (1958–63), and Thanom Kittikachorn (1963–73), political repression was the most common and effective means of removing political opponents, maintaining comprehensive control over the entire population, and thus perpetuating military rule.

Although the legitimation messages of the new regime were directed at the narrow urban middle class and government officials, its leaders recognized the need to secure the support, or at least the acquiescence, of the other power centers. Thus while they sought to exclude members of the royal family from the new power structure, the new leaders compromised with certain factions of the old aristocratic elites. Phaya Mano, a senior judge in the last years of the absolute monarchy, was appointed the first prime minister. The members of the first cabinet included seven former aristocrats of Phaya rank. There was no systematic confiscation of the wealth of most royal family members.

Despite the populist overtone of the first proclamation after the coup, its promoters denied freedom of political association and organization. A leading newspaper at the time reported that after June 1932 there were as many as 10,000 people signing up for membership in the People's Party.[18] Instead of extending mass participation, the leaders of the coup claimed that the people were not yet ready for democracy and a tutelage of ten years was needed before full political participation could be granted. The coup group remained the only legal political organization during the first five years after 1932.

The new rulers decided to consolidate their regime by relying on the support of the armed forces and the bureaucracy. The increased salience of the already powerful armed and civil bureaucracies had far-reaching consequences for political development in Thailand. Until 1973, the civil-military bureaucratic elite enjoyed almost absolute power in Thai politics. Most constitutions granted extensive power to the executive branch. Major policy decisions were made by the military-civilian bureaucratic elite while democratic institutions such as an elected parliament, political parties, and political participation were shunted aside and their development thwarted. There was no meaningful extrabureaucratic force or civil society. These were controlled and suppressed. Politics was depoliticized. It should, however, be noted that there was no substantive indigenous bourgeoisie in Thailand before the early 1950s. Most local entrepreneurs were ethnic Chinese who usually played the role of "go-between" compradores of the ruling class during the early years of capitalist development in Siam.[19] In the absence of such forces the ruling bureaucrats controlled all state apparatuses as well as significant economic wealth. This has since been termed a "bureaucratic polity."[20]

In this respect, the political change in 1932 was in essence only a transfer of power from the king and his royal circle to the commoner civil-military bureaucrats. As observed by Ben Anderson: "The real political problem in Siam was—and is—precisely this: that there was no decisive popular break with absolutism, fueled by social radicalism and indeed mass nationalism."[21] With the removal of high-ranking members of the royal family from the political arena, the armed forces and the civilian bureaucrats became the omnipotent political force.

As early as 1933, coup d'état had become the primary means of settling political conflict. From then on, change of government was accomplished more often through military coup than democratic procedures. In justifying their action, coup promoters usually cited a number of reasons including political instability, economic crisis, corruption, national security, and protection of revered institutions. Studies of the Thai military have pointed out that the real motive behind a military coup often lay in the military establishment's institutional interests or power struggles among the various factions.[22] Public consent seemed not to matter. As noted earlier, the Thai people neither approved nor disapproved of the various coups. Most of the time they remained indifferent. Voter turnout in elections between 1932 and 1957 never exceeded 44 percent. There was no social unrest or widespread demonstration or protest. There was also no serious attempt by the military leaders to mobilize the masses in support of their political activities. Although ideology has been employed from time to time to support their claim to authority, these efforts were not serious and not sustained. In the final analysis, the ability of the elites to neutralize or win support from the other centers of power was crucial to political legitimation.

During his final years, Phibul sought to rely on popular mandate to maintain his position vis-à-vis rivals Phao and Sarit. Beginning in 1955, public rallies and political parties were allowed. Although general elections were held in 1957, the major opposition parties as well as the press and the students vigorously protested the government's blatant rigging of the election. The Phibul government lost its legitimacy rapidly as a result of many factors: public discontent over the rigged elections; its poor handling of the drought crisis and famine in the northeast; and the abuse of power by Phao, the police chief.

The political crisis confronting Phibul's government set the stage for the "popular" coup led by Sarit, who tactfully capitalized on the discontent expressed by students and the press. It is possible to argue, citing the 1957 coup, that the masses were no longer indifferent and had become a crucial factor in political legitimation. Yet it was not until the 1973 uprising that the public became a significant force for major political change. Phibul's government was toppled in 1957 mainly because of internal conflict and rivalry among the army elites themselves. The growing popular discontent was a pretext for the coup. Sarit's accession to power was welcomed by the urban educated. In his speech to the demonstrators who gathered to lend moral support, Sarit emphasized that his actions were taken in the pursuit of popular will and to advance the interests of the people. The 1957 coup, therefore, marked a new era in Thai politics with conse-quences for the substance of the legitimizing principles. It also altered the nature of the legitimacy problem.[23]

Sarit and the Changing Basis of Legitimacy

Sarit, an army general, had been one of the most powerful figures since the early 1950s, building his power through various illegal business ac-tivities. American military assistance during the Cold War had strength-ened the Thai military establishment in general and Sarit in particular.[24] His claim to power in 1957 was supported by the students and the urban educated public and also had royal approval. Sarit did not immediately establish an authoritarian-paternalistic rule. The coup was justified as a move to save the country from a corrupt and inefficient government, not to radically change the nature of the regime. In one observer's view, "it also appears that the Sarit clique had not yet formulated any definite ideas on national administration and thus had to rely temporarily on old politi-cal practices."[25]

Yet after little more than one year of parliamentary politics in which the army leaders played an active political role through their political party, Sarit became impatient with the opposition parties, the press, and the factionalism within the government party itself. His impatience led to the 1958 coup, which ended all political activities and dissolved constitu-tional rule. The rationales for the 1958 coup offered in Proclamation 4 read:

The Revolutionary Party wishes to elaborate further on the reasons for this action:
—First is the internal situation. Communism is a grave danger. . . . They seek to undermine the monarchy, they have tried to destroy Buddhism, they have at-tempted to overthrow all the institutions the Thais cherish. . . .
—Some people, thinking only of themselves, have used constitutional govern-ment to cause disturbances and destroy the nation. They have used their rights and freedoms to oppose the work of the nation.[26]

Sarit cited the growing communist threat in Indochina and the animos-ity between Thailand and Cambodia as additional reasons. The Thai mil-itary's perception of the "communist threat" was influenced significantly by the American containment policy. Before any real communist threat to Southeast Asia had emerged, Edward Stanton, the U.S. ambassador to Thailand, warned Phibul and other senior generals of communist subversion, especially among the intellectuals and "left-of-center" politicians and unionists. In early 1951, in a warning to the Thai people of the consequences of a communist invasion, Stanton stated publicly: "Your good and noble king and your democratic constitution would be overthrown."[27]

Sarit ruled the country as a despotic paternal leader. The 1958 constitution granted the executive, the prime minister in particular, unlimited power to rule by decree. According to Article 17 of the Interim Constitution: "Whenever the prime minister deems it appropriate for the purpose of repressing or suppressing actions, whether of internal or external origin, which jeopardize the national security or the monarchy or subvert or threaten law and order, the prime minister, by resolution of the Cabinet, is empowered to issue orders to take steps accordingly. Such orders or steps shall be considered legal." Sarit used these provisions to the full in order to assert political control.

Thousands of people were arrested during his five years in office on various charges ranging from hooliganism to communist-related subversion. Among the hundreds accused of being communist and tried by military tribunals were politicians, journalists, union leaders, student activists, lawyers, government officials, farmers, priests, and hill tribesmen. Another target of repression was the rural insurgency led by the Communist Party of Thailand (CPT). Brutal counterinsurgency operations were routinely carried out by relatively autonomous local Communist Suppression Operation units. The local officials often abused their power: there were innumerable cases of rural people arbitrarily charged as being communist sympathizers simply because they were in personal conflict with local authorities. Many joined the CPT simply because they could not tolerate the abuse of power by local officials. Meanwhile, less blatant suppression was directed against local peasant leaders, student activists, "progressive" union leaders, and socialist politicians.

In addition to emphasizing national security, Sarit sought legitimacy on the basis of a Thai-centric ideology.[28] Sarit belonged to a generation of leaders educated entirely in Thailand. Unlike the 1932 coup's promoters, he had no exposure to the Western ideals of democracy and constitutionalism. His ideas about politics were home grown and rooted in Thai history and tradition. Sarit asserted that Western democracy was not suitable to Thai society at that stage of development. Thanat Khoman, one of his close associates, elaborated: "The fundamental cause of our political instability in the past lies in the sudden transplantation of alien institutions onto our soil without careful preparation and more particularly without proper regard to the circumstances which prevail in our homeland, the nature and characteristics of our own people."[29] While previous military governments had retained certain democratic elements such as limited political participation and parliamentary procedures, Sarit did not hesitate to do away with all the trappings of democracy. He did not believe in loyalty to an abstract state or constitution.[30] Instead he attempted to restore a moral, social, and political order based on traditional Thai values with the monarchy at its apex. The king became the focus of loyalty and cohesion as well as a key source of legitimacy for Sarit's government.

Revival of the Monarchy

Although politically weakened by the coup of 1932, the Thai monarchy continued to enjoy widespread popular affection. Sarit was quick to recognize the political potential of this traditional institution. The rise of Sarit and his clique to power by a path different from that of Phibul made it easier for them to accommodate King Bhumipol (Rama IX). (They were not antiroyalists and had not directly participated in the overthrow of the absolute monarchy in 1932.) Unlike the 1932 coup leaders, Sarit had no eloquent democratic justification, and public support for him came mostly from resentment over the corrupt Phibul regime. Hence the support of the revived monarchy was crucial for the consolidation of Sarit's power and the legitimation of his rule.

Immediately after the 1957 coup, Sarit made it known to the public that he had already informed the king of his actions. He openly projected himself as the guardian of the monarchy, which he described as the indispensable pillar of the nation. The government made it possible for the king and royal family to have more access to the public. Many traditional royal ceremonies were revived; the national day was changed to coincide with the king's birthday. Sarit also encouraged the king and his family to visit various outlying parts of the country. As the king made several speeches on behalf of the government, official programs and policies became more credible and acceptable. The king approved the central themes of the Sarit government: economic development and national security. In the New Year address of 1961, for example, the king noted: "Regarding the domestic scene, I am glad that you live in peace and happiness. Also, the government is trying to promote national development in a most competent way. . . . The government has drawn up a plan to revitalize the economy. . . . I believe that it will be useful for the nation. I hope you will cooperate with the government on these matters in the future."[31] Since 1962, moreover, the king had always reminded the people of the threat of communism. As one analyst observes: "This naturally, if implicitly, underscored the importance of the military and police in national administration. . . . The king in effect helped to legitimize the role of the military in Thai politics by strongly urging the public to support the government's internal security policies."[32]

Sarit also arranged extensive state visits for the king to foreign countries around the world to gain international support and legitimacy. But the popularity and admiration the king regained during the 1950s and 1960s under the patronage of the military regime outgrew what the military elite had expected. After 27 years of his reign and having survived seven constitutions, half a dozen elections, and a score of cabinets, by 1973 the beloved king as "head of state, the focus of his people's loyalty and cohesion, [and] the fount of legitimacy" had become a center of power in his own right.[33] In fact according to David Morell and Chai-anan Samudavanija the king had become "the most powerful figure in the [Thai] political system."[34] Thus royal approval, or at least royal acquiescence, became an indispensable basis of legitimacy. Withdrawal of royal support was the crucial final act in the delegitimation of the Thanom-Praphat government and resolution of the October 1973 political crisis.

Thai-Style Democracy

Concurrently Sarit redefined democracy. His new "democracy Thai style" must

1. Fit into the Thai way of life. The constitution must not be a duplication of the West; it must be practical and relevant to the Thai environment. Elections are not necessary.
2. Contribute to political stability.
3. Be accompanied by a liberal economic system that is minimally guided by the government.
4. Uphold the monarchy.
5. Facilitate national development.[35]

In keeping with "Thai-style democracy," there were neither elections nor an autonomous legislative body during the 1958–63 period. Priority was given to stability, law and order, and national development. At the center of a "Thai-style democracy" was Sarit's role as head of the nation: "The nation is like a big family. If members of the family have quarrels, the family could not be happy."[36] Following this line of thought, the leader is the father who is responsible for the well-being and happiness of the family members. The leader rules with compassion and decisiveness; the people must strictly obey him.

Democracy in Sarit's view meant, not popular sovereignty, but the responsiveness of the king and his government to the needs and aspiration

of the people. Thus even after open politics was suddenly and sharply cur-
tailed, Sarit sought mass support through numerous short-term populist
measures: reducing electricity rates, providing free tap water, providing
low-cost commodities for the people, reducing prices of basic consumer
goods and foodstuffs. These programs projected the image of Sarit as decisive solver of practical problems.

"Developmentalism" as a Source of Legitimacy

Sarit made extensive use of "developmentalism" both as economic goal
and as ideology to reinforce the sociopolitical order he sought to construct
and to justify his right to rule. He set up the National Economic Development Board (NEDB) and launched the first National Economic Development Plan based on the recommendations of the World Bank. Several
leading technocrats were placed in key policy positions in the NEDB, the
Bank of Thailand, and the Board of Investment. Sarit's main concern,
however, was the fulfillment of the population's immediate needs such as
the improvement of roads, irrigation, sanitation, electricity, clean water,
and health care. Macroeconomic planning was left to the technocrats and
bureaucrats of various development agencies. The economic nationalism
of Phibul's government was largely abandoned. Domestic private enterprise as well as foreign investment, in the form of joint ventures with local
capital, steadily replaced state-led capitalist development strategy.

Starting in the Sarit era, economic policy began to be redefined toward
a more liberal capitalist orientation. Rather than intervening directly in
the economy, the government concentrated on developing public infrastructure to facilitate the growth of private industries. By strictly prohib-
iting all political activity and ruthlessly disciplining labor unions, the government created a favorable climate for investment and industrialization.
With an average annual growth rate of 7 or 8 percent during the 1960s,
Thailand became one of the world's fastest-growing economies.

The business community had a stake in this growth and began to support the military regime. Indeed, networking among top-level military
leaders and large business groups thrived during the Sarit and Thanom
governments. During the long years of Phibul's nationalistic government,
businesspeople, most of them ethnic Chinese, were subjected to many restrictions and pressures. They therefore found it imperative to establish
ties with influential bureaucrats in order to secure privileges and ensure
protection. In return, the Chinese business community became a source of
wealth and economic power for the bureaucratic elite. This collaboration
was largely on an individual basis, however, and partnerships emerged in
the context of clique rivalry among leading elements of the military. As

this relationship spawned nepotism and patronage, it was resented by the public and contributed to an erosion of legitimacy.

Decline of the Regime's Legitimacy

Sarit's authoritarian restructuring of the Thai sociopolitical order, emphasis on development, and commitment to a free market economy gained him the support of the monarchy, military and civilian bureaucrats, and the economic elite. Those who opposed Sarit (leftist intellectuals and rural political leaders, especially from the northeast) were suppressed and eliminated. Although this formula did initially legitimate the Sarit government, what it entailed—particularly economic development and the revived monarchy—in the long run undermined the military regime's legitimacy. The 1973 student-led uprising that brought about the downfall of the Thanom-Praphat government and the military regime was in the main rooted in the large and growing gap between, on the one hand, the unmet aspirations of the new groups that emerged from the economic development in the 1950s and 1960s and, on the other, the stagnant political institutions.[37] The military was unable and unwilling to accommodate the demands of the new socioeconomic groups for political participation.

Comprehensive development programs launched under Sarit's leadership contributed to economic and social changes. In 1950 agriculture employed four-fifths of the total workforce and provided more than half the gross domestic product (GDP). By 1968 the share of agriculture had strikingly declined to less than one-third.[38] Under Sarit's industrial promotion policy, there was a steady growth of the mining, manufacturing, construction, and transport sectors. Industrialization was accompanied by the growth of urbanization and substantial increases in the number of managerial professionals and white-collar workers as well as workers in both the manufacturing and service sectors. While leading bankers, industrialists, and businesspeople still relied to a certain extent on clientelistic relationships with the military elite in power, newly emerging business groups began to feel that their vested interests were blocked by a small group of businesspeople who were well connected with the power holders.

Economic growth without due concern for equitable distribution of the benefits had negative consequences for a high percentage of the rural population. Only the well-to-do peasant families with large holdings and enough capital could afford modern agricultural equipment and better marketing facilities. The result was a widening gap between the rural elite and the poor peasants. The growing hardship in the rural area—which included landlessness, indebtedness, tenancy, poverty, unemployment, and generally poor living conditions—politicized and even radicalized some marginal peasants.[39] But their efforts to organize themselves as effective pressure groups were kept under tight control. Before the emergence of the Farmer Federation of Thailand in 1974, all peasant organizations had to be set up by the Ministry of Interior or the Ministry of Agriculture and Cooperatives. Prospective leaders had to be approved by the ministry and their activities were closely controlled.

The expansion of primary, vocational, and higher education throughout the country led to a growing number of students and professionals. In the 1960s, universities and teachers' colleges were set up in regional centers. More people, especially professionals, technocrats, and academics, began to seek education abroad, in the United States and Western Europe in particular, and were thus exposed to the lifestyle, the values, and the liberal democratic political systems of those countries.

Given the magnitude and comprehensiveness of all these changes, politics could no longer be confined to civil-military bureaucratic groups. New forces emerged whose political views were imbued with the ideology of political participation. The military governments were unable and unwilling, however, to face up to these new challenges. With the death of Sarit in 1963, political power passed on almost automatically to his closest associate in the armed forces: Thanom Kittikachorn. As Thanom was not a strong personality like Sarit, military rule became vulnerable. Indeed, after Sarit no single military leader was able to attain unquestioned control of the armed forces. Leadership had to be shared among several generals: Thanom, Praphat, Prasert Charusathien, Krit Sivara, and Dawee Chulasap. Thanom had to yield to the demand for constitutional rule and limited political contestation. Political parties—weak, unorganized, and without mass support—were allowed to contest in the general election of May 1969. But parliamentary politics, as before, had a rather short lifespan. Though Thanom's party held a majority in the House of Representatives, the tension between the government and the elected parliament increased when the members of parliament tried to exert more control over the military-backed government. Thanom therefore decided to stage a coup and end parliamentary democracy once again in 1971—an action that fueled resentment among various groups, especially the students, academics, urbanites, and opposition politicians. Indeed, outspoken leaders of the opposition parties took the military to court on the charge of overthrowing the constitution.

Since the late 1960s, public support for the principle of constitutional rule, representative government, civil liberties, and public accountability has been growing. Students in leading universities began to form discussion groups on social and political issues. In 1968, a small number of Thammasat University students together with a few politicians requested the government to lift martial law to ensure a fair election. In 1969, there was a student demonstration against the increase in bus fares. The National Student Center of Thailand (NSCT) organized a week of "Anti-Japanese Goods" rallies in 1972. The campaign gained wide support from the public and the king explicitly approved it as an "excellent" idea.

The student force was significantly strengthened when Ramkhamhaeng University was founded in 1971 as an open university run by the government. In the first year after its establishment, 28,611 students enrolled— almost the same number of students as all the other universities in the country combined. In 1973, nine Ramkhamhaeng students were expelled on the charge of issuing illegal magazines criticizing the government. Students of various universities joined the demonstration. For the first time principles of democracy and idealism figured prominently in public debates. University students may be regarded as the proxy of the nonbureaucratic middle class in Thailand. Though they come from different social and economic backgrounds and have no specific interests that could be classified as middle-class interests, their politics and idealism are decidedly liberal.

The legitimacy of the Thanom government was undermined not only by the growing force of democratic principles, but also by its poor performance. Corruption and nepotism caused public resentment against the armed forces and also created rifts within the military. Certain senior officers (and the king), for example, became disenchanted with the meteoric rise of Thanom's son, Colonel Narong Kittikachorn. Further, the public was experiencing economic hardship. People had to line up to buy rice for the first time in the country's history as a result of natural disasters as well as government mismanagement. The Thais now openly showed their intolerance of the government's inefficient and corrupt bureaucratic rule.

It can be said, then, that it was the military regime's poor performance as well as the growing force of democratic principles that led to the October 1973 uprising. It should, however, be noted that the elite's disunity and royal intervention were decisive factors leading to the removal of the Thanom government. Though hundreds of thousands of students and citizens vigorously joined the demonstration, such a loosely organized movement could not have withstood the use of brute force. Had senior military officers, especially General Krit, not decided to withdraw their support from the ruling clique and had not the king withdrawn his backing, the October 1973 incident would not have resulted in victory for the people.

The 1973–76 Democratic Regime

With the ouster of the military regime, the interim Sanya Dharmasakti government appointed by the king had the onerous task of constructing a democratic regime. The long preparation time,[40] the exclusion of students and young people from the appointed national convention and the national assembly to draw up the new constitution, and the protracted haggling among the traditional elite that led to the deletion of the more progressive sections of the draft constitution tempered the initial enthusiasm of the politically conscious public and gradually gave way to frustration and disenchantment.[41] Nevertheless, the April 1975 elections were the cleanest in Thai history and the relatively high caliber of persons who contested the elections enhanced the prestige of elected institutions. The legitimacy of the democratic regime, however, was soon undermined by a number of developments: weak coalition governments, their poor performance, and intraparty strife; the dramatic growth in extraparliamentary forces and interest groups and the heavy demands they placed on the weak governments; the uncertainty and insecurity created by the extremism and polarization that pervaded Thai society during this period; factional strife within the military; and the alliance of the king with conservative forces. Ultimately all these elements contributed to the public's loss of confidence in the democratic system—setting the stage for a violent military coup d'état in October 1976.

Weak Coalition Governments

A total of 42 parties fielded 2,199 candidates for 269 seats in the April 1975 elections. In addition to the confusion caused among voters by the bewildering number of parties and candidates, no single party emerged with even a slim majority. The first coalition government, headed by Seni Pramoj, lasted less than two weeks. The second government under Kukrit Pramoj lasted more than a year, but this fourteen-party coalition was shaky throughout its tenure in office. Coalition partners had no mutual trust and maneuvered against each other constantly. The agreement among the three major parties in the coalition to divide the cabinet positions in proportion to the seats they held in the parliament and not to interfere in the ministries under each other's jurisdiction in effect meant there were three mini-governments. While this agreement produced some stability, it implied there could be no common long-range policies to address the many key socioeconomic problems facing Thai society.

The Seni and Kukrit governments did undertake a number of reforms (land control act, initiation of minimum wage and labor legislation, anti-corruption measures, a subdistrict development fund), but these were limited and did not meet the expectations of the students, farmers, and workers. The ability of the Kukrit government to undertake reform was further hampered by the opposition of the three leftist parties, which drove Kukrit into closer alliance with the rightist parties, as well as by the bureaucracy's inability and unwillingness to effectively implement even the limited reforms. Faced with certain defeat in the no-confidence motion tabled by the Democrat Party—and an ultimatum from the military, which by now had recovered from its fall in 1973, that it would not tolerate a socialist-oriented government—Kukrit dissolved the parliament in January 1976 and called for fresh elections.

The April 1976 elections were the most violent in Thai history. More than 30 people were killed and dozens were injured. The public was relieved when the elections were finally over. Although the four-party coalition that emerged did have a sizable majority controlling 206 of the 269 seats in the parliament, its potential to provide stability and govern effectively was undermined by two developments: a deep split in the Democrat Party between the conservative and progressive elements and the death of General Krit Sivara, which stimulated factional strife within the military—a development that dashed the Democrat Party's hopes of forging an alliance with the Krit faction to prevent a coup. As it was, the death of General Krit made possible the return of Thanom and Praphat with far-reaching consequences for Thai politics. An alliance comprising the conservative wing of the Democrat Party, the Thai Nation Party, and the Thanom-Praphat factions in the military engineered a political crisis in the months leading up to the October 1976 coup.

Polarization of Thai Society

Excluded from the preparation of the new constitution, unable to identify with any political party and therefore excluded from the parliamentary process, and dissatisfied with the extent of the reforms undertaken by the Seni and Kukrit governments, the students took to the streets to express their grievances and demands. They also reached out to the masses, propagated democracy, and were instrumental in forming labor unions and farmer organizations throughout the country, thereby contributing to the dramatic growth of extraparliamentary and extrabureaucratic groups. The latter were no longer awed by the political center and the traditional political elite. With the support of the students, the labor unions and farmer organizations, joined by progressive monks, staged numerous strikes and protests demanding higher wages, higher rice prices, return of agricultural land to the tillers, and so forth—demands that the governments could not satisfy, at least not to the extent desired by the activists. This unprecedented alliance of students, workers, farmers, and leftist monks created a sharp reaction from the right.

The fears of the right were exacerbated by the radicalization of the student movement.[42] The National Student Center of Thailand (NSCT) was captured by a small group of radical students who believed that the progress of Thai society could only be ensured through revolution. Over the next year they firmly rejected the democratic process as a route to social reform and concentrated their efforts in bringing about a true cultural revolution in Thailand. This campaign was perceived by the conservative sections of Thai society (military, police, royalty, bureaucrats, middle class, businesspeople) as a communist threat that must be dealt with quickly and firmly. Their apprehension was exacerbated by the NSCT's protests against the United States, which culminated in the massive demonstration of March 1976, the successive victories of communist movements in Laos, Cambodia, and South Vietnam in 1975, and the abolition of the monarchy in Laos.

Several new rightist organizations (Nawaphon, Red Gaurs, Village Scouts), supported by the traditional elite and the business community, emerged to counter the power of the progressive groups. The rightists deployed the slogan "nation, religion, monarchy" in support of their movement. Claiming that the progressives were out to destroy these traditional pillars of Thai society, they attempted to mobilize a broad cross section of Thai society. Nawaphon concentrated on organizing supporters in the bureaucracy and business communities at the provincial level; the Red Gaurs were concentrated in Bangkok with the express purpose of disrupting student protests and breaking strikes; the Village Scouts focused on inculcating nationalistic values in the rural areas. By late 1975 Nawaphon claimed to have over a million members, and the Village Scouts under royal patronage had by late 1978 trained more than 2.5 million men and women. This ultranationalist cause was supported by militant rightist monks—principally by Kitthiwuttho Bhikkhu, who argued that while killing leftists and communists did produce demerit, this was more than compensated by killing the devil.[43] The forces of the right gained strength, too, from the public's fear and Thailand's increasingly insecure international situation.

The proliferation of progressive and rightist movements, their nonintegration into the formal political system, and their preference for the politics of the street exposed the weakness and increasing irrelevance of political parties and the parliamentary system. Ultimately the extreme polarization of Thai society and frequent and massive political violence discredited the democratic order. The Thai public, especially the Bangkok middle class, "was quite willing to trade chaotic parliamentary democracy for stable military dictatorship, to exchange individual freedom for national security and domestic tranquility, and to adopt short-run pragmatic solutions to problems rather than the troublesome pursuit of long-run reforms."[44]

Return of the Traditional Institutions

Though discredited after the 1973 revolution, the military quickly recovered and by 1975 had become a formidable political force again. Faced with sharp criticism from the public on several fronts (failure to deal with the communist threat, corruption, links with U.S. imperialism) and the emergence of several factions within the military,[45] the armed forces under the leadership of General Krit were initially reluctant to play a direct political role. Krit, whose interests lay more in the commercial world and who through his previous appointments had an understanding of electoral politics, concentrated his efforts on strengthening his faction within the military and in exercising his influence through electoral politics. As it recovered, the military began to exert its political influence more directly—as, for example, in 1975 when Krit delivered an ultimatum to Kukrit. Unable to return to political power directly through a coup, the military worked to bring about the defeat of Kukrit and his Social Action Party in the April 1976 elections. The death of General Krit in April 1976, however, created a power vacuum and intensified the struggle for supremacy within the military establishment. Concerned that state power might be seized by the other factions, the Krit faction—by then firmly identified with Generals Serm Na Nakhon and Kriangsak Chomanan and supported by the Young Turks—launched a coup d'état after crushing a student rally at Thammasat University on October 5, 1976.

Although the king had sided with the students in the October 1973 revolution, he was not for radical change. As a conservative institution, the monarchy advocated gradual reform, law and order, national security, and, of course, preservation of the institution of the monarchy itself. Developments within Thailand and in neighboring countries, particularly the abolition of the Laotian monarchy in early 1976, appeared to have convinced the king that there was a distinct threat to the monarchy. He— some argue at the behest of his wife who was politically more involved— decided to side with the conservative forces and support the military's seizure of power. The return of Thanom to Bangkok in September 1976 sparked a massive student protest demanding his departure from Thailand. A series of events—leftist and rightist demonstrations, the announcement of a new cabinet by Seni Pramoj, a mock hanging at Thammasat (one of the two effigies bore a startling resemblance to the crown prince), and the rightists' call to crush the leftist demonstrations—culminated in the bloody conclusion of the democratic period. More than 46 persons were dead, hundreds were wounded, and arrests totaled some 3,000.

Clearly there was no sustainable support for democracy in Thai society. Democracy was valued, as it was 40 years earlier, only as an ideology that could be used to contest the legitimacy of the incumbent regime. As a political system it was incapable of responding to the exploding demands of the changing society. Democratic procedures could not satisfy the conflicting demands of several groups. The bureaucratic elite, business groups, and the less politicized public feared that excessive demonstrations and protests would lead to political instability. Even if they did not go along with the mobilization of the extreme right, they preferred to stand aside because they were skeptical about the motives and benefits of these radicalized mass movements. The victory of the communists in neighboring countries in 1975 further reinforced the public's anxiety and to some extent confirmed the military's argument that the communists were going to take over all of Southeast Asia and Thailand was the next target. All left-of-center groups that were active in politics were perceived as communist agents or sympathizers. Political violence and polarization of the society intensified. In these turbulent circumstances, the elected civilian governments could not maintain law and order. Support for the democratic regime declined rapidly.

The armed forces moved quickly to regain their omnipotent status. The alleged communist threat to the revered institutions of Buddhism and monarchy was the rallying cry for the conservative mass organizations to crack down on the left. Though the communist threat had been cited in earlier coups (1951, 1957, 1958, and 1971), it became the central theme of the 1976 bloody coup.

While the 1976 coup was a setback for democracy, the military elite could not turn the clock back to the 1950s. The fall of the ultraconservative Thanin Kravichien government within one year showed that anticommunist doctrine and ultraconservative ideology were not a sufficient basis for legitimation in light of the rapid social and economic changes that had transpired. Moreover, the Thanin government could not cope with the powerful threat of the Communist Party of Thailand. Nor could it gain the support of the intellectuals, the middle class, the business community, the workers, even the military. In October 1977, the same military group that had staged the 1976 coup removed Thanin from office in order to ease political tensions.

The 1978–88 Quasi-Democratic Regime

The term "quasi-democracy" is used here to denote the salient characteristics of Thai politics in the 1980s, which evinced a liberal policy toward
political parties and political activity while at the same time accommodating the interests of the civil-military bureaucratic forces. An attempt was
made to include all political forces in the political process and policymaking. The newly emerging nonbureaucratic forces could exert their influence through parliamentary process and political parties while the bureaucrats could be appointed to government positions.

   Although General Kriangsak Chomanan, the army's former supreme
commander-in-chief, assumed political power through a military coup, he
recognized the need to share power with the increasingly strong nonbureaucratic forces. He relied on political liberalism as the primary basis of
his government's legitimacy. General amnesty was offered to political de-
tainees and to those who had defected from the CPT. The theme of "democracy" was widely held as the most effective way to end the communist
insurgency. The commander-in-chief of the army, General Prem Tinsulanonda, reiterated the policy that "placed political cause and democratic actions ahead of military actions in combating communist insurgencies."[46]
These political moves effectively neutralized the communist sympathizers.
Further, General Kriangsak did not play the role of an autocratic ruler as
previous military leaders had done. He instead allowed certain forms and
degrees of popular representation and political contestation.

   The 1978 constitution represented a fusion of the old and new forces
of Thai politics. It allowed full-fledged political contestation among political parties; but at the same time it left channels open for prominent
figures of the armed forces and the bureaucracy to constitutionally enter
the political decision-making arena. Prior to the 1983 amendment, the
prime minister and cabinet ministers did not need to be members of the
House of Representatives and could concurrently hold their position in
the bureaucracy. The House of Representatives comprised a government-
appointed Upper House of 225 members and a popularly elected Lower
House of 301 members. The Upper House was entitled to vote in joint
session on matters of national security, the monarchy, the economy, the
budget, and on motions of no confidence.

   Certainly this constitution cannot be regarded as truly democratic. Earlier charters contained more extensive democratic principles and procedures. But they did not take into account the true power configuration in
Thai politics and unrealistically excluded the military-bureaucratic elite.
According to Anek Laothammatas, General Kriangsak provided Thailand

with a constitutional framework that offered the means for a gradual transition to a more democratic government.[47] The 1978 constitution embraced all the key players as well as providing the basis for parliamentary politics. Of particular interest here are the principles and practices of political legitimation during the period of the governments headed by Prem Tinsulanonda. An inclusionary approach (facilitated by Prem's personality and support base), his emphasis on development with due concern for distributive justice, the support of the monarchy—all underscored the legitimacy of the quasi-democratic regime.

Inclusionary Approach

General Prem Tinsulanonda, who succeeded General Kriangsak as another nonpartisan prime minister, was a well-respected commander-in-chief of the army with a clean professional record and the personal trust of the king and queen. He had strong support from the powerful Young Turks.[48] His prestige and integrity, as well as his tactful management of rifts within the army, helped him to secure control over the armed forces. He appointed trusted men to powerful posts and played one faction against another with great success. As a result, ambitious or frustrated officers were prevented from organizing successful coups.

Prem capitalized on the army's growing desire to become more professional in order to regain the prestige of the military establishment, which had been deteriorating steadily since the 1970s. Some officers deeply resented the nepotism, corruption, and clientelistic business links. Despite the call for professionalism, however, some military leaders wanted to regain political power while others preferred the role of guardian or power broker lending support to those they considered fit.[49] Notwithstanding this difference, there was general agreement that the military had a legitimate role in the political process to set the course for political development as part of national development.[50] During the 1980–88 period, this role was largely satisfied by the appointment of Prem, their master, as prime minister.

Prem used his integrity and professionalism as well as his personal connections to secure legitimacy for his government.[51] Deftly he played a balancing role among contending forces in the Thai polity—notably the armed forces, political parties, and the monarchy—within the framework of constitutional rule. During his eight-year tenure, Prem reshuffled his cabinets several times as well as dissolved the parliament twice and refused to use military force to settle political conflict in 1981 and 1986. Constitutionalism evolved gradually and became an independent basis for legitimacy.

The nature of Thai political parties had undergone significant change since the 1973–76 period. The new parties were not based entirely on personalities. Increasingly, their organization reflected specific concerns and interests. Business groups formed their own political parties to further their interests. Renowned businessmen like Boonchu Rojanasathien, Pramarn Adireksarn, and Pongse Sarasin actively entered politics. Apart from an increase in the numbers of elected business-politicians at national and provincial levels, influential local businessmen also became involved in party activities as candidates and major contributors. Close relations between political parties and the business community began to replace traditional clientelistic alliances between military elites and businessmen. Moreover, local politics was invigorated with grassroots politicians providing the link between the rural populace and the government in Bangkok.

Notwithstanding the change in the nature of political parties, conflicts among them prevented Thai politics from moving toward full-fledged democracy. After each election between 1980 and 1988, ruling parties could not find a politician acceptable to all of them to assume the post of prime minister. General Prem was thus reappointed again and again—the only person regarded as qualified and acceptable to the political parties as well as the military establishment. This situation gave Prem room to maneuver and facilitate (intentionally or not) the institutionalization of political parties and participatory politics amidst the skeptical attitudes of the military. Equally important, civil rights and freedom of expression and association were maintained throughout the Prem years. His emphasis on achieving reconciliation with communist defectors proved to be fruitful initially in curtailing the expansion of the CPT and subsequently in its collapse.[52]

Though he allowed relatively open politics, Prem did not permit political parties to push the civil-military bureaucrats into a corner. In his first cabinet, three-fourths of the members were from three major parties whereas certain key portfolios—defense, interior, and foreign affairs—were reserved for nonpartisan appointees of his own choice. In his successive cabinets, the finance portfolio was held by former high officials of the Bank of Thailand. While elected members of the parliament performed a wider range of functions in aggregating demands from the populace, leading members of the bureaucratic organs, especially the National Economic and Social Development Board (NESDB), were highly influential in the decision-making process with respect to economic development policy and planning. Prem also appointed a team of advisers to help him handle economic matters. His reliance on technocrats and academics not only made him legitimate in this important stratum of society but also contributed to a rational reorientation of policymaking for enhanced performance that secured domestic and international support.[53]

Economic Development and Distributive Justice

The legitimacy of Prem's quasi-democratic regime was rooted, too, in the ability of ruling groups to articulate as their own the interests of various social and economic groups. Compared to previous prime ministers, Prem had considerable interest in rural development programs. The growth of the Thai economy in the 1960s resulted in development that benefited mainly the rich, the upper middle class, and the better-off local elite in certain rural areas. Many peasant families, however, became heavily indebted and frequently lost their land to moneylenders. Prem's redirection of development policy toward a more equitable distribution of benefits to the rural population was viewed as necessary to make government legitimate in the perception of rural dwellers. Prem often expressed concern over the people's hardship in the provincial areas, especially in the northeast. A special plan for rural poverty alleviation was launched by the NESDB.

Prem also responded to the business community's desire to gain a more prominent role in economic policymaking. As a result of drastic structural change in the Thai economy since the 1970s, businesspeople who had for decades relied on military and bureaucratic patronage to promote their interests now sought to translate their demands into policy actions in a more institutionalized way. The leading business associations—the Thai Bankers' Association, the Thai Chamber of Commerce, and the Association of Thai Industries—finally succeeded in lobbying the government for the creation of a Joint Public and Private Sector Consultative Committee in 1981. By incorporating business associations into economic policy, the Prem administration gained much credibility in the private sector. Moreover, such an inclusionary approach to policymaking bore economic fruit. By 1986, Thailand began to surge economically and was widely called Asia's Fifth Tiger. Thus Prem enjoyed legitimacy not only by securing the support of the various strategic groups and through conformity with institutions that were becoming gradually established but also on the basis of performance as well as the monarchy's support.

The move against Prem's premiership did not come from these powerful strategic groups in Thai politics. He still had strong support from the king, from the military and business leaders, and from most of the major political parties. It was the educated urban middle class, student organizations, academics, and certain groups of politicians who advocated the principle that the prime minister should come from among the ranks of elected members of parliament, that "forced" Prem to refuse another term as unelected prime minister after the 1988 elections.

The Post-1988 Democratic Regime

When Chatichai Choonhavan became Thailand's first elected prime minister in twelve years, the urban educated middle class, professional executives, academics, and independent media heralded the event as a major step toward full-fledged democracy, which they depicted as the primary source of regime legitimacy. But within two years, the same groups responded quite favorably to the coup in February 1991 that returned the military to the corridors of power. Within months, however, the popularity and credibility of the military declined rapidly as it became clear that it wished to hold onto power permanently. General Suchinda Kraprayoon, who masterminded the 1991 coup, assumed the premiership after the April 1992 elections despite his repeated vows never to do so. Protests spread like wildfire throughout Bangkok and several provinces. The cry of the demonstrators was: "Down with the nonelected prime minister! Down with the illegitimate regime!" With the king's appointment of Anand Panyarachun, former prime minister and respected bureaucrat, as interim prime minister with responsibility to organize new elections, the political crisis was resolved.

This series of developments suggests that legitimacy in contemporary Thai politics must be seen as a dynamic and multifaceted issue. With the emergence of numerous competing power centers and interest groups adhering to competing values about a legitimate political order, the question of "legitimacy in whose eyes" has become of much greater importance than ever before. Although the 1991 coup must be seen primarily as a defensive maneuver of the military against the expanding role of elected politicians and political parties and their intervention in military affairs,[54] it also reflected the erosion of the legitimacy of the incumbent government and to a lesser degree the parliamentary system.

The Chatichai government when it assumed office enjoyed considerable legitimacy, as it was the first fully elected government in twelve years. It derived its authority from conformity with democratic principles and procedures that were becoming more important as the basis for political legitimacy. Moreover, the Thai economy continued to register impressive double-digit growth rates. Yet these advantages alone appeared insufficient. From the perspective of the urban middle class, "the measure of good government was not only economic performance but also integrity and honesty, and one cannot substitute one for the other."[55] The impact of these middle-class groups had a multiplier effect because they were influential opinion leaders in the society.

Commentary in major newspapers and by leading academics encouraged and reflected the public's resentment of the rampant corruption, cronyism, and unprincipled behavior of politicians, especially the cabinet members. The government's claim that it had a popular mandate was largely rejected on the ground of the alleged vote-buying practices in the previous election. Thus while the middle class supported a democratic regime in theory, it was unhappy with the incumbent government. For the middle class, Chatichai's claim to legitimacy based on democratic principles could not be sustained because his government was using state power for private gain. Critical and cynical as they might have been, the middle class did not directly invite the military to step in. Most of its representatives reminded the public that the problems should be resolved through democratic means. But their impatience and call for immediate action to "purify" Thai politics could not help but pave the way for the military's return.

The 1991 coup was thus justified by the military as an act in the name of the people. The coup's leaders officially cited eradication of rampant corruption as one of the major rationales for their usurpation of power. The general public welcomed the coup at first. Their expectation, however, was that the military would quickly return to barracks once political order had been restored and democratic principles reestablished. Indeed, the early declarations of the military and its actions reinforced this belief. Though parliament was dissolved and martial law was proclaimed, the coup leaders allowed a considerable degree of political and economic liberalism. Political parties were not banned, press freedom remained largely untouched, and public criticism was tolerated. The most important move to gain domestic as well as international support was to appoint an interim civilian government comprising a number of well-respected business executives, technocrats, and former senior bureaucrats.

Within a few months, however, the sincerity of the coup group began to be questioned. It became obvious that the military leaders sought to perpetuate their political control through a new constitution that would pave the way for military officers to assume the highest political offices. A new political party, Sammakkitham, was set up by retired officers as a front party to support Suchinda as the next prime minister. For the business community and the professional middle class, the adverse effect of continued military rule on the economy was another major concern. Because of the highly internationalized character of the Thai economy, the world's reaction to the coup was now a major consideration. After the coup the European Community issued a statement expressing regret at the demise of the democratic government. The United States suspended $16.4 million of economic and military aid. Further, by the end of 1991 the economy had slowed to a growth rate of 7 or 8 percent. Though the Gulf Crisis and the slowdown of world trade in general were undeniably major causes of the reduced growth rate, the Thai middle class, according to at least one political analyst, placed the blame elsewhere: "The educated public held the military responsible for this economic downturn, believing that the coup had inevitably led to a serious decline in international trade, investment, and tourism on the one hand and mounting hardship in international trade negotiation on the other. The middle class and the business community understood that, amidst the worldwide democratization trend, any military takeover was bound to be ostracized by Western democracies."[56]

Opposition to the military's attempt to retain political power had been the focus of the campaign of various nonbureaucratic groups since November 1991. But now, unlike the early 1970s, a much wider spectrum of people was involved in the anti-military-rule movement of the 1990s. Political awareness was to be found not only among political activist groups such as students, labor unionists, and grassroots nongovernmental organizations but also among the educated and resourceful middle and upper classes. A survey by the Social Science Association of Thailand, conducted during the month of May 1992, showed that 45.5 percent of the demonstrators earned a lower-middle-class or middle-class income (10,000 to 49,000 baht per month); 36.5 percent were between the ages of 30 and 39; 13.7 percent were self-employed; 45.7 percent were employees in the private sector.[57]

That the urban middle class contributed greatly to the return of democracy in May 1992 is beyond doubt. But the key question is this: What will prevent them from calling for the return of the military should an elected government in the future fall short of the ideal standards of government—integrity and competence—they have set? Here it is necessary to review the different understandings of democracy and democratic procedures among the electorate. There are at least two distinct ways of thinking about democracy in Thailand: one is the view of the urban, educated middle class; the other is the view of the rural voters. The parliamentary system of Thai democracy leaves the question "Who should be elected to govern the country?" to the rural voters who outnumber the urban, educated middle and upper classes. For the rural voters who are still deprived of simple necessities, democratic rights are usually limited to their votes at election time. Democracy, therefore, simply means the responsiveness of politicians and political parties to local needs and immediate problems:

roads, water reservoirs, electricity, public safety, some extra income. Vote buying is a fact of Thai electoral life.

After elections, however, the survival of political leaders depends on their acceptance by the educated urbanites, most of whom belong to professional groups and the business community. These groups apply a different set of criteria to assess the performance and legitimacy of the elected government. For them, efficiency, integrity, and honesty are additional elements essential for political legitimacy. Corrupt, inefficient, and self-seeking politicians will not be tolerated. This is not to say that the middle class is ready to sanctify an authoritarian or autocratic regime. The middle class is in a dilemma: they need a third way out.

Thai politics is now facing a situation of unprecedented pluralism where heterogeneous forces have been unleashed. Profound socioeconomic changes have inevitably created new social and economic forces outside the bureaucracy, leading to a more complex and politicized society, something missing during the first 40 years after 1932.[58]

Conclusion

The challenge for Thailand is to construct a political system that can accommodate all the key new and old forces and their interests and at the same time provide a framework for the peaceful acquisition and exercise of political power. Military absolutism, democracy, and quasi-democracy were tried with varying degrees of success, but ultimately all were delegitimated and displaced. Developments in 1973 and 1992 demonstrate beyond doubt that military absolutism and even quasi-democracy under military tutelage are no longer acceptable as permanent political systems. The lack of opposition to the 1991 coup d'état, as demonstrated by the developments in 1992, cannot be interpreted as evidence of support for military rule. It is better viewed as a negative reaction to the abuse of power by a democratic government rather than as dissatisfaction with the democratic system. At the same time, a democratic regime that appears incapable of ensuring security and stability (as was the case during the 1973–76 period) or one that abuses power (as did the Chatichai government) will not be acceptable either. To be legitimate, the political system of contemporary Thailand must be rooted in democratic principles, the government must have acquired power in conformity with the institutions and procedures of the system, it must exercise power effectively within the law and for public rather than private gain, and it must be acceptable to the military and the monarchy.

Despite the negative experiences of the 1973–76 period, the democratic principle has progressively gained strength and has become a necessary though not sufficient condition for political legitimation. The growing strength of this principle is rooted in the rapid socioeconomic development that has taken place over the last 30 years as well as in the internationalization of the Thai economy. This process cannot be reversed. If anything, further industrialization is likely to make the Thai body politic even more complex, sophisticated, politically conscious, and concerned about political participation and the government's performance. The growing force of the democratic principle does not imply that the democratic system reinstituted in 1992 has become established. The system continues to suffer many weaknesses—weak political parties, a shaky coalition government, the lackluster performance of Prime Minister Chuan Leepkai, his government's inability to pass the necessary constitutional reforms to move the democratic process forward,[59] and the continued existence of strong extraparliamentary political forces.[60] Rumors of a possible coup have resurfaced. Notwithstanding these weaknesses, the democratic regime has not been discredited—at least not yet. The government of Chuan Leepkai is still viewed as legitimate. There is no alternative organizing principle.

But for a long time to come the democratic principle alone, while necessary, will not be sufficient. The government of the day must perform effectively and within the law to satisfy the legitimacy criteria set by the Bangkok elite, and it must also be acceptable to the extraparliamentary political forces, particularly the military and the monarchy. As the democratic regime matures in a Thai context—this may take decades and the process will not be free of conflict—the political power and influence of the military and monarchy may be expected to decline. The decline in the political role of the military, if one takes a long historical view from 1932, is evident. This trend is likely to continue, but the military is certain to resist and contest the decline. Unlike the military, the power and prestige of the monarchy has progressively strengthened. The role expansion of the monarchy, however, is related to the weakness of the political systems introduced after absolute monarchy. The inability of the military elite to find alternative legitimizing principles—and subsequently the political conflict between the forces of status quo and change—provided opportunities for the monarchy to play an enlightened balancing role that enhanced its power and influence. As the system becomes stronger and less conflict ridden, however, the monarchy's political influence is likely to decline. Further, there is also the personality element. Forty-eight years on the throne and his caring approach have conferred respect and authority on the present king. Whether Rama X can command similar respect and moral authority remains to be seen.[61]

The other bases of legitimacy—nationalism, religion, security, international support, and coercion—that were significant in the early years have become much less important if not irrelevant in the contemporary period. Security could become important again, especially in a law and order context, but it is unlikely to be the overriding basis of political legitimation it was in the early post-1932 period. The brute suppression employed by Phibul, Sarit, Thanom, and Thanin will no longer be acceptable. Indeed, the use of massive coercion now is more likely to demonstrate a loss of authority rather than contribute to its consolidation. The changing basis of legitimacy—the growing force of democratic principles and performance and the declining relevance of other bases—is related to broadening of the politically conscious public and the growing importance of the masses in political legitimation as well as delegitimation.

This chapter also suggests that although performance becomes more significant in the absence of established norms, institutions, and procedures for the acquisition of political power, it is not an enduring basis for political authority. It has the potential both to build and to undermine the legitimacy of an authoritarian regime. Economic development shored up the legitimacy of the Sarit and Thanom governments, but in the long run it undermined the legitimacy of the military regime. Poor performance has the potential to discredit a democratic regime, as well, as exemplified by the developments during the 1973–76 period, while abuse of power can delegitimate a democratic government like that of Chatichai. Poor performance is a minus for the Chuan government; but because he is regarded as a man of honesty and integrity, because there is no alternative acceptable political leader, and because his government is rooted in democratic principles, Chuan's government continues to be perceived as legitimate.[62] To the extent that democratic principles and the institutions and procedures associated with them become established, the salience of other bases will gradually decline.

9

Indonesia

Historicizing the New Order's Legitimacy Dilemma

MOCHTAR PABOTTINGI

> The truth is that we have been set free from the colonial hypnosis and
> have therefore become self-confident. From here we can see the *colonial*
> truth clearly. And this is what our action is based on.
> —Mohammad Hatta, 1928

HAD Clifford Geertz, the great Indonesianist, waited twenty years, would he still characterize Indonesia as "a state manqué"?[1] Since the fall of Sukarno, Indonesia has emerged as one of the few politically stable and economically dynamic countries in the Third World, a state with a strong government and a cohesive bureaucracy.[2] However, this has been achieved through a drastic departure of the New Order from the original 1945 conception of Pancasila,[3] which simultaneously constitutes the national consensus, the ultimate ideals of the nation, and hence the moral basis for political authority in Indonesia. The New Order's present legitimacy dilemma is underscored by its violation of key elements of the national consensus and ideals.

Political suppression, mystification, and a degree of confusion have so far prevented the majority of Indonesians from realizing the illegitimacy of many government policies and practices. Certainly a wide spectrum of social life has improved as a result of political stability, economic growth, and shifts in political orientation. Despite the impressive economic growth, more and more Indonesians perceive an increasing discrepancy between the nation's ideals and the naked realities they face. How profound is the discordance between the ideals of the nation and reality under the New

Order? Is the eroding legitimacy likely to deteriorate to crisis proportions, affecting the performance and survival of the regime?

These central questions concerning political legitimacy in contemporary Indonesia cannot be satisfactorily answered unless one considers the historical, economic, and cultural forces that affect Indonesian politics. Legitimacy is a dynamic politico-historical concept that endlessly evolves with time. The ideals that emerge from a nation's history—ideals that are not only continuously tested and contested but also preserved and remembered—constitute a basis for claiming, acknowledging, and resisting the right to rule. Thus legitimacy must be seen in the light of the politically meaningful in a nation's history.[4]

In the case of Indonesia, the essential determinant of legitimacy has always been the historically shared and cherished ideals prompting its people to form their nation. All four constituent elements of legitimacy identified by Alagappa—"shared normative ideals and values," "conformity with established rules in acquiring power," "proper exercise of power," and "consent of the governed"—are informed by this historical consideration. It is the ideals of the *nation* that are the repository of moral authority in Indonesia.[5] A nation of course is not a fixed and unchanging entity. But being born out of a long history, it naturally possesses a relatively durable character. While the historically shared and cherished ideals may be temporarily displaced by adverse crises or circumstances, they will always resurface and assert themselves. In examining the questions posed earlier, this chapter begins with a discussion of the current debate in Indonesia over the legitimacy of the New Order.

Controversy over the New Order

Incumbents and supporters of the New Order argue its legitimacy on two key grounds: political stability and economic development. They claim that the endless political strife in the previous systems of parliamentary democracy and guided democracy created acute political instability that rendered development efforts impossible and even threatened the survival of the state of Indonesia.

Aliran politics of the 1950s,[6] seen as the main cause of the fifteen-year political quagmire, has created in the military a deep suspicion of politics and particularly political contestation. It has been used by President Soeharto as a pretext to ward off "extreme ideologies," assert a selective interpretation of Pancasila, and generally depoliticize Indonesian society. It is also regarded as a sufficient reason to concentrate all power and decision making within central state structures and for the New Order government to dominate all the country's political institutions. The New Order and its supporters claim that *aliran* politics must end if the nation and country are to remain united. The political controls instituted by the New Order are, in their view, a necessary price for the sake of unity and economic development. Political stability and economic growth constitute the dual leitmotif of the New Order in justifying its entitlement to rule.

Increasingly, the New Order's economic achievements are given pride of place in justifying continuation of its rule. The New Order has not only halted but reversed the rapid deterioration of the economy; it has also led Indonesia into the rank of middle-income countries, created self-sufficiency in rice, significantly reduced dependence on oil exports by enhancing the manufacturing sector, and commendably increased the facilities for primary school education. With such cumulative achievements, the New Order government deserves, in the eyes of its supporters, to continue ruling the country for another 25 years.

Critics of the New Order, however, see it differently. With regard to politics, they are dissatisfied with the way in which the principle of representative government, enshrined in both Pancasila and the 1945 constitution, has been operationalized. Their criticism has focused on the stipulation that 20 percent of the DPR and 60 percent of the MPR be appointed by the president.[7] The opponents are also critical of the executive branch's domination of the rules and practices governing general elections and its discrimination against political parties to the advantage of the government "party," Golkar.[8] These rules guarantee the continued dominance of the New Order government, regardless of public consent.

Off the record, critics have called for amendments to the 1945 constitution to curb the unbridled presidential powers that Sukarno and Soeharto have exploited to their advantage. They have also advocated the establishment of new political parties. In their view, the PPP and PDI have been co-opted by the government and function merely as "sparring partners" to Golkar in an attempt to project a democratic image.

The government has been urged to formulate and make public the basic guidelines of "Demokrasi Pancasila,"[9] to reduce the number of military representatives in the legislative bodies, to make the presidency a genuinely elected institution with clear limits on the number of terms, to guarantee the freedom of workers to establish their own labor unions while freeing branches of the Indonesian Unitary Workers' Association (SPSI)—the only labor union thus far allowed by the government—from bureaucratic interference, and to reduce, if not discontinue, the depoliticization of the rural masses. In their eyes, the absence of genuine people's representation in the DPR and MPR directly affects political participation and the distribution of economic opportunities.

Critics demand that the government be held accountable to the public. Many Indonesians were angered by the attempt to muzzle news of the killings in East Timor in 1991 and similar cover-ups of atrocities committed by the authorities. Most Indonesians were enraged as the press disclosed in early 1994 a state bank's megascandal involving fraudulent credit of over $600 million going to an obscure Chinese businessman. Dozens of similar cases involving embezzlement of public funds by state banks are still being kept quiet. But most intolerable to critics was the arbitrary shutdown of Indonesia's outspoken magazine *Tempo* along with two other weeklies in mid-1994. *Tempo* had grown with the New Order to become one of the few credits to democracy in the regime's era; above all, it had acquired a reputation for fair coverage. The story prompting *Tempo*'s termination had to do with the tainted purchase of former German warships in 1994—despite the government's countless pronouncements advocating openness and condemning corruption.

The economy—distributive justice in particular—is the second major criticism of the New Order. Indonesia's "success story" has benefited the urban and modern sectors considerably while marginalizing the rural and traditional ones. Critics disagree with the government's claim that there has been a significant reduction in the number of people living below the poverty line. They contend that the reduction will be much less significant if other criteria—such as medical care and old-age security—are included or the standard of minimum income is fixed according to actual needs. Critics also cite innumerable evictions of the poor from lands they have cultivated for decades, the substantial increase in the number of strikes in industrial complexes, the burgeoning of unemployment, the economic injustice faced by the indigenous majority as well as minorities in the periphery, and countless instances of terror, torture, and mutilation of the powerless in land and wage disputes. Not only legal aid activists but many university students and ordinary people as well expressed their anger at the brutal killing of Marsinah, a woman labor activist, at Sidoardjo, East Java, in 1993.

From the perspective of the critics, the state of the Indonesian economy is far from bright. Rampant monopoly, oligopoly, and nepotism increase inefficiency and hobble the national economy. Indonesia's foreign debt has reached a critical level, with a disproportionate percentage of new aid receipts used to pay debt installments and interest.[10] The malfeasance and resulting kleptocracy are perceived to issue from the subordination of the rule of law to the interest of the power holders and their cronies.

Critics believe that the non-*pribumi* group is best served by the present economic arrangements at the expense of the *pribumi*.[11] Economic policies and practices of the New Order, critics say, have resulted in an inordinate predominance of non-*pribumi* in the national economy, particularly in the urban and modern sectors. They claim that if prior to 1965 the government's economic policy was geared toward lifting the position of the *pribumi* entrepreneurs vis-à-vis their Chinese counterparts, from the time of the New Order there has been a definite reversal in favor of the latter.[12]

Pribumi businessmen have a deep-seated feeling that they are being unfairly pushed aside by their non-*pribumi* counterparts, a feeling that is widely shared by other indigenous Indonesians. They view this unequal development as resulting not from fair competition, but from favoritism, collusion between the politically and economically predominant, and the perpetuation of an economic structure inherited from colonial times.[13] This resentment harks back to the old, bitter, and—in Furnivall's words—"loaded dice" competition between Indonesian and Chinese businessmen, which reached its peak at the beginning of the twentieth century.[14] Critics observe that the same "loaded dice" competition is being repeated in the New Order.[15] Such a course of development has a chilling impact on many Indonesians, for it runs counter to their historical understanding of the ideals of their nation.

This outline of the current debate shows that the legitimacy of the New Order is significantly contested. While readily conceding that Indonesia has enjoyed political stability for more than two decades, critics are apprehensive about the course of development under the New Order. They believe the economy enriches too few too much. They worry that the widening gap between the *pribumi* and non-*pribumi* has been such that, short of major economic and political adjustments, reconciling the two groups would be almost impossible. Many predict that this antagonism could well be the Achilles' heel of the New Order.

The debate also reflects the present democratic ferment in Indonesia. The extent of this ferment can be gauged by the unprecedented richness and complexity of issues raised, discussed, and polemicized in the media. Open public scrutiny spares no issue or position—including Soeharto's fifth reelection and the monopolies of his children, topics that only a few years ago were taboo. But this change toward democratization is uncertain and comes as much from the government's own haphazard predilection for a more open process as from the drive of liberalism unleashed by socioeconomic changes wrought by the New Order.

History, Economy, and Legitimizing Ideals

Indonesia's ideals of legitimacy must be understood in conjunction with the evolution of the country's economy. The economy of precolonial Indonesia flourished in what W. F. Wertheim calls "harbor principalities" and "bureaucratic inland-states."[16] Unlike the portrayal in much of the colonial literature in the early twentieth century,[17] the economy of the vast archipelago, at least from the thirteenth to the sixteenth centuries, was neither autarkic nor backward. This period coincided with the spread of the Malay language throughout maritime Southeast Asia and the generally peaceful, trade-mediated spread of Islam in most of the Malay-speaking world.[18]

Using a monetized system, the precolonial economy had a large base of artisans, cultivators, manufacturers, traders (both land-bound and ocean-crossing), and internationally valued produce and products. In fact, the archipelago was an integral part of a thriving economy in the East, whose commerce was superior to that of the West in both quality and quantity of merchandise. Having their own *popolo grosso*, "Indonesians" traded actively among themselves and with the wider world.[19] Despite the centuries-old presence of foreign traders—Chinese, Indians, Arabs, Persians, and Europeans—indigenous rulers by and large controlled political and economic affairs in their land.

But beginning in 1599, Dutch military intrusion gradually changed the economy of the archipelago. By the middle of the eighteenth century, major trades and trade lanes in the archipelago were already under the tight control of the colonizers. Colonial monopoly in key trade items, the list of which changed according to circumstances, accompanied exploitive practices of forced deliveries, forced cultivation, and contract coolies from the seventeenth to the nineteenth centuries. These measures destroyed indigenous economic arrangements and gravely impoverished the people.[20] Through gradual, deceptive, and piece-by-piece land acquisition, the Dutch practically colonized the entire land by the end of the nineteenth century, destroying the ancient economy.

Throughout the colonial era, Indonesians were no passive pawns of destiny. The colonial government had to face numerous, if intermittent, uprisings and wage costly, sometimes protracted, wars up till the end of Dutch rule in 1942. Most of the resistance by local rulers or peoples was carried out in the name of Islam,[21] whether or not faith was the prime mover. Only through adeptness in political manipulation, superiority in armament, and above all dexterity in carrying out the policy of divide-and-rule were the Dutch capable of holding onto and taking the utmost advantage of this exceptionally rich land for over three centuries. The efficiency and extent of their profit-gathering were made possible by symbiotic cooperation between the Dutch, the *priyayi* (native colonial bureaucracy), and the local Chinese businessmen.[22]

The colonial economic arrangement, however, made for unequal growth. The economic power of the Europeans—owners of big companies and plantations—grew by leaps and bounds, followed at some distance by that of the Chinese, who functioned largely as an extension of the Dutch exploiters, and then, far behind, by that of the native peoples. Sumitro Djojohadikusumo maintains that in 1936 Indonesians comprised 98 percent of the total populace but received only 20 percent of the national income. Another 20 percent went to the Chinese, who constituted less than 2 percent of the population. The Europeans, who made up 0.5 percent of the total populace, gathered 60 percent of the national income.[23]

By the third decade of the twentieth century, the negative impact of Dutch monopolistic exploitation had become clear. First, the indigenous class of artisans and manufacturers had been weakened and indigenous traders were marginalized. Unlike in British India,[24] the indigenous middle class in Indonesia was supplanted by the Chinese, who were structurally separated from the indigenous people. Second, the indigenous precolonial economy disintegrated. Third, the skewed colonial division of labor prevented industrialization. Finally, a socioeconomic stratification emerged in which Europeans occupied the highest stratum, followed by foreign Asians. The majority of indigenous people at the bottom of the social ladder lived on the crumbs of the colonial enterprise.

Despite the defeat or subordination of local rulers and the exploitive practices of the Dutch, organized resistance from among the Javanese peasantry did not materialize for over a century.[25] The political atmosphere changed drastically, however, as the Dutch resorted to the practice of direct rule: villagers taking orders directly from Dutch officials. Moreover, an influx of Chinese arrived from mainland China who gradually outnumbered the *peranakan*, the partly assimilated Chinese.[26] These immigrants established their own schools and associations in the cities. Adopting the nationalistic zeal of their compatriots and realizing their increasing power and wealth, the Chinese ended up treating Indonesians as pariahs.[27]

The birth of national consciousness in Indonesia followed the concurrent political deprivation, economic exploitation, and cultural marginalization. The feeling of being cornered instigated Indonesians, and their leaders in particular, to define their situation, to perceive themselves as one people, and to pursue their struggle accordingly. "Indonesian" consciousness began to germinate during the era of the *pergerakan* as it was manifested in *Boedi Oetomo, Indische Partij,* and *Sarekat Islam* in the years between 1908 and 1912.[28]

Based on the Islamic confession and constituting a vigorous economic and political movement, Sarekat Islam was the largest organization to challenge the colonial establishment and its policies. Its original objective was to foster the economic interests of Muslim entrepreneurs, perhaps the most severely deprived group. As the movement grew, so did the scope of its struggle. It took the side of small workers and farmers, established labor unions, organized strikes. It also sought to better people's representation in the Volksraad—the colonial parliament—and showed an initial desire to establish its own government. At times, Sarekat Islam already appeared to be representing the nation in embryo as its membership spanned ethnic and ideological categories.[29]

But as in the case of Filipino nationalism,[30] the first true Indonesians appeared overseas, in this case in the Netherlands within the association of Indonesian students called Perhimpoenan Indonesia. By 1925, the organization led by Mohammad Hatta began to advocate its four-point political agenda: national unity, national solidarity, noncooperation, and self-initiative.[31] The imperative of unity loomed large in the minds of Hatta and his colleagues as they learned from history that Indonesians' own divisiveness made possible centuries of colonization and exploitation by the Dutch. This explains why from the very beginning ethnic-based nationalism was ruled out and a strong emphasis was placed on unity and solidarity in equality. Soon the cause of Perhimpoenan Indonesia was adopted by the Indonesian Nationalist Party, led by Sukarno in Bandung, during the heyday (1927–29) of Indonesian nationalism.

A number of meaningful events predated the nation's "politically defining moment." One was the pronouncement of Soempah Pemoeda (Youth Pledge) in 1928, in which representatives of Indonesian youth in Jakarta declared their commitment to "one country, one nation, one language." The second was Hatta's defense speech before the colonial court in The Hague, also in 1928,[32] in which he disclosed the discriminating realities of Dutch colonialism and the impossibility of peaceful coexistence between the colonized and the colonizer. The third was Sukarno's distinctive oration before a similar court in Bandung in 1929. There Sukarno traced Dutch colonialism to Europe's industrial revolution and exposed the exploitive practices throughout the colonial period.[33] Despite the increasing severity of Dutch suppression and Japanese fascism during the 1930s and early 1940s, Indonesia's founding fathers kept their struggle alive.

The time to define their ideals arrived when the Japanese, aware of impending defeat by the Allied forces, allowed Indonesian leaders to hold a series of meetings under the Investigating Committee for the Preparation of Indonesian Independence (BPUPKI) in Jakarta.[34] The purpose of the committee was to formulate a philosophical foundation as well as a constitution for the prospective republic. With the exception of the communist elements, Indonesian political elites from Java and the Outer Islands—party members, professionals, bureaucrats, women, and minorities, including Chinese and Christians—were represented. The over-all atmosphere of the meetings approximated Habermas's "ideal-speech situation."[35]

There was a long heated debate between Muslim representatives and the nationalists over whether Islam or some secular ideology was to be the foundation of the state. Sukarno ended this debate on June 1, 1945, with his ingenious proposal of Pancasila: the five principles on which the nation was to stand. It was unanimously accepted by the committee. Embodying the national consensus, this proposal and its adoption by the founding fathers constitute Indonesia's politically defining moment and the moral basis on which the right to rule can be claimed, acknowledged, and resisted.

Demystifying Pancasila

Although unanimously accepted in 1945, Pancasila has in later years been arbitrarily appropriated and subject to serious contestation. With regard to the interpretation of the principle of people's representation, Sukarno's proposal seems to have had much in common with Western democratic tradition. Proximity also obtains between his reading of the principle of belief in one deity and, for instance, Americans' understanding of the credo "In God we trust." Both end up promoting the equality of religions.

But Sukarno is unique in his advocacy of a broad-minded national-ism—one that emphasizes an encompassing national brotherhood and ex-plicitly rejects xenophobia in both national and international relations.[36] Similarly unique was Sukarno's dream of a "political-economic" democ-racy. What he had in mind was a political system "capable of bringing social prosperity" particularly to Indonesia's common people. The prin-ciple of social justice implied to him the upholding of both political and economic equality.[37] This nationalism of Sukarno underscored the eco-nomic struggle of Indonesians to rise from the bottom of colonial stratifi-cation and was shared by the rest of the founding fathers.[38]

There was an ideological tendency, however tenuous, to read Pancasila as rooted in the people's own cultural heritage. Such a reading is not peculiar to Indonesians. Benedict Anderson, for instance, observes that "Pancasila, Indonesia's 'modern' political ideology, was originally a set of Buddhist principles, mentioned in the earliest known Javanese epic, the Nagarakrtagama."[39] But when Sukarno delivered his famous address on Pancasila, it was clear that his use of a Sanskritized term had nothing to do with any notion of preexisting ideals by that name. He was merely looking for a decorous title for the five principles and was accordingly advised by his language expert.[40] Later, Indonesians also read the term as an ingenious construct of an outstanding "solidarity maker." In this case the text was taken to be simply an *alat pemersatu* (a unifying stratagem)— a compromise to overcome conflicting ideologies and political streams in Indonesia. This is just another way of saying that Pancasila was incoherent and a facade. Western scholars tend to share this view.[41]

To understand Pancasila, however, we must first clarify its "philosophical" and "ideological" character. Then we need to put it back in its historical context and read it as a political agenda, uncover the cultural dynamics at work in its making, and try to gauge its underlying assumptions. The problems of political legitimacy in Indonesia are constituted in that discussion.

The confusion around Pancasila is for the most part a result of its simultaneous treatment by Indonesians as a philosophical foundation, a state ideology, and a unifying stratagem. But this confusion is more apparent than real. In the context of Pancasila, the word *ideology* is used to signify ideals that people seek to materialize. This meaning of ideology coincides with one of the meanings of philosophy—a set of principles an individual or a collectivity wants to uphold. In other words, ideal objectives (in Pancasila as ideology) and ultimate principles (in Pancasila as philosophy) are taken here as synonymous.[42] As a unifying stratagem, the emphasis has mistakenly been on the third principle of Pancasila—the unity of Indonesia—when in fact the national ideology is only valid as a unifier if all five principles are applied as an integrated whole. It would be unwarranted to compel the people to unite if they perceive that the principles upholding social justice or genuine representation are continuously betrayed.[43] As we shall see, such a compulsion had indeed happened during the period of guided democracy and in the New Order.

Second, Pancasila should be read in the context of the history of Indonesia's *pergerakan* (national movement) and the nation's meaningful events. Its text was primarily devised to overcome Indonesians' own divisiveness before and during the colonial period. The ideals of political and economic equality of Sarekat Islam are certainly well encoded in the text. At least two of the four themes of Hatta's Perhimpoenan Indonesia—national unity and national solidarity—are strongly represented in Pancasila. Likewise, one can sense in it the ghost of a long and painful colonial experience.

Thus Pancasila constitutes as much a testimony against colonial dehumanization as a crystallization of all the national ideals that emerged during the *pergerakan* era. For all its weaknesses, it is the summation of Indonesian nationalism and the essence of Indonesian republicanism. The founding fathers managed to free themselves from the bitterness of the colonial experience to arrive at a set of progressive and universal ideals answerable not only to the plight of their people but to humanity in general—an exceptional political phenomenon one might call "universality in particularity," captured very well by Jean Cohen and Andrew Arato.[44] Unlike James Mayall's portrayal of nationalism as invariably reactive and chauvinistic,[45] Indonesian nationalism has from 1925 been open and liberal. Sukarno saw in imperialism, not certain people, but the working of particular economic laws at particular economic stages, just as he placed his struggle not against the Dutch but against exploitive practices in general. This historicization represents Pancasila as constituting not only the ultimate political agenda of the nation, but its social contract as well.

Third, Pancasila can only be comprehended within a dynamic conception of culture.[46] Pancasila is by no means a monocultural text. It was not intended as such by its formulators. Nor was it meant to be internally consistent. The first principle, belief in one deity, is ambiguous. Literally it conveys monotheism; but from the very beginning it was accepted as a profession of belief in God encompassing all world religions.[47] The culture at work in Pancasila is a dynamic one that transcends any such differentiating labels as "orientalism" versus "occidentalism" or "traditionalism" versus "modernism." The text provides intricate coalescing possibilities in culture.[48] As Sukarno tersely depicts himself:

I am a follower of Karl Marx, but, on the other hand, I am also a religious man, so I can grasp the entire gamut between Marxism and theism. . . . I know all the trends and understand them. . . . I have made myself the meeting place of all trends and ideologies. I have blended, blended, and blended them until they finally became the present Sukarno.[49]

Consistent with our dynamic conception of culture, Pancasila is a blend comprising elements of socialist thought, traditional Indonesian notions of a good community, Islamic modernism, and late-nineteenth-century European liberalism. Much as in the Vietnamese experience,[50] all four worldviews were spreading and overlapping throughout the country from the third decade of the twentieth century. This period witnessed a high degree of religious and ideological tolerance.[51] But motivation for liberation was stronger. In the midst of severe impoverishment by the colonial scheme, people were forced to employ any symbolic—cultural or ideological, "indigenous" or "foreign"—weapons available to mobilize resistance against the colonizer.[52] This may be called the politics of the mobilization of meanings,[53] Sukarno's forte.

Thus far we have focused on the five formal principles of Pancasila. Yet there are two major unstated assumptions—the existence of political order and economic sufficiency—on which Pancasila rested. A sentence in the preamble of the constitution—"And the struggle for Indonesia's independence has reached the happy moment, peacefully leading to the gate of independent Indonesia, which is free, united, sovereign, just, and prosperous"—discloses precisely these assumptions. The immense wealth extracted by the Dutch from Indonesian soil, the "long continuance of established government and general tranquillity," or the many decades of colonial *rust en orde* in most parts of the archipelago may have influenced the perceptions of Indonesia's founding fathers and made them less cautious in the way the state was to be administered, particularly during the early years of the republic.[54] It is equally plausible that the founding fathers' assumptions of order and sufficiency resulted from the predominance in their mind of democratic models in the West—where scarcity and disorder have generally been eliminated.[55]

Regardless of their origins, acceptance or denial of these assumptions has led successive leaders of the republic to commit serious errors in devising expedient political arrangements, giving rise to a continuing legitimacy dilemma. Despite these adverse consequences, the force of Pancasila in embodying national consensus and ideals—and hence the basis of moral authority—should not be minimized. It is an embodiment of both a bitter past and an ideal future for a long-subjugated people and an emerging nation. To explore the legitimacy problem confronting the New Order and to speculate on the future, we turn now to some dynamics of tradition relevant to the problem of legitimacy.

The Tradition-Modernity Equation

Tradition and modernity are not antagonistic; rather, they form a dynamic and complex continuum. Besides, the actions of social groups need not correspond with their cherished values. Benedict Anderson made perhaps the strongest case for the bulwark of tradition in contemporary Indonesia: "Power does not raise the question of legitimacy."[56] In other words, a ruler does not require the consent of his people to rule. Since power is "divine energy which animates the universe," there is no such thing as a social contract.[57] A ruler rules because he is chosen by the divine; moral consideration is therefore irrelevant. Anderson sees this conception of power at work, for instance, in Sukarno's populism and in the refusal of both Sukarno and Soeharto to give autonomy to the Outer Islands. He sees it, too, in the building of massive monuments, in the blurring of the public and private sectors, and in the necessity of widespread corruption to maintain political stability in Indonesia. Above all, he sees it in the so-called reemergence of patrimonialism.

Anderson's thesis rests on seriously contestable assumptions.[58] First, it views power in a monocultural perspective, neglecting the contested na-

ture of power in Javanese tradition.[59] Second, its analysis is entrapped by
the coherence principle of explanation: cultural incoherences as well as
social phenomena whose meanings cannot yet be fathomed are simply left
out of the analysis. Third, it has only tenuous historical support. We know
that even in traditional Javanese kingdoms, power was dispersed and
openly contested. Fourth, it is based on an old Indic—cyclical and cos-
mocentric—notion of time. The use of this notion overlooks certain cultural facts and historical developments. Anderson's "idea of power" is
accepted by many foreign scholars in part because of the erroneous view
that Islam has not taken deep root in Java.[60] Finally, Anderson downplays
the fact that the Javanese are capable of being either intensely devout or
elusively syncretic in their practice of Islam, with both attitudes incorporating many universally accepted values.

The illustrations Anderson cites to support his "idea of power" can be
explained on the basis of other factors. Sukarno's and Soeharto's refusal
to grant autonomy to provinces outside Java has to do with the prevalence
of separatist movements and sentiments in the Outer Islands. Sukarno's
populism was directly related to the egalitarian discourses of liberalism,
Marxism, and reform Islam in the first decades of the twentieth century.
The building of massive monuments should be read as part of Sukarno's
nation-building obsession to overcome the people's colonized mentality;
for Soeharto, monuments instilled in the minds of Indonesians the primacy of Pancasila and the unity of a country that had just escaped civil
war. The blurring of the public and private sectors stemmed to a great
extent from the mode of Indonesians' resistance against Dutch forces, in
which Indonesian army personnel smuggled opium and harnessed villagers' economic resources to buy weapons and support their combat units.

The correlation of corruption with political stability makes sense only
in the context of minimal political consensus, as in the mid-1950s. But
even during the period of parliamentary democracy, charges of corruption
led to the downfall of cabinets. At the time of the New Order, particularly
in its early stage, the army deemed corruption a necessary evil in its effort
to consolidate power. To some extent it was simply a continuation of
the army's fundraising practices during the revolution as well as the subsequent lack of accountability in both governance and development.[61]
Nonetheless, all this corruption has not been accepted with impunity. Students' riots and demonstrations as well as efforts to impeach Soeharto by
leading politicians and statesmen, including his former fellows-in-arms,
might have brought about his downfall had not the army remained united.
The widespread propensity to corruption among Indonesian civil servants
should be traced not to "the idea of power," but to the absence of accountability and to the racist and stingy salary system of colonial rule.

Patrimonialism in independent Indonesia stems from the lack of political consensus among the egalitarian forces during the *pergerakan*, the revolutionary, and the postrevolutionary periods. It works only because the egalitarian and potentially modern-oriented parties and groups—each commanding a sizable membership and some even substantial economic power and significant numbers of educated people—have been mutually undermining. Patrimonialism prevails accidentally, not independently.

Javanese Culture

To read Javanese traditional culture into Indonesian politics, we have to consider the different ideas of power, authority, and justice in its major subcultural variants.[62] Notions about high political ideas between God-fearing *santri* and status-obsessed *priyayi* would serve as a case in point. Insofar as the former emphasize the Islamic teleological view of life and the latter the Indic cyclical conception, the translation of their contending views into real life would tend to cancel each other out. With this consideration in mind, we can speculate that only ideas commonly shared by the three cultural variants in Java—*priyayi* (the nominal Muslims closely associated with the colonial bureaucracy), *abangan* (the nominal Muslims), and *santri* (the entrepreneurial Muslims, both modernists and traditionalists)—have a greater chance of influencing the course of politics.

Cultural variants among the Javanese put high value on the grace and refinement of human behavior, customs, and actions. The *alus*—the refined—is by no means the monopoly of the *priyayi*. It also pervades the symbolic systems of both *santri* and *abangan*. Inseparable from the primacy of the *alus* is the high priority given to *kerukunan* (peaceful coexistence), since both *alus* and *rukun* emphasize equanimity. In other words, average Javanese are basically averse to roughness, intemperance, and disorder. *Keselarasan* (harmony) and *keseimbangan* (fine balance) are not empty words to most Javanese.[63] So important are the principles of the *alus* and *rukun* that the Javanese have acquired what can be called "ethnicity-transcending values." In fact, to cultured Javanese, the word "Jawa" has ceased to connote ethnicity; instead it embodies all those values they admire. To them these values are much more important than ethnicity. The expression *durung Jawa*—not yet Javanese—is used to refer to Javanese and non-Javanese alike who have not acquired these values.[64] Sukarno and Soeharto were graceful and refined in their respective ways. Both were capable of winning—and losing—gracefully in rough political struggles. In fact, Sukarno's "March 11 Letter" transferring power to Soeharto was an exemplary act of losing gracefully in Indonesian politics.[65]

These cultural traits tend to deter rough attempts at seizing power and thus tend to support the incumbent. A government may therefore endure not because it is legitimate, but because of the absence of a graceful and refined way to replace it. This does not mean that control mechanisms are completely absent, for the people would expect similar grace and refinement in the mode of governance. It cannot be denied that the Javanese have experienced bloodshed. But it has generally come only during times of great cultural change or confusion.[66]

Compared to Indonesian Malays of the Outer Islands, whose culture is more cosmopolitan, commercialized, and homogeneously Islamic, the Javanese, particularly in the hinterland, tend to be more respectful of institutionalized power and more conscious of the importance of institutionalized authority. This attitude is related to the strong predilection among the Javanese to identify a king with God or to see a king as God's *wahana* on earth.[67] The word *gusti* in Javanese applies to both God and king. If to a traditional Javanese obeying a king constitutes one of the highest virtues, a "traditional" Malay would follow the maxim of *raja adil raja disembah, raja lalim raja disanggah*—a popular teaching exhorting obedience only to a just king.[68] The frequency of rebellions in the Outer Islands and putsches by army officers in the 1950s can be largely explained in this context. None of these, however, is to be taken as permanent. As the cases of Mangoenkoesoemo and Misbach in the heart of Javanese culture clearly indicate,[69] deference to *gusti* has undergone an irreversible erosion with the influx of the egalitarian worldviews of Islamic modernism, communism, and Western liberalism.

The persistence of Javanese respect for power must have something to do with the profound internalization of the *alus* in their symbolic system. It might also be influenced by the continuous functioning of *kraton* during colonial times, when relations between king and subject were largely undisturbed by Dutch indirect rule. But the New Order has brought into both urban and rural Java an unprecedented increase in commercialization, in the changing modes and relations of production, and in capital-intensive technology—all vigorously dislocating traditional social relations.

The magnitude of changes flowing from these socioeconomic innovations is perhaps rivaled only by the vigorous spread of *pergerakan* and the independence revolution in earlier periods. These developments are likely to have altered the Javanese view of power, moving them closer to that of their Malay compatriots. Hildred Geertz observes that even in Java the *priyayi*'s refined and courtly ways have long been challenged by the practical commercial ethics of the *santri*. Moreover, the higher *priyayi* find it more and more difficult to maintain their inner superiority, excellence in artistic matters, and penchant for mysticism as the colonial government is no longer there to support their exclusiveness. Now other social groups have similar opportunities.

Norbert Elias writes that "the structure of psychological functions, the particular standard of behavioral controls at a given period, is connected to the structure of social functions and the change in relationships between people."[70] He further argues that the patterns of behavior "were transmitted not only from above to below but, in line with the shift in the social center of gravity, from below to above."[71] This explains why even the most self-conscious Javanese in 1928 had to accept Bahasa Indonesia, not Javanese, as the national language. It also explains why a process of "santrinization" among the *priyayi* and *abangan* has been going on throughout Java in the past ten years.

Changes in Indonesian Islam

Indonesian Islam shares egalitarianism and a propensity for commercial activities with the rest of the Islamic world. What makes it distinct, however, is the predominance of its dynamism,[72] openness, and resilience. Even the "traditional" Islamic groups in Java increasingly send their children to modern schools and accept nontraditional ideas. Their intellectuals are now indistinguishable from those of the modernists. An equally distinctive feature of Indonesian Islam is that its two dominant schools—the modernist Muhammadiyah and the traditionalist Nahdatul Ulama (NU)—are both moderate and both by and large promote tolerance in religious matters.

Despite its dynamism and demographic majority, Indonesian Islam has never ruled the entire country. Furnivall writes that twice during the distant past—at the end of the fifteenth century and toward the end of the sixteenth—Islam would have swept the entire archipelago under its religio-political hegemony had it not been for the Portuguese and Dutch interventions.[73] Two more recent opportunities—one during the heyday of Masyumi in the early 1950s and the second during the formative years of the New Order around 1965–67—were also frustrated. The New Order turned against political Islam as soon as the communists were eliminated. Nevertheless, during the first years of the New Order a new devout and enlightened movement of Muslim intellectuals emerged. Led by Nurcholish Madjid in 1969, this *gerakan pembaharuan Islam* (Islamic renewal movement) reasserted the orthodox understanding of Islamic *tauhid*, which stresses that God is "the complete Other" whom humankind can only approach but never reach.[74] This new vision in Indonesian Islam is original in that it uniquely combines Islamic orthodoxy with a grasp of modernity without compromising either. Here modernity has a deeper and more essential meaning, that is, as an approach to the ultimate truth, to God. God, the representation of the ultimate truth, is at once the representation of the ultimate modernity.[75] This view is shared by many Muslim intellectuals.

One aspect in the new theology highly pertinent to our discussion is the doctrine of the "unreachability" of God. The belief that God can never be appropriated renders it impossible for any mortal to claim God as his own. This implies that sociopolitical arrangements should be based not on the appropriation of God but on the mutual predictability of humankind. Legitimacy ceases to be a mandate from heaven. Hence the Islamic intellectuals' concern for democratization, rationality, and common rules.

This new vision in Indonesian Islam has had its critics. Early on Madjid's articulation of Islam was attacked for spreading secularism in Indonesia. More recently, it has been accused by a group Liddle calls "scripturalist" of being allied to the Jewish lobby or advocating Christian-Chinese interests.[76] Some also suspect that the movement has been supported from the beginning by the Soeharto government.

With the struggle and influence of Madjid and, during the past few years especially, of Abdurrahman Wahid, a new political vision averse to religious and political absolutism has emerged from within Indonesian Islam. This vision embraces non-Muslim communities on the basis of equality and has renounced the goal of post-*pergerakan* Islam to establish an Islamic state. It remains to be seen how this new theology in Indonesian Islam will fare in the long run. In religion, behavior often runs counter to tenets. Still, during the past two decades an unmistakable potentiality has developed from within Indonesian Islam to break cultural and political bonds that have stultified the country's progress.

Pancasila and Postcolonial Reality

Postrevolutionary Indonesia was soon confronted with grave legitimacy problems. These were perhaps the inevitable result of the formidable tasks following the transfer of sovereignty from the Dutch—tasks including the formation of a government from the debris of revolutionary liberation and establishing civilian control over the revolutionary army.[77] When the five-year undeclared war between Dutch and Indonesians finally ended at the Round Table Conference,[78] the revolutionary psyche was still predominant.

Parliamentary Democracy, 1949–57

The scale and pace of economic, political, and social change—as well as the challenges related to the end of revolution and assumption of sovereignty—barely allowed time to build an effective administration. Indeed, much of the effort to improve the country's politics and economy worked the opposite way. During the first four years of independence, the successive cabinets of Hatta, Natsir, Sukiman, and Wilopo were concerned "to legitimize a whole regime,"[79] to establish a rule-based government, and to abide by the articles of the constitution.[80] But the young republic was soon immobilized by conflicting tensions: the urgent need to create an effective government, a commitment to practice democracy, and a desperate need to revive the nation's economy with additional programs to distribute economic resources and opportunities. Throughout the period, steps to implement these policies largely canceled each other out.

The period of parliamentary democracy was generally characterized by the weakness of both state and society.[81] Cabinets based on fragile coalitions collapsed in quick succession. Their emphasis on the rule of law and respect for international conventions alienated many groups that had played important roles in the revolution. These groups viewed such practices as contrary to the spirit of the revolution and the ideals of the nation.[82] The flabby civilian bureaucracy was virtually paralyzed by widespread corruption and divisive factions. This process reached a dangerous level in the mid-1950s with hyperinflation. Simultaneously, *aliran* politics took command of various government bodies. Moreover, the Indonesian army was far from integrated and was unprepared for peace.[83]

The weakness of the state was reinforced by the fissiparous tendencies of political parties and rampant ethnocentrism in the society itself. Although parliament functioned well as a check on the executive, its non-elected character and the stigma of colonialism limited its authority and legitimizing function. The three-year-long general campaign prior to the 1955 election, viewed earlier as a panacea for the many ills of the young republic, had adverse political consequences. In the course of the long and heated campaign, the Nationalist Party (PNI) appropriated Pancasila as its symbol,[84] while Masyumi resorted to its call for an Islamic state. This Pancasila-versus-Islamic-state controversy was one of the main sources of tension in Indonesian politics until the early 1980s.

Since the nationalists and Muslims had reached an agreement on June 1, 1945, the fresh rift between them was likely the result of the active reentry, toward the end of 1945, of the Indonesian Communist Party (PKI) into national politics under the guise of nationalism.[85] With the reentry of the PKI, the meaning of the theistic, democratic, and justice principles in Pancasila became problematic. As Sukarno and PNI members came largely from the *abangan* variant of Javanese Islam, they did not seem to mind that a de facto ideological readjustment in favor of the PKI had taken place. But members of Masyumi and, to a lesser extent, members

of the Socialist Party saw this change as an affront to the national ideology.[86] Those who refused to accept the de facto readjustment silently
returned to their pre-1945 political positions. Masyumi, which had hith-
erto cooperated well with the socialists and Christian minorities, now advocated an Islamic state.[87] That the antagonism originated from a new and
unanticipated turn in politics was indicated by the bitter contention even
among Islamic parties.

Moreover, among the Javanese, who comprise about 45 percent of the
nation's population, a similar contest arose between the *santri*, the *abangan*, and the *priyayi*.[88] Factionalism and petty interests undermined national morale and cohesiveness, contributing to a desperate inertia among
the elite as well as the society at large. As Feith notes:

> Movement-type politics and mob-like collective behavior appeared in many areas
> of social tension. Political unrest seemed to be rising, just when government au-
> thority was at an ebb. To many in the political elite, civil order and the cohesion
> of the state seemed threatened. Anarchy, territorial disintegration, civil war, for-
> eign intervention—each of these appeared on the horizon of possibility for some
> members of the political elite, and so did Communist take-over.[89]

The rebirth of the PKI toward the end of 1945 had indeed seriously complicated the political situation. Not only did it fuel the strife between the
nationalist and Muslim parties, but it also changed the overall power
relations, contributing to radical politics. In turn, these developments
increased the army's quest for power and recharged regional demands
for autonomy, igniting rebellions in Aceh, West Sumatra, West Java, and
South Sulawesi, all Islamic strongholds.

David Steinberg and others are right when they observe that Indonesia's first experiment in democracy was doomed by the complication of a
backward economy and an unfortunate political ecology.[90] As indicated
earlier, the colonial government never intended to industrialize the country. At the conclusion of the national revolution in December 1949, the
bulk of Indonesia's economy remained agrarian. Worse, its production fell
way below the standard reached by the colonial administration prior to
World War II.

Guided Democracy, 1958–65

Guided democracy was an attempt to recapture not so much the revolution as meaningful politics, which had so strongly characterized the
emergence of the nation.[91] This aspiration was not Sukarno's alone. It was
shared, if for different reasons, by important sections of the army, a sizable
number of politicians, the *pamong praja* (the inherited core of colonial
bureaucracy), and the majority of nonpartisan political elites.

The move toward some kind of controlled democracy appeared as early as 1953. With the fading of independence euphoria and disillusionment with democratic government, calls for democracy with leadership increased and found a strong proponent in Sukarno. His *konsepsi* contained the main outline of guided democracy. In place of the elected parliament, which Sukarno dissolved in 1959, he created in 1960 the Gotong Royong Parliament (GRP).[92] By appointing the members of GRP, he laid the foundation for the subordination of the legislature to the executive.

Sukarno's rhetoric and symbolism formed the core of Indonesian politics during the period of guided democracy. His symbolism reinforced the position of the "state" in all matters and discontinued the program of previous democratic governments. The new regime rejected the principle of representative government. Press harassment and the rituals of indoctrination became more frequent. Sukarno's call for a return to "the rails of the revolution" emphasized politics at the expense of economic rationality. Efforts to rehabilitate the economy were abandoned. The destruction of Dutch economic enterprises, overregulation, high deficit spending (coupled with a headlong drop in production), a major reduction in the power and wealth of the Chinese minority, victimization of businessmen in general, galloping inflation, rampant corruption—all soon led to total economic ruin.

Meanwhile the 1958–65 period witnessed the rise and consolidation of authoritarianism.[93] The elected parliament was dissolved, incapacitating the political parties. The enactment of martial law in 1957 extended authoritarianism to the village level. The power of the presidency increased sharply. With the army's appropriation of the management of all nationalized Dutch companies, its coercive power also increased. As with the decline of parliamentary democracy, the consolidation of authoritarianism was facilitated by a number of factors. Sukarno quickly exploited the 1945 constitution, which gave the presidency virtually unlimited power. Since he did not have a party of his own, he cooperated with the army. The convergence and divergence of interests among Sukarno, the PKI, the army, and the *pamong praja* contributed in a complex way to the consolidation of authoritarianism.[94]

The ideology of unfinished revolution propagated by Sukarno and accepted by his allies rendered all opposition antirevolutionary and subject to suppression. To balance the army's power, Sukarno turned to the PKI. He also resorted to ideological manipulation as a device to control the course of politics and obscure the insecurity of his government. For his cultural anchorage, he took up Javanism, which made him a captive of messianic politics. With the economy in serious disarray and no organized political force at his disposal, he fell back on the politics of the "mobilization of meanings."

The most important transformation in the period of guided democracy was the strengthening of the institutions of the state. Of crucial importance in this respect was the consolidation of the armed forces, the army in particular. The introduction of martial law and the expeditious quelling of PRRI "rebellion" greatly enhanced the authority of the army's central command.[95] It quickly secured a pledge of allegiance from regional commanders who had earlier sympathized with the rebels' cause. Revenue from smuggling and nationalized Dutch companies provided the army with the finances to strengthen itself as an institution and appease the material needs of its senior officers. The unprecedented inclusion of 34 armed forces personnel as representatives of the functional group in the 283-member GRP legalized the army as a political force in its own right. In Sukarno's cabinet, representation of the armed forces jumped from two ministers to eleven.[96] These developments reinforced the army's doctrine of dual function, a doctrine based on the army's key role in the national revolution.[97]

Similarly, the army's social base and ideological orientation changed significantly. At the outset, the army's ethnic representation fairly reflected the ethnic composition of the country, and its ideological orientation was strongly Islamic.[98] But after the quelling of regional rebellions, its social base became more Javanese and its ideological orientation shifted toward secularism and the *abangan* strand.[99] In the second half of the 1950s, the army became disillusioned with political parties and ideologies that did not hold the unity and defense of the country as their primary goals.

A parallel development occurred in the bureaucracy. Guided democracy increased the recruitment of apolitical or PNI-oriented *priyayi* into the bureaucracy. Although senior civil servants and those entrusted with high positions in government enterprises were obliged to resign their party affiliations, the barrier between politics and administration disappeared as the political elite were to an extent also dependent on the bureaucracy. With the removal of political supervision, the bureaucracy became more self-centered and less effective.[100]

If the state became stronger, the society became weaker. To increase his control over societal forces, in 1960 Sukarno reduced the number of parties from 25 to 10, grouping them into nationalist (PNI, Partindo, IPKI), Islam (NU, PSII, Perti), Christian (Parkindo, Partai Katolik), and Marxist (PKI, Murba). Soon the parties discovered that under the new regime their existence meant very little. With an appointed parliament, they were powerless. As both the president and the army condemned parliamentary democracy, freedom of expression and party initiatives were suppressed. It would be wrong, however, to argue that the disempowering of the parties was primarily the work of Sukarno and the army, given the parties' inca-

pacity to reach agreement among themselves. PNI was co-opted by Sukarno. To survive, the NU and lesser parties became subservient. Only the
PKI took advantage of the new situation and thrived with the revolutionary symbolism of Sukarno. Indeed, the PKI claimed to have 20 million
members by 1965. Because of its formal acceptance of Sukarno's nationalism, however, the PKI was not able to fully implement its doctrine of
class struggle.[101] Thus, despite its phenomenal growth, the PKI fitted well
in the "flaccid colossus" of guided democracy.

The end of guided democracy was directly related to the limits of Sukarno's politics of "mobilization of meanings." There was an important
difference between the 1958–65 period and the 1918–30 or 1945–49
periods, when such politics was more successful. In the earlier situations,
Indonesia was under colonial rule and the mobilization of all available
cultural and ideological values had one goal: ousting the alien power and
liberating the nation. But even with a common enemy, certain ideological systems cannot coexist in constructive competition. The irreversible
breach between Muslims and communists in Sarekat Islam in 1922 is a
case in point that was to lead to the victimization of Masyumi members in
the Madiun Revolt in 1948 and the massacre of mostly Indonesian communists and others in 1965. In both cases, we have a tragic transformation
of the "mobilization of meanings" into a "contestation of meanings"—
between the Muslims and the communists in particular.

There was another important difference: the symbolic mobilization
during the period of guided democracy was largely confined to Sukarno
and his communist ally. Beginning with the "rediscovery of our revolution," he pounded the country with endless symbolic and ideological ex-
hortations. Manipol-Usdek, Panca Azimat Revolusi, and Jas Merah were
some of his radical formulations.[102] However, in the case of the army on
the one hand and the PKI on the other, what occurred was a mobilization
and subsequently a contestation of real power. Sukarno overlooked or ignored this reality, a mistake for which he and the country were to pay
dearly.

In conclusion, then, both the parliamentary and guided democracy regimes faced serious legitimacy problems. The political elites failed to uphold the ultimate ideals of the nation. The various governments violated
the principles embodied in Pancasila. The theistic principle was undermined by the communists' reentry into national politics. The humanistic
principle was neglected. Economic and political uncertainties brought the
nation's morale to its nadir. The unity principle was violated by divisive
political discourse and practices within the government and without. The
performance of the various governments was poor. Although the democratic governments formally implemented the democratic principle, it was

soon perceived as devoid of meaning and discredited by a sizable section of its own supporters. All parties were finally entrapped by narrow interests. The guided democracy regime's claim to practice a better democracy was negated by its authoritarianism and lack of "the virtue of wisdom in representative consultations." The justice principle was abandoned as efforts at economic recovery as well as rule-based administration faltered amid the political struggle among key groups and the emphasis on the continuation of revolution. This failure was exacerbated by the absence of a competent and independent judiciary and the military's refusal to submit to civilian control.

The inability of the governments in the two regimes to realize the ideals of Pancasila had a great deal to do with the two unstated assumptions underlying the ideology.[103] Political order was fragile at best, but the excessively long campaign period before the 1955 election assumed that political order was unproblematic. Largely absent were the necessary precautions, for instance, to avoid the negative and self-defeating features of such a long campaign. Proponents of the regime seemed oblivious to the lingering dissensions and revolutionary psyche among their compatriots at large. The same can be said of their dealings with foreign companies, domestic interest groups, and paramilitary units. Of similar effect was their determination to live by the words of the constitution and abide by the agreements of the Round Table Conference. All this amounted to an unfortunate commitment to conventional thought and behavior in the face of widespread abnormality and irrationality.[104]

The leaders of the guided democracy understood the situation well and acted accordingly; hence their swift rise to power. But they were unable to control the tide of revolutionary politics and wrongly believed that the nation's economic resources were capable of supporting the many "years of living dangerously." They assumed economic sufficiency. Sukarno stated in 1963: "My feelings and ideas about the economic question are simple, very simple indeed. They can be formulated as follows: If nations who live in a dry and barren desert can solve the problems of their economy, why can't we?"[105] Yet the guided democracy failed to create a *durable* political system, just as the parliamentary democracy fell short of devising a *working* one.

Pancasila and the New Order

Guided democracy collapsed following the abortive coup of September 30, 1965, and strong opposition from the army-led ad hoc coalition of religious leaders, students, and intellectuals. Islamic students and religious

leaders played a major role in mobilizing the masses to oust Sukarno; intellectuals and students made significant contributions in defining the rationale for the new regime. Hence both groups had great expectations. But
the architects of the New Order had their own objectives. Unlike its predecessors, the New Order government did not take political order and
economic sufficiency for granted. In fact, it explicitly recognized their absence and articulated their achievement as its primary goal. As soon as
Sukarno was rendered powerless, the New Order distanced itself from
groups that had strong ideological orientations, including its ad hoc allies,
both for its own benefit and for fear of leading the country into another
tragic impasse. Its principal concern was to establish political stability and
reconstruct the economy.[106]

With the ousting of Sukarno and the destruction of the PKI, the army
emerged as the only effective political force. It further strengthened its
hold on state power by creating a responsive and supportive bureaucracy,
loyal and well-integrated armed forces, a legislature subservient to the executive, a simplified and weakened party system, a powerful presidency,
and a controlled press.[107] To substantiate the superstructural transformation, the New Order centralized the process of decision making at the
top, broadened the scope of executive authority, and increased the government's presence at the lowest levels. These objectives were secured by appointing military officers to key positions in ministries and bureaucratic
departments. The purpose was to facilitate a system of centralized mobilization—and allocation—of state resources.

Turning to the armed forces, Soeharto moved to end old factional divisions. He adopted five measures. Leftist officers and Sukarno loyalists
were dismissed. Leaders locked in conflict with each other were transferred to remote areas or noninfluential civilian positions. The military's
internal institutions were used to solicit constructive suggestions and
criticisms. Loyalists were generously rewarded. The armed forces—now
called ABRI—were reorganized on the principle of unified command under Soeharto's full control.

Soeharto followed Sukarno's practice of executive appointment of
members of the legislature. In 1967 he reached a crucial agreement with
the leaders of the remaining parties. It was now decided that the elections
were to be carried out with a list system that gave Soeharto control over
who could be elected; the membership of parliament was increased from
347 to 460; and the president had the right to appoint one-fifth of the
members of the DPR and three-fifths of the members of the MPR.[108] Since
by the constitution only the MPR could initiate major changes in governance and state structure, the appropriation of at least three-fifths of the
seats in the highest state institution guaranteed government stability and

continuity. These decisions as well as the superstructural transformation were essentially exigent. And yet they molded the character of the New Order and constitute its political format. Based on the politics of distrust, they were valid and justifiable only insofar as they were deployed in the country's political and economic emergency of the 1960s.

Perhaps the most important development in New Order politics was the consolidation in 1969 of hundreds of disparate functional groups, including the civil servants, and their transformation into a single political party: Golkar.[109] Intended to provide an alternative to the seemingly insurmountable divisiveness of the political parties, Golkar was essentially the child of guided democracy, which both Sukarno and the army competed to nurture from 1958 to balance the weight of political parties in the parliament.[110] With the backing of the army, Golkar scored resounding victories in the five general elections under the New Order.

Before the 1967 agreement with political parties, Ali Moertopo and his cohort consistently attacked the political parties for concentrating on ideology rather than programs and for being the main source of political instability.[111] These attacks were orchestrated by the founders of the New Order to check the power of the people's representatives in the legislature. Beginning in 1970, Soeharto urged the merger of the ten parties into two groups: the Group for Democracy and Development and the Group for Unity and Development.[112] With increasing pressure from the government and the harsh treatment they received from the military and its civilian associates in the 1971 election, the ten parties finally merged in 1973 into two parties, PPP and PDI. With the prerogative to appoint significant numbers of the DPR and MPR members, the establishment of Golkar, and the neutralization of political parties, coupled with the use of coercion when necessary, the New Order was assured of at least a four-fifths majority in the MPR.

Under the New Order, the power of the presidency increased dramatically. Two years after the discreet ouster of Sukarno in 1966, Soeharto was sworn in as president. With the help of his own think tank he identified critical areas to be addressed, allocating tasks to each member of his personal staff at the expense of his own cabinet members and the strategic institution at army headquarters (MBAD). Soon after the attempted coup in 1965 he had created Kopkamtib—a special body to uproot the remnants of communism and control demonstrations or possible insurgencies.[113]

With the necessary legal powers and full control of strategic groups, Soeharto's next move was to acquire a financial base. Nonbudgetary funds were soon extracted from lucrative state enterprises (such as Pertamina and Bulog),[114] from monopolies farmed out, following the colonial practice, primarily to Chinese businessmen, and from highly taxed pilgrimages to Mecca. Above all the massive inflow of foreign capital and the oil boom accompanying the rise of the New Order flooded the presidential office with virtually unlimited funds. Soeharto easily ousted his rivals, co-opted prospective troublemakers, and distributed presidential favors from nonbudgetary funds like Banpres and Inpres throughout the country,[115] thus expanding his patronage up and down the social ladder.

With respect to the press, the New Order took advantage of both the colonial tradition and the practice of guided democracy. Unacceptable coverage, condemned for instigating instability, was suppressed. The government had the authority to close down any periodical or ban any publication—and indeed did so on many occasions—without having to go to court. Editors and publishers were forced to practice self-censorship. The result was a severely controlled press that gave wide coverage to government pronouncements and policies, but little else. On top of all this, the New Order stressed the primacy of Pancasila as the national ideology and ruled that it should be the only foundation of all political and social organizations (*asas tunggal*). No other ideology, including Islam, was allowed to serve as the basis of political organization. Thus while the government claimed to uphold Pancasila democracy, it adhered only to a fragment of Pancasila and some semblance of democracy.

This tight control of society enabled the New Order to formulate and implement economic policies without opposition. The severity of economic conditions led the government to adopt a judicious mix of controlled, open-door, and liberal policies. Fearing social unrest, the government fixed the prices of daily necessities. The open-door policy was designed to secure large amounts of foreign capital to stem the tide of inflation and revive the economy. The liberal approach was introduced to lure domestic and foreign investors to redress the headlong drop in productivity. With this combination of policies, the New Order achieved its major economic objectives. Productivity increased sharply and self-sufficiency in rice was achieved in 1984. The national economy grew an average of 7 percent a year from 1969 to the 1980s. Even more amazing was the government's ability to overcome the economic crisis despite the Pertamina debacle in the 1970s and the fall of oil prices in 1982.

In spite of this outstanding achievement in both political stability and economic growth, the basic problem of legitimacy remained. The elimination of the communists and the silencing of vocal Islamic modernists left the army as the primary political force. Yet statism supported by the coalition of the military, the civilian bureaucracy, and Golkar was not all that survived in the New Order. Nationalism or republicanism became the focal point for the coalescence of the interests of various groups, including

the bulk of Indonesian Islam. With the liberalization of the economy, capitalism became a significant force as well. Politics and economics in the
New Order have been influenced by the interaction of these three streams.
A closer look at each will reveal the intricacy of political-economic development in contemporary Indonesia and show how it contributes to the
legitimacy dilemma of the New Order.

As we have seen, the New Order inherited and then further reinforced
statism. This process was strongly reflected in the protracted practice of
discretionary controls in fixing prices, controlling supplies of fertilizer and
kerosene, setting licensing arrangements for imported goods, and imposing arbitrary ceilings on bank credits.[116] Economic planning and programs
were prepared by a handful of economists and powerful military bureaucrats. This concentration of political and economic power in the hands of
a few enabled development programs to move fast. But it also bred favoritism, excessive corruption, and executive-conglomerate collusion to the
detriment of the government's own concerns over distributive justice. The
gap between socioeconomic groups and between the eastern and western
parts of the country widened inordinately.

While the New Order welcomed export-oriented industrialization, it
maintained political control over the domestic market.[117] Deregulation
during the past five years largely benefited the owners of capital. The goal
of the New Order appears to be an integrated industrial economy in which
political-bureaucratic power is closely allied with private domestic capital.[118] This objective underlies the much-coveted dream of Indonesia Inc.
and the appetite for high-tech industries.

Yet concentration of power in the government, particularly in the chief
executive, and the dynamics of industrialization and capitalism have had
unanticipated effects. The introduction of modern agricultural equipment,
the abandonment of sharecropping, the discontinuation of the old system
of tenancy, and the renting of smallholdings by large private estates have
multiplied the number of landless peasants, displaced labor, and changed
the economic situation in the countryside.[119] Geertz's famous "agricultural involution" has in general become a thing of the past. In big cities,
particularly in Jakarta and the surrounding areas, industrial plants have
mushroomed with capital-intensive projects, buildings, and golf courses.
This sudden growth has sharpened income inequalities. The steep increases in land prices have multiplied the cases of land disputes and led to
forceful evictions of the poor.

Economic growth under the New Order has reinforced the economic
dualism of the colonial era—prosperity and economic advancement for
the foreign/modern sector and retardation or extinction for the indige-
nous/traditional sector. The "Sadli principle" of Bappenas,[120] and with it

the massive inflow of capital, exacerbated this dualism. The same principle encouraged domestic capital formation from the early 1970s. The decline in state economic power in the early 1980s due to the oil glut led to a heavier reliance on the now transformed and much bigger private sector—a shift that gave the latter greater leverage on the government. This private sector forced the government to deregulate the state-capital relationship and privatize state enterprises.[121]

With the convergence of the interests of statism and capitalism, not much was left for Indonesia's indigenous people. Economic nationalists and democrats were confronted with formidable challenges. An increasing number of *pribumi* entrepreneurs in rural and urban areas were forced to close their small businesses. If the economic fortunes of the *pribumi* were quickly declining, those of the non-*pribumi* were rapidly ascending. Citing figures reminiscent of Djojohadikusumo in 1936, an economist has calculated that in 1993 about 1 percent of the population secured 80 percent of the national income whereas the remaining 99 percent at the bottom and middle levels obtained only 20 percent.[122] Clearly this has been a major setback for indigenous people.

What especially embitters the *pribumi* is that statism and capitalism have directly benefited the Indonesian Chinese at the *pribumi*'s expense. Lucrative projects, licenses, monopolies, and megacredits—most of which are scandalous—as well as expensive malls, preferred recreation sites, and exclusive residential areas have become virtually exclusive privileges of the non-*pribumi* and, to a lesser extent, the foreigners, provoking the kind of spiteful sense of day-to-day deprivation that galvanized the Indonesian *pergerakan* during the first decades of the twentieth century. This deterioration in the position of native Indonesians has led to numerous protests, petitions, demonstrations, riots, and instances of popular resistance—some of them exacting high death tolls. Although this resistance has been intermittent, it has nonetheless been broad-ranging and consistent, encompassing rural and urban areas, the poor and the better off, the less- and the well-educated, religious leaders, both Islamic and Christian, certain statesmen, retired generals, elements of the civilian bureaucracy, nongovernmental organizations, and university students.

The year 1974 witnessed major student unrest in Jakarta and a major uprising by the fishing community at Muncar, East Java. This resistance was followed by another major anti-Soeharto student movement in Bandung in 1978; the Petisi 50 in 1980;[123] the Banteng riot and Priok uprising in 1984; the Kedungombo and Lampung resistances in 1989–90; the rather muted challenge of Forum Demokrasi in 1991; the petition of the Forum for the Purification of People's Sovereignty in 1992; the armed resistances in Aceh, Irian Jaya, and East Timor and numerous strikes in the country's industrial quarters over the years; a strong statement of concern from the Petisi 50 delivered to the chairman and members of the MPR on February 15, 1993; farmers' resistance in West Java and Madura, ruthlessly suppressed in 1993; and a big labor demonstration that cost the life of a local Chinese businessman in Medan in 1994.

The government has deployed a combination of measures to counter social unrest, ranging from persuasion and co-optation to the use of naked force and heavy punishment. Important policy changes, designed largely to provide for the economic share of native Indonesians, did follow the major student unrest of 1974. Given the structure of Indonesia's economy and the ineffectiveness of the bureaucracy, however, these changes and others were hardly consistent and were never effectively carried out. Thus the collusion between statism and capitalism that further expanded in the wake of the oil boom went on unchecked.

The economic and political marginalization of native Indonesians continued. Many began to feel the urgency of this situation as their sense of inordinate deprivation increasingly turned into a sense of betrayal of the nation's ideals. This urgency was reflected by Sritua Arief:

It is hardly exaggerating to suggest that should this situation continue without a fundamental correction, Indonesia would likely retain its stamp as *de natie van koelies.* . . . Likewise, it is hardly exaggerating to suggest that the foreign and non-*pribumi* domination of the private sector on which the bulk of Indonesians depend for their living would give birth to a feeling of superiority and disparagement of the minority toward the majority. Two kinds of psychological state would visit the majority—an inferiority complex and an urge to brutally destroy the stifling conditions. Both would be fatal to the life of the people and the state.[124]

Arief's recovery of the pejorative colonial label *de natie van koelies* evinces the anguish that many Indonesians feel because their nation was in fact founded to overcome that very label. Perhaps the anguish was rooted too in the knowledge that the bulk of the Indonesian Chinese were an integral part of the colonial exploitive scheme. For the majority of Indonesians, therefore, their present political-economic position is a negation of their cherished ideals. Once again they are confronted with the big question of the meaningfulness of their national politics.

Certainly the New Order has been single-minded in its determination to establish political stability and pursue economic growth. In view of the serious mistakes committed by earlier governments, this determination was warranted. But the present government seems to emphasize stability and development as the ultimate goals rather than the basis for achieving the ideals embodied in Pancasila. In the name of political stability and economic development, the New Order has systematically violated Pancasila's humanitarian, democratic, and justice principles. Moreover, unless the New Order checks the serious political and economic marginalization of native Indonesians, it will sooner or later threaten the unity of the nation and country and is thus on the brink of violating the third principle as well.

The violation of three of the nation's ideals may not be as serious as the failure of earlier governments to maintain political order and rehabilitate the economy. Perhaps nothing could be worse than the regional rebellions of the 1950s, the collapse of the economy during the early 1960s, and the draconian massacre of 1965. The big difference, however, is that while most Indonesians today do not fear impending tragedy, they increasingly feel that the nation is abandoning its original ideals at an accelerating speed. As these violations were committed to guarantee the perpetuation of the army-led regime, they have inevitably stigmatized the army, which for over two decades has claimed to be faithful to Pancasila. Although all the country's major political groups have in one way or another shared in violating the nation's ultimate ideals, the criticisms cited here are now more and more directed at Soeharto and ABRI.

The Legitimacy Dilemma: Crisis or Solution?

The New Order confronts a threefold dilemma: between economic growth and distribution, between political stability and participation, and between apparent and substantive democracy. While this dilemma is characteristic of many developing countries, in Indonesia it has the potential to unravel the nation. Rooted as it is in history, the New Order's dilemma should always be read against the dilemmas faced by the two predecessor regimes. The present government's goals of political stability and economic growth are a direct result of the inability of parliamentary democracy to create a working political system *and* a delivering economy and the failure of guided democracy to build the economy *and* a durable political system. All the rest follows from this.

Yet given their respective situations, aspirations, and limitations, the primary goals of the first two regimes were apt. The parliamentary democracy was committed to restoring normalcy and the rule of law, but the revolutionary situation overwhelmed it. With an eye on the failure of its predecessor, the guided democracy reinvoked the spirit of the revolution, but put too much emphasis on it. Neglect of the economy and the conflicting understanding of "revolution" among its principal players brought about its collapse.[125] The unfortunate end of both regimes resulted not from wrong intentions but from wrong assumptions. This may also prove to be the case with the New Order. If it intends to preserve its positive achievements and to bequeath a solid foundation to the republic, the New Order should correct its assumption that all the country needs is political stability and economic growth, where "stability" and "growth" are deprived of the historical intention of, and the politically meaningful in, the nation.

Despite the serious legitimacy dilemma confronting the New Order, a major political crisis seems unlikely for a number of reasons. First, the political system is becoming, if inconsistently, more tolerant of free expression. Further, the middle class is still too small and dependent, thanks to the collusion of statism and capitalism, to contest the status quo and function as a reliable agent of democratization. Second, the two most likely political contenders—the Indonesian military and political Islam—are unlikely to challenge the present government overtly. Soeharto has removed General Benny Moerdani, a potential challenger to his position, and installed his own appointees to key army posts, including the intelligence service.[126] Moreover, a significant section in the military still believes that ABRI is the principal defender of the nation's unity and stability. With respect to the perpetuation of Soeharto's administration, Indonesian Islam is divided between ICMI under Minister Habibie and Abdurrahman Wahid, the chairman of NU.[127] Soeharto appears to be backing ICMI, but this does not necessarily mean his support is limited among the *pesantren* leaders. Besides, we still need to assess Muhammadiyah's position on this issue.

Third and perhaps most significant is a combination of psychological, cultural, and historical factors. Psychologically, people have not completely forgotten the instability of the democratic period and the tragic consequences of 1965. Culturally, most followers of Islam and, overlappingly, most Javanese seem to prefer moderation in politics. Historically, attempts at rebellions and putsches have been crushed, despite the frequency of such attempts, particularly in the 1950s when the state was weakest. Finally, Soeharto with a strong state at his command has begun to address, again inconsistently, some of the problems.

Having said that, one still must underscore the illegitimacy of the New Order. Its political goals were valid in the 1960s in light of the state of emergency surrounding Indonesia's politics and economy. But this situation has long been overcome. The monopoly of political power stems from distrust of the people and is therefore illegitimate. Not only does it violate the ideals of the republic, but it is laden with potential crisis. The monopoly of political power has been translated into an even more contentious monopoly in the economic sphere. The sharp and increasingly perilous contradictions provide fertile ground for a violent crisis. The huge foreign debt, flagrant inconsistencies in policies and practices, collusions leading to some fifty cases of megascandals involving state banks, and the inordinate gap between the *pribumi* and the non-*pribumi* as well as between the poor and the rich could easily spark a political catastrophe.

Political succession, which has to take place sometime soon, could trigger a political crisis. Try Sutrisno, the newly appointed vice president, holds significant advantages. He was Soeharto's adjutant and was endorsed by ABRI for the vice presidency. He is also a Javanese and on good terms with the Islamic community. But many doubt his political leadership. With Soeharto's term in office approaching its actuarial limit and perhaps also the limit of Indonesians' political tolerance, succession will become critical.

Anticipation of a succession crisis is based on two practical considerations. First, the tradition of constitutionality is weak in independent Indonesia. The New Order, which claims to be the defender of the 1945 constitution, has in fact violated it at several important points. Second, the stakes in the politics of succession have become very high, and the collusion of the monopolists in the economy and in politics has multiplied them. As the economic-political monopoly extends its reach and power, the betrayal of the nation's original ideals will soon be ultimate and irreversible. And as more and more Indonesians realize this, considerations about moderation in culture, the memory of the 1950s and 1960s, and the failure of past rebellions will become secondary.

To preclude the possibility of another political tragedy, both the state and the society must devise a firm political foundation upon which the republic can stand rather than return the nation to the trauma of the 1960s. There are four broad guidelines for achieving this. First, contending groups in Indonesia must promote civility and cohesiveness among themselves and then reassert their republican consensus on ideals. Each major contender in the spheres of politics and the economy must extend itself beyond its parochial camp. The New Order's politics of distrust must be discontinued. Civilian and democratic forces, particularly from among Muslims, Christians, and Chinese, must prove they are capable of constructive cooperation. The Chinese in the forefront of the business sector must learn to support the ideals of the republic rather than the powers that be.

Second, Indonesians should establish genuine democratic institutions and practices. The political system should be based on the principle of government of the people, by the people, and for the people through proper elections and genuine representation. For this to happen the ambiguous articles in the 1945 constitution should be freed from the New Order's exigent reading or, better still, be amended to ensure that sovereignty indeed resides with the people. There should be freedom of expression and freedom of association. As such, the politics of depoliticization must end. There should also be a fixed limit to presidential terms in office. ABRI needs to readjust the doctrine and practices of dual function: its representation in DPR and MPR should be eventually phased out. In short, the present government will have to abandon its political monopoly and its exigent character, both of which have become markedly anachronistic over the past fifteen years.

Third, both the state and the society need to take the principle of clean government seriously. Fairness and accountability should be the rule in the bureaucracy itself, in extrabureaucratic institutions, and in development projects using public funds. The military should stop its business activities. Those involved in collusive practices should be punished severely. Clean government means cultivating the integrity of judiciary institutions and releasing them from continual interference by the executive branch.

Finally, distributive justice should be made tangible by adopting an economic policy that puts growth and fair distribution in one package. Economic equalization must become part of every development plan. To achieve this, the government needs to introduce regional autonomy so that regions contributing significantly to national economic growth receive fair benefits in return. Moreover, lucrative licenses, economic facilities, and development projects should be deployed in such a way that both economic growth and economic equity are simultaneously achieved. This policy implies slower growth but ensures a much better economic and political situation in the long run. This will be an arduous task for the government, but given the magnitude of the danger the nation is now facing, it looks like the only option.

The sequence of these steps is all-important. No democracy is possible without trust among contending political groups. Clean government is impossible without democratic practices that are tempered by civility. Economic equality is impossible without nationwide trust and clean government. But to follow these guidelines would inevitably mean to undo the New Order. Clifford Geertz's "state manqué" is still very much with us.

10

Vietnam

The Changing Models of Legitimation

THAVEEPORN VASAVAKUL

DURING the 1980s, communist regimes in Eastern Europe and the Soviet Union experienced a crisis of legitimacy in the eyes of certain sectors of the public as well as a crisis of political leadership that culminated in the collapse of communism as a state ideology. During the same period, despite the political and ideological debacles in the socialist bloc and chronic economic difficulties at home, socialist Vietnam witnessed comparatively small-scale political challenges at both leadership and public levels. Furthermore, compared with its Southeast Asian neighbors, Vietnam did not undergo the political upheavals experienced in Thailand (1973, 1976, and 1992), the Philippines (1972 and 1986), and Burma (1962 and 1988). Vietnam's sustained stability suggests that the Vietnamese leadership and the socialist regime have always enjoyed a certain degree of legitimacy. This chapter explores the models of political legitimation in socialist Vietnam, focusing on the period from the August uprising of 1945 to the 1989–91 crisis in the socialist bloc and the Seventh National Congress of the Vietnamese Communist Party in 1991.

The literature in English on post-1945 Vietnam rarely discusses the legitimacy of the socialist regime. This is not surprising, however, given the Cold War context in which Vietnam scholarship developed. Scholars who disapproved of American involvement in Vietnam accorded legitimacy to the Hanoi government, while those who supported American intervention and sympathized with the anticommunist Saigon government questioned the legitimacy of the Hanoi government on the grounds of its communist ideology.

There are exceptions, however. A number of scholars have emphasized the role of tradition in buttressing Marxism in the eyes of Vietnamese leaders and the public. Nguyen Khac Vien, a French-educated Vietnamese intellectual-turned-communist, argues that Vietnamese Confucians viewed Marxism as similar to Confucianism in that both "concentrated man's thoughts on political and social problems" and "considered the highest aim of man to be the fulfillment of his social obligations."[1] William Duiker also argues that Marxism attracted followers in Vietnam because of its similarities with Confucianism: the belief in one truth embodied in quasi-sacred texts; the concept of an anointed elite trained in an all-embracing doctrine with responsibility for leading the broad masses; the stress on personal ethics and selfless service to society; the subordination of the individual to the community; the belief that pursuit of material wealth should be firmly subordinated to social goals; and the conviction that human nature is malleable and can be improved through corrective action.[2]

Paul Mus and John McAlister, in their discussion of the 1945 Vietnamese revolution, argue that this social and political revolution "was not merely imposed from the top down but had local antecedents that gave it real roots in the countryside." These writers conclude: "Because the Communists have gone beyond the partial political programs of their competitors and tried determinedly, though not always successfully, to grapple with the symbols and idiom of traditionalist politics, they have had the most effective revolutionary movement in Vietnam."[3]

Stephen Young, however, in examining reunified Vietnam, argues that Hanoi lacks legitimacy because the goals and aims of the Vietnamese Communist Party cannot be affirmed by the values held by most Vietnamese. Young contends that "Vietnamese invest true authority with those who possess the quality of *uy tin* (moral legitimacy), consisting of *tai* (ability), *duc* (virtue), and *so* (destiny)."[4] According to Young, the "core philosophic rationalization of the Vietnamese cultural pattern is the notion of *phuc duc*, an amalgam of Buddhist and Confucian notions, with pre-Confucian origins, stressing individualism and private economic incentive in the context of family."[5] He thus concludes that "a Vietnamese leader who does not promote *phuc duc* inhibits the people from doing what they most want to do in that inner part of their being by which they identify themselves as 'Vietnamese.' Such a leader has no *duc* and therefore, no *uy tin*."[6]

Since legitimacy involves belief in the moral right of rulers to rule, these writings provide useful insights into the basis of the Vietnamese socialist regime's legitimacy. They fall short, however, in explaining political legitimacy in socialist Vietnam in the wake of the collapse of socialism. If Vien is correct, what then accounts for the policy of political and economic renovation (*doi moi*) adopted in 1986? If Mus and McAlister are correct in arguing that there is a compatibility between the values held by the Vietnamese socialist leadership and the society, how does one explain the postreunification economic and popular resistance to the Hanoi government in the Mekong delta? And if Young's argument that the goals and aims of the Vietnamese leadership departed from the values of almost all Vietnamese is right, how can one explain the comparative success of the North Vietnamese government in mobilizing popular support in both North and South Vietnam and achieving its reunification goal? If socialist collectivism was so alien, as Young suggests, why did provincial party cadres and even northern Vietnamese rural producers oppose complete land privatization in the wake of the Seventh Party Congress?

The inadequacies of the works just cited stem from their adherence to four premises. First is the notion that Vietnamese "tradition" is the main, if not the sole, factor in the consideration of political legitimacy. This premise runs into a number of difficulties. For example, Vietnam did not become a unified country under one central government until the early nineteenth century. Regionalism was more common and was exacerbated by the French division of Eastern Indochina into Tonkin, Annam, and Cochin China. Thus one "tradition" to be reckoned with is that of regionalism and patriotism, but not "nationalism." The logic of this tradition will be to turn to anything except a modern nation-state. Second, these writings assume that there is one Vietnamese tradition shared by all Vietnamese, especially all Vietnamese peasants. Recent studies on Vietnamese culture question this generalization. David Marr, for example, in discussing the resurgence of Vietnamese "tradition" between 1925 and 1945, implicitly points to diverse strands and interpretations of tradition.[7] Ho Hue Tam Tai's and Jayne Werner's studies on the Hoa Hao and the Cao Dai sects present a complex cultural picture of the Mekong River delta.[8] James Scott's "moral economy" of the peasantry in the Red River delta and Samuel Popkin's "rational" peasantry in the Mekong delta illustrate rural populations' diverse economic ethics, stemming from such factors as settlement patterns and differing ecologies; while these authors generalize about peasants' economic thinking, their writings actually serve to caution us against making such generalizations.[9] Third, these writings assume that the ideologies of the leadership and those of the society are separate. This premise ignores the interpenetration between what Tran Quoc Vuong, a Hanoi archaeologist and historian, calls "popular culture" and "high culture." Vuong argues that throughout Vietnamese history there existed a process of interaction between village-based and officially sanctioned cultures.[10] Fourth, these writings assume that legitimacy is determined by the degree of compatibility or incompatibility between the values held by the leadership and those held by the society. This premise restricts the study of legitimacy to an either/or argument without taking into consideration the many-faceted process of legitimation.

In analyzing political legitimacy in socialist Vietnam, one can instead put forth the following modified premises. First, modern, nontraditional ideologies are the basis of regime legitimacy. Second, there is no single Vietnamese tradition, no single Vietnamese people, and no single Vietnamese peasantry: Vietnamese "traditional" values vary from region to region, even from village to village. Third, the concept of "Vietnamese tradition" itself may be a construct created by power holders to legitimize their control of political authority.[11] The invention of "tradition" involves the selection of a wide range of "traditional" values to form *the* tradition, as well as the connection of this tradition with the official ideology to legitimize the hegemonic view. Fourth, the quality of legitimacy is determined not only by the proportionate increase or decrease of the compatibility or incompatibility of values held among the leadership or between the leadership and the society but also by the ability of the power holders to neutralize, accommodate, and co-opt conflicting values and traditions.

This exploration of political legitimation in Vietnam is divided into three parts. The first part considers the legitimation model in the Democratic Republic of Vietnam (DRV) from 1945 to 1975. The second part examines the legitimacy crisis of this model in reunified Vietnam between 1975 and 1985. The last part analyzes the legitimation model in the era of renovation, which officially began in 1986. In each section we shall examine how modern ideologies were connected with selected traditions, how the new ideology buttressed legitimacy of the Vietnamese state socialist system both at leadership and public levels, and how and why the model of legitimation changed over time.

The DRV Model: 1945–75

Scholars studying the Vietnamese communist movement tend to highlight either the goal of national independence or the goal of socialist revolution as the main factor in legitimizing the party's claim to leadership. Huynh Kim Khanh, for example, argues that the failure of the Indochinese Communist Party to expand its mass base between 1930 and 1941 stemmed from the party's blind adherence to the Comintern's class-against-class revolutionary strategy under the leadership of the proletariat.[12] Ken Post, on the other hand, argues that it was the class-against-class policy, rather than nationalism, that provided the party with a much needed mass base and brought about its eventual victory in 1975.[13]

Goal Rationality

The crucial point is not which goal was strategically more useful in buttressing the legitimacy of the Vietnamese communist/nationalist movement prior to 1975, but whether, from the leadership's perspective, the goal of national independence and reunification could be achieved without capitalizing on the ideology of socialism. In "The Path That Led Me to Leninism," written in 1960 for the Soviet review *Problems of the East*, Ho Chi Minh stated: "At first, it was patriotism (*chu nghia yeu nuoc*), not yet communism (*chu nghia cong san*), which led me to have confidence in Lenin, in the Third International."[14] Ho reminisced that when he observed the heated discussions in the branches of the French Socialist Party in 1920, he was most concerned with the question of "which International sides with the peoples of colonial countries?"[15] While these statements presumably described how Ho justified his affiliation with communism in the 1920s, they were also relevant in highlighting the symbiotic relationship between nationalism and communism prior to 1975.

From the very beginning, Nguyen Ai Quoc/Ho Chi Minh assigned the Vietnamese communist movement the task of liberating Vietnam from French colonialism. In founding the Vietnamese Revolutionary Youth Association (Thanh Nien) in 1925 and in unifying communist factions in Tonkin, Annam, and Cochin China under the banner of the Vietnamese Communist Party in 1930, Nguyen Ai Quoc emphasized that their main task was to struggle for national independence and their main strategy was to unite all forces to serve this cause. As Huynh Kim Khanh points out, the Nguyen Ai Quoc revolutionary line was overridden by the Comintern line, which advocated the goals of proletarian revolution and world revolution, to be achieved through a class-against-class strategy. It was not until 1941 when Nguyen Ai Quoc returned to Vietnam as Ho Chi Minh that the national liberation revolution (*cach mang giai phong dan toc*) again received priority. The Eighth Plenum of the Indochinese Communist Party set up the League for the Independence of Vietnam (Viet Nam Doc Lap Dong Minh), or Viet Minh, consisting of members from different social groups.[16]

Yet the Vietnamese nationalist movement could not have won independence without capitalizing on the ideology of socialism. In the first place, the movement gained both ideological and material support from the socialist camp. As Khanh argues, the Indochinese Communist Party could not have survived successive French suppressions had it not exploited Leninist organizational tactics. The Vietnamese nationalist movement, after 1945, could not have consolidated its newly won independence without reviving the ideology of socialism that the Viet Minh had shelved. During the 1945–46 years, Ho's diplomatic efforts to secure recognition from the United States and the West failed.[17] France, with the assistance of Britain and the Kuomintang Chinese, returned to Cochin China and Tonkin and, with indirect assistance from the United States, was determined to fight the Viet Minh.

Only the People's Republic of China and the Soviet bloc countries recognized the DRV state and the Ho Chi Minh government as legitimate (officially in 1950). After 1954, when Vietnam was partitioned and the United States intervened to support noncommunist South Vietnam, the socialist connection helped buttress the legitimacy of the DRV as a state as well as that of the Communist Party as the nationalist leader. In the 1960s, the Vietnamese leadership employed the language of proletarian internationalism to solicit support for its nationalist cause and for development programs from its socialist allies.[18] Integrated into the socialist bloc when the Soviet policy toward the United States vacillated between peaceful coexistence and détente and the Sino-Soviet split became permanent, the DRV leadership nonetheless realized that its allies' foreign policy and support were conditioned by their own "national interests," which might or might not agree with what the DRV wished. The leadership thus was forced to retain an independent position in order to advance national reunification objectives, one of the goals on which its claim for legitimacy was based.

Furthermore, from the leadership's perspective, the party could not have gained the enthusiastic support for the national liberation war and could not have tapped rural resources for state-building efforts had it not advocated a socialist revolution. In 1952, Ho Chi Minh asserted that mass mobilization campaigns for rent reduction were justified because poor peasants were sacrificing for the war. Thus, beginning in 1953, the leadership launched mass mobilization campaigns for rent reduction and land reform to unleash peasant support for the last stage of the war of resistance.[19] After 1958, it moved to transform the relations of production in the countryside; it considered agricultural cooperativization not only a means to improve socioeconomic conditions but also a means to reorganize the state-society relationship and a precondition for state building through socialist industrialization. Yet nationalism modified the party's class-against-class policy, downplaying the role of class antagonism in cooperativization campaigns. Agricultural cooperativization and industrialization—the epitome of the Stalinist model of development—strengthened the DRV state in competing politically and militarily with the U.S.-backed Saigon government.

The twin goals of national independence and reunification justified, and were buttressed by, the leadership's advocacy of socialism and the

building of the state socialist system. The twin goals of national liberation
and socialist egalitarianism underscored the legitimacy of the Vietnamese
communist movement and granted it popular support, both in the North
and in the South. These goals became the party's ideological weapons in
competing with noncommunist political organizations under French colonialism, the French-backed State of Vietnam, and finally the U.S.-backed
South Vietnamese governments.

Party and State Authority

After the declaration of independence in 1945, the Indochinese Communist Party dissolved itself in order to appease noncommunist elements.
Reemerging in 1951 at the Second Party Congress, it was renamed Dang
Lao Dong Viet Nam (Vietnam Labor Party). The Lao Dong Party exercised political power by appointing its own rank-and-file to fill the offices
of state apparatuses, representative institutions, and mass organizations.
Although party leaders perceived national reunification and socialist revolution as their goals, they disagreed over intermediate goals and implementation strategies. Unlike the organized party in other socialist countries, however, the Lao Dong Party suffered neither major purges as in the
Soviet Union under Stalin nor the destructive polarization and succession
struggle experienced by the party in China. The DRV state was never exposed to attacks such as those by Mao in China during the Cultural Revolution; on the other hand, it never received the complete authority granted
the Soviet state during Stalin's rule. The party's monopoly of political
power was sustained by collective leadership and the claim to moral and
intellectual leadership.

The stability of the Lao Dong Party was sustained, first and foremost,
by its early shift of the basis for legitimacy from the personal authority of
Ho Chi Minh to collective leadership. While charismatic authority functioned as the basis of Stalin's government until his death, and the basis of
the CPC's control until Mao's death, in the DRV it was superseded by the
"collective leadership" system that was put in place just after the August
revolution and institutionalized at the Third Party Congress in 1960.[20]
"Collective leadership" refers to the decision-making process within the
party in which high-ranking members, through bargains and compromises on goal priorities, achieved unanimity in endorsing policy guidelines
and carried collective responsibility for their consequences. It was this
unity of leadership that sustained the legitimacy of the party among both
the political elite and the rank-and-file.

Three principles underscored the Lao Dong Party's collective leadership concept. The first principle was the maintenance of factional repre-

sentation in the Politburo and regional and ethnic representation in the Central Committee. Ho Chi Minh introduced this principle in his handling of the party leaders who committed errors during the last wave of land reform in 1956. While demoting Truong Chinh from the position of secretary-general, Ho kept him in the Politburo and, in 1958, appointed him vice prime minister. At the Third Party Congress in 1960, Truong Chinh was appointed chairman of the National Assembly. Ho's move set a precedent for the inclusion of leaders with different policy orientations at the senior leadership level. The second principle that underlined the collective leadership system was bargaining and compromise on policies and implementation strategies.[21] The results of the process were synthetic policies and implementation strategies. The third principle was power sharing among key personalities and political institutions. Nobody except Ho exercised control of more than one political institution.[22] These three principles, by preventing a monopoly of power by one person and averting political polarization, fostered unity and consensus among the leadership. These principles were confined, however, to the senior leadership level.

The party justified its monopoly of political power on the grounds of its moral and intellectual leadership. As early as 1947, Ho Chi Minh put forth the following five revolutionary ethics (*dao duc cach mang*): humanity (*nhan*), a sense of duty (*nghia*), knowledge (*tri*), courage (*dung*), and integrity (*liem*).[23] Emphasizing the need to assist comrades and compatriots, to reject personal preoccupation, to know how to reason, to endure suffering, and to relinquish aspirations to wealth, Ho warned that "a revolutionary lacking morality will never accomplish his role of leading the people."[24] To ensure this moral superiority, the Vietnamese leadership relied heavily on campaigns such as ideological rectification, criticism, and self-criticism to periodically rejuvenate party/state cadres. Nguyen Khac Vien, as noted earlier, wrote on various occasions that party teachings on revolutionary ethics were drawn from Confucian teachings. The place of "Confucian tradition" in the legitimation of the party should not be exaggerated, however. Under the Vietnamese state socialist system, the party underscored the self-perfecting and self-improving morality of cadres because there was no alternative mechanism through which the populace could control or impeach power holders.

Thus the legitimacy of the party and the state rested on unity through collective leadership and on the party's claim to moral and intellectual superiority. These principles explain why the party's authority was legitimate in the eyes of Politburo members, Central Committee members, and party cadres and why, despite disagreements, there was not an overt leadership conflict, which would have resulted in the collapse of the party.

Legitimation at the Societal Level

In 1945 the party leadership entered into a compact with the Vietnamese peasantry, which constituted 90 percent of the population.[25] Ho Chi Minh was well aware that for the majority of the rural population, the language of modern nationalism and socialism required translation. Ho himself was particularly adept at employing lay language, casting abstract concepts in the vocabulary of folk poems or giving traditional sayings new meanings.[26] Ho evoked positive Vietnamese "traditional culture" to refute what he considered negative Confucian teachings and used international examples—modernity so to speak—to buttress or criticize popular wisdom.[27]

Ho linked nationalism (literally *chu nghia ai quoc* or *chu nghia dan toc*) with traditional Vietnamese patriotic spirit (*tinh than yeu nuoc*). Since North Vietnam was the cradle of premodern Vietnam's resistance against invasion from the North, its villages worshiped local deities, some of which were symbols of heroic and patriotic engagements in the defense of the fatherland. To energize the resistance to French colonialism, Ho evoked the memory of resistance against the Chinese invasion and the Vietnamese fighting spirit (*tinh than dau tranh*).[28] He called the Trung sisters, Lady Trieu, Tran Hung Dao, Le Loi, and Quang Trung, all of whom fought Chinese invasion, "*anh hung dan toc,*" or national heroes. According to Ho, they were symbols of *dan toc anh hung*, a "heroic nation."[29] During the political and military confrontation with the United States (1954–73), Ho proclaimed that nothing was more precious than independence and freedom (*khong co gi qui hon doc lap tu do*). In his last will and testament (*di chuc*), which was read to the public on September 10, 1969, a week after his death, Ho asked for his compatriots' determination to fight against the United States until Vietnam achieved complete victory.[30] In discussing socialism, Ho avoided complex Marxist-Leninist doctrines; he defined socialism as a system in which the Vietnamese would "have enough food to eat and enough clothes to wear in cold weather" (*an no mac am*), a system in which there was no human exploitation (*che do nguoi boc lot nguoi*).

The state-party-peasantry relationship developed in distinct phases: the Viet Minh phase (1941–51), the socialist land revolution phase (1953–57), the agricultural collectivization phase (1958–65), and the American War period (1965–73). During each phase, the leadership's policy toward the rural population defined and redefined the meaning of legitimacy, laying the foundation for future legitimation. During the first phase, the 1941–51 years, the Viet Minh government, adhering to the united front

strategy, invited and did in fact receive support from all peasants. Prior to
1953, it had adopted a reformist land strategy because most landowners,
especially the medium and small landlords, had supported the war effort.[31]
As a result, the Viet Minh government was able to sustain the resistance
effort during the "isolated national revolution" period from 1946 to 1949
when the Chinese Red Army reached the Vietnamese border.

During the last stage of the War of Resistance, however, beginning in
1951, the party changed its alliance policy by moving closer to the land-
poor and landless strata of the peasantry. During this phase, which lasted
from 1953 to 1957, the Vietnamese communist movement linked the legitimacy of the nation-state with the legitimacy of socialist revolution. On
December 19, 1952, on the sixth anniversary of the war, Ho Chi Minh
criticized the slow implementation of the interest and rent reduction policies promulgated since the late 1940s as "unjust" because "nearly 90 percent of soldiers in the National Defense Army, local guards, and militia-
men are guerrillas of poor peasant stock."[32] He announced that the party,
the government, and the National United Front would "launch a movement to urge peasants to implement the policy on reduction of land rent
and interest rates in order to protect their legitimate interests."[33] The
party's move offended the rich and the landlords who had joined the Viet
Minh rank-and-file and enthusiastically supported the war effort.

Determined not to abandon the middle and rich peasants and cadres
who had supported the Viet Minh government, the party leadership called
for an alliance with them and set up guidelines using contributions to the
War of Resistance as classification criteria.[34] This consideration notwithstanding, at the end of 1955 during the last wave of land reform, which
covered 1,720 villages in newly liberated areas, local land reform cadres
committed a "leftist" error. They discriminated against party members
who had been recruited during the early period of the war. They also
wrongly classified the rural population by assigning the "landlord" label
to many rich and even middle peasants.[35]

In the eyes of the landless and land-poor peasants, the fundamental
principle underlying the party's socialist land policy—*nguoi cay co ruong*,
or land to the tiller—was legitimate. As a result of the reform, 810,000
hectares of land, 1,846,000 farm tools, 106,448 head of cattle, and
148,565 houses were reportedly confiscated, with or without compensa-
tion, and redistributed to 8,323,636 peasants, 72.8 percent of the rural
population.[36] Several writings on land reform point out that mass mobili-
zations for rent reduction and the first wave of land reform not only inspired peasant soldiers to prepare for the Dien Bien Phu battle but also
motivated villagers in the Viet Minh–controlled areas to send men and
rice supplies to support the front.[37] In the eyes of the once marginalized

groups, the leadership's policy of mass mobilization for rent reduction and land reform also contributed to creating a culturally egalitarian country-side. By undercutting the hierarchical sociocultural and political relations in Vietnamese villages, it allowed land-poor and landless peasants, women in particular, to challenge the authority of the traditional power elite.[38]

Yet the errors committed during the last wave of land reform put in question the leadership's commitment to national unity. They brought about a confrontation between the party's new allies, poor and landless peasants, and the middle and rich peasants and cadres who had enthusiastically contributed to the War of Resistance. In the eyes of landlords and rich peasants who had strongly supported the Viet Minh and formed the core of Viet Minh village organizations, land reform cast doubts on the leadership's emphasis on national unity and created tension and mistrust among individuals.

The party leadership attempted to surmount the land reform crisis by evoking national unity to mend the rift among local cadres and the rural population. It practiced self-criticism in public, a move unprecedented in the socialist bloc.[39] Ho Chi Minh, in August 1956, publicly called for rectification of errors, including rehabilitation of cadres wrongly expelled from the party and reclassification of those who had been misclassified. Ho called for both old and newly recruited cadres—that is, those from middle/rich peasant backgrounds and those from poor/landless peasant backgrounds—to adopt "an identity of ideas, to be united and single-minded, and to compete to serve the people."[40] Ho demoted Truong Chinh, then secretary-general of the Lao Dong Party, who had been in charge of the reform. Vo Nguyen Giap, enjoying prestige from the Dien Bien Phu victory, stepped in to restore national unity and minimize class struggle. Giap attributed land reform errors to a policy of discrimination and a failure to take precautions against "leftist deviations and unjust punishment."[41] In 1957, the party completed the rectification of errors that officially began with the Central Committee's decree entitled "Correcting Errors Committed in the *Chi Bo* Rectification During Wave Five (1956)."[42]

The relationship between the party and the rural population entered a new phase when the leadership launched cooperativization campaigns in 1958.[43] The party evoked peasants' patriotism to mobilize support for its cooperativization policy. The building of a strong state through industrialization, it argued, had to rely on internal accumulation extracted from the agricultural sector. The cooperative as an institution would enable the state to mobilize surpluses from the agricultural sector to expedite industrial undertakings.[44] The party also evoked peasants' economic interests to mobilize support for its socialist collectivism policy in the countryside. It claimed that the cooperative would reduce socioeconomic differences. Assuming that the amalgamation of production units and specialization of labor in cooperatives would increase production efficiency and output, the leadership also argued that the cooperative would help offset a hostile production environment in North Vietnam caused by droughts and floods. Finally, the party argued that the development of cooperatives would create a socialist/collectivist and egalitarian culture in the Vietnamese countryside.[45]

The structural features of the North Vietnamese countryside made it receptive to at least a mild form of socialist collectivism. Densely populated, yet low in surplus and regularly hit by natural calamities, it was an area where the institution of communal land was well entrenched and where the ideology of communalism gave birth to mechanisms that helped maintain the collective interests of villagers.[46] These socioeconomic and cultural features of northern villages offered fertile ground for socialist collectivism. A recent Vietnamese writing on cooperativization called the 1961–65 period the "golden age" (*thoi dai hoang kim*) of the cooperative movement, pointing to such positive outcomes as increases in gross agricultural product, cultivated land, and domestic animals.[47]

Yet there was also a certain incompatibility between the values of the socialist regime and those of northern rural producers. From the latter's perspective, the merging of hamlets to form commune-based advanced cooperatives and the merging of several communes to form large-scale cooperatives led to chronic cultural tension among hamlets or villages placed under the same cooperative. In Hy Van Luong's study, a villager of Son Duong reported that the high-level cooperative in Son Duong had fewer problems than cooperatives elsewhere because it had only one "father." Another high-level cooperative close to Son Duong had "three different contests at the annual village festivals: rice cooking, wrestling, and group singing." According to him, it had "three different traditions; hence the problems with a high-level cooperative."[48] Industrially patterned division of agricultural tasks that separated rural producers from end products gave rise to freeloaders and hampered production enthusiasm. The egalitarian principle of distribution, which became an entrenched principle during the war years, further drove rural producers away from cooperative works. Finally, the leadership's overemphasis on heavy industry meant that the state was neither motivated to invest in agriculture nor capable of fulfilling the rural population's need for consumption goods and services.[49]

Despite management and organizational problems during the American War period, the ideology of nationalism, in both its military and economic aspects, legitimized the leadership's cooperativization policy in the eyes of the rural population. Between 1966 and 1972, when military conflict with the United States intensified, cooperatives accepted the state's low procurement prices, the so-called service price (*gia nghia vu*), in order to contribute to the national war effort. Adam Fforde points out that comparatively high levels of procurement did occur during the war years, and in the early 1970s the North Vietnamese collectivized sector was meeting its basic target of procurement.[50] It was not until after the reunification of Vietnam that the management and organizational problems in the collective sector resurfaced to directly challenge the legitimacy of the regime in the eyes of the public.

Between 1945 and 1975, in addition to relying on the rural population to achieve its goals, the leadership also entered into an alliance with Vietnamese intellectuals. The relationship between the party and the intellectuals underwent stages of development. During the first years of the War of Resistance, the Viet Minh solicited and received substantial support from both noncommunist and communist Vietnamese intellectuals trained during the French colonial period.[51] This alliance, however, crumbled in 1949–50 when the party leadership imported Maoist practices of ideological rectification (*chinh huan*). Unable to tolerate criticism and self-criticism sessions when they were asked to discard their petty bourgeois political position, to hate landlords and the French, to learn from the peasant masses, and to devote their works to serving the needs of the party at particular moments, many Vietnamese intellectuals left for French-controlled areas. Those who remained in the DRV-controlled areas were split into those who enthusiastically supported the party line and those who became dissatisfied with the party's definition of intellectual freedom.[52]

The adverse reaction of the dissidents surfaced after the end of the war. According to Georges Boudarel, intellectual dissidence began in the army as early as 1955 and became widespread in 1956.[53] Dissenters called for the party to expand freedom and democracy, to strengthen legal institutions, to respect human rights, and to liberalize all fields of research.[54] Several intellectuals attributed the land reform errors to the party's ban on open criticism of policies. Nguyen Manh Tuong, a French-trained lawyer, charged that the lack of a legal basis for land reform allowed local cadres to ignore the rights of the accused.[55]

While Vietnamese intellectuals challenged the legitimacy of the party and the socialist regime on legal and democratic grounds, Ho rebutted their accusations on moral grounds. Avoiding Marxist terminology, Ho framed his arguments around the good/evil (*thien/ac*) theme to buttress the party's authority. He distinguished the DRV, which he asserted served the interests of the people, from the colonial and the U.S.-backed Ngo Dinh Diem governments, which he described as serving individual gain. Despite the errors committed, Ho argued that the DRV government was "good" (*thien*) because it served the people.[56] After 1958, the party leadership launched systematic attacks on dissidents. Communist intellectuals, who collaborated with the party, criticized dissenters in public.[57]

Between 1958 and 1965, a number of novels and short stories portrayed how rich peasants, intellectuals, and the petty bourgeoisie struggled to survive under socialism.[58] No major writings, however, overtly challenged the authority of the party and the emerging state socialist regime. As Boudarel concludes, in the 1960s and 1970s patriotism played an important role in curbing French-trained Vietnamese intellectuals' challenges to the regime.[59] In early 1970, Nguyen Khac Vien both explained and demanded compliance from the intellectuals when he stated that "Marxism came to Vietnam not as just another doctrine, but as an instrument of liberation after the Confucian scholars had failed to liberate the country and the efforts of bourgeois intellectuals against the colonial and feudal regimes had proved feeble and without promise."[60]

With the eventual waning of dissidence, the state educational and cultural apparatuses, with their means of cultural and ideological production and their educational and cultural cadres, reified and corroborated the party's ideologies of nationalism and socialism. Educators wrote textbooks, trained teachers, and administered examinations. Researchers defined research topics and boundaries relevant to state policies and goals.[61] Cultural cadres, writers, artists, and the media echoed the leadership's intermediate and long-term goals, propagated implementation strategies, and popularized successful models.[62]

Collectively and cumulatively, these groups of intellectuals contributed to the making of the official ideology. Essentially the hegemonic ideology asserted that there existed a compatibility between the party's nationalist goal and peasant patriotism on the one hand and the interlocked and mutually enhancing nature of peasant and state economic interests on the other. The party's aspiration to the goal of national liberation was compatible with that of the Vietnamese population—both the ethnic Vietnamese (*kinh*) and the minorities, who, throughout history, had actively resisted foreign invasion. The party also pushed to eliminate class exploitation and advance state building through socialist industrialization. This goal was compatible with that of the peasantry, which had struggled against the ills of feudalism and French colonial capitalism. The new social compact, cast in the vocabulary of peasant patriotism and selected peasant economic ethics, underscored the national political discourse. It connected the past to the present and tradition to socialism, both to legitimize the party and its goals and to provide ideological guidance for present and future action.[63] It was the ideology of socialist nationalism developed prior to 1975 that defined the parameters within which claims and counterclaims to legitimacy would emerge at both leadership and societal levels.

The DRV Model in Reunified Vietnam: 1975–85

After 1975, the state socialist system, which had functioned well in mobilizing support for pre-1975 political institutions, plummeted into crisis, a crisis that brought into question the party's leadership role, the rationale of the state socialist system, and even the legitimacy of a reunified Vietnam. Why did the same generation of leadership that had led Vietnam from one victory to another lose credibility in the eyes of party members and the public? Why did the DRV legitimation model fail to work in reunified Vietnam?

With reference to the leadership crisis, Huynh Kim Khanh correctly points to "objective conditions" inherent in the nature of revolutionary movements as the major cause. These objective conditions were deradicalization of the communist movement after the war, fragmentation of the international communist movement, loss of ideological certainty, absence of common enemies, and the inability of the old revolutionary generation to transfer their revolutionary ideals.[64] While Khanh's arguments shed some light on the causes of the postreunification leadership crisis, they are one-sided in that they focus exclusively on the role of the Vietnamese Communist Party, ignoring the changing relationship between the VCP and other political institutions as well as the larger socioeconomic structural problems of reunified Vietnam. In fact, the legitimacy problems of postreunification Vietnam stemmed from the inadequacy of the DRV model as the legitimation model for reunified Vietnam.

At the leadership level, the legitimacy problem was precipitated by inadequate political inclusion when the established party leadership of the North expanded its control to include the entire country's major political institutions. At the Fourth Party Congress of 1976, the first party congress after reunification, Le Duan and Le Duc Tho took control of the party apparatuses.[65] Between 1976 and 1980, Truong Chinh rewrote the constitution of the Socialist Republic of Vietnam, giving enormous power to the State Council (Hoi Dong Nha Nuoc), which replaced the presidency. Termed the collective presidency, the State Council was "the highest continually functioning body of the National Assembly."[66] In July 1981, Truong Chinh became chairman of the new State Council.[67] This meant that the old guard of the North remained the dominant players in the new national government.

The postreunification legitimacy problem stemmed also from the inefficiency of expanding state apparatuses. The 1980 constitution granted the state apparatus more administrative, allocative, and management power than the 1960 constitution had allowed.[68] Even so, the Fifth Party Congress in 1982 admitted that "our state apparatuses at all levels are weak" and that Vietnam needed to "reform and strengthen (*tang cuong*) the state apparatuses."[69] Vietnamese state cadres and researchers argued that a strong state apparatus could effectively implement policies because it was organized rationally and had an appropriate number of qualified personnel, unlike a "big and cumbersome (*cong kenh*) state."[70] The strength of the socialist state would derive from a clear division of labor among different state apparatuses, strict recruitment rules and regulations, a tight organization, preservation of socialist law and order, and a system of checks and balances between the state and the National Assembly and the State Council.[71] However, the expansion of the state apparatus gave rise to bureaucratic inefficiency and thus could not accomplish the enormous tasks required after reunification. Under a state socialism in which party leadership did not have to report to an electorate, the leadership's legitimacy was based only on the ability of power holders to retain a public perception of their intellectual and moral superiority. During the years following the reunification of Vietnam, this moral and intellectual leadership disintegrated. The collapse was manifested by rampant corruption, a quest for personal privileges, injustice, bribery, and the rise of communist "village notables."[72]

Finally, the leadership's move to use military means to reunify the country in 1975 called into question its claim to cherish national harmony. Prior to 1975, the Provisional Revolutionary Government of the Republic of South Vietnam and the DRV leadership had agreed that reunification would proceed step by step.[73] South Vietnamese political leaders and party cadres subsequently criticized the party for violating this principle of national reconciliation. By 1986, southern party members had gathered to form the Club of Resistance Fighters (*cau lac bo nhung nguoi khang chien cu*), demanding that the leadership launch extensive political and economic reform. In subsequent years it circulated a newspaper criticizing the party's monopoly of political power and its postreunification policy.[74]

The crisis of political legitimacy was further exacerbated by economic crises resulting from the imposition of the DRV's socialist economic model on the newly liberated South. At the Fourth Party Congress of 1976, the party endorsed the move toward large-scale socialist development for the entire country.[75] This model had evolved in the North in the early 1970s.

The performance problems of the collectivized agricultural sector in the North, manifested in its limited productivity, had cast doubt upon leadership's ability to manage a socialist economy. Since political and economic control were interdependent, economic stagnation and autarky at the local level showed that the leadership had also to some extent lost political control. In response, the Thai Binh Conference (1974) endorsed the New Management System (NMS), which increased state investment, enlarged the size of cooperatives, entrusted power to Cooperative Management Committees, promoted the use of technocrats or outside cadres in agricultural management, and advocated an increasingly complex division of labor. Making the basic production unit the district or the cluster of villages instead of the individual village, the central government attempted to break the local political network that had been the source of cooperative cadres' power. Relying on the Cooperative Management Committee, staffed by technocrats from the central government, to control cooperatives' production, resource utilization, and distribution, the state hoped to offset any formation of local power blocs. In 1976, this DRV model was extended to include South Vietnam.

The DRV model of socialist development, however, proved inadequate to maintain postreunification legitimacy in both North and South. In the North, its weakness was a collectivization model based on unequal terms of trade between the state and rural producers. Prior to 1975, in the North, the relationship between the state and rural producers was sustained in large measure by foreign aid and the importation of food and consumer goods from the socialist bloc. Foreign loans from the Soviet Union allowed the DRV to pursue a lenient policy toward the peasantry; consumer goods from China helped to lessen the negative effects of the bias toward heavy industry. China cut commodity aid in 1975 and all construction aid in 1978, however, while the Soviet bloc hardened its terms of loans and grants.[76] The Hanoi government thus had to rely more on domestic resources for its large-scale development projects. Its increasing pressure on the collectivized sector by administrative means discouraged rural producers from cooperating with the state.

In the newly liberated South, the state socialist economic policies encountered different difficulties. In southern central Vietnam, where a communal tradition was entrenched, the DRV model developed rather smoothly: by 1980, in the coastal plains of northern South Vietnam, 83 percent of households had formed work exchange teams and 76 percent of the cultivated land belonged to agricultural cooperatives. But in the Mekong delta, the state met with large-scale resistance. In 1980, only 31 percent of the households joined work exchange teams and only 24 percent of the land under cultivation belonged to cooperatives.[77]

This resistance in the Mekong River delta sprang from a series of socioeconomic and cultural factors—above all the middle class's size, values, and perceptions. First, both rural and urban areas in the Mekong delta boasted a high percentage of the population belonging to the middle class. In rural areas, this was a product of the Viet Minh land reform program in the 1940s, the NLF's land policy, and the U.S.-supported "land to the tiller" program in the 1970s during Nguyen Van Thieu's administration. In urban areas, it was a product of lavish American military spending and the rise of entrepreneurs engaged in services and retail trade. Second, the economic activities of the South Vietnamese rural and urban middle classes had been sustained by the Commercial Import Program of the United States. Not only had this program distorted the southern economy by providing it with artificial economic growth but it had also helped to create a middle class that was more prone to consumption than production.

The party's attempt to consolidate the state socialist system in reunified Vietnam in the context of decreasing foreign aid offended the new ethic of consumerism that had emerged as a product of the economic development of both Vietnams prior to 1975. In the South, agricultural collectivization attacked the interest of the middle peasant group, which had found satisfaction in the land distribution schemes of the Saigon governments. Moreover, the nationalization of commerce and industry in urban areas adversely affected both Vietnamese and Chinese who had been engaged in entrepreneurial activities and also disrupted the flow of supplies between urban and rural areas. In the North, large-scale cooperativization exacerbated management problems. The decline in production was made worse by natural calamities that struck the North in 1978, so severe that food riots reportedly occurred. The period between 1979 and 1981 was a time of economic crisis characterized by shortages of food, consumer goods, and services.[78]

To surmount the crisis and restore the party's credibility, the Sixth Plenum of the Central Committee, which met in September 1979, officially recognized the need to adjust its economic strategy. It endorsed a multisectoral economy (*kinh te nhieu thanh phan*) consisting of five elements: state, collective, state/private, private, and individual sectors. In the countryside it moved to revive the individual household economy.[79] In 1981 an end-product system (*khoan san pham*) was implemented, allowing households to sign contracts directly with cooperatives to transplant rice seedlings, tend the crop, and harvest it, linking remuneration to the quality of work. In 1985, the leadership called for the collective sector to apply the end-product system to all other agricultural tasks.[80]

In the cities it was not until June 1985, when Nguyen Van Linh returned to the Politburo at the Eighth Central Committee Plenum, that the party attempted to improve poor economic performance: it dismantled the state subsidy system and allowed basic economic units to have financial autonomy in order to lessen the burden on the state budget.[81] A follow-up measure was to apply the principle of socialist business accounting (*hach toan kinh te xa hoi chu nghia*)—that is, to apply stricter budget constraints to state enterprises.

Between 1975 and 1978, Vietnam's military conflict with Cambodia, culminating in the invasion of that country in December 1978, as well as its clashes with China in 1979, helped sustain the legitimacy of the party leadership and that of the nation-state in times of disintegrating domestic consensus and popular discontent.[82] Responses to external military threats, from both the northern and southern borders, illustrated the leadership's commitment to the goal of national defense. To rouse nationalistic feelings, the party circulated documents revealing several "facts" regarding Sino-Vietnamese relations since the mid-1950s, all of which pointed to the PRC's strategy of using Vietnam as a pawn in its conflict with other great powers, with damaging effects on the Vietnamese Revolution and national reunification.[83] The Fifth Party Congress, which met in 1982, stated clearly that China's hegemonic ambitions in Southeast Asia threatened Vietnam's national security.[84]

Vietnamese intellectuals and writers, who had been dissatisfied with the party's political and economic policy after 1975, temporarily shelved their grievances. Historians directed their energies to extensive research on historical wars between Vietnam and China.[85] Writers wrote short stories and plays describing the 1979 battle, Chinese atrocities, and Vietnamese heroism.[86] Ho Chi Minh City, the place where anger had smoldered most, opened a war crimes museum to show the development of the Sino-Vietnamese conflict and China's support of the Khmer Rouge.

Socialist Vietnam's nationalist policies, while buttressing legitimacy at home, damaged Vietnam's international legitimacy in the eyes of the non-Soviet bloc. ASEAN countries opposed Vietnam's invasion of Cambodia; the Western countries and China imposed trade and diplomatic embargoes. The diplomatic and economic isolation of socialist Vietnam by the capitalist camp continued throughout the 1980s, impeding the economic recovery on which legitimacy, to a large extent, depended.

The New Model: 1986–91

The Sixth Congress of the Vietnamese Communist Party, which met in December 1986, endorsed the policy of renovation: *doi moi*. In the political realm, *doi moi* referred to the need for reform in the political process:

to rejuvenate the party ideologically and organizationally, to improve the managerial efficiency of the state, to uphold the role of the National Assembly, the State Council, and People's Councils at all levels, and to revive mass organizations.[87] In the economic realm, *doi moi* marked the first step toward the abolition of Stalinist economic development principles. While the previous development goals endorsed by the Third (1960), Fourth (1976), and Fifth (1982) Party Congresses had been biased in favor of heavy industry, the resolution of the Sixth Party Congress stressed the development of three major economic sectors (*ba chuong trinh kinh te lon*): foodstuffs (*luong thuc, thuc pham*), consumer goods (*hang tieu dung*), and export goods (*hang xuat khau*). While previous congresses had adhered to the principles of central planning and state ownership of the means of production, the Sixth Congress endorsed the development of structured market relations and multisectoral economic activities. In foreign policy, *doi moi* meant looking outward for international economic cooperation. While earlier congresses had situated Vietnam in the socialist economic bloc and had emphasized Vietnam's economic autarky, the Sixth Congress endorsed the need for Vietnam to establish economic exchanges with the world's capitalist economic system.[88]

In sum, then, the policy of *doi moi* signified the party's reliance on a more inclusionary political process to restore the legitimacy of one-party rule, as well as its reliance on economic liberalization to restore leadership credibility and the legitimacy of Vietnam as a unified nation-state.

Renewing Party and State Legitimacy

The leadership sought to restore the legitimacy of the political system in the eyes of its own members and the public by revitalizing the party apparatuses and other political institutions such as the state apparatuses, the National Assembly, and mass organizations.

The first sign of party reform was the arrival of Nguyen Van Linh, a Southerner, as the secretary-general in 1986.[89] The succession process was smoothed by an institutional innovation: the party had set up an advisory committee (*ban co van*) attached to the Central Committee; its members were Le Duc Tho, Pham Van Dong, and Truong Chinh, the old guards.[90] Once in power, Nguyen Van Linh began his campaign for party reform; he relied on the "mass line," calling for the press, the media, writers, and artists to attack corrupt and anti-reform party and state cadres. By 1991, the party had reportedly disciplined 127,000 party members and expelled 78,200 others.[91] Linh's attack on corrupt cadres aimed to restore the party's image of intellectual and moral leadership as well as to ease the move toward a new economic order.

To rejuvenate the political process, the party granted autonomy to the state apparatuses. The Sixth Plenum of the Central Committee, which met in March 1989, announced plans to reduce party supervision over state bodies by cutting the number of Central Committee departments from 32 to 12.[92] In early 1990, in the name of efficiency, ministries merged and made large cuts in personnel (*giam bien che*). Finally, to renovate popular representative bodies, the leadership revised regulations governing National Assembly elections and granted more power to National Assembly representatives in debating policy issues, making decisions, and criticizing state cadres.[93] It also moved to reorganize the People's Councils and Committees, attempting to minimize party control over local popular representatives. In 1989, two new laws were issued to expand popular involvement in the activities of the councils.[94] Although mass participation was not synonymous with political democratization, the attempt to revive the "mass line" concept encouraged popular attacks against conservative party and state cadres.

Political turmoil in China and the move toward multiparty pluralism in Hungary and Poland in the summer of 1989 cast serious doubts on the legitimacy of socialism and one-party rule. To cope with these challenges, the VCP leadership moved to elevate Ho Chi Minh's thought to the position of an official ideology.[95] In August 1989, during the Seventh Plenum of the Central Committee, the leadership disclosed to the Vietnamese public "certain problems regarding Ho Chi Minh's last will and testament (*di chuc*)." It revealed that the document officially presented to the public in 1969 had merely contained excerpts drawn from Ho's 1965 testament and related documents.[96] Since Vietnam was at war with the United States, the earlier version had emphasized Ho's evocation of patriotism, international communism, and solidarity. His suggestions on how socialism could be built in Vietnam, especially after the end of the war, had been excluded.[97] These excluded portions were now presented to the public.

The Central Committee's release of Ho's last will and testament, coupled with the printing of the original in booklet form, served important legitimizing functions. The document evoked the memories of Ho as a nationalist leader with an internationalist outlook. It justified socialism on the grounds that it was the path that Ho had chosen. It also suggested that Ho's view of socialism differed from that of the previous party leaders, whose policies had brought about the economic crisis. The release of the document was thus used to delegitimize the policies pursued by the leadership from 1975 to 1986. The release of Ho's last will and testament reflected the political leadership's attempt to capitalize on his authority, his nationalist ideology, his international outlook, and his conception of socialism as the basis on which to renew the party.

While the release of Ho's last will and testament restored the credibility of the party's leadership among the rank-and-file, the collapse of communism and one-party rule in Eastern Europe made political renovation more urgent. Just prior to the Eighth Plenum of the Central Committee, scheduled for March 1990, members criticized the party's monopoly of power, calling for party reform, intraparty democracy, and political pluralism. Most of the critics recognized the leadership role of the party as rooted in history. Yet they called for the party to assume genuine moral and intellectual leadership and to share power with other political institutions.

Tran Xuan Bach, for example, a Politburo member, asserted that in order to avoid a debacle similar to that in Eastern Europe, Vietnam had to rethink Marxism, promote democratization, and diversify political ideas—what he called the democratization of socialism.[98] Nguyen Ho, head of the Club of Former Resistance Fighters, argued that developments in the Soviet bloc showed that abject poverty, lack of democratic freedom, repression, dissatisfaction, injustice, indignation, and lack of confidence in the party could lead to revolution even under socialism. According to him, such grievances were accumulating in Vietnam. Nguyen Ho called for the party to allow mass participation in the political process as well as to "shed its skin" (lot xac minh). He argued for a personnel revolution, an organizational revolution, and a democratic revolution. As part of political reform, he demanded that the party grant the club the status of an "association." These demands notwithstanding, Nguyen Ho claimed that he recognized the vanguard role of the party.[99]

The communiqué of the Eighth Plenum of the Central Committee, which met in mid-March 1990, confirmed the leading role of the party and rejected multiparty democracy. It cited the need for economic development to justify one-party domination, arguing that political change would undermine the economic progress achieved in past years. It ordered the dismissal of Tran Xuan Bach from the Politburo on the grounds that he had violated party organizational and disciplinary principles.[100] The party exerted pressure on executive committee members of the Club of Resistance Fighters to vote out its chairman, Nguyen Ho, and vice-chairman, Ta Ba Tong. In an attempt to co-opt less radical club members, the party set up an alternative organization called the Vietnam War Veterans' Association (Hoi Cuu Chien Binh Viet Nam). It was considered a mass organization affiliated with the Vietnam Fatherland Front under the guidance of the VCP.[101]

Another wave of political criticism was delivered when the Ninth Plenum of the Central Committee, which met in November 1990, circulated two draft documents to solicit opinions from party cadres and the public:

the "Platform for National Construction in the Period of Transition to Socialism" and the "Strategy of Socioeconomic Stabilization and Development to the Year 2000." Both were prepared for discussion at the Seventh Party Congress scheduled for 1991.[102] In his speech delivered at the Seventh Party Congress in June 1991, Nguyen Van Linh claimed that "more than 80 percent of party members, hundreds of veteran revolutionaries, thousands of scientists and intellectuals, and millions of members of various mass organizations" had commented on the political platform and the economic blueprint and, moreover, that the majority agreed with them.[103] While it is not possible to ascertain the accuracy of this claim, widely circulated documents criticized the drafts for their continued adherence to a conservative ideology and strategy. The criticisms came from prominent middle-ranking party members and prominent intellectuals. Questioning the party's conservative ideology and strategy, they challenged the basis for its claim to legitimacy and called for a shift in the basis of legitimation.

The first group of criticisms dealt with the rationale for the party's socialist policies. Critics suggested that the main goal of the regime should be "national reconciliation," not class struggle. Hoang Minh Chinh, for example, former head of the Institute of Philosophy, demanded that the party adhere to Ho Chi Minh's slogan *dai doan ket* (great unity) to mobilize all social forces regardless of class background. Chinh contrasted Nguyen Ai Quoc's political thesis, which called for a united front, with Tran Phu's political thesis, which called for class struggle. He criticized the party's past and present political policies based on class struggle, such as land reform, ideological rectification, reeducation, attack on anti-Maoist intellectuals, and cooperativization in the South, which had brought about national disunity. He argued that the united front strategy—manifested in the Viet Minh front, the August revolution, the Provisional Central Government of 1945–46, the National Liberation Front, and the Provisional Revolutionary Government of South Vietnam—had brought unity, popularity, and success. Chinh challenged the party's socialist goal on the grounds that Vietnam could not reach the socialist stage of development without first going through the capitalist stage. What was needed, then, was a "bourgeois-democratic revolution" (*cach mang tu san dan quyen*), a concept originally proposed by Nguyen Ai Quoc.[104] Phan Dinh Dieu, a mathematician, echoed a similar line when he criticized the party's class struggle policy after 1975 and suggested that the party promote a democratic political regime characterized by national unity (*doan ket*) and national harmony (*hoa hop dan toc*). Bui Tin, deputy editor-in-chief of the *Nhan Dan Sunday Weekly*, agreed and made the additional demand that the party change the country's name back to Democratic Republic of

Vietnam (Viet Nam Dan Chu Cong Hoa) and the party's name back to the Vietnam Labor Party (Dang Lao Dong Viet Nam).[105]

The second group of criticisms dealt with the need to reform the political system through institutional separation of power and promotion of popular freedom. Hoang Minh Chinh called for a political system with a division of power between the state, the presidency, and the National Assembly, with guaranteed pluralism and freedom of the press.[106] In his petition to Nguyen Huu Tho, the chairman of the Fatherland Front, Nguyen Khac Vien called for the strengthening of the state apparatus and criticized the party's intrusion into the state, the Council of Ministers, the National Assembly, and other government branches.[107] These institutional reforms needed to go hand in hand with the expansion of popular freedom. Vien suggested that the masses set up a popular democratic front that would defend democratic freedom and maintain social equality in the form of equal pay, antistratification measures, guaranteed education, and a public health service.[108]

The third group of criticisms dealt with the role of the state in the economy. Critics suggested that central planning be replaced with a multisectoral economy and privatization. Bui Tin warned that as socialist economic organization contained serious shortcomings, the party should rely on nonsocialist measures to restore economic performance.[109] Phan Dinh Dieu suggested that the party promote "a developed market economy" in which private citizens were allowed to control the means of production. Dieu suggested that the state should limit its role to macroeconomic management in order to create favorable conditions for the development of a market economy. The state sector should be limited to infrastructural industries such as energy, transportation, and certain revenue-raising industries such as beer and tobacco.[110] The final group of criticisms dealt with the relationship between Vietnam and the world. Critics pointed out that the world was moving toward a scientific revolution; the Cold War had ended, nuclear war had been restrained, and the information revolution had begun. It was imperative that Vietnam open its doors and benefit from world peace and a global technology.

While the party leadership rejected many of these ideas, it did incorporate several of them into the party platform in an attempt to renew the legitimacy of party and regime. At the Seventh Party Congress, Nguyen Van Linh asserted that socialism remained the ultimate goal of Vietnam, but the means to achieve a socialist society would be modified to reflect a hybrid model of state socialism and market economy.[111] Linh affirmed that the party would advocate the policy of a multisectoral economy with socialist orientation. While the state sector would continue to be dominant in this system, all Vietnamese would be free to do business according to law and their rights to ownership and legally derived income would be protected.[112]

In claiming legitimacy for the leadership role of the party, Linh asserted that the VCP was a historically rooted movement that had brought both national independence and specific revolutionary gains. He rejected a return to the period of "people's democratic revolution" and multiparty pluralism, pointing to the political experiences of South Vietnam before 1975.[113] "The presence or absence of democracy does not depend on the one-party or multiparty system," he argued, because "under the former Saigon puppet regime, there were dozens of political parties and factions, but no one thought there was much democracy then."[114] Linh also used national security to justify the ban on multiparty competition, as it would "create conditions favorable for the reactionary forces of revenge within the country and from abroad to rear their heads immediately and legally to operate against the homeland, the people, and the regime."[115]

According to Linh, the crucial question was this: what could the party do to secure adequate democracy under the one-party system? One solution was to seek various mechanisms to allow for accomplishing adequate democracy within the party.[116] The relationship between the party and people would be manifested through the roles of the state, the Vietnam Fatherland Front, and mass organizations.[117] The state would first play a role in macroeconomic management—creating macroeconomic balances, regulating the market, creating favorable conditions for production and business operations, and ensuring compatibility between economic growth and social justice and progress. Linh emphasized the need to reform the administrative system, building a strong executive system from the top down to grassroots levels.[118] In other words Linh called for a new type of state activities, one that would change the means of control from direct management to legislative and administrative regulation.

To the intellectuals Linh offered full acceptance. The socialist state would rest on "the worker-peasant-intellectual alliance" (*lien minh giai cap cong nhan voi giai cap nong dan va tang lop tri thuc*).[119] According to him, "socialism cannot be built if the working class does not have its own contingent of intellectuals and if the worker/peasant alliance itself fails to improve its knowledge or to attain intellectualization" (*duoc tri thuc hoa*).[120] Finally, Linh declared that Vietnam would "advocate cooperation on an equal footing for mutual benefit with all other countries, regardless of their different political and social systems."[121]

Undoubtedly, the Seventh Party Congress endorsed change in the nature of the state socialist system, which had been developed during the DRV period and imposed on reunified Vietnam after 1975. It shifted the goal of the regime, at least temporarily, from building socialism to stabilizing postwar socioeconomic and political conditions. It replaced the state socialist system—with its central planning and state owner-ship of the means of production—with a multisectoral economy. It re-lied on party reform to rejuvenate the image of the party as the moral and intellectual leader of society. It allowed limited political liberaliza-tion and called for the strengthening of the state apparatuses by stream-lining their administrative role and improving their efficiency. It offi-cially recognized the importance of contributions from intellectuals and technocrats.

The party's policy outline was "legalized" by the 1992 constitution of the SRV and passed by the National Assembly in April 1992. The consti-tution modified the SRV political arrangements by institutionalizing the separation of power. Unlike the 1980 constitution, which referred to the VCP as the only leading force (*duy nhat*), Clause 4 of the 1992 consti-tution merely stated that it "is a leading force of the state and the soci-ety."[122] It abolished the State Council, replacing it with the presidency (*chu tich*). It renamed the Council of Ministers "the government" (*chinh phu*), reflecting the party's rejection of the collective character of the ad-ministrative body. The constitution also reorganized the "government" by drawing clear boundaries to separate ministerial functions. The Law Or-ganizing the Government, promulgated in September 1992, granted the government administrative power over provincial and local People's Com-mittees.[123] Finally, there was a reduction in the number of party members–cum–state cadres, security cadres, central planners, and cadres in heavy industry and agriculture represented in the Seventh Central Committee.[124] The Seventh Congress Politburo represented a wide range of sectoral in-terests in the areas of security, ideology, technocratic expertise, and agri-culture.[125] Its members also represented major municipalities (Hanoi and Ho Chi Minh City), geographical areas (north, central, and south Viet-nam), and ethnic groups.[126]

As the policy of renovation and change in party goals could be taken to imply that party leadership had been wrong in conducting policy, the party sought to legitimize the changes by invoking Ho Chi Minh's thoughts and the memory of his pragmatic nationalist revolutionary line. In Linh's words: "Ho Chi Minh's thought resulted from his creative appli-cation of Marxism-Leninism to the specific conditions of our country and to reality."[127] Linh characterized Ho as the symbol of "the combination of class and nation, nationalism and internationalism, national indepen-dence and socialism."[128] The party leadership as well as critics who advocated renovation used the concepts of "national harmony" and "na-tional reconciliation" to legitimize regime change. "National reconciliation" meant the accommodation of groups in the South that had been alienated by the class-against-class policy. The multisectoral economy reflects the attempt to create an economic system acceptable to former North and South Vietnam.

Yet the party justified the continuation of one-party rule, as well as limited political liberalization, on the basis of "national security" and "economic security." Finally, it claimed that the "force of history" legitimized its political supremacy: history had proved that the communist movement was the only one able to bring about national independence.

The Societal Perspective

After 1986, the party leadership moved to reform land allocation and landownership policy. Resolution 10, issued in April 1988, guaranteed land allocation in the form of single parcels. While land still belonged to the state, peasants were granted fixed cultivation rights for a period of fifteen to nineteen years. The state also began to use bargaining to determine state prices for food procurement.[129] In the industrial sector, the leadership moved to renovate management of state enterprises, increase incentives, grant financial autonomy, and change the type of ownership to state/private joint venture for enterprises incapable of making profits. The National Assembly promulgated a foreign investment law in 1987, providing material incentives to foreign companies and protecting their rights in economic undertakings in Vietnam.[130] In 1989, Vietnam opened its northern borders and resumed trading relations with China. With the waning of the Cambodian problem, Vietnam could improve its trading relationship with ASEAN, Japan, the European Economic Community, and other European states.

In 1989, Vietnam experienced one of its best economic upturns since 1975. The GNP increased by an estimated 3.5 percent. Agricultural production reached an all-time high, transforming Vietnam from a net importer of food to the world's third-largest grain exporter after the United States and Thailand. Annual inflation was drastically reduced—from over 700 percent in early 1987 and 300 percent in 1988 to 33.8 percent in 1989.[131] Consumer goods were relatively abundant, purchasing power rose, and private business, both local and foreign, mushroomed.

Would *doi moi* be sufficient to legitimize the regime in the eyes of the populace? In addressing this question, it is first necessary to sketch the distribution of the population by occupation. According to the 1989 census, 71.2 percent of the Vietnamese population was engaged in agriculture and forestry, 11.7 percent in industry, 6.5 percent in trade and business,

2.02 percent in construction, 2 percent in transport and communications, 3.8 percent in scientific research, education, culture, sports, and social services, and 1.06 percent in management of state and party organizations. In 1989, only 20.11 percent of the population lived in urban areas.[132]

The attitude toward renovation differs by social group and even within each group by region. Rural producers in different parts of the country reacted differently to the policy of agricultural renovation. Peasants in the Mekong delta, who had earlier protested against the arbitrary appropriation of their land, welcomed the new land policy and the prospect of land (re)privatization. Their northern counterparts, however, were more ambivalent. Rapid economic stratification after the implementation of Resolution 10 in 1988 prompted rural producers from various areas to demand a slower move toward land privatization. Provincial party cadres in the northern provinces reportedly objected to a complete dismantling of collectives and complete privatization of land. Pressure came from poor peasants and invalid war veterans who relied on cooperative arrangements to earn their living.[133]

In the industrial sector, the party's reluctance to issue bankruptcy laws and its selective dismantling of the bureaucratic subsidy system helped minimize negative effects on the working class. While the party's move to reorganize agriculture had yielded both economic and political benefits, its complete dismantling of state socialist enterprises would have meant a major dislocation of the workforce and a blow to the social groups whose economic survival depended on their perpetuation. For private entrepreneurs, who comprised about 7 percent of the workforce, the party's multisectoral economy allowed a renewal of private economic engagement after a long hiatus in the North (since 1950) and the post-1975 disruption in the South. The relationship between the state and these entrepreneurs remained problematic because the state had attempted, directly and indirectly, to control private commercial freedom. While the constitution guarantees the right of private entrepreneurs to exist, this group is not yet represented in political bodies that defend its interests.[134]

Different occupational groups not only responded differently to the party's economic reforms but they were also restrained and selective in following the party's call to participate in political reform. The public was cautious in making alliances with the party/state to fight corrupt cadres or alliances with local cadres to evade the party/state's new restrictive economic regulations. Writings on popular involvement in evaluating state managers and state officials reported a high degree of indifference, for example, and even evinced support for officials whom the higher echelon perceived as unsuitable. Vietnamese workers in state enterprises tended to give positive evaluations of those considered corrupt cadres by the upper echelons, since "bad" managers tolerated moonlighting and "illegal" business deals. Some accepted the easygoing attitudes of old cadres for fear that competent ones would apply state regulations more strictly.[135]

University students, at one point, seemed concerned with the questions of political participation, democratic freedom, and freedom of thought. Students, both in Hanoi and Ho Chi Minh City, reportedly complained about the obsolete study programs, poor living conditions, and lack of institutional autonomy. Since there had been few senior secondary graduates and university graduates in pre-1975 North and South Vietnam, Vietnamese intellectuals amounted to no more than 3 percent of the population in 1989, and their attitudes toward the party leadership varied because the Vietnamese intellectual community was by no means monolithic. Researchers at state institutions and professionals working in social and natural sciences were willing to cooperate, provided that the party was willing to continue its reform program and they were granted more autonomy. Nguyen Xuan Oanh, a Harvard-trained South Vietnamese economist interviewed by an overseas Vietnamese newspaper during his trip to the United States in May 1991, pointed to South Korea, Singapore, and Taiwan to support his argument that political stability was a prerequisite for economic growth.[136]

Vietnamese writers-cum-intellectuals were critical of the regime's policies. They were supported by Nguyen Van Linh, who in 1987 encouraged writers, the press, and the media to criticize middle-level party and state cadres.[137] Linh, however, withdrew his support in 1989 when the political situation in Eastern Europe became unstable and one-party rule was challenged.[138] Many literary works appearing after 1987 belonged to the "critical socialist realism" category. Writers attacked corrupt officials in party and state apparatuses while presenting alternative ethics. They attacked economic inefficiency in both collective and state sectors, as well, attributing the causes to neglect of individual economic interests. Luu Quang Vu's plays, which became big hits in 1987 and 1988, exemplified these themes.

While many writings supported the party's aims of economic renovation, others challenged the ideology of socialist nationalism that had developed during the DRV period.[139] Nguyen Huy Thiep's writings questioned the party's monopoly of truth. Challenging the assumption that there was only one truth, Thiep discarded the good/bad (*thien/ac*) narrative structure employed by orthodox communist writers and replaced it with multistructural and multidimensional themes. Tran Manh Hao's *Ly than* (Alienation) depicted the party's intrusion into the private life of its cadres. Vietnamese writers did not restrict their criticism to the party; some even attempted to put Ho Chi Minh on trial. Tran Huy Quang's

"Linh nghiem" (Prophecy), published in *Van Nghe* in July 1992, was the first piece alluding directly to Ho Chi Minh, interpreting his "discovery journey" as a failure.[140]

Writers not only attacked the party's monopoly of truth and power, they also questioned the benefits of class struggle that the party had emphasized. Duong Thu Huong's *Nhung thien duong mu* (Foggy paradises) portrayed the impact of the class war waged during land reform and the impact of its errors on the lives of three women. Contrary to the conventional view of nationalism that depicted war as a glorious and heroic act, Bao Ninh's *Noi buon chien tranh* (Sorrow of war) / *Than phan tinh yeu* (Fate of Love) described war as a source of misery, sorrow, separation, inhumanity, and atrocities. War, once portrayed as a collective heroic undertaking, was recast in terms of individual loss and suffering. Writers also wrote about individualism, individual freedom, family relationships, humanism, love, and female sexual freedom. Pham Thi Hoai's short stories focused on the lives of women, their connubial difficulties, and their personal sexual freedom. Xuan Quynh, a famous Vietnamese poet and Luu Quang Vu's wife, glorified personal feelings between mother and children, between husbands and wives, and among women. All these topics were once thought to reflect the "petty bourgeois" mentality.

These writings undoubtedly defied certain crucial aspects of the hegemonic ideology that had been entrenched in socialist Vietnam prior to the era of renovation. They questioned the party's monopoly of truth, derided party cadres, challenged the value of socialist collectivism, and redefined nationalism. Yet, while challenging the hegemonic ideology, these writings, all together, did not yet form a coherent and powerful body of thought that could serve as an alternative to the official ideology. The weakness of dissident literature stemmed from the fact that writers were themselves unable to separate the party's leadership role from the existence of Vietnam as an independent and unified country. In other words, they hesitated to negate the "historical" role of the communist movement through fear of negating the importance of national independence itself.

The absence of large-scale popular uprisings in the wake of the crisis in the socialist bloc in 1989–91 resulted from the historical specificities that gave birth to the Vietnamese communist movement and to Vietnam as a reunified modern nation-state. It resulted, too, from the regime's willingness to move toward renovation. In the short run, this move was sufficient to appease the rural producers who formed the majority of the population. The party's willingness to recognize the intelligentsia as an important social group, as well as its grant of limited civil liberties, wooed a substantial number of Vietnamese intellectuals to its side while neutralizing others. The absence of large-scale popular uprisings in the wake of the socialist bloc's crisis also resulted from the "undemocratic" legacy of the system itself. Limited public freedom of speech, state censorship of mass media, and self-censorship curbed the formation of public opinion. Moreover, fear that political democratization would damage economic gains and the investment climate dampened popular resistance.

Yet McAlister and Mus, commenting on Vietnamese moral notions, warn that it is a mistake to conclude that the Vietnamese common man is concerned about nothing but his bowl of rice. They contend: "The *dan* chooses between systems and thus with his collective strength decides between the 'virtues' that come into conflict before him and about him. It is up to him through that choice to sanction the system, or 'virtue,' that is in harmony with fate; Westerners have a suitable expression for this choice: the historical moment."[141]

Future political change depends on several questions: whether or not the party can restore its moral and intellectual superiority so that direct mass participation and political competition would seem unnecessary; whether or not the development of a multisectoral economy under the leadership of the state will eventually necessitate a reorganization of political interests; and how long the party's traditional and historical role can be used to legitimize its continued control and neutralize political challenges.

Conclusion

The ideology of nationalism has played an important role in Vietnam's political legitimation. The Vietnamese communist movement evoked nationalism to legitimize the state socialist system in North Vietnam (1945–75), to delegitimize post-1975 state socialism in reunified Vietnam, and more recently to legitimize the policy of renovation (*doi moi*). To strengthen its claim to legitimacy, the leadership capitalized on the compatibility between modern and traditional Vietnamese values. With a regime change, however, it accommodated and co-opted new values held among the leadership and different social groups in order to renew political legitimation.

During the 1945 to 1975 period, the DRV's state socialist system rested on five principles: rule by a single Leninist party; strong commitment to nation building through rapid socioeconomic development; state ownership of the means of production; central planning; and political mobilization. The legitimacy of the Vietnamese state socialist system was fused with and buttressed by the legitimacy of Vietnam as a nation. This model of political legitimation emerged in the context of the Indochinese Communist Party's role in the long struggle against French colonialism, the War of Resistance between 1945 and 1954, and the resistance to the American attempt to establish and perpetuate a separate southern state between 1954 and 1973.

At the leadership level, the state socialist system's claim to legitimacy was sustained by a collective leadership that neutralized attempts by leading political personalities to monopolize power. It also rested on the party's claim to intellectual and moral leadership. At the societal level, socialist collectivism along with nationalism helped mobilize support from the peasantry of North and South Vietnam in resisting political and military pressure from France and the United States. This effort was facilitated by the compatibility between socialist collectivism and nationalism as well as the communalism and patriotism of peasants in the Red River delta. The goal of national reunification and the military conflict with the United States in the 1960s played an important role in sustaining the social compact between the party and society. Party leadership was restrained in its pursuit of the extreme class-against-class policy for fear it would alienate prosperous peasants.

Rural cooperatives supported the state by providing both labor and food for its goals. The economic compact between the party and the society also indirectly benefited from and was sustained by two crucial contextual variables. First, conflict between the Soviet Union and China allowed the DRV to play one ally against the other. Second, aid from both countries made socialist development in Vietnam less traumatic than it was in other countries. Aid-financed development allowed the leadership to be less rigorous with the peasant majority in its collectivization campaigns without seriously sacrificing its goals of state building through rapid industrialization.

After the reunification, between 1975 and 1985, the imposition of the North's legitimation model on the newly liberated South created a post-reunification crisis with three major dimensions. First, while state socialism fulfilled the task of mobilizing resources for war and industrialization and provided basic economic and social security for the North, it contained the seeds of chronic systemic crises. The system's bias in favor of heavy industry failed to respond to the demands placed on it by an increasingly consumption-oriented society. Its reliance on central planning and administrative mechanisms in managing the economy dampened the enthusiasm of producers in all sectors. Second, changes in international conditions exacerbated the system's declining effectiveness after the war. With the waning of foreign aid, the system could no longer allocate sufficient resources for both its rural constituency and its industrialization program. Third, the socioeconomic and cultural features of South Vietnam, especially in the Mekong delta, differed from those in the North, making the northern model for legitimation impractical.

Thus the socialist model imposed on the South was in fact an attack on the southern commercial class, both rural and urban, a move that contradicted the principle of national harmony. The resulting economic performance crises in 1978 and 1979 created a major strain in the party/society relationship. Vietnam's conflict with the Pol Pot government between 1975 and 1978, culminating in its invasion of Cambodia in 1978, and Vietnam's deteriorating relations with China, culminating in the 1979 border clashes, helped the party to mobilize popular support for national defense from both the North and the South and temporarily alleviated the legitimacy crisis of the socialist regime.

The reform movement in the socialist bloc that began in the late 1970s, coupled with Vietnam's chronic economic crises, forced the Vietnamese Communist Party to rethink socialism. The results can be seen in the policy of renovation (*doi moi*), which was officially endorsed in 1986. In the context of *doi moi*, the party leadership moved to redistribute power among major political institutions, strengthening the power of the state apparatus and the National Assembly. It revived the ideology of Ho Chi Minh to buttress the regime's legitimacy. Under pressure from reformist party members in the South, the party redefined its goals, shifted its policy, and launched limited sectoral reform. Recognizing the increasing importance of Vietnamese intellectuals, the party leadership emphasized the need to create a worker-peasant-intellectual alliance. The ideology of nationalism was employed to justify *doi moi*, which represented a compromise between the Northern and Southern models. It deterred the conservatives from becoming reactionary while co-opting certain members of the moderate opposition into its camp.

While the collapse of communism in the Soviet Union and Eastern Europe, and the challenge to communism in China, questioned the very foundation of the Vietnamese state socialist system, the Vietnamese Communist Party appears to have been successful, at least for the moment, in coping with the crisis and in renewing its legitimacy at both the leadership and society levels.

PART III

CONCLUSIONS AND OBSERVATIONS

11

Seeking a More Durable
Basis of Authority

MUTHIAH ALAGAPPA

THE country studies in Part II of this book support the central proposition advanced in Part I: in the absence of an established normative order, the procedural element cannot be the primary basis on which political authority is claimed, acknowledged, or resisted. Other rationales (normative goals, performance, personal authority, politically defining moment, and international support) will be more important in the legitimation of governments. Legitimation on the basis of these rationales, however, is highly contingent and subject to periodic erosion and crisis. Only when legitimation turns primarily on the procedural element will it become less problematic. For this to be the case, progress will have to be made in forging ideological unity between ruler and ruled and translating the shared norms and values into acceptable institutions, procedures, and practices.

In the postindependence period, governments in the Philippines, Burma, Indonesia, Singapore, and Malaysia did claim their authority on the basis of the procedural element rooted in versions of popular sovereignty and democracy. These governments, however, as well as the political system they represented, were subsequently displaced (Philippines, Burma, Indonesia) or substantially modified (Malaysia and Singapore). Drawing upon a politically defining moment or manipulating an atmosphere of crisis, successor governments deployed personal authority (Burma, Indonesia, Philippines) or goal rationality (Malaysia and Singapore) and invoked performance (security and economic development) as a key supplementary rationale or even as a goal in itself in projecting their legitimacy. Goal rationality has been the primary basis on which the Vietnamese Communist Party (VCP) claimed its authority from the outset, though economic performance became a crucial rationale in the post-1986 period. Personal authority and performance (security and development) were the key rationales deployed by the military governments in Thailand during the 1957–73 period, whereas inclusiveness and power sharing underscored the claim to authority by the quasi-democratic governments during the 1978–91 period.

The outcomes of these legitimation projects have been mixed. While most governments have been relatively successful in legitimating themselves, at least initially and in some cases for quite extended durations, the quest for regime legitimation has been much less successful. At best, governments like that led by UMNO in Malaysia have been able to accommodate the demands of subordinate groups. None, however, has yet been able to synthesize competing values and create ideological unity between ruler and ruled. In most cases, regime legitimation efforts have failed.

Drawing upon the framework outlined in Part I and the country studies presented in Part II, this concluding chapter explores two central questions raised in the Introduction: What accounts for the success or failure of these legitimation projects? And what progress has been made in the legitimation of political authority in the long term? The chapter begins by analyzing the failed legitimation projects of governments claiming their authority on the basis of procedures rooted in popular sovereignty and democracy.

Democratic Authority

The democratic systems instituted at independence in the Philippines (1946), Burma (1948), and Indonesia (1949) were relatively new to these societies, especially in Burma and Indonesia.[1] Indeed, the choice of constitutional democracy in these countries was to some extent fortuitous. Very few among the elite were committed to democratic values. In Indonesia, for example, expediency (in order to gain international support), national self-respect, the difficulty of securing the elite's agreement on any other system of government, and commitment to liberal-democratic values by a handful of power holders in 1949 underscored the adoption of constitutional democracy.[2] As noted by Herbert Feith, "although the symbol of democracy enjoyed very great acclaim, constitutional democracy was accepted only tentatively by the great part of the political public."[3] Further, democracy as conceived by Indonesian leaders had only tenuous links with the Western constitutional system.

Thus, at least initially, the democratic system was quite alien, constituting only a superficial overlay on traditional and colonial experiences. In contrast to the notions of participation, contestation, institutionalized opposition, and rule of law associated with a democratic system, the traditional as well as the colonial layers in all three countries tended toward concentration of power in the executive, absolutism, just rule, passive consent, and, in the absence of participatory channels, rebellion. Certain political leaders in these countries also viewed a strong executive as essential in the postindependence period in order to keep the nation united and undertake the socioeconomic policies needed to improve the welfare of the people. Thus the 1935 constitution in the Philippines, for example, was an amalgam of two contradictory tendencies: "one leaning toward liberal democracy and the other towards authoritarianism."[4]

Further, in all three countries the governments were weak and their writ did not extend to all parts of the society, especially those in the outlying regions. Regional and ethnic leaders, as well as local bosses, operated outside the formal political system. Drawing their power from local constituencies and traditions, these leaders contested the authority of the "national" government at the local level. Regional political and military leaders together with leading politicians from the Masyumi and Socialist parties rebelled against the Javanese-dominated central government in Indonesia from 1956 to 1958. Liberation movements in Aceh, West Irian, and East Timor continue to resist their integration into the Indonesian nation-state while contesting the legitimacy of the Jakarta government at the local level. In Burma the Rakhine and Karen communities challenged the authority of the Burman government in Rangoon from the time of independence and were joined in the late 1950s by other minority communities. In the Philippines *datus* (local chieftains) continue to enjoy power and authority, often in opposition to the state, especially in parts of the country least affected by Spanish and American colonial rule. Some of these groups have been fighting to secede from the Philippines (Moro National Liberation Front) or in pursuit of autonomy (Cordillera People's Liberation Army).

At the national level, the democratic political system did not embrace all centers of power. Several key actors and the politics associated with them remained outside the democratic process as, for example, with Sukarno and the military in Indonesia. Through their roles in the national revolution, they had become key political actors commanding relatively independent bases of power, but the democratic process in Indonesia did not effectively integrate them. In Burma, the left wing of the Anti-Fascist People's Freedom League (AFPFL) chose self-exclusion and viewed the system as a "sellout to the imperialists" (Chao-Tzang Yawnghwe in Chapter 7). The Burmese military, which progressively became more involved in administering the country at the regional level, was formally excluded from politics. Because of the exclusion of key individuals and groups, the democratic political systems in these countries were not the sole or even the primary repository of power. Those who gained power through the democratic process had to come to terms with those who remained outside it and who often did not view the regime as legitimate. Resenting their exclusion or seeking a monopoly of power, these actors deployed their power to subvert and eventually displace the system.

Even among those who embraced the regime, the consensus was rather fragile. Economic and political developments after independence produced conflicts of interest within the elite that further eroded consensus. Moreover, these developments created new socioeconomic forces that challenged the elite's domination of politics. In the Philippines, for example, the import substitution industrialization (ISI) strategy of the 1950s and 1960s diversified the recruitment base of political leadership at both the national and local levels.[5] This diversification undermined the previous monopoly of economic and political power by the landed aristocracy. At the same time, however, the extension of the oligarchic concentration of wealth in land and commerce to industry contributed to the creation of private economic-political power bases with potential to influence the formulation of state policy and challenge the authority of the chief executive of the government.[6] The attempts by Presidents Macapagal and Marcos to concentrate power in the office of the chief executive were opposed by these power centers, resulting in an impasse between the executive and the legislature and, ultimately, the paralysis of government.

Concurrently, there was a sharp rise in inequity and poverty and a resurgence of nationalism in the late 1960s. From the perspective of the student left, industrial workers, nationalist industrializers, segments of the Catholic church committed to reform, and the newly formed Communist Party of the Philippines, the two key institutions of the country—the Congress and the president—had lost their legitimacy because of their greed and inaction.[7] Radicalism and nationalism added a second cleavage to Philippine politics that manifested itself in the form of street protests and rallies contributing to an atmosphere of crisis and instability, a situation that President Ferdinand Marcos manipulated to his advantage, laying the context for his 1972 declaration of martial law.

Several other accounts have been advanced to explain the failure of democracy in the Philippines.[8] Moreover, some question whether democracy did fail in the Philippines or whether its expansion from the elite to the popular level was forestalled by Marcos.[9] From the perspective of this study, the crucial point is that the key actors were not committed to democratic ideals. Most of them viewed democratic institutions and procedures in terms of narrow self-interest. When these institutions ceased to serve their purpose, the incumbents as well as their opponents undermined and in due course destroyed them. Further, Philippine democracy in practice reflected "the interplay of money, violence, and the manipulation of state resources" (Sidel in Chapter 6). A great majority of Filipinos tended to view the government as predatory and were highly skeptical about its claim to legitimacy on the basis of democratic procedures. This widespread belief helps to explain the lack of public opposition to the declaration of martial law. In fact, the elite and the middle class welcomed martial law because they believed that authoritarian rule would promote political stability and economic development.[10]

As noted earlier, the commitment to democratic values in Indonesia was limited to a small Western-educated group led by Mohammad Hatta. Although this "administrator" group did make some headway in creating and legitimating a constitutional democratic system between 1949 and 1953, the regime remained continuously under threat from revolutionary political groups that it could not integrate.[11] The weakness and frequent collapse of cabinets (seven cabinets in as many years) and their inability to satisfy material, status, and political expectations, coupled with increasing political unrest, undermined the credibility of the democratic system among large segments of the Indonesian elite.

The 1955 elections, the first in Indonesia since independence, were viewed as a means to arrive at a master solution to many of the country's political problems. Instead the three-year-long election campaign accelerated the disintegration of national consensus, contributing to the polarization of society along ideological lines (the Javanese-aristocratic versus Islamic-entrepreneurial political cultures—Pancasila versus Islam) as well as regional lines (Mochtar Pabottingi in Chapter 9). In the absence of common goals, there was no basis for compromise. Ineffective governments, a polarized society, and apprehension among many in the political elite over civil disorder discredited the democratic system of government, weakening the power of groups advocating democratic values.

Concurrently the power and influence of the army and President Sukarno, supported for its own reasons by the Partai Kommunis Indonesia (PKI), increased. Although initially the central leaders of the army cooperated with the "administrators," the army resented its diminished position after 1952 and became actively hostile to civilian politicians and resolved to destroy their dominance. Sukarno, from the beginning, did not subscribe to Western democratic values.[12] With the discrediting of the democratic system and the growing atmosphere of crisis, Sukarno's criticism of liberal democracy, his advocacy of national solidarity, and his *konsepsi* (democracy with leadership) had wide appeal. The alliance of

Sukarno and the army—the former providing the ideology and the latter providing the coercive power—proved to be formidable. Ultimately it led to the replacement of the democratic system by "guided democracy."

In Burma, the Anti-Fascist People's Freedom League (AFPFL) government projected its legitimacy by deploying multiple resources: nationalist credentials, a federalist image, and the future goal of a prosperous, just, and equitable Burmese society (Yawnghwe in Chapter 7). It sought to consolidate its legitimacy on the basis of the political system rooted in the 1947 Constitution. This system, founded upon liberal-democratic principles with ultimate authority resting in the people via the Parliament, was quite inclusive. It was, however, from the outset contested by the Burmese Communist Party (BCP/CPB), the AFPFL's most important partner-cum-rival during the struggle against colonialism. Accusing the AFPFL of abandoning the goals of the revolution, the BCP/CPB openly challenged the democratic system as well as the incumbent government. Yet another challenge came from the Karen, who deeply distrusted the Burman. From their perspective the Burman-based nation-state and the incumbent government were both illegitimate.

Despite these challenges, the AFPFL government did make progress in legitimating itself and the system. The success of the National United Front in the 1956 elections convinced even the allies of BCP/CPB of the possibilities for carrying out reform through the parliamentary system. The 1961–62 federal movement was another indication of the growing confidence of the non-Burman people in the federal structure and parliamentary system. This growing legitimacy was negated, however, by two developments: the disintegration of the AFPFL and the military's rejection of civilian political dominance and the democratic system.

In all three countries, the commitment to democratic values was shallow. The democratic regime and the incumbent government were challenged from the beginning by those advocating different political ideologies as well as by charismatic figures and groups like the politically active military who could not be accommodated within the system. Political and economic developments contributed to divisions among the elite, eroding the national consensus forged at the time of independence. They also created new groups that challenged the legitimacy of the incumbent power holders if not the whole system itself. The disenchanted elite as well as the new groups used the political space provided by the democratic system and its weaknesses to mobilize and articulate their interests—all of which contributed to an atmosphere of crisis. Moreover, the political system failed to embrace those in the outlying regions who challenged national authority at the local level.

The inability of the incumbent governments to address the many political and economic problems of their countries—coupled with concern in the respective body politic over deteriorating law and order and threats to the unity of their countries—discredited the democratic system and undermined the legitimating value of its procedural element. Governments acquiring power through the democratic process did not command moral authority among certain key groups or from a majority of the politically aware public. In all three countries, the mounting atmosphere of crisis presented an opportunity for those advocating competing ideologies to usurp political power.

The commitment to democratic values in Singapore and Malaysia was qualified, and in Thailand it was almost nonexistent. Although the stated goal of the 1932 "revolution" in Thailand was "democratic" government (as opposed to absolute monarchy) and every government since then has felt duty bound to proclaim its commitment to democracy and promulgate a constitution, these gestures have had no bearing on the actual conduct of politics. The acquisition and exercise of power in Thailand had little regard for the formal rules, which were honored more by their breach than by their observance.[13] In Singapore, too, there was no commitment among the competing parties to preserve the democratic system (Cho-Oon Khong in Chapter 5). The democratic process was used in the 1950s and early 1960s by all political parties in a Hobbesian fashion to capture the key institutions of state. Having captured power through the system, the PAP proceeded to amend the rules of the game, neutralizing and eliminating political opposition on the grounds of stability and, later, survival. In Malaysia, the parliamentary democratic system was suspended after the racial riots that followed the May 1969 elections. The Malay community believed that the results of the election challenged the principle of Malay dominance—the core element, from its perspective, of the bargain struck among the three major ethnic communities in 1957. Many in UMNO—including Mahathir Mohamad, then an UMNO backbencher and presently prime minister—advocated the permanent closing of the Parliament and continuation of emergency rule (William Case in Chapter 4). Reinstitution of the parliamentary system in 1971 was accompanied by constitutional amendments to enshrine the goal of Malay political dominance, which was to become the overriding basis of authority from the perspective of the Malay community.

For the reasons outlined here, the legitimacy of the democratic systems in all these countries, which constituted only a thin veneer to begin with, was increasingly contested and led eventually to the regime's displacement or modification. The successor governments relied more heavily on other rationales in justifying their right to rule—personal authority, goal rationality, and performance—as popular sovereignty and democratic procedures assumed a subordinate role. Although all the governments deployed multiple rationales in projecting their legitimacy, in some cases personal authority weighed more heavily while in others goal rationality was stressed as the primary basis of authority.

Personal Authority

Personal authority figured quite prominently in the legitimacy projection of governments led by Sarit in Thailand, Marcos in the Philippines, and Ne Win in Burma and continues to be the case with the Soeharto government in Indonesia. The personal authority referred to here is not the charismatic authority defined by Weber but, rather, the authority of the "strong man" (in the case of Sarit and Marcos) and the new patrimonial authority (in the case of Soeharto and Ne Win). Although it is difficult to determine the precise salience of personal authority in the legitimation formula, the fact that these governments have been so closely tied to the fortunes of the leaders suggests that it must be substantial.

In no case, however, has personal authority alone been sufficient. In addition to his strong man credentials, Sarit deployed the goals of security and development, the moral authority of the monarchy, and the ideology of Thai-style democracy to legitimate his autocratic rule. Marcos deployed "constitutional authoritarianism," popular sovereignty (plebiscites and elections), and socioeconomic reform and development (the goal of a new, more egalitarian society). Ne Win invoked restoration of order, preservation of national unity, resolution of economic problems, the historic role of the Tatmadaw (the Burmese military), and the Burmese Way to Socialism. Political stability and reconstruction of the economy formed the core of the early legitimacy projection of Soeharto's New Order government. Moreover, all four governments sought to constrict the political arena through selective interpretation or construction of new national ideologies, control of political activities and organizations, and, with the exception of Burma, depoliticization of the economy and certain contentious issues that were then subjected to technocratic management. In all four countries, state coercion—rule by decree, arrests and detention without trial, confiscation of property, restriction or denial of civil liberties, torture and killing—was used liberally to suppress and exclude political opposition.

The legitimacy projections of these governments, except for that of Ne Win, did enjoy a measure of initial success. In time, however, the widening gap between projection and reality (in the case of the Marcos government) and the unintended consequences of certain rationales (in the case of the

Sarit-Thanom governments) undermined their legitimacy and led eventually to their ouster. Marcos's emphasis on constitutional authoritarianism, the organization of plebiscites, and *barangay* democracy, his commitment to socioeconomic reform, and the shift to an export-oriented economic strategy appealed to the urban middle class, to technocrats in the bureaucracy, to entrepreneurs in the private sector, and to ordinary Filipinos (whose welfare Marcos claimed was being addressed for the first time), generating considerable support for his authoritarian government at the outset. Concurrently he silenced or co-opted the traditional opposition by attacking its economic and institutional bases of power. In the first five years, Marcos's martial law government registered substantial advances in a number of areas: law and order was restored, land reform was being implemented, the economy posted impressive growth (an average annual expansion of 6.5 percent), the communist insurgency was being rolled back, an agreement providing for autonomy was signed with the Muslim secessionists in the south, and foreign policy was being diversified in the wake of the Vietnam War.[14] His policies also appealed to international investors and lending agencies, especially in the United States.

But these initial successes were not sustained. From about 1977 the gap between promise and reality with respect to most of Marcos's claims began to widen, exposing the emptiness of his rhetoric and undermining the legitimacy of his government. Indeed, his rhetoric was seized by the politically dissatisfied, including the traditional opposition, to contest the legitimacy of Marcos and his government.[15] Marcos's frequent revision of the constitution and his blatant manipulation of referenda and plebiscites undermined the credibility of his claim to constitutional authoritarianism. The deep economic crisis and the hardship it created, coupled with Marcos's personal corruption and lust for power, exposed the hollowness of his claim that his rule was in the interest of ordinary Filipinos and, more generally, the justification of authoritarian rule for the sake of "developmentalism." The economic crisis together with Marcos's attempt to suppress student, labor, and peasant unrest as well as abuse by government troops contributed to the intensification of the challenges mounted by the Communist Party of the Philippines (CPP/NPA) and Muslim liberation fronts, challenges the government appeared unable to overcome.

Concurrently, Marcos's support base was shrinking. In addition to the traditional elite and the left, who were alienated from the beginning of martial law, the policies of Marcos eventually alienated the students, the professional elite, the business community, and the Catholic church. Increasingly Marcos relied on the military and international support, but these buttresses too proved undependable. Its new mission to defend the regime politicized the Armed Forces of the Philippines (AFP) and led to factionalism.[16] The "Reform the Armed Forces Movement" (RAM), which grew out of the faction loyal to Defense Minister Juan Ponce-Enrile, played a crucial role in the ouster of Marcos. Compelled to review its policy because of the growing communist threat, the deepening economic crisis, the gross violation of human rights, and more immediately the assassination of Benigno Aquino in 1983, the United States urged Marcos to undertake socioeconomic reform and to hold elections to renew his mandate. Adding to his problems, Marcos's own health was failing. His projection of "big man" authority was no longer credible. There was growing concern about succession.

By 1985 Marcos and his authoritarian rule had been thoroughly discredited, but they continued to survive because of state coercion, disunity among the opposition, and the absence of means to displace them. The opportunity came when Marcos, attempting to recapture legitimacy, called for snap presidential elections in February 1986. Having had considerable success in the past in manipulating elections and national referenda,[17] Marcos was hoping he could do the same with the 1986 elections and stem the mounting U.S. pressure for reform. He was counting on disunity among the opposition as well as his control of the state machinery to ensure his victory.[18] He miscalculated on both counts. Although neither he nor Corazon Aquino could claim absolute victory, the closeness of the results and the belief that despite international scrutiny Marcos was able to manipulate the election's outcome gave the moral victory to Aquino. The mutiny by key segments within the AFP and the massive "people power" rally led to the final ouster of Marcos.

The Sarit government in Thailand, like that of Marcos in the Philippines, was welcomed by the conservative urban middle class. Ordinary Thais, especially those living outside Bangkok, were not active participants in the political process. Two key elements in Sarit's legitimation formula (economic development and support of the monarchy) had wide appeal, but their very success conflicted with other key elements of the legitimation formula (order and stability and the need for a strong man), contributing to contestation and erosion and eventually a crisis of legitimacy of the government and regime.

The success of the comprehensive development programs launched by General Sarit and continued by General Thanom made for rapid socioeconomic transformation of Thai society (Saitip Sukatipan in Chapter 8). While this transformation produced a few conservative groups (the business community with links to the military, co-opted segments of the urban middle class, rich peasants), the vast majority of the new socioeconomic forces (students, independent businesspeople, professionals, industrial workers, farmers) were progressively demanding greater equity and political participation. These demands not only conflicted with the order and stability goals of the Thanom government but challenged its very nature. At base there was a tension between the power holders who continued to emphasize security and stability and the new groups who demanded political and socioeconomic reform. The unwillingness of the Thai military to modify its legitimation formula in order to incorporate popular sovereignty and equity elements led to the largely student-led popular uprising in October 1973—which, as was the case later in the Philippines (1986), Burma (1988), and once again in Thailand itself (1992), publicly confirmed the Thanom government's lack of moral authority.

The final ouster of the Thanom government was due to the monarchy's withdrawal of support—the monarchy had outgrown the symbiotic relationship with the military governments to become the most powerful political institution in the country—and disunity within the army, the primary support base of Sarit and later Thanom. The tension between order and stability, on the one hand, and equity and participation on the other also underscored the contestation of the ensuing democratic regime's legitimacy, this time by the conservative forces with the support of the monarchy and the acquiescence of the ordinary people who were apprehensive about the radical demands of the progressive forces. This tension was temporarily resolved by the 1978 constitution, which accommodated the key groups on both sides on the basis of power sharing.

In Burma, by way of contrast, the Ne Win government (initially the Revolutionary Council and later the Burma Socialist Program Party until 1988) was not successful in legitimizing itself even at the outset (Yawnghwe in Chapter 7). The Revolutionary Council's attempt to justify its monopoly of political power on the basis of goal rationality (building Burmese socialism) failed miserably. As a goal, socialism was not new to Burma and the military's version did not appeal to any other audience. Despite its declared intention to become mass based, the Burma Socialist Program Party (Lanzin), which became the sole legal party after 1964, remained a hollow organization and could not serve a legitimizing function. All power was concentrated in the military—in fact in Ne Win, who through patronage and purges kept absolute control of the army and the Lanzin Party.

The legitimacy of Ne Win's government was contested almost universally from its inception in 1962. The political parties refused to cooperate with the Revolutionary Council.[19] Beginning in July 1962 students periodically demonstrated against the military government, as did workers in the state enterprises. The economic policies of the Revolutionary Council alienated the urban middle class, as well, and later the peasants. Initially the peasants did benefit from the cancellation of debts and abolition of land rents, but by 1981 some 86 percent of the country's rural families were living in poverty. The Sanggha (Buddhist church) contested the military's attempt to control religious organizations and activities. The ethnic minorities, viewing the 1962 coup as a violation of the 1947 Panglong Agreement and tantamount to dissolution of the Union of Burma, refused to acknowledge the legitimacy of the Burman-based nation-state as well as the military government. The BCP/CPB continued its war against Rangoon. Economic mismanagement, decline, and corruption caused enormous suffering for all but the military officers and well-connected civilians. Thus, except for the armed forces and the bureaucracy, the military's projection of legitimacy was rejected by nearly everyone.

Nevertheless the military-socialist regime continued to survive for well over two decades because of the unity of the armed forces and their loyalty to Ne Win. Ultimately, however, the accumulated resentment against military rule, ignited by the 1988 Sanda Win incident, burst into a countrywide "people power" uprising. Faced with moral bankruptcy and widespread popular demand for change, the military promised a multiparty system. In an effort to silence domestic opposition and gain international legitimacy—and, more significantly, confident that the military-backed National Unity Party (NUP) would win—the State Law and Order Restoration Council (SLORC) organized national elections in May 1990. But, as in the Philippines, the results clearly confirmed the lack of legitimacy of the military rulers. The military, however, has refused to hand over power. SLORC, which is seen as a continuation of the previous military-socialist government, continues to suffer a legitimacy crisis. Worse, the legitimacy of the military as a patriotic institution, a key element of SLORC's legitimation formula, has been seriously compromised. Even so, with international support from China and the ASEAN countries as well as the use of state coercion, SLORC continues to control Burma.

In contrast to the other three governments, all of which have been thoroughly discredited and displaced or remain at an impasse, Soeharto's government has achieved considerable success in legitimating itself and continues to survive. It should be noted here that goal rationality (political stability and economic development) continues to be a key component of the Soeharto government's claim to authority. Soeharto's personal authority was in fact rather tenuous to begin with. Only later, through the persistent deployment of patronage, coercion, and tradition, did his personal authority assume greater significance, capturing a central position in the political legitimation of the New Order.[20] Although personal authority became more central, giving the regime an autocratic character, development continued to be a key component of the legitimation formula. The

New Order's legitimacy projection has a hegemonic content, as well, in that an effort has been made to universalize a selective interpretation of Pancasila. And ABRI (the military) seeks to legitimize its sociopolitical role and continued domination of Indonesian politics by depicting *dwifungsi* ("dual function"—security and sociopolitical) as a right that is in the interest of the whole nation.

In light of the continuous political upheaval from 1950 through 1965, as well as the sharp deterioration in people's living standards, especially during the guided democracy era, the goals of political stability and economic development had great appeal to most sections of the Indonesian polity—except, of course, the members of the PKI, whose massacre was justified in terms of these same two goals. The New Order government had the support of religious leaders, students, and intellectuals. But this alignment, born of common disenchantment with the PKI's dominant position in the previous political arrangements, was short-lived. As the New Order consolidated its position, it neutralized the other groups. These groups, however, continued to support the New Order because they believed in its commitment to the goals of political stability and economic development; besides, they had no choice. As Soeharto did not have an independent power base to begin with, the New Order government was firmly rooted in ABRI. There was unity of purpose, therefore, between Soeharto and ABRI.

The New Order concentrated power in the chief executive and constricted the political arena. Depoliticization in Indonesia continues to be extensive: all groups have been compelled to accept Pancasila as the *asas tunggal* (sole basis of political organization) and the government arrogates to itself the right to define the meaning of the national ideology; all other "extreme" ideologies have been banned; electioneering is confined to narrowly defined issues and limited to a very short duration; nongovernment political parties have been excluded from the rural areas through the floating mass concept; senior appointments in the political parties are made by the president, who also makes appointments to the legislature and gubernatorial posts; political activities and organizations are tightly controlled through the territorial defense system, pervasive intelligence organizations, and admonitory killings; freedom of expression and the media are controlled. Despite the extensiveness and severity of these measures, many accepted them as necessary in the interest of ensuring political stability and economic growth. The realization of these two goals, therefore, appears to have conferred moral authority on Soeharto and his New Order government from the perspective of a majority of the Indonesian people.[21]

From about the middle to late 1980s, however, nearly all the key underlying principles of the New Order (a strong chief executive, Pancasila

as *asas tunggal*, managed participation and contestation), the military's
sociopolitical role, as well as the New Order's dual goals of political stability and economic development, were contested by a number of groups
including Forum Democracy, the Indonesian Muslim Intellectual Association (ICMI), Nahdatul Ulama (NU), human rights organizations, Christian minorities, and critics within ABRI itself. These groups have challenged various principles and goals of the New Order or, more commonly,
their implementation. In arguing their case, critics draw upon the 1945
ideals as well as the languages of legitimation advanced by the government
itself.[22] Islamic and democratic groups, for example, claim to accept Pancasila but contend that Soeharto has contravened or deviated from the
1945 interpretation. National ideology here is deployed by the critics to
challenge the legitimacy of the government and regime, lending support to
James Scott's observation that the process of seeking to legitimate a social
order by idealizing it provides the tools for resistance.[23] While Soeharto
has managed to keep effective control over the army by appointing loyalists to senior positions, since the late 1980s a breach has developed between Soeharto and the military. Soeharto's attempt to create a power
base of his own has undermined, though not destroyed, the unity of purpose created earlier between the president and ABRI, contributing to the
erosion of support from a key pillar of the New Order government.[24] In
attempting to curb Soeharto's unbridled power (as opposed to the authority of the New Order), critics within ABRI, preferring not to confront Soeharto directly, advocate the strengthening of the DPR and MPR.

With political stability assured and Soeharto's personal authority subject to increasing criticism,[25] the emphasis in projecting legitimacy appears
to have shifted to developmentalism (now defined as economic growth,
equalization, and industrialization).[26] But this goal too has become the
focus of criticism. Indonesia's economic performance since 1965 has been
impressive, and by most accounts the benefits of growth appear to have
reached all social classes: by some measures, consumption expenditure of
even the lowest income group has increased while the absolute number of
those living below the poverty line has declined.[27] This claim, however, is
contested by critics who contend that economic growth has increased inequity, benefiting the non-*pribumi* (ethnic Chinese) at the expense of the
pribumi (native Indonesians) (Pabottingi in Chapter 9). The same groups
also contest the *dwifungsi* principle that underlies the military domination
of politics. Not only political stability and economic growth, they argue,
but democracy, Islam, and equity must now underpin the political system
in Indonesia.

Although Soeharto's legitimacy and that of his government are contested, for a number of reasons the challenges appear unlikely to reach

critical proportions in the immediate future. The demand for democratic government is not yet widespread, and the negative experiences of the 1950–57 period created a strong distrust of democratic politics that is still quite pervasive. Moreover, there is a strong constituency for development. While critical of Soeharto, the army is not against the New Order and is unlikely to move against him. Further, Soeharto has taken several measures to recapture legitimacy: displaying greater concern for equity and nationalism in formulating economic policy, alignment with modernist Islamic organizations to counterbalance the army, promotion of loyalists within the army, and increasing the civilian element in the government and Golkar (the government party, or, more correctly, the government mechanism for winning elections).

It is pertinent to observe here that despite its self-serving character, the accommodation of Islam and Islamic groups by Soeharto does in a limited way contribute to the enhancement of not only his personal authority but also that of the government and regime. Despite the cynical perceptions of the political elite, the increasing Islamic character of Soeharto, his government, and its policies—for example, the increased support for *Haj* and cancellation of the SDSB lottery—has increased their appeal to the ordinary, especially Javanese, Muslims. Through the inclusion of the dominant religion in the country, the base of government and regime has been inadvertently broadened. Islamic groups need no longer feel proscribed and excluded from the system.

While enhancing the legitimacy of the New Order government from the perspective of one key segment of the population, the accommodation of Islam also creates apprehensions in minority religious communities and ABRI and could erode the New Order's legitimacy from their perspectives. By raising concerns in neighboring Singapore and the Western international community, greater accommodation of Islam could also undermine the international support for the New Order government. More fundamentally, if Islam is accorded a privileged status, even if it is only unofficial and on pragmatic grounds, the New Order will be confronted with the dilemma of reconciling this with the 1945 understanding of Pancasila, which does not accord a privileged position to any religion—an interpretation that the government has chosen thus far to stress. The key question is whether Soeharto, like UMNO in Malaysia, can accommodate and manage Islam without subjecting his government and regime to fundamental change. Further, will partial accommodation of Islam be sufficient or will it expose the New Order government to additional demands and challenge from groups who could argue that the interpretation of Islam favored by Soeharto is incorrect or insist that his government and regime are not Islamic enough?

Although serious challenges to the legitimacy of Soeharto and his government may be unlikely, at least in the short to medium term, the legitimacy of successor governments is not at all assured. Increasing contestation of goals (especially if economic development further aggravates inequity), of principles (such as concentration of power in the chief executive and *dwifungsi*), and of the selective interpretation of Pancasila suggests that the present goals and principles alone cannot form the basis for long-term ideological unity between ruler and ruled. Other ideologies—Islam and democracy, for instance—may become more potent in influencing the structure of domination. This likelihood is supported by the fact that nearly all groups appear to be positioning themselves for the post-Soeharto era. Thus, unlike government legitimation, regime legitimation has made only limited progress in Indonesia. Future governments will have to find a new formula to legitimate themselves. In addition to emphasizing development with equity and modifying *dwifungsi*, the new formula would have to accommodate Islam without alienating the minority religious communities, it would have to provide for greater political participation and choice, and the government would have to be more inclusive. Personal authority, at least to begin with, will be less important.

This discussion of the legitimacy projections of autocratic governments and their reception suggests at least four conclusions. First, it supports the observation in Part I regarding the difficulty of routinizing personal authority and its unsuitability as the primary basis for regime legitimation. None of the four leaders has made much effort to deploy his personal authority to institutionalize a political system.[28] Indeed, the tendency has been to subvert institutions and procedures to enhance personal authority. Thus transfer of power and the legitimacy of successor governments remain problematic. The Ne Win government, for example, did not adopt a constitution until 1974. Even after that the constitution and the Lanzin Party were really a front for patrimonial rule. Power rested not in the office of the chief executive but in the person of Ne Win, who prevented the development of other autonomous centers of power. Moreover, until recently the Burmese military made no serious effort to legitimate and institutionalize its political role. Like Ne Win, Marcos's concern was to strengthen his position and later to ensure his political survival. He did not anoint a successor or institute a system for succession. Thus his failing health set off a struggle for power among his own supporters and reinvigorated the opposition. Although Thailand's Sarit advocated Thai-style democracy, he did not attempt to institutionalize the idea. From 1958 he ruled by decree. The weaker Thanom, who succeeded Sarit upon his death, had to yield to demands for constitutional rule and political contestation. But in 1971, two years after national elections, Thanom launched an auto-coup ending parliamentary democracy. From 1932 the

Thai military had no clear idea which political system it preferred or how to institutionalize its political role. Thanom's attempt to groom his son Narong Kittikachorn to succeed him accentuated disunity within the army and drew a negative reaction from the king.

In contrast to these three cases, there has been an attempt in Indonesia to institutionalize a political system based on the principles cited earlier. Since 1973 there have been regular elections and regular meetings of the DPR and MPR. The constitution specifies a procedure for presidential succession should the incumbent die in office. Very few, however, believe that it will be observed. The problem is that the system hinges on the person of Soeharto as opposed to the office of the president. Soeharto has done very little to give the institutions and procedures a life of their own. Manipulation to serve his immediate political concerns rather than principles and policies has guided Soeharto's actions. He has dealt harshly with those who have advocated depersonalizing the system. In fact, some of the measures deployed by Soeharto to enhance his personal authority contradict principles that underlie the New Order—strengthening forces (like ICMI) that are opposed to the nature of the regime, while antagonizing or weakening those (like ABRI and NU) that support it. His alliance with modernist Islamic groups to counterbalance the army, for example, contradicts the principles of *asas tunggal* and *dwifungsi*. As noted earlier, however, these measures, particularly the accommodation of Islam, may contribute to an inadvertent broadening of the government but at the same time they may create apprehension in minority groups. The basic point is that irrespective of how these developments are viewed, there is much reason to doubt that the system in its present form will survive Soeharto.

In all four cases, then, the requirements of the leader's power and authority have overridden those of government and regime. Leader, government, and regime have remained fused. Hence the legitimacy of the governments and regimes has paralleled the fortunes of the leaders. The autocratic regimes in the Philippines and Thailand did not survive the ruler; in Burma the regime has been repudiated; the likelihood of the regime in Indonesia surviving Soeharto remains in doubt.

Second, there is an inherent tension between personal authority and political stability on the one hand and the rationales of performance and popular sovereignty on the other. While performance and popular sovereignty may contribute to the legitimacy of autocratic (and authoritarian) governments in the short run, in the long term they are likely to undermine their authority. Good economic performance enhanced the authority of Marcos and Sarit in the short term, but failure to sustain success and increasing inequity contributed to the contestation of Marcos's legitimacy, while continued success gave rise to equity concerns and produced new forces that challenged the legitimacy of the Thanom government. Similarly, while good performance has contributed to the legitimacy of the Soeharto government, the New Order's legitimacy has been challenged on grounds of inequity and corruption—and the growth of more independent middle and working classes is likely to accentuate this contestation. In Burma, failure to perform deepened the legitimacy problem of the Ne Win government.

These observations support Samuel Huntington's assertion that authoritarian governments face a perpetual performance dilemma.[29] In fact, one can even argue that unless authoritarian governments are willing to accommodate change (address equity concerns and share power) in a timely fashion, the negating potential of performance is greater than its legitimating potential. There is, moreover, an inherent tension between political stability and economic development. While political stability is necessary for economic growth, the institutions responsible for the stability are essentially conservative and stand to lose in relative terms as a consequence of growth. Hence they view change with apprehension. The forces emerging from the socioeconomic transformation that accompanies economic development, however, view the political status quo as unacceptable and demand change. This tension between stability and change produces political conflict and may, as in Thailand in 1973, lead to crisis.

Popular sovereignty poses another dilemma for autocratic rulers. Because of the moral authority that is believed to attach to popular mandate, most rulers deem it necessary to rule for and in the name of the people; but they are unable and unwilling to cope with the demands of this principle, which challenges the very core of autocratic rule. To serve their purpose, rulers have attempted to indigenize ideologies and institutions associated with popular sovereignty (Thai-style democracy, guided democracy, Pancasila democracy, Burmese socialism, *barangay* democracy) or to manipulate them through managed participation and contestation. Such formulations, however, are readily transparent and easily penetrated, producing skepticism and cynicism. Socioeconomic transformation and the transnational flow of ideas make self-serving indigenous formulations of "universal" ideologies and controlled participation even more difficult. The institutional mode of legitimation (affecting the practical social conduct of the body politic through resource allocation and structuring of rules) is also weak in autocratic regimes because of the arbitrariness that characterizes such rule. Commitment to the objective of democracy, however weak, and exposure to elections and parliaments, however controlled, will in the long run, as in Thailand, inculcate belief in such values and practices, making them indispensable elements of the legitimation formula. International pressure can also increase the salience of these values and practices. The unexpected outcomes of the 1986 elections in the Philippines and the 1990 elections in Burma illustrate in stark

terms the dangers of deploying popular sovereignty to legitimate autocratic regimes.

Third, as suggested in Chapter 2, multiple-rationale strategies have
both positive and negative consequences for political legitimation. Marcos's constitutional authoritarianism appeased the urban middle class; his
export-oriented economic development strategy appealed to technocrats,
to entrepreneurs in the private sector, and to international development
agencies; his anticommunism appealed to the army; and his socioeconomic reform and "big man" projection appealed to the ordinary people.
In Indonesia, a multiple-rationale strategy has facilitated a shift in emphasis from the less relevant or weakening components (political stability and
personal authority) to the stronger one (developmentalism). On the negative side, multiple rationales expose the government to contestation from
a wide array of groups, as was the case in the last stage of Marcos's rule.
More significant, the inherent tensions among the various rationales discussed earlier expose the government in the long term to contestation
and erosion of its legitimacy, making regime legitimation all the more
problematic.

And fourth, the survival of the Marcos and Ne Win governments even
after they were thoroughly discredited strongly argues against using survival as the sole or even the primary indicator of legitimacy. The case of
the Ne Win government demonstrates that with solidarity among power
holders and the threat of coercion, a government can hold onto power for
quite a long time. Apathy, coercion, fear, the lack of means to displace
it—all can sustain a government. Hence other indicators must also be
used in evaluating a government's legitimacy. The continued survival of
governments even after they have been thoroughly discredited also suggests the limits of the explanatory and even more the predictive potential
of the theory of legitimacy with regard to regime change. While the loss of
legitimacy is a necessary condition for government/regime change, it is not
sufficient. Other factors—coercion, apathy, unavailability of alternatives,
lack of opportunity for public expression, international support—may
sustain a government and must be factored into the explanation. In contrast to legitimacy projections based on personal authority, those based
on pertinent and enduring goals, as we shall see, have had relatively
greater success in regime legitimation.

Goal-Rational-cum-Hegemonic Authority

The legitimacy projections of governments led by the United Malays National Organization (UMNO), the People's Action Party (PAP), and the
Vietnamese Communist Party (VCP) have been distinctly goal-rational.

The goal of ethnic protection underscored UMNO's claim to authority from the outset (Case in Chapter 4). After May 1969, this rationale (the commitment to protect and promote Malay dominance) became even more explicit in UMNO's claim to the right to rule. In Vietnam the Communist Party claimed monopoly of political power on the basis of its moral and intellectual superiority in achieving the goals of national liberation and building socialism (Thaveeporn Vasavakul in Chapter 10). With reunification in 1975, building socialism became the sole goal, and since 1986 economic renovation has been the key theme of the VCP. Survival (political and economic) was the primary basis on which the PAP government claimed its authority upon the separation of Singapore from Malaysia (Khong in Chapter 5). Although survival is no longer precarious, the government periodically reminds Singaporeans that survival cannot be taken for granted.

Legitimacy projections in Malaysia and Vietnam were hegemonic as well, in that sectional goals were articulated as embodying the interests of the whole society. In addition to asserting the rightfulness of Malay dominance, UMNO, in its effort to secure the consent of the non-Malay communities, contends that the principle of Malay dominance is in the interest of the entire Malaysian society. Without Malay dominance, it is argued, instability will reign and the political and economic rights of the non-Malay communities cannot be guaranteed. In Vietnam, although the VCP projected its two goals in nationalist terms and presented them as symbiotic, the goal of building socialism was a sectional value clothed in nationalist language. Since 1975, the VCP's projection of legitimacy has been distinctly hegemonic, based on the goal of building socialism. In Singapore the goal of survival was initially shared by the rulers and the bulk of the country's population. But its continued deployment even after survival became much less problematic and the recent deployment of a national ideology based on a selective interpretation of the Confucian ethic have introduced hegemonic overtones into the PAP's legitimation project.

The legitimacy projections of UMNO, the VCP, and the PAP have been relatively successful. Their success is due to the contextual pertinence of the goals and their consequent appeal to the targeted audiences. In Malaysia, belief in their special rights as "sons of the soil," as well as apprehension of being dominated by non-Malays, underscored the Malay appeal for ethnic protection and political dominance (Case in Chapter 4). Developments in 1969 confirmed to the Malay community the importance of ethnic unity and protection. Since then the goal of Malay dominance has been its overriding concern. A majority of the Malays, rural and urban, believe that UMNO is the right vehicle to achieve this goal. This belief confers moral authority on UMNO.

Even when certain Malay leaders believed that the UMNO-led government failed to deliver on this goal, they did not contest the legitimacy of UMNO but worked from within the party to rededicate it and the government to the goal of Malay dominance by seeking changes in leadership and policies. This was the case after 1969 when Tunku Abdul Rahman was replaced and several changes were introduced in the constitution and government policies to broaden and deepen Malay dominance. The successful implementation of these policies further reinforced UMNO's moral authority from the perspective of a majority of the Malays.

While goal rationality was highly successful in relation to the Malay community and UMNO could genuinely claim to represent the interests of that community, its hegemonic projection in relation to the other communities has been less successful. After 1969 UMNO adopted the strategy of marginalizing non-Malay political parties while simultaneously accommodating certain non-Malay interests. It continued, in a more limited way, the inclusionary approach instituted at independence by allowing participation and representation of non-Malays in government. UMNO has not, however, attempted to create ideological unity between itself and the non-Malay communities. In the absence of alternatives—and given a perception that things could be worse—many non-Malays have accepted the principle of Malay dominance. Despite its rhetoric, even the Democratic Action Party (DAP) has accepted Malay dominance as demonstrated by its junior partner status in the Semangat '46 coalition. The acceptance of Malay dominance by non-Malays is largely pragmatic. UMNO does not command a high degree of moral authority among the non-Malays. At the same time, except for certain groups, it is not completely devoid of moral authority either. Malay dominance is increasingly resented by indigenous communities in East Malaysia, principally by the Kadazan community in Sabah. This resentment has fueled Kadazan nationalism and antifederal sentiments. The United Sabah Party (PBS) has openly contested the legitimacy of the Malay-dominated central government as it affects Sabah.

In Vietnam, commitment to the goals of national liberation and building socialism, coupled with the system of collective leadership, ensured the leadership's legitimacy within the party (Vasavakul in Chapter 10). Despite the many hardships they had to endure, nearly all the people could relate to the goal of national liberation, which therefore had broad-based support. Receptivity to the goal of building socialism was less broad and deep, but this goal, especially its egalitarian aspect, did have appeal in rural areas as demonstrated by the support for land reform and cooperativization policies. The socialist goal also enabled the VCP to secure international legitimacy and support from other socialist countries for its liberation goal. While the two goals were projected as symbiotic and did have certain mutually reinforcing elements, there were also contradictions between them. When this occurred, as it did in the implementation of the land reform policy after 1951, the conflicts were resolved in favor of the demands of national liberation, which on balance was the higher goal until 1975.

To mobilize the entire country against France and later the United States, the VCP adopted an inclusive united front strategy as opposed to a class struggle approach. In line with this strategy, the party changed its name from Vietnamese Communist Party to Vietnamese Labor Party, forged an alliance with intellectuals, and took into account the interests of rich and middle-class peasants in its land reform policy. The VCP's goal-rational projection of legitimacy was virtually uncontested in pre-1975 North Vietnam. Even those opposed to the VCP on ideological grounds did not contest its legitimacy or at least muted their challenge because of their support for the goal of national liberation.

Similarly, the goal of survival was shared by ruler and ruled in Singapore (Khong in Chapter 5). Internal political turbulence before joining Malaysia, political experiences during the 1963–65 period, perception of an external security threat from its two large Malay-Muslim neighbors, economic vulnerability—all underscored the survival "ideology" that served as a powerful force uniting the PAP and the majority of the people. The PAP justified its single-party dominance and its "no nonsense, no compromise" approach on the grounds that Singapore, as a small and vulnerable country, could not afford the luxury of political competition and policy failures. This outlook was accepted by most people. Belief in the PAP government's commitment to survival and its success in transforming the sense of isolation and vulnerability underlies the moral authority conferred on Lee Kuan Yew and his government.

Apart from the contextual pertinence of the goals and the receptivity of the targeted audiences, success of the legitimation projects was also due to the deployment of a number of other resources including personal authority, performance, popular sovereignty, and state power. These resources were deployed in a supplementary fashion, however, harnessed in support of the primary goal on the basis of which authority was claimed. While these supplementary rationales have contributed to legitimation, they have in the long term also had, in some cases, the unintended effect of eroding legitimacy.

In Vietnam, Ho Chi Minh successfully deployed his personal authority as well as selected aspects of Vietnamese history, tradition, and culture to reinforce the primacy of the two goals and the VCP's historic, moral, and intellectual leadership role in realizing them. The collective leadership system instituted by Ho facilitated a relatively smooth leadership change even after his death. The VCP continues to invoke him to justify changes in goals and policy and to legitimize the party's continued monopoly of power. In Singapore, Lee Kuan Yew deployed his enormous moral authority to emphasize the continued salience of the goal of survival and to legitimate the single-party dominant regime and, now, his chosen successors. His continued presence, however, is also problematic, for it raises questions about the authority of second-generation leaders and casts doubt on the regime's viability in the post-Lee era. In Malaysia, Tunku Abdul Rahman's considerable personal authority enhanced the legitimacy of the UMNO-led Alliance government, but he was later accused of failing to protect and promote Malay interests and was unceremoniously replaced after 1969. Since then personal authority has been much less important in the legitimation formula in Malaysia. In fact, personality conflicts and leadership challenges within UMNO have intensified.

Performance has been a key supporting rationale in both Singapore and Malaysia. In Singapore, the PAP has invoked competence, integrity, sustained rapid economic growth, and the vision of an industrialized society to justify its continuation in power as well as its tight control over society. While there can be no question about the impressive economic performance of the PAP government, this performance has not achieved the desired result in terms of political allegiance, at least not to the anticipated degree. Popular support for the PAP, measured in terms of the percentage of total votes cast in its favor, has on the contrary continued to decline. At one level, the disaffection may be explained in terms of distributive justice: not all have shared equally in the growth. At a more fundamental level, declining support may indicate that material progress, while important, is not a sufficient basis for political authority. The first explanation suggests that equity must accompany growth if economic development is to be an effective legitimating rationale; the second interpretation supports the proposition that economic performance is not a sufficient or durable basis for political authority.

In Malaysia, economic performance assumed greater importance in UMNO's projection of legitimacy after 1969. But it was explicitly tied to the goal of uplifting the economic position of the Malays. UMNO's success in achieving these goals further enhanced its legitimacy within the Malay community. As this success was achieved primarily through rent seeking, however, it has also intensified the leadership struggle within UMNO, produced conflict between UMNO leaders and hereditary rulers, and given rise to the phenomenon of money politics and large-scale corruption. These developments, coupled with the assurance of Malay dominance, have damaged party unity, contributed to cynicism, skepticism, and irreverence toward authority among the laypeople, and subjected

UMNO to greater challenges from the PAS. Good economic performance has contributed to increased support for the UMNO-led government from certain sections of the non-Malay population. The Chinese business community benefited substantially from the massive spending undertaken by the government, for example, though the poorer sections of the non-Malay communities benefited only marginally.

In Vietnam, economic performance, except in terms of egalitarian policies such as land reform and cooperativization, was not a key factor in legitimacy projection until 1975. Despite increased productivity in certain regions and assistance from China and the Soviet Union that helped ease economic problems, the Vietnamese people had to endure severe hardships. This, however, did not affect their support for the VCP, which rested largely on the goal of national liberation. But in the post-1975 period, poor economic performance had a strong negating effect, especially in South Vietnam, calling into question the validity of the socialist goal, the moral and intellectual superiority of the party, and its monopoly of political power.

Popular mandate has become a key supplementary element in the legitimation of governments in Malaysia and Singapore. Despite frequent amendments to the constitution, the reduction of the Parliament to a rubber stamp, the emasculation of the judiciary, and the exponential increase in the power of the executive, elections have become an indispensable element of the legitimation formula in Malaysia. The limiting condition is that the results must not challenge Malay political dominance. Within this constraint, elections do have meaning. Political leaders believe that their mandate must come from the *raakyat* (the people) and elections do provide genuine political choice, especially at the state level. Had the Semangat '46 multiethnic coalition fared better in the 1990 elections, political choice would have become a reality at the national level as well. The political leadership and the public have come to accept the idea that political power is achieved through elections. Thus Mahathir could quite effectively deploy the "mandate of the people" argument to reduce the power and privileges of the hereditary rulers. The salience of popular mandate also belies the cynical manner in which his action to curtail the independence of the judiciary was viewed by many urban groups, Malay as well as non-Malay.

In Singapore, too, the PAP leadership views victory in elections as a key element of its legitimation and has organized regular elections that have been scrupulously clean.[30] But, like the subordination of elections in Malaysia to Malay dominance, elections in Singapore have been subordinated to PAP control of state power. It is unclear whether the PAP would respect the results of an election that voted it out of office.[31] In any case, the PAP government has taken several measures to prevent such an out-come. The elected presidency is designed to cope with a situation in which, despite the many preventive measures, the people elect an "irresponsible" government. Although opposition parties contest elections, there is no real choice in Singapore. Hence elections have become a referendum on the people's confidence in the government, as the PAP tries to secure a high percentage of the total votes and the opposition parties try to reduce this percentage (Khong in Chapter 5). Despite the certainty of the outcome, elections have in recent years become an effective way for the alienated to demonstrate their dissatisfaction with the PAP government and thus question its legitimacy, if only indirectly.

In Vietnam, as in other communist countries, popular sovereignty has not been a key element of the VCP's claim to authority except in the mobilization mode to demonstrate that the party is representing the collective will of the workers and peasants. The public has no control over the choice of political leaders. The leaders, claiming their authority on the basis of the projected goals and their personal moral and intellectual superiority, are not accountable to the people. Yet the people were frequently mobilized to identify with and support the VCP's goals, its political platform, and its policies (as, for example, with rent reduction, land reform, and cooperativization). Despite increasing criticism and calls from inside and outside the party for greater democracy and pluralism, the VCP in 1990 rejected multiparty democracy, opting for democracy under a one-party system on grounds of national and economic security and the historic role of the VCP. In the post-1986 *doi moi* era, some managed political liberalization has been attempted on paper (Vasavakul in Chapter 10). But mass campaigns in support of the party's goals and policies—as, for example, in the campaign against corrupt and anti-reform officials and later to endorse *doi moi* and the new party political platform in 1991—are still a feature of the system.

All three governments have systematically concentrated power in the structures of the state and deployed this power in support of their quest for legitimation. While there are differences of detail, in general the strategies employed by the governments include the following elements: co-optation of, strategic alliance with, or neutralization and elimination of other centers of power; construction of a national ideology; socialization; and coercion. The purpose of these strategies has been to shrink the political arena—structuring it in favor of the government, preventing socio-political mobilization and organization by other groups—with the net effect of reducing choice. In the absence of alternatives, the governments hope that the ruled will become socialized into the system.

In Malaysia, the political arena has been constricted by excluding "sensitive" issues from politics, by discreet interelite bargaining and compromises within the Barisan, by limiting politics to groups exclusively registered as political organizations (thereby excluding unions, nongovernment organizations, students, and other blocs from the political process), by banning certain political ideologies and organizations (communism, certain interpretations of Islam), by controlling the press, and by deploying structural coercion and fear.[32] Moreover, federal resources have been denied to states and constituencies that elect opposition parties and candidates. In Singapore, the PAP depoliticizes contentious issues through technocratic management, co-opts the civil service, unions, armed forces, police, and intelligentsia, exercises strict control over the press, employs political, legal, and security regulations to marginalize if not eliminate political opposition, and channels the best talent into the PAP government.

In both countries, the electoral systems have been legally crafted in favor of the ruling parties. The state has also substantially expanded its role in many sectors—economy, health, education, housing, pensions, and, in the case of Malaysia, religion. State power touches nearly every aspect of the average citizen's life. Through the allocation of resources and the structuring of rules in these areas as well as in the political arena, the governments seek to socialize the citizens into accepting their right to rule. This is especially true in the case of socialist Vietnam, where most aspects of daily life were subject to state regulation. Considerable effort was made in the 1960s and 1970s to indoctrinate the public with the state ideology. The state's educational and cultural apparatuses "reified and corroborated the party's ideologies of nationalism and socialism" (Vasavakul in Chapter 10). Combining tradition and socialism and linking the past to the present and future, the state ideology was deployed to control national political discourse. Dissenting intellectuals were systematically attacked— publicly criticized, forced to attend ideological rectification classes, and made to work in public enterprises or in the countryside.

The success of these efforts has been mixed. At the discursive level, for example, the deployment of national ideologies has not had the desired effect. Governments have not been able to completely control the content of political discourse. While the UMNO-led Barisan government was able to proscribe communal issues—though not completely, as evidenced by their continuing salience in intraparty politics—it could not do likewise with Islam without being labeled anti-Islamic.[33] Islam is now emerging as a key basis of political discourse in Malaysia. Increasing criticism of the Soeharto government on the basis of Islam and democracy, as well as the continuing debate between Asian (read Confucian) and Western values in Singapore, all reflect the inability of governments to limit political discourse to defined areas. More than two decades of ideological indoctrination has not prevented the emergence of alternative bases for political discourse in Vietnam. In addition to drawing upon democracy and capitalism, critics of the government have also seized upon Ho Chi Minh's last will and testament (deployed by the government in the first place to justify *doi moi*) to argue against the party's monopoly of truth and political power.

The institutional mode would appear to have had a greater effect in conditioning people's behavior and hence their acceptance of the government in Malaysia and Singapore. Believing they have no alternative, the majority of Malays, at least until now, have come to accept UMNO despite its many weaknesses. Support for the PAS, except in Kelantan, was, until recently, essentially a protest vote. Even the non-Malays, persuaded that they have no alternative and perceiving the prevailing system, though not to their liking, as tolerable, have come to accept Malay dominance. Similarly, Singapore's dominant-party political system is largely accepted as a given, even as necessary and desirable by some. The effectiveness of government in these two countries in providing security and economic welfare has also enhanced their standing, although these achievements are not without negative consequences as noted earlier. Further, to the extent that state power is effectively deployed to curb developments that could lead to a breakdown of law and order, it has enhanced the people's acceptance of the government and its policies. The use of the Internal Security Act (ISA) in Malaysia in 1987, for example, was generally welcomed or at least not opposed because many believed that such use of state power was in the collective interest of society. Where the "threat" is not clearly grounded in reality—as, for example, the arrest of "communist conspirators" in 1987 in Singapore—the deployment of state power becomes controversial. The public in this case, or at least certain segments, was skeptical about the accuracy of the implied motives (to overthrow the ruling regime and establish a communist state) as well as the capacity of those arrested to execute them.

While UMNO, the VCP, and the PAP have been relatively successful with their legitimation projects, their legitimacy has not been uncontested. Challenges have issued not only from the unintended consequences of the supplementary rationales, as noted earlier, but also from the declining relevance of the goals themselves due to their successful attainment, their negative effects, or changing circumstances. As goals are crucial for their legitimation, these governments have attempted to recapture their waning authority by invoking additional goals, reinterpreting current ones, or shifting to another basis of authority.

In Malaysia, assurance of Malay dominance has contributed to intense intraparty struggles and contestation of the legitimacy of specific power holders within UMNO (Case in Chapter 4). More seriously, UMNO's right to lead the Malay community has been challenged, primarily on the basis of Islam. In responding to the Islamic challenge posed by PAS, which controls Kelantan and has growing support in several other states, UMNO has attempted to project its own Islamic credentials while depicting the Islam of PAS as extremist and not suited to contemporary realities. Indeed, PAS is portrayed as incapable of governing Kelantan, let alone multiracial Malaysia. Ultimately, UMNO may even seek to bring PAS into the Barisan fold. This move to counter the appeal of PAS by projecting UMNO's Islamic credentials poses two problems, not dissimilar to the situation in Indonesia. First, it has raised apprehension among the minority non-Malay communities who fear that their political position would be further eroded if Islam became the organizing political principle. Second, can UMNO manage the inclusion of Islamic values without itself undergoing fundamental change? Are the fundamentalists getting a free ride? While no definitive answer can be given to these questions, it is pertinent to observe here that the progressive accommodation of the interests of the moderate Muslim majorities in Tunisia, Algeria, and even Egypt has in the long term contributed to the erosion of government legitimacy, fueling legitimacy contestations by fundamentalist groups.

On a long-term basis, UMNO appears to be in the early stage of recasting its legitimacy projection in developmental terms to appeal to Malay as well as non-Malay constituencies (Case in Chapter 4). The New Development Policy, which emphasizes growth over distribution and the articulation of a long-range vision of an industrialized Malaysian society by the year 2020, indicates movement in this direction. While this trend is likely to be welcomed by most in the non-Malay communities and some in the Malay community, it is likely to be contested by those still wedded to Malay dominance as well as by those who deploy Islam to support their claim to authority.

In Vietnam, the goal of national liberation became irrelevant with reunification. After 1975, the VCP's claim to legitimacy rested almost exclusively on the hegemonic goal of building socialism (Vasavakul in Chapter 10). This goal, and the class struggle approach it dictated, alienated significant groups (especially the ethnic Chinese) not only in the South but also in North Vietnam. In the South, the socialist policies contributed to an economic crisis. The poor performance in the North, previously tolerated because of the war effort, became a cause of public grievance. The economic difficulties were aggravated by the termination of Chinese and later Soviet economic and military assistance. Coupled with infighting and corruption within the party, these developments undermined the VCP's claim to moral and intellectual superiority. The wars in Cambodia and with China, by resurrecting nationalism, temporarily alleviated the legitimacy problem but they also had negative consequences. Not only was Vietnam's international legitimacy adversely affected, but the social and economic cost of the wars further aggravated domestic economic and political problems. From the perspective of certain segments inside and outside the party, these wars raised doubts about the VCP's ability to lead the country. In short, the VCP's legitimacy suffered considerable erosion in the post-1975 period.

To recapture legitimacy, the VCP reinterpreted socialism more broadly, making it a long-term goal. The immediate goal is *doi moi* (political and economic renovation). Through a more inclusionary approach and better economic performance, the VCP seeks to justify continuation of one-party rule. Despite this recasting, socialism remains important: without it the party's claim to the monopoly of political power cannot be justified. The response to the policy of renovation has been mixed (Vasavakul in Chapter 10). Critics from inside and outside the party have challenged crucial aspects of the political renovation and more generally the party's hegemonic ideology—including its monopoly of truth and power, the benefits of class struggle, the role of the state in the economy, and the control of mass organizations by the state. Economic performance is generally improving, but the benefits have not been shared equally. There are many fundamental economic problems in the transition to a market economy that have yet to be dealt with. Moreover, the expertise required to manage a market economy will challenge the party's claim to intellectual superiority. Even if these problems are overcome, there is a question as to whether the party can manage capitalist development to reinforce its authority without creating challenges to its monopoly of political power. It appears likely that while in the short term *doi moi* may shore up the VCP's legitimacy, it could lay the basis for contestation of its legitimacy at a fundamental level in the long term.

In Singapore, despite the government's insistence, survival in the political, economic, and security sense is much less precarious. Thus its power to unify ruler and ruled is much more limited than it was in the 1960s and 1970s, although it is not without resonance in the body politic. While Lee Kuan Yew's personal authority and the government's impressive performance have contributed significantly to political legitimation, as noted earlier, there are clear limits to their potential. They might even become liabilities. Recognizing the increasingly pragmatic foundations of its legitimacy, the PAP government deployed Confucianism and a national ideology comprising five shared values to develop an ideological foundation for its claim to authority.

The preceding discussion suggests several observations. First, while all

three governments have been successful in legitimating themselves, their
success in legitimating their respective regimes has been less impressive.
They have not been able to forge an enduring ideological unity between
ruler and ruled, and there is no essential connection between the goals and
the procedural elements being cultivated. Among the three countries, regime legitimation is relatively more advanced in Malaysia. Malay dominance and the articulation of certain non-Malay interests to this principle,
as well as the institutions and procedures associated with it, have now
been accepted by a majority of the Malaysian people. Indeed, the principle
of Malay dominance is likely to endure for some time to come in light of
Malaysia's demographic makeup. Further, the institutions and procedures
being cultivated have been relatively successful in meeting the aspirations
of a majority of the people. It should, however, be noted that while ideological unity characterizes relations between UMNO and a majority of the
Malay population, UMNO's legitimacy in relation to the non-Malay communities is largely pragmatic. The situation is comparable to the instrumental alliance layer in the Gramscian conception of hegemony, where
each group maintains its own identity as well as its own ideology but the
demands of the subordinate groups are accommodated by the fundamental group. As long as ethnic dominance constitutes the hegemonic principle, it will be impossible for UMNO to advance beyond the instrumental
level to the higher plane of ideological unity with respect to the non-
Malays. Nevertheless, the regime based on Malay dominance is not totally
devoid of moral authority from the perspective of most non-Malays in
peninsular Malaysia.

While prime ministers have changed, the ruling party has remained the
same since independence. So far, UMNO has found it advantageous to
deliberately fuse the institutions of party, government, and regime as well
as, at times, the nation-state. UMNO depicts contestation by the PAS as
not only challenging UMNO but also undermining Malay dominance as
well as national unity and stability. The DAP challenge is depicted as challenging the right of Malays to their homeland. Because the challenge of
the DAP, the PAS, and the Kadazan community is directed toward the
principle of Malay-UMNO dominance, from their perspective the government and regime are one and the same. To contest the legitimacy of the
UMNO-led government is to contest the legitimacy of the system. In the
case of the Kadazan community, the challenge may also extend to the legitimacy of the Malaysian nation-state. Had the Semangat '46 coalition
been more successful, government and regime might have become more
distinct because of that coalition's embodiment of the principle of Malay
dominance as well. Contestation of the legitimacy of the UMNO-led government cannot then be construed as contestation of the regime. At the

state level, government and regime have become more distinct. Opposition parties have acquired power in several states. The attempt by the PAS to transform Kelantan into an Islamic state, however, suggests that even at this level the distinction must be qualified.

In Singapore, as noted earlier, the potential of the survival ideology to justify continued single-party dominance has declined. To buttress the foundations of regime legitimacy, the PAP government deployed a conservative interpretation of the Confucian ethic, but this effort has had little success (Khong in Chapter 5). Deployment of the Confucian ethic and the increasing emphasis on the Chineseness of Singapore also undermined the PAP's earlier multiracial projection, alienating the non-Chinese communities. Thus while the PAP has been successful in legitimating itself, increasingly this success has been founded on instrumental rather than ideological grounds. According to Lee Kuan Yew, the second-generation leaders have yet to establish their own moral compact with the people as the first generation did in the 1950s and 1960s.[34] Although party and government leadership has passed to the second generation, as yet there is no acceptable ideological foundation of the regime in Singapore. Increasingly the thrust of the government appears to be on managing conformity. Hence the legitimacy of the one-party dominant regime in Singapore, while not contested in any fundamental sense, is far from established. Party, government, and regime are still fused. To contest the legitimacy of the PAP, therefore, is to contest the legitimacy of the government and the regime but not the nation-state, which has now been accepted both at home and abroad.

In Vietnam, similarly, after reunification the ideological unity within the VCP as well as between the VCP and the ordinary people dissipated. The VCP's pursuit of hegemony on the basis of socialism failed and the regime's legitimacy has declined. To recapture its authority, the VCP has made *doi moi* the central feature of its legitimacy projection, invoking Ho Chi Minh's authority to justify this change (Vasavakul in Chapter 10). But this is a pragmatic approach lacking the basis for ideological unity that is necessary to justify continued rule by the VCP and especially its Leninist structure of domination. In Vietnam, even more than in Singapore, the party, government, and regime are fused. Notwithstanding the recent attempt to separate party and government, the VCP still claims de facto if not de jure monopoly of political power.

Legitimation of the regime in these three countries is further hampered by the fact that there is no essential connection between the posited principles or goals and the structures of domination being cultivated. The unity between UMNO and the Malay community is based on the need for Malay political dominance, not on how the Malays and the country should be governed. Similarly, while there is agreement in Singapore on the goal of survival, a one-party dominant regime is not necessarily a logical consequence of this goal. In Vietnam, while there may be broad-based support for *doi moi*, this support need not extend logically to the VCP or the Leninist system of domination. Stated alternatively: the quasi-parliamentary, dominant-party, and Leninist systems are not necessarily the only or even the best routes to achieve Malay dominance, Singapore's survival, and Vietnam's *doi moi*.

Indeed, even the incumbent power holders are not fully committed to these systems. This is the case, for example, in Malaysia and Singapore where frequent changes to the constitution—changes that have concentrated power in the executive at the expense of the parliament, the judiciary, and, in the case of Malaysia, the hereditary rulers—undermine the legitimating value of the procedural elements. The government's effective performance in these two countries over a prolonged period does, to some degree, validate their respective structures of domination. This, however, makes the procedural element contingent and detracts from its development into an independent legitimating element. The problem is more acute in Vietnam where the VCP has a poor record of performance in the post-1975 period and cannot claim moral and intellectual superiority in pursuit of the goal of economic renovation. Further, developments in the former Soviet bloc countries have considerably undermined the credibility of the Leninist system. The basic point here is that in goal-rational authority the procedural element is subordinated to task achievement, subjecting it to frequent changes and preventing it from developing into a more independent and durable basis of legitimation. Thus legitimation remains at the level of goals and performance, both of which are contingent. While some goals (such as Malay dominance) may be more enduring, others (such as survival) may become less relevant and still others (such as reunification and building socialism) may cease to be relevant altogether.

Second, based on the relative success of these three governments, one can specify the key elements for successful goal-rational legitimacy projects. To succeed, the goal must be situationally pertinent, a dominant political organization (party, group, or movement) must be committed to realizing the goal, the target audience must believe in this political organization, and some progress must be made in attaining the goal. If certain segments of the population do not identify with the goal or the political organization, the organization must be capable of accommodating some of their demands and providing a unifying vision that incorporates some of their values. To the extent that it succeeds in presenting itself as inclusionary and representing the collective interest, the organization will be deemed legitimate by these groups. Personal authority, performance, the procedural element, and international support may be crucial elements of the formula, but only in a subordinate role. The goal and its attainment must be the primary basis of authority.

Third, the need to formulate new goals or reinterpret existing ones in order to conform to changing circumstances—and more generally the need to recast legitimacy projections—demonstrate the point made in Part I of the book regarding the dynamic nature of legitimacy and the need for its constant cultivation. Past and present success does not guarantee future success, especially in light of the weakness of the procedural element. As noted, the legitimacy of all three governments is contested in varying degrees. If they are not successful in recapturing their authority, they may suffer further erosion of their legitimacy and eventually cease to be legitimate. This is especially the case with the VCP. There is a fundamental tension between an open economic system and a closed political system—a tension that will continue to pose a dilemma for the VCP as it has for many other authoritarian systems. The VCP will almost certainly have to modify the system continually, provide greater choice, share power with other groups, and in the process be willing to transform itself and the regime, if its effort to recapture legitimacy is to be successful and enduring.

Fourth, the discussion confirms the assertion in Part I that legitimacy is multifaceted—not all groups have to be equally committed and different rationales may appeal to different groups—and that a certain measure of contestation is inevitable. As long as the government is accepted by key segments of the population, contestation does not delegitimize it. Stated alternatively, governments can get by even when they do not command a high degree of moral authority from all segments of the society. Instrumental acceptance by disaffected groups and the deployment of state coercion can compensate for what a government lacks in legitimacy.

Finally, the three case studies suggest that power does have legitimating potential, although it has been more effective in the institutional mode than in the discursive. Through an extensive incentive and repression system and a broad socialization network, the governments in all three countries quite successfully persuaded a majority of the people to believe that they have no alternative and that, given the circumstances, the present structure of domination is proper. This argument is particularly revealing with respect to the non-Malay acceptance of Malay dominance. But the legitimating potential of power is limited and quite contingent upon the pertinence of the goal, the relationship between goal and structure, and the progress made in realizing the goal.

Malay dominance, Singapore's survival, and Vietnam's national liberation were contextually pertinent goals, and the relative success of the institutions, rules, and practices in realizing these goals contributed to their acceptance and hence legitimation of the structures of domination and the parties advocating them. Yet the legitimating potential of the very same structures declined in Vietnam after 1975 and in Singapore when survival became less problematic. The legitimating potential of power in the autocratic governments of Ne Win and Marcos was minimal in view of the wide gap between projection and reality. Their goals and ideologies were not inspiring, and their structures of domination were intended not to realize the stated goals but to keep these men in power. In such situations power may command obedience through fear but it cannot command authority. Even where the goals are pertinent and the structures are effective, political thought and action cannot be completely governed by the power of the state. Despite their overwhelming power, the PAP, VCP, and Indonesia's New Order governments have failed to gain acceptance of the national ideologies or the interpretations they advocate. This point supports Anthony Giddens's observation that the agent, capable and knowledgeable, has a measure of freedom to act differently. Structure is both enabling and constraining but not determining.[35]

Unlike the legitimacy projections of the governments discussed in the preceding two sections, the projections of the governments in Thailand during the 1978–91 period do not fit well into the categories of democratic, personal, or goal-rational authority. No single rationale was dominant in their legitimation formulas. From the perspective of the strategic groups, these governments were legitimate because of their own inclusion. Their inclusion, however, was based not on any goal, principle, or vision but on pragmatic grounds.

Authority Based on Pragmatic Accommodation

By Thai standards, the 1978 quasi-democratic constitution was remarkably resilient.[36] This constitution and the governments associated with it were viewed, for the most part, as legitimate by the key institutions and groups in Thai society (Sukatipan in Chapter 8). Acceptance, however, was underscored by a high degree of pragmatism. Political developments in 1973, 1976, and 1977 had confirmed to the military-led conservatives as well as the "new" social forces that neither could govern to the total exclusion of the other: power had to be shared among the strategic groups—the armed and unarmed bureaucrats, the technocrats, the business community, and the political parties.

The 1978 constitution, drafted with the military holding the reins of government, balanced the power of the elected Lower House with that of a military-appointed Upper House.[37] The first government under General Kriangsak Chomanan and the subsequent three governments under General Prem Tinsulanonda included representation from all key groups, which were allowed sufficient space to advance their corporate interests. In addition to the constitutional foundation, the legitimacy of Prem-led governments was also underscored by the support of the monarchy, Prem's personal authority, and his governments' impressive performance (sustained economic growth, increasing concern for distributive justice, defeat of the communist insurgency, effective handling of the Cambodian conflict).

While this legitimation formula was relatively successful, it was also weak in a number of respects. It was not underscored by any agreement on goals or values among the strategic groups. Although the component groups (political parties, the military, and business) claimed to be committed to democracy, their conceptions of democracy differed substantially. Each group was in government for its own narrow interests and tolerated the others only because it had no choice. Prem himself was not committed to democracy and made no particular effort to institutionalize the system. To preserve his authority, he sought to remain above politics as an arbiter. Further, power did not fully reside in the system. The military's acceptance of the constitution and support for Prem was not total. The Young Turks (who engineered the ouster of Thanin Kravichien in 1977, the installation and later ouster of Kriangsak, and the subsequent accession to power by Prem in 1980) and General Arthit Kamlangek (then chief of the army) wielded substantial power that they deployed, though not successfully, to oust Prem's government on several occasions. With the support of the monarchy, Prem was able to abort the coup attempts by the Young Turks in 1981 and 1985 and weather the constitutional and extraconstitutional challenges posed by General Arthit.

The power-sharing formula embodied in the constitution was increasingly viewed as unsatisfactory by the military as well as certain political parties. The military wanted to continue the four-year transition clause in the constitution that allowed bureaucrats to hold political office without resigning their bureaucratic positions. The elected members of the Lower House wanted to curb the power of the military by reducing the number of appointed senators and passing a constitutional amendment that would require the prime minister to be elected as well as oblige him to appoint half his cabinet from elected MPs. As Prem's style of politics was exercised at their expense, the political parties became disenchanted with him. The public (the growing numbers of urban workers, students, intellectuals, and independent businesspeople who were not fully integrated into the

quasi-democratic regime) had also swung against Prem and more generally against the bureaucrats, who by now had a poor public image. Not
only was the public mood strongly in favor of democracy, but the growing
demand that Prem be replaced by an elected prime minister was supported
by the print media, which had become a powerful force in the 1980s.
Stung by the growing criticism, Prem declined the invitation to lead a new
government after the 1988 elections.

General Chatichai, leader of the Chart Thai Party, became the first
elected prime minister in twelve years. While the regime continued to be
based on the 1978 constitution, the power of the political parties increased substantially at the expense of the military. Chatichai claimed the
right to rule on the basis of popular mandate. The strong democratic
mood in the country, augmented by Chatichai's style of politics, accorded
his government a high degree of legitimacy, but this was not to be enduring. Over the next two or three years, the legitimacy of Chatichai's government was increasingly contested by the military, civilian bureaucrats,
businesspeople who were shut out of massive government projects, opposition political parties, intellectuals, professionals, and students.

Although Chatichai was careful at first not to antagonize the military,
his subsequent policies and actions (cabinet appointments, Cambodia
policy), as well as those of certain cabinet ministers, alienated the military.
Not only was the military concerned about being marginalized, but it was
also worried about the increasing dominance of ethnic Chinese in government and business, which was perceived to be at the expense of the bureaucrats. Given the strong public support for Chatichai, however, the
military initially had to accept its diminished position, adopting a defensive posture to protect its corporate integrity and focusing on rural development. But abuse of power, infighting among the government coalition,
and the slowdown in the economy (due largely to the Gulf Crisis) undermined the legitimacy of Chatichai and his government. Nearly all his early
supporters (students, intellectuals, workers, the press) and the civilian bureaucrats, who had been alienated from the beginning, became harshly
critical of Chatichai's government. The military seized this opportunity
and launched a coup in February 1991 that brought the thirteen-year-old
quasi-democratic regime to an end. Although the ouster of Chatichai was
welcomed, it did not signify public support for a return to military rule or
even to quasi-democratic rule as practiced by Prem. The military's attempt
to consolidate its position through the March 1992 elections led to political conflict in May 1992 between the military and the new social forces
and then intervention by the king to resolve it.

Although a democratic government acceded to power following the
September 1992 elections and the notion of an elected prime minister has

become quite firmly entrenched in public thinking, the democratic system, for several reasons, is far from established in Thailand. First, political parties are still regional and weak. As no single party can gain an absolute majority in parliament, the pattern of coalition governments, vulnerable to crisis and collapse, is likely to continue. Second, because of rampant vote buying in rural areas, the victors in elections cannot genuinely claim to represent the popular will (Sukatipan in Chapter 8). Their claim to popular mandate will be contested especially by the urban middle class and the students who apply stringent performance criteria in judging the success of governments. Further, there are serious differences between the expectations of government held by the rural people who command the votes and those of the urban middle class whose support, as demonstrated in 1991 and 1992, is crucial for the continued survival of governments— and these differences will continue to pose problems for democratically elected Thai governments. Third, the military is still a formidable political force with which any elected government must contend. Recognizing this, Prime Minister Chuan Leepkai, despite the public's antipathy toward the military, has stepped carefully in dealing with that institution—on the issues of the generals accused of ordering the shooting in May 1992, for example, and the composition of the Upper House. The latter in conjunction with the opposition parties in the Lower House has been successful in defeating the government's proposals for constitutional reform in 1994.[38] So long as the military does not fully accept the principle of civilian control, the democratic system in Thailand will not be the sole repository of power. Finally, the political parties, the business community, the rural people, and even the urban middle class are not fully committed to democratic ideals. Certainly the military and civilian bureaucrats are not. Moreover, as noted earlier, there is a wide gap between the conception and expectations of government held by the rural people and those of the urban middle class. Thus while democratic values and procedures are likely to continue to gain ground, other legitimating factors—performance, support of the monarchy, and power sharing with extraparliamentary forces—will continue to be crucial for political legitimation.

The Thai experience during the 1978–91 period illustrates the transitory nature of political legitimation on the basis of pragmatic considerations. In the absence of common political goals and values, the political coalition based on power sharing was fragile, each group seeking to manipulate the system to its advantage. Increasing tension between the conservative military and certain political parties both inside and outside the parliamentary framework weakened the system, preventing its institutionalization. Further, while the system did, at least initially, take into account the distribution of power among key groups, it did not embrace certain

forces that subsequently came to influence public opinion in favor of democracy. Although democratic values and procedures are gaining ground,
no dominant group is committed to their realization. The groups advocating democracy have been essentially reactive and intolerant of the en-
cumbrances of the democratic system. They are not sufficiently committed to democratic values and institutions to resolve political problems—
such as that relating to the Chatichai government—through the democratic process.

The monarchy, which has become the most powerful political institution in the country, plays a crucial role in political legitimation, but the
king himself is not committed to a democratic political system. In fact, he
is generally conservative and pragmatic in orientation. In the absence of a
common political value system and a dominant group, tension among factions with conflicting interests and differing values is inevitable, leading
to periodic conflict and crisis. And changes in the distribution of power
among groups due to rapid capitalist development are likely to intensify
the conflict. Under these circumstances, progress in forging shared norms,
to the extent that it occurs, is likely to be gradual and beset by crisis and
frequent setbacks.

Quest for a More Enduring Basis of Authority

Political legitimation, particularly regime legitimation, continues to be
problematic in Southeast Asia. Not only were they not rooted in the political traditions of the countries concerned, but the initial democratic governments could not cope with the many political and socioeconomic problems of the postindependence period. Their legitimacy was contested and
eventually they were displaced or modified. Personal authority, while it
did contribute to government legitimation in several countries, could
make only a limited contribution to regime legitimation. Even when genuinely motivated, as in Singapore, it is difficult to routinize and transfer
personal authority to anointed successors. More often, as in Thailand, the
Philippines, Burma, and, to a lesser degree, in Indonesia, autocratic rulers
have been more concerned with preserving their own power rather than
institutionalizing a regime.

Goal-rational legitimacy projects in Malaysia, Singapore, and Vietnam
appear to have had greater success in regime legitimation. This lends support to the proposition in Part I that authority based on goal rationality
has the potential to be more durable and therefore ranks higher than personal authority and performance. The superior potential of goal-rational
authority, however, must be qualified. Not all goals have the power to

constitute an enduring normative order. Goals like survival, national liberation, and development are more contingent than, for example, Malay
dominance. Further, because of the overriding importance of goals, the
procedural element in goal-rational authority is incapable of developing
into an independent basis for legitimation, although it can play an important supplementary role. For a goal to legitimate a regime, in addition to
being pertinent it must have the potential to produce shared political values. Only rarely—as in Malaysia where the goal of ethnic protection has
been translated into the organizing principle of Malay political dominance—have the goals deployed in Southeast Asian countries contributed
to the development of an institutionalized normative order. Even in Malaysia, the principle of Malay political dominance, as noted earlier, is limited in its capacity to forge ideological unity between UMNO and several
segments of the Malaysian population.

While no basis is valid in perpetuity, a fundamental political challenge
for the countries of Southeast Asia is the development of a more durable
basis for political authority. Most goals, personal authority, performance,
politically defining moment, and international support are highly contingent and cannot serve this function, although they can play a crucial supplementary role in regime legitimation. The requirement is for shared political principles or an ideology on the basis of which acceptable political
institutions, procedures, and practices can be constructed. This is not to
argue that shared political principles alone will be sufficient, but that this
is a fundamental requirement for regime legitimation. Only when political
legitimation turns primarily upon the procedural element will it become
less problematic. The need for such an ideological foundation appears to
have been recognized by many political leaders in Southeast Asia, as most
governments have attempted to articulate one.

The problem lies in gaining acceptance of the articulated "national"
ideologies and their institutionalization. Governments have had little success in this regard. Several reasons, some of which have been noted earlier,
underscore this lack of success. First, identification with the nation-state
(as opposed to allegiance to other social groups and formations), the antecedent condition for the forging of shared political values, is still tentative in most countries and nonexistent with respect to some groups.[39] The
multiethnic and multireligious composition of many of these countries
further limits the range of acceptable ideologies and their legitimation potential. Malay political dominance, for example, is at base incapable of
creating ideological unity between UMNO and the non-Malay communities. Islam alienates the other religious groups in Malaysia and Indonesia; the Confucian ethic alienates the Malays and Indians in Singapore.

Second, even when the antecedent condition is satisfied—as in Indonesia where, except on the margins, considerable progress has been made in creating a national sense of identity—the forging of shared values and their translation into widely accepted institutions, rules, and procedures are not guaranteed. The five principles of Pancasila (belief in Almighty God, humanity, unity of Indonesia, peopleness and able leadership based on consultation and representation, and social justice for all Indonesians), while accepted by most Indonesians and certainly crucial in the forging of national identity and the continued unity of the Indonesian nation-state, are abstract, all embracing, and far too diffuse to provide any specific guidance on the actual structure of domination. Thus they have been deployed to justify or contest almost any regime form (democracy, guided democracy, patrimonialism, authoritarianism). In the absence of an authoritative body to define and give them specific content, these principles will continue to be debated at the abstract level with little immediate consequence for the actual structure of domination. Further, they will continue to be more relevant in contesting the legitimacy of incumbent governments (on the ground that they have contravened or deviated from Pancasila) than in providing the foundation of an enduring political system. Similarly, the five "shared values" that comprise the national ideology of Singapore, while certainly not objectionable from the perspective of most Singaporeans, do not provide specific guidance on the regime form. They may with equal plausibility be deployed to justify democracy, authoritarianism, fascism, or communism.

A third reason lies in the conservative and self-serving approach taken by governments in the formulation and interpretation of national ideologies with intent to justify and freeze the status quo in the face of contending ideas and forces. The revival of the Confucian ethic in Singapore, for example, is rooted in the leadership's belief that the Chinese segment of the population is losing its moral bearings and the conviction that Chinese political traditions and cultural values can provide a moral foundation for the continuation of the PAP in power. This deployment of the Confucian ethic in a conservative form to justify a one-party-dominant regime and reject Western values and political systems—particularly democracy—equates tradition with authoritarianism. It had little appeal to those Chinese Singaporeans who were already alienated from the government; it created unease among the English-educated Chinese supporters of the government; and it alienated Malay and Indian Singaporeans. The growing salience of popular sovereignty and democratic developments in other Confucian societies (South Korea and Taiwan) makes it difficult to sustain the Confucian ideology, especially its conservative interpretation, in modern Singapore.

Individual and collective political consciousness and attitudes are constituted on the basis of contemporary sociopolitical realities as well as historical experiences. While the ancient political traditions of China and Chinese cultural values are important, they cannot be deployed to erase by fiat a century of English education and exposure to Western traditions and values, especially in an increasingly interdependent world. Tradition and culture, as observed in Part I, are not static and there is no single "national" culture. Further, as demonstrated by the political swings in China itself and by the recent political developments in South Korea and Taiwan, Confucian culture can support more than one way of political life. The challenge for Singapore and the other Southeast Asian countries is to forge shared political principles that take account of past experiences as well as contemporary sociological realities in a world undergoing profound change.

The forging of such shared norms and values can only be accomplished incrementally and over a long period of time. And the process is likely to be marked by tension, conflict, crises, and accommodation or collapse. Progress in forging shared values, as in forging a nation-state, will inevitably be checkered. Developments in Thailand illustrate this contention well. While democratic principles have gradually gained ascendance, this is the result of contestation and accommodation among the competing interests in Thai society over six decades. Although the approach taken in Malaysia has been hegemonic, as in Thailand, the principle of Malay political dominance has indigenous roots (both historical and contemporary) and its acceptance has been gradual and marked by periodic tension and conflict. The organizing political principles in both these countries are still evolving and will not be free of further tension and conflict.

Until a more durable basis for political authority is established and legitimacy turns on widely accepted institutions and procedures, government legitimation in the Southeast Asian countries is not assured. Each government will have to expend considerable effort on legitimating itself while remaining flexible enough to recast its legitimation formula to adapt to changing circumstances. In this process, periodic legitimacy crises, especially during times of leadership succession, are likely.

Although this investigation has confined itself to Southeast Asia, political legitimacy is a problem throughout Asia, Africa, Latin America, Eastern Europe, and the successor states of the Soviet republics. While different in magnitude, the problems of political authority confronting Russia, China, and India, for example, are not dissimilar from those in the Southeast Asian countries. The framework for this study, and its conclusions, are applicable to them as well as most other countries. It should be noted here that while regime legitimacy has been remarkably durable in the Western countries, the continued legitimacy of their democratic systems cannot be taken for granted. There is growing concern in these countries that excessive emphasis on individualism at the expense of the larger community, and on freedom of expression without due attention to responsibility, has contributed to a collapse of moral standards and rise in antisocial behavior that may be endangering the system. Coupled with economic insecurity and a perception that democratic systems cannot cope with international economic competition from nondemocratic states, these concerns may undermine public faith in democratic values and institutions, fuel authoritarian tendencies, and increase the appeal of rightist movements—as, for example, with the neo-Nazi and neofascist movements in Germany and Italy. Democratic systems may well be able to overcome these dangers; the point is that their future legitimacy—and indeed the legitimacy of any system—cannot forever be taken for granted.

REFERENCE MATTER

Notes

ALAGAPPA, INTRODUCTION

1. The estimate for the number of missing persons is from nongovernmental sources. The Ministry of Interior's figure is only 47. Although the fate of the missing remains a mystery, most are believed to have been shot and their bodies removed by the army. The report prepared by the Ministry of Defense—the basis of former Prime Minister Anand Panyarachun's action against several army officers—is believed to contain information about the missing, but it has not been released. See *Far Eastern Economic Review* (hereafter *FEER*), May 27, 1993, p. 16.

2. The opposition groups were not formally organized. Chamlong Srimuang, the controversial leader of the opposition Palang Dharma party, galvanized the various groups into action through his vow to fast unto death if General Suchinda did not resign from the post of prime minister.

3. For an account of the political and economic conditions leading to the September 18, 1988, coup d'état and its aftermath, see Steinberg, *Future of Burma*, pp. 1–48.

4. SLORC convened a national convention of 700 hand-picked delegates representing political parties, ethnic minorities, and professional groups on January 9 and again on February 1, 1993, with the purpose of drafting a new constitution that would institutionalize the political role of the military. This effort was resisted by the delegates and the convention has been adjourned. See Lintner, "Conventional Wisdom," p. 20.

5. For an account of the removal of Ferdinand Marcos, see Mackenzie, "People Power or Palace Coup," pp. 1–57.

6. Barker, *Political Legitimacy*, p. 11.

7. Following the Weberian tradition, this usage contrasts power and authority. Others have defined power more broadly to encompass authority as well as force, manipulation, and persuasion. In the latter usage, authority relations are viewed as one form of power relations. For a discussion of these different approaches to power and authority, see Wrong, *Power*, chaps. 2 and 3. These differences in approach, while significant, are not critical in terms of the central concern of this book. Regardless of whether authority is power transformed or is a special case of

power, it does not affect the proposition that legitimacy is a critical precondition for the effective exercise of authority.

8. The importance of and the recurring challenges to political legitimacy in Southeast Asian countries were noted more than two decades ago by Leifer, *Dilemmas of Statehood in Southeast Asia*, pp. 105–14.

9. Paul Lewis argues that legitimacy is as important as the monopoly of physical power. See his introduction to the section on power, legitimacy, and the states in Held, *States and Societies*, p. 413.

10. Compulsory jurisdiction and monopoly over the legitimate use of force, advanced by Max Weber as the essential characteristics of the modern state, have now become key ingredients of the definition of the state. For a discussion of these characteristics see Weber's *Theory of Social and Economic Organization*, pp. 154–56. For a good discussion of the nature of political authority see Green, *Authority of the State*, chaps. 1–3.

11. Weber, *Theory of Social and Economic Organization*, p. 325.

12. For a definition of discourse, see the introduction to Giddens and Turner, *Social Theory Today*, pp. 21–22. See also Lindstrom and White, "Introduction: Custom Today," p. 469.

13. The phrase "language of legitimacy" is that of John Sidel. See Chapter 6 in this volume.

14. Merquior, *Rousseau and Weber*, p. 123.

15. Crone, "State, Social Elites, and Government Capacity," pp. 252–68.

16. Wrong, *Power*, pp. 103–13.

17. It has, however, been implicit in writings on nation building, political participation, political succession, revolution, regime change, and security.

18. Although there is great variety within each current, there are enough common elements for each to be termed a "school."

19. For an overview of the political development literature see Huntington, "Political Change," pp. 3–6.

20. Skocpol, "Bringing the State Back In," p. 5.

21. For a review of dependency theses see Packenham, *Dependency Movement*.

22. Ibid., p. 29. For the other key features of this school, see ibid., pp. 30–31.

23. Huntington, "Political Change," pp. 10–11.

24. The present wave of theories on democratization, the primary focus of which is transition from authoritarianism and totalitarianism to democratic rule, while more discriminating, is still in the same vein. Guillermo O'Donnell, Philippe C. Schmitter, and Laurence Whitehead contend that "legitimate political domination can only be an expression of popular sovereignty or, in exceptional cases, the issue of revolutionary mandate for dramatic political transformation." See their *Transitions from Authoritarian Rule*, pt. 4, p. 15.

25. Talcott Parsons, for example, in noting the persistence of "particularism" in industrialized Japan, predicted that "I would expect this situation to be seriously unstable and to show marked tendency to change in the expected direction with further industrial development." Quoted by Casanova, "Legitimacy and the Sociology of Modernization," p. 223.

26. Huntington, *Third Wave*, pp. 304–5.

27. These dynamics are the product of the interaction of an array of factors and processes. Harold Crouch and James W. Morley, for example, find that their model positing economic growth as driving political change through social and political mobilization cannot explain all cases. They cite a number of other factors—geographic (size, regionalism), social (inherited class structure, communalism), and political (institutions, elite cohesion)—as additional elements that may be necessary to explain "deviant" cases. See their "Dynamics of Political Change," pp. 277–310.

28. This theme is also reflected in the conclusion reached by Crouch and Morley. Citing the cases of Japan, Korea, and Taiwan, they argue that the continuation of economic growth will ultimately lead to a Western democratic form, but "there is no guarantee that full democracy will be achieved. Many other factors . . . can slow or even reverse this process." Ibid., p. 309.

29. For one account of the limitations of the theory of legitimacy, see Bensman, "Max Weber's Concept of Legitimacy," pp. 17–48. See also Merquior, *Rousseau and Weber*, chap. 7, pp. 104–30.

30. For a recent statement of these problems and the limitation of legitimacy's explanatory power, see O'Kane, "Against Legitimacy," pp. 471–87.

31. Some of these criticisms, especially that relating to tautology, are difficult to refute in the abstract. For a criticism based on circularity, see O'Kane, "Against Legitimacy," pp. 475–76. David Beetham counters O'Kane's criticism of his work by arguing that his construction is not circular but highlights the complex nature of legitimacy. See his "In Defence of Legitimacy," pp. 488–89.

32. Anthony Giddens quoted in Cohen, "Structuration Theory," p. 283. For a discussion of the shortcomings of the attempt at general theory, see Giddens, *Central Problems*, chap. 7, pp. 234–60.

33. Cohen, "Structuration Theory," p. 285.

34. Adam Przeworski argues that what matters for stability is not the legitimacy of a particular system of domination but the absence or presence of alternatives. See his "Some Problems," pt. 3, pp. 512–15.

35. Mohammed Ayoob argues that "it is this dissonance between the loci of authority and of power which lies at the heart of the Third World state's security problematic, especially as it relates to the intrastate dimension of this problem." See Ayoob, "The Security Predicament of Third World States," p. 66.

36. The political-cultural change in Eastern Europe is explained using the concept of legitimacy in Di Palma, "Legitimation from the Top," pp. 49–80. On legitimacy and political revolution see Schutz and Slater, *Revolution and Political Change in the Third World*, especially the first three chapters; and Kaufeler, *Modernization, Legitimacy and Social Movement*.

37. See Huntington, *Third Wave*, p. 46.

38. Giddens, *Central Problems*, p. 258.

39. This is acknowledged by O'Kane. See her "Legitimacy and Political Science," p. 104.

40. Barker, "Legitimacy," pp. 101–2.

1. ALAGAPPA, THE ANATOMY OF LEGITIMACY

1. Weber's idea of belief informs the definitions of legitimacy advanced by many scholars including C. J. Friedrich, S. M. Lipset, Reinhard Bendix, and David Apter. Friedrich defines legitimacy as "whether a given rulership is believed to be based on a good title by most of those subject to it"; see *Man and His Government*, p. 246. According to Lipset, "legitimacy involves the capacity of the system to engender and maintain the belief that the existing political institutions are the most appropriate ones for the society"; see *Political Man*, p. 77. Bendix states: "Legitimation achieves what power alone cannot, for it establishes the belief in the rightness of rule which, as long as it endures, precludes massive challenges"; see *Kings or People*, p. 17. Apter contends that legitimacy is related "to a set of conceptions held by significant members of the polity about the rightfulness of a political pattern"; see *The Politics of Modernization*, p. 235.

2. Weber, *Theory of Social and Economic Organization*, p. 382.

3. Ibid., p. 327.

4. Wrong, *Power*, p. 49.

5. For a critique of Weber's formulation of legitimacy, see Schaar, *Legitimacy in the Modern State*, pp. 19–25; Bensman, "Max Weber's Concept of Legitimacy," pp. 17–48; Merquior, *Rousseau and Weber*, pp. 130–36; Stillman, "Concept of Legitimacy," pp. 32–56; and Beetham, *Legitimation of Power*, pp. 8–13.

6. Although the following discussion defends Weber on several points, this is not my primary purpose. Weber's work on legitimacy, while useful, should be considered as a starting point that demands explication and considerable development to make the concept analytically relevant. Hence the effort in the first part of this book at elaborating the concept.

7. Weber, *Theory of Social and Economic Organization*, pp. 130–32.

8. Stillman, "Concept of Legitimacy," p. 39.

9. Ibid.

10. Barker, *Political Legitimacy*, p. 36.

11. Weber, *Theory of Social and Economic Organization*, p. 127.

12. Ibid., p. 125.

13. Beetham, *Legitimation of Power*, pp. 14–15.

14. Giddens, *Central Problems*, p. 5.

15. The term "judgmental dope" was coined by Harold Garfinkel in referring to analysts' treatment of the actor's understanding and reasoning in concrete situations as irrelevant to an analytical approach to social action. See Heritage, "Ethnomethodology," p. 229. Mutual knowledge is "a knowledge that is shared by all who are competent to engage in or recognize the appropriate performance of a social practice or range of practices"; see Cohen, "Structuration Theory," p. 287.

16. Beetham, *Legitimation of Power*, pp. 12–13.

17. Weber, *Theory of Social and Economic Organization*, p. 131. Weber's treatment of belief in legality as an independent basis of authority, however, is questionable. The authority of law derives from normative beliefs that underlie

the political system. Hence legality can only be an intermediate source of authority and is better viewed as an element of legitimacy. Beetham is correct in identifying legality as an element of legitimacy in addition to normative belief and consent.

18. Ideology is used here to refer to a system of beliefs or attitudes held by a social group. For a discussion of the various meanings of ideology see the introduction in De Crespigny and Cronin, *Ideologies of Politics*, pp. 5–22.

19. Heritage, "Ethnomethodology," p. 227; Giddens, *Central Problems*, p. 101.

20. Giddens, *Contemporary Critique of Historical Materialism*, vol. 1, pp. 64–68.

21. Ibid., p. 103. See also Held, *Political Theory*, p. 126.

22. Thus socialization, which is closely tied to structure, should not be interpreted as the passive imprinting of society on the individual or as a single process that stops at a particular point in time, but as a continuous process in which the agent (capable and knowledgeable) and the structure are mutually dependent. For a good discussion of socialization see Giddens, "Institutions, Reproduction and Socialization," in his *Central Problems*, pp. 69–73 and 96–130.

23. A strategic group may be defined as one that has the power—physical, moral, or both—to directly or indirectly challenge and bring about change in the composition and authority of the government.

24. For a good discussion of Gramsci's conception of hegemony see Mouffe, "Hegemony and Ideology in Gramsci," pp. 168–204.

25. Ibid., pp. 182–83.

26. Ibid., pp. 189–90.

27. For the various definitions of culture see Geertz, *Interpretation of Cultures*, pp. 4–5.

28. Parekh, "Cultural Particularity of Liberal Democracy," p. 167.

29. Geoffrey White, quoted in Tonkinson, "Understanding 'Tradition,'" p. 604, n. 4.

30. The seminal critique of the static conception of culture as an integrated and consensual symbolic system is Wagner's *Invention of Culture*.

31. Keesing, "Kastom Re-examined," p. 587; Tonkinson, "Understanding 'Tradition,'" p. 599.

32. Sahlins, *Islands of History*, p. 153.

33. On the relationship between history and culture see Sahlins, *Islands of History*, intro. and chap. 5, and Sahlins, *Historical Metaphors and Mythical Realities*, intro. and chap. 4.

34. Luhmann, *Sociological Theory of Law*, p. 169. For good discussions of force and legitimate authority see Luhmann, pp. 83–90, 168–69, and 199–206; and Wrong, *Power*, pp. 84–123.

35. Weber says that monopoly over the legitimate use of force is as important a component of the modern state as compulsory jurisdiction and continuous organization. See his *Theory of Social and Economic Organization*, p. 156.

36. Wrong, *Power*, pp. 86–87.

37. This theme has been explicit in the works of several Southeast Asia schol-

ars. See, for example, Anderson, "Idea of Power in Javanese Culture," pp. 17–77; Crouch, "Patrimonialism and Military Rule in Indonesia," pp. 571–87; Lande, *Leaders, Factions, and Parties*; Liddle, "Soeharto's Indonesia," pp. 68–90; and Steinberg, *Future of Burma*, pp. 1–2.

38. Clapham, *Third World Politics*, p. 48.

39. For discussion of a politically defining moment and charismatic authority, see Chapter 2 of this volume.

40. Irving Louis Horowitz contends that "when authority can neither be institutionalized through the mechanism of class/mass, nor through law/authority, then illegitimacy exists." He has characterized this as the "norm of illegitimacy" and argues that it has a wide range of applicability in the Third World. See Horowitz, "The Norm of Illegitimacy," pp. 23–30.

41. Weber, *Theory of Social and Economic Organization*, p. 325.

42. Barker, *Political Legitimacy*, p. 23.

43. Held, *Political Theory*, pp. 100–101.

44. Beetham, *Legitimation of Power*, pp. 136–42.

45. Friedrich argues that the capacity to deliver in terms of economic welfare is an important source of legitimacy. See Friedrich, *Man and His Government*, p. 244. Arthur J. Vidich argues more forcefully that "in our world of advanced industrial civilization none of these [subjective belief in the validity of charisma, tradition, or legality] seem necessary in the maintenance of authority. They have been supplemented by or perhaps even replaced by either promises of rewards or the actual rewards of industrialization. . . . The rational calculation of self-interest may be a more powerful force than credence in higher spiritual, cultural or judicial values." See Vidich, "Legitimation of Regimes in World Perspective," p. 301. A similar thesis has been advanced more recently by Scalapino, "National Political Institutions," p. 171.

46. With the passage of time, communist governments, for example, laid increasing emphasis on performance as the basis for their claim to legitimacy. See White, "Economic Performance and Communist Legitimacy," p. 463.

47. Latent ideology refers to everyday political words that express attitudes and behavior that can be raised to the conceptual level by social research. Forensic ideology refers to "elaborate, self-conscious word systems, formulated at a rather abstract level." These concepts are discussed in De Crespigny and Cronin, *Ideologies of Politics*, pp. 12–13.

48. Green, *Authority of the State*, p. 159.

49. While the individual's free will is important in creating the duty to obey, as Green points out, "it is wrong to think of our most important duties as being consequences only of our own wills; this is to drain them of the social dimension which explains their form and content." Membership in a political community carries rights and duties that a good citizen is bound to observe. Thus, through willing membership in a community, the individual also assumes role-bound duties. See Green, *Authority of the State*, pp. 188–219.

50. For a discussion of these and other types of obedience see Held, *Political Theory*, pp. 101–2, and Barker, *Political Legitimacy*, pp. 35–38. See also Claessen, "Changing Legitimacy," pp. 24–26.

51. Beetham, *Legitimation of Power*, pp. 151–56.

52. Conscientious objection to military service is a case in point. Yet even this disobedience need not involve legitimacy. The person concerned is not rejecting the general authority of the government but only a specific provision. By disobeying a specific provision and accepting the legal penalties for doing so, one can argue, the act actually helps to assert legitimacy. I am grateful to Rodney Barker for this observation.

53. Friedman, "On the Concept of Authority," pp. 127–31.

54. For a discussion of the different meanings of the term "state," see Benjamin and Duvall, "The Capitalist State in Context," pp. 22–29.

55. This characterization of the state is drawn from Fishman, "Rethinking State and Regime," p. 428.

56. For a discussion of the distinction between state, regime, and government see Lawson, *Some Conceptual Issues*, pp. 3–7.

57. Ra'anan, "Nation-State Fallacy," p. 5.

58. Renan, "What Is a Nation?" pp. 408–9.

59. Anderson, *Imagined Communities*, pp. 6–7.

60. Ibid., p. 135.

61. Fishman, "Rethinking State and Regime," p. 428.

62. For different uses of the term "government" see Finer, *Comparative Government*, chap. 1, especially pp. 3–4.

63. Lawson, *Some Conceptual Issues*, p. 7.

64. Rothschild, "Political Legitimacy in Contemporary Europe," p. 50.

65. Stinchcombe, *Constructing Social Theories*, p. 162.

66. Fishman, "Rethinking State and Regime," pp. 425–26, 437–38. Di Palma argues that in states where legitimation issues from the top, the decisive operative relationship is not between ruler and ruled but between rulers and the administrative staff. See his "Legitimation from the Top," p. 57.

67. Weber, *Theory of Social and Economic Organization*, p. 383.

68. Lipset, *Political Man*, pp. 78–80.

69. Reinhard Bendix observed two decades ago that "in our time, not only democracies but military regimes, dictatorships, and even constitutional monarchies are legitimized by claims of popular mandate. Indeed other means of justifying are becoming inconceivable." See Bendix, *Kings or People*, p. 4.

2. ALAGAPPA, THE BASES OF LEGITIMACY

1. For Weber's three types of authority see his *Theory of Social and Economic Organization*, pp. 130–32 and 328–29.

2. Talcott Parsons, introduction to Weber, *Theory of Social and Economic Organization*, p. 64.

3. On the development of normative frameworks see Cohen, "Legitimacy, Illegitimacy and State Formation," p. 3.

4. Cohen, "Structuration Theory," p. 287. Resources are bases of power employed by legitimators and other strategic groups to influence the outcome of interactions in their favor.

5. Giddens, *Central Problems*, pp. 190–93.

6. For a discussion of legitimacy in communist states see the essays in Rigby and Fehrer, *Political Legitimation in Communist States*. See also Di Palma, "Legitimation from the Top," pp. 55–63.

7. Brunner, "Legitimacy Doctrine and Legitimation Procedures," pp. 27–44.

8. Ibid., p. 31.　　　　　　　　　　9. Ibid., pp. 32–34.

10. Taylor, *State in Burma*, p. 364.　　11. Ibid., pp. 362–63.

12. Marcos, *Ideology for Filipinos*, p. 27.

13. Ibid., p. 27.

14. Giddens, *Central Problems*, pp. 184–93.

15. Ibid., pp. 193–97.

16. Scott, *Weapons of the Weak*, p. 338.

17. For a discussion of the conditions for effective hegemony, see ibid., pp. 336–37.

18. See Di Palma, "Legitimation from the Top," pp. 73–77.

19. Weber, *Theory of Social and Economic Organization*, p. 127.

20. For a discussion of this point see Barker, *Political Legitimacy*, pp. 49–52.

21. Ibid., p. 9.

22. Bendix, *Kings or People*, pp. 8–9.

23. Ibid., pp. 595–97.

24. Mostov, *Power, Process, and Popular Sovereignty*, pp. 5–18. Mostov argues for the process-oriented conception.

25. On the feasibility of popular sovereignty (identifying a popular will and devising institutional arrangements) see Nelson, *On Justifying Democracy*, pp. 53–70. For other criticisms of the outcome-oriented approach, see Mostov, *Power, Process, and Popular Sovereignty*, pp. 5–10.

26. Quoted in Mostov, ibid., p. 7.

27. Ibid., pp. 7–9.

28. Ibid., p. 10.

29. Such considerations underscore the questioning by Lee Kuan Yew of the principle of universal suffrage, the institution of the office of the elected president in Singapore, and the qualifications stipulated as necessary to run for that office.

30. For a good discussion of the relationship between power and human rights—a concept that is closely linked to popular sovereignty—and how human rights may be deployed to sustain or challenge power relations, see Stammers, "Human Rights and Power," pp. 70–82.

31. Huntington, *Third Wave*, p. 45.

32. Youngblood, *Marcos Against the Church*.

33. For a discussion of political legitimacy in Islam see Lewis, *Political Languages of Islam*, chaps. 3 and 5; and Mozaffari, *Authority in Islam*. There is more than one school of thought on what constitutes political legitimacy in Islam. The version presented here is close to the traditionalist version, which according to Clive Kessler is in the ascendant in Malaysia. See his "Reactualizing Islam in Our Times."

34. Lewis, *Political Languages of Islam*, pp. 92–93.

35. At the conceptual level, Islamic political community excludes slaves, women, and non-Muslims.

36. Weber, *Theory of Social and Economic Organization*, p. 125.

37. An organic link between effectiveness—that is, continuous economic development—and legitimacy in the long term was suggested by Lipset, *Political Man*, pp. 81–83.

38. The possibility that such threats can recur, especially in multiethnic and multireligious states, may be used to justify continued authoritarian rule. See Brown, *Legitimacy of Governments in Plural Societies*.

39. On the Thai experience see Morell and Samudavanija, *Political Conflict in Thailand*.

40. Dominguez, "Political Change," pp. 76–77.

41. This observation must be qualified—especially in democratic regimes where reelection considerations often make political leaders pander to the short-term interests of pressure groups, making long-range policies extremely difficult except in grave situations.

42. Weber, *Theory of Social and Economic Organization*, p. 358. For a good account of charismatic authority see Wilner, *Spellbinders*. For a good discussion of the conditions and qualifications relating to charismatic authority see Bendix, "Reflections of Charismatic Leadership."

43. Benedict Anderson argues that charismatic authority has been quite routine in the political cultures of Southeast Asian countries. See his "Further Adventures of Charisma," in *Language and Power*, pp. 78–93.

44. The relevance of personal authority for political legitimation is reflected in concepts like personal rule, neo-patrimonialism, paternalism, and patron-client relations that have been coined to describe such governments and authority relationships.

45. See, for example, the excellent discussion in Anderson, "Idea of Power in Javanese Culture," pp. 17–77.

46. Ibid., p. 72.

47. Pye, *Asian Power and Politics*, p. vii; see chaps. 1 and 2 for a discussion of power, authority, and legitimacy in Asian countries based on the cultural dimension.

48. See, for example, Lande, *Leaders, Factions, and Parties*; Machado, "Changing Aspects of Factionalism," pp. 1182–99. The patron-client approach, deficient on several counts, was discredited by several developments in the 1980s including the durability of the authoritarian rule of Marcos, ethnic and class conflict, and the restoration of formal democracy. See Kerkvliet, *Everyday Politics in the Philippines*. See also Chapter 6 in this volume.

49. Roth, "Traditional Patrimonialism and Personal Rulership," pp. 582–83.

50. For a discussion of legitimacy in classical Southeast Asia see the essays in Hall and Whitmore, *Explorations in Early Southeast Asian History*.

51. Samuel Huntington contends that with the fading of colonialism and the assumption of positions of authority by locally trained elites, indigenous values and beliefs are reasserting themselves and a process of de-Westernization is under

way. Hence, he argues, culture will become more important in explaining political development in these societies. He notes, however, that culture has all too often been a soft residual category and that political scientists have not done a good job of linking cultures to patterns of political development. See Huntington, "Goals of Development," pp. 26–28.

52. This contention is forcefully advanced in Thompson, Ellis, and Wildavsky, *Cultural Theory*, especially the introduction and chaps. 11 and 12.

53. Lucian Pye, for example, explains the dramatic political shifts in China by positing two cultures that, according to him, share certain important qualities. See Pye, *Mandarin and Cadre*, pp. 38–43.

54. Hobsbawm, "Introduction: Inventing Traditions," p. 9. Hobsbawm defines invented tradition as a "set of practices, normally governed by overtly or tacitly accepted rules and of ritual or symbolic nature, which seek to inculcate certain values and norms of behavior by repetition, which automatically implies continuity with the past"; ibid., p. 1.

55. Geertz, *Interpretation of Cultures*, p. 314.

56. Weber's discussion of routinization of charisma is relevant here. See Weber, *Theory of Social and Economic Organization*, pp. 363–73.

57. Atul Kohli argues that the populist actions and policies of Indira Gandhi and Rajiv Gandhi, designed to strengthen their personal positions, in fact contributed to fragmentation and conflict within the Congress Party, weakening its ability to govern effectively in the long run. See his *Democracy and Discontent*, chap. 13.

58. On the meaning of political revolution and its distinction from a social revolution see Wurfel, *Filipino Politics*, pp. 303–4.

59. Ibid., pp. 305–24.

60. See, for example, the text of the *Report of the Regional Meeting for Asia of the World Conference on Human Rights*, UN General Assembly A/CONF.157/ASRM/8, dated Apr. 7, 1993, pp. 1–16.

61. Di Palma argues that the persistence and vitality of capitalism, the enemy of the promised global order, was decisive in the loss of confidence by communist leaders in the former Soviet Union and the Eastern European states, leading to a loss of faith in their "mandate from heaven." See Di Palma, "Legitimation from the Top," p. 74.

62. Interaction capacity, defined as "the absolute quality of technological and societal capabilities across the system," has been advanced as a key level of analysis in the ongoing paradigmatic debate in international relations theory. See Buzan, Jones, and Little, *The Logic of Anarchy*, pp. 66–80.

63. While arguing that the herd effect in Latin American countries is a consequence of the impact of the international environment (the global economic situation, American policy), Dominguez asserts that this environment's effect must not be exaggerated. To illustrate his point he cites the transition to democracy in South America in the early 1980s despite the willingness of the Reagan administration to cooperate with authoritarian regimes. See Dominguez, "Political Change," pp. 79–80.

64. See the chapters on the international dimension and its relationship to democratization in Taiwan and South Korea in Robinson, *Democracy and Devel-*

opment in East Asia. Philippe C. Schmitter makes the same point with respect to Southern Europe. According to him the transitions from authoritarian rule and the prospects for democracy can be explained largely in terms of national forces and calculations; international forces play only an indirect and frequently a marginal role. See his "Introduction to Southern European Transitions," in O'Donnell, Schmitter, and Whitehead, *Transitions from Authoritarian Rule*, p. 3. This is the conclusion reached by Samuel P. Huntington as well. See his *Third Wave*, p. 86.

65. For a contrary viewpoint see Gills and Rocamora, "Low Intensity Democracy," pp. 501–23.

66. Wrong makes a similar point, but in relation to the advantage of a mixed power base. See Wrong, *Power*, pp. 70–72.

67. Beetham, *Legitimation of Power*, pp. 240–41.

68. It should be noted here that Beetham qualifies his acceptance of the end-of-history thesis; ibid., pp. 189–90. On the end-of-history thesis see Fukuyama, "End of History," pp. 3–18, and "Reply to My Critics," pp. 21–28.

69. John Hall quoted in Gaddis, "International Relations Theory and the End of the Cold War," pp. 47–48.

70. Hall, "Consolidations of Democracy," p. 288.

71. For a discussion of state capabilities in these areas see Migdal, *Strong Societies and Weak States*, pp. 3–41.

3. ALAGAPPA, CONTESTATION AND CRISIS

1. Beetham, *Legitimation of Power*, p. 117.

2. For an elaboration of some of these difficulties see ibid., pp. 117–60.

3. The substantive conditions are inferred from the discussion in Rueschemeyer, Stephens, and Stephens, *Capitalist Development and Democracy*, pp. 291–96.

4. According to Kohli a "crisis of governability" should be understood "not only in growing political violence but also in the state's developmental incapacity." See his *Democracy and Discontent*, p. 401.

5. In the Western industrialized states, with a few exceptions, the nation-state as constituted and the nature of the regime are relatively well established and their legitimacy is not in question. Although the philosophical orientation (liberals versus conservatives in a democratic regime) and effectiveness of specific governments may be contested—and may indeed account for changes in government—the nature of the regime itself is not controversial. The regimes in some of these states have been remarkably durable. It should, however, be noted here that the identity function of the state has in recent times been called into question. Some have argued that local institutions and affiliations are becoming more significant in the construction of political and social identity in Western European countries.

6. Geertz, *Interpretation of Cultures*, pp. 317–19.

7. For a discussion of the factors that contributed to this transformation see Anderson, *Imagined Communities*, pp. 113–40.

8. For a discussion of the formation of national-territorial states in the Third World see Smith, *State and the Nation in the Third World*, chap. 7. The multi-ethnic character of states is also rooted in precolonial migration and settlement.

9. The phrase "internal colonialism" is used by Hechter, *Internal Colonialism.*

10. The right to national self-determination in Africa and Asia has been limited to people under colonial domination. For a recent explicit statement of this see the *Report of the Regional Meeting for Asia of the World Conference on Human Rights,* UN General Assembly A/CONF.157/ASRM/8. The norm of territorial integrity has become entrenched in Africa. See Foltz, "Organization of African Unity," p. 352.

11. International support for norms of juridical statehood was important for the survival of weak states after World War II. See Jackson and Rosberg, "Why Africa's Weak States Persist," pp. 1–24.

12. Vatikiotis, "Local Hero," pp. 26–27.

13. In a few cases colonial rule strengthened traditional institutions, but these were intended to serve the needs of colonial authorities. Their relevance to post-independent states has been relatively marginal. Colonial powers, particularly the United States and Britain, did create and support political processes for self-government toward the end of colonial rule. Conformity with them was quite helpful in political legitimation in the early years after independence.

14. For a discussion of social control and state capabilities in developing countries, see Migdal, *Strong Societies and Weak States,* pp. 3–41.

15. Held views the first as a "crisis with transformative potential" and the second as a partial crisis and a recurrent feature of a system—much like the booms and recession in a business cycle. See his *Political Theory,* p. 118.

16. "Legitimacy strain" is preferable to "legitimacy deficit." The latter term gives the impression of concreteness and measurability whereas in reality one can only offer a subjective assessment. On legitimacy deficit see Beetham, *Legitimation of Power,* pp. 18, 207–9.

17. A good recent work on capitalist development and democracy is Rueschemeyer, Stephens, and Stephens, *Capitalist Development and Democracy.* An older pioneering work in this area is Moore, *Social Origins of Dictatorship and Democracy.* For a good summary of the theory see Potter, "Democratization in Asia," pp. 355–60.

18. According to Rueschemeyer, Stephens, and Stephens, the contradictions issuing from capitalist development create the pressures for democratic development. See their *Capitalist Development and Democracy,* particularly chaps. 1, 3, and 7.

19. The two principal works on this theory are those by Claus Offe and Jürgen Habermas. For a summary of their approaches see Held and Krieger, "Accumulation, Legitimation and the State," pp. 487–97. See also Barker, *Political Legitimacy,* chap. 5, especially pp. 87–98.

20. Connolly, "Dilemma of Legitimacy," pp. 222–49.

21. For an account of this theory see Held, *Political Theory,* pp. 119–20.

22. For a good account of military intervention in politics, see Finer, *Man on Horseback.*

23. For an extended discussion of the legitimacy problem of authoritarian regimes see Huntington, *Third Wave,* pp. 46–59.

24. President William Clinton in his address to the United Nations General

Assembly on September 27, 1993, stated: "In a new era of peril and opportunity, our overriding purpose must be to expand and strengthen the world's community of market-based democracies." For the text of his address see Clinton, "Confronting the Challenges," pp. 649–53. The enlargement doctrine, which has been advanced as the replacement for the strategy of containment, involves strengthening major market democracies, countering aggression by states hostile to democracy and supporting their liberalization, and promoting a humanitarian agenda to nurture democracy and market economies. See Lake, "From Containment to Enlargement," pp. 658–64. On the promotion of good governance by multilateral financial institutions, see Leftwich, "Governance, Democracy and Development in the Third World," pp. 608–9.

25. It should be noted here that one school of thought argues that the democratic system has the tools for internal and international conflict resolution. Robert L. Rothstein cautions against extending these propositions to democracies in the Third World. See his "Democracy and Conflict," pp. 20–21.

26. Kohli, *Democracy and Discontent*, p. 393.

27. Huntington, *Third Wave*, p. 41.

28. For a good account of the legitimacy crisis of communist regimes see Di Palma, "Legitimation from the Top," pp. 49–80.

29. Consociational arrangements have been advanced as a more promising way of achieving democracy as well as a considerable degree of political unity in multiethnic states. The four defining features of such an arrangement are government by a grand coalition, mutual veto, proportional representation, and a high degree of autonomy for each community to run its own affairs. See Lijphart, *Democracy in Plural Societies*, chap. 2. A reasonably high level of per capita income has also been suggested as a prerequisite for democratic development. For a good survey of the literature on the causal links between economic development and democracy see Diamond, "Economic Development and Democracy Reconsidered," pp. 450–99. Although they do not claim such a causation, Crouch and Morley suggest that rapid economic growth and democratic development tend to be associated; see Crouch and Morley, "Dynamics of Political Change," p. 282.

4. CASE, MALAYSIA

1. Barker, *Political Legitimacy*, p. 160.

2. For a full exposition of the Malaysian government's coercive resources see Barraclough, "Dynamics of Coercion," pp. 797–822. See also Crouch, "Malaysia," especially pp. 136–40.

3. Bourchier, "Crime, Law and State Authority in Indonesia," p. 177.

4. Von Vorys, *Democracy Without Consensus*. See also Lijphart, *Democracy in Plural Societies*, pp. 153–57.

5. Barker, *Political Legitimacy*, p. 28.

6. Horowitz, *Ethnic Groups in Conflict*, pp. 202–3.

7. Crouch, "Malaysia," p. 151.

8. As one example, Mahathir was quoted by the MCA-owned *Star* (Apr. 20, 1979) as saying: "We practice Islam within our means and it is not possible to

practice it to the extent of 100 per cent when the country has a sizeable non-Malay population." While this posture may have mostly to do with UMNO's rivalry with the Parti Islam Se-Malaysia (Pan-Islamic Party of Malaysia), it redounds nevertheless to the advantage of the Chinese.

9. Kok Wee Kiat, former MCA vice president and vice chairman of the MCA think tank, INSAP, wrote: "Despite the rhetoric of power sharing, the Malaysian Chinese see the reality as an increasingly Malay-dominated political administrative system which reacts harshly to the calls for greater political equality, justice and fair play. Loyal Malaysian Chinese increasingly feel that the aim of restructuring Malaysian society and nation building is to be borne solely through sacrifices made by the non-Malays, including the creeping erosion of their cultural identity." See Kok Wee Kiat, "Facing the Future," p. 14.

10. Lim Kit Siang, "Introduction," p. x.

11. Zakaria Haji Ahmad, "Evolution and Development of the Political System in Malaysia," p. 235.

12. *Far Eastern Economic Review* (hereafter *FEER*), Sept. 27, 1990. In a personal communication, Mar. 31, 1993, Michael Ong suggests that the Barisan government was rapidly "coming up" in the eyes of Chinese, shedding its image of illegitimacy.

13. Chung, *Mahathir Administration*, p. 49.

14. Milner, "Inventing Politics," pp. 112–13.

15. Chung, *Mahathir Administration*, p. 52.

16. Lim Kit Siang, "Introduction," pp. xiii–xiv.

17. In a brief discussion (MCA headquarters, Kuala Lumpur, Nov. 2, 1989), an MCA parliamentarian spoke of his admiration for Malay political skills—"we cannot hope to match them"—in dealing with the Chinese community. He then outlined his "boiling kettle theory," which portrays UMNO leaders as knowing precisely when and how much to lift the "lid" in order to keep Chinese resentments from boiling over. (The lid is then replaced.) The respondent suggested that his metaphor was particularly apt at election time, for UMNO offered various concessions (usually over education) in order to strengthen Chinese support for the MCA, then stalled or reneged after the election was won.

18. Loh, "Modernization," p. 226. Loh also notes (p. 225) that because the government introduced an obfuscatory, amalgamating category of "Pribumi" in Sabah in the early 1970s that includes all non-Chinese groups, one can only project the relative size of ethnic communities from earlier data.

19. Kahin, "Crisis on the Periphery," pp. 33–34.

20. Ibid., pp. 30–31.

21. For analyses of the 1994 Sabah state election and its aftermath see "The Sabah Elections in 1994: Probing the Larger Issues," *Aliran Monthly* 14(2) (1993 [incorrectly dated]): 2–6, and "Settling Scores: Defections Doom PBS Government in Sabah," *FEER*, Mar. 24, 1994, p. 23.

22. Loh, "Modernization," pp. 225 and 241–48.

23. For a brief discussion of the recent revival of Iban nationalism, see Shafruddin Hashim, "Malaysia 1991," pp. 189–91.

24. Lee, "Symbols of Separatism," p. 34.

25. For an interpretation of the UMNO conflict during the 1980s as growing

out of unfinished business during the 1970s, see Shamsul A. B., "'Battle Royal,'" pp. 170–72.

26. See Nagata, *Malaysian Mosaic*, pp. 188–89. See also Loh and Kahn, "Introduction," pp. 9–12.

27. Horowitz, *Ethnic Groups in Conflict*, pp. 185–86.

28. Strauch, "Multiple Ethnicities," p. 235; Nagata, *Malaysian Mosaic*, p. 177.

29. Kessler, "Archaism and Modernity," p. 134.

30. Milner, *Kerajaan*.

31. Nagata, *Malaysian Mosaic*, p. 149; see also Milner, "Inventing Politics," pp. 108–9.

32. Chandra, *Protector?* passim.

33. *Malay Annals*; quoted in Andaya and Andaya, *History of Malaysia*, pp. 44–45.

34. Nagata, *Malaysian Mosaic*, p. 149.

35. *Malay Annals*; quoted in Andaya and Andaya, *History of Malaysia*, p. 48.

36. Andaya and Andaya, *History of Malaysia*, p. 48.

37. Sadka, *Protected Malay States*, p. 32.

38. Gullick, "Role of the Malay Ruler," p. 2.

39. Kessler, "Archaism and Modernity," p. 141.

40. Sadka, "State Councils," p. 105.

41. Gullick, "Role of the Malay Ruler," p. 3.

42. Chandra, *Protector?* p. 57.

43. Khasnor, *Emergence of the Modern Malay Administrative Elite*, p. viii.

44. Stockwell, "White Man's Burden," p. 62. Stockwell (p. 63) also speculates that after invigorating Islamic customs in order to give the rulers greater authority over a more cohesive Malay community, the British sought to temper Islam's reformism and fundamentalism with a revival of Malay literature (led by R. J. Wilkinson and R. O. Winstedt) and the "softer and moderating aspects of folklore."

45. Chandra, *Protector?* p. 66.

46. Ibid. Indeed, while such awards and offices were once coupled with state pensions, today they attract business offers, which are essential for undergirding contemporary elite statuses in Malaysia.

47. Milner, "Inventing Politics," p. 109.

48. See, for example, Gale, *Politics and Public Enterprise in Malaysia*. See also Chandra, *Protector?* passim; and Kessler, "Archaism and Modernity," pp. 148 and 155. In some measure, argues Nagata, these UMNO appeals may also have been reinforced by traditional Muslim precepts that "discouraged the formation of associations . . . between the wider religious community (*ummat*) and the individual, for fear of creating too many intervening loyalties to worldly institutions, especially political." After presenting this view, however, Nagata sharply dissents from it. See Nagata, *Malaysian Mosaic*, pp. 90–91.

49. Fan Yew Teng, *UMNO Drama*, p. 98.

50. See Mauzy, "Malaysia in 1987," pp. 213–22.

51. Pye, *Asian Power and Politics*, p. 251.

52. Strauch, "Multiple Ethnicities," p. 242.

53. Nagata, *Malaysian Mosaic*, p. 238.

54. Sadka, *Protected Malay States*, p. 308.

55. Tan Liok Ee, "Dongjiaozong and the Challenge to Cultural Hegemony," p. 184.

56. Strauch, "Multiple Ethnicities," p. 41.

57. Wang Gungwu, "Chinese Politics in Malaya," pp. 173–200.

58. Pye, *Asian Power and Politics*, p. 251.

59. See, for example, Jesudason, *Ethnicity and the Economy*. See also Bowie, *Crossing the Industrial Divide*.

60. Strauch, "Multiple Ethnicities," p. 241; see also Kessler, "Archaism and Modernity," pp. 140–41.

61. See, for example, Abraham, "Manipulation and Management," pp. 1–27. See also Jomo, *A Question of Class*.

62. For a game theory approach to these outcomes see Rabushka and Shepsle, *Politics in Plural Societies*.

63. Sadka, "State Councils," p. 116.

64. See Stockwell, "White Man's Burden," pp. 61–62. Horowitz writes that "the preference for multiethnic organizations in the colonies became something of British policy in the 1950s as the British came to grips with emerging nationalist movements"; *Ethnic Groups in Conflict*, p. 401n.

65. Allen, *Malayan Union*, pp. 8–9.

66. Heng Pek Koon, *Chinese Politics in Malaysia*, p. 154.

67. Means, *Malaysian Politics*, p. 393.

68. Safeguards for Chinese business activities are contained in article 153, section 9, of the Malaysian Constitution, which states that "nothing in this article shall empower Parliament to restrict business or trade solely for the purpose of reservations for Malays."

69. Horowitz, *Ethnic Groups in Conflict*, p. 406.

70. The best account of the July 1959 crisis is given by Haas, "MCA, 1958–59."

71. Milne, *Government and Politics in Malaysia*, p. 41.

72. Andaya and Andaya, *History of Malaysia*, p. 44.

73. Funston, *Malay Politics*, p. 17.

74. Stubbs, *Hearts and Minds in Guerrilla Warfare*, p. 211.

75. Funston, *Malay Politics*, p. 175.

76. Chandra, *Protector?* p. 126; Funston, *Malay Politics*, p. 174.

77. See Crouch, "UMNO Crisis," pp. 11–36 and 53–55. See also Funston, *Malay Politics*, p. 208.

78. Jesudason, *Ethnicity and the Economy*, p. 52.

79. Funston, *Malay Politics*, p. 66.

80. Lau Teik Soon writes that "the unwritten law regarding communal issues was violated by both the Alliance and the Opposition parties when they indulged in open, public and heated debate over such subjects." See "Malaysia: The May 13 Incident," p. 1.

81. The classic account of the May Thirteenth rioting is given by von Vorys, *Democracy Without Consensus*. See also Slimming, *Death of a Democracy*.

82. Quoted in von Vorys, *Democracy Without Consensus*, p. 373.

83. Means, *Malaysian Politics*, p. 398.

84. Quoted from Tengku Razaleigh, a central figure in the design and implementation of the NEP during the 1970s, in *Malaysian Business*, July 1976, p. 14.

85. Gomez, *Money Politics*, p. vi.

86. Gomez, *Politics in Business*.

87. See, for example, Jesudason, *Ethnicity and the Economy*, and Gomez, *Money Politics* and *Politics in Business*. See also Mehmet, *Development in Malaysia*.

88. For a good study of this issue in Malaysia, see Jesudason, *Ethnicity and the Economy*. See also Searle, "Rent-Seekers or Real Capitalists?" This debate now spans the region. See Clad, *Behind the Myth*; Doner, "Approaches to the Politics of Economic Growth"; and Yoshihara, *Rise of Ersatz Capitalism in Southeast Asia*.

89. Quoted in Scott, "Where the Quota Is King," p. 66.

90. Jesudason thus concludes that "Chinese businesses [did] not appear to have lost out markedly, certainly not as much as they initially feared"; *Ethnicity and the Economy*, p. 160. See also Fong Chan Onn's remarks about increased non-Bumiputra participation in the corporate sector after 1970; Fong, *Malaysian Economic Challenge in the 1990s*, p. 113.

91. Quoted in Loh and Kahn, "Introduction," p. 13.

92. Crouch, *Malaysian Government*.

93. Crouch, "UMNO Crisis," p. 17.

94. Ibid., p. 13.

95. Crouch, *Malaysian Government*.

96. Means, *Malaysian Politics*, pp. 316–17.

97. See, for example, Jomo, *Growth and Structural Change in the Malaysian Economy*. See also Khoo Kay Jin, "Grand Vision," pp. 44–77.

98. *Asiaweek*, Feb. 19, 1988.

99. For an account of these events see Means, *Second Generation*, pp. 199–222.

100. *FEER*, Mar. 3, 1988.

101. The original UMNO was founded in 1946. Hari Singh writes that "the connection with UMNO continued to provide legitimacy among the Malays to the Semangat '46 movement as an alternative to the present leadership, more so given that Tunku Abdul Rahman, the founding father of the nation and UMNO's president for 19 years, was associated with the group"; "Political Change in Malaysia," p. 717.

102. Khoo Kay Jin, "Grand Vision," p. 45.

103. Quoted in *FEER*, Nov. 26, 1992.

104. See "Mara Unit Trust Opens Door to Non-Bumiputeras," in *New Straits Times*, Apr. 21, 1992, p. 1.

105. See "The Language Lobby: Mahathir in Clash Over Use of Malay," in *FEER*, Oct. 8, 1992, p. 31; see also *New Straits Times*, Aug. 22, 1990.

106. In an interview with *FEER* (Sept. 3, 1992), an UMNO official stated that "Malays in the civil service and other middle class occupations [were frequently] neutral to UMNO's economic appeals because they already have everything, but they would like to do something holy and look after the hereafter. [Many were

thus attracted by PAS] campaigns for clean government, free of greed, corruption and money politics" (p. 13).

107. For an account of the revitalization of Malaysia's democratic procedures during this period see Khong Kim Hoong, *Malaysia's General Election 1990*.

108. See Halim Salleh, "Peasants, Proletarianization, and the State," pp. 107–32. See also *FEER*, Sept. 24, 1992, pp. 100–102.

109. See Armstrong, "Identity Manipulation by Urban Malays," pp. 104–27. See also Kahn, "Class, Ethnicity, and Diversity," pp. 158–78.

110. Nagata, *Malaysian Mosaic*, p. 168. In an interview with Margaret Scott, Mahathir observed: "In offices we work together, in the factories we work together, but we don't play together. Unfortunately, we go back to our own homes"; "Where the Quota Is King," p. 64.

111. See, for example, Loh and Kahn, "Introduction."

112. *FEER*, May 20, 1993, p. 32.

113. Milner, "Inventing Politics," pp. 115 and 129.

5. KHONG, SINGAPORE

1. See Lee Kuan Yew's remarks in *Straits Times* (Singapore), Nov. 15, 1988; and Goh Chok Tong quoted in Vasil, *Governing Singapore*, pp. 123–24.

2. Trends in income distribution in Singapore have engendered some debate in recent years. The figures do not allow for a straightforward interpretation, and there is no clear consensus. Lee Hsien Loong, in attempting to show that all social groups have benefited from PAP rule, revealed that lower-level groups increased their incomes at a significantly lower rate than higher-level groups; *Straits Times*, July 29, 1991. See also Ibrahim, "Will Income Gap Divide S'pore?," and the letters by Paul Cheung in *Straits Times*, June 8, 1993, and by Bhanoji Rao in *Straits Times*, June 11, 1993.

3. Huntington, *Third Wave*.

4. Lee Kuan Yew, "Text of a Speech by the Prime Minister, Mr. Lee Kuan Yew, at the Official Opening of the Civil Service Study Center," Singapore government press statement, Aug. 15, 1959.

5. See the depiction by Goh Keng Swee, *Practice of Economic Growth*, pp. 95–96.

6. Barker, *Political Legitimacy*, p. 114.

7. Chan Heng Chee, *Politics in an Administrative State*.

8. See O'Donnell, *Modernization*, pp. 55, 89–91, 113–14. He distinguishes between "exclusion" of a popular sector that has been politically active and "incorporation" of the popular sector as a deliberate government policy. An "inclusionary" regime, by contrast, may consciously incorporate part of the popular sector although the political system remains authoritarian.

9. Quoted by Bogaars, "Public Services," p. 73.

10. Chan Heng Chee, *Dynamics of One Party Dominance*.

11. Quoted by Vasil, *Governing Singapore*, pp. 145–46.

12. See Khong, "Leadership and National Security," pp. 22–24.

13. Minchin, *No Man Is an Island*, p. 228.

14. See Cheung, "Soldiers and Scholars," pp. 15–18; and the Singapore government's response in the Letters column of *FEER*, Dec. 19, 1991, pp. 4–6.

15. O'Donnell, *Modernization*, pp. 79–83.

16. See Collier's discussion of the bureaucratic-authoritarian model; *New Authoritarianism in Latin America*, pp. 19–32. For official views of recent changes to the Chinese Chamber of Commerce see *Sunday Times* (Singapore), Aug. 22, 1993, and *Straits Times*, Aug. 26, 1993.

17. Report of the Economic Committee, *Singapore Economy: New Directions*.

18. See Bello and Rosenfeld, *Dragons in Distress*, pp. 295–97, 301–2.

19. See the discussion by Pang Eng Fong, Tan Chwee Huat, and Cheng Soo May, "Management of People," pp. 129–30.

20. Krause, "Government as Entrepreneur," p. 439.

21. Discussion of the trade union movement remains sensitive. A standard text on Singapore politics has the following note by the editors: "A significant omission from this book . . . is the trade union movement. . . . In all, a total of four persons were invited (one after the other) to write the chapter. . . . The first person who was approached gave up after a few months and was replaced by someone else. The same pattern was observed in all the four cases and the chapter on trade unions remained unwritten." See Jon S. T. Quah, Chan Heng Chee, and Seah Chee Meow, "Editors' Introduction," p. xviii, n. 15. On leadership changes at the NTUC see *Straits Times*, Sept. 6, 1993.

22. Chan Heng Chee, "Role of Intellectuals in Singapore Politics," p. 64.

23. Rao notes the constant use of the word "good" as both description and explanation of government policy. See Rao, "Role of Government in Singapore's Economic Development."

24. As Michael Leifer argues, the people are deemed responsible to the government, not vice versa. See Leifer, "Triumph," p. 27.

25. A case in point is the dismissal of the failed opposition candidate Chee Soon Juan from his university lectureship, a move interpreted by many as politically motivated though the grounds for dismissal were an alleged misuse of research funds. See *Straits Times*, Apr. 3, 1993. For a vivid account of the fear cited here see Selvan, *Singapore*, pp. 300–303.

26. See, for example, Pye, *Asian Power and Politics*, pp. 339–41.

27. Figures based on total votes cast, including spoiled and blank votes.

28. Ow Chin Hock, "Role of Government in Economic Development," p. 234.

29. The Asian-Western debate is incisively analyzed by Clammer, *Singapore: Ideology, Society, Culture*, pp. 22–29.

30. See Goh Keng Swee's remarks in *Straits Times*, Feb. 4, 1982.

31. Balakrishnan, "Esprit de Core," p. 27.

32. Malay members of Parliament could not restrain themselves from expressing concern that the proposed national ideology would reinforce Chinese dominance. Having voiced their reservations, however, they publicly affirmed the propounded core values. See *Straits Times*, July 19, 1989.

33. Cotton, "Political Innovation," p. 13.

34. Jon S. T. Quah's suggested modifications to the government-sponsored values were not taken up; see Quah, *In Search of Singapore's National Values*.

35. Pye, *Asian Power and Politics*, p. vii.

36. See the discussion in Wade, *Governing the Market*, p. 375.

37. There is still an external threat in the leadership's perception, however. Note its reaction to a joint Malaysian-Indonesian military exercise in southern Johore; *Straits Times*, Aug. 10, 1991.

38. Cotton, "Political Innovation," p. 3. The following discussion on the elected presidency draws on Cotton.

39. The president will have to be a Singapore citizen, with ministerial, senior executive, or senior-level civil service experience. See the analysis "The New President: Will He Rewrite the Script?" *Sunday Times*, Aug. 8, 1993.

40. See Rajaratnam's comments in *Straits Times*, Nov. 7, 1990.

41. Balakrishnan, "Forked Tongues," pp. 19–20.

42. *Straits Times*, Aug. 11, 1991.

43. Brown, "Singapore PM Puts Reform Plans on Hold," p. 4.

44. See the discussion in Singh, *Whither PAP's Dominance?* pp. 135–48. Note also the survey findings by Kuo, Holaday, and Peck, *Mirror on the Wall*, pp. 13, 99.

45. See the comments by Lee Hsien Loong, *Straits Times*, Oct. 24, 1991.

46. See Cheung, "Summary of Census Findings" and "Discussion," pp. 6, 64; and Chiew Seen Kong, "Social Mobility in Singapore," p. 214.

47. See the comments by Lee Hsien Loong, *Straits Times*, May 18, 1987.

48. Li, *Malays in Singapore*, pp. 178–79.

49. Ibid., pp. 173–76.

50. Almond and Verba, *Civic Culture*.

51. Quah and Quah, "Limits of Government Intervention," pp. 120–21.

52. See Lee Kuan Yew's comments on the 1984 general elections, *Straits Times*, Dec. 24, 1984.

53. Leifer, "Triumph," p. 28.

54. For evidence of alienation, note a survey conducted by the Institute of Policy Studies in Singapore on the government's proposal for an elected presidency, which found 68 percent of respondents aware of the proposal, but only 3.2 percent stating that they were interested in it. Half the respondents said they were not interested in any local (presumably political) issues at all. See *Sunday Times* (Singapore), Oct. 14, 1990.

55. This survey, also carried out by the Institute of Policy Studies, devised a political alienation index and found that respondents with higher scores on the index (meaning more alienated) were much more likely to have considered emigrating. See *Straits Times*, Oct. 4, 1990. The points on emigration, which follow in the text, also derive from this study.

56. Khong, "Politics of Bureaucracy," p. 19.

57. *Straits Times*, Sept. 27, 1990.

58. Quoted by Vasil, *Governing Singapore*, pp. 212–13.

59. "Lee States His Case," *FEER*, Oct. 12, 1989, p. 15.

60. *Straits Times*, June 14, 1986.

61. See First Deputy Prime Minister Goh Chok Tong's statement to Parliament in *Straits Times*, July 30, 1987.

62. Balakrishnan, "Leg Up for Friends," p. 15. See also *Straits Times*, Aug. 25, 1993, which gives details of the program.

63. Taylor, "Quiet Grumbles Among the Partners," p. 2.

64. See the discussion of corporatism in Held, *Political Theory*, pp. 64–67 and 75–77; see also Held, *Foundations of Democracy*.

6. SIDEL, THE PHILIPPINES

1. For a comprehensive discussion of the symbolic functions of analogous, pre-colonial memorial and reliquary monuments elsewhere in Southeast Asia, see Snodgrass, *Symbolism of the Stupa*.

2. See Pemberton, "The Appearance of Order."

3. For an extremely thoughtful and well-documented discussion of the career of Ramon M. Durano, Sr., see Cullinane, "Patron as Client," pp. 163–241.

4. As Reynaldo C. Ileto has noted, precolonial leaders "who distinguished themselves [attributed] their prowess to divine forces and [took] pains to select burial sites that would become centers of ancestor worship." See "Rizal," p. 322.

5. Durano, *Ramon M. Durano*.

6. Przeworski, "Some Problems," p. 52.

7. Weber, *Economy and Society*, vol. 1, p. 213.

8. Ibid., vol. 3, p. 953.

9. Scott, *Weapons of the Weak*, p. 317; italics in the original.

10. Thompson, *Whigs and Hunters*, p. 265.

11. Anderson, *Imagined Communities*, pp. 80–128.

12. "Within the constitutional framework," argues David Wurfel, "popular elections periodically reinforced the legitimacy of the regime." See *Filipino Politics*, p. 37.

13. See Del Carmen, "Constitutionality and Judicial Politics," especially pp. 87–90.

14. See Abueva, "Ideology and Practice in the 'New Society.'"

15. See, for example, Glang, *Muslim Secession or Integration?* See also Finin, "Regional Consciousness and Administrative Grids."

16. For accounts of the emergence of the radically "nationalist" student movement in the late 1960s, see Lacaba, *Days of Disquiet*, and Pimentel, *Edjop*.

17. See Anderson, *Imagined Communities*, pp. 12, 144–47.

18. Guerrero, *Philippine Society*.

19. See "Philippine Trade Unionism: A Situationer," *Philippine Labor Monitor* 1(2) (1985): 3–82.

20. See de los Reyes and Jopillo, *Pursuing Agrarian Reform in Negros Occidental*.

21. See, for example, Parnell, "Time and Irony in Manila Squatter Movements."

22. Guerrero, *Philippine Society*, p. iii.

23. Marcos, *Democratic Revolution in the Philippines*, pp. 9–10.

24. See Wurfel, *Filipino Politics*, pp. 24–27.

25. Silliman, "Folk Legal Culture," p. 225. See also Fegan, "Between the Lord and the Law," pp. 113–28.

26. For a deeper understanding of the imposition of formal democratic institutions upon Philippine society, see the insightful and well-researched articles in Paredes, *Philippine Colonial Democracy.*

27. The literature on the Philippines' "dependent independence" and "neo-colonial" ties to the United States is extensive. See, in particular, the works of Renato Constantino as well as Bonner, *Waltzing with a Dictator*; Broad, *Unequal Alliance*; Karnow, *In Our Image*; and Shalom, *The United States and the Philippines.*

28. Rafael, "Patronage and Pornography," p. 283.

29. As E. P. Thompson notes: "Paternalism as myth or as ideology is nearly always backward-looking. It offers itself in English history less as actuality than as a model of an antique, recently passed, golden age from which present modes and manners are a degeneration. . . . Always paternalist actuality appears to be receding into an ever more primitive and idealized past." See *Customs in Common*, pp. 23–24.

30. Monographs written in the 1960s by sociologists and political scientists popularized a "patron-client" model that has long dominated discussions of Philippine society and politics. See, for example, Hollnsteiner, *Dynamics of Power*; and Lande, *Leaders, Factions, and Parties.*

31. Nowak and Snyder, "Clientelist Politics in the Philippines," p. 1147.

32. For accounts revealing greater dissonance in the collective memory, see Larkin, *Sugar and the Origins of Modern Philippine Society*, pp. 124–34.

33. Crisanto-Ortega, *Vanishing Breed*, p. 44.

34. Kerkvliet, *Huk Rebellion*, p. 6.

35. Blanc-Szanton, "Change and Politics in a Western Visayan Municipality," p. 106.

36. Agpalo, *Pandanggo sa Ilaw*, p. 3.

37. Rafael, "Patronage and Pornography," p. 298.

38. See Yambot, *How to Win in the 1992 Local Elections*, pp. 61–65. The term "KBL" is a play on words based on the acronym of the Kilusang Bagong Lipunan (New Society Movement), Marcos's political machine.

39. In fact, Makati's public coffers provided the funds for these social services. Political opponents have charged the current mayor with overpricing the goods donated and pocketing the difference, which amounts to millions of pesos. See Corotan, "It's Back with Binay," p. 10.

40. See Kerkvliet, "Classes and Class Relations in a Philippine Village," pp. 31–50; and Kerkvliet, *Everyday Politics in the Philippines*, especially pp. 202–41.

41. See Scott, *Weapons of the Weak*, p. 266.

42. See Kerkvliet, *Huk Rebellion*; Scott, "Patron-Client Politics," pp. 91–113; Scott, "Erosion of Patron-Client Bonds," pp. 5–37; and Scott and Kerkvliet, "How Traditional Rural Patrons Lose Legitimacy," pp. 439–58.

43. Scott, *Weapons of the Weak*, pp. 1–27.

44. Reynaldo Ileto describes *pulitika* as mere "jockeying for position among the old political oligarchy." See Ileto, "Past in the Present Crisis," p. 9.

45. These terms, long featured in popular political discourse in the Philippines, are most thoughtfully discussed in Hutchcroft, "Oligarchs and Cronies in the Philippine State," pp. 414–50.

46. Holston, "Misrule of Law," p. 695.

47. Stone, *Philippine Urbanization*, p. 83.

48. Ibid., p. 84; emphasis added.

49. A retired high-ranking constabulary officer has noted: "The credibility of the officer of the law is all but zero. The average tao looks at a policeman and invariably sees a *parak* or *lespu* or *pondying* or *alat*." See Gutang, *Pulisya*, p. 1.

50. Silliman, "Folk Legal Culture," p. 234.

51. See Wurfel, "Philippines," pp. 757–73. See also Ravenholt, "Peso Price of Politics"; and Navarro, "How Much to Get Elected."

52. Baterina, "Study of Money," p. 169.

53. It is widely suspected that Senator Joseph "Erap" Estrada abandoned his own bid for the presidency and agreed to be the running mate of presidential candidate Eduardo "Danding" Cojuangco, Jr., in exchange for a payment of 200 million pesos. See "Erap Denies P200M Payoff from Danding," *Philippine Daily Globe*, Jan. 9, 1992, p. 2.

54. "The Toll: Jan. 12–May 24," *Philippine Daily Globe*, May 25, 1992, p. 2.

55. The months preceding the May 11, 1992, elections saw a dramatic rise in the number of kidnappings, for example, as well as a noticeable increase in the "vigilance" of authorities involved in the enforcement of antigambling statutes. See "GAB Raiders Raising Funds for Presidentiables' Bids?" *Manila Standard*, Feb. 19, 1992, p. 14.

56. See, for example, "Franchises Rushed by Congress? Pols May Be Raising Funds," *Philippine Daily Globe*, Jan. 19, 1992, p. 6. Also worthy of note is the controversy that dominated Manila newspaper headlines on May 4–5, 1992, based on a photograph of a vice-presidential candidate holding a box containing 4.5 million pesos in cash supposedly extorted from a garment firm applying for renewal of its export quota. See Juan V. Sarmiento, "Ramos Camp Accused of P4.5-M Extortion," *Philippine Daily Inquirer*, Mar. 4, 1992, pp. 1, 12.

57. Throughout the 1992 campaign, the Aquino administration was persistently accused of selectively delaying and expediting the release of budgetary allocations for local government units (BALGUs) and the countryside development funds (CDF) in order to secure promises of support for the administration's candidate.

58. The most systematic attempt to analyze the role of fraud in Philippine elections is Luzviminda Tancangco's controversial study, *Anatomy of Electoral Fraud*.

59. See Simmel, *Philosophy of Money*, pp. 255–57. Simmel defines the blasé attitude as "not the devaluation of things as such, but indifference to their specific qualities from which the whole liveliness of feeling and volition originates"; p. 256.

60. Kerkvliet and Mojares, "Themes in the Transition from Marcos to Aquino," in *From Marcos to Aquino*, p. 7.

61. Narding Suario, "Votes for Sale," *Philippine Daily Inquirer*, May 6, 1992, p. 5.

62. Ileto, "Rizal," p. 488.

63. See Wolters, *History, Culture, and Region*; and Sahlins, "Poor Man, Rich Man."

64. Scott, *Slavery in the Spanish Philippines*, pp. 51–52.

65. As Marshall Sahlins notes: "The indicative quality of big-man authority is everywhere the same: it is *personal* power. Big-men do not come to office; they do not succeed to, nor are they installed in, existing positions of leadership over political groups. The attainment of big-man status is rather the outcome of a series of acts which elevate a person above the common herd and attract about him a coterie of loyal, lesser men." See Sahlins, "Poor Man, Rich Man," p. 289.

66. Aguilar, "Phantoms of Capitalism," pp. 29–34. See also McCoy, "*Baylan.*"

67. Where Islam penetrated, it favored the closer association of political leadership with certain lineages and the stabilization of succession through the establishment of genealogies and rules for leadership transition. See, for example, Majul, "Succession in the Old Sulu Sultanate."

68. May, "Civic Ritual," p. 13.

69. See Bankoff, "Big Fish in Small Ponds."

70. On this process see Larkin, *Pampangans*, especially chap. 4, as well as Wickberg, *Chinese in Philippine Life*, especially chaps. 2 and 3.

71. De Azcarraga y Palmero, *La Reforma*, pt. 4, p. 14; Fenner, *Cebu Under the Spanish Flag*, p. 155; Hollnsteiner, *Dynamics of Power*, p. 38; Legarda, "Foreign Trade, Economic Change and Entrepreneurship," p. 368; and May, "Civic Ritual."

72. In the early twentieth century, by contrast, colonial officials in Burma, Malaya, and the Netherlands Indies began to incorporate native elites into centralized bureaucratic state apparatuses, while in Siam the Crown embarked on an "absolutist" project in roughly the same period.

73. For three colorful and illuminating accounts of these aspects of the American colonial period, see Concepcion, "*La Tragedia*" *del Banco Nacional Filipino*; Kelly, *His Majesty King Torrens*; and "La Oficina de Aduanas Sigue Siendo una Mina de Oro," *Chismes y Escandalos*, May 19, 1934, pp. 11, 16. See also Wolters, "Rise and Fall of Provincial Elites," pp. 54–74.

74. The literature on this subject is extensive. For particularly insightful accounts see Ileto, *Pasyon and Revolution*; McCoy, "*Baylan*"; Medina, "Cavite Before the Revolution," pp. 120–210; and Sturtevant, *Popular Uprisings in the Philippines*.

75. See, for example, Abinales, "Marcos, Pendatun, Matalam and Toothpick"; Bentley, "Dispute, Authority, and Maranao Social Order"; Kiefer, *Tausug*; and Mednick, "Sultans and Mayors."

76. See, for example, Barton, *Kalingas*; and Rosaldo, *Ilongot Headhunting 1883–1974*.

77. On the role of the *pangat* in Kalinga society see Barton, *Kalingas*, pp. 138–48.

78. See, for example, Lieban, *Cebuano Sorcery*.

79. For the most well-researched, sympathetic, and thoughtful account of a contemporary religious cult, see Pesigan, *Dulang-Buhay ng Bundok Banahaw*.

80. See Melissa G. Contreras, "Pop Catholicism," *Sunday Chronicle*, Mar. 21, 1993, pp. 1 and 8, as well as her article "Godfather" on p. 9 of the same issue.

81. See Love, "*Samahan* of Papa God," pp. 300–333.

82. See Reyes, *Romance Mode in Philippine Literature*, pp. 287–98.

83. Eric Hobsbawm defines social bandits as "peasant outlaws whom the lord and state regard as criminals, but who remain within peasant society, and are considered by their people as heroes, as champions, avengers, fighters for justice, perhaps even leaders of liberation, and in any case men to be admired, helped, and supported." See *Bandits*, p. 17.

84. "Poor Folk Bury Kidnap Gang Chief as 'Hero of New Age,'" *Philippine News*, Mar. 17–23, 1993, p. 6.

85. See Chapman, *Inside the Philippine Revolution*; and Jones, *Red Revolution*.

86. See the thoughtful discussion of Irish "hardmen" in Feldman, *Formations of Violence*, pp. 46–56.

87. See Nid Anima, "Tattoo, Anyone," *Philippines Free Press*, Jan. 8, 1972; Edward R. Kiunsala, "The End of Boy Golden," *Philippines Free Press*, Jan. 4, 1964, pp. 6, 63–64; and "Tattoos: The Underworld's Badge of Honor," *Veritas*, July 8–14, 1984, p. 12. As Francisco Colin, S.J., wrote in 1663: "Besides the exterior clothing and dress, some of these nations wore another inside dress, which could not be removed after it was once put on. These are the tattooings of the body so greatly practiced among the Visayans, whom we call Pintados for that reason. For it was a custom among them, and was a mark of nobility and bravery, to tattoo the whole body from top to toe when they were of an age and strength sufficient to endure the tortures of the tattooing." See Colin, "Native Races," p. 63.

88. See, for example, Lorenzo-Abrera, *Ang Numismatika*; Covar, "Potensiya, Bisa, at Anting-Anting"; Ileto, *Pasyon and Revolution*, p. 23; Ileto, "Rizal," p. 322; and McCoy, "Baylan," pp. 357–58.

89. Lorenzo-Abrera, *Ang Numismatika*, p. 38.

90. "Faced by a superior physical/spiritual power, the islanders understandably comprehended colonial conquest in terms of the Spaniards' rapport, alliance and support derived from *their* spirit world. . . . The paraphernalia used by the friars in their shamanic ensemble were thereby seen as potent objects . . . [which] became novel media for the transference of power from the spiritual to the human domain." See Aguilar, "Phantoms of Capitalism," pp. 39–43.

91. Ileto, "Rizal," p. 285.

92. Ileto, *Pasyon and Revolution*, p. 25. Ileto notes the similarity to the Javanese notions of power cited by Anderson: "the direct relationship between the state of a person's inner being and his capacity to control the environment" (Anderson, "Idea of Power in Javanese Culture," pp. 16–17).

93. "Ang taong may anting-anting, ayon sa mga karaniwang tao, ay matulungin, madasalin, mapagpakumbaba, at tahimik, subalit matapang kung magkasubukan. . . . Mahigpit ang pagkakaugnay ng anting-anting sa 'loób' ng tao, sa katatagan at kagandahan ng kanyang pagkatao"; Lorenzo-Abrera, *Ang Numismatika*, pp. 63–66.

94. Reyes, *Romance Mode in Philippine Literature*, p. 293.

95. For a thoughtful reevaluation of "social bandits" and insightful discussion of the significance of "protection," see Anton Blok's classic essay, "Peasant and Brigand."

96. See Orentlicher and Takiff, *Vigilantes in the Philippines*; and Porter, *Politics of Counterinsurgency*.

97. In fact, the very origins and survival of the armed revolutionary movement in the late 1960s and 1970s were very much linked to relationships with local politicians. On this point see Jones, *Red Revolution*, pp. 27–29, 47.

98. See, for example, "Ex-NDF Chief Is Surigao Town Mayor," *Philippine Daily Globe*, May 20, 1992, p. 8.

99. Kerkvliet, *Everyday Politics in the Philippines*, p. 221.

100. Victor Turner defines communitas as "a moment in and out of time" that "reveals, however fleetingly, some recognition (in symbol if not always in language) of a generalized social bond that has ceased to be and yet has simultaneously yet to be fragmented into a multiplicity of structural ties . . . of society as an unstructured or rudimentarily structured and relatively undifferentiated comitatus, community, or even communion of equal individuals who submit together to the general authority of the ritual elders." See *Ritual Process*, p. 96.

101. Kirsch, *Feasting and Social Oscillation*, p. 10.

102. O. W. Wolters, citing Kirsch, argues that in the procedure of feast giving, "the successful feaster is actually demonstrating his 'innate virtue,' showing his 'internal potency,' and his control over external supernatural forces." See Wolters, "Khmer 'Hinduism,'" p. 436.

103. Crisanto-Ortega, *Vanishing Breed*, p. 53.

104. Ibid., p. 44.

105. Wolters, "Khmer 'Hinduism,'" p. 429.

106. Rex Aguado, "Pasay City's Sleazy Politics," *Manila Chronicle*, May 9–15, 1992, p. 2.

107. See Guggenheim, "Cock or Bull"; and Lansang, *Cockfighting in the Philippines*.

108. Aguilar, "Odds on the Future."

109. As Antonio Pigafetta noted, "the kings know more languages than the other people." See Blair and Robertson, *Philippine Islands*, vol. 33, p. 115.

110. On the importance of political commentary on radio talk shows, see Mojares, "Talking Politics."

111. *Brod* is the term commonly used to refer to a college fraternity brother. 'Pare is short for *kumpare* or *kumpadre*, terms used in the Philippines for a ritual cofather. 'Pare is also used informally as a friendly or even intimate form of address among men.

112. Mojares, "Talking Politics," p. 131.

113. Siegel, *Solo in the New Order*, p. 18.

114. Crisanto-Ortega, *Vanishing Breed*, p. 46.

115. Desabelle, *Lapulapu City*, p. 40.

116. Scott, *Weapons of the Weak*, p. 308, cited in Kerkvliet, *Everyday Politics in the Philippines*, p. 266.

117. For colorful accounts of this gruesome subculture, see Paredes, *Philippine Colonial Democracy*, pp. 135–36; and De Quiros, "Guns, Goons, and Government," p. 27.

118. This paragraph borrows heavily from Vicente L. Rafael's insightful and witty essay, "Patronage and Pornography," pp. 282–304.

119. See Spence, *For Every Tear a Victory*, pp. 7–10.

120. On the elaboration of the "Si Malakas At Si Maganda" theme, see Rafael, "Patronage and Pornography," p. 282.

121. See Doronila, "Transformation of Patron-Client Relations," pp. 111–13.

122. This theme is well treated in Shantz, "Political Parties."

123. Polotan, *Imelda Romualdez Marcos*, p. 235, cited in Rafael, "Patronage and Pornography," p. 299; emphasis added.

124. Rafael, "Patronage and Pornography," p. 299.

125. Ibid., p. 295.

126. For a striking reminder of Marcos's eagerness to legitimate his authoritarian rule in American eyes, see the 32-page paid advertisement, "Philippine Prospects," that comprises Section 11 of the June 10, 1973, issue of the *New York Times*.

127. See the three volumes of Marcos, *Tadhana*, which were written in the 1970s under President Marcos's direction.

128. Ironically the notion of the New Society mirrored a program of the same title promoted by South Vietnamese dictator Nguyen Cao Ky and allegedly ghostwritten by CIA operative Edward Lansdale. This ghost writing, it is well worth noting, took place during the administration of U.S. president Lyndon B. Johnson, who at the time was promoting a domestic program under the rubric of "The Great Society." See Kahin, *Intervention*, p. 353.

129. See Ileto, "Past in the Present Crisis."

130. Aquino's presidential campaign coincided with the celebration of the Marian Year and the world pilgrimage of Our Lady of Fatima, an image of the Madonna, to the Philippines. See Noli Alparce, "1.5-M Join Family Rosary Rally," *Malaya*, Dec. 9, 1985, pp. 1 and 6; Butch Francisco, "Hail, Mary!," *Sunday Magazine* 2(25) (Dec. 8, 1985): 8–9; and Teresita Elena P. Mapa, "How Antipolo Folk Honor the Blessed Virgin," pp. 10–12 of the same issue.

131. See the various participant accounts and photographs in Mercado, *Eyewitness History*.

132. Columnist Hilarion M. Henares, Jr., commented on this spectacle during the election campaign: "Entertainers are so popular that even NUCD Senate bets are mimicking them. Frank Chavez sings, Letty Shahani dances, Gem Carague plays the mouth organ, Alran Bengzon marches, and Buddy Gomez stands on his bald head. . . . If Erap Estrada and this bunch of ham actors win, the Senate will be known as the Balcony, the Lower House as the Orchestra, and Malacanang as the Loge. . . . It's showtime, folks." See "Nikki, Orly, Roger, Wilson, Nora, Morato, RJ," *Philippine Daily Inquirer*, Apr. 22, 1992, p. 5.

133. Thompson, *Customs in Common*, p. 28. This theme is treated extensively in Hedman, "In the Name of Civil Society."

134. Wurfel, "Bell Report and After"; Coquia, *Philippine Presidential Election of 1953.*

135. See Thompson, "Cory and 'the Guy.'"

136. For accounts of this phenomenon see the May 9–16 issues of various Manila tabloids, as well as Chula Sicam, "'Manananggal' Season," *Manila Chronicle,* May 9–15, 1992, pp. 32, 34; and Constantino C. Tejero, "The Manananggal of Tondo: 'Dugo! Dugo!'" *Sunday Inquirer Magazine,* May 24, 1992, pp. 3–4, 6–7.

137. Crisanto-Ortega, *Vanishing Breed,* p. 40.

138. Rafael, "Patronage and Pornography," pp. 283, 297.

139. "Una cuadrilla de mujercillas *Catolonas* . . . las cuales tenian casi tiranizado el pueblo de secreto"; see Chirino, *Relacion de las Islas Filipinas,* pp. 65, 302.

140. Simmel, *Philosophy of Money,* p. 257.

141. Krueger, "Political Economy of the Rent-Seeking Society," p. 302.

142. See "Angry, Frustrated 'Winners,'" *Philippine Daily Inquirer,* May 29, 1992, p. 8.

7. YAWNGHWE, BURMA

1. This coup did not signify a change of rulers, for it was staged against the government of Dr. Maung Maung, installed by the same ruling military establishment controlled by Ne Win and Sein Lwin. The coup of General Saw Maung was aimed at salvaging military predominance and saving Ne Win rather than "saving the country," as claimed.

2. The NUP is the reincarnation of the ruling Lanzin (BSPP) Party.

3. Aungsan Suukyi (born 1945) is the daughter of Bogyoke (General) Aungsan, mythologized as the father of Burma's independence, and Daw Khin Kyi (a Christian, part-Karen nurse, and one-time Burmese ambassador to India). She studied and lived outside Burma for most of her adult life, but happened to be in Rangoon during the 1988 uprising because her mother was ill. Like Aung Gyi, U Nu, and other nonmilitary figures, she took a stand against the military's massacre of unarmed civilian protesters and was transformed overnight into a national leader and "savior." Her political thoughts have been collected in Aungsan Suukyi, *Freedom from Fear.* Aungsan Suukyi has been detained by the military since 1989. She was awarded the Nobel Peace Prize in 1992 for her staunch role in the democracy movement and for her nonviolent stance.

4. Mranmaa Soshei-lit Lanzin, the Burmese Way to Socialism Program Party (BSPP), will be referred to hereafter as Lanzin or the BSPP. In writing Burmese terms, I will use the transliteration mode, as in Thai studies, rather than the phonetics: instead of "Myanmar" (phonetics), I write "Mranmaa." But I will use the conventional English spellings for familiar places and terms. (Coincidentally "Sanda Win," the teashop where a fight between students and local party thugs took place, is the name of the daughter of Ne Win, regarded by many as the power behind General Khin Nyunt, the present SLORC leader. On Sanda Win and Aungsan Suukyi, see Badgley, "Clear Gathering of Miraculous Success," pp. 10–11.)

5. For accounts of the effect of the 1987 demonetization measures, see Mya Maung, *Totalitarianism in Burma*, pp. 93–135.

6. The 1988 uprising is comprehensively covered by Bertil Lintner in *Outrage*.

7. "Ne Win" is the name adopted by Maung Shu-maung, a former postal clerk, when he underwent military training under Japanese instructors on Hainan Island together with Aungsan and other young Bama nationalists just prior to the Japanese invasion of Burma in 1942. After independence (1948) and following the resignation (due to the Karen rebellion) of the Karen commander of the Burma Army, Ne Win became chief of the armed forces (the Tatmadaw). From 1958 to 1960 Ne Win headed a military caretaker government and won high praise from many (especially outside observers) as a modernizing, professional military-political leader. In 1962, he staged a coup against the government of U Nu and instituted the Lanzin socialist regime. He resigned from the military in 1974 to become president of the country. In 1981 Ne Win gave up the presidency, but he retained chairmanship of the Lanzin Party. Following the 1988 countrywide uprising, he relinquished all positions. Nonetheless, it is widely believed by both the Burmese and outsiders that Ne Win still controls SLORC and has a hand in all important matters. For the open letters see Committee for the Restoration of Democracy in Burma (CRDB), *Aung Gyi's Letter* and *The Day Blood Flowed on the Inya Embankment*.

8. In responding to these protests, the *lon-htein* killed over 2,000 people. See U.S. State Dept., *Country Reports on Human Rights Practices for 1988: Burma*.

9. Aungsan, born in 1915, first gained attention in 1936 as leader of the first mass strike by university students. Together with Thakin Soe he formed the Communist Party of Burma in 1939, but was forced in 1940 to flee abroad. The Japanese provided him and 29 other young Burmans with military training, and Aungsan was able to raise a ragtag force, the Burma Independence Army (BIA), which followed the victorious Japanese into Burma. When Japan granted Burma its "independence," Aungsan served as defense minister under Dr. Ba Maw. When the tide turned against Japan, Aungsan and his forces turned against the Japanese and were recognized by the British as an ally. After the war he entered politics as leader of the AFPFL, a front composed of left-wing parties including the communists.

The British—unable to hold onto Burma after the Congress Party's successful struggle for Indian independence (and the looming partition of the Indian subcontinent into India and Pakistan)—negotiated the terms of Burma's independence with Aungsan and the AFPFL. In 1947, while an independence constitution was being drafted, Aungsan and members of the interim government were gunned down by a rival, U Saw. Aungsan became a national hero, and his name has since been used by successive Burmese governments, especially by Ne Win's Lanzin regime, to support their legitimacy.

10. Burma is a multiethnic, multicultural country configured in a majority-minority equation. The majority are the Bama (or Mranmaa), said to comprise more than half the population. Politically important minorities are the Karen, Shan (Tai/Thai), Mon, Kachin, and Rakhine. Conventionally, "Burmese" denotes all inhabitants of Burma. I will use "Bama" for Burman and "non-Bama" for oth-

ers. After the massacres it was rumored that non-Bama soldiers (Chin or Kachin) were responsible.

11. The massacres, especially the one in front of the U.S. Embassy, were video-taped. This videotape has been circulating among Burmese overseas ever since and has reinforced the illegitimacy of the military in general and SLORC in particular. For a concise but excellent account of the 1988 massacres, including the disposal of bodies, see Sesser, "Rich Country Gone Wrong."

12. There is a widespread but incorrect impression that the Western countries imposed economic sanctions. While they did suspend programs and cut back on assistance, no restrictions were imposed on corporations doing business with SLORC. No sanctions like those against South Africa were ever imposed upon Burma.

13. According to Theda Skocpol, social revolution is a basic transformation in state and class structures resulting in a change in the composition of the ruling class, state structures and apparatus (or "state order"), and the dominant ide-ology. Skocpol's insistence that a "social revolution" must be class-based is quite problematic and dogmatically Marxist in flavor. She circumvents this problem by discussing social revolutions in terms of "the dominant class" and "subordinated" classes. See Skocpol, *States and Social Revolutions*, especially pp. 3–5, 29–30.

14. For comments on the chances of opposition parties winning the contest, see Brunnstrom, "Democracy Under the Gun"; Loeb, "Despite Fear, Democracy's 'Fire' Burns"; Erlanger, "Burmese Are Going to Vote."

15. For examples of such works see Tinker, *Union of Burma*; Trager, *Burma*; Cady, *History of Modern Burma*. Cady's study is comprehensive, analytical, and skeptical and avoids Trager's wildly optimistic enthusiasm.

16. For example, the Karen resistance was attributed to British imperialist (neoimperialist) interests and missionaries. The Shan resistance was blamed on Taiwan-Kuomintang interests, Thailand, and the Southeast Asian Treaty Organi-zation (SEATO), a U.S.-backed anticommunist regional body. The 1988 uprising and subsequent armed Bama resistance are blamed on communists, unspecified foreign interests, U.S. congresspersons, and scholars.

17. Huntington, *Political Order in Changing Societies*, especially pp. 1–92 and 192–263. His prescription for political order and stability in "changing societies" is the organization of society via an authoritarian political party led by strong leaders, preferably in military garb, capable of taming praetorian or indisciplined forces and tendencies in modernizing Third World societies.

18. SLORC's desperate desire for external approval can be gauged from the prominence given in the *Working People's Daily* to the arrivals of ambassadors, delegations, UN personnel, and scholars such as Robert Taylor and David Stein-berg. The message it wishes to convey to the public is that it is recognized by the outside world as unquestionably legitimate. (The name of the official news organ, the *Working People's Daily*, was changed to *Myanma Alin*, the *New Light of Burma*, in 1993.)

19. One reason given by SLORC is that since Burma is a multiethnic country, "Myanmar" is more suitable because it encompasses all ethnic groups (implying that "Burma" was not inclusive). However, Mranmaa/Myanmar is the literary version of "Bama," the majority Burman. Domestically, the name change is a ploy

by SLORC to gain support by cloaking itself in the mantle of Bama ethno-nationalism.

20. Taylor, *State in Burma*; Aung-Thwin, "British 'Pacification'"; and Aung-Thwin, "1948 and Burma's Myth of Independence," pp. 19–34.

21. See, for example, the review article on Taylor's book *State in Burma* by Victor Lieberman. He himself has written a valuable study of the state and the dynamics of power in precolonial Burma: *Burmese Administrative Cycle*. For critical reviews of Taylor's *State in Burma*, see Gordon Means's review in *Contemporary Southeast Asia* and Bertil Lintner's review in *Asian Studies Review*. See also the review by Hugh Tinker in *Third World Quarterly*, which questions Taylor's contention that Ne Win's state is the recognized authority throughout Burma.

22. Taylor, *State in Burma*, pp. 1, 3–5, and 8. This is a simplified summary of Taylor's thesis on the state in Burma.

23. In regard to the AFPFL government, see ibid., pp. 243–49.

24. Ibid., "Introduction," especially pp. 1–12.

25. Taylor's confusion regarding resistance to the colonial state in Burma is evident from his assertion that the colonial state, with "its utility in terms of its progressive, efficiency-oriented nature," is illegitimate for those concerned with "emotion, sentiment and personal bonding, an 'imagined community,' which a merely utilitarian movement or institution could not create." The implication here is that anticolonial, "nationalistic" resistance is legitimate. By this same criterion, ethnic-based resistance to the Burman state can also be viewed as legitimate, but Taylor contends that resistance, especially ethnic-based resistance, to the "contemporary" Lanzin state (and demands for autonomy) are illegitimate. His contention ignores the dynamics of political relations that lies at the heart of political legitimacy. See ibid., pp. 151–52; see also Taylor, "Perceptions of Ethnicity in the Politics of Burma."

26. Taylor appears to have had second thoughts about the efficacy of a "strong," highly autonomous state in Burma; see "Military in Myanmar," pp. 139–52.

27. Aung-Thwin, "British 'Pacification,'" and "1948 and Burma's Myth of Independence."

28. Aung-Thwin, "British 'Pacification,'" p. 261; the italics are his.

29. See Taylor, "Perceptions of Ethnicity in the Politics of Burma."

30. Mya Maung, a distinguished Bama economist who once worked with the Bama military (at Maymyo Military Academy), likens Aung-Thwin's writings on the military-socialist regime to the eulogies of *hpaw-lan-hpa* (sycophantic) court chroniclers of old. He asserts that Aung-Thwin's excessive idealization of the past has blinded him to the military's construction of an "Orwellian" Burma. See Mya Maung, *Burma Road to Poverty*, pp. xxii–xxiii.

31. Leach, *Political System of Highland Burma*.

32. Sao Saimong Mangrai, *Shan State*, p. 111. In a letter from the Muangnai *chaofa* to the Hsipaw *chaofa* in 1886, he refers to the plan to form a confederation similar to that formed by German states.

33. See Sao Saimong Mangrai, *Shan State*, which essentially covers the successful rebellions of the Shan princes of Hsenwi, Hsipaw, Kengtung, Muangnai, and so forth against King Thibaw from the mid-1880s to the final British annexation. See also Furnivall, *Colonial Policy and Practice*, p. 12.

34. Maung Maung Gyi, a Bama, provides a less romantic view of traditional rulership. See his *Burmese Political Values*, pp. 21–35. See also Sarkisyanz, *Buddhist Background*, p. 78, and Sangermano, *Burmese Empire*. Bama kingship follows the general pattern of other precolonial autocracies. It is no better or worse— a point that must be recognized, not glossed over or viewed as a Western slur on Bama civilization or culture.

35. Sarkisyanz, *Buddhist Background*, pp. 10–15.

36. Taylor, *State in Burma*, p. 55. He interprets the word *elected* to mean superior or superordinate.

37. Chai-anan Samudavanija provides an insightful analysis of "Thai identity" in which "history/traditions" are used selectively. See his "State Identity Creation, State-Building and Civil Society." See also Terwiel, "Thai Nationalism and Identity," and Jackson, "Thai Buddhist Identity," in the same collection.

38. Silence of the populace in non-Western states is often interpreted as acquiescence, even support. It is also presumed to stem from a unique communal-traditional political culture. The possibility that it might be due to repression of the institutions for articulation and action is often ignored. Taylor and Aung-Thwin, for example, equate silence with a culturally and historically conditioned support for violent, coercive rulership.

39. See MacDougall and Wiant, "Burma in 1985"; Tilman, "Burma in 1986"; Guyot and Badgley, "Myanmar in 1989"; Steinberg, "Myanmar 1991."

40. For example, the pre-1990s Marxist-Leninist states were viewed as models of strength and purpose. There is undoubtedly a significant, even causal, correlation between coercion and illegitimacy. In Burma, however, although the coercion is not denied, no connection has been made between the two. The failure to link coercion and illegitimacy may have something to do with an unwillingness to concede that illegitimate regimes may long endure if power holders are determined to retain power or pursue a certain goal at all cost.

41. The tragic irony of it all is that the final cost of illegitimate rulership is borne largely by its victims. Power holders may lose their privileges and even their heads, but as in Somalia, Liberia, and the former Yugoslavia, the ultimate victims are the "people" and the country as a whole.

42. The necessity of military control to keep Burma from becoming a "Yugoslavia" is precisely the argument SLORC now employs for both internal and external consumption. (Events in Bosnia are given prominent attention on SLORC's television programs.) This fear, with reference to Burma and the Kachin, Karen, Shan, and others, is also expressed by Lee Kuan Yew in "Democracy and Human Rights." For an analysis and rebuttal of the fear of "national disintegration" in Burma see Yawnghwe, "Burma: 'Constructive Engagement.'"

43. Clark and Dear, *State Apparatus*, p. 188.

44. "Thakin" (meaning "master") was used by the Bama to address the white man in general and colonial officers in particular. Reacting to this tradition, nationalists (who entered politics in the early 1930s) belonging to the Dobama Asi-Ayone (We Bama Confederation) affixed the term to their names. Maung Nu, Burma's first prime minister, thus became Thakin Nu.

45. Ne Win is regarded by both officers and lowly soldiers as "Ahba" (Father)

and looked up to as the Great Benefactor and Patron (Kyesu-shin Gyi). The military intelligence chief, "Lumbaa" (or "Lanky") Tin Oo, who was dismissed and imprisoned in 1982, was on his release in 1990 given a large "loan" and continues to enjoy the usual perks and privileges such as a house, land, and access to special medical care.

46. The consensus among Burma watchers, diplomats, and the general public in Burma is that Ne Win is still in control. See, for example, McCullough, "Terror Continues."

47. For an excellent attempt to understand the insurgency, see Smith, *Burma*. Difficult as it is to follow the convoluted account of rebel leaders, armies, alliances, fronts, rivalries, and clashes, this book deserves thoughtful reading, especially by Burma scholars.

48. Born in 1905, Thakin Soe together with Aungsan, Thakin Ba Tin (Goshal), and other Bama nationalists (the Thakins) formed the Communist Party of Burma in 1939. Unlike the other Thakins, Thakin Soe did not collaborate with the Japanese but was in charge of the communist and Rakhine resistance groups that co-operated with Allied forces. After the war he set up his own Red Flag communist party and opposed negotiation with the British for independence. From 1948 he led the Red Flag in rebellion against both the AFPFL and the Lanzin governments until his "capture" in 1970. He was sentenced to death in 1973, but the sentence was not carried out. He lived to witness the 1988 countryside uprising against Ne Win.

49. Formally the Burmese Communist Party (BCP), which later called itself the CPB, or Communist Party of Burma. The White Flag's name change from BCP to CPB is linked to the Beijing-Moscow ideological struggle: it was made in the late 1960s when the White Flag obtained substantial aid from Beijing. As Sai Aung-win, a senior CPB member, explained it to me, BCP denotes a Moscow-revisionist stance whereas CPB was revolutionary-Maoist.

50. Born in 1911 and assassinated in 1968, Thakin Than Tun was one of Burma's top politicians, although he never ruled. A good organizer and able administrator, he performed well as minister of land and agriculture in the Japanese-sponsored government of Dr. Ba Maw. He began his political career in the 1930s, together with Aungsan, U Nu, and Thakin Soe, as a Thakin nationalist. When the tide of war turned against the Japanese, Than Tun played a pivotal role in setting up the AFPFL and was its first general secretary. After the war, he fell out with Aungsan (his brother-in-law) and condemned the independence negotiated with Britain as a sham. In 1948, well after Aungsan's death, he led the White Flag BCP/CPB communists in a revolutionary struggle against the AFPFL government and almost toppled it. Than Tun's greatest mistake was his failure to control the "cultural revolution" (imported from Mao's China), which decimated the top leadership in the White Flag. Consequently, Ne Win's forces were able to drive the White Flag from its strongholds. Thakin Than Tun was shot by a disgruntled cadre.

51. Lintner, *Rise and Fall*, p. 14.

52. For a good account of the Karen struggle see Falla, *True Love and Bartholomew*.

53. For a firsthand account of resistance in the Shan highlands see Yawnghwe, *Shan*.

54. See Sesser, "Rich Country Gone Wrong."

55. These are the explanations for rebellions and unrest with which political scientists are most familiar. Furnivall's dictum about communities that "mingle but do not mix" describes one aspect of colonialism. His thesis, however, has been distorted by Taylor, for example, who attributes ethnic plurality or non-Bama national or ethnic consciousness to British strategy or to colonial "simplistic pseudo-anthropology" (Taylor, *State in Burma*, p. 93). Though Furnivall's plural-societies thesis deals with Burma and Netherlands India, the "plural-societies phenomenon" can also be seen as the product of capitalist-monetized economic transformation of premonetized economies. It occurs everywhere (even in England during the early industrial revolution). At any rate, all societies and states are to various degrees and in different ways plural, especially precolonial Burma. See Furnivall, *Netherlands India*, especially pp. 446–69.

56. Most non-Bama, especially the Karen and Kachin, were loyal to the British. This put them in armed opposition to the AFPFL Thakins, who became Burma's new rulers in 1948.

57. The AFPFL signed a number of agreements with the British to ensure an orderly transfer of power and protect remaining British interests: the London Agreement, the Nu-Atlee Agreement, and the Letya-Freeman Defense Agreement, all signed in 1947.

58. For the crucial role played by foreign donors—Britain, India, Pakistan, certain Commonwealth countries, and the United States—see *Foreign Relations of the United States* (Washington: U.S. State Department): vol. 9/1949 (pp. 573–74); vol. 5/1950 (p. 149); vol. 6/1950 (pp. 12, 49, 70, 232–35, 240–44, 247–48, 751).

59. Sao Shwe Thaike became the union's first president and went on to become speaker of the Upper House. He was the leader of the federal movement, was detained by the military in 1962, and died the same year.

60. For an insightful account of Bama and non-Bama relationships and politics, see Silverstein, *Burmese Politics*.

61. The Kachin state legislature opted to give up this right, however, much to the dissatisfaction of Kachin "nationalists."

62. The BCP/CPB was also a member of the AFPFL, a hastily patched-up umbrella organization. For details of the AFPFL, its structure, and its factions, see Butwell, *U Nu*, pp. 146–56.

63. Martin Smith, *Burma*, p. 67; Cady, *History of Modern Burma*, pp. 447, 579.

64. Aungsan formed the PVO from demobilized members of the Thakin armies who were not incorporated into the reformed Burma Army in 1946.

65. Lintner, *Rise and Fall*, p. 9.

66. This is a rudimentary account of the BCP/CPB's reasons for revolution. Other reasons had to do with personal, factional politics within the AFPFL, of which it was a member until expelled in 1947. Aungsan's assassination in July 1947, five months before independence, may have exacerbated "socialist-communist" rivalries. Moreover, there is evidence that the AFPFL planned to violently repress the BCP/CPB and kill or imprison its leaders. See ibid., pp. 13–14.

67. Aungsan was assassinated by U Saw, a former prime minister of Ministerial Burma.

68. Maung Maung Gyi, *Burmese Political Values*, p. 233.

69. Furnivall, *Colonial Policy and Practice*, pp. 104, 180.

70. Much has been made of the Karen's service in the colonial military and the Bama's exclusion. This point, however, is irrelevant with regard to power and privilege. Colonial soldiers did not enjoy special rights; they were mostly confined to barracks, treated as servants of the state, and highly subordinated to civil authority. In fact, few Shan, Mon, Arakan, and so forth served in the colonial military or police force.

71. According to Dorothy Guyot, the Karen were overrepresented only in the education service but underrepresented elsewhere. See Guyot, "Communal Conflict," p. 201. Also see Taylor, *State in Burma*, table 2.2, p. 130.

72. These riots were also fueled by competition for jobs. In post-1948 Burma, an anti-Chinese rampage in Rangoon and other towns was partially provoked by the military regime to win mass support. It was also in response to the pro-Mao fervor of Chinese students, encouraged by Red Guard elements in the Chinese embassy.

73. This assumption is just as valid as the idea that the whole Bama "nation" viewed colonial rule as illegitimate or supported the national struggle. Claims made by the AFPFL and its successors can be viewed as part of their legitimation message to the outside world.

74. See Guyot, "Communal Conflict."

75. During those years there was much banditry, pillage, and killing by armed roving bands claiming affiliation with the AFPFL, BCP/CPB, and Red Flag in the rural areas. But it was not AFPFL policy to target the Karen for extermination, as Karen extremists have claimed. After the Karen insurrection in 1949, however, the Burma Army subjected the non-Bama population to a reign of terror throughout the country. See Amnesty International, *Extrajudicial Execution*.

76. The Karen and other non-Bama perceived the AFPFL as "traitors" not only for going over to the Japanese, but also for stabbing their mentors in the back when the tides of war favored the Allies.

77. For a brief account of Bama–non-Bama political relations, rebutting the military's claim that it prevented Burma's disintegration, see Yawnghwe, "Burman Military," pp. 81–101.

78. See *Foreign Relations of the United States* (Washington: U.S. State Department): vol. 9/1949 (pp. 573–74); vol. 5/1950 (p. 149); vol. 6/1950 (pp. 12, 49, 70, 232–35, 240–44, 247–48, 751).

79. The leftist coalition won 44.8 percent of the popular vote in the 1956 elections. See Butwell, *U Nu*, p. 139; see also Maung Maung, *Burma and General Ne Win*, p. 226.

80. These organizations included the PVO, the Arakan (Rakhine) People's Liberation Party (led by the monk U Seinda), the Pa-O National Liberation Organization (led by Thaton Hla Pe), the Mon People's Front, the Shan State Communist Party, and some BCP/CPB and Red Flag units. According to official figures, 5,500 insurgents surrendered. Martin Smith believes that many "simply returned home to their villages"; see his *Burma*, p. 168.

81. Butwell, a biographer and admirer of U Nu, devotes only a paragraph to

the 1956 elections. See Butwell, *U Nu*, p. 139; Maung Maung, *Burma and General Ne Win*, p. 226.

82. Trager, *Burma*, pp. 173–75.

83. This episode is dealt with in all standard works on post-1948 Burma. However, scholars disagree on whether U Nu's handover of power to Ne Win was made under military duress or otherwise. Knowledgeable Bama observers say that Ne Win was not politically engaged at the time and that the takeover, backed by threat of a military coup, was engineered by Brigadiers Aung Gyi and Tin Pe.

84. For example, the head of Shan State was the Hsenwi prince Chao Suahom Hpa. He was the elder brother of the Yawnghwe Mahadevi (or Yawnghwe princess-consort). She was a member of Parliament (until the 1958 handover of power), a vocal Shan nationalist, and founder of the SSA (Shan State Army), which he chaired from 1964 to 1969.

85. Yawnghwe, "Rebellions in Burma," especially pp. 197–99.

86. Amnesty International first compiled its report of army atrocities against non-Bama only in 1988. (Previous reports of atrocities were dismissed as rebel propaganda.) Until 1988 the Bama did not believe Bama soldiers capable of such brutal violence. See Amnesty International, *Extrajudicial Execution.*

87. See Tun Myint, *Syam-Pry Bae Lae?* He was an anti-*chaofa* politician with close links to Bama leaders, politicians, writers, and journalists.

88. *Taunggyi Conference, Meetings Record* (*Pry-Ne Baungzone Nyila Khan Gyi*), Shan State Government, Taunggyi, June 1961.

89. Yawnghwe, "Rebellions in Burma." By 1959 the Shan government had extended its administrative reach to all the princely states. The only privilege the princes enjoyed was to nominate from among themselves 25 members to the Shan State Council (and concurrently to the Union Chamber of Nationalities). See also Taylor, *State in Burma*, p. 269.

90. Abstracted from "Shan State Army: Position Paper on the Union of Burma, 1948–1962," a communiqué of the Office of the Chairman, Shan State War Council, Shan State Army, June 1964.

91. Karen leaders took a similar stand in February 1993 in a message transmitted to Manerplaw, headquarters of the Burmese opposition—the NCGUB (National Coalition Government of the Union of Burma), the DAB (Democratic Alliance of Burma), and the NDF (Nationalities Democratic Front).

92. The falling out of early postcolonial leaders is quite common. Had U Nu remained above the fray, he might have kept the AFPFL from shattering, but he was not a politician, as his autobiography shows. See U Nu, *Saturday's Son.*

93. Aungsan and other military leaders (including Ne Win) began their careers as Thakin politicians. After 1948 senior military officers, such as Ne Win, Aung Gyi, Tin Pe, and Maung Maung, were associated with AFPFL factions. In the late 1950s the military was believed to be part of, or closely tied to, the Stable (Swe-Nyein) faction.

94. The 1958–60 military caretaker government will not be dealt with here. It was only of short duration and did not represent a break with the practice of the 1948 parliamentary democracy.

95. See, for example, von der Mehden, "Burmese Way to Socialism."

96. This is a synthesis of the coup makers' pronouncements as observed or attributed to them by Maung Maung and Taylor. See Taylor, *State in Burma*, pp. 291–92, 296–97, 300–301; Maung Maung, *Burma and General Ne Win*, pp. 295–300.

97. For a less idealized account of the role of the Tatmadaw see Ba Maw, *Breakthrough in Burma*, p. 145. See also Donnison, *Burma*, p. 128; Allen, "Leaving a Sinking Ship," pp. 65–78.

98. Maung Maung, *Burma and General Ne Win*, p. 298.

99. Von der Mehden, "Burmese Way to Socialism."

100. As noted by Dr. Myint Maung, a Buddhist scholar who initially welcomed the 1962 coup.

101. See Committee for the Restoration of Democracy in Burma (CRDB), *Aung Gyi's Letter*.

102. After reading Darwin in the 1950s, the monk wrote *Lu-The, Lu-Pyit*, arguing that when a human being dies (Lu The), he will automatically be reborn a human being (Lu Pyit), contradicting the Burmese belief that only those with sufficient karma will be reborn as human. The soft-porn author Chit Hliang explains his work, which portrays white women as sex objects, as "repaying a debt of history"—in revenge, that is, for when Bama women were similarly treated by white men.

103. See Aung-Thwin, "British 'Pacification'" and "1948 and Burma's Myth of Independence." See also Steinberg, *Burma*, p. 93; Badgley and Wiant, "The Ne Win–BSPP Style of Bama-Lo," pp. 43–62. All except Aung-Thwin have revised their favorable view of military rule.

104. Eastern bloc analysts made favorable comparisons, extolling it as representing the Burmese *Lup-tha-Prythu* (working people). The military was praised as the best-organized anti-imperialist progressive force. See Iskenderof, "The Army, Politics, and the People," pp. 149–56; and Mirsky, "Role of the Army," pp. 327–38.

105. Wiant, "Tradition in the Service of Revolution," pp. 59–72.

106. Ibid., p. 66. See also Steinberg, *Burma's Road Toward Development*, p. 74; Maung Maung Gyi, *Burmese Political Values*, p. 222, n. 54; Lintner, *Outrage*, p. 79.

107. This sarcastic slang term for former military officers means "those who have discarded their trousers."

108. This account is synthesized from works by indigenous Burmese on the Lanzin Party's structures and political system. See Maung Maung Gyi, *Burmese Political Values*; Mya Maung, *Burma Road to Poverty*; U Nyun Han, "Burma's Experiment in Socialism"; Yawnghwe, "Ne Win's Tatmadaw Dictatorship."

109. Walter, *Terror and Resistance*.

110. For a picture of Ne Win's pivotal role in the state-party-military structure and his exercise of power like despotic Bama kings of old, see Badgley, "Burmese Ideology," pp. 63–79.

111. As Walter notes, the "king's knives" (torturers, informants, and spies) are not spared the uncertainties of arbitrary power and the unpredictable thrust of court politics. In Burma many MI officers became victims of their own terror ma-

chine. When the MI chief Tin Oo was purged, over a thousand MI personnel were also sacked and imprisoned.

112. For an analysis of the decay of institutions in Burma and the establishment of a patrimonial pyramid of arbitrary power, see Yawnghwe, "Ne Win's Tatmadaw Dictatorship," pp. 136–59.

113. Yawnghwe, *Shan*, pp. 15–17.

114. For details of the KKY program and the opium-heroin trade, see Lintner, "Shans and the Shan State of Burma." See also Yawnghwe, *Shan*, pp. 23, 127–28.

115. The term "economic insurgents" is applied to anyone engaged in private commerce after the regime's outlawing of such activities.

116. U Nu, certain prominent AFPFL figures, and other leaders—all of whom had spent some years in prison—were asked to advise on "building internal unity" in 1968, but Ne Win summarily rejected their advice.

117. Maung Maung Gyi, *Burmese Political Values*, pp. 193–94.

118. Silverstein, *Burma*, pp. 49, 141.

119. Steinberg, *Burma's Road Toward Development*, pp. 79, 128.

120. The black economy has been mentioned in almost every analysis of Lanzin socialism, but no systematic study has been undertaken. For journalistic accounts see Fawthrop, "Burma's Rebel Economy"; and Lintner, "All the Wrong Moves," p. 83.

121. For an economist's detailed, authoritative analysis of Burma's decline into poverty see Mya Maung, *Burma Road to Poverty*, especially pp. 117–43, 171–204, and 205–31.

122. Perhaps it was only the main power holders who were being delegitimized by the "people power" movement. Had Saw Maung's coup really been against Ne Win et al., the military's claim to power might have won the support of a large section of the politically important mobilized urban masses.

123. Until 1988 the Bama public as a rule differentiated between military rulers and the Tatmadaw. The former were hated; the latter was associated with heroism, Aungsan, and the independence struggle. The Tatmadaw's image is now tarnished.

124. SLORC's position, vis-à-vis its justification for holding onto power and its future superordinate political role, is based on SLORC Order 13/92 (Oct. 2, 1992), as translated in *Burma Alert* 3(10) (Nov. 1992): 3–5.

125. Sein Lwin and Maung Maung were "heads of state" between May and September 1988 (the post-Lanzin, pre-SLORC period).

126. See Lintner, "New Dealers" and "Border Heroin Trade."

127. Most of these "insurgents" are Sino-Bama or Indo-Bama based in such places as Singapore, Bangkok, Kunming, and Hong Kong and connected to such figures as Sanda Win (Ne Win's daughter), her husband (Aye Zaw Win), Khin Nyunt, Tin Oo (SLORC deputy secretary), and other military officers and families. This statement is based on interviews with Burmese businessmen based in Singapore and Bangkok.

128. For a brief account of the warlords' mutiny and their subsequent marriage of convenience with SLORC see Lintner, *Territory Briefing (No. 1)*, especially pp. 22–23.

129. According to a frequent visitor to Rangoon (connected with the pre-1988

military), military officers have been buying up land and property with "loans" from SLORC and profits from "business" deals. They now own land in almost every major town, making them the new landed class. Those with cash have been buying at highly inflated prices, owing mainly to the lack of confidence in both the Kyats and the economy.

130. SLORC Declaration 10/90 (July 27, 1990), in *Burma Alert* 3(7) (July 1992): 5–6.

131. For a succinct definition of ASEAN's "constructive engagement" policy toward Burma, see "ASEAN Should Follow Japan and Disavow Burma's SLORC," Editorial, *Nation*, Apr. 5, 1993.

132. See "Bangkok Declaration of the Asian Regional Meeting on Human Rights," *Bangkok Post*, Apr. 3, 1993; see also Lee Kuan Yew, "Democracy and Human Rights."

133. These aspirations are expressed by the 1961–62 federal movement and the NDF declaration in 1976 in support of a "genuine, federal union."

8. SUKATIPAN, THAILAND

1. On the Malay-Muslim contestation of the Thai nation-state see Pitsuwan, "Islam and Malay Nationalism."

2. See, for example, Samudavanija, *Thai Young Turks*, chap. 1, pp. 1–6.

3. For an insightful and well-documented analysis of the 1932 regime change, see various chapters in Mektrairatana, *Karn Patiwat Sayam.*

4. There are many studies of the Chakri Reformation during the reign of King Rama V that focus on various aspects of the reform. For an overview see Dhirave-gin, *Thai Politics.* For the study of educational reform and its political implications, see Wyatt, *Politics of Reform in Thailand.* On the hundredth anniversary of the administrative reform, Chai-anan Samudavanija published his new study on the bureaucratic and administrative reform in 1892: *Nuang Roi Pee Haenng Karn Patiroop Rabob Rachakarn.*

5. For the complete text of the petition see Samudavanija and Kannasootara, *Ekasarn Karn Muang Karn Pokrong Thai Por Sor 2417–2477,* pp. 75–77.

6. Since 1932 there have been ten successful coups and seven abortive coups.

7. Civilian elite factions and the constitution were politically significant from 1932 through 1946. But from 1947 the military became the dominant political force and the coup d'état the primary means of acquiring political power. This situation lasted until 1973.

8. The coup proclamation reads: "The king ruled in an absolute manner without heeding the wishes of the people, who had no chance to voice their plight. . . . It must be remembered that this country belongs to the people, not to the selfish royalty and their favorites as a place for them to achieve their own desires. Remember that our ancestors gained freedom for us and therefore the country must be governed by the people and for the people." For an English translation of the text of the Announcement of the People's Party see Chaloemtiarana, *Thai Politics,* pp. 4–7.

9. Batson, *End of Absolute Monarchy,* p. 211.

10. For details of the disputes between the king and the government and the

acceptance of the abdication by the national assembly, see Chaloemtiarana, *Thai Politics*, pp. 238–40.

11. For details of the government effort to promote nationalism see Documents 1 to 4 in Nakhata, "National Consolidation and Nation-Building," pp. 244–321.

12. See Piewnual, *Prachatippatai Bab Thai*, pp. 42–43.

13. For a historical overview of Thailand during World War II see Kasetsiri, "First Pibul Government"; Numnonda, *Thailand and the Japanese Presence 1941–1945*. For a detailed and well-researched study of the power struggle among competing political elites during World War II, see Ngamkajornkulkij, *Kabuankarn Seri Thai Kab Kwam Kad Yaeng Tang Karn Muang Pai Nai Prathet Thai Rawang Por Sor 2481–2492*.

14. Subsequently Phibul Songkram defended his collaboration with Japan as a stratagem to save Thailand from destruction and prevent Japanese cultural domination. See Songkram, "Cooperation with and Resistance Against Japan During the War," pp. 348–70.

15. Suksamran, *Buddhism and Politics*, p. 12.

16. Chaloemtiarana, *Thai Politics*, pp. 716–17.

17. Ibid., pp. 717–18.

18. See endnote 13 in Batson, *End of Absolute Monarchy*, pp. 265–66.

19. For a comprehensive study of the Chinese community in Thailand before the 1960s, see Skinner, *Leadership and Power in the Chinese Community in Thailand*. Anek Laothammatas's study of business associations in Thailand reviews the Chinese role in the Thai political economy; see Laothammatas, *Business Associations and the New Political Economy of Thailand*.

20. Riggs, *Thailand*.

21. Anderson, "Studies of the Thai State," p. 225.

22. For a comparative analysis of military coups in Thailand see Bungbongkarn, *Military in Thai Politics*, and Samudavanija, *Thai Young Turks*, chap. 2.

23. Chaloemtiarana, "Sarit Regime," p. 160.

24. Bumroongsuk, *United States Foreign Policy and Thai Military Rule*, chap. 3.

25. Chaloemtiarana, "Sarit Regime," p. 195.

26. Ibid., p. 216.

27. *Bangkok Post*, Jan. 24, 1951, p. 3.

28. The works of Luan Wichit Wathakan, particularly his "Strategies to Achieve Greatness," deeply influenced Sarit and underscored the political order he sought to create. For an extract from Luan's "Strategies to Achieve Greatness," see Chaloemtiarana, *Thai Politics*, pp. 794–802.

29. *Bangkok Post*, Jan. 24, 1961, p. 3.

30. Wyatt, *Thailand*, p. 281.

31. Adulyadej, "Phra Rhat Cha Damras Pra Rhat Chathan Kae Puang Chon Chao Thai Nai O Kat Wan Khun Pee Mai Por Sor 2504," p. 110.

32. Chaloemtiarana, "Sarit Regime," p. 406.

33. Morell and Samudavanija, *Political Conflict in Thailand*, p. 68.

34. Ibid.

35. Samudavanija and Wongtrangan, *Bhasa Kab Karn Muang*, pp. 93–94.

36. Quoted in Chaloemtiarana, "Sarit Regime," pp. 168–69.

37. Morell and Samudavanija, *Political Conflict in Thailand*, p. 6.

38. Girling, *Thailand: Society and Politics*, p. 72.

39. The NESDB admitted that there were "undesirable" consequences of the earlier development effort. See NESDB, *Fifth National Social and Development Plan*, chap. 1.

40. Promulgation of a new constitution and the holding of elections took fifteen months after the October 1973 revolution.

41. This section draws extensively on the definitive work of Morell and Samudavanija, *Political Conflict in Thailand*, chaps. 5–10. See also Girling, *Thailand: Society and Politics*, chap. 5, pp. 187–230, and Wyatt, *Thailand*, pp. 297–302.

42. By 1974 the student movement had splintered into three main student groups and many smaller ones.

43. On Kitthiwuttho Bhikkhu and his mass mobilization against the left see Suksamran, *Buddhism and Politics*, pp. 132–57.

44. Morell and Samudavanija, *Political Conflict in Thailand*, pp. 251–52.

45. Despite their exile, Thanom and Praphat continued to have influence in certain sections of the army; the Phibul-Phin-Phao faction reemerged along with a new faction comprising high-ranking officers in the supreme command with close ties to the United States.

46. On Prem's policy toward the communist insurgency see Bungbongkarn, *Military in Thai Politics*.

47. Laothammatas, "Politics of Structural Adjustment," p. 33.

48. On the Young Turks and their goals see Samudavanija, *Thai Young Turks*, chaps. 3–6.

49. Bungbongkarn, *Military in Thai Politics*, pp. 49–50.

50. Ibid., p. 70.

51. Yos Santasombat, among others, recognizes Prem as a rare army leader who could tolerate parliamentary democracy and party politics. See his "End of Premocracy in Thailand," p. 317.

52. The withdrawal of the PRC support for the Communist Party of Thailand following the Vietnamese invasion and occupation of Cambodia was a crucial factor in the defeat of the Thai communist insurgency.

53. Anek Laothammatas's study on the politics of structural adjustment in Thailand commends Prem's ability to insulate economic officials from the pressures of various groups by building coalition links to countervailing groups; he says this is the key to the success of the economic structural adjustment of the 1980s. See Laothammatas, "Politics of Structural Adjustment," p. 32.

54. A large number of military elites still have a hostile attitude toward political parties and especially business-politicians. They will tolerate parliamentary democracy only to the extent that elected politicians do not pose a threat to their corporate interests. The military felt that Chatichai disregarded their interests and even attempted to intimidate the military establishment. Certainly there was a series of clashes between Chatichai's ministers and senior military officers. Most analysts point out that it was Chatichai's bitter relationship with the military that caused his downfall.

55. Laothammatas, "Sleeping Giant Awakens?"

56. Ibid., p. 23.

57. Reported in *Poo Chat Karn Daily*, May 27, 1992.

58. Samudavanija and Paribatra describe what emerged after 1978 as "liberalization without democracy"—that is, a mixed system with considerable political and social freedom but without the substance of Western-style liberal democracy. See Samudavanija and Paribatra, "Liberalization Without Democracy."

59. Tasker, "Anti-Reform Club," p. 17.

60. On the weaknesses of the Chuan government see Bungbongkarn, "Thailand in 1992," pp. 220–23; and Snitwongse, "Thailand in 1993," pp. 147–50.

61. According to Clark Neher Crown Prince Vachiralongkorn is not held in high esteem by the Thai public. See note 1 in his "Political Succession in Thailand," p. 585.

62. Snitwongse, "Thailand in 1993," p. 149.

9. PABOTTINGI, INDONESIA

1. "If Indonesia gives any overall impression, it is of a state manqué, a country which, unable to find a political form appropriate to the temper of its people, stumbles on apprehensively from one institutional contrivance to the next." See Geertz, *Interpretation of Cultures*, p. 315.

2. This observation is largely due to Liddle, "Merekayasa Demokrasi di Indonesia," pp. 4–5.

3. Pancasila is the name given to the five principles proposed by Sukarno on June 1, 1945: belief in one deity; just and civilized humanity; unity of Indonesia; people-ness led by wisdom in representative consultations; and social justice for the entire people of Indonesia. Western scholars tend to read them as simply belief in God, humanity, nationalism, democracy, and social justice. Although Pancasila has been widely called Indonesia's "state ideology," it emerged largely during the era of the *pergerakan* and thus predates Indonesia as a state. It is, therefore, more appropriate to call it a national ideology. For a textual understanding of Pancasila see Pabottingi, "Pancasila."

4. Though I disagree with Liah Greenfeld's Eurocentric and Nietzschean view of nationalism, I fully share her conviction of the importance of *the meaningful* in a nation's politics. See Greenfeld, *Nationalism: Five Roads to Modernity*, pp. 17–18.

5. For Ernest Renan's definition of a nation see Renan, "What Is a Nation?" pp. 408–9.

6. *Aliran* politics refers to the time when the nation's political community was bitterly divided into antagonistic political streams. See Geertz, *Religion*.

7. The DPR—Indonesia's house of representatives—ratifies presidential bills and the annual budget proposal as a mechanism to control the executive branch; however, its authority is not above the president. It also has the right to interpellate and propose bills of its own. The DPR meets at least once a year. By the 1945 constitution, the MPR—Indonesia's people's consultative assembly, the highest state institution in the country—elects a president and draws basic guidelines of state policy. It convenes at least once in five years.

8. "Golkar" stands for Golongan Karya (Functional Group). For a brief reference see Krissantono, "Ali Moertopo di Atas Panggung Orde Baru," pp. 146–50.

9. Virtually throughout the New Order, the government has played hide-and-seek with the national ideology. The same is true of its derivative "Demokrasi Pancasila." Perhaps they are left deliberately vague to accommodate the many inconsistencies in governmental policies and practices.

10. Professor Djojohadikusumo, the country's senior economist, has maintained that Indonesia's 32 percent debt service ratio is much too high and should be put at 20 percent. Rachbini, a younger economist, wrote in *Tempo* about the danger of Indonesia's becoming a net capital exporter to the wealthy North. See Rachbini, "Bumerang Utang," p. 6.

11. For want of a better term, we use *pribumi* and non-*pribumi* to distinguish native Indonesians from Indonesians of Chinese descent.

12. See Thee Kian Wie, "Impact of the Colonial Past on the Indonesian Economy," pp. 39–40.

13. For a good example see Arief, "Perjalanan Nasionalisme," pp. 3–15. For a recent critique featuring the Chinese and the executive entanglement as well as the dependence of Indonesian conglomerates, mostly Chinese, see Ramli, "Industrialisasi di Indonesia."

14. See Furnivall, *Netherlands India*, p. 48. See also Kartodirdjo, *Protest Movements in Rural Java*; and his "Agrarian Radicalism in Java." Also indispensable is McVey, *Rise of Indonesian Communism*.

15. See Arief, "Perjalanan Nasionalisme." As in colonial times, the Chinese are again favored by the military-dominated regime simply because their cooperation is mutually beneficial. See Robison, *Indonesia*, chap. 9.

16. Wertheim, *Indonesian Society in Transition*, p. 53.

17. Two examples stand out: Angelino, *Colonial Policy*, vol. 2; and Boeke, *Economics and Economic Policy of Dual Society*.

18. See Reid, *Southeast Asia in the Age of Commerce*, p. 7. We should distinguish this wave from the later spread of Islam, which involved proselytizing wars. See Reid, "Kings, Kadis, and Charisma in the 17th-Century Archipelago," in *Making of an Islamic Political Discourse*.

19. See the rich and detailed comments on Asian trade in Van Leur, *Indonesian Trade and Society*, p. 121. See also Vlekke, *Nusantara*, p. 338; and Raffles, *History of Java*, vol. 1, pp. 203–4.

20. A few scholars hold that the forced cultivation, which began in 1830 and lasted at least 50 years, did not really impoverish Indonesians. See, for instance, Elson, "Peasant Poverty and Prosperity." For a detailed discussion of Dutch monopoly, exploitation, and distortion in Indonesia, see Pabottingi, "Nationalism," chaps. 1 and 2. For a broad historical reading of the impact of Western colonization see Panikkar, *Asia and Western Dominance*.

21. This statement is more or less consistent with P. J. Zoetmulder's observation that by the end of the seventeenth century, Java's transition to Islam was complete. See Zoetmulder, *Kalangwan*, p. 22. Raffles also writes that although the Javanese were generally unacquainted with Islamic doctrine, Java had apparently been converted to Islam during the sixteenth century and its institutions were "still

gaining ground." See Raffles, *History of Java*, p. 2. The process of Islamization in the archipelago began in the thirteenth century. See Hall, *A History of Southeast Asia*, p. 221.

22. See Kahin, *Nationalism and Revolution*, pp. 7–8, 84. See also Furnivall, *Netherlands India*, pp. 45, 397.

23. Quoted in Arief, "Perjalanan Nasionalisme," pp. 5–6.

24. The British colonizers encouraged the growth of India's own middle class in order to increase India's capacity to buy British industrial products. See, for example, Desai, *Social Background of Indian Nationalism*; Mukherjee, *Rise and Fall of the East India Company*; and Nehru, *Discovery of India*.

25. This lack of resistance resulted largely from three related factors: the Dutch policy of divide and rule; the absence of effective leaders among the villagers as local rulers were subordinated or replaced; and the fact that the expropriation and exploitation were carried out, not directly by the Dutch, but indirectly through the orders of the villagers' own superiors.

26. Efforts by these fresh immigrants—the *totok* Chinese—to preserve their language and culture effectively resinified the Indonesian Chinese in general.

27. See Mackie, "Anti-Chinese Outbreaks in Indonesia," in *Chinese in Indonesia*, pp. 130–31.

28. *Pergerakan*, "movement," is Indonesia's brief expression for its national movement. For a vivid discussion see Shiraishi, *Age in Motion*, p. 32. For the movements cited here see Van Niel, *Emergence of a Modern Indonesian Elite*; Wertheim, *Indonesian Society in Transition*; Nagazumi, *The Dawn of Indonesian Nationalism*; McVey, *Rise of Indonesian Communism*; Korver, *Sarekat Islam*; and Shiraishi, *Age in Motion*.

29. See Korver, *Sarekat Islam*, p. 274.

30. The first expression of Filipino nationalism appeared not in the Philippines but in Spain. See Steinberg et al., *In Search of Southeast Asia*, p. 259.

31. For a fine account of Perhimpoenan Indonesia, or Indonesische Vereeniging, see Ingleson, *Jalan Ke Pengasingan*.

32. See Hatta, *Indonesia Merdeka*, or see his "Indonesia Free," in *Portrait*.

33. Sukarno made it clear that colonialism and exploitation were by no means practices peculiar to Western powers. Using the rhetoric of Marxism, he exposed the contradictions of imperialism and ended his defense by expressing a firm belief in the inevitability of national independence for Indonesians. For Sukarno's defense see Paget, *Indonesia Accuses*.

34. These meetings were held in Jakarta several times at irregular intervals between May 29 and August 18, 1945. BPUPKI stands for Badan Penyelidik Usaha-Usaha Persiapan Kemerdekaan Indonesia.

35. It was a Habermasian "ideal-speech situation" because the meetings were carried out in the relative absence of political pressures from without or from within the convening parties. The Japanese military was still in control, but it encouraged the meetings. Eager to see the agelong dream of their nation realized, the founding fathers had arrived at a balanced foundation—duly attentive to the historical reality and diversity of Indonesian society—for an Indonesian state. For Habermas's ideal of political consensus, see his discussion of "universal pragmat-

ics," "communicative competence," and "legitimation problems" in Habermas, *Communication and the Evolution of Society*, pp. 26–29 and 199–205.

36. Sukarno writes: "Internationalism cannot flourish if it is not rooted in the soil of nationalism. Nationalism cannot flourish if it does not grow in the flower garden of internationalism." In the same vein, he contends: "We have not only to establish the state of Indonesia Merdeka, but also have to proceed toward the familyhood of nations." See Sukarno, "Pantja Sila," p. 44.

37. Ibid., p. 47.

38. Hatta, for instance, holds that Article 33 of the 1945 constitution is meant to overcome the extremely unequal growth between economic groups in Indonesia. Hence Indonesian nationalism was taken to consist of two tangled and equally important components: political nationalism and economic nationalism. The founding fathers' understanding of nationalism was also inseparable from their dream of democracy. They advocated both political and economic democracy.

39. Anderson, "Languages of Indonesian Politics," p. 111.

40. See Sukarno, *Lahirnja Pantja Sila*.

41. Clifford Geertz and Allan A. Samson are two of them. See Geertz, *Interpretation of Cultures*, p. 225. "An sich," writes Samson, "war *Pancasila* als ideologie begrenzt und verschwommen." See Opitz, *Profile und Programme der Dritten Welt*, pp. 165–66. Donald E. Weatherbee glosses over Pancasila as mere rhetoric. See Weatherbee, "Indonesia."

42. For an early analysis of the confusing use of Pancasila see Pabottingi, "Pancasila."

43. Ibid., p. 124.

44. Influenced by the Habermasian perspective, Cohen and Arato write: "Universality does not mean neutrality with respect to a plurality of values or forms of life but rather refers, in the first instance, to the metanorms of symmetric reciprocity that are to act as regulative principles guiding discursive processes of conflict resolution and, in the second instance, to those norms or principles to which all those who are potentially affected can agree. The procedure of universalization defended here involves an actual rather than a hypothetical dialogue." See Cohen and Arato, *Civil Society and Political Theory*, p. 21.

45. See Mayall, *Nationalism and International Society*. Despite my disagreement with Francis Fukuyama's "end-of-history" thesis, he is right to observe that "there is nothing inherently incompatible between nationalism and liberalism." See Fukuyama, *End of History and the Last Man*, p. 215.

46. I understand "culture" as a never-wholly-integrated pattern of human behavior. The integration is neither static nor completely coherent. Culture is being renewed every day in the myriad bargainings of human thoughts, actions, and other social exchanges. It contains ambiguities, contradictions, and incoherences as well as dark sides whose definitions are suspended and whose meanings are emergent. For the social origin of this understanding see Pabottingi, "Nationalism," pp. 291–304. This understanding of "culture" largely coincides with that of Clifford, *Predicament of Culture*, and Rosaldo, *Culture and Truth*.

47. One might consider the acceptance of this principle as a concession to the Islamic community for three reasons. First, the community represents In-

donesia's absolute majority. Second, Dutch economic suffocation, exploitation, and deprivation by and large fell on that community. Third, the bulk of the resistance and wars against the Dutch, even down to the ferocious battle involving the Allied forces in Surabaya in November 1945, was waged mostly by that community.

48. In fact, this broad-minded view of culture is written in the formal explication of the 1945 constitution: "Cultural efforts should be to promote civilization and unity, not denying new materials from foreign cultures to develop and enrich our own as well as to emancipate the degree of Indonesians' humanity." Translated from Joeniarto, *Undang-Undang Dasar 1945*, p. 129.

49. Quoted in Geertz, *Islam Observed*, p. 85.

50. For the concurrence of various ideologies in Vietnam, see Marr, *Vietnamese Tradition on Trial*.

51. See Kahin, *Nationalism and Revolution*, p. 477.

52. Nevertheless, the modern cultural outlook does permeate the entire text of Pancasila as well as most of the *pergerakan*, and traditional elements are recast in a modern perspective. Just as Pancasila is not entirely Western in outlook, there is nothing decidedly indigenous in it. Here modernity and traditionalism are blurred, mixed, or complemented by each other, without relegating the one as necessarily inferior to the other.

53. Such a phenomenon runs counter to the Marxian dictum that "the ruling idea was the idea of the ruling class." The "mobilization of meanings" characterized a number of struggles for liberation by colonized peoples. For an elaboration of this phenomenon, see Pabottingi, "Nationalism," pp. 264–77.

54. The quote is from Raffles, *History of Java*, p. 252. For *rust en orde* see Anderson, "Old State, New Society." On the subject of wealth, Hatta writes: "Indonesia is a producing and exporting country par excellence. Her exports amount to some two thousand millions of florins per annum. And every year she supplies the world community with a surplus of on an average 500 million florins. It is this wealth which has been the cause of Indonesia's subjugation by the Dutch State." See Hatta, *Portrait*, p. 166. Allusions to the country's surplus can also be found in Sukarno, *Dibawah*.

55. Kahin notices the same phenomenon in the postrevolutionary years. See Kahin, *Nationalism and Revolution*, p. 477.

56. See Anderson, "Idea of Power in Javanese Culture," p. 8.

57. Ibid., p. 7.

58. See Pabottingi, "Nationalism," pp. 305–28.

59. Anderson's "idea of power" is actually that of the *priyayi*—the deeply mystical variant in the trichotomy of what Geertz calls "the religion of Java." The idea of power of the *santri kolot* and *santri moderen* is silenced or overridden. Unlike the *priyayi*, both groups of *santri* are similarly preoccupied with the moral aspect of human conduct. Both also see time as linear and history as teleological.

60. This view has been nullified by authoritative observations. See Zoetmulder, *Kalangwan*, p. 22, and Raffles, *History of Java*, p. 2. See also Geertz, "Indonesian Cultures and Communities," p. 43; and Ricklefs, *War, Culture and Economy in*

Java, pp. 10–11. According to these scholars, even though Islamic rituals have not been practiced in full by the majority of Javanese, neither is Islam just a thin veneer covering the Javanese Indic flesh.

61. This judgment coincides with that of R. William Liddle, who writes that "the seriousness of the corruption problem [in Indonesia] has less to do with culture than with the political needs and also, of course, the financial wants of the rulers and the lack of popular accountability in the political system." See Liddle, *Politics and Culture in Indonesia*, p. 23.

62. This understanding of Javanese culture is based largely on the works of Geertz, *Religion*; Soemardjan, *Perubahan Sosial di Yogyakarta*; Moertono, *Negara dan Usaha Bina Negara di Jawa Masa Lampau*; Koentjaraningrat, *Javanese Culture*; Kartodirdjo, *Tjatatan Tentang Segi-Segi Mesianistis Dalam Sedjarah Indonesia*; and Kayam, "Transformasi Budaya Kita." Despite their rather too strong interpretive bent, I also learn much about Javanese culture from Anderson's important works.

63. In general, they have learned to internalize exceptional maxims like "winning without humiliating [the adversary], attacking without force"; "courage to concede would be rewarded with honor"; "carrying up high, keeping deep inside" (*mikul dhuwur, mendem jero*); "deference to God, teacher, government, and parents"; and "those who remember God and stay alert are superior to those who forget and go astray."

64. This might explain why the Javanese do not seem reluctant to marry exogamously. It is impossible to understand Sukarno's inclusive nationalism, ideological blend, or belief that "at bottom all things are one" without considering the internalization of the values mentioned.

65. Similar examples can be found in the struggles of Ki Hadjar Dewantara, Dr. Soetomo, and Tjipto Mangoenkoesoemo.

66. For instance, the great cultural and political confusion during the early 1960s led to the apocalyptic massacre of members of the PKI and innocent people in 1965. The exceptional stability of the New Order has much to do with the sobering impact of this massacre. Most Indonesians still seem to feel that "we have had enough."

67. The word *wahana* is difficult to translate. It simultaneously connotes "embodiment," "agent," "means," and "manifestation." See also Moertono, *Negara dan Usaha Bina Negara*, p. 42.

68. For the political view of the Malays in general, see a seminal article by Abdullah, "Formation of a Political Tradition in the Malay World."

69. For an elaborate account of the struggle of Tjipto Mangoenkoesoemo and Haji Misbach in the 1910s and 1920s, see Shiraishi, *Age in Motion*.

70. Elias, *Power and Civility*, p. 324.

71. Ibid.

72. On the dynamism of Indonesian Islam see Noer, *Modernist Muslim Movement in Indonesia*; Peacock, *Muslim Puritans*; and Geertz, *Religion*.

73. Furnivall, *Netherlands India*, pp. 15, 17. This statement implies that the advance of Islam was not really checked by the Hindu-Buddhistic followers flour-

ishing earlier in the country, as many Indonesianists believe. Hinduism and Buddhism had been either relegated to the periphery or incorporated into the Sufic blend of Islam. See Marshall G. S. Hodgson's criticism of Geertz's observation of Islam in Java in Hodgson, *Venture of Islam*, vol. 2, p. 551.

74. For the significant contribution of Nurcholish Madjid to Indonesian Islamic thinking see Pabottingi, "Tentang Visi, Tradisi, dan Hegemoni Bukan-Muslim," in *Islam*.

75. Ibid., p. 235.

76. See Liddle, "Skripturalisme *Media Dakwah*."

77. As Herbert Feith vividly records, Indonesia's independence from the Netherlands involved "a process of far-reaching disruption of old social relationships and substitution of new ones." He concludes: "If this was not a revolution in the sense in which the word is used for the French, Russian, and Chinese revolutions, it certainly involves a deeper shattering of social foundations than occurred in the independence struggle of any other new nation of the postwar period—with the possible exception of Vietnam." See Feith, *Decline*, p. 1.

78. For a good account of this conference, see Kahin, *Nationalism and Revolution*, chap. 8. See also Feith, *Decline*, passim.

79. See Feith, *Decline*, p. 573.

80. Hence the designation "constitutional democracy." Thus far Indonesia has known three constitutions: the 1945 constitution; the 1949 constitution, which was designed for the Republic of the United States of Indonesia (RUSI) under a parliamentary system; and the 1950 constitution.

81. The term "parliamentary democracy" is used because during most of the period parliament strongly influenced the regime's attempt at democratization. For the richest and most penetrating work dealing with Indonesia's parliamentary democracy, see Feith, *Decline*.

82. A succession of prime ministers under Masyumi—the party of modernist Muslims—became unpopular for staunchly defending fair play in politics and the economy. See Noer, *Partai Islam di Pentas Nasional*, pp. 433–34.

83. See Feith, *Decline*, pp. 77–78. The Indonesian army was a fusion of Republican troops, former soldiers of the Netherlands Indies, youth defense organizations established by the Japanese, and paramilitary units founded largely by Islamic communities during the revolution.

84. In Feith's words, Pancasila "had lost much of its umbrella role and become a partisan symbol"; *Decline*, p. 325.

85. The same argument comes from Robert C. Bone, Jr., as quoted in Fachry Ali's introduction to Compton, *Kemelut Demokrasi Liberal*, p. xlviii.

86. See, for example, Natsir, "Dangers of Secularism," p. 218.

87. Ibid., p. 219.

88. For an elaborate account of these three variants of Islam in Java and their political contestation, see Geertz, *Religion*.

89. Feith, *Decline*, p. 575.

90. Steinberg et al., *In Search of Southeast Asia*, pp. 382–84.

91. An excellent reference for this period is Feith, "Dynamics."

92. The Indonesian word *gotong royong* is difficult to render in English. It emphasizes communality and cooperation in undertaking a big task.

93. This authoritarianism, however, fell short of dictatorship or totalitarianism. Most of the government's policies were formalistic in that what mattered were the symbols, meanings, and intentions, not the implementation. See Feith, "Dynamics," pp. 372–74.

94. Sukarno needed the army to maintain order in the rebellion-stricken regions just as he needed the PKI to be an ally in the propagation of his revolutionary ambitions. The army and the PKI needed Sukarno as the foremost symbol of legitimacy; he was, after all, the principal architect of the nation. Both Sukarno and the army needed the civilian bureaucracy to carry out the routines of governance. And the bureaucracy needed Sukarno and the army to end the parties' violation of its integrity and privileges as civil servants.

95. The rebellion of the Revolutionary Government of the Republic of Indonesia (PRRI) broke out in West Sumatra and North Sulawesi in 1958.

96. See Feith, "Dynamics," p. 362. Nonetheless, by making the operational commands of the four forces independent of each other in 1960 and then establishing himself as Supreme Commander in the State of War and Siege (Peperti), Sukarno was able to make each force depend more on him than on the military's central command.

97. The doctrine of dual function rests on the belief that the army personifies the spirit of the 1945 revolution, in which it was not merely a coercive tool of the state but a social and political force as well. For the genealogy of the doctrine, see Feith, "Dynamics." For a more recent and comprehensive account of the army, see Crouch, *Army and Politics*. For a discussion of the development of army ideology, see ibid., pp. 26–27.

98. See Feith, "Dynamics," p. 330.

99. Crouch, *Army and Politics*, pp. 36–37. Crouch writes: "By the 1960s it was estimated that some 60 to 80 percent of army officers were Javanese" (p. 37).

100. See Feith, "Dynamics," pp. 393–94, 397.

101. Feith writes that "the PKI is probably further from power in 1962 than it was in 1958" (ibid., p. 340). For an incisive analysis of the PKI in this period see Anderson, "Rewinding 'Back to the Future.'"

102. For Manipol-Usdek, see Feith, "Dynamics." Panca Azimat Revolusi literally means the five amulets of the Indonesian revolution. Jas Merah is an Indonesian acronym whose meaning in English would be "Never Forget the Course of History"—the title of one of Sukarno's speeches. More important, however, the acronym literally means "Red Jacket," which strongly connotes communism.

103. For an excellent study on the necessity of looking into unstated assumptions, see Scott, *Domination and the Arts of Resistance*.

104. The speeches and writings of Natsir and Sjafruddin Prawinegara during the period of parliamentary democracy clearly reflect this conventionalism. See, for instance, Natsir, "Restoring Confidence in Democracy."

105. Sukarno, "Economics of a Nation in Revolution," pp. 392–93.

106. Soeharto's condemnation in 1966 of three sorts of deviation—the PKI's

left radicalism, political opportunism, and economic adventurism—was a good indication of the direction the New Order wanted to follow. See Soeharto, "Ending Three Deviations," pp. 146–47.

107. For a systematic account of the techniques used by the New Order to consolidate its power, see Mas'oed, *Ekonomi*, pp. 150ff.

108. The DPR's allotment consists of 75 from the military and 25 from the functional groups. Later DPR membership increased to 500.

109. Proponents of the New Order refuse to refer to Golkar as a political party because of the unsavory reputation of political parties in general since the mid-1950s. Among Indonesianists, similar objections can be found. Ruth McVey, for one, objects to calling Golkar "a government party." It is, she says, "more an anti-party, a political organization whose goal was to depoliticize." See McVey, "The Beamtenstaat in Indonesia," p. 86. Despite objections to calling it a political party, it has the characteristics of one and should be treated as such. Perhaps it is not so much an "anti-party," as McVey calls it, as an "anti-*aliran*-politics party."

110. See Feith, "Dynamics," p. 360.

111. Ali Moertopo is a former intelligence officer whose contribution to establishing the New Order is perhaps second only to Soeharto's. For an account of these attacks see Liddle, "Modernizing Indonesian Politics," pp. 182–85.

112. The Group for Democracy and Development comprises PNI, IPKI, Murba, Parkindo, and the Partai Katolik; the Group for Unity and Development includes all the surviving Islamic parties (NU, Parmusi, PSII, and Perti).

113. Kopkamtib is an acronym for Komando Operasi Pemulihan Keamanan dan Ketertiban (Command for the Restoration of Peace and Order).

114. Pertamina is Indonesia's state oil company. Bulog is the state's logistic body responsible for ensuring the supply of people's daily needs.

115. Banpres, literally "presidential help," was used to win over potential political challengers. Inpres, "presidential instruction," is an annual extrabudgetary allocation of development funds. For further details see Mas'oed, *Ekonomi*, pp. 182, 190.

116. See Booth and McCawley, *Indonesian Economy During the Soeharto Era*, p. 17.

117. See Robison, *Indonesia*, pp. 387–88. See also Sjahrir, *Kebijaksanaan Negara*, pp. 162–63.

118. Robison, *Indonesia*, p. 389.

119. Budiman rightly observes that "peasants are losing their land, people who work in the informal sectors in . . . big cities are losing their jobs, and industrial workers are being laid off." See Budiman, "Indonesian Politics in the 1990s," p. 135.

120. Bappenas stands for Badan Perencana Pembangunan Nasional—Indonesia's national planning board. The "Sadli principle" was the board's decision to give priority to foreign investors and provide them with the necessary facilities. See Robison, *Indonesia*, pp. 144–45.

121. Ibid., p. 375.

122. Rachbini, "Alih Saham," p. 6.

123. This petition, which strongly criticized Soeharto's appropriation of Pan-

casila, was signed by 50 prominent figures, intellectuals, and retired generals. See Jenkins, *Suharto and His Generals*, p. 162.

124. Translated from Arief, "Perjalanan Nasionalisme," pp. 14–15. Arief was by no means the only economist to express his concern over Indonesia's economic situation. See, for instance, Pamungkas, "Akankah Terjadi Perubahan-Perubahan," and Rachbini, "Alih Saham." Equally strong statements can be found in the writings of active economists such as M. Dawam Rahardjo, Kwik Kian Gie, Sarbini Soemawinata, Sri-Edhi Swasono, Rizal Ramli, and Mubyarto.

125. To the army, revolution was limited to the period relating to the actual establishment of an independent state. To the PKI, revolution was strictly communistic: the founding of the dictatorship of the proletariat. To Sukarno, revolution was much more complex and encompassed nationalism, Islam, and communism.

126. See "Current Data on the Indonesian Military Elite," *Indonesia* 55 (Apr. 1993): 177–98.

127. ICMI stands for Ikatan Cendekiawan Muslim Indonesia (Indonesian Muslim Intellectual Association), founded in 1991. For an insightful account of ICMI see Hefner, "Islam, State, and Civil Society."

10. VASAVAKUL, VIETNAM

1. Nguyen Khac Vien, *Tradition and Revolution in Vietnam*, p. 47.
2. Duiker, *Communist Road to Power*, p. 26.
3. McAlister and Mus, *Vietnamese and Their Revolution*, pp. 59–60 and 114–15.
4. Young, "Unpopular Socialism," p. 228.
5. Ibid., p. 229; see also Young, "Vietnamese Marxism," pp. 770–79.
6. Young, "Unpopular Socialism," pp. 229–30.
7. Marr, *Vietnamese Tradition on Trial*.
8. Tai, *Millenarianism and Peasant Politics in Vietnam*; Werner, "Cao Dai."
9. Scott, *Moral Economy of the Peasant*; Popkin, *Rational Peasant*.
10. Tran Quoc Vuong, "Dan gian va bac hoc" and "Loi truyen mien dan gian ve noi bat hanh cua mot so tri thuc nho gia," in *Trong coi*, pp. 159–95 and 233–61 respectively.
11. As Eric Hobsbawm puts it: "'Traditions' which appear or claim to be old are often quite recent in origin and sometimes invented." See Hobsbawm, "Introduction: Inventing Traditions," p. 1.
12. Huynh Kim Khanh, *Vietnamese Communism*, chap. 3.
13. Post, *Revolution, Socialism and Nationalism*.
14. Ho Chi Minh, "Con duong dan toi den chu nghia Le-Nin," p. 701.
15. Ibid., p. 700.
16. Huynh Kim Khanh, *Vietnamese Communism*, chaps. 1, 2, 5; Duiker, *Communist Road to Power*, pp. 1–87.
17. See Hammer, *Struggle for Indochina*, chaps. 4–8; Tonnesson, "The Outbreak of War in Indochina 1946."
18. See Porter, "Vietnam and the Socialist Camp," in Turley, *Vietnamese Communism*, pp. 225–64; Smyser, *Independent Vietnamese*.

19. White, "Agrarian Reform," especially chaps. 5–6.

20. In the field of Vietnamology, there are two interpretations of Vietnamese leadership politics. The *factional* model, first advocated by P. J. Honey and later elaborated by Thai Quang Trung, views the Vietnamese politburo as being divided into several factions vying for personal power. See, for example, Honey, *Communism in North Vietnam*; Thai Quang Trung, *Collective Leadership and Factionalism*, pp. 63–96. The *collegial* model, advocated by Carlyle Thayer, emphasizes the continuity of leadership and the cohesiveness of the elite and argues that there is basic agreement over ends and disagreements only on the means to achieve them. This collegial system has evolved and remained stable because its ultimate ends, national reunification and national survival, have remained relatively constant despite a powerful adversary. Analyzing the Central Committees of the Lao Dong Party (1951–76) and the Vietnamese Communist Party (1976–86), Thayer argues that power gradually moved away from the old guard and military officials to provincial party and state cadres and, further, that this regularization of politics caused the collegial model to break down. See Thayer, "Political Development in Vietnam," pp. 59–77; Thayer, "Vietnamese Perspectives," pp. 57–76; and Thayer, "Regularization of Politics," pp. 177–93.

21. After 1954 contention centered on the following issues: building socialism in the North and supporting political struggle in the South; strategies for constructing a socialist economy, culture, and education; strategies for the revolution in the South; and policies toward the Sino-Soviet split.

22. See the 1946 and the 1959 constitutions of the Democratic Republic of Vietnam in Vien Luat Hoc, *Hien phap nuoc Cong Hoa Xa Hoi Chu Nghia Viet Nam (binh luan)*, vol. 2, pp. 397–405 and 412–23.

23. Ho Chi Minh, *Ho Chu Tich ban ve giao duc*, pp. 43–44.

24. Ibid.

25. Tong Cuc Thong Ke, *So lieu thong ke 1930–1984*, p. 17.

26. See his criticisms of party/state cadres who used abstract language with the Vietnamese masses in Ho Chi Minh, "Sua doi loi lam viec" (Changing the working method), especially the section titled "Chong thoi ba hoa," pp. 50–58.

27. For examples of Ho's style see Vasavakul, "Schools and Politics."

28. "Letter from Abroad," in Fall, *Ho Chi Minh on Revolution*, p. 133.

29. Ho Chi Minh, "Tinh than yeu nuoc cua dan ta," pp. 1–2.

30. Ban Chap Hanh Trung Uong Dang Cong San Viet Nam, *Di chuc cua Chu Tich Ho Chi Minh*, p. 49.

31. For a detailed discussion see Moise, *Land Reform*, pp. 146–66.

32. Ho Chi Minh, "Appeal on the Occasion of the Sixth Anniversary of the National Resistance War," pp. 377–78.

33. Ibid.

34. See Moise, *Land Reform*, pp. 167–204; White, "Agrarian Reform," chap. 3; Truong Chinh, *Cach mang dan toc dan chu nhan dan Viet Nam*, vol. 2, pp. 307–402; Van Tao, "Cai cach ruong dat," pp. 1–4.

35. See Porter, *Myth of Bloodbath*; Van Tao, "Cai cach ruong dat," pp. 5–10.

36. Van Tao, "Cai cach ruong dat," pp. 3–4.

37. See Lockhart, *Nations in Arms*, chap. 7.

38. In his study of Son Duong village in Phu Tho province, Hy Van Luong points to a changing power relationship during land reform—manifested in poor and female villagers' omission of status-oriented personal pronouns in addressing the traditional village elite and elder family members. See Hy Van Luong, *Revolution in the Village*, pp. 188–91.

39. In China, for example, the errors of the Great Leap Forward were never debated openly in the party. Local officials took the blame. See Shue, *Reach of the State*, pp. 137–38.

40. White, "Agrarian Reform," p. 430.

41. Le Thanh Khoi, *Socialisme et développement au Viet Nam*, pp. 60–68.

42. Moise, *Land Reform*, pp. 237–68.

43. On the cooperativization movement in the 1960s see Vickerman, *Fate of the Peasantry*, chaps. 4–6; Fforde and Paine, *Limits of National Liberation*, chap. 6; Chaliand, *Peasants of North Vietnam*, pp. 38–46 and 71–242; Vo Nhan Tri, *Croissance économique de la République Démocratique du Vietnam*; "Sau 30 nam hop tac hoa nong nghiep," pp. 27–69.

44. The role of the state in regulating the relationship between agriculture and industry was stipulated in Articles 9–21 of the 1959 constitution. See *Hien phap nuoc Cong Hoa Xa Hoi Chu Nghia Viet Nam*, pp. 413–15. See also White, "Agricultural Planning," pp. 97–114.

45. Truong Chinh, *Resolutely Taking the North Vietnam Countryside to Socialism*; Nguyen Lai Van, "Battle of Rice."

46. See Rambo, *Comparison of Peasant Social Systems*; Scott, *Moral Economy of the Peasant*; Hy Van Luong, *Revolution in the Village*; and McAlister and Mus, *Vietnamese and Their Revolution*, pp. 88–89 and 95–98.

47. "Sau 30 nam hop tac hoa nong nghiep," p. 31.

48. Hy Van Luong, *Revolution in the Village*, p. 200.

49. With the arrival of the policy of renovation (*doi moi*) in 1986 and the official endorsement of a multisectoral economy (*kinh te nhieu thanh phan*), Vietnamese economists have begun to review the country's agricultural policies. According to them the cooperativization movement had the following shortcomings: first, it was too "hasty" (*nong voi*) and "voluntaristic" (*duy y chi*) in mobilizing peasant households into low-level cooperatives, transforming low-level into advanced cooperatives, and enlarging advanced cooperatives to facilitate the industrial pattern of division of labor; second, the leadership favored poor and lower-middle peasants, who "had little capital and little experience in economic management," allowing them to become cooperative chairpersons, inspectors, accountants, and heads of production teams; third, cooperativization dampened individual initiative in its exclusive emphasis on benefits to the collective; and fourth, the cost of production was increasing more rapidly than cooperative income over the past decades. Heavy state investment in irrigation works, chemical fertilizers, agricultural implements, and agricultural mechanization, based mostly on foreign loans, did not bring about the desired economic results.

50. Fforde, *Agrarian Question*, p. 24.

51. See *Cach mang khang chien va doi song van hoc.*

52. For a detailed analysis of intellectual dissidence see Boudarel, "Intellectual Dissidence"; and Kurihara, "Changes in the Literary Policy," pp. 165–93.

53. Boudarel, "Intellectual Dissidence"; Thayer, *War by Other Means*, pp. 95–96. Boudarel and Thayer argue convincingly that intellectual dissidence took place in Vietnam before it appeared in China. They point to domestic political development in Vietnam as the main cause of the dissidence.

54. For writings by the Nhan Van Giai Pham group see *Tram hoa dua no tren dat Bac.*

55. Ibid., pp. 293–318.

56. Ho Chi Minh, *Ho Chu Tich ban ve giao duc*, p. 157.

57. See the early 1958 issues of *Nhan Dan.*

58. In the early 1960s, for example, Ha Minh Tuan's *Vao doi* (Enter life) depicted the hard lives of a man and a woman who resisted "injustices" under the new regime. Socialist critics attacked *Vao doi* on the grounds that it portrayed too bleak a picture of life under socialism. See *Tram hoa van no tren que huong*, p. 26.

59. See Boudarel, "Intellectual Dissidence," p. 173.

60. Nguyen Khac Vien, *Tradition and Revolution in Vietnam*, p. 46.

61. For Vietnamese history see Uy Ban Khoa Hoc Xa Hoi Viet Nam, *Lich su Viet Nam.*

62. See *Truyen ngan Viet Nam, 1945–1985.* For a discussion of the state's role in cultural production and the organization of Vietnamese writers, see Nguyen Hung Quoc, *Van hoc Viet Nam duoi che do cong san*, pp. 15–85.

63. Vasavakul, "Schools and Politics," chaps. 10–11.

64. Huynh Kim Khanh, "Revolution at an Impasse," pp. 11–16.

65. See Thai Quang Trung, *Collective Leadership and Factionalism*, pp. 79–93; Thayer, "Vietnamese Perspectives," pp. 61–63.

66. *Hien phap nuoc Cong Hoa Xa Hoi Chu Nghia Viet Nam*, p. 450.

67. Thai Quang Trung, *Collective Leadership*, pp. 91–92.

68. See Articles 104–112 of the 1980 constitution, *Hien phap nuoc Cong Hoa Xa Hoi Chu Nghia Viet Nam*, pp. 453–55.

69. Vien Luat Hoc, *Tang cuong hieu luc nha nuoc xa hoi chu nghia cua chung ta*, p. 12.

70. Ibid., p. 18.

71. Ibid., pp. 47–132.

72. Huynh Kim Khanh, "Revolution at an Impasse," p. 4.

73. For the post-1975 period see Duiker, *Vietnam Since the Fall of Saigon*, pp. 3–90.

74. Thayer, *Political Developments in Vietnam.*

75. DCSVN, *Nghi quyet Dai hoi dai bieu toan quoc lan thu IV*; Thayer, "Development Strategies in Vietnam"; Fforde, *Agrarian Question*, pp. 59–85.

76. Duiker, *Vietnam Since the Fall of Saigon*, pp. 63–91.

77. Hy Van Luong, *Revolution in the Village*, p. 227; Ngo Vinh Long, "Some Aspects of Cooperativization," pp. 163–76.

78. Duiker, *Vietnam Since the Fall of Saigon*, pp. 31–51; Beresford, *National Unification.* See also the following chapters in Marr and White's *Postwar Viet-*

năm: Melanie Beresford, "Issues in Economic Unification: Overcoming the Legacy of Separation," pp. 95–110; Suzy Paine, "The Limits of Planning and the Case for Economic Reform," pp. 91–94.

79. To liberate the individual enthusiasm of cooperative members, the Sixth Plenum endorsed agricultural price reform. It also allowed cooperative members to sell the remainder of their produce after meeting procurement quotas and agricultural taxes either to state trading agencies or to the free market. It allowed individual households cultivating land unused by the cooperatives to retain the harvest in full.

80. See Vo Nhan Tri, "Party Policies and Economic Performance," pp. 77–90.

81. Porter, *Vietnam*, chap. 5.

82. For the "Third Indochina" conflict see Chanda, *Brother Enemy*; and Evans and Rowley, *Red Brotherhood at War*.

83. Bo Ngoai Giao, *Su that ve quan he Viet Nam Trung Quoc trong 30 nam qua*.

84. "Bao cao chinh tri tai Dai hoi dai bieu toan quoc lan thu V cua Dang (Political report for the Fifth National Party Congress)," in Le Duan, *Cach mang xa hoi chu nghia o Viet Nam*, pp. 9–172.

85. See, for example, Hong Nam and Hong Linh, *Nhung trang su ve vang cua dan toc Viet Nam chong phong kien Trung Quoc xam luoc*.

86. The late Luu Quang Vu, a famous short story writer and dramatist, wrote "The Postman" describing the impact of Chinese attacks on villages along the border. Vu's commitment to nationalism was an exemplary case; his plays and short stories attacking corrupt party cadres and the ills of the state socialist system were often best-sellers. See *Back to His Home Village*, pp. 31–50.

87. "Draft Resolution of the Sixth CPV Congress," Sixth Congress of the Communist Party of Vietnam, Dec. 15–18, 1986, *Foreign Broadcast Information Service*, May 7, 1987, pp. 144–45.

88. For a comparative discussion of Vietnam's party congresses see Le Mau Han, *Cac dai hoi Dang ta*. On the Sixth Party Congress see Tran Duc Nguyen, *Mot so quan diem kinh te cua Dai hoi VI*.

89. Do Muoi, a Northerner, became chairman of the Council of Ministers; Vo Chi Cong, from central Vietnam, became chairman of the State Council.

90. Many Vietnamese historians likened this advisory committee to the position of "*thai thuong hoang*," which was established during the Tran dynasty (thirteenth and fourteenth centuries). To eliminate power struggles during succession periods, Tran kings would retire early to become "advisers" to their sons. In the process the son would be able to consolidate his power and gradually learn the craft of rulership.

91. Thayer, "Challenges Facing Vietnamese Communism," p. 349.

92. Thayer, "Political Reform in Vietnam," pp. 110–29.

93. A number of studies show that in the case of the National Assembly elections, full or alternate members of the Central Committee and ministers whose positions required National Assembly membership were automatically nominated. Moreover, although party membership was not required, provincial, municipal, and district party committees tended to select party members as candi-

dates. Of the Eighth National Assembly deputies, only about 7 percent were not party members. See Thayer, *Political Developments in Vietnam.*

94. Turley, "Party, State, and People," pp. 257–75.

95. A close reading of party documents and the party's newspaper, *Nhan Dan,* published in the 1950s and 1960s suggests that the party had not emphasized Ho's socialist credentials until 1989. The party had referred to Ho's writings and speeches as advice (*loi dan*), whereas Marx's and Lenin's catechisms were "isms" (*chu nghia*) and Mao's teaching was "thought" (*tu tuong*). More obvious was the use of Ho Chi Minh as a national symbol. The party endorsed the building of a Ho Chi Minh mausoleum and a Ho Chi Minh museum to commemorate his hundredth birthday in 1990.

96. In May, Ho's secretary in the 1960s, Vu Ky, told *Nhan Dan Chu Nhat* that Ho had begun his writing as early as 1965 and only finished the last related document in 1968. His interviews were republished in Vu Ky, *Bac Ho viet di chuc.*

97. The Politburo admitted that Ho's successors had deliberately changed Ho's death date because the real date, September 2, happened to be the nation's Independence Day. The announcement also explained that the Politburo had violated Ho's wish that his body be cremated because they had seen the importance of preserving the body of Vietnam's beloved leader. See "Thong bao cua Bo Chinh Tri Ban Chap Hanh Trung Uong Dang Cong San Viet Nam ve mot so van de lien quan den di chuc va ngay qua doi cua Chu Tich Ho Chi Minh" (The Politburo's announcement on problems related to President Ho's death date and his last will and testament), in Ban Chap Hanh Trung Uong Dang Cong San Viet Nam, *Di chuc*, pp. 5–9; for the edition released in 1969 see pp. 47–50.

98. In 1978 Tran Xuan Bach was in charge of the organization responsible for Vietnamese party ties with Cambodia under Le Duc Tho. In 1982 he returned to the Central Committee and in 1986 was appointed to the Politburo. He was in charge of the party's foreign relations and was given responsibility for arts and culture.

99. The speech was reprinted in *Tieng noi dan chu*, pp. 58–62.

100. *Nhan Dan*, Mar. 31, 1990.

101. *FEER*, Mar. 29, 1990, pp. 18–20; Thayer, *Political Developments in Vietnam.*

102. See DCSVN, *Chien luoc on dinh va phat trien kinh te-xa hoi den nam 2000;* and DCSVN, *Cuong linh xay dung dat nuoc trong thoi ky qua do len chu nghia xa hoi.* Another indication of the intraparty disagreement could be seen in *Tap Chi Cong San*'s publication of comments against the party's political and economic platforms in March 1991. The Central Committee's culture and ideology department called a meeting of print media editors and warned them against going too far in reporting the views of party critics. In the April issue, *Tap Chi Cong San* (Communist review) published a self-critical article entitled "Some Things That Need to Be Discussed Again"; *FEER*, May 2, 1991, pp. 17–18.

103. Nguyen Van Linh, "Tiep tuc dua su nghiep doi moi tien len theo con duong xa hoi chu nghia," in DCSVN, *Van kien Dai hoi dai bieu toan quoc lan thu VII*, p. 107.

104. Hoang Minh Chinh, "Gop y ve du thao cuong linh." Born in 1925, Chinh attended a party school in the Soviet Union in 1957. After his return to Vietnam he became head of the Institute of Philosophy. According to *Dien Dan Nguoi Viet,*

a Vietnamese monthly magazine in the United States, in 1964 he was confined owing to his pro-Khruschev stance during the Maoist era of Vietnamese politics, accused of being "revisionist" and "antiparty." He was released in 1981, but after criticizing top party leadership, he was again confined from 1981 to 1986.

105. Phan Dinh Dieu received his Ph.D. in mathematics. He was head of the Institute of Mathematical and Engineering Sciences, vice-director of the Institute of Science, and a National Assembly deputy. See *Dien Dan Nguoi Viet* (Spring 1991): 11–15. "Ban kien nghi cua mot cong dan" (A citizen's proposal) was sent to the party through the Vietnamese embassy in Paris. Bui Tin went to Paris for a conference, then asked for permission to reside in France to receive medical treatment. See *Thanh Tin tran tinh*, pp. 3–5.

106. Hoang Minh Chinh, "Gop y ve du thao cuong linh."

107. In 1981 Vien sent a petition to Truong Chinh criticizing the economic policies endorsed by the Fourth Party Congress, the inefficiency of the state apparatuses, and the party's meddling with tasks assigned to the state. See "Kien nghi Dai hoi DCSVN," *Dien Dan Nguoi Viet* (Spring 1991): 30. For his 1990 petition see *Dien Dan Nguoi Viet* (Spring 1991): 19–20.

108. Ibid., pp. 19–20.

109. *Thanh Tin tran tinh*, pp. 3–4.

110. *Dien Dan Nguoi Viet* (Spring 1991), pp. 11–15.

111. Nguyen Van Linh, "Tiep tuc dua su nghiep doi moi," pp. 111–12.

112. Ibid., pp. 115–19.

113. Ibid., pp. 109–10.

114. Ibid., p. 125.

115. Ibid.

116. Ibid., p. 126.

117. Ibid., p. 124.

118. Ibid., p. 145.

119. Ibid., p. 113.

120. Ibid., pp. 113–14.

121. Ibid.

122. *Hien phap nuoc Cong Hoa Xa Hoi Chu Nghia Viet Nam 1992*, p. 13.

123. *Luat to chuc chinh phu nuoc Cong Hoa Xa Hoi Chu Nghia Viet Nam*, pp. 6–34.

124. Elliott, "Vietnam's 1991 Party Elections." The only increase, according to Elliott, was in the number of provincial party members: from 23.7 percent in 1986 to 32.2 percent in 1991.

125. *Nhan Dan*, June 28, 1991. The Seventh Congress Politburo retained five members from the previous Politburo and had eight new members. Security cadres were Le Duc Anh and Doan Khue from the army and Bui Thien Ngo from the police; ideological cadres were Dao Duy Tung from the Central Ideological Apparatus, Nguyen Duc Binh from the Nguyen Ai Quoc Party School, and Vu Oanh from the Mass Mobilization Department; technocratic cadres were Le Phuoc Tho from the Agricultural Apparatus and Phan Van Khai from the State Planning Commission.

126. Municipal cadres were Pham The Duyet, who was secretary of the Hanoi's People Committee, and Vo Tran Chi, secretary of the Ho Chi Minh City People's

Committee. The only party member from a minority group was Nong Duc Manh, president of the National Assembly. Old revolutionaries retained in the Politburo were Do Muoi, the general secretary, and Vo Van Kiet, the prime minister.

127. Nguyen Van Linh, "Tiep tuc dua su nghiep doi moi," p. 127.

128. Ibid., p. 128.

129. Porter, *Vietnam*, chap. 5.

130. See Bo Kinh Te Doi Ngoai, *Luat dau tu nuoc ngoai tai Viet Nam*, pp. 89–139.

131. See Ronnas and Sjoberg, "Economic Reform in Vietnam," p. 12; and see their *Doi Moi*.

132. Banister, *Vietnam Population Dynamics and Prospects*, pp. 54–55.

133. Ngo Vinh Long, "Reform and Rural Development," pp. 191–204.

134. See Gillespie, "Evolution of Private Commercial Freedoms," pp. 129–47.

135. These examples are cited in Turley, "Party, State, and People," p. 267.

136. *Tieng noi dan chu*, p. 75.

137. In 1987 Linh began to write for a column in *Sai Gon Giai Phong* and *Nhan Dan*. He criticized bureaucrats, mid-level party officials, and rampant corruption and urged the public to submit letters to the editors and petitions to state bodies. See *Nhan Dan* and *Sai Gon Giai Phong*, 1987–88; see also *Van kien cua Dang Cong San Viet Nam ve van hoa van nghe*.

138. *FEER*, May 4, 1989, p. 15. For information on the party's crackdown on "excesses" see Thayer, *Political Developments in Vietnam*.

139. For example, *Tram hoa van no tren que huong*; Luu Quang Vu's *Toi va chung ta* (I and we); Nguyen Huy Thiep's *Tac pham va du luan* (Works and comments), *Nhung ngon gio hua tat* (A gust of wind from Hua Tat), and *Con gai thuy than* (The daughter of the river god); Tran Manh Hao's *Ly than* (Alienation); Pham Thi Hoai's *Thien su* (The crystal messenger), *Me lo* (Labyrinth), and *Tu Man Nuong den AK va nhung tieu luan* (From Man Nuong to AK and other essays); Duong Thu Huong's *Nhung thien duong mu* (Foggy paradises); and Bao Ninh's *Than phan tinh yeu* (Fate of love)/*Noi buon chien tranh* (Sorrow of war). Some of the short stories are translated into English. See, for example, Peter Zinomon's translation of Nguyen Huy Thiep's "Vang lua," in *Vietnam Generation Inc.* 4(1–2) (Spring 1991): 58–61, and his translation of Pham Thi Hoai's "Chin bo lam muoi" in *Vietnam Generation Inc.* 4(3–4) (Summer–Fall 1992): 37–40. See especially Greg Lockhart's translation of Nguyen Huy Thiep's short stories in *General Retires*.

140. Tran Huy Quang, "Linh nghiem." The Central Committee of the Association of Vietnamese Writers later practiced self-criticism for overlooking the content of the story and allowing it to be published in *Van Nghe*.

141. McAlister and Mus, *Vietnamese and Their Revolution*, pp. 64–65.

11. ALAGAPPA, SEEKING A MORE DURABLE BASIS

1. The democratic system has a longer history in the Philippines. An elected legislature was authorized in the Philippines in 1907. For a brief overview of the increasing role of the Filipino elite in the political process during the American colonial period see Wurfel, *Filipino Politics*, pp. 8–12.

2. Feith, *Decline*, pp. 43–45.

3. Ibid., p. 45.

4. See Doronila, *State*, pp. 37–38.

5. For the impact of the economic transformation on the political process see ibid., especially chaps. 4–6.

6. Ibid., p. 89.

7. Ibid., p. 163.

8. For a summary see Timberman, *Changeless Land*, pp. 67–70.

9. Wurfel, *Filipino Politics*, pp. 330–32.

10. Lande, "Political Crisis," pp. 116–17.

11. This discussion draws extensively from Feith, *Decline*, chap. 11.

12. Ibid., p. 38.

13. Chantornvong and Chenvidyakarn, "Constitutional Rule," p. 144.

14. Timberman, *Changeless Land*, pp. 75–91. According to Bernardo Villegas economic policy during the first five years of martial law rule was sound and contributed to good economic performance. See Villegas, "The Economic Crisis," pp. 156–61.

15. For a good discussion of growing opposition to the Marcos government see Lande, "Political Crisis," pp. 116–44; see also Mackie and Villegas, "Unusual Case," pp. 102–10.

16. Lande, "Political Crisis," pp. 134–39.

17. See Noble, "Politics in the Marcos Era," pp. 70–113.

18. Mackie and Villegas, "Unusual Case," pp. 108–10.

19. Steinberg, *In Search of Southeast Asia*, pp. 401–2.

20. The gradual jettisoning of key "old guard" figures like General Nasution, Adam Malik, General Benny Moerdani, and most recently Admiral Sudomo; the refutation in 1980 of "Petisi 50" (a petition from 50 prominent members of the 1945 generation) without any significant backlash; the selection in 1988 of Sudharmono to the vice presidency despite opposition from ABRI; his own growing ability and self-confidence; the general public perception that no one has equal standing with Suharto—all reflect the growth in Suharto's personal authority, which reached a climax in the mid-1980s.

21. Liddle, "Useful Fiction."

22. A good example of this is Mochtar Pabottingi (Chap. 9) in this book.

23. Scott, *Weapons of the Weak*, p. 338.

24. Suharto's personal intervention to ensure the selection of Information Minister Harmoko as the first nonmilitary chairman of Golkar in October 1993 and the subsequent statement by Major General Sembiring Meliala, the deputy leader of the military faction in the DPR, that the military will not let the presidency go to a civilian illustrate the breach between Suharto and ABRI. See *FEER*, Nov. 25, 1993, pp. 25–26.

25. Paradoxically, as Suharto's personal authority grew, it was also subject to increasing criticism from ABRI and other groups. The privileged business activities and outright corruption of the first family tarnished the image and authority of Suharto, contributing further to the criticism.

26. This definition of developmentalism is drawn from Liddle, "Useful Fiction."

27. For details of these claims see Bresnan, *Managing Indonesia*, pp. 286–87.

28. In contrast there has been considerable effort to develop structures and procedures for public administration, especially in the socioeconomic domain.

29. Huntington, *Third Wave*, p. 50.

30. In responding to criticism about press censorship in Singapore and its impact on government legitimacy, the press secretary to the Singapore prime minister stated: "The legitimacy of the People's Action Party (PAP) government depends not on the endorsement of writers to the Letters column of the Review, but on the support of citizens expressed in secret elections. Any citizen is free to join or form a political party to challenge the government. That the opposition parties lack the substance reflects the strength of the PAP's support." See *FEER*, June 4, 1992, p. 6.

31. When the popular vote for the PAP declined by 12.6 percent to 62.9 percent in the 1984 general election, Lee questioned the principle of one man one vote. In fact throughout his political career Lee has always inveighed against the one man one vote principle. In 1984 he attacked the idea several times before the December general election. After 1984 the theme has also been aired by Goh Chok Tong. I am grateful to Cho-Oon Khong for pointing this out to me.

32. Chee, "Consociational Political Leadership," pp. 75–77.

33. Ibid.

34. Responding to a question from Chinese journalists as to whether the PAP would lose the next election, Lee Kuan Yew recently stated: "The older generation went through fire with me. They were immensely relieved that they all came through in one piece and they stayed committed to the PAP thereafter. The younger generation has grown up in secure, comfortable circumstances. They are less committed to the younger leadership. They have not had to face a major crisis. When they do, leaders and people will forge enduring bonds of loyalty." See *Straits Times*, Weekly Edition, Dec. 4, 1993, p. 2.

35. Giddens, *Central Problems*, pp. 67–73.

36. It withstood two major coup attempts, three general elections, five cabinet reshuffles, and numerous constitutional crises as well as extraparliamentary challenges during its thirteen-year life span.

37. In fact the balance was tilted in favor of the traditional forces: the prime minister did not have to come from the lower house; bureaucrats could concurrently hold political office during the first four years of the constitutional period; and important bills had to be approved in a joint session of the house. See Chantornvong and Chenvidyakarn, "Constitutional Rule," pp. 156–60.

38. Tasker, "Anti-Reform Club," p. 17.

39. This is not to deny that in some cases prior commitments to beliefs may help mold a group or nation. On the need for antecedent conditions in the development of group beliefs see Bar-Tal, *Group Beliefs*, pp. 63–69.

Bibliography

Abdullah, Taufik. "The Formation of a Political Tradition in the Malay World." In Anthony Reid, ed., *The Making of an Islamic Political Discourse in Southeast Asia*. Monash Papers on Southeast Asia 27. Clayton, Vic., Australia: Center of Southeast Asian Studies, Monash University, 1993.

Abinales, Patricio N. "Marcos, Pendatun, Matalam and Toothpick: Political Violence in Pre–Martial Law Mindanao." Paper presented at the 45th annual meeting of the Association for Asian Studies, Mar. 26, 1993, Los Angeles.

Abraham, Colin. "Manipulation and Management of Racial and Ethnic Groups in Colonial Malaysia: A Case Study of Ideological Domination and Control." In Raymond Lee, ed., *Ethnicity and Ethnic Relations in Malaysia*. De Kalb: Northern Illinois University, Center for Southeast Asian Studies, 1986.

Abueva, Jose V. "Ideology and Practice in the 'New Society.'" In David A. Rosenberg, ed., *Marcos and Martial Law in the Philippines*. Ithaca: Cornell University Press, 1979.

Adulyadej, Bhumipol. "Phra Rhat Cha Damras Pra Rhat Chathan Kae Puang Chon Chao Thai Nai O Kat Wan Khun Pee Mai Por Sor 2504" (Royal new year address to the Thai people in 1961). In *Phra Rhat Cha Damras lae Pra Borom Rachowat kong Phra bat Somdej Phra Chao Yu Hua lae Somdej Phra Nang Chao Sirikit Phra Borom Rajini* (Speeches and advice of His Majesty King Bhumipol and Queen Sirikit). Bangkok: Bandarn Sarn, 1966.

Agpalo, Remigio. *Pandanggo sa Ilaw: The Politics of Occidental Mindoro*. Quezon City: University of the Philippines, 1965.

Aguilar, Filomeno V., Jr. "Odds on the Future: Gambling and State Making in the Philippines." Paper prepared for the conference "Development in the Philippines: What's Next?" sponsored by the Program for Southeast Asian Studies, Arizona State University, Tempe, Mar. 21–22, 1992.

———. "Phantoms of Capitalism and Sugar Production Relations in a Colonial Philippine Island." Ph.D. dissertation, Cornell University, 1992.

Allen, James. *The Malayan Union*. New Haven: Yale University, Southeast Asian Studies, 1967.

Allen, Louis. "Leaving a Sinking Ship: A Comment on the End of Empire." In

D. K. Basset and V. T. King, eds., *Britain and Southeast Asia*. Hull: University of Hull Press, 1986.

Almond, Gabriel A., and Sidney Verba. *The Civic Culture*. Princeton: Princeton University Press, 1963.

Amnesty International. *Extrajudicial Execution and Torture of Members of Ethnic Minorities*. London: Amnesty International, 1988.

Andaya, Barbara Watson, and Leonard Y. Andaya. *A History of Malaysia*. London: Macmillan, 1982.

Anderson, Benedict R. O'G. "The Idea of Power in Javanese Culture." In Claire Holt, ed., *Culture and Politics in Indonesia*. Ithaca: Cornell University Press, 1972.

————. *Imagined Communities: Reflections on the Origin and Spread of Nationalism*. Rev. ed. London: Verso, 1991.

————. *Language and Power: Exploring Political Cultures in Indonesia*. Ithaca: Cornell University Press, 1990.

————. "The Languages of Indonesian Politics." *Indonesia* 1 (Apr. 1966): 89–116.

————. "Old State, New Society: Indonesia's New Order in Comparative Historical Perspective." *Journal of Asian Studies* 42(3) (May 1983): 477–96.

————. "Rewinding 'Back to the Future.'" Paper presented at the Conference on Indonesian Democracy of the 1950s and 1990s, Dec. 17–20, 1992, CSEAS, Monash University, Melbourne, Australia.

————. "Studies of the Thai State: The State of Thai Studies." In E. B. Ayal, ed., *The Study of Thailand: Analyses of Knowledge, Approaches and Prospects*. Athens: Ohio University Center for International Studies, Southeast Asia Program, 1978.

Anderson, Benedict R.O'G., and Audrey Kahin, eds. *Interpreting Indonesian Politics: Thirteen Contributions to the Debate*. Interim Report 62. Ithaca: Cornell Modern Indonesia Project, Southeast Asia Program, Cornell University, 1982.

Angelino, A. D. A. de Kat. *Colonial Policy*. Vol. 2. The Hague: Martinus Nijhoff, 1931.

Apter, David. *The Politics of Modernization*. Chicago: University of Chicago Press, 1965.

Arief, Sritua. "Perjalanan Nasionalisme Ekonomie Indonesia: Sebuah Tinjauan Kritis." *Prisma* 2 (Feb. 1991): 3–15.

Armstrong, M. Jocelyn. "ASEAN Should Follow Japan and Disavow Burma's SLORC." *Nation* (Bangkok), Apr. 5, 1993.

————. "Identity Manipulation by Urban Malays." In Raymond Lee, ed., *Ethnicity and Ethnic Relations in Malaysia*. De Kalb: Northern Illinois University, Center for Southeast Asian Studies, 1986.

Aungsan Suukyi. *Freedom from Fear*. London: Penguin, 1991.

Aung-Thwin, Michael. "The British 'Pacification' of Burma: Order Without Meaning." *Journal of Southeast Asian Studies* 16(2) (1985): 245–61.

————. "1948 and Burma's Myth of Independence." In Josef Silverstein, ed., *Independent Burma at Forty Years: Six Assessments*. Ithaca: Cornell University Press, 1989.

Ayoob, Mohammed. "The Security Predicament of Third World States: Reflections on State Making in a Comparative Perspective." In Brian Job, ed., *The Insecurity Dilemma: National Security of Third World States*. Boulder: Rienner, 1992.

Ba Maw. *Breakthrough in Burma*. New Haven: Yale University Press, 1968.

Badgley, John. "Burmese Ideology: A Comment." In Josef Silverstein, ed., *Independent Burma at Forty Years: Six Assessments*. Ithaca: Cornell University Press, 1989.

———. "A Clear Gathering of Miraculous Success." *Peace and Security* (Spring 1992): 10–11.

Badgley, John, and Jon A. Wiant. "The Ne Win–BSPP Style of Bama-Lo." In Josef Silverstein, ed., *The Future of Burma in Perspective: A Symposium*. Athens: Ohio University Center for International Studies, 1974.

Balakrishnan, N. "Esprit de Core." *Far Eastern Economic Review*, Feb. 7, 1991, pp. 27–28.

———. "Forked Tongues." *Far Eastern Economic Review*, Jan. 24, 1991, pp. 19–20.

———. "A Leg Up for Friends." *Far Eastern Economic Review*, May 14, 1992, p. 15.

Ban Chap Hanh Trung Uong Dang Cong San Viet Nam. *Di chuc cua Chu Tich Ho Chi Minh* (President Ho Chi Minh's last will and testament). Ho Chi Minh City: n.p., 1989.

Bangkok Post. "Bangkok Declaration of the Asian Regional Meeting on Human Rights." Apr. 3, 1993.

Banister, Judith. *Vietnam Population Dynamics and Prospects*. Berkeley: University of California Press, 1993.

Bankoff, Greg. "Big Fish in Small Ponds: The Exercise of Power in a Nineteenth-Century Philippine Municipality." *Modern Asian Studies* 26(4) (1992): 679–700.

Barker, Rodney. "Legitimacy: The Identity of the Accused." *Political Studies* 42(1) (Mar. 1994): 101–2.

———. *Political Legitimacy and the State*. Oxford: Clarendon Press, 1990.

Barraclough, Simon. "The Dynamics of Coercion in the Malaysian Political Process." *Modern Asian Studies* 19(4) (1985): 797, 822.

Bar-Tal, Daniel. *Group Beliefs*. New York: Springer-Verlag, 1990.

Barton, R. F. *The Kalingas: Their Institutions and Custom Law*. Chicago: University of Chicago Press, 1949.

Baterina, Virginia F. "A Study of Money in Elections in the Philippines." *Philippine Social Sciences and Humanities Review* 20(2) (June 1985): 39–172.

Batson, Benjamin. *The End of Absolute Monarchy in Siam*. Singapore: Oxford University Press, 1984.

Beetham, David. "In Defence of Legitimacy." *Political Studies* 41(3) (Sept. 1993): 488–89.

———. *Legitimation of Power*. Atlantic Highlands, N.J.: Humanities Press International, 1991.

Bello, Walden, and Stephanie Rosenfeld. *Dragons in Distress: Asia's Miracle*

Economies in Crisis. San Francisco: Institute for Food and Development Policy, 1990.

Bendix, Reinhard. *Kings or People: Power and the Mandate to Rule*. Berkeley: University of California Press, 1978.

———. "Reflections of Charismatic Leadership." In Reinhard Bendix, ed., *States and Societies*. Berkeley: University of California Press, 1968.

Benjamin, Roger, and Raymond Duvall. "The Capitalist State in Context." In Roger Benjamin and Stephen L. Elkin, eds., *The Democratic State*. Lawrence: University Press of Kansas, 1985.

Bensman, Joseph. "Max Weber's Concept of Legitimacy: An Evaluation." In Arthur J. Vidich and Ronald Glassman, eds., *Conflict and Control: Challenge to Legitimacy of Modern Governments*. Beverly Hills: Sage, 1979.

Bentley, G. Carter. "Dispute, Authority, and Maranao Social Order." In Resil B. Mojares, ed., *Dispute Processing in the Philippines*. Quezon City: Ministry of Local Government, 1985.

Beresford, Melanie. *National Unification and Economic Development in Vietnam*. New York: St. Martin's Press, 1989.

Blair, Emma Helen, and James Alexander Robertson. *The Philippine Islands 1493–1803*. Cleveland: Clark, 1919.

Blanc-Szanton, Cristina. "Change and Politics in a Western Visayan Municipality." In Benedict J. Kerkvliet and Resil B. Mojares, eds., *From Marcos to Aquino: Local Perspectives on Political Transition in the Philippines*. Quezon City: Ateneo de Manila University Press, 1991.

Blok, Anton. "The Peasant and the Brigand: Social Banditry Reconsidered." *Comparative Studies in Society and History* 14(4) (Sept. 1972): 494–503.

Bo Kinh Te Doi Ngoai. *Luat dau tu nuoc ngoai tai Viet Nam, tap I* (Laws of foreign investment in Vietnam, vol. 1). Hanoi: BKTDN, 1988.

Bo Ngoai Giao. *Su that ve quan he Viet Nam Trung Quoc trong 30 nam qua* (The truth about Vietnam-China relations over the past thirty years). Hanoi: Su That, 1979.

Boeke, J. H. *Economics and Economic Policy of Dual Society*. New York: Institute of Pacific Relations, 1953.

Bogaars, G. E. Quoted in "Public Services." In *Towards Tomorrow: Essays on Development and Social Transformation in Singapore*. Singapore: National Trades Union Congress, 1973.

Bonner, Raymond. *Waltzing with a Dictator: The Marcoses and the Making of American Policy*. New York: Times Books, 1987.

Booth, Anne, and Peter McCawley, eds. *The Indonesian Economy During the Soeharto Era*. Kuala Lumpur: Oxford University Press, 1981.

Booth, Anne, W. J. O'Malley, and Anna Weideman, eds. *Indonesian Economic History in the Dutch Colonial Era*. Monograph Series, No. 35. New Haven: Yale University Southeast Asia Studies, 1990.

Boudarel, Georges. "Intellectual Dissidence in the 1950s: The *Nhan Van Giai Pham* Affair." *Vietnam Forum* 13 (1990): 154–74.

Bourchier, David. "Crime, Law and State Authority in Indonesia." In Arief Budiman, ed., *State and Civil Society in Indonesia*. Clayton, Vic., Australia: Monash University, Center of Southeast Asian Studies, 1990.

Bowie, Alasdair. *Crossing the Industrial Divide: State, Society, and the Politics of Economic Transformation in Malaysia*. New York: Columbia University Press, 1991.

Bresnan, John. *Managing Indonesia: The Modern Political Economy*. New York: Columbia University Press, 1993.

———, ed. *Crisis in the Philippines*. Princeton: Princeton University Press, 1986.

Broad, Robin. *Unequal Alliance: The World Bank, the International Money Fund, and the Philippines*. Berkeley: University of California Press, 1988.

Brown, David. *The Legitimacy of Governments in Plural Societies*. Occasional Paper 43. Singapore: Department of Political Science, National University of Singapore, 1984.

Brown, Kevin. "Singapore PM Puts Reform Plans on Hold." *Financial Times* (London), Sept. 5, 1991, p. 4.

Brunner, George. "Legitimacy Doctrine and Legitimation Procedures in East European Systems." In T. H. Rigby and Ferenc Fehrer, eds., *Political Legitimation in Communist States*. London: Macmillan, 1982.

Brunnstrom, David. "Democracy Under the Gun." *Nation* (Bangkok), Apr. 25, 1989.

Budiman, Arief. "Indonesian Politics in the 1990s." In Harold Crouch and Hal Hill, eds., *Indonesia Assessment 1992*. Canberra: Research School of Pacific Studies, Australian National University, 1992.

Bumroongsuk, Surachat. *United States Foreign Policy and Thai Military Rule 1947–1977*. Bangkok: Duangkamol, 1985.

Bungbongkarn, Suchit. *The Military in Thai Politics 1981–1986*. Singapore: Institute of Southeast Asian Studies, 1987.

———. "Thailand in 1992: In Search of a Democratic Order." *Asian Survey* 33(2) (1993): 220–23.

Butwell, Richard. *U Nu of Burma*. Stanford: Stanford University Press, 1969.

Buzan, Barry, Charles Jones, and Richard Little. *The Logic of Anarchy: Neorealism to Structural Realism*. New York: Columbia University Press, 1993.

Cach mang khang chien va doi song van hoc, 1945–1954, tap II (Revolution, resistance, and literary life, 1945–54, vol. 2). Hanoi: Tac Pham Moi, 1987.

Cady, John F. *The History of Modern Burma*. Ithaca: Cornell University Press, 1958.

Casanova, Jose. "Legitimacy and the Sociology of Modernization." In Arthur J. Vidich and Ronald Glassman, eds., *Conflict and Control: Challenge to Legitimacy of Modern Governments*. Beverly Hills: Sage, 1979.

Chaliand, Gerard. *The Peasants of North Vietnam*. Baltimore: Penguin, 1968.

Chaloemtiarana, Thak. "The Sarit Regime 1957–1963: The Formative Years of Modern Thai Politics." Ph.D. dissertation, Cornell University, 1974.

———. *Thailand: Politics of Despotic Paternalism*. Bangkok: Social Science Association, 1979.

———, ed. *Thai Politics 1932–1957*. Bangkok: Social Science Association, 1978.

Chan Heng Chee. *The Dynamics of One Party Dominance: The PAP at the Grass-roots.* Singapore: Singapore University Press, 1976.

———. *Politics in an Administrative State: Where Has the Politics Gone?* Occasional Paper 11. Singapore: Department of Political Science, National University of Singapore, 1975.

———. "The Role of Intellectuals in Singapore Politics." *Southeast Asian Journal of Social Science* 3 (1975): 64.

Chanda, Nayan. *Brother Enemy: The War After the War.* Orlando: Harcourt Brace Jovanovich, 1986.

Chandra Muzaffar. *Protector? An Analysis of the Concept and Practice of Loyalty in Leader-Led Relationships Within Malay Society.* Penang: Aliran, 1979.

Chantornvong, Sombat, and Montri Chenvidyakarn. "Constitutional Rule and the Institutionalization of Leadership and Security in Thailand." In Stephen Chee, ed., *Leadership and Security in Southeast Asia.* Singapore: Institue of Southeast Asian Studies, 1991.

Chapman, William. *Inside the Philippine Revolution: The New People's Army and Its Struggle for Power.* New York: Norton, 1987.

Chee, Stephen. "Consociational Political Leadership and Conflict Regulation in Malaysia." In Stephen Chee, ed., *Leadership and Security in Southeast Asia.* Singapore: Institute of Southeast Asian Studies, 1991.

Chen, King. *Vietnam and China, 1938–1954.* Princeton: Princeton University Press, 1969.

Cheung, Paul. "Summary of Census Findings" and "Discussion." In Yap Mui Teng, ed., *Report of the IPS Forum on the Census of Population 1990.* Report No. 4. Singapore: Institute of Policy Studies, 1991.

Cheung, Tai Ming. "Soldiers and Scholars." *Far Eastern Economic Review,* Dec. 5, 1991, pp. 15–18.

Chiew Seen Kong. "Social Mobility in Singapore." In Stella R. Quah, Chiew Seen Kong, Ko Yiu Chung, and Sharon Mengchee Lee, *Social Class in Singapore.* Singapore: Times Academic Press, 1991.

Chirino, Pedro, S.J. *Relacion de las Islas Filipinas.* Manila: Historical Conservation Society, 1969. Originally published in 1604.

Chung Kek Yoon. *Mahathir Administration: Leadership and Change in a Multi-Racial Society.* Petaling Jaya, Malaysia: Pelanduk, 1987.

Clad, James. *Behind the Myth: Business, Power, and Money in Southeast Asia.* London: Hyman Press, 1990.

Claessen, Henri J. M. "Changing Legitimacy." In Ronald Cohen and Judith D. Toland, eds., *State Formation and Political Legitimacy.* Vol. 6 of *Political Anthropology.* New Brunswick: Transaction Books, 1988.

Clammer, John. *Singapore: Ideology, Society, Culture.* Singapore: Chopmen, 1985.

Clapham, Christopher. *Third World Politics.* Madison: University of Wisconsin Press, 1985.

Clark, Gordon L., and Michael Dear. *State Apparatus: Structures and Language of Legitimacy.* Boston: Allen & Unwin, 1984.

Clifford, James. *The Predicament of Culture.* Cambridge, Mass.: Harvard University Press, 1988.

Clinton, William. "Confronting the Challenges of a Broader World." *Dispatch* 4(39) (1993): 649–53.

Cohen, Ira J. "Structuration Theory and Social Praxis." In Anthony Giddens and Jonathan H. Turner, eds., *Social Theory Today.* Stanford: Stanford University Press, 1987.

Cohen, Jean L., and Andrew Arato. *Civil Society and Political Theory.* Cambridge, Mass.: MIT Press, 1992.

Cohen, Ronald. "Legitimacy, Illegitimacy and State Formation." In Ronald Cohen and Judith D. Toland, eds., *State Formation and Political Legitimacy.* Vol. 6 of *Political Anthropology.* New Brunswick: Transaction Books, 1988.

Colin, Francisco, S.J. "Native Races and Their Customs." In Emma Helen Blair and James Alexander Robertson, eds., *The Philippine Islands 1493–1803.* Vol. 40. Cleveland: Clark, 1919.

Collier, David, ed. *The New Authoritarianism in Latin America.* Princeton: Princeton University Press, 1979.

Committee for the Restoration of Democracy in Burma (CRDB). *Aung Gyi's Letter: The Truth Revealed.* Falls Church: CRDB, 1988.

————. *The Day Blood Flowed on the Inya Embankment: The Second Letter of Aung Gyi.* Falls Church: CRDB, 1988.

Compton, Boyd R. *Kemelut Demokrasi Liberal.* Jakarta: LP3ES, 1993.

Concepcion, Venancio. *"La Tragedia" del Banco Nacional Filipino.* Manila: n.p., 1927.

Connolly, William. "The Dilemma of Legitimacy." In William Connolly, ed., *Legitimacy and the State.* New York: New York University Press, 1984.

Coquia, Jorge R. *The Philippine Presidential Election of 1953.* Manila: Philippine Education Foundation, 1955.

Corotan, Gemma Luz. "It's Back with Binay." *Manila Chronicle,* Mar. 14–20, 1992.

Cotton, James. "Political Innovation in Singapore: The Presidency, the Leadership and the Party." In Garry Rodan, ed., *Singapore Changes Guard: Social, Political and Economic Directions in the 1990s.* Melbourne: Longman Cheshire, 1993.

Covar, Prospero. "Potensiya, Bisa, at Anting-Anting (Decoding Belief System Encoded in Folklore)." *Asian Studies* 18 (1980): 71–78.

Crisanto-Ortega, M. J. *The Vanishing Breed: Francisco I. Ortega: A Biography.* Manila: Philippine Daily Express Commercial Press, 1977.

Crone, Donald. "State, Social Elites, and Government Capacity in Southeast Asia." Review article. *World Politics* 40(2) (1988): 252–68.

Crouch, Harold. *The Army and Politics in Indonesia.* Rev. ed. Ithaca: Cornell University Press, 1988.

————. "Malaysia: Neither Authoritarian nor Democratic." In Kevin Hewison, Richard Robison, and Garry Rodan, eds., *Southeast Asia in the 1990s: Authoritarianism, Democracy, and Capitalism.* Sydney: Allen & Unwin, 1992.

————. *Malaysian Government: Authoritarian Repression and Democratic Responsiveness.* Canberra: Australian National University, n.d.

————. "Patrimonialism and Military Rule in Indonesia." *World Politics* 31(4) (1979): 571–87.

————. "The UMNO Crisis: 1975–77." In Harold Crouch, Lee Kam Hing, and Michael Ong, eds., *Malaysian Politics and the 1978 Election.* Kuala Lumpur: Oxford University Press, 1980.

Crouch, Harold, and Hal Hill, eds. *Indonesia Assessment 1992.* Canberra: Research School of Pacific Studies, Australian National University, 1992.

Crouch, Harold, and James W. Morley. "Dynamics of Political Change." In James W. Morley, ed., *Driven by Growth: Political Change in the Asia-Pacific Region.* Armonk, N.Y.: M. E. Sharpe, 1993.

Cullinane, Michael. "Patron as Client: Warlord Politics and the Duranos of Danao." In Alfred W. McCoy, ed., *An Anarchy of Families: State and Family in the Philippines.* Madison: University of Wisconsin Center for Southeast Asian Studies, 1993.

DCSVN. *Chien luoc on dinh va phat trien kinh te-xa hoi den nam 2000* (Strategy of socioeconomic stabilization and development until the year 2000). Hanoi: Su That, 1991.

————. *Cuong linh xay dung dat nuoc trong thoi ky qua do len chu nghia xa hoi* (Platform for national construction in the period of transition to socialism). Hanoi: Su That, 1991.

————. *Nghi quyet Dai hoi dai bieu toan quoc lan thu IV* (Resolution of the Fourth National Party Congress). Hanoi: Su That, 1976.

————. *Van kien Dai hoi dai bieu toan quoc lan thu VII* (Documents on the Seventh Congress). Hanoi: Su That, 1991.

De Azcarraga y Palmero, Manuel. *La Reforma del Municipio Indigena en Filipinas.* Madrid: Imp. de J. Noguera, 1871.

De Crespigny, Anthony, and Jeremy Cronin, eds. *Ideologies of Politics.* London: Oxford University Press, 1975.

de los Reyes, Romana P., and Sylvia Ma. G. Jopillo. *Pursuing Agrarian Reform in Negros Occidental.* Quezon City: Institute of Philippine Culture, Ateneo de Manila University, 1991.

De Quiros, Conrado. "Guns, Goons, and Government: Pre–Martial Law Politics and Elections." In *1992 and Beyond: Forces and Issues in Philippine Elections.* Quezon City: Philippine Center for Investigative Journalism and Ateneo Center for Social Policy and Public Affairs, 1992.

Del Carmen, Rolando V. "Constitutionality and Judicial Politics." In David A. Rosenberg, ed., *Marcos and Martial Law in the Philippines.* Ithaca: Cornell University Press, 1979.

Desabelle, Gerry Yuan. *Lapulapu City (Mactan Island): Its Role in the Birth of the Filipino Nation.* Cebu City: n.p., 1988.

Desai, A. R. *Social Background of Indian Nationalism.* Bombay: Popular Press, 1948.

Dhiravegin, Likhit. *Thai Politics: Selected Aspects of Development and Change.* Bangkok: Tri Science, 1985.

Diamond, Larry. "Economic Development and Democracy Reconsidered." *American Behavioral Scientist* 55(4/5) (May/June 1992): 450–99.

Di Palma, Giuseppe. "Legitimation from the Top to Civil Society: Politico-Cultural Change in Eastern Europe." *World Politics* 44(1) (1991): 49–80.

Dominguez, Jorge I. "Political Change: Central America, South America and the Caribbean." In Myron Weiner and Samuel P. Huntington, eds., *Understanding Political Development*. Boston: Little, Brown, 1987.

Doner, Richard. "Approaches to the Politics of Economic Growth in Southeast Asia." *Journal of Asian Studies* 50(4) (1991): 818–49.

Donnison, F. S. V. *Burma*. New York: Praeger, 1970.

Doronila, Amando. *The State, Economic Transformation, and Political Change in the Philippines, 1946–1972*. Singapore: Oxford University Press, 1992.

———. "The Transformation of Patron-Client Relations and Its Political Consequences in Postwar Philippines." *Journal of Southeast Asian Studies* 16(1) (Mar. 1985): 99–116.

Duiker, William J. *The Communist Road to Power in Vietnam*. Boulder: Westview Press, 1981.

———. *Vietnam Since the Fall of Saigon*. Rev. ed. Athens: Ohio University Center for International Studies, 1985.

Durano, Ramon M. *Ramon M. Durano: An Autobiography*. Cebu City: Ramon Durano Foundation, 1987.

Elias, Norbert. *Power and Civility*. New York: Pantheon, 1982.

Elliott, David W. P. "North Vietnam Since Ho." *Problems of Communism* (July–Aug. 1975): 35–52.

———. "Vietnam's 1991 Party Elections." *Asian Affairs* 19(3) (Fall 1992): 159–68.

Elson, R. E. "Peasant Poverty and Prosperity Under the Cultivation System in Java." In Anne Booth, W. J. O'Malley, and Anna Weideman, eds., *Indonesian Economic History in the Dutch Colonial Era*. Monograph Series, No. 35. New Haven: Yale University Southeast Asia Studies, 1990.

Erlanger, Steven. "The Burmese Are Going to Vote; the Army Tells Them To." *New York Times*, Apr. 1, 1990.

Evans, Grant, and Kevin Rowley. *Red Brotherhood at War: Vietnam, Cambodia and Laos Since 1975*. Rev. ed. London: Verso, 1990.

Fall, Bernard, ed. *Ho Chi Minh on Revolution: Selected Writings, 1920–66*. Boulder: Westview Press, 1984.

———. *The Viet Minh Regime*. Data Paper 14. Ithaca: Southeast Asia Program, Cornell University, 1954.

Falla, Jonathan. *True Love and Bartholomew: Rebels on the Burmese Border*. New York: Cambridge University Press, 1991.

Fan Yew Teng. *The UMNO Drama*. Kuala Lumpur: Egret, 1989.

Fawthrop, Tom. "Burma's Rebel Economy." *Insight* (July 1979).

Fegan, Brian. "Between the Lord and the Law: Tenants' Dilemmas." *Philippine Sociological Review* 20(1–2) (1972): 113–28.

Feith, Herbert. *The Decline of Constitutional Democracy in Indonesia*. Ithaca: Cornell University Press, 1962.

————. "Dynamics of Guided Democracy." In Ruth T. McVey, ed., *Indonesia.* New Haven: Southeast Asia Studies, Yale University, by arrangement with HRAF Press, 1963.

Feith, Herbert, and Lance Castles, eds. *Indonesian Political Thinking, 1945–1965.* Ithaca: Cornell University Press, 1970.

Feldman, Allen. *Formations of Violence: The Narrative of the Body and Political Terror in Northern Ireland.* Chicago: University of Chicago Press, 1991.

Fenner, Bruce Leonard. *Cebu Under the Spanish Flag, 1521–1896: An Economic-Social History.* Cebu City: San Carlos Publications, 1985.

Fforde, Adam. *The Agrarian Question in North Vietnam, 1974–1979: A Study of Cooperator Resistance to State Policy.* Armonk, N.Y.: M. E. Sharpe, 1989.

Fforde, Adam, and Suzanne H. Paine. *The Limits of National Liberation: Problems of Economic Management in the Democratic Republic of Vietnam with a Statistical Appendix.* London: Croom Helm, 1987.

Finer, S. E. *Comparative Government.* Baltimore: Penguin, 1970.

————. *The Man on Horseback: The Role of the Military in Politics.* Baltimore: Penguin, 1975.

Finin, Gerard Anthony. "Regional Consciousness and Administrative Grids: Understanding the Role of Planning in the Philippines' Gran Cordillera Central." Ph.D. dissertation, Cornell University, 1991.

Fishman, Robert. "Rethinking State and Regime: Southern Europe's Transition to Democracy." *World Politics* 42(3) (1990): 422–40.

Foltz, William J. "The Organization of African Unity and the Resolution of Africa's Conflicts." In Francis M. Deng and I. William Zartman, eds., *Conflict Resolution in Africa.* Washington, D.C.: The Brookings Institution, 1991.

Fong Chan Onn. *The Malaysian Economic Challenge in the 1990s: Transformation and Growth.* Singapore: Longman, 1989.

Friedman, Richard B. "On the Concept of Authority in Political Philosophy." In Richard E. Flathman, ed., *Concepts in Social and Political Philosophy.* New York: Macmillan, 1973.

Friedrich, C. J. *Man and His Government: An Empirical Theory of Politics.* New York: McGraw-Hill, 1963.

Fukuyama, Francis. "The End of History." *National Interest* (Summer 1989): 3–18.

————. *The End of History and the Last Man.* New York: Free Press, 1992.

————. "A Reply to My Critics." *National Interest* (Winter 1989–90): 21–28.

Funston, John. *Malay Politics in Malaysia: A Study of the United Malays National Organization and Party Islam.* Kuala Lumpur: Heinemann, 1980.

Furnivall, John S. *Colonial Policy and Practice.* Cambridge: Cambridge University Press, 1948.

————. *Netherlands India: A Study of the Plural Economy.* Cambridge: Cambridge University Press, 1939.

Gaddis, John Lewis. "International Relations Theory and the End of the Cold War." *International Security* 17(3) (Winter 1992–93): 47–48.

Gale, Bruce. *Politics and Public Enterprise in Malaysia.* Singapore: Eastern Universities Press, 1981.

Geertz, Clifford. "The Integrative Revolution: Primordial Sentiments and Civil Politics in the New States." In Clifford Geertz, ed., *Old Societies and New States: The Quest for Modernity in Asia and Africa*. New York: Free Press, 1963.

———. *The Interpretation of Cultures*. New York: Basic Books, 1973.

———. *Islam Observed*. Chicago: University of Chicago Press, 1969.

———. *The Religion of Java*. Chicago: University of Chicago Press, 1960.

Geertz, Hildred. "Indonesian Cultures and Communities." In Ruth T. McVey, ed., *Indonesia*. New Haven: Southeast Asian Studies, Yale University, by arrangement with HRAF Press, 1963.

Giddens, Anthony. *Central Problems in Social Theory*. Berkeley: University of California Press, 1984.

———. *A Contemporary Critique of Historical Materialism*. Berkeley: University of California Press, 1981.

Giddens, Anthony, and Jonathan H. Turner, eds. *Social Theory Today*. Stanford: Stanford University Press, 1987.

Gillespie, John. "The Evolution of Private Commercial Freedoms in Vietnam." In Carlyle Thayer and David Marr, eds., *Vietnam and the Rule of Law*. Political and Social Change Monograph 19. Canberra: Department of Political and Social Change, Australian National University, 1993.

Gills, Barry, and Joel Rocamora. "Low Intensity Democracy." *Third World Quarterly* 13(3) (1992): 501–23.

Girling, John. *Thailand: Society and Politics*. Ithaca: Cornell University Press, 1981.

Glang, A. C. *Muslim Secession or Integration?* Quezon City: R. P. Garcia, 1969.

Goh Keng Swee. *The Practice of Economic Growth*. Singapore: Federal Publications, 1977.

Gomez, Edmund Terence. *Money Politics in the Barisan Nasional*. Kuala Lumpur: Forum, 1991.

———. *Politics in Business: UMNO's Corporate Investments*. Kuala Lumpur: Forum, 1990.

Green, Leslie. *The Authority of the State*. Oxford: Clarendon Press, 1990.

Greenfeld, Liah. *Nationalism: Five Roads to Modernity*. Cambridge, Mass.: Harvard University Press, 1992.

Guerrero, Amado. *Philippine Society and Revolution*. Hong Kong: Ta Kung Pao, 1971.

Guggenheim, Scott. "Cock or Bull: Cockfighting, Social Structure, and Political Commentary in the Philippines," *Pilipinas* 3(1) (June 1982): 1–35.

Gullick, John. "The Role of the Malay Ruler Between 1850 and 1950." *Kajian Malaysia* 9(2) (1991): 1–23.

Gutang, Red B. *Pulisya: The Inside Story of the Demilitarization of the Law Enforcement System in the Philippines*. Quezon City: Daraga Press, 1991.

Guyot, Dorothy Hess. "Communal Conflict in the Burma Delta." In Ruth McVey, ed., *Southeast Asian Transitions*. New Haven: Yale University Press, 1978.

Guyot, James F., and John Badgley. "Myanmar in 1989: Tatmadaw V." *Asian Survey* 30(2) (1990): 187–95.

Haas, Roy C. "The MCA, 1958–59: An Analysis of Differing Conceptions of the

Malayan Chinese Role in Independent Malaya." Unpublished thesis, Northern Illinois University, 1967.

Habermas, Jürgen. *Communication and the Evolution of Society*. Boston: Beacon Press, 1979.

Halim Salleh. "Peasants, Proletarianization, and the State: FELDA Settlers in Pahang." In Joel S. Kahn and Francis Loh Kok Wah, eds., *Fragmented Vision: Culture and Politics in Contemporary Malaysia*. Sydney: Allen & Unwin, 1992.

Hall, D. G. E. *A History of Southeast Asia*. 4th ed. New York: St. Martin's Press, 1981.

Hall, John A. "Consolidations of Democracy." In David Held, ed., *Prospects for Democracy: North, South, East, West*. Stanford: Stanford University Press, 1993.

Hall, Kenneth R., and John K. Whitmore, eds. *Explorations in Early Southeast Asian History: The Origins of Southeast Asian Statecraft*. Michigan Papers on South and Southeast Asia, No. 11. Ann Arbor: Center for South and Southeast Asia, University of Michigan, 1976.

Hammer, Ellen. *The Struggle for Indochina, 1940–1955*. Stanford: Stanford University Press, 1966.

Han, U Nyun. "Burma's Experiment in Socialism." Ph.D. dissertation, University of Colorado, 1970.

Harding, Neil. *The State in Socialist Society*. Oxford: St. Anthony's College, 1984.

Hatta, Mohammad. *Indonesia Merdeka*. Jakarta: Bulan Bintang, 1976.

———. *Portrait of a Patriot: Selected Writings*. The Hague: Mouton, 1972.

Hechter, Michael. *Internal Colonialism: The Celtic Fringe in British National Development*. Berkeley: University of California Press, 1975.

Hedman, Eva-Lotta E. "In the Name of Civil Society: Participatory Crises, Critical Elections, and Transformist Mobilization in the Postwar Philippines." Ph.D. dissertation, Cornell University, 1994.

Hefner, Robert W. "Islam, State, and Civil Society: ICMI and the Struggle for the Indonesian Middle Class." *Indonesia* (Oct. 1993): 2–35.

Held, David. *Foundations of Democracy: The Principle of Autonomy and the Global Order*. Cambridge: Polity Press, 1993.

———. *Political Theory and the Modern State: Essays on State, Power and Democracy*. Stanford: Stanford University Press, 1989.

Held, David, and Joel Krieger. "Accumulation, Legitimation and the State: The Ideas of Claus and Jurgen Habermas." In David Held, ed., *States and Societies*. New York: New York University Press, 1983.

Heng Pek Koon. *Chinese Politics in Malaysia: A History of the Malaysian Chinese Association*. Kuala Lumpur: Oxford University Press, 1988.

Heritage, John C. "Ethnomethodology." In Anthony Giddens and Jonathan H. Turner, eds., *Social Theory Today*. Stanford: Stanford University Press, 1987.

Hien phap nuoc Cong Hoa Xa Hoi Chu Nghia Viet Nam (binh luan), tap I–II (Constitutions of the Socialist Republic of Vietnam [comments], vols. 1–2). Hanoi: Khoa Hoc Xa Hoi, 1985.

Hien phap nuoc Cong Hoa Xa Hoi Chu Nghia Viet Nam 1992 (Constitution of the Socialist Republic of Vietnam, 1992). Hanoi: Phap Ly, 1992.

Ho Chi Minh. "Appeal on the Occasion of the Sixth Anniversary of the National Resistance War." In *Selected Works*, vol. 3. Hanoi: Foreign Language Publication House, 1961.

———. "Con duong dan toi den chu nghia Le-Nin" (The path that led me to Leninism). In *Ho Chi Minh toan tap, 1958–1960* (Ho Chi Minh's writings, 1958–1960). Hanoi: Vien Mac-Lenin, 1989.

———. *Ho Chu Tich ban ve giao duc* (President Ho discussing education). Hanoi: Giao Duc, 1962.

———. "Tinh than yeu nuoc cua dan ta" (The patriotic spirit of our people). In *Van tuyen, lop bay, tap II* (Literary excerpts, grade 7, vol. 2). Hanoi: Giao Duc, 1959.

Hoang Minh Chinh. "Gop y ve du thao cuong linh" (Comments on the draft platforms). *Dien Dan Nguoi Viet* (Spring 1991): 16–18.

Hoang Van Hao, Pham Hong Thai, and Tran Ngoc Duong. *Tim hieu ve doi moi to chuc va hoat dong cua bo may nha nuoc theo hien phap nam 1992* (On renovating the organization and activities of the state apparatus as stated in the 1992 Constitution). Hanoi: Chinh Tri Quoc Gia, 1994.

Hobsbawm, Eric J. *Bandits*. New York: Pantheon, 1969.

———. "Introduction: Inventing Traditions." In Eric J. Hobsbawm, ed., *The Invention of Tradition*. New York: Cambridge University Press, 1983.

Hodgson, Marshall G. S. *The Venture of Islam*. Vol. 2. Chicago: University of Chicago Press, 1974.

Hollnsteiner, Mary R. *The Dynamics of Power in a Philippine Municipality*. Quezon City: University of the Philippines, Community Development Research Council, 1963.

Holston, James. "The Misrule of Law: Land and Usurpation in Brazil." *Comparative Studies in Society and History* 33(4) (Oct. 1991): 695.

Holt, Claire, ed. *Culture and Politics in Indonesia*. Ithaca: Cornell University Press, 1972.

Honey, P. J. *Communism in North Vietnam: Its Role in the Sino-Soviet Dispute*. Cambridge, Mass.: MIT Press, 1963.

———. "The Death of Ho Chi Minh and After." *China News Analysis* 785 (Dec. 12, 1969): 1–7.

———, ed. *North Vietnam Today: Profile of a Communist Satellite*. New York: Praeger, 1962.

Hong Nam and Hong Linh. *Nhung trang su ve vang cua dan toc Viet Nam chong phong kien Trung Quoc xam luoc* (Glorious historical episodes of the Vietnamese nation in its resistance against the feudalist Chinese invasion). Hanoi: Su That, 1984.

Horowitz, Donald. *Ethnic Groups in Conflict*. Berkeley: University of California Press, 1985.

Horowitz, Irving Louis. "The Norm of Illegitimacy: Ten Years Later." In Bogdan Denitch, ed., *Legitimation of Regimes*. Beverly Hills: Sage, 1979.

Houtart, François, and Genevieve Lemercinier. *Hai Van: Life in a Vietnamese Commune*. London: Zed Books, 1984.

Huntington, Samuel P. "The Goals of Development." In Myron Weiner and Samuel P. Huntington, eds., *Understanding Political Development*. Boston: Little, Brown, 1987.

———. "Political Change in the Third World." In Myron Weiner and Samuel P. Huntington, eds., *Understanding Political Development*. Boston: Little, Brown, 1987.

———. *Political Order in Changing Societies*. New Haven: Yale University Press, 1968.

———. *The Third Wave: Democratization in the Late Twentieth Century*. Norman: University of Oklahoma Press, 1991.

Hutchcroft, Paul D. "Oligarchs and Cronies in the Philippine State: The Politics of Patrimonial Plunder." *World Politics* 43(3) (Apr. 1991): 413–50.

Huynh Kim Khanh. "Revolution at an Impasse: Impressions of Vietnamese Communism Circa 1990." In Richard Stubbs, ed., *Vietnam Facing the 1990s*. Toronto: Joint Center for Asia Pacific Studies, 1989.

———. *Vietnamese Communism, 1925–1945*. Ithaca and London: Cornell University Press, 1980.

Hy Van Luong. *Revolution in the Village: Tradition and Transformation in North Vietnam, 1925–1988*. Honolulu: University of Hawaii Press, 1992.

Ibrahim, Zuraidah. "Will Income Gap Divide S'pore?" *Straits Times*, May 29, 1993.

Ileto, Reynaldo Clemeña. "The Past in the Present Crisis." In R. J. May and Francisco Nemenzo, eds., *The Philippines After Marcos*. New York: St. Martin's Press, 1985.

———. *Pasyon and Revolution: Popular Movements in the Philippines, 1840–1910*. Quezon City: Ateneo de Manila University Press, 1979.

———. "Rizal and the Underside of Philippine History." In David K. Wyatt and Alexander Woodside, eds., *Moral Order and the Question of Change: Essays on Southeast Asian Thought*. New Haven: Yale University Southeast Asia Studies, 1982.

Ingleson, John. *Jalan Ke Pengasingan*. Jakarta: LP3ES, 1983.

Iskenderof, A. "The Army, Politics, and the People." In H. Bienen, ed., *The Military and Modernization*. New York: Atherton, 1971.

Jackson, Peter A. "Thai Buddhist Identity." In Craig J. Reynolds, ed., *National Identity and Its Defenders*. Victoria: Aristoc Press, 1991.

Jackson, Robert, and Carl G. Rosberg. "Why Africa's Weak States Persist: The Empirical and the Juridical in Statehood." *World Politics* 35(1) (1982): 1–24.

Jamieson, Neil L. *Understanding Vietnam*. Berkeley: University of California Press, 1993.

Jenkins, David. *Suharto and His Generals: Indonesian Military Politics, 1975–1983*. Monograph Series. Ithaca: Cornell Modern Indonesia Project, 1984.

Jesudason, James V. *Ethnicity and the Economy: The State, Chinese Business, and Multinationals in Malaysia*. Singapore: Oxford University Press, 1989.

Joeniarto. *Undang-Undang Dasar 1945 sebagai Hukum Negara Tertinggi*. Jakarta: PT. Bina Aksara, 1982.

Jomo, K. S. *Growth and Structural Change in the Malaysian Economy*. London: Macmillan, 1990.

———. *A Question of Class: Capital, the State, and Uneven Development in Malaya*. New York: Monthly Review Press, 1988.

Jones, Gregg R. *Red Revolution: Inside the Philippine Guerrilla Movement*. Boulder: Westview Press, 1989.

Kahin, Audrey R. "Crisis on the Periphery: The Rift Between Kuala Lumpur and Sabah." *Pacific Affairs* 65(1) (1992): 30–49.

Kahin, George McTurnan. *Intervention: How America Became Involved in Vietnam*. New York: Knopf, 1986.

———. *Nationalism and Revolution in Indonesia*. Ithaca: Cornell University Press, 1952.

Kahn, Joel S. "Class, Ethnicity, and Diversity: Some Remarks on Malay Culture in Malaysia." In Joel S. Kahn and Francis Loh Kok Wah, eds., *Fragmented Vision: Culture and Politics in Contemporary Malaysia*. Sydney: Allen & Unwin, 1992.

Karnow, Stanley. *In Our Image: America's Empire in the Philippines*. New York: Random House, 1989.

Kartodirdjo, Sartono. "Agrarian Radicalism in Java: Its Setting and Development." In Claire Holt, ed., *Culture and Politics in Indonesia*. Ithaca: Cornell University Press, 1972.

———. *Protest Movements in Rural Java*. Kuala Lumpur: Oxford University Press, 1973.

———. *Tjatatan Tentang Segi-Segi Mesianistis Dalam Sedjarah Indonesia*. Yogyakarta: Penerbitan Lustrum ke-II, Universitas Gadjah Mada, 1959.

Kasetsiri, Charnwit. "The First Pibul Government and Its Involvement in World War II." *Journal of Siam Society* 70(2) (1974): 121–73.

Kaufeler, Heinz. *Modernization, Legitimacy and Social Movement*. Zurich: Ethnologische Seminar der Universität, 1988.

Kayam, Umar. "Transformasi Budaya Kita." Professorial address. Yogyakarta: Universitas Gadjah Mada, 1989.

Keesing, Roger M. "Kastom Re-examined." *Anthropological Forum* 6(4) (1993): 587–96.

Kelly, Amzi B. *His Majesty King Torrens: An Impartial Constructive Criticism of Our Land Registration Under the Torrens Title System*. Manila: n.p., 1920.

———. "La Oficina de Aduanas Sigue Siendo una Mina de Oro." *Chismes y Escandalos*, May 19, 1934.

Kerkvliet, Benedict J. "Classes and Class Relations in a Philippine Village." *Philippine Sociological Review* 28 (1980): 31–50.

———. *Everyday Politics in the Philippines: Class and Status Relations in a Central Luzon Village*. Berkeley: University of California Press, 1990.

———. *The Huk Rebellion: A Study of Peasant Revolt in the Philippines*. Berkeley: University of California Press, 1977.

Kerkvliet, Benedict J., and Resil B. Mojares, eds. *From Marcos to Aquino: Local Perspectives on Political Transition in the Philippines*. Quezon City: Ateneo de Manila University Press, 1991.

Kessler, Clive S. "Archaism and Modernity: Contemporary Malay Political Culture." In Joel S. Kahn and Francis Loh Kok Wah, eds., *Fragmented*

Vision: Culture and Politics in Contemporary Malaysia. Sydney: Allen & Unwin, 1992.

———. "Reactualizing Islam in Our Times: Faith, Law and the State in Malaysia." Paper presented to the conference on Islam and the Social Construction of Identities: Comparative Perspectives on Southeast Asian Muslims, organized by the University of Hawaii and the East-West Center in Honolulu, Aug. 4–6, 1993.

Khasnor, Johan. *The Emergence of the Modern Malay Administrative Elite.* Singapore: Oxford University Press, 1984.

Khong, C. O. "Leadership and National Security: The Search for Institutional Control." In Stephen Chee, ed., *Leadership and Security in Southeast Asia: Institutional Aspects.* Singapore: Institute of Southeast Asian Studies, 1991.

———. "The Politics of Bureaucracy." *Far Eastern Economic Review*, Sept. 19, 1991, p. 19.

Khong Kim Hoong. *Malaysia's General Election 1990: Continuity, Change, and Ethnic Politics.* Singapore: Institute of Southeast Asian Studies, 1991.

Khoo Kay Jin. "The Grand Vision: Mahathir and Modernization." In Joel S. Kahn and Francis Loh Kok Wah, eds., *Fragmented Vision: Culture and Politics in Contemporary Malaysia.* Sydney: Allen & Unwin, 1992.

Kiefer, Thomas M. *The Tausug: Violence and Law in a Philippine Moslem Society.* New York: Holt, Rinehart & Winston, 1972.

Kirsch, A. Thomas. *Feasting and Social Oscillation: Religion and Society in Upland Southeast Asia.* Ithaca: Cornell University Southeast Asia Program, 1973.

Koentjaraningrat. *Javanese Culture.* Singapore: Oxford University Press, 1985.

Kohli, Atul. *Democracy and Discontent: India's Growing Crisis of Governability.* New York: Cambridge University Press, 1990.

Kok Wee Kiat. "Facing the Future." In Dato' Dr. Ling Liong Sik et al., *The Future of Malaysian Chinese.* Kuala Lumpur: Malaysian Chinese Association, 1988.

Kornai, Janos. *Economics of Shortage.* Amsterdam: North-Holland, 1980.

Korver, A. P. E. *Sarekat Islam, 1912–1916.* Amsterdam: Historische Seminarium van de Universiteit van Amsterdam, 1982.

Krause, Lawrence B. "Government as Entrepreneur." In Kernial Singh Sandhu and Paul Wheatley, eds., *Management of Success: The Moulding of Modern Singapore.* Singapore: Institute of Southeast Asian Studies, 1989.

Krissantono. "Ali Moertopo di Atas Panggung Orde Baru." *Prisma*, Edisi Khusus 20 Tahun. Jakarta: LP3ES, 1991.

Krueger, Anne O. "The Political Economy of the Rent-Seeking Society." *American Economic Review* 64(3) (June 1974): 302.

Kuo, Eddie C. Y., Duncan Holaday, and Eugenia Peck. *Mirror on the Wall: Media in a Singapore Election.* Singapore: Asian Mass Communication Research and Information Centre, 1993.

Kurihara, Hirohide. "Changes in the Literary Policy of the Vietnamese Workers' Party, 1956–1958." In Takashi Shiraishi and Motoo Furata, eds., *Indochina in the 1940s and 1950s.* Ithaca: Southeast Asia Program, Cornell University, 1992.

Lacaba, Jose F. *Days of Disquiet, Nights of Rage: The First Quarter Storm and Related Events.* Manila: Asphodel Books, 1986.

Lake, Anthony. "From Containment to Enlargement." *Dispatch* 4(39) (1993): 658–64.

Lande, Carl H. *Leaders, Factions, and Parties: The Structure of Philippine Politics.* New Haven: Yale University Southeast Asia Studies, 1965.

———. "The Political Crisis." In John Bresnan, ed., *Crisis in the Philippines.* Princeton: Princeton University Press, 1986.

Lansang, Angel J. *Cockfighting in the Philippines.* Quezon City: Progressive Printing Palace, 1966.

Laothammatas, Anek. *Business Associations and the New Political Economy of Thailand.* Boulder: Westview Press, 1992.

———. "The Politics of Structural Adjustment in Thailand: A Political Explanation of Economic Success." In Andrew J. MacIntyre and Kanishka Jayasuriya, eds., *The Dynamics of Economic Policy Reform in South-East Asia and the South-West Pacific.* Singapore: Oxford University Press, 1992.

———. "Sleeping Giant Awakens?: The Middle Class in Thai Politics." Paper prepared for the Conference on Democratic Experience in Southeast Asian Countries, Dec. 7–8, 1991, at Thammasat University, Bangkok.

Larkin, John A. *The Pampangans: Colonial Society in a Philippine Province.* Berkeley: University of California Press, 1972.

———. *Sugar and the Origins of Modern Philippine Society.* Berkeley: University of California Press, 1993.

Lau Teik Soon. "Malaysia: The May 13 Incident." *Australia's Neighbors* 4(65) (1969): 1–4.

Lawson, Stephanie. *Some Conceptual Issues in the Study of Regime Change.* Discussion Paper 3, Political and Social Change. Canberra: Research School of Pacific Studies, Australian National University, 1991.

Le Duan. *Cach mang xa hoi chu nghia o Viet Nam, tap IV* (The socialist revolution in Vietnam, vol. 4). Hanoi: Su That, 1984.

Le Mau Han, ed. *Cac dai hoi Dang ta (1930–1986)* (Our party congresses, 1930–1986). Hanoi: Su That, 1991.

Le Thanh Khoi. *Socialisme et développement au Viet Nam.* Paris: Presses universitaires de France, 1978.

Leach, Edmund. *The Political System of Highland Burma.* London: G. W. Bell, 1964.

Lee Kuan Yew. "Democracy and Human Rights by Lee Kuan Yew." *Australia and World Affairs* 16 (Autumn 1993): 5–15.

———. "Text of a Speech by the Prime Minister, Mr. Lee Kuan Yew, at the Official Opening of the Civil Service Study Center." Singapore government press statement, Aug. 15, 1959.

Lee, Raymond. "Symbols of Separatism: Ethnicity and Status Politics in Contemporary Malaysia." In Raymond Lee, ed., *Ethnicity and Ethnic Relations in Malaysia.* De Kalb: Northern Illinois University, Center for Southeast Asian Studies, 1986.

Leftwich, Adrian. "Governance, Democracy and Development in the Third World." *Third World Quarterly* 14(3) (1993): 605–24.

Legarda, Benito Fernandez, Jr. "Foreign Trade, Economic Change and Entrepreneurship in the Nineteenth-Century Philippines." Ph.D. dissertation, Harvard University, 1955.

Lehman, F. K., ed. *Military Rule in Burma Since 1962: A Kaleidoscope of Views.* Singapore: Maruzen Asia, 1981.

Leifer, Michael. *Dilemmas of Statehood in Southeast Asia.* Singapore: Asia Pacific Press, 1972.

———. "Triumph of the Will." *Far Eastern Economic Review*, Nov. 15, 1990, pp. 27–34.

Lewis, Bernard. *The Political Languages of Islam.* Chicago: University of Chicago Press, 1988.

Lewis, Paul. "Introduction" to the section on power, legitimacy, and the state. In David Held, ed., *States and Societies.* New York: New York University Press, 1983.

Li, Tania. *Malays in Singapore: Culture, Economy, and Ideology.* Singapore: Oxford University Press, 1989.

Liddle, R. William. "Merekayasa Demokrasi di Indonesia." *Kompas*, Feb. 2–3, 1990, pp. 4–5.

———. "Modernizing Indonesian Politics." In R. William Liddle, ed., *Political Participation in Modern Indonesia.* Monograph Series, No. 19. New Haven: Yale University Southeast Asia Studies, 1973.

———. *Politics and Culture in Indonesia.* Ann Arbor: Center for Political Studies, Institute for Social Research, University of Michigan, 1988.

———. "Skripturalisme *Media Dakwah*: Satu Bentuk Pemikiran dan Aksi Politik Islam Masa Orde Baru." *Ulumul Qur'an* 3(4) (1993): 53–65.

———. "Soeharto's Indonesia: Personal Rule and Political Institutions." *Pacific Affairs* 58 (1985): 68–90.

———. "A Useful Fiction: Democratic Legitimation in New Order Indonesia." Paper presented at a conference on Elections in Southeast Asia at the Woodrow Wilson Center, Washington, D.C., Sept. 13, 1993.

———, ed. *Political Participation in Modern Indonesia.* Monograph Series, No. 19. New Haven: Yale University Southeast Asia Studies, 1973.

Lieban, Richard W. *Cebuano Sorcery: Malign Magic in the Philippines.* Berkeley: University of California Press, 1967.

Lieberman, Victor. *Burmese Administrative Cycle: Anarchy and Conquest.* Princeton: Princeton University Press, 1984.

———. "Review of Robert Taylor's *The State in Burma*." *Journal of Asian Studies* 7(4) (Nov. 1988): 952–53.

Lijphart, Arend. *Democracy in Plural Societies: A Comparative Exploration.* New Haven: Yale University Press, 1977.

Lim Kit Siang. "Introduction." In Democratic Action Party, *25 Years of Struggle: Milestones in DAP History.* Petaling Jaya, Malaysia: Democratic Action Party, 1991.

Lindstrom, Lamont, and Geoffrey M. White. "Introduction: Custom Today." *Anthropological Forum* (University of Western Australia) 4(4) (1993): 467–74.

Lintner, Bertil. "All the Wrong Moves: Only the Black Economy Is Keeping Burma Afloat." *Far Eastern Economic Review*, Oct. 27, 1988, p. 83.

———. "Border Heroin Trade." *Far Eastern Economic Review*, Feb. 28, 1992, pp. 23–24.

———. "Conventional Wisdom: Junta's Attempt to Amend Constitution Fails." *Far Eastern Economic Review*, Feb. 18, 1993, p. 20.

———. "The New Dealers." *Far Eastern Economic Review*, Mar. 28, 1991, p. 26.

———. *Outrage: Burma's Struggle for Democracy*. Hong Kong: Review Publishing House, 1989.

———. "Review of Robert Taylor's *The State in Burma*." *Asian Studies Review* 13(3) (1990): 178–80.

———. *The Rise and Fall of the Communist Party of Burma (CPB)*. Ithaca: Cornell University Press, 1990.

———. "The Shans and the Shan State of Burma." *Contemporary Southeast Asia* 5(4) (1984): 403–50.

———. *Territory Briefing (No. 1): Crossborder Drug Trade in the Golden Triangle (S.E. Asia)*. Durham: Boundary Research Press, 1991.

Lipset, S. M. *Political Man*. New York: Doubleday, 1960.

Lockhart, Greg. *Nations in Arms: The Origins of the People's Army of Vietnam*. Sydney: Allen & Unwin, 1989.

Loeb, Vernon. "Despite Fear, Democracy's 'Fire' Burns." *Miami Herald*, May 6, 1989.

Loh Kok Wah, Francis. "Modernization, Cultural Revival and Counter-hegemony: The Kadazans of Sabah in the 1980s." In Joel S. Kahn and Francis Loh Kok Wah, eds., *Fragmented Vision: Culture and Politics in Contemporary Malaysia*. Sydney: Allen & Unwin, 1992.

Loh Kok Wah, Francis, and Joel S. Kahn. "Introduction: Fragmented Vision." In Joel S. Kahn and Francis Loh Kok Wah, eds., *Fragmented Vision: Culture and Politics in Contemporary Malaysia*. Sydney: Allen & Unwin, 1992.

Lorenzo-Abrera, Ma. Bernadette G. *Ang Numismatika ng Anting-Anting: Panimulang Paghawan ng Isang Landas Tungo Sa Pag-Unawa ng Kasaysayan at Kalinangan Pilipino*. Quezon City: Unibersidad ng Pilipinas, Programang Kaalamang Bayan, Tanggapan ng Dekano, Dalubhasaan ng Agham Panlipunan at Pilosopiya, 1992.

Love, Robert S. "The *Samahan* of Papa God: Tradition and Conversion in a Tagalog Religious Movement." Ph.D. dissertation, Cornell University, 1977.

Luat to chuc chinh phu nuoc Cong Hoa Xa Hoi Chu Nghia Viet Nam (Law organizing the government of the Socialist Republic of Vietnam). Hanoi: Phap Ly, 1992.

Luhmann, Niklas. *A Sociological Theory of Law*. Boston: Routledge, 1985.

Luu Quang Vu. *Back to His Home Village*. Hanoi: FLPH, 1981.

McAlister, John T., Jr., and Paul Mus. *The Vietnamese and Their Revolution*. New York: Harper Torchbooks, 1970.

McCoy, Alfred W. "*Baylan*: Animist Religion and Philippine Peasant Ideology." In David K. Wyatt and Alexander Woodside, eds., *Moral Order and the Question of Change: Essays on Southeast Asian Thought*. New Haven: Yale University Southeast Asia Studies, 1982.

McCullough, Erskine. "Terror Continues Under Secret Rule of Ne Win." *Bangkok Post*, Sept. 9, 1991.

MacDougall, Hugh C., and Jon A. Wiant. "Burma in 1985: Consolidation Triumphs over Innovation." *Asian Survey* 26(2) (1986): 186–95.

Machado, K. G. "Changing Aspects of Factionalism in Philippine Local Politics." *Asian Survey* (Dec. 1971): 1182–99.

Mackenzie, Ann. "People Power or Palace Coup: The Fall of Marcos." In Mark Turner, ed., *Regime Change in the Philippines: The Legitimation of the Aquino Government*. Political and Social Change Monograph 7. Canberra: Australian National University, Research School of Pacific Studies, 1987.

Mackie, J. A. C., ed. *The Chinese in Indonesia*. Honolulu: University of Hawaii Press, 1976.

Mackie, Jamie, and Bernardo M. Villegas. "The Philippines: An Unusual Case." In James W. Morley, ed., *Driven by Growth: Political Change in the Asia-Pacific Region*. Armonk, N.Y.: M. E. Sharpe, 1993.

McVey, Ruth T. "The Beamtenstaat in Indonesia." In Benedict Anderson and Audrey Kahin, eds., *Interpreting Indonesian Politics: Thirteen Contributions to the Debate*. Interim Reports Series 62. Ithaca: Cornell Modern Indonesia Project, Southeast Asia Program, Cornell University, 1982.

———. *The Rise of Indonesian Communism*. Ithaca: Cornell University Press, 1965.

———, ed. *Indonesia*. New Haven: Southeast Asia Studies, Yale University, by arrangement with HRAF Press, 1963.

———, ed. *Southeast Asian Transitions*. New Haven: Yale University Press, 1978.

Majul, Cesar A. "Succession in the Old Sulu Sultanate." *Philippine Historical Review* 1(1) (1964): 252–71.

Marcos, Ferdinand E. *The Democratic Revolution in the Philippines*. Manila: n.p., 1977.

———. *An Ideology for Filipinos*. Manila: n.p., 1980.

———. *Tadhana: A History of the Filipino People*. 3 vols. Manila: n.p., 1976–.

Marr, David G. *Vietnamese Tradition on Trial, 1920–1945*. Berkeley: University of California Press, 1981.

Marr, David G., and Christine White, eds. *Postwar Vietnam: Dilemmas in Socialist Development*. Ithaca: Southeast Asia Program, Cornell University, 1988.

Mas'oed, Mohtar. *Ekonomi dan Struktur Politik: Orde Baru 1966–1971*. Jakarta: LP3ES, 1989.

Maung Maung. *Burma and General Ne Win*. New Delhi: Asia Publishing House, 1969.

Maung Maung Gyi. *Burmese Political Values: The Sociopolitical Roots of Authoritarianism*. New York: Praeger, 1965.

Mauzy, Diane K. "Malaysia in 1987: Decline of 'the Malay Way.'" *Asian Survey* 28(2) (1988): 213–22.

May, Glenn A. "Civic Ritual and Political Reality: Municipal Elections in the Late Nineteenth Century." In Ruby Paredes, ed., *Philippine Colonial Democracy*. Quezon City: Ateneo de Manila University Press, 1989.

Mayall, James. *Nationalism and International Society*. Cambridge: Cambridge University Press, 1990.

Means, Gordon P. *Malaysian Politics*. 2nd ed. London: Hodder & Stoughton, 1976.

———. *Malaysian Politics: The Second Generation*. Singapore: Oxford University Press, 1991.

———. "Review of Robert Taylor's *The State in Burma*." *Contemporary Southeast Asia* 10(3) (Dec. 1988): 328–30.

Medina, Isagani R. "Cavite Before the Revolution, 1571–1896." Ph.D. dissertation, University of the Philippines, 1985.

Mednick, Melvin. "Sultans and Mayors: The Relation of a National to an Indigenous Political System." In Abdullah T. Madale and Mamitua Saber, eds., *The Maranao*. Manila: Solidaridad Publishing House, 1975.

Mehmet, Ozay. *Development in Malaysia: Poverty, Wealth, and Trusteeship*. Petaling Jaya, Malaysia: INSAN, 1988.

Mektrairatana, Nakharin. *Karn Patiwat Sayam*. Bangkok: Moolanithi Krongkarn Tamra, 1992.

Melendez-Cruz, Patricia, and Apolonio Bayani Chua, eds. *Himalay: Kalipunan ng mga Pag-aaral kay Jose Rizal*. Manila: Sentrong Pangkultura ng Pilipinas, 1991.

Mercado, Monina Allarey, ed. *An Eyewitness History: People Power: The Philippine Revolution of 1986*. Manila: Reuter Foundation, 1986.

Merquior, J. G. *Rousseau and Weber: Two Studies in the Theory of Legitimacy*. London: Routledge, 1980.

Migdal, Joel. *Strong Societies and Weak States: State-Society Relations and State Capabilities in the Third World*. Princeton: Princeton University Press, 1988.

Milne, R. S. *Government and Politics in Malaysia*. Boston: Houghton Mifflin, 1967.

Milner, A. C. "Inventing Politics: The Case of Malaysia." *Past and Present* 132 (1991): 104–29.

———. *Kerajaan: Malay Political Culture on the Eve of Colonial Rule*. Tucson: University of Arizona Press, 1982.

Minchin, James. *No Man Is an Island*. Sydney: Allen & Unwin, 1986.

Mirsky, Georgy I. "The Role of the Army in the Sociopolitical Development of Asian and African Countries." *International Political Science Review* 2(3) (1981): 327–38.

Moertono, Soemarsaid. *Negara dan Usaha Bina Negara di Jawa Masa Lampau*. Jakarta: Yayasan Obor Indonesia, 1985.

Moise, Edwin. *Land Reform in China and North Vietnam: Consolidating the Revolution at the Village Level*. Chapel Hill: University of North Carolina Press, 1983.

Mojares, Resil B. "Talking Politics: Political Commentaries on Cebuano Radio." In Soledad Reyes, ed., *Reading Popular Culture*. Quezon City: Ateneo de Manila University, Office of Research and Publications, 1991.

Moore, Barrington. *Social Origins of Dictatorship and Democracy: Lord and Peasant in the Making of the Modern World*. Boston: Beacon Press, 1966.

Morell, David, and Chai-anan Samudavanija. *Political Conflict in Thailand: Reform, Reaction, Revolution*. Cambridge, Mass: Oelgeschlager, Gunn & Hain, 1981.

Mostov, Julie. *Power, Process, and Popular Sovereignty.* Philadelphia: Temple University Press, 1992.

Mouffe, Chantal. "Hegemony and Ideology in Gramsci." In Chantal Mouffe, ed., *Gramsci and Marxist Theory.* London: Routledge, 1979.

Mozaffari, Mehdi. *Authority in Islam: From Muhammad to Khomeini.* New York: M. E. Sharpe, 1987.

Mukherjee, Ramkrishna. *The Rise and Fall of the East India Company: A Sociological Approach.* 2nd ed. Berlin: VEB Deutscher Verlag der Wissenschaften, 1958.

Mya Maung. *The Burma Road to Poverty.* New York: Praeger, 1991.

———. *Totalitarianism in Burma: Prospects for Economic Development.* New York: Paragon House, 1992.

Nagata, Judith. *Malaysian Mosaic: Perspectives from a Poly-Ethnic Society.* Vancouver: University of British Columbia Press, 1979.

Nagazumi, Akira. *The Dawn of Indonesian Nationalism: The Early Years of Boedi Oetomo.* Tokyo: Institute of Developing Economies, 1972.

Nakhata, Thinaphan. "National Consolidation and Nation-Building, 1939–1947." In Thak Chaloemtiarana, ed., *Thai Politics 1932–1957.* Bangkok: Social Science Association, 1978.

Natsir, Mohammad. "The Dangers of Secularism" and "Restoring Confidence." In Herbert Feith and Lance Castles, eds., *Indonesian Political Thinking, 1945–1965.* Ithaca: Cornell University Press, 1970.

Navarro, Napoleon Gabriel Y. "How Much to Get Elected." *Manila Chronicle,* July 15–20, 1992, pp. 13, 15.

Neher, Clark. "Political Succession in Thailand." *Asian Survey* 32(7) (1992): 585–605.

Nehru, Jawaharlal. *The Discovery of India.* New York: Anchor Books, 1960.

Nelson, William N. *On Justifying Democracy.* London: Routledge, 1980.

NESDB. *The Fifth National Social and Development Plan.* Bangkok: Prime Minister's Office, 1981.

Ngamkajornkulkij, Sorasak. *Kabuankarn Seri Thai Kab Kwam Kad Yaeng Tang Karn Muang Pai Nai Prathet Thai Rawang Por Sor 2481–2492.* Bangkok: Chulalongkorn Institute of Asian Studies, 1992.

Ngo Vinh Long. *Before the Revolution: The Vietnamese Peasants Under the French.* Cambridge, Mass.: MIT Press, 1973.

———. "Reform and Rural Development: Impact on Class, Sectoral, and Regional Inequalities." In William Turley and Mark Selden, eds., *Reinventing Vietnamese Socialism: Doi Moi in Comparative Perspective.* Boulder: Westview Press, 1993.

———. "Some Aspects of Cooperativization." In David G. Marr and Christine White, eds., *Postwar Vietnam: Dilemmas in Socialist Development.* Ithaca: Southeast Asia Program, Cornell University, 1988.

Nguyen Hung Quoc. *Van hoc Viet Nam duoi che do cong san, 1945–1990* (Vietnamese literature under communism, 1945–1990). Stanton, Calif.: Van Nghe, 1991.

Nguyen Huy Thiep. *The General Retires and Other Stories.* Translated by Greg Lockhart. Singapore: Oxford University Press, 1992.

Nguyen Khac Vien. *Tradition and Revolution in Vietnam.* Comp. and trans. David Marr et al. Washington: Indochina Resource Center, 1974.

Nguyen Lai Van. "The Battle of Rice." *Vietnamese Studies* 13(6) (1967): 6–35.

Nguyen Van Linh. "Tiep tuc dua su nghiep doi moi tien len theo con duong xa hoi chu nghia" (Continuing the tasks of renovation along the socialist path). In DCSVN, *Van kien Dai hoi dai bieu toan quoc lan thu bay* (Documents of the Seventh National Party Congress). Hanoi: Su That, 1991.

———. *Van kien cua Dang Cong San Viet Nam ve van hoa van nghe (tu Dai hoi VI den Dai hoi VII)* (The VCP's statements on culture and the arts [from the Sixth to the Seventh Congress]). Hanoi: Su That, 1991.

Noble, Lela Garner. "Politics in the Marcos Era." In John Bresnan, ed., *Crisis in the Philippines.* Princeton: Princeton University Press, 1986.

Noer, Deliar. *The Modernist Muslim Movement in Indonesia, 1900–1942.* Kuala Lumpur: Oxford University Press, 1973.

———. *Partai Islam di Pentas Nasional.* Jakarta: Grafiti Pers, 1987.

Nowak, Thomas C., and Kay A. Snyder. "Clientelist Politics in the Philippines: Integration or Instability?" *American Political Science Review* 68(3) (Sept. 1974): 1147–70.

Numnonda, Thamsook. *Thailand and the Japanese Presence 1941–1945.* Singapore: Institute of Southeast Asian Studies, 1977.

Nyun Han, U. "Burma's Experiment in Socialism." Ph.D. dissertation, University of Colorado, 1970.

O'Donnell, Guillermo A. *Modernization and Bureaucratic-Authoritarianism: Studies in South American Politics.* Berkeley: Institute of International Studies, University of California, 1973.

O'Donnell, Guillermo, Philippe C. Schmitter, and Laurence Whitehead. *Transitions from Authoritarian Rule: Prospects for Democracy.* Baltimore: Johns Hopkins University Press, 1986.

O'Kane, Rosemary H. T. "Against Legitimacy." *Political Studies* 41(3) (1993): 471–87.

———. "Legitimacy and Political Science." *Political Studies* 42(1) (1994): 103–4.

Opitz, Peter J., ed. *Profile und Programme der Dritten Welt.* Munich: List Verlag, 1970.

Orentlicher, Diane F., and Pamela K. Takiff. *Vigilantes in the Philippines: A Threat to Democratic Rule.* New York: Lawyers Committee for Human Rights, 1988.

Ow Chin Hock. "The Role of Government in Economic Development: The Singapore Experience." In Lim Chong Yah and Peter J. Lloyd, eds., *Singapore: Resources and Growth.* Singapore: Oxford University Press, 1986.

Pabottingi, Mochtar. "Nationalism and Egalitarianism in Indonesia, 1908–1980." Ph.D. dissertation, University of Hawaii at Manoa, 1991.

———. "Pancasila dan Demitologi." *Prisma* (Aug. 1977).

———, ed. *Islam: Antara Visi, Tradisi, dan Hegemoni Bukan-Muslim.* Jakarta: Yayasan Obor Indonesia, 1986.

Packenham, Robert A. *The Dependency Movement: Scholarship and Politics in Development Studies.* Cambridge, Mass.: Harvard University Press, 1992.

Paget, Roger L., ed. *Indonesia Accuses: Sukarno's Defense Oration in the Political Trial of 1930*. Kuala Lumpur: Oxford University Press, 1975.

Pakulski, Jan. "Legitimacy and Mass Compliance: Reflections on Max Weber and Soviet-Type Societies." *British Journal of Political Science* 16 (1986): 35–56.

Pamungkas, Sri-Bintang. "Akankah Terjadi Perubahan-Perubahan." *Merdeka*, Mar. 1, 1993.

Pang Eng Fong, Tan Chwee Huat, and Cheng Soo May. "The Management of People." In Kernial Singh Sandhu and Paul Wheatley, eds., *Management of Success: The Moulding of Modern Singapore*. Singapore: Institute of Southeast Asian Studies, 1989.

Panikkar, K. M. *Asia and Western Dominance*. New York: Collier Books, 1969.

Paredes, Ruby, ed. *Philippine Colonial Democracy*. Quezon City: Ateneo de Manila University Press, 1989.

Parekh, Bhiku. "The Cultural Particularity of Liberal Democracy." In David Held, ed., *Prospects for Democracy*. Stanford: Stanford University Press, 1993.

Parnell, Philip C. "Time and Irony in Manila Squatter Movements." In Carolyn Nordstrom and JoAnn Martin, eds., *The Paths to Domination, Resistance, and Terror*. Berkeley: University of California Press, 1992.

Parsons, Talcott. "Introduction." In Max Weber, *Theory of Social and Economic Organization*. New York: Free Press, 1964.

Peacock, James L. *Muslim Puritans: Reformist Psychology in Southeast Asian Islam*. Berkeley: University of California Press, 1978.

Pemberton, John. "The Appearance of Order: A Politics of Culture in Colonial and Postcolonial Java." Ph.D. dissertation, Cornell University, 1989.

Pesigan, Guillermo M. *Dulang-Buhay ng Bundok Banahaw: Karanasan ng Cuidad Mistica*. Quezon City: Unibersidad ng Pilipinas, Programang Pangkaalamang Bayan, Dalubhasaan ng Agham Panlipunan at Pilosopiya, 1992.

Piewnual, Chalermkiat. *Prachatippatai Bab Thai*. Bangkok: Thai Khadi Institute, 1990.

Pimentel, Benjamin, Jr. *Edjop: The Unusual Journey of Edgar Jopson*. Quezon City: Ken Inc., 1989.

Pitsuwan, Surin. "Islam and Malay Nationalism: A Case Study of the Malay-Muslims in Southern Thailand." Ph.D. dissertation, Harvard University, 1982.

Polotan, Kerima. *Imelda Romualdez Marcos*. New York: World, 1969.

Popkin, Samuel L. *The Rational Peasant: The Political Economy of Rural Society in Vietnam*. Berkeley: University of California Press, 1979.

Porter, Gareth. *The Myth of Bloodbath*. Interim Report 2. Ithaca: Cornell University, International Relations of East Asia Project, 1972.

———. *The Politics of Counterinsurgency in the Philippines: Military and Political Options*. Honolulu: University of Hawaii, Center for Philippine Studies, 1987.

———. *Vietnam: The Politics of Bureaucratic Socialism*. Ithaca: Cornell University Press, 1993.

———. "Vietnam and the Socialist Camp: Center or Periphery?" In William S. Turley, ed., *Vietnamese Communism in Comparative Perspective*. Boulder: Westview Press, 1980.

Post, Ken. *Revolution, Socialism and Nationalism in Vietnam.* 3 vols. Hants, England: Dartmouth, 1989.

Potter, David. "Democratization in Asia." In David Held, ed., *Prospects for Democracy.* Stanford: Stanford University Press, 1993.

Przeworski, Adam. "Some Problems in the Study of the Transition to Democracy." In G. O'Donnell, P. C. Schmitter, and L. Whitehead, eds., *Transitions from Authoritarian Rule.* Baltimore: Johns Hopkins University Press, 1986.

Pye, Lucian W. *Asian Power and Politics: The Cultural Dimensions of Authority.* Cambridge, Mass.: Belknap Press, 1985.

————. *The Mandarin and Cadre: China's Political Cultures.* Michigan Monographs in Chinese Studies No. 59. Ann Arbor: Center for Chinese Studies, University of Michigan, 1988.

Quah, Jon S. T., ed. *In Search of Singapore's National Values.* Singapore: Institute of Policy Studies, 1990.

Quah, Jon S. T., Chan Heng Chee, and Seah Chee Meow, eds. "Editors' Introduction." In *Government and Politics of Singapore.* Singapore: Oxford University Press, 1987.

Quah, Jon S. T., and Stella R. Quah. "The Limits of Government Intervention." In Kernial Singh Sandhu and Paul Wheatley, eds., *Management of Success: The Moulding of Modern Singapore.* Singapore: Institute of Southeast Asian Studies, 1989.

Ra'anan, Uri. "The Nation-State Fallacy." In Joseph V. Montville, ed., *Conflict and Peacemaking in Multiethnic Societies.* Lexington, Mass.: Lexington Books, 1990.

Rabushka, Alvin, and Kenneth Shepsle. *Politics in Plural Societies: A Theory of Democratic Instability.* Columbus: Merrill, 1972.

Race, Jeffrey. *War Comes to Long An: Revolutionary Conflict in a Vietnamese Province.* Berkeley: University of California Press, 1972.

Rachbini, Didik J. "Alih Saham Sebagai Program Nasional." *Republika,* July 19, 1993, p. 6.

————. "Bumerang Utang." *Tempo,* June 5, 1993, p. 6.

Rafael, Vicente L. *Contracting Colonialism: Translation and Christian Conversion in Tagalog Society Under Early Spanish Rule.* Quezon City: Ateneo de Manila University Press, 1988.

————. "Patronage and Pornography: Ideology and Spectatorship in the Early Marcos Years." *Comparative Studies in Society and History* 32(2) (Apr. 1990): 282–304.

Raffles, Thomas Stamford. *The History of Java.* Vol. 1. Kuala Lumpur: Oxford University Press, 1965. Originally published in 1817.

Rambo, A. Terry. *A Comparison of Peasant Social Systems of Northern and Southern Vietnam: A Study of Ecological Adaptation, Social Succession, and Cultural Evolution.* Carbondale: Center for Vietnamese Studies at Southern Illinois University, 1973.

Ramli, Rizal. "Industrialisasi di Indonesia: Tantangan untuk PJPT II." Paper delivered at the Seminar on Indonesian Democracy Since 1945 in Jakarta, May 24–25, 1993, arranged by Akademi Ilmu Pengetahuan Indonesia, YIIS, and LIPI.

Rao, V. V. Bhanoji. "Role of Government in Singapore's Economic Development." Paper presented at a conference on The Fiscal System of Singapore: Trends, Issues, and Future Directions, Singapore, Feb. 8–10, 1990.

Ravenholt, Albert. "The Peso Price of Politics." *American University Field Staff Reports*, May 17, 1958.

Reid, Anthony. *Southeast Asia in the Age of Commerce, 1450–1680*. New Haven: Yale University Press, 1988.

———, ed. *The Making of an Islamic Political Discourse in Southeast Asia*. Monash Papers on Southeast Asia 27. Clayton, Victoria: Center of Southeast Asian Studies, Monash University, 1993.

Renan, Ernest. "What Is a Nation?" In Robert A. Goldwin, ed., *Readings in World Politics*. New York: Oxford University Press, 1970.

Report of the Economic Committee. *The Singapore Economy: New Directions*. Singapore: Ministry of Trade and Industry, 1986.

Reyes, Soledad S. *The Romance Mode in Philippine Literature and Other Essays*. Manila: De La Salle University Press, 1991.

Reynolds, Craig J., ed. *National Identity and Its Defenders: Thailand, 1939–1989*. Victoria: Aristoc Press, 1991.

Ricklefs, M. C. *War, Culture and Economy in Java 1677–1726*. Southeast Asia Publication Series. Sydney: ASAA, 1993.

Rigby, T. H., Archie Brown, and Peter Reddaway. *Authority, Power and Policy in the USSR*. New York: St. Martin's Press, 1980.

Rigby, T. H., and Ferenc Fehrer, eds. *Political Legitimation in Communist States*. London: Macmillan, 1982.

Riggs, Fred W. *Thailand: The Modernization of a Bureaucratic Polity*. Honolulu: East-West Center, 1966.

Robinson, Thomas, ed. *Democracy and Development in East Asia*. Washington, D.C.: AEI Press, 1991.

Robison, Richard. *Indonesia: The Rise of Capital*. North Sydney: Allen & Unwin, 1986.

Ronnas, Per, and Orjan Sjoberg. "Economic Reform in Vietnam: Dismantling the Centrally Planned Economy." *Journal of Communist Studies* 7(1) (1991): 7–19.

———, eds. *Doi Moi: Economic Reforms and Development Policies in Vietnam*. Stockholm: SIDA, SSSE/CIEM, 1990.

Rosaldo, Renato. *Culture and Truth: The Remaking of Social Analysis*. Boston: Beacon Press, 1989.

———. *Ilongot Headhunting, 1883–1974*. Stanford: Stanford University Press, 1980.

Rosenberg, David A., ed. *Marcos and Martial Law in the Philippines*. Ithaca: Cornell University Press, 1979.

Roth, Guenther. "Traditional Patrimonialism and Personal Rulership." In Reinhard Bendix, ed., *States and Societies*. Berkeley: University of California Press, 1968.

Rothschild, Joseph. "Political Legitimacy in Contemporary Europe." In Bogdan Denis Denitch, ed., *Legitimation of Regimes: International Framework for Analysis*. Beverly Hills: Sage, 1979.

Rothstein, Robert L. "Democracy and Conflict." In Edy Kaufman, Shukri D. Abed, and Robert L. Rothstein, eds., *Democracy, Peace and the Israeli-Palestinian Conflict.* Boulder: Rienner, 1993.

Rueschemeyer, D., E. Stephens, and J. Stephens. *Capitalist Development and Democracy.* Cambridge: Polity Press, 1992.

Sadka, Emily. *The Protected Malay States, 1874–1895.* Kuala Lumpur: University of Malaya Press, 1968.

———. "The State Councils in Perak and Selangor." In K. G. Tregonning, ed., *Papers on Malayan History.* Singapore: Journal of South-East Asian History, 1962.

Sahlins, Marshall. *Historical Metaphors and Mythical Realities.* Ann Arbor: University of Michigan Press, 1981.

———. *Islands of History.* Chicago: University of Chicago Press, 1985.

———. "Poor Man, Rich Man, Big-Man, Chief: Political Types in Melanesia and Polynesia." *Comparative Studies in Society and History* 5(3) (Apr. 1963): 285–303.

Samudavanija, Chai-anan. *Nuang Roi Pee Haenng Karn Patiroop Rabob Rachak-arn: Wiwatana Karn Kong Amnat Rat Lae Amnat Karn Maung.* Bangkok: Chulalongkorn Research Unit, 1992.

———. "State Identity Creation, State-Building and Civil Society." In Craig J. Reynolds, ed., *National Identity and Its Defenders: Thailand, 1939–1989.* Victoria: Aristoc Press, 1991.

———. *The Thai Young Turks.* Singapore: Institute of Southeast Asian Studies, 1982.

Samudavanija, Chai-anan, and Kattiya Kannasootara, eds. *Ekasarn Karn Muang Karn Pokrong Thai Por Sor 2417–2477.* Bangkok: Moolanithi Krongkarn Tamra, 1972.

Samudavanija, Chai-anan, and Sukhumbhand Paribatra. "Liberalization Without Democracy: Growth, Development and Political Change in the Asia-Pacific Region." Paper presented at a conference organized by the East Asian Institute, Columbia University, June 20–22, 1988, at Hua Hin, Thailand.

Samudavanija, Chai-anan, and Kanok Wongtrangan. *Bhasa Kab Karn Muang* (Language and politics). Bangkok: Chao Phraya, 1983.

Sangermano, Fr. V. *The Burmese Empire.* London: S. Gupta, 1966.

Santasombat, Yos. "The End of Premocracy in Thailand." In *Southeast Asian Affairs 1989.* Singapore: Institute of Southeast Asian Studies, 1990.

Sao Saimong Mangrai. *The Shan State and the British Annexation.* Ithaca: Cornell University, Southeast Asia Program, 1965.

Sarkisyanz, E. *Buddhist Background of the Burmese Revolution.* The Hague: Martinus Nijhoff, 1965.

"Sau 30 nam hop tac hoa nong nghiep: doi song nong dan va van de quan ly san xuat nong nghiep hien nay" (Thirty years of agricultural cooperativization: peasants' living conditions and the present problems of agricultural production). In *Thuc trang kinh te xa hoi Viet Nam giai doan 1986–1990* (Vietnam's socioeconomic conditions, 1986–1990). Hanoi: Tap Chi Thong Ke, 1990.

Scalapino, Robert A. "Legitimacy and Institutionalization in Asian Socialist Society." In Robert Scalapino et al., eds., *Asian Political Institutionalization.* Berkeley: Institute of East Asian Studies, University of California, 1986.

———. "National Political Institutions and Leadership in Asia." *Washington Quarterly* 15(4) (Autumn 1992): 157–72.

Schaar, John H. *Legitimacy in the Modern State.* New Brunswick: Transaction Books, 1981.

Schutz, Barry M., and Robert O. Slater, eds. *Revolution and Political Change in the Third World.* Boulder: Rienner, 1990.

Scigliano, Robert. *South Vietnam: Nation Under Stress.* Westport, Conn.: Greenwood Press, 1964.

Scott, James C. *Domination and the Arts of Resistance: Hidden Transcripts.* New Haven: Yale University Press, 1990.

———. "The Erosion of Patron-Client Bonds and Social Change in Rural Southeast Asia." *Journal of Asian Studies* 32(1) (Nov. 1972): 5–37.

———. *The Moral Economy of the Peasant: Rebellion and Subsistence in Southeast Asia.* New Haven: Yale University Press, 1976.

———. "Patron-Client Politics and Political Change in Southeast Asia." *American Political Science Review* 66(1) (Mar. 1972): 91–113.

———. *Weapons of the Weak: Everyday Forms of Peasant Resistance.* New Haven: Yale University Press, 1985.

Scott, James C., and Benedict J. Kerkvliet. "How Traditional Rural Patrons Lose Legitimacy." In Steffen W. Schmidt, Laura Guasti, Carl H. Lande, and James C. Scott, eds., *Friends, Followers, and Factions: A Reader in Political Clientelism.* Berkeley: University of California Press, 1977.

Scott, Margaret. "Where the Quota Is King." *New York Times Magazine,* Nov. 17, 1991, pp. 62–67, 111.

Scott, William Henry. *Slavery in the Spanish Philippines.* Manila: De La Salle University Press, 1991.

Searle, Peter. "Rent-Seekers or Real Capitalists? The Riddle of Malaysian Capitalists." Forthcoming thesis, Department of Political and Social Change, Australian National University.

Selvan, T. S. *Singapore: The Ultimate Island.* Melbourne: Freeway Books, 1990.

Sesser, Stan. "A Rich Country Gone Wrong." *New Yorker,* Oct. 9, 1989, pp. 55–96.

Shafruddin Hashim. "Malaysia 1991: Consolidation, Challenges, and New Directions." In *Southeast Asian Affairs 1992.* Singapore: Institute of Southeast Asian Studies, 1992.

Shalom, Stephen Rosskam. *The United States and the Philippines: A Study of Neocolonialism.* Quezon City: New Day, 1986.

Shamsul A. B. "The 'Battle Royal': The UMNO Elections of 1987." In Mohammed Ayoob and Ng Chee Yuen, eds., *Southeast Asian Affairs 1988.* Singapore: Institute of Southeast Asian Studies, n.d.

Shan State Government. *Pry-Ne Baungzon Nyila-Khan Gyi* (Taunggyi Conference, Meeting Records). Taunggyi: Shan State Government, 1961.

Shan State War Council, Shan State Army. *Shan State Army: Position Paper on the Union of Burma 1948–1962.* Liberated Area: Office of the Chairman, 1964.

Shantz, Alan Arthur. "Political Parties: The Changing Foundations of Philippine Democracy." Ph.D. diss., University of Michigan, 1972.

Shiraishi, Takashi. *An Age in Motion: Popular Radicalism in Java, 1912–1926.* Ithaca: Cornell University Press, 1990.

Shue, Vivienne. *The Reach of the State.* Stanford: Stanford University Press, 1988.

Siegel, James T. *Solo in the New Order: Language and Hierarchy in an Indonesian City.* Princeton: Princeton University Press, 1986.

Silliman, G. Sidney. "The Folk Legal Culture of the Cebuano Filipino." *Philippine Quarterly of Culture and Society* 10 (1982): 225–44.

Silverstein, Josef. *Burma: Military Rule and the Politics of Stagnation.* Ithaca: Cornell University Press, 1977.

———. *Burmese Politics: The Dilemmas of National Unity.* New Brunswick, N.J.: Rutgers University Press, 1980.

———, ed. *Independent Burma at Forty Years: Six Assessments.* Ithaca: Cornell University Press, 1989.

Simmel, Georg. *The Philosophy of Money.* London: Routledge, 1990.

Singh, Bilveer. *Whither PAP's Dominance? An Analysis of Singapore's 1991 General Elections.* Petaling Jaya, Malaysia: Pelanduk, 1992.

Singh, Hari. "Political Change in Malaysia: The Role of Semangat '46." *Asian Survey* 31(8) (1991): 712–28.

Sjahrir. *Kebijaksanaan Negara: Konsistensi dan Implementasi.* 2d ed. Jakarta: LP3ES, 1988.

Skinner, G. William. *Leadership and Power in the Chinese Community in Thailand.* Ithaca: Cornell University Press, 1958.

Skocpol, Theda. "Bringing the State Back In: Strategies of Analysis in Current Research." In Peter Evans et al., eds., *Bringing the State Back In.* Cambridge: Cambridge University Press, 1989.

———. *States and Social Revolutions.* Cambridge: Cambridge University Press, 1979.

Slimming, John. *Death of a Democracy.* London: John Murray, 1969.

Smith, Anthony D. *State and the Nation in the Third World.* New York: St. Martin's Press, 1983.

Smith, Martin. *Burma: Insurgency and the Politics of Ethnicity.* London: Zed Books, 1991.

Smyser, W. R. *The Independent Vietnamese: Vietnamese Communism Between Russia and China, 1956–1969.* Papers in International Studies, Southeast Asia, No. 55. Athens: Ohio University Center for International Studies, 1980.

Snitwongse, Kusuma. "Thailand in 1993: Politics of Survival." *Asian Survey* 34(2) (1994): 147–50.

Snodgrass, Adrian. *The Symbolism of the Stupa.* Ithaca: Cornell University Southeast Asia Program, 1985.

Soeharto. "Ending Three Deviations." In Herbert Feith and Lance Castles, eds., *Indonesian Political Thinking, 1945–1965.* Ithaca: Cornell University Press, 1970.

Soemardjan, Selo. *Perubahan Sosial di Yogyakarta.* Cetakan Kedua. Yogyakarta: Gadjah Mada University Press, 1986.

Songkram, Phibul. "Cooperation with and Resistance Against Japan During the War." In Thak Chaloemtiarana, ed., *Thai Politics 1932–1957*. Bangkok: Social Science Association, 1978.

Spence, Hartzell. *For Every Tear a Victory*. New York: McGraw-Hill, 1964.

Stammers, Neil. "Human Rights and Power." *Political Studies* 41 (1993): 70–82.

State Law and Order Restoration Council (SLORC). "SLORC Declaration 10/90 (27 July 1990)." *Burma Alert* 3(7) (July 1992).

Steinberg, David I. *Burma: A Socialist Nation in Southeast Asia*. Boulder: Westview Press, 1981.

———. *Burma's Road Toward Development: Growth and Ideology Under Military Rule*. Boulder: Westview Press, 1981.

———. *The Future of Burma: Crisis and Choice in Myanmar*. New York: University Press of America, 1990.

———. "Myanmar 1991: Military Intransigence." *South-East Asian Affairs* (1992): 221–37.

Steinberg, David Joel, ed. *In Search of Southeast Asia: A Modern History*. Honolulu: University of Hawaii Press, 1987.

Stillman, Peter G. "The Concept of Legitimacy." *Polity* 7(1) (Fall 1974): 32–56.

Stinchcombe, Arthur L. *Constructing Social Theories*. New York: Harcourt, Brace, 1968.

Stockwell, A. J. "The White Man's Burden and Brown Humanity: Colonialism and Ethnicity in British Malaya." *Southeast Asian Journal of Social Science* 10(1) (1982): 44–68.

Stone, Richard L. *Philippine Urbanization: The Politics of Public and Private Property in Manila*. De Kalb: Northern Illinois University Center for Southeast Asia Studies, 1973.

Strauch, Judith. "Multiple Ethnicities in Malaysia: The Shifting Relevance of Alternative Chinese Categories." *Modern Asian Studies* 15(2) (1981): 235–60.

Stubbs, Richard. *Hearts and Minds in Guerrilla Warfare: The Malayan Emergency, 1948–1960*. Singapore and New York: Oxford University Press, 1989.

———, comp. *Vietnam: Facing the 1990s*. Toronto: Joint Centre for Asia Pacific Studies, 1989.

Sturtevant, David R. *Popular Uprisings in the Philippines, 1840–1940*. Ithaca: Cornell University Press, 1976.

Sukarno. *Dibawah Bendera Revolusi*. Jakarta: Panitya Penerbit, 1963.

———. "The Economics of a Nation in Revolution." In Herbert Feith and Lance Castles, eds., *Indonesian Political Thinking, 1945–1965*. Ithaca: Cornell University Press, 1970.

———. *Lahirnja Pantja Sila*. Jakarta: Ministry of Information, 1960.

———. "The Pantja Sila." In Herbert Feith and Lance Castles, eds., *Indonesian Political Thinking, 1945–1965*. Ithaca: Cornell University Press, 1970.

Suksamran, Somboon. *Buddhism and Politics in Thailand*. Singapore: Institute of Southeast Asian Studies, 1982.

Tai, Hue Tam. *Millenarianism and Peasant Politics in Vietnam*. Cambridge, Mass.: Harvard University Press, 1983.

Tan Liok Ee. "Dongjiaozong and the Challenge to Cultural Hegemony 1951–

1987." In Joel S. Kahn and Francis Loh Kok Wah, eds., *Fragmented Vision: Culture and Politics in Contemporary Malaysia.* Sydney: Allen & Unwin, 1992.

Tancangco, Luzviminda. *The Anatomy of Electoral Fraud: Concrete Bases for Electoral Reforms.* Manila: MJAGM, 1992.

Tasker, Rodney. "Anti-Reform Club: Opposition and Senate Defeat Government Bills." *Far Eastern Economic Review,* May 12, 1994, p. 17.

Taylor, Paul. "Quiet Grumbles Among the Partners." *Financial Times,* Apr. 30, 1991, Singapore Survey, sec. iii.

Taylor, Robert H. "The Military in Myanmar: What Scope for a New Role?" In Viberto Selochan, ed., *The Military, the State, and Development in Asia and the Pacific.* Boulder: Westview Press, 1991.

———. "Perceptions of Ethnicity in the Politics of Burma." *Southeast Asian Journal of Social Science* 10(1) (1982): 7–22.

———. *The State in Burma.* London: C. Hurst, 1987.

Teiwes, Frederick C. *Leadership, Legitimacy, and Conflict in China: From a Charismatic Mao to the Politics of Succession.* Armonk, N.Y.: M. E. Sharpe, 1984.

Terwiel, B. J. "Thai Nationalism and Identity." In Craig J. Reynolds, ed., *National Identity and Its Defenders.* Victoria: Aristoc Press, 1991.

Thai Quang Trung. *Collective Leadership and Factionalism: An Essay on Ho Chi Minh's Legacy.* Singapore: Institute of Southeast Asian Studies, 1985.

Thanh Tin tran tinh (Thanh Tin expresses his opinions). Paris: Doan Ket, 1991.

Thayer, Carlyle. "The Challenges Facing Vietnamese Communism." In *Southeast Asian Affairs 1992.* Singapore: Institute of Southeast Asian Studies, 1992.

———. "Development Strategies in Vietnam: The Fourth National Congress of the Vietnamese Communist Party." *Asian Profile* 7(3) (June 1979): 275–86.

———. "Political Development in Vietnam, 1975–1985." In Colin Mackerras, Robert Cribb, and Allan Healty, eds., *Contemporary Vietnam: Perspective from Australia.* North Wollongong: University of Wollongong Press, 1988.

———. *Political Developments in Vietnam: From the Sixth to Seventh National Party Congress.* Regime Change and Regime Maintenance in Asia and the Pacific, Discussion Paper 5. Canberra: Department of Political and Social Change, Research School of Pacific Studies, Australian National University, 1992.

———. "Political Reform in Vietnam: Doi Moi and the Emergence of Civil Society." In Robert F. Miller, ed., *The Developments of Civil Society in Communist Systems.* Sydney: Allen & Unwin, 1992.

———. "The Regularization of Politics: Continuity and Change in the Party's Central Committee, 1951–1986." In David G. Marr and Christine White, eds., *Postwar Vietnam: Dilemmas in Socialist Development.* Ithaca: Southeast Asia Program, Cornell University, 1988.

Thayer, Carlyle. "Vietnamese Perspectives on International Security: Three Revolutionary Currents." In Donald H. McMillen, ed., *Asian Perspectives on International Security.* New York: St. Martin's Press, 1984.

———. "Vietnam's Sixth Party Congress: An Overview." *Contemporary Asia* 9(1) (June 1987): 12–22.

———. "Vietnam's Two Strategic Tasks: Building Socialism and Defending the

Fatherland." In *Southeast Asian Affairs 1983*. Singapore: Institute of Southeast Asian Studies, 1983.

————. *War by Other Means: National Liberation and Revolution in Vietnam 1954–60*. Sydney: Allen & Unwin, 1989.

Thayer, Carlyle, and David Marr, eds. *Vietnam and the Rule of Law*. Political and Social Change Monograph 19. Canberra: Department of Political and Social Change, Research School of Pacific Studies, Australian National University, 1993.

Thee Kian Wie. "The Impact of the Colonial Past on the Indonesian Economy." Paper presented at the Conference on the Socioeconomic Foundations of the Late Colonial State of Java Circa 1880–1930: Towards an Explanation, NIAS, Wassemaar, June 12–14, 1989.

Thompson, Edward P. *Customs in Common*. New York: Basic Books, 1991.

————. *Whigs and Hunters: The Origins of the Black Act*. New York: Pantheon, 1975.

Thompson, Mark Richard. "Cory and 'the Guy': Reformist Politics in the Philippines." UFSI Field Staff Report 16. Indianapolis: Universities Field Staff International, 1988–89.

Thompson, Michael, Richard Ellis, and Aaron Wildavsky. *Cultural Theory*. Boulder: Westview, 1990.

Tieng noi dan chu cho Viet Nam (Democratic voices for Vietnam). Irvine, Calif.: Saigon Press, 1992.

Tilman, Robert O. "Burma in 1986: The Process of Involution Continues." *Asian Survey* 26(2) (1987): 254–63.

Timberman, David G. *A Changeless Land*. Singapore: Institute of Southeast Asian Studies, 1991.

Tinker, Hugh. "Review of Robert Taylor's *The State in Burma*." *Third World Quarterly* 10(3) (1988): 1399–1401.

————. *The Union of Burma: A Study of the First Years of Independence*. London: Oxford University Press, 1967.

Tong Cuc Thong Ke. *So lieu thong ke 1930–1984* (Statistics 1930–84). Hanoi: Thong Ke, 1985.

Tonkinson, Robert. "Understanding 'Tradition'—Ten Years On." *Anthropological Forum* 6(4) (1993): 597–606.

Tonnesson, Stein. "The Outbreak of War in Indochina, 1946." Ph.D. dissertation, University of Oslo, 1982.

Trager, Frank N. *Burma: From Kingdom to Republic*. London: Praeger, 1966.

Tram hoa dua no tren dat Bac (Hundred flowers bloom in the northern land). Paris: Que me, 1983.

Tram hoa van no tren que huong: cao trao van nghe phan khang tai Viet Nam, 1986–1989 (Hundred flowers still bloom in the fatherland: the high tide of dissident literature in Vietnam, 1986–1989). Reseda, Calif.: Le Tran, 1990.

Tran Duc Nguyen. *Mot so quan diem kinh te cua Dai hoi VI* (Several economic concepts of the Sixth Party Congress). Hanoi: Su That, 1988.

Tran Huy Quang. "Linh nghiem." *Van Nghe* 27 (July 4, 1992): 12–13.

Tran Quoc Vuong. *Trong coi: nhung y kien ve lich su, truyen thong va hien trang dan toc cua mot su gia trong nuoc* (Inside the country: opinions on history, tradition, and ethnic phenomena by a historian in the country). Garden Grove, Calif.: Tram Hoa, 1992.

Truong Chinh. *Cach mang dan toc dan chu nhan dan Viet Nam, tap I–II* (The Vietnamese people's democratic national revolution, vols. 1–2). Hanoi: Su That, 1976.

———. *May van de ve nha nuoc Cong Hoa Xa Hoi Chu Nghia Viet Nam* (Several problems about the state of the Socialist Republic of Vietnam). Hanoi: Su That, 1985.

———. *Resolutely Taking the North Vietnam Countryside to Socialism Through Agricultural Cooperation.* Hanoi: FLPH, 1959.

Truyen ngan Viet Nam, 1945–1985 (Vietnam's short stories, 1945–85). Hanoi: Van Hoc, 1985.

Tucker, Robert. *Stalinism: Essays in Historical Interpretation.* New York and London: Norton, 1977.

Tun Myint, U. *Syam-Pry Bae Lae?* (Whither the Shan State?) N.p., n.d.

Turley, William. "Party, State, and People: Political Structure and Economic Prospects." In William Turley and Mark Selden, eds., *Reinventing Vietnamese Socialism: Doi Moi in Comparative Perspective.* Boulder: Westview Press, 1993.

———. "Vietnam Since Reunification." *Problems of Communism* 26(2) (Mar.–Apr. 1977): 36–54.

———, ed. *Vietnamese Communism in Comparative Perspective.* Boulder: Westview Press, 1980.

Turley, William, and Mark Selden, eds. *Reinventing Vietnamese Socialism: Doi Moi in Comparative Perspective.* Boulder: Westview Press, 1993.

Turner, Victor. *The Ritual Process: Structure and Anti-Structure.* Ithaca: Cornell University Press, 1977.

U Nu. *Saturday's Son.* New Haven: Yale University Press, 1975.

U.S. State Department. *Country Reports on Human Rights Practices for 1988: Burma.* Washington: GPO, 1989.

———. *Foreign Relations of the United States (1949–1957).* Washington: GPO, 1975.

Uy Ban Khoa Hoc Xa Hoi Viet Nam. *Lich su Viet Nam, tap I* (Vietnamese history, vol. 1). Hanoi: Khoa Hoc Xa Hoi, 1976.

Van kien cua Dang Cong San Viet Nam ve van hoa van nghe tu Dai hoi VI den Dai hoi VII (Vietnamese Communist Party's documents on culture and arts from the Sixth to the Seventh Congress). Hanoi: Su That, 1991.

Van Leur, J. C. *Indonesian Trade and Society.* Bandung: W. van Hoeve, 1955.

Van Niel, Robert. *The Emergence of a Modern Indonesian Elite.* Bandung: W. van Hoeve, 1960.

Van Tao. "Cai cach ruong dat—thanh qua va sai lam" (Land reform—achievements and errors). *Nghien Cuu Lich Su* 2(267) (1993): 1–10.

Vasavakul, Thaveeporn. "Schools and Politics in South and North Viet Nam, 1945–1965: A Comparative Study of State Apparatus, State Policy, and State Power." Ph.D. dissertation, Cornell University, 1994.

Vasil, Raj. *Governing Singapore.* Rev. ed. Singapore: Mandarin, 1992.

Vatikiotis, Michael. "Local Hero: Drive to Topple Sabah Leader Stalls." *Far Eastern Economic Review*, May 27, 1993, pp. 26–27.

Vickerman, Andrew. *The Fate of the Peasantry: Premature "Transition to Socialism" in the Democratic Republic of Vietnam*. Monograph Series, No. 28. New Haven: Yale University Southeast Asia Program, 1984.

Vidich, Arthur J. "Legitimation of Regimes in World Perspective." In Arthur J. Vidich and Ronald Glassman, eds., *Conflict and Control*. Beverly Hills: Sage, 1979.

Vien Kinh Te Hoc. *45 nam kinh te Viet Nam (1945–1990)* (45 years of Vietnam's economy [1945–90]). Hanoi: Khoa Hoc Xa Hoi, 1990.

Vien Luat Hoc. *Hien phap nuoc Cong Hoa Xa Hoi Chu Nghia Viet Nam (binh luan), tap I–II* (Constitutions of the Socialist Republic of Vietnam [comments], vols. 1–2). Hanoi: Khoa Hoc Xa Hoi, 1985.

———. *Tang cuong hieu luc nha nuoc xa hoi chu nghia cua chung ta* (Strengthen the effectiveness of our socialist state). Hanoi: Khoa Hoc Xa Hoi, 1983.

Villegas, Bernardo. "The Economic Crisis." In John Bresnan, ed., *Crisis in the Philippines*. Princeton: Princeton University Press, 1986.

Vlekke, Bernard H. M. *Nusantara*. Brussels: Editions A. Manteau, 1961.

Vo Nhan Tri. *Croissance économique de la République Démocratique du Vietnam*. Hanoi: Editions en langues étrangères, 1967.

———. "Party Policies and Economic Performance: The Second and Third Five-Year Plans Examined." In David G. Marr and Christine White, eds., *Postwar Vietnam: Dilemmas in Socialist Development*. Ithaca: Southeast Asia Program, Cornell University, 1988.

———. *Vietnam's Economic Policy Since 1975*. Singapore: Institute of Southeast Asian Studies, 1990.

von der Mehden, F. R. "The Burmese Way to Socialism." *Asian Survey* 3(3) (1963): 129–35.

von Vorys, Karl. *Democracy Without Consensus: Communalism and Political Stability in Malaysia*. Princeton: Princeton University Press, 1975.

Vu Ky. *Bac Ho viet di chuc* (Uncle Ho writing his last will and testament). Hanoi: Su That, 1989.

Wade, Robert. *Governing the Market: Economic Theory and the Role of Government in East Asian Industrialization*. Princeton: Princeton University Press, 1990.

Wagner, R. *The Invention of Culture*. Englewood Cliffs, N.J.: Prentice-Hall, 1975.

Walter, Eugene V. *Terror and Resistance: A Study of Political Violence*. New York: Oxford University Press, 1969.

Wang Gungwu. "Chinese Politics in Malaya." In Wang Gungwu, *Community and Nation: Essays on Southeast Asia and the Chinese*. Sydney: Allen & Unwin, 1981.

Weatherbee, Donald E. "Indonesia: The Pancasila State." In *Southeast Asian Affairs 1985*. Singapore: Institute of Southeast Asian Studies, 1985.

Weber, Max. *Economy and Society: An Outline of Interpretive Sociology*. Berkeley: University of California Press, 1978.

———. *Theory of Social and Economic Organization*. Edited by Talcott Parsons. New York: Free Press, 1964.

Werner, Jayne. "Cao Dai: The Politics of a Vietnamese Syncretic Religious Movement." Ph.D. dissertation, Cornell University, 1976.

Wertheim, W. F. *Indonesian Society in Transition.* Bandung: W. van Hoeve, 1959.

White, Christine. "Agrarian Reform and National Liberation in the Vietnamese Revolution: 1920–1957." Ph.D. dissertation, Cornell University, 1981.

———. "Agricultural Planning, Pricing Policy and Co-operatives in Vietnam." *World Development* 13(1) (1985): 97–114.

White, Stephen. "Economic Performance and Communist Legitimacy." *World Politics* 38 (Apr. 1986): 462–82.

Wiant, Jon. "Tradition in the Service of Revolution: The Political Symbolism of Taw-hlan-ye-khit." In F. K. Lehman, ed., *Military Rule in Burma Since 1962: A Kaleidoscope of Views.* Singapore: Maruzen Asia, 1981.

Wickberg, Edgar. *The Chinese in Philippine Life, 1851–1898.* New Haven: Yale University Press, 1965.

Wilner, Ann Ruth. *The Spellbinders: Charismatic Political Leadership.* New Haven: Yale University Press, 1984.

Wolters, Oliver W. *History, Culture, and Region in Southeast Asian Perspectives.* Singapore: Institute of Southeast Asian Studies, 1982.

———. "Khmer 'Hinduism' in the Seventh Century." In R. B. Smith and W. Watson, eds., *Early South East Asia: Essays in Archaeology, History and Historical Geography.* New York: Oxford University Press, 1979.

Wolters, Willem. "Rise and Fall of Provincial Elites in the Philippines: Nueva Ecija from the 1880s to the Present Day." *Sojourn* 4(1) (Feb. 1989): 54–74.

Woodside, Alexander. *Community and Revolution in Vietnam.* Cambridge and Boston: Houghton Mifflin, 1976.

Wrong, Dennis H. *Power: Its Form, Bases and Uses.* New York: Harper & Row, 1979.

Wurfel, David. "The Bell Report and After: A Study of the Political Problems of Social Reform Stimulated by Foreign Aid." Ph.D. dissertation, Cornell University, 1960.

———. *Filipino Politics: Development and Decay.* Ithaca: Cornell University Press, 1988.

———. "The Philippines." Special issue, "Comparative Studies in Political Finance," *Journal of Politics* 25(4) (Nov. 1963): 757–73.

Wyatt, David K. *The Politics of Reform in Thailand: Education in the Reign of King Chulalongkorn.* New Haven: Yale University Press, 1969.

———. *Thailand: A Short History.* New Haven: Yale University Press, 1982.

Yambot, Reuben. *How to Win in the 1992 Local Elections.* Quezon City: Active Research Center, 1992.

Yawnghwe, Chao-Tzang. "Burma: 'Constructive Engagement.'" *Thai-Yunnan Project Newsletter* 21 (June 1993): 7–10.

———. "The Burman Military: Keeping the Country Together?" In Josef Silverstein, ed., *Independent Burma at Forty Years: Six Assessments.* Ithaca: Cornell University Press, 1989.

———. "Ne Win's Tatmadaw Dictatorship." Master's thesis, University of British Columbia, 1990.

———. "Rebellions in Burma: An Overview." *B.C. Asian Review* 5 (1991): 169–203.

———. *The Shan of Burma: Memoirs of a Shan Exile*. Singapore: Institute of Southeast Asian Studies, 1987.

Yoshihara, Kunio. *Rise of Ersatz Capitalism in Southeast Asia*. Singapore: Oxford University Press, 1988.

Young, Stephen. "Unpopular Socialism in United Vietnam." *Orbis* 22(2) (Summer 1977): 227–36.

———. "Vietnamese Marxism: Transition in Elite Ideology." *Asian Survey* 19(8) (Aug. 1979): 770–79.

Youngblood, Robert. *Marcos Against the Church: Economic Development and Political Repression in the Philippines*. Ithaca: Cornell University Press, 1990.

Zakaria Haji Ahmad. "Evolution and Development of the Political System in Malaysia." In Robert A. Scalapino, Seizaburo Sato, and Jusuf Wanandi, eds., *Asian Political Institutionalization*. Berkeley: Institute of East Asian Studies/University of California, 1986.

Zoetmulder, P. J. *Kalangwan*. The Hague: Martinus Nijhoff, 1974.

Index

In this index an "f" after a number indicates a separate reference on the next page, and an "ff" indicates separate references on the next two pages. A continuous discussion over two or more pages is indicated by a span of page numbers, e.g., "pp. 57–58." *Passim* is used for a cluster of references in close but not continuous sequence.

Abangan (nominal Muslims), 237, 242
Abdul Rahman, Tunku, 44, 92 ff, 98 f, 313, 315, 353 n101
Abdul Razak, Tun, 97–98 f
ABRI (Indonesian armed forces), 247, 254, 256, 305
Aceh, 242, 295
Adireksarn, Pramarn, 216
AFP (Armed Forces of the Philippines), 2, 301–2
AFPFL (Anti-Fascist People's Freedom League, Burma), 173, 178, 180–85 f, 295, 298, 369 n50, 370 n57, 372 n92
Agriculture: Thai developmentalism and, 206–7, 217; Vietnam's cooperativization of, 262, 267–74 *passim*, 288, 389–90 n49, 391 n79
Alagappa, Muthiah, 78, 225
Aliran politics, 225–26, 241, 378 n6
Alliance coalition (Malaysia), 79, 93–94, 352 n80
Alus principle, 237 f
American colonialism, 151
American War period (1965–73, Vietnam), 265–69 *passim*
Amnesty International, 372 n86
Amulets, 154–55
Anand Panyarachun, *see* Panyarachun, Anand
Ananda Mahidol Mahidol, King, *see* Mahidol, Ananda Mahidol
Andaya, Barbara, 90
Andaya, Leonard, 90

Anderson, Benedict, 26–27, 44, 199–200, 232, 235–36, 345 n43, 361 n92, 382 n59
Anek Laothammatas, *see* Laothammatas, Anek
Anticommunist Act (1952, Thailand), 198
Anti-Japanese Goods campaign (1972, Thailand), 208
Anting-anting (magical powers), 154 f, 162, 167, 361 n90
Apter, David, 340 n1
Aquino, Benigno, 164, 302
Aquino, Corazon, 47, 71, 164–65 f, 302, 359 n57
Arato, Andrew, 234, 381 n44
Arief, Sritua, 252, 387 n124
Arms for Democracy program (1958, Burma), 183, 371 n80
ASEAN, 191, 275
Asian-Western debate: in Singapore, 124–25
Aung Gyi, 171, 364 n3, 372 nn83,93
Aungsan, 44, 171, 180 f, 364 n3, 365 n9, 369 nn48,50, 370 nn64,66–67, 372 n93
Aungsan Suukyi, 2, 170 f, 173, 189, 364 n3
Aung-Thwin, Michael, 174–77, 367 n30
Authoritarian regimes: consent in, 24, 28, 343 n66, 368 n38; popular sovereignty dilemma in, 38 f, 62, 293, 310–11; in Southeast Asia, 44–45, 127; international norms and, 48–49, 55, 62, 120–21, 171–72, 174, 190–91, 220, 276,

307, 346–47nn61–64, 348–49n24, 366nn12,18; reliance on performance by, 61–63, 223, 309–10
Authority: moral leadership basis of, 2, 103, 264, 269–70, 314f; power vs., 2, 4, 44, 326, 337–38n7; Max Weber on, 11, 22, 31, 35, 41, 43, 341n35; force and, 18–19, 42, 341n35; performance element of, 22–23, 41–43, 61–62, 64, 342nn45–46, 345nn37,41, 348n38; normative rationales for, 31, 32–41; personal, 43–46, 345n44, 345n48; cultural basis of, 45, 82–86, 237–39, 345–46n51, 346nn53–54, 351n44, 383n63; of politically defining moment, 46–48; international dimension of, 48–49, 346nn61–63; democracy as basis of, 294–300; based on pragmatic accommodation, 326–30. *See also* Legitimacy
Ayoob, Mohammed, 339n35

Ba Maw, Dr., 365n9
Ba Nyein, U, 186
Bama (or Mranmaa), 174, 176–77, 365–66n10
Bama military, *see* Tatmadaw
Bama Thakins (masters), 178, 183, 368n44
BANDA (Border Areas New Democratic Army, Burma), 187, 190, 374n127
Bangkok, 1, 194f, 337nn1–2
Bangkok Times, 196
Banomyong, Pridi, 196–97
Bao Ninh, 286
Bappenas (Badan Perencana Pembangunan Nasional, Indonesia), 250–51, 286n120
Barisan Nasional (National Front, Malaysia), 70–76 *passim*, 80, 102
Barisan Sosialis (Singapore), 113
Barker, Rodney, 22, 114, 343n52
Batson, Benjamin, 196
BCP/CPB (White Flag Communist Party, Burma), 179, 181–82, 187, 190, 298, 304, 369nn49–50, 370n60
Beetham, David, 14, 51–52, 347n68
Belief, 11–12ff, 46, 340n1. *See also* Normative element
Bendix, Reinhard, 340n1, 343n69
Bhikkhu, Kitthiwuttho, 211
Bhumipol Adulyadej Mahidol, King, *see* Mahidol, Bhumipol Adulyadej
BIA (Burma Independence Army), 183
Boudarel, Georges, 269f, 390n53
Bowaredt, Prince, 197
BPUPKI (Investigating Committee for the Preparation of Indonesian Independence), 231–32, 380n34
British colonialism, 79, 83–90 *passim*, 182, 352n64, 371n70, 371n71, 380n24
British residential system, 83–84
BSPP (Mranmaa Soshei-lit Lanzin, Burmese Socialist Program Party), 34, 170–71, 187, 188–89, 303, 364n4, 374n122
Buddhism, 186, 198, 383–84n73
Bui Tin, 279–80, 393n105
Bumiputra ("sons of the soil"), 73, 95
Burma: 1988 uprising in, 2, 170–72, 188–89, 364n1, 366n11, 374n122; goal-rational ideology of, 33–34, 172, 178, 300, 303; international norms and, 48f, 171–74 *passim*, 190–91; ethnic-based resistance in, 174–79 *passim*, 183–84, 295, 304, 367n25; name change for, 174, 366–67n19; resistance to colonialism in, 175, 367n25; statist model of legitimacy in, 175–76f; parliamentary system of, 178, 183–84f; multicolored insurgents in, 178–80; during AFPFL period, 180–85; under military-socialist regime, 185–89; failed democratic system in, 294f, 298; majority-minority configuration of, 365–66n10. *See also* AFPFL; SLORC; Tatmadaw
Burma Rifles units, 182
Burmese Communist Party, *see* BCP/CPB
Burmese Constitution (1947), 181
Burmese military, *see* Tatmadaw
Burmese Way to Socialism, 33–34, 172, 178, 300
Bush, George, 23

Cambodia, 3, 33, 49, 58, 275, 289
Cao Dai sect (Vietnam), 259
Capitalism, 151, 167–68, 205–7, 222, 250–51, 386n120
Capitalist development theory, 60f, 348n18
Capitalist state theory, crisis of, 60
Catholic church, 39–40, 135, 137, 153, 159
Cebu City, 136–37, 154, 156
Chai-anan Samudavanija, *see* Samudavanija, Chai-anan
Chan Heng Chee, 122
Charisma, 31f, 43–46 *passim*, 345n43. *See also* Personal authority
Charusathien, Praphat, 207, 210, 377n45
Charusathien, Prasert, 207
Chatichai Choonhavan, *see* Choonhavan, Chatichai

Chee Soon Juan, 355n25
China, 3, 48f, 172, 191, 262, 273, 275, 288, 391n86
Chinese: business community role of, 72f, 79, 89–90, 96f, 106, 119–20; UMNO and, 72–74, 79, 86, 89–90, 96, 104, 106, 316, 350nn9,12,17; cultural alienation of, 75–76; authority patterns of, 85–86; under British colonialism, 87–90; and May Thirteenth riots, 93–97; economic policies and, 96, 102, 205–6, 230, 251, 353n90; and Singapore identity, 129–30; Bama riots against, 182, 371n72
Chinese Red Army, 266
Chinh, *see* Hoang Minh Chinh
Chit Hliang, 373n102
Chomanan, Kriangsak, 212–15 *passim*, 327
Choonhavan, Chatichai, 22, 218, 222f, 328, 329
Chuan Leepkai, *see* Leepkai, Chuan
Chulasap, Dawee, 207
Civil service: in Singapore, 117–22 *passim*
Clark, Gordon, 178
Class struggle, 279, 286, 314
CLC (Communities Liaison Committee, Malaysia), 88
Clinton, William, 348–49n24
Club of Resistance Fighters (*cau lac bo nhung nguoi khang chien cu*, Vietnam), 272, 278
Cockfighting, 158
Cohen, Jean, 234, 381n44
Cojuangco, Danding, 169
Cold War, 48f, 56–57
Colin, Francisco, 363n87
Collective leadership principle, 263–64, 388n21
Collective will, 37–38, 52. *See also* Popular sovereignty
Collegial model of leadership, 388n20
Colonialism: legitimation impact of, 56f, 175f, 348n13, 367n25; in Malaysia, 79, 83–90 *passim*, 352n64; in Philippines, 150–51, 360n67; in Burma, 182, 371nn70–71; plural-societies phenomenon and, 182, 370n55; in Indonesia, 229–34 *passim*, 241, 379n20, 380n25, 384n77; in Vietnam, 261, 265, 314
Comintern, 260f
Commercial Import Program (United States), 274
Communism: as threat to Thailand, 201–4 *passim*, 213f; Sukarno's alliance

with, 241–45 *passim*, 385n102; Vietnamese nationalism goal and, 260–66 *passim*, 270–71, 313–14
Communist Party of Burma, *see* BCP/CPB
Communist Suppression Operation units (Thailand), 202
"Communitas," 157, 362nn100,102
Confucianism, 125, 127, 258, 264, 321, 323, 332–33
Connolly, William, 60
Consent element, 14f, 23–29 *passim*, 296, 342n49, 343n66, 368n38
Consociational arrangements, 72, 349n29
Cooperativization, agricultural, 262, 267–74 *passim*, 288, 389–90n49, 391n79
"Correcting Errors Committed in the *Chi Bo* Rectification During Wave Five (1956)," 267
Cotton, James, 127f
CPB (Communist Party of Burma), 369nn48–49. *See also* BCP/CPB
CPP (Communist Party of the Philippines), 142f, 301
CPT (Communist Party of Thailand), 202, 213f, 216, 377n52
Crouch, Harold, 96, 339nn27–28
Culture: as dynamic construction, 17–18, 107, 234, 333, 341n30, 381n46, 382n48; political development role of, 45, 345–46n51, 346n53; traditional Javanese, 237–39, 383nn63–64; diverse Vietnamese, 259
Cuneta, Pablo, 157

Dang Lao Dong Viet Nam (Vietnam Labor Party), *see* Lao Dong Party
DAP (Democratic Action Party, Malaysia), 76f, 94, 313, 322
Daw Khin Kyi, 364n3
De Leon, Alfredo (pseud. Ka Benjie/Joey/Boyet), 153–54
Dear, Michael, 178
Defensor Santiago, Miriam, 166, 169
Democrat Party (Thailand), 210
Democratic regimes: political development theories on, 4–5, 338n24; performance element in, 22–23; popular sovereignty and, 37f; self-regulation in, 54–55; legitimacy crisis in, 63–64f, 349n25; Singapore's limited procedural, 111–12, 123, 132f, 355n25; contradictory Philippine, 137–38, 141–44, 148–49, 296; Filipinos' skepticism about, 147–49, 161, 167, 297; in Burma, 178, 183–84f, 294–98 *passim*; Sarit Thanarat's Thai-style, 202–5

passim; Thai societal conflict over, 207–13 *passim*, 218–21, 302–3, 328, 329–30, 377n42; Thai inclusionary, 214–17, 222, 326–27; of Sukarno, 232, 242–46, 253, 295, 297–98, 381n38, 387n125; in postrevolutionary Indonesia, 240–42, 294, 297; failed legitimacy of, 294–300; in Western countries, 333–34

The Democratic Revolution in the Philippines (Marcos), 143

Demokrasi Pancasila, 226, 379n9. *See also* Pancasila

Department of Agrarian Reform (Philippines), 163

Dependency school of political theory, 4–5, 338n18

Developing countries: legitimacy studies on, 4–6, 338n17; political transition in, 5, 174, 339n27, 366n17; ideological conflict in, 18; power acquisition in, 20–21; regime-government relationship in, 27–28, 59, 115–16; legitimacy crises in, 59–65, 348nn15–16,18, 349n25

Development theory, 4f, 338n18

Dharmasakti, Sanya, 209

Di Palma, Giuseppe, 35, 343n66, 346n61

Djojohadikusumo, Sumitro, 230, 379n10

Doi moi (renovation policy), 275–76, 289, 321

Dominance, 312–13, 322

Dominant groups, *see* Hegemonic groups

Dominguez, Jorge I., 346n63

DPR (Indonesia's house of representatives), 226, 247f, 256, 306, 378n7

DRV (Democratic Republic of Vietnam) model: of nationalism–socialist revolution, 260–66 *passim*, 270–71, 287–88; Ho Chi Minh on, 269–70; for reunified Vietnam, 271–75, 288–89; of developmentalism, 272–74. *See also* Lao Dong Party; VCP

Duiker, William, 258

Dulag, Macliing, 153

Duong Thu Huong, 286

Durano, Ramon M., Sr., 136f, 145, 159, 357n4

Dutch colonialism, 229–34 *passim*, 241, 379n20, 380n25, 384n77

East Asian countries, 5, 48, 339nn27–28

East Timor, 227, 295

Eastern European countries, 3, 57, 278

Economic performance: as basis of authority claim, 22–23, 41–43, 61–62, 64, 223, 315, 342nn45–46, 345nn37–38,41; UMNO's entrepreneurism aims and, 72–73, 95–102 *passim*, 315–16; Singapore's development strategy for, 109, 113, 119–22, 127, 130, 315, 354n2; under Thai developmentalism, 205–7, 217, 300, 302–3, 377n39; under New Order, 226, 227–28, 249–56 *passim*, 379n10; VCP's postreunification strategies for, 272–75, 276, 280, 283, 316, 320–21; under Ferdinand Marcos, 301, 309, 395n14; political stability and, 309f; as supplementary rationale, 315–16

Eighth Plenum of the Central Committee (1990, VCP), 278

Elections: participation in, 20, 23–24; popular sovereignty and, 38, 316–17; in Malaysia, 76, 316; in Singapore, 123–24, 130–34 *passim*, 316–17, 396nn30–31; in Philippines, 141–43f, 148–49, 157, 168f, 359nn53,55–57; in Burma, 172–73; in Thailand, 209f, 216

Elias, Norbert, 239

Elite groups: consent role of, 16–17, 28–29f, 35f; and Malaysia's relational legitimation, 72–78, 82–85, 89–90, 104; Singapore leadership's incorporation of, 116–23, 354n8. *See also* Hegemonic groups; Strategic groups

Emigration, 133, 356n55

Enlargement doctrine, 348–49n24

Escario clan (Philippines), 156, 159

Estrada, Joseph, 165, 169, 359n53

Ethnic minorities: non-Bama, 56f, 174–84 *passim*, 295, 304, 366n16, 367n25, 370n56, 371nn70–71,75–76; Malaysia's relational legitimacy and, 72–81 *passim*, 103–4; adjustable character of, 81–82, 104–5, 107; in colonial Malaysia, 87–89f, 352n64; Singapore's commonality ideology and, 126, 129–30, 355n32; in Philippines, 152–56, 295

European Community, 220

External elites, *see* International support

Far Eastern Economic Review, 75

Farmer Federation of Thailand, 207

Federal Land Development Authority (Malaysia), 105

Feith, Herbert, 242, 294, 384n77, 385n101

Fforde, Adam, 269

Fifth Party Congress (1982, VCP), 272, 275f

For Every Tear a Victory (Spence), 162
Force: and authority, 18–19, 42, 341n35
Forum Democracy (Indonesia), 306
Fourth Party Congress (1976, VCP),
    271f, 276
French colonialism, 261, 265, 314
French Indochina, 197
Friedrich, C. J., 340n1, 342n45
Furnivall, John S., 239, 370n55

Gandhi, Indira, 38, 346n57
Gandhi, Mohandas, 52
Gandhi, Rajiv, 38, 346n57
Geertz, Clifford, 45, 224, 256, 378n1,
    381n41
Geertz, Hildred, 238
Gerakan pembaharuan Islam (Islamic re-
    newal movement), 239–40
Giddens, Anthony, 16, 326
Goal-rational ideologies: legitimating po-
    tential of, 33, 34–36, 322–24, 330–
    31; of VCP, 33, 203–4, 260–63, 275,
    293, 312–13, 317, 320–21; of Burma,
    33–34, 172, 178, 300, 303; of UMNO-
    led government, 78f, 81, 94–99 pas-
    sim, 103–4, 293, 312–13, 319–20,
    331; of PAP campaign, 124–27, 312,
    314; supplementary rationales to, 314–
    19; recasting of, 319–21
Goh Chok Tong, 118, 130, 134f, 396n31
Golkar (Golongan Karya, Functional
    Group), 226, 248, 386n109
Governments: and force-legitimacy rela-
    tionship, 19–20, 42; exercise of power
    by, 20–23, 103; defined, 27; legitimacy
    challenges to, 55–59 passim, 347n4,
    348n15; incumbency issue for, 173–
    74; successful legitimation of, 294, 308
Gramsci, Antonio, 16f, 110, 322
Green, Leslie, 342n49
Greenfeld, Liah, 378n4
Gregorio, Tomas, 156
GRM (Gerakan Rakyat Malaysia, People's
    Movement of Malaysia), 73, 77, 94
Group for Democracy and Development
    (Indonesia), 248, 386n112
Group for Unity and Development (Indo-
    nesia), 248, 386n112
GRP (Gotong Royong Parliament, Indo-
    nesia), 243
Gulf Crisis, 220
Gullick, John, 83
Guyot, Dorothy, 371n71

Habermas, Jürgen, 60, 232, 380–81n35
Habibie, B. J., 254
Hall, John, 52

Harun Idris, 94–99 passim
Hatta, Mohammad, 231, 241, 297,
    381n38
Hegemonic groups, 16–18, 35. *See also*
    Elite groups; Strategic groups
Hegemony, 16f, 34–35, 110
Held, David, 22, 348n15
Henares, Hilarion M., Jr., 363n132
Hikayat Hang Tuah (myth of Hang Tuah),
    82
Hinduism, 383–84n73
Ho Chi Minh, 44, 52; early anticolonial
    goal of, 261; collective leadership prin-
    ciple of, 264–65, 314–15; peasantry alli-
    ance policy of, 265f; authority claims by,
    269–70; VCP's endorse-
    ment of, 277–82 passim, 315, 319,
    392nn95–97; intellectuals' criticism of,
    285–86, 394n140
Hoa Hao sect, 259
Hoang Minh Chinh, 279f, 393n104
Hobsbawm, Eric, 346n54, 361n83
Honasan, Gregorio, 165
Honey, P. J., 388n20
Horowitz, Donald, 82, 352n64
Horowitz, Irving Louis, 342n40
Huntington, Samuel, 5, 6–7, 39–40, 64,
    310, 345–46n51, 366n17
Hussein Onn, 97ff
Huynh Kim Khanh, 260f, 271
Hy Van Luong, 268, 389n38

ICMI (Indonesian Muslim Intellectual As-
    sociation), 254, 306
Ideology, 15, 16–18, 23, 341n18, 342n47.
    See also Goal-rational ideologies
Ileto, Reynaldo C., 357n4, 358n44,
    361n92
Illegitimacy: and coercion, 177, 368nn40–
    41. *See also* Legitimacy
IMP (Independence of Malaya Party), 88,
    352n64
India, 63, 171–72, 380n24
Indians: in Malaysia, 73, 104, 107
Indochinese Communist Party, 260f, 263,
    287–88. *See also* Lao Dong Party; VCP
Indonesia: national ideology of, 34, 48, 58,
    230–34, 380–81nn34–36, 38; percep-
    tion vs. reality in, 224–25; marginalized
    indigenous peoples of, 227–28, 250ff,
    386n119; precolonial economy of, 228–
    29; Islamization of, 229, 230–31, 379–
    80n21; colonial economy of, 229–30,
    242, 379n20; corruption in, 236, 250,
    383n61; parliamentary democracy in,
    240–42, 294, 384n81; under guided de-
    mocracy, 242–46; limited democratic

commitment in, 295, 297–98; depoliticization in, 305; regime legitimation in, 308. *See also* New Order; Pancasila
Indonesian army: under Sukarno, 243–48 *passim*, 385nn94,96–97,387n125; under Soeharto, 247, 254, 256, 305
Indonesian Constitution (1945), 226, 255, 382n48
Indonesian Nationalist Party, 231
Industrial Relations Ordinance (Singapore), 121
Institute of East Asian Philosophies (Singapore), 125
Institute of Policy Studies (Singapore), 356nn54–55
Institutionalization: personal authority and, 46, 52, 115–16, 128–29, 308, 330, 346n57; of national ideologies, 331–33, 396n39
Intellectuals, Vietnamese, 269–70, 281, 285–86, 390nn53,58
Interim Constitution, Article 17 (Thailand), 202
International support: as legitimacy resource, 31–32, 48–49, 52, 62, 190–91, 198, 348–49n24; domestic reliance on, 120–21, 220, 276, 307, 346–47nn61–64; of authoritarian regimes, 171–72, 174, 366nn12,18
Invented tradition, 45, 346n54
ISA (Internal Security Act, Malaysia), 71, 80, 319
Islam: command-obedience relationship of, 40–41, 344n33; Malaysian contestation over, 75, 105f, 318, 320, 353n106; in Philippines, 159, 360n67; in Java, 229, 236, 379–80n21, 382–83n60; economic interests of, 230–31; Pancasila advocacy and, 234, 241–42, 307, 309, 381–82n47; dynamism of Indonesian, 239–40, 383–84n73

Jakarta meetings, 231–32, 380–81nn34–35
Japan, 197, 376n14
Java, 230, 236, 237–40, 382–83n60, 383nn63–64, 383–84n73. *See also* Indonesia
Jesudason, James V., 353n90
Joint Public and Private Sector Consultative Committee (Thailand), 217
Juridical statehood, 56–57, 348n11

Kachin minority, 179, 370n61
Kadazan community, 77, 313, 322
Kamlangek, Arthit, 327

Kampong Memali, 75
Kapangyarihan (big-man authority), 150–64 *passim*, 360n65
Kapitan Cina system (Malaysia), 85
Karen minority, 179–83 *passim*, 295, 298, 366n16, 371nn70–71, 371nn75–76
KBL ceremonies (Philippines), 146
Kessler, Clive, 82, 344n33
Khanh, *see* Huynh Kim Khanh
Khin Nyunt, 172, 189
Khomeini, Ayatollah, 40
Kinship: as legitimacy basis, 156–57, 160
Kittikachorn, Narong, 208, 309
Kittikachorn, Thanom, 198–99, 205–12 *passim*, 223, 302, 308–9, 377n45
KKY (Ka-Kwe-Ye, Homeguard), 187
KNU (Karen National Union), 182f
Kohli, Atul, 63, 346n57, 347n4
Kok Wee Kiat, 350n9
Korean War, 198
Kraprayoon, Suchinda, 1, 218f, 337n2
Krause, Lawrence, 121
Kravichien, Thanin, 213, 327
Kriangsak Chomanan, *see* Chomanan, Kriangsak
Kuala Lumpur, 88, 115
Kukrit Pramoj, *see* Pramoj, Kukrit
Kuok, Robert, 96

Labor Party (Malaysia), 89
Labor unions, 121f, 226, 355n21
Language identity, 85, 129f, 158
Lansdale, Edward, 363n128
Lanzin Party, *see* BSPP
Lao Dong Party (Vietnam Labor Party): nationalism–socialist revolution goals of, 260–63, 266, 270–71; cooperativization policy of, 262, 267–69, 389–90n49; collective leadership concept of, 263–64, 388n21; legitimacy claims of, 264, 269–70; peasantry alliance policy of, 265–71; rent reduction policy of, 266–67, 389n38; intellectuals and, 269–70, 390nn53,58. *See also* VCP
Laos, 3, 33, 58
Laothammatas, Anek, 214–15, 377n53
Latin America, 42–43
Lau Teik Soon, 352n80
Law Organizing the Government (1992, VCP), 282
Law Society (Singapore), 135
Le Duan, 271
Le Duc Tho, 271, 276
Le Loi, 265
Leach, Edmund, 176
League for the Independence of Vietnam

(Viet Nam Doc Lap Dong Minh), 261–69 *passim*

Lee Hsien Loong, 119f, 354n2

Lee Kuan Yew: personal authority of, 44, 52, 115, 128f, 314f; political beliefs of, 111, 117, 344n29, 396n31; at independence celebration, 113; on second-generation leadership, 134–35, 143, 323, 396n34

Leepkai, Chuan, 222f, 329

Legal validity, 14, 340–41n17. *See also* Procedural element

Legitimacy: defined, 2, 29, 337–38n7; fundamental importance of, 3–4, 338n9; limited scholarship on, 4–6, 338n17; explanatory value of, 6–7; belief/acknowledgment elements of, 11–14 *passim*, 340nn1,15; Weber's formulation of, 11–14 *passim*, 22, 31, 41, 141, 340nn1,6, 340–41n17; normative element of, 13, 15–16, 20, 30; dynamic nature of, 13–14, 25–26, 55–56, 79, 225, 325; consent element of, 14, 23–24, 343n52; legal validity element of, 14, 340–41n17; procedural element of, 14, 21–22, 30f, 53, 293, 340–41n17; key elements of, 14–15, 29–30, 293–94; use of power and, 14–15, 20–23, 342nn40,45–46; use of force and, 18–19, 341n35; performance element of, 22–23, 30, 31–32, 41–43, 52, 103, 309–10, 345nn37–38; international dimension's role in, 31–32, 48–49, 346–47nn61,63–64; personal authority resource of, 31–32, 43–46 *passim*, 138; politically defining moment and, 31–32, 46–48; multiple rationales strategy for, 50–53, 311, 325; in postcolonial nations, 56–57, 348n13; as problematic for regimes, 57, 58–59, 294, 308, 322–24, 330f; vs. illegitimacy, 177, 368nn40–41. *See also* Authority; Consent element; Legitimacy crisis; Legitimacy strain; Normative element; Performance element; Procedural element

Legitimacy crisis: in Southeast Asian countries, 1–3; defined, 59, 348n15; vs. legitimacy strain, 59, 348n16; theories on, 60–61; in regimes, 61–65

Legitimacy strain, 59, 71, 79, 103, 348n16

Leifer, Michael, 132

Lewis, Paul, 338n9

Liddle, R. William, 383n61

Lim, Alfredo, 168

Lim Boon Heng, 122

Lim Goh Tong, 96

Liminal moments, 157, 362n100

Linguistic identity, 85, 129f, 158

"Linh nghiem" (Prophecy, Tran Huy Quang), 286, 394n140

Lipset, Seymour Martin, 28, 340n1

Local business community: in Malaysia, 72, 75–76, 79, 99–102 *passim*; in Singapore, 119–20; in Thailand, 205–6, 213, 216f

Local politicians: in Philippines, 156–61

Loh Kok Wah, 77, 350n18

Lon-htein (special riot police, Burma), 170–71

Lotteries: in Philippines, 168–69

Lu-The, Lu-Pyit (U Okkata), 373n102

Luu Quang Vu, 285f, 391n86

Ly than (Alienation, Tran Manh Hao), 285

McAlister, John, 258f, 287

McVey, Ruth, 386n109

Madiun Revolt (1948), 245

Madjid, 240

Magsaysay, Ramon, 147, 165

Mahathir Mohamad, 75, 77, 94–102 *passim*, 107, 299, 316, 349–50n8

Mahidol, Ananda Mahidol (King Rama VIII), 197

Mahidol, Bhumipol Adulyadej (King Rama IX), 1, 203–4

Majlis Amanah Rakyat (Council of Trust for Indigenous People, Malaysia), 102

Malay Administrative Service, 84, 87

Malay Annals (*Sejarah Melayu*), 82

Malaya, British, 79, 83–89, 352n64

Malayan Emergency (1948–60), 88–89

Malayan Union scheme (1946), 83, 88

Malays: UMNO's commitment to dominance of, 72–73, 89–90f, 104, 312–13, 322; middle-class identity of, 73, 105; authority patterns of, 82–90 *passim*; and UMNO legitimacy, 91–104 *passim*; economic self-reliance of, 95–96; as Singapore ethnic minority, 126, 130, 355n32

Malaysia: political stability in, 70–71; May Thirteenth riots in, 72, 79–80, 91–97 *passim*, 102; Chinese business community in, 72f, 79, 89–90, 96f, 106; elite-mass relations in, 72–73, 82–85; political legitimacy in, 73–77, 322; ethnic delineation in, 75–76, 81–82, 103f; elections in, 76, 316; British administration of, 79, 83–89, 352n64; under Mahathir's economic policy, 99–102 *passim*; societal fragmentation in, 106–7; Singapore's separation from, 113; state power in, 317–18f. *See also* UMNO

Malaysian Institute for Islamic Under-
standing (IKIM), 106
Mandalay, 179
Mandarin dialect, 129f
Manecio, Leonardo, 154
Manila, 151
Mano, Phaya, 199
Marcos, Ferdinand: constitutional authori-
tarianism of, 34, 141, 300, 301–2;
intrinsic personal power of, 44, 162–
63f; Corazon Aquino vs., 47; and elections, 142; institutionalization subverted by, 143, 296–97, 308; economic
performance under, 301, 309, 395n14;
multiple-rationale strategies of, 311
Marcos, Imelda, 162–64
Marr, David, 259
Marsinah (labor activist), 227
Marxism: and Confucianism, 258
Marxist school, 4f, 338n18
Marxist-Leninist regimes, 33, 38f, 48–49,
64–65, 346n61
Mass audiences: consent role of, 29f,
343n69; Malaysian elites and, 72–78,
82–85 *passim*; alienation of Singapore's, 112–17 *passim*, 132–33,
356nn54–55; skepticism of Philippine,
143–44, 161, 167; role of Thai, 195,
199, 200–201, 207–11 *passim*; VCP
renovation response by, 284–87 *pas-
sim*. See also Popular sovereignty
Masyumi (modernist Muslim party),
239–45 *passim*, 295, 384n82
Maung Maung, Dr., 171, 189, 364n1
Maung Maung Gyi, 182
Maung Shu-maung, *see* Ne Win
May Thirteenth riots (1969, Malaysia),
72, 79–80, 91–97 *passim*, 102
Mayall, James, 234
MCA (Malaysian Chinese Association),
73–79 *passim*, 85f, 90–96 *passim*,
350n9
Mekong River delta, 259, 273–74, 284
Melaka Sultanate (Malaysia), 82, 90
Memali incident (1985), 75
Merdeka Constitution (Malaysia), 79, 89
MI (Military Intelligence, Burma), 187,
373n111
MIC (Malayan/Malaysian Indian Con-
gress), 73, 89
Middle class, 73, 74–75, 105–6, 218–21
passim
Milne, R. S., 90
Milner, A. C., 84, 107
Minchin, James, 119
Mindanao, 152

Ministry of Education (Malaysia), 96
Ministry of Information (Philippines), 163
Min-tara (just king) tradition, 177
Mitra, Ramon, Jr., 169
MNLF (Moro National Liberation Front,
Philippines), 142, 153
Modernity: of Islamism, 239–40
Moerdani, Benny, 254
Moertopo, Ali, 248, 386n111
Monarchy: consent element in, 24, 39; in
Thailand, 194–97, 199, 203–4, 212,
222, 303, 330, 375n8
Montemayor, Isabelo, 154
Morell, David, 204
Morley, James W., 339nn27–28
Mostov, Julie, 37
MPR (Indonesian people's consultative
assembly), 226, 247f, 256, 306, 378n7
Muhammad, 40
Muhammadiyah school of Islam, 239
Multicolored insurgents (*Yaungzon Thu-
bon*, or *Yaungzon-thaunggyan-thu*),
178–80
Mus, Paul, 258f, 287
Musa Hitam, 97
Mutual knowledge, 13, 340n15
Mya Maung, 367n30
Myanmar (*formerly* Burma), 174, 366–
67n19. *See also* Burma

Nagarakartagama (Javanese epic), 232
Nagata, Judith, 82, 351n48
Narong Kittikachorn, *see* Kittikachorn,
Narong
National Assembly (Vietnam), 276f
National Equity Corporation (Permodalan Nasional Bhd.), 95
National ideologies: as policy justifica-
tion, 34, 332; problematic institutional-
ization of, 318–19, 331–33, 396n39.
See also Goal-rational ideologies
National Wages Council (Singapore), 122
Nation-state: and force-legitimacy rela-
tionship, 19, 175; as basis for political
community, 26–27; multi-ethnic terri-
torialisms of, 56f, 116, 142; legitimacy
challenges to, 57–58; Malaysian, 76–
77; Philippine, 140–44, 150–52, 165;
tentative identification with, 331–32,
396n39. *See also* State
Natsir, 241
Nawaphon (Thailand), 211
NCP (National Culture Policy, UMNO),
74, 96
NDF (National Democratic Front, Philippines), 142

NDP (New Development Policy, Malaysia), 80, 102, 106, 320

Ne Win: patrimonial authority of, 44, 187, 300, 308; and 1988 uprising, 171, 364n1; and U Nu, 184; perceptions of, 186, 368–69nn45,46; contested legitimacy of, 303–4; background of, 365n7

NEDB (National Economic Development Board, Thailand), 205

Nehru, Jawaharlal, 52

NEP (New Economic Policy, Malaysia), 72–73, 80, 95–96, 102, 105

NESDB (National Economic and Social Development Board, Thailand), 216f

New Order (Indonesia): violation of Pancasila by, 224, 226, 249, 252–53, 306f; legitimacy dilemma of, 224–25; legitimacy claims of, 225f, 300, 304–5, 383n66; *aliran* politics vs., 225–26, 378n6; challenges to economic performance of, 227–28, 254–55, 306, 379n10; order and sufficiency policies of, 238, 247–53 *passim*; Islamic renewal under, 239–40, 307, 309; presidential powers under, 247, 248–49; parliamentary system under, 247–48; depoliticization under, 249, 305; economic dualism of, 250–55 *passim*, 386n120; statism-capitalism under, 250–51; guidelines for, 255–56

New Order (Malaysia), 97–99

New Society Movement (Kilusang Bagong Lipunan, Philippines), 164, 363n128

Newspaper and Printing Presses Act (1986, Singapore), 134–35

Newsweek, 69

Ngo Dinh Diem, 270

Nguyen Ai Quoc (*later* Ho Chi Minh), 261, 279. *See also* Ho Chi Minh

Nguyen Cao Ky, 363n128

Nguyen Ho, 278

Nguyen Huu Tho, 280

Nguyen Huy Thiep, 285

Nguyen Khac Vien, 258, 264, 270, 280, 393n107

Nguyen Manh Tuong, 269

Nguyen Van Linh, 276–81 *passim*, 285, 394n137

Nguyen Van Thieu, 274

Nhan Dan Chu Nhat (VCP newspaper), 392n95

Nhung thien duong mu (Foggy paradises, Duong Thu Huong), 286

Ninth Plenum of the Central Committee (1990, VCP), 278–79

Nixon, Richard M., 22

NLD (National League for Democracy, Burma), 2, 170, 173

NMS (New Management System, Vietnam), 273

Noe buon chien tranh/Than phan tinh yeu (Sorrow of war/Fate of love, Bao Ninh), 286

Non-Bamas, 56f, 174–84 *passim*, 295, 304, 366n16, 367n25, 370n56, 371nn70–71,75–76

Non-Malays: UMNO and, 72–76, 88–90, 96, 104, 106, 313, 316, 350nn9,12,17. *See also* Chinese

Non-*pribumi*, 227–28, 251f, 306

Non-system-defining goals, 32–33

Normative element: limitations of, 15–16, 333, 341n22; cultural construction of, 17, 45, 333, 345–46nn51,53–54; indicators of, 18–20; in legitimacy hierarchy, 24–25, 30, 50; as legitimation resource, 31–33, 343n4. *See also* Goal-rational ideologies

North Vietnam, 265–74 *passim*, 288. *See also* DRV model; Vietnam

NPA ("Nice People Around," Philippines), 153f

NSCT (National Student Center of Thailand), 208, 211

NTUC (National Trades Union Congress, Singapore), 122

Nu, U, 181–86 *passim*, 372nn83,92, 374n116

NU (Nahdatul Ulama) school of Islam, 239, 245, 306

NUF (National United Front, Burma), 183

NUP (National Unity Party, Burma), 170, 172f, 304

O'Donnell, Guillermo, 119, 338n24

Okkata, U, 186, 373n102

Ong, Michael, 350n12

Ong Teng Cheong, 122

Onn bin Jaafar, 79

Ortega, Francisco, 159

Outer Islands (Indonesia), 238

Outlaws: in Philippines, 153–56, 361n83, 363n87

Overloaded government theory, 60–64 *passim*

Ow Chin Hock, 124

Packenham, Robert, 5

Pancasila: as policy justification, 34, 305, 332; New Order's departure from, 224, 226, 249, 252–53, 306f; misunder-

standings of, 232–33, 381n41; as anti-colonial mobilization, 233–34, 382n53; principles of, 233–34, 245–46, 332, 378n3, 381–82nn44,46–48,52; Islam and, 234, 241–42, 307, 309, 381–82n47; order and sufficiency assumptions of, 234–35, 246, 382n54
Panglong Agreement (1947), 180, 304
Panyarachun, Anand, 1–2, 218, 337n19
PAP (People's Action Party, Singapore): contingent legitimacy of, 112–13; de-politicization by, 114–17 *passim*, 299, 318; elites' incorporation by, 117–23 *passim*, 354n8; as cadre-based institution, 118; election legitimation and, 123–24, 132, 316–17, 396nn30–31; voter opposition to, 123–24, 130–34 *passim*; goal-rational ideology of, 124–27, 312, 314; Confucian campaign by, 125, 127, 321, 323, 332–33
Parekh, Bhiku, 17
Paris Peace Accords (October 1991), 49
Parliamentary system: popular sovereignty and, 38; of Burma, 178, 183–84f; in Thailand, 196, 201–12 *passim*, 218; in Indonesia, 241–48 *passim*, 253, 384n81
Parsons, Talcott, 338n24
Parti Rakyat (People's Party, Malaysia), 89
Participation: and commitment, 19–20; and consent, 23–24; alienation vs., 131–34
PAS (Parti Islam Se-Malaysia, Pan-Islamic Party of Malaysia), 75, 76–77, 93, 320, 322, 349–50n8
"The Path That Led Me to Leninism" (Ho Chi Minh), 261
Patron-client relationships: in Philippines, 44, 145–62 *passim*, 166, 345n48, 358n30
PBS (Parti Bersatu Sabah, United Sabah Party, Malaysia), 77, 313
PCSO (Philippine Charity Sweepstakes Office), 168
PDI (Indonesian party), 226, 248
People Power Revolution (Philippines), 164
People's Party (Thailand), 194–97, 199, 375n8
Pepsi-Cola lottery, 168–69
Performance element: as basis of authority claim, 22–23, 42, 61–62, 64, 103, 223, 309–10, 342nn45–46; in legitimacy hierarchy, 24–26, 52; legitimation's connection to, 41–43, 345nn37–38,41. *See also* Economic performance; Power
Pergerakan movement (Indonesia), 230, 238, 380n28

Perhimpoenan Indonesia, 231, 233
Personal authority: charisma and, 43–46 *passim*; of Soeharto, 44, 300, 304–9 *passim*, 395nn20,25; as legitimation basis, 44–45, 300–311, 345nn43–44, 396n28; institutionalization and, 46, 52, 115–16, 128–29, 308, 330, 346n57; of Tunku Abdul Rahman, 92–93; in Philippines, 149–58 *passim*, 162, 167, 360n65
"Petisi 50," 251f, 386–87n123
Pham Thi Hoai, 286
Pham Van Dong, 276
Phan Dinh Dieu, 279f, 393n105
Phanfa bridge (Bangkok), 1, 337nn1–2
Phibul Songkram, *see* Songkram, Phibul
Philippine Constitution, 141
Philippines: political crisis in, 2; goal-rational ideology of, 33–34, 300; religion's legitimating force in, 40, 159, 164, 363n130; patron-client relationships in, 44, 145–62 *passim*, 166, 345n48, 358n30; politically defining moment in, 47; contradictory democratic system in, 137–38, 141–44, 148–49, 295, 296–97; paternalist power in, 138, 144–47, 358nn29–30; personal authority projection in, 138, 149–50, 161–63, 308; nation-state power in, 140–44, 165–66; elections in, 141–43f, 148–49, 168f, 302, 359nn53,55–57; legitimacy skepticism in, 147–49, 167, 296f; as colonial regime, 150–51; big-man authority in, 150–58 *passim*, 162, 167, 300, 360n65; ethnic resistance in, 152–56, 295; kinship-based legitimacy claims in, 156–57, 160
Phuc duc notion, 258
PKI (Partai Kommunis Indonesia, Indonesian Communist Party), 241–45 *passim*, 297, 305, 385nn94,101, 387n125
"Platform for National Construction in the Period of Transition to Socialism" (Ninth Plenum), 279, 392n102
PNI (Nationalist Party, Indonesia), 241, 244f
Pol Pot, 289
Police: in Philippines, 147–48, 155, 359n49
Politburo of the Seventh Party Congress (VCP), 282, 393–94nn125–26
Political development theory, 4f, 338n18
Political legitimacy, *see* Legitimacy
Politically defining moments, 46–47, 52, 78–79, 103, 231–32
Ponce-Enrile, Juan, 47, 302
Popkin, Samuel, 259
Popular sovereignty: significance of, 36–37; and legitimation claims, 37–39, 62; in

authoritarian regimes, 38 f, 62, 293, 310–11; in multiple-rationales strategy, 50–52, 316–17

Post, Ken, 260.

Power: vs. authority, 2, 4, 44, 326, 337–38 n7; exercise of, 14–15, 20–23, 54–55, 103; depoliticization process and, 114–15; Philippine structure of, 140–47; intrinsic personal, 154–63 *passim*, 167, 361 n92; capital accumulation and, 167–68; Benedict Anderson on, 235–36, 382 n59; Javanese view of, 237–38. *See also* Performance element

PPP (Indonesian party), 226, 248

Prachathipok, King (Rama VII), 196–97

Pramoj, Kukrit, 209–10, 212

Pramoj, Seni, 209–10

Praphat Charusathien, *see* Charusathien, Praphat

Prem Tinsulanonda, *see* Tinsulanonda, Prem

Presidential Arm for Community Development (Philippines), 162

Presidential Commission on Good Government (Philippines), 166

Pribumi, 227–28, 251, 306

Priestesses: in Philippines, 153, 166

Priyayi (native colonial bureaucracy), 229, 237 f, 242, 382 n59

Problems of the East (Soviet review), 261

Procedural element, 14, 24–25, 31, 53, 141, 293, 324, 331, 340–41 n17

Provisional Revolutionary Government of the Republic of South Vietnam, 272

Pry-daungzu (Union Party, Burma), 185 f

Przeworski, Adam, 339 n34

Pulitika (jockeying for position), 147, 358 n44

Puwesto (position), 150–51

PVO (People's Volunteer Organization, Burma), 181 f, 370 n64

Pye, Lucian, 44, 85 f, 127, 346 n53

Quah, Jon, 131

Quah, Stella, 131

Quang Trung, 265

Rachbini, 379 n10

Raffles, Thomas Stamford, 379–80 n21, 382 n54

Rajaratnam, Sinnathamby, 118

Rakhine, Burma, 176, 179, 295

RAM ("Reform the Armed Forces Movement," Philippines), 302

Rama V (king of Thailand), 194, 197

Rama VII (king of Thailand), 196–97

Rama VIII (king of Thailand), 197

Rama IX (king of Thailand), 1, 203–4

Rama X (king of Thailand), 222

Ramkhamhaeng University (Thailand), 208

Ramon M. Durano Sr. Home, 136

Ramos, Fidel, 165, 169

Rangoon, 170–72, 179, 190, 295, 366 nn11,13

Razaleigh Hamzah, 97, 100 f

Red Flag Communist Party, 179, 183

Red Gaurs (Thailand), 211

Red River delta, 259, 288

Red Scorpion Group (Philippines), 154

Regimes: participatory, 23–24; defined, 27; performance consequences in, 42–43; international recognition of, 48–49; multiple rationales strategy for, 50–53 *passim*; problematic legitimation of, 57, 58–59, 294, 308, 322–24, 330 f; legitimacy crisis of, 59, 348 n15; government's fusion with, 115–16, 322–23; personal authority legitimation in, 308–11, 396 n28. *See also* Authoritarian regimes; Democratic regimes; Monarchy; Totalitarian regimes

Religion: as political legitimation basis, 39–41, 51, 159, 164, 198, 240, 307, 363 n130. *See also* Islam

Rent reduction, 262, 266–67

Resolution 10 (VCP), 283 f

Revilla, Ramon, 155, 165

Revolutionary Council (Burma), 303

Rojanasathien, Boonchu, 216

Rothstein, Robert L., 349 n25

Round Table Conference, 240, 246

Royal Thai Army, 1

Rukun principle, 237

Sabah, 77 f, 350 n18

Sabungero (cockfighting aficionado), 158

Sadka, Emily, 87

Sadli principle, 250–51, 386 n120

Sahlins, Marshall, 17–18, 360 n65

Sammakkitham party (Thailand), 219

Samson, Allan A., 381 n41

Samudavanija, Chai-anan, 204

Sanda Win incident (1989, Burma), 170, 304, 364 n4

Santri (entrepreneurial Muslims), 237 f, 242

Sao Shwe Thaike, 180, 370 n59

Sarasin, Pongse, 216

Sarekat Islam (Indonesia), 230–31, 233, 245

Sarit Thanarat, *see* Thanarat, Sarit

Saw, U, 370 n67

Saw Maung, 171 f, 189, 364 n1

Schmitter, Philippe C., 338 n24, 346–47 n64

SCME, *see* System of Correlation of Man and His Environment
Scott, James C., 34, 139, 259, 306
Second Party Congress (1951, Lao Dong Party), 263
Sein Lwin, 189, 364n1
Sein Win, 170f
Seinda, U, 179
Semangat '46 (Spirit of '46, Malaysia), 100, 316, 322, 353n101
Seni Pramoj, *see* Pramoj, Seni
Serm Na Nakhon, 212
Seventh Party Congress (1991, VCP), 257, 259, 280–82
Seventh Plenum of the Central Committee (1989, VCP), 277
Shan minority, 176–87 *passim*, 366n16, 372n89
Shared norms and values, *see* Normative element
Singapore: vulnerable legitimacy in, 108–10, 133, 135; economic development strategy in, 109, 113, 119–22, 127, 130, 315, 354n2; limited procedural democracy in, 111–12, 123, 132f, 293, 299, 355n25; independence of, 113, 115; popular alienation in, 114–17 *passim*, 129–33 *passim*, 318, 356nn54–55; government-regime fusion in, 115–16, 322–23; civil servants' role in, 117–22 *passim*; local business access in, 119–20; trade union movement in, 121f, 355n21; election legitimation in, 123–24, 130–34 *passim*, 316–17, 396nn30–31; linguistic/ethnic division in, 129–30; emigration from, 133, 356n55; state power deployment in, 317–18f. *See also* PAP
Sivara, Krit, 207–12 *passim*
Sixth Party Congress (1986, VCP), 275–76
Sixth Plenum of the Central Committee (1989, VCP), 277
Skocpol, Theda, 366n13
SLORC (State Law and Order Restoration Council, Burma): military establishment ties of, 2, 178, 189–90, 304, 337n4, 364n1; legitimacy crisis of, 170–73, 189–92 *passim*, 304, 366n11; Burma's name change by, 174, 366–67n19; international legitimacy claim by, 174, 190–91, 366–67nn18–19; BANDA alliance with, 190
Social Action Party (Thailand), 212
Social bandits: in Philippines, 153–56, 361n83
Socialism: nationalism's symbiosis with, 260–63, 266, 270–71, 313–14; democratization of, 278, 279–83

Socialist Front (Malaysia), 89
Socialist Republic of Vietnam, *see* Vietnam
Socialization: vs. structural determinism, 16, 341n22
Soeharto: personal authority of, 44, 300, 304–9 *passim*, 395nn20,25; *aliran* politics and, 225–26; Benedict Anderson's "power" and, 235ff; parliamentary control by, 247–48; political succession to, 254f; order and sufficiency goals of, 300, 304–5, 385–86n106; ABRI and, 305f, 395nn24–25; Islamic accommodation by, 307, 309
Soempah Pemoeda (Youth Pledge, Indonesia), 231
Son Duong village, 268, 389n38
Songkram, Phibul, 196–200 *passim*, 205, 376n14
South Africa, 49
South Vietnam, 3, 257, 272–74, 288–89, 316, 320. *See also* Vietnam
Southeast Asian countries: goal-rational ideology of, 33–34; religious basis of authority in, 39–41, 51, 159, 164, 198, 307, 363n130; personal authority in, 44–45, 345nn43–44; legitimacy challenges in, 57–59; regime legitimation in, 294, 308, 322–24, 330f; institutionalized national ideologies in, 331–33
Southeast Asian Treaty Organization, 198
Soviet Union, 49, 262, 273, 288
Spanish colonialism, 150–51, 360n67
SPSI (Indonesian Unitary Workers' Association), 226
Srimuang, Chamlong, 1, 337n2
Sriyanon, Phao, 196
Stalin, Joseph, 263
Stanton, Edward, 201–2
State: as structure of domination, 3, 26, 175–76, 317–18f, 325–26, 338n10. *See also* Nation-state
State Council (Hoi Dong Nha Nuoc, VCP), 271, 282
Steinberg, David, 242
Stillman, Peter, 12
Stockwell, A. J., 351
Strategic groups, 16–17, 28–29f, 35f, 341n23. *See also* Elite groups; Hegemonic groups
"Strategy of Socioeconomic Stabilization and Development to the Year 2000" (Ninth Plenum), 279, 392n102
Strauch, Judith, 82, 85
Structural determinism, 16, 341n22
Student movements, 207–13 *passim*, 251, 285, 303, 377n42, 386–87n123
Suchinda Kraprayoon, *see* Kraprayoon, Suchinda

Suharto, *see* Soeharto
Sukarno: authoritarianism of, 44 f, 226, 243, 385 nn93–94; on colonialism, 231, 380 n33; inclusive nationalism of, 232, 381 nn36,38, 383 n64; Pancasila proposal of, 232–35, 378 n3, 381–82 nn44,46–48,52; cultural construction of, 234, 237, 382 n48, 383 n64; Benedict Anderson's "power" and, 235 f; communist alliance with, 241–42, 245, 385 n102; guided democracy of, 242–46, 253, 295, 297–98, 387 n125; ousting of, 246–47
Sukiman, 241
Sulu archipelago, 152
Sutrisno, Try, 255
System of Correlation of Man and His Environment (*Anya-manya Th'baw-tra,* Burma), 34, 185–86
System-defining goals, 32

Ta Ba Tong, 278
Tagalog, 150, 155
Tai, Ho Hue Tam, 259
Talmon, J. L., 37
Tatmadaw: atrocities by, 2, 184, 372 n86, 373 n111; 1988 uprising and, 2, 170–72, 188–89, 364 n1, 366 n11, 374 n122; SLORC ties to, 2, 178, 189–90, 374 nn123–24,129; legitimation claims by, 185–86, 189; economic insurgents and, 187 f, 190, 374 n115. *See also* SLORC
Taunggyi Federal Conference (1961), 184
Taylor, Robert H., 174–75, 367 n25, 370 n55
Tempo (Indonesian magazine), 227
Thai Binh Conference (1974), 273
Thai Constitution (1932), 196
Thai Constitution (1978), 214–15, 326–27, 396 n37
Thai Nation Party, 210
Thai Quang Trung, 388 n20
Thailand: Phanfa bridge demonstration in, 1, 48, 58, 337 nn1–2; authoritarianism-parliamentarianism cycle in, 193–95 f, 201–2, 207–12 *passim,* 218–21, 294, 375 n7; monarchical legitimacy in, 194, 195–96, 203–4, 303, 330, 375 n8; military legitimation claims in, 195–200, 375 n8; Thai-centric ideology of, 202–3; developmentalism promotion in, 205–7, 217, 300, 302–3, 377 n39; anti-military movement in, 207–8, 212–13, 220–21, 329; societal conflict in, 207–8, 210–13, 220–21, 302–3, 329–30, 377 n42; democratic regime in, 209–13; democratic principles

in, 213, 221–22 f, 327, 329 f; quasi-democratic regime in, 214–18, 326–28, 396 nn36–37; post-1988 democratic regime in, 218–21, 328–29; subverted institutionalization in, 308–9
Thakin Ba Tin, 369 n48
Thakin Nu, 368 n44
Thakin Soe, 179, 365 n9, 369 n48
Thakin Than Tun, 179, 181, 369 n50
Thammasat University (Thailand), 208, 212 f
Than Shwe, 189
Thanarat, Sarit, 196–207 *passim,* 223, 300, 302–3, 308
Thanom Kittikachorn, *see* Kittikachorn, Thanom
Thayer, Carlyle, 388 n20, 390 n53
Theocratic regimes, 24
Third Party Congress (1960, Lao Dong Party), 263 f, 276
Third World, *see* Developing countries
Thompson, E. P., 140, 358 n29
Tinsulanonda, Prem, 214, 215–17, 327–28, 377 n53
Totalitarian regimes: consent in, 24; international norms and, 55
Trade Union Act (1983, Singapore), 122
Trade unions, 121 f, 226, 355 n21
Tran Hung Dao, 265
Tran Huy Quang, 285–86, 394 n140
Tran Manh Hao, 285
Tran Phu, 279
Tran Quoc Vuong, 259
Tran Xuan Bach, 278, 392 n98
Transnational enterprises, 120–21. *See also* International support
Tribal chiefs: in Philippines, 152–53
Trieu, Lady, 265
Truong Chinh, 265, 267, 271, 276, 393 n107
Turner, Victor, 362 n100
Twenty Points (Malaysia), 77

UMNO (United Malays National Organization): governing authority of, 70 f, 76–77, 84–85, 351 n48; Malay dominance commitment of, 72–73, 89–90 f, 104, 312–13, 319–20, 322; New Economic Policy of, 72–73, 95–96, 105; non-Malay relationships with, 72–76, 89–90, 96, 104, 106, 313, 316, 350 n9, 12, 17; and elite-mass relations, 72–78; cultural appeal of, 73–74, 105–6, 349–50 n8; PAS denouncement of, 75, 320, 322; interethnic legitimacy strains on, 77–78, 79–81, 104–5; goal-rational ideology of, 78 f, 81, 94–99 *passim,* 103–4, 293, 312–13, 331; founding of,

79; New Development Policy of, 80, 102, 106, 320; intra-Malay legitimacy strains on, 91–97 *passim*, 299; high political culture period of, 91–93; entrepreneurism aims of, 95–102 *passim*; deregistration of, 100; middle-class Malays and, 105–6; legitimacy expansion by, 106–7, 319; and regime legitimacy, 322–23
United front strategy, 279, 314
United States, 151, 198, 201–2, 220, 262, 265, 269, 314
Unity, ideological, 16–17
Universality: of Pancasila, 234, 381n44

Values, *see* Normative element
VCP (Vietnamese Communist Party): goal-rational ideology of, 33, 203–4, 260–63, 275, 293, 312–13, 317, 320–21; and tradition-based legitimacy, 258–60; nationalism–socialist revolution goals of, 260–63, 266, 270–71, 313–14, 318; intellectuals and, 269–70, 275, 281, 285–86, 390n53, 390n58, 391n86, 394n137, 394n140; postreunification leadership crisis of, 271–75, 288–89; handling of state apparatuses by, 272, 277, 280f, 391–92n93, 393n107; postreunification economic strategies of, 272–75, 276, 280, 283, 316, 320–21; renovation goals of, 275–76, 281–83, 289, 320f, 323; succession process in, 276, 391n90; Ho Chi Minh's endorsement by, 277, 279, 282, 315, 319, 392nn95–97; membership criticism of, 278–80, 317, 392n102, 393n107; united front strategy of, 279, 314; separation of powers in, 282, 393–94nn125–126; Constitution of (1992), 282; response to renovation policies of, 284–87, 321, 394n137, 394n140; and regime legitimation, 323, 325. *See also* Lao Dong Party
Vidich, Arthur J., 342n45
Vien, *see* Nguyen Khac Vien
Viet Minh, 261f, 265–66, 269
Vietnam, 58; cultural diversity of, 258, 259–60; nationalism-socialism symbiosis in, 260–63, 266, 270–71, 313–14, 318; cooperativization in, 262, 267–69, 272–74, 288, 313, 389–90n49, 391n79; state-party-peasantry relationship in, 265–71; rent reduction policies in, 266–67, 389n38; intellectual dissidence in, 269–70, 275, 281, 285–86,

390nn53,58, 391n86, 394nn137,140; China's conflict with, 275, 321, 391n86; land allocation reform in, 283; occupational distribution in, 283–84; renovation response in, 284–87, 321, 394nn137,140; postreunification economy in, 320f; political leadership models in, 388n20. *See also* DRV model; Lao Dong Party; VCP
Vietnam Labor Party, *see* Lao Dong Party
Vietnam War Veterans' Association (Hoi Cuu Chien Binh Viet Nam), 278
Vietnamese revolution (1945), 258
Vietnamese Revolutionary Youth Association (Thanh Nien), 261
Village Scouts (Thailand), 211
Villegas, Bernardo, 395n14
Visayan, 150, 154
Vo Nguyen Giap, 267
Vu Ky, 392n96
Vuong, *see* Tran Quoc Vuong

Wahid, Abdurrahman, 240, 254
Wan Azmi Wan Hamzah, 96
War of Resistance (Vietnam, 1945–54), 266
Weber, Max: on structure of domination, 3, 139; on authority, 11, 22, 31, 35, 41, 43, 341n35; legitimacy formulation of, 11–14 *passim*, 22, 31, 41, 141, 340–41nn1,6,17
Werner, Jayne, 259
Wertheim, W. F., 229
West Irian, 295
Western countries, 48, 171–72, 333–34, 347n5, 366n12
White Flag Communist Party (Burma), *see* BCP/CPB
Whitehead, Laurence, 338n24
Wilopo, 241
Wolters, O. W., 362n102
Wong Kan Seng, 134f
Working People's Daily (Burma), 366n18
World Bank, 198, 205
World War II, 183

Xuan Quynh, 286

Yeltsin, Boris, 49
Yorac, Haydee, 166, 169
Young, Stephen, 258f
Young Turks, 212, 215, 327

Zoetmulder, P. J., 379–80n21

Library of Congress Cataloging-in-Publication Data

Political legitimacy in Southeast Asia : the quest for moral
    authority / edited by Muthiah Alagappa.
        p.   cm. — (Contemporary issues in Asia and the Pacific)
    Includes bibliographical references and index.
    ISBN 0-8047-2504-7 (cloth). — ISBN 0-8047-2560-8 (pbk.)
    1. Legitimacy of governments—Asia, Southeastern.   2. Asia,
Southeastern—Politics and government.   I. Alagappa, Muthiah.
II. Series.
JQ750.A91P65   1995
320.959—dc20   95-1075
                                                               CIP

⊗ This book is printed on acid-free, recycled paper.

Original printing 1995
Last figure below indicates year of this printing:

04 03 02 01 00 99 98 97 96 95